MANAGING FINANCIAL RISK

Also Available from the Irwin Library of Investment & Finance:

Risk Management and Financial Derivatives by Satyajit Das
Valuing Intangible Assets by Robert F. Reilly and Robert P. Schweihs
Convertible Securities by John P. Calamos
Pricing and Managing Exotic and Hybrid Options by Vineer Bhansali

MANAGING FINANCIAL RISK

A Guide to Derivative Products, Financial Engineering, and Value Maximization

Charles W. Smithson
CIBC World Markets
School of Financial Products

McGraw-Hill
New York   San Francisco   Washington, D.C.   Auckland   Bogotá
Caracas   Lisbon   London   Madrid   Mexico City   Milan
Montreal   New Delhi   San Juan   Singapore
Sydney   Tokyo   Toronto

Library of Congress Cataloging-in-Publication Data

Smithson, C. W. (Charles W.)
    Managing financial risk : a guide to derivative products
financial engineering, and value maximization / Charles W. Smithson.
— 3rd ed.
        p.   cm. — (Irwin library of investment & finance)
    Includes bibliographical references and index.
    ISBN 0-07-059354-X
    1. Business enterprises—Finance.   2. Risk management.
3. Derivative securities.   I. Title.   II. Series.
HG4026.S58   1998
658.15—dc21   98-17711
                                                        CIP

McGraw-Hill

A Division of The McGraw·Hill Companies

    3 4 5 6 7 8 9 0   FGR/FGR   9 0 2 1 0 9

ISBN 0-07-059354-X

The sponsoring editor for this book was Stephen Isaacs, the editing supervisor was
John M. Morriss, and the production supervisor was Suzanne W. B. Rapcavage. It
was set in Times by BookMasters.

Printed and bound by Quebecor/Fairfield.

McGraw-Hill books are available at special quantity discounts to use as premiums
and sales promotions, or for use in corporate training programs. For more
information, please write to the Director of Special Sales. McGraw-Hill, 11 West
19th Street, New York, NY 10011. Or contact your local bookstore.

 This book is printed on recycled, acid-free paper containing a
minimum of 50% recycled de-inked fiber.

ABOUT THE AUTHOR

Charles W. Smithson is a Managing Director of CIBC World Markets where he is responsible for the *CIBC School of Financial Products.*

Charles Smithson's career has spanned the gamut, with positions in academe and in government, as well as in the private sector. In academe, Charles taught for nine years at Texas A&M University, where (not surprisingly) his primary interests were in natural resource economics and regulation. In government, Charles served with both the Federal Trade Commission and the Consumer Products Safety Commission. In the private sector, Charles was the Managing Director for Risk Management Research at Continental Bank (1988–90). He served two stints with the Chase Manhattan Bank, as the developer of Chase's education program for derivatives (1985–87) and as the Managing Director for Risk Management Research and Education (1990–95).

The author of a half-dozen books and scores of articles in professional and academic journals, Charles is best known as the originator of the "building block approach" to financial products.

Charles Smithson served as a member of the Working Group for the Global Derivatives Project sponsored by the Group of Thirty. He currently serves on the boards of directors of the International Swaps and Derivatives Association and the International Association of Financial Engineers.

Charles Smithson received his Ph.D. in Economics from Tulane University in 1976.

To my parents

PREFACE

Almost ten years have passed since the first edition of *Managing Financial Risk* was written.

That ten-year period of time has witnessed dramatic changes in the derivatives markets. Early in the 1980s, **derivatives** was almost a "nerdy" word. (At the time, derivatives were something that only a few "rocket scientists" understood.) In 1994 and 1995, **derivatives** almost became a "dirty" word (following the losses reported by Gibson Greetings, P&G, and all the rest); indeed, many people referenced derivatives as the "d-word." By 1998, **derivatives** has become a word that you will hear in an ever-increasing number of general business discussions.

Ten years ago, an easily defensible position would be for the managers of the firm to elect *not* to use derivatives—". . . we are a conservative firm; and derivatives are risky. . . ." Today, such a position is much harder to defend. Derivatives have come to be recognized simply as a corporate finance **tool**—albeit a powerful tool and one that could do damage if used incorrectly. Today, the question is *not* whether the firm will use derivatives, but is instead *how* these tools can be used to enhance shareholder value—and will avoid the firm being featured in one of those unfortunate stories.

The evolution of this book has traced the evolution of the market. The first edition, which contained 18 chapters, was focused on descriptions of the financial products—forwards, futures, swaps, and options—and how they work. The second edition, which had grown by one chapter, included discussion of some new financial products; but the primary addition was discussions about the way that financial products are used by nonfinancial corporations and how a derivatives dealer manages the risks that result from acting as the intermediary. In addition to adding a few more financial products to the list, this edition, now 24 chapters long, expands the discussion of risk management by the dealer, adds risk management to the discussion of how nonfinancial corporations use these products, and adds a discussion of how the products are used by financial institutions and institutional investors.

A feature that was introduced in the second edition and has been continued in this edition are the applications written by practitioners. I very much appreciate the hard work of these people:

Roger Burge, Eurotunnel

George Crawford, Stanford Law School

Dan Cunningham, Cravath, Swaine & Moore

Kosrow Dehnad, Citibank

Peter D. Hancock, J.P. Morgan

R. K. Hinkley, British Petroleum

Walter D. Hosp, Ciba Specialty Chemicals

Ira G. Kawaller, Chicago Mercantile Exchange

Claude R. Lamoureux and Robert G. Bertram, Ontario Teachers' Pension Plan

Ronald G. Layard-Liesching, Pareto Partners

Kenneth Lehn, University of Pittsburgh

Carleton Pearl, McDonald's Corporation

Lisa K. Polsky, Morgan Stanley

Matthew Pritsker, Federal Reserve Bank

Jacques Tierney

Ronald D. Watson, Custodial Trust Company

The people I work with and for at CIBC have been instrumental in the production of this edition. Particular thanks is owed to my colleagues at the CIBC School of Financial Products: Caroline Choe, François Gagnon, Joanne Galluscio, George François, Greg Hayt, John LeGrand, John Rozario, and Christine Stackpole, Ziad Zakharia, and David Zhang, as well as people who have moved from the School to other positions in CIBC World Markets, Lyle Minton in New York and Shang Song in Hong Kong, and to other financial institutions, William Chan to Bank of America and Tyrone Po to Chase. Moving beyond the School, other CIBC colleagues who deserve particular mention are: Michael Davis, Charles Henry, Mike Judge, Bill Mansfield, Bob Mark, Ken Minklei, Shaun Rai, Gerson Riddy, and Eric Salzman. I owe a special thanks to my managers for their support of the School of Financial Products and this book—the global managers of CIBC

Financial Products, Frank Gelardin and Bruce Berger, the chairman and CEO of CIBC Oppenheimer Corp., Mike Rulle, the President of CIBC World Markets, John Hunkin, and the chairman of CIBC, Al Flood.

In addition to people at CIBC, a number of practitioners at other firms helped with this book. For their help with the discussion of "hybrid" securities in Chapter 15, I owe thanks to Don Chew (Stern Stewart Management Services, Inc. who co-authored the article that forms the basis for this chapter), John Finnerty of KMPG Peat Marwick who created much of the literature on hybrid securities, and Gary Gastineau who is currently creating the newest of these hybrid securities at the American Stock Exchange. With respect to the Value-at-Risk discussion in Chapter 19, I wish to thank Jitendra Sharma of Arthur Andersen, Jacques Longerstaey of J.P. Morgan, and Cathy Cole of the US Securities and Exchange Commission for their contributions. I also want to recognize the assistance of Alfredo Bequillard of Lehman Brothers, Phelim Boyle of the University of Waterloo, David Mengle of J.P. Morgan, Yves de Montaudouin of Goldman Sachs, and Serge Marquie of Deutsche Morgan Grenfell.

I also want to thank Don Chance and Robert Mackay (VPI), and Jack Clark Francis (Baruch Colllege, City University of New York) for their help in identifying and correcting errors that were in the second edition.

Three people have taught me most of what I know about finance in general and risk management in particular. Lee Wakeman coauthored a number of the articles which are the precursors to chapters of this book and had a profound impact on the way that I look at the risk management business. Clifford W. Smith, Jr. (W. E. Simon Graduate School of Business, University of Rochester) and D. Sykes Wilford (CDC Investment Management Corporation) were coauthors of the first two editions of this book. While they elected not to continue as coauthors, their influence on this book and the way I think about finance remains.

My biggest debt is, as always, to my wife, Cindy. She has suffered and supported me through three editions—each time with me promising her that "this will be the last edition."

Charles W. Smithson

CONTENTS

Preface

**1 The Evolution of Risk
Management Products   1**

The World Becomes a Riskier Place   2
   Volatility of Foreign Exchange Rates   3
   Volatility of Interest Rates   4
   Volatility of Commodity Prices   4
The Impact of Increased Financial Price
   Risk on Firms   5
   Exchange Rate Risk   7
     Illustration 1–1: Laker Airlines
      an FX Risk   7
     Illustration 1–2: Caterpillar's
      FX Whammy   8
     Illustration 1–3: A Summer of Discontent
      for Japanese Manufacturers   9
   Interest Rate Risk   11
     Illustration 1–4: Time to
      Blame FX?   12
     Illustration 1–5: From Money
      Machines to Money Pits:
      U.S. S&Ls   13
     Illustration 1–6: Inherent Exposures
      to Interest Rates: Residential
      Construction   14

   Commodity-Price Risk   11
     Illustration 1–7: A Gulf War Casualty:
      Continental Airlines   14
The Forecasters Flunk   15
     Illustration 1–8: Making Millions
      Trading Wheat Futures   17
The Markets' Response: Tools to Manage
   Financial Price Risk   18
   Exchange Rate Risk
     Management Products   18
   Interest Rate Risk
     Management Products   20
   Commodity-Price Risk
     Management Products   22
How Much Is Really New?   23
Concluding Remarks   25

**2 An Overview of the Risk
Management Process   27**

A Building-Block Approach to Forwards,
   Futures, Swaps, Options, and
   Hybrid Securities   27
An Overview of the Risk
   Management Products   27
Forward Contracts   29
Futures Contracts   30

Swap Contracts   31
Option Contracts   34
The Box of Financial Building Blocks   39

3   Impact of the Introduction of the Risk Management Products   42

The Impact of Risk Management
    on the Markets for the
    Underlying Assets   42
    The Impact on Price Volatility   43
Authored Box: Less Is Brewing
    in Witching Hours
    John Rozario, CIBC
    World Markets   45
    The Impact on Adjustment Speed   48
    The Impact on the Bid-Ask Spread   49
    The Impact on Trading Volume of the
        Underlying Assets   49
    Summary   50
The Impact of Risk Management on
    the Economy   51
The Impact of the Derivative Markets on
    Each Other   52

4   Forward Contracts   54

The Structure of a Forward Contract   54
    ASIDE: Notional Principal   56
A Framework for Forward Pricing   57
    Forward Prices Must Reflect Costs
        and Benefits   58
    Forward Prices Must Be
        Arbitrage-Free   58
Forward Contracts and Default   60
Foreign Exchange Forwards   60
    The Contract   61
    The Forward Foreign Exchange
        Rate   62
        ASIDE: Interest Rate Parity   64
        Illustration 4–1: Pricing an FX
            Forward Contract   65
    Bid-Ask Spreads   66
        Illustration 4–2: Pricing an FX
            Forward Contract Again   66
Forward-Rate Agreements   67

The Contract   67
The Forward Interest Rate   68
    Illustration 4–3: Deriving a
        Forward Rate   68
Bid-Ask Spreads   69
Authored Box: Pricing an FRA
    George François,
    CIBC World Markets   71

5   Applications of Forwards   74

The Markets   74
    Foreign Exchange Forwards   74
    FRAs   76
The Trading Rooms   77
    Foreign Exchange Forward Trading   77
        Illustration 5–1: Laying Off
            an FX Forward   77
    FRA Trading   79
        Illustration 5–2: Using FRAs for
            Asset-Liability Management   79
End Users   81
    Managing Foreign Exchange Risk   81
        Illustration 5–3: Hedging
            Transaction Exposures   81
    Managing Interest Rate Risk   83
        Illustration 5–4: Using FRAs in an
            Insurance Company   86

6   Futures   89

The Futures Contract   89
Institutional Features That Reduce
    Credit Risk   91
    Illustration 6–1: Implementing
        Daily Settlement   92
    Daily Settlement   91
    Margin Requirements   93
        Illustration 6–2: Tracing
            Margin Balances   95
    The Clearinghouse   94
    Price Limits   96
Institutional Features That
    Promote Liquidity   100
    Standardized Contracts   100
    Organized Exchanges   100

Futures Prices   101
Future Prices and the Cost
of Carry   101
Illustration 6–3: Cash and Carry
Limits on Wheat Futures
Prices   104
Futures Prices and Expected Future
Spot Prices   106
Cost of Carry versus Expectations   107
Illustration 6–4: Speculation and the
Expectations Model   106
Illustration 6–5: Backwardation and
Contango in Bond Futures   108
Futures Prices and the Cost of
Hedging: Basis   109
Changes in the Convergence of the
Futures Price to the Cash Price   110
Changes in Factors That Affect the Cost
of Carry   111
Mismatches between the Exposure Being
Hedged and the Futures Contract
Being Used as the Hedge   111
Random Deviations from the Cost-of-
Carry Relation   113

7   Applications of Futures   116

*Authored Box: To Hedge or Not
to Hedge   119
Ira G. Kawaller, Kawaller &
Co.   119*
Using Futures to Hedge an
Underlying Exposure   120
Illustration 7–1: No Basis Risk   122
Mismatches on Maturities: Basis
Risk   123
Illustration 7–2: Basis Risk   123
Mismatches on Maturities: Strip and
Rolling Hedges   124
Mismatches in the Asset:
Cross-Hedging   124
Illustration 7–3: A Strip Hedge   125
Illustration 7–4: A Rolling Hedge   125
Illustration 7–5: A Rolling
Hedge Again   126

Illustration 7–6A: A Cross-Hedge:
Selecting the Appropriate
Futures Contract   127
Illustration 7–6B: A Cross-Hedge:
Selecting the Appropriate Number
of Contracts, Part 1   129
Illustration 7–6C: A Cross-Hedge:
Selecting the Appropriate Number
of Contracts Part 2   129
Illustration 7–6D: A
Cross-Hedge   130
Illustration 7–6E: The Results
of the Cross-Hedge   131
Adjusting for the Margin Account:
"Tailing" the Hedge   132
Illustration 7–7: A "Tailed"
Hedge   134
*Authored Box: Waging War against
Currency Exposure
Ira G. Kawaller, Chicago
Mercantile Exchange   135*
Managing a Futures Hedge   138

8   Swaps   140

Evolution of the Swap Contract   140
From Parallel Loans to
Currency Swaps   141
Illustration 8–1: Hedging a U.S.
Parent/UK Subsidiary with a
Parallel Loan   142
ASIDE: Currency Swap versus
FX Swaps   146
From Currency Swaps to Interest Rate,
Commodity, and Equity Swaps   145
Development of the Swap Market   150
Growth of the Swap Market   151
Comparative Advantage   153
ASIDE: Comparative Advantage   153
Underpriced Credit Risk
(Risk Shifting)   153
Differential Cash Flow Packages   154
Illustration 8–2: Embedded Interest
Rate Options   154
Information Asymmetries   155

Tax and Regulatory Arbitrage   156
   Illustration 8–3: Arbitraging Japan's
      Tax and Regulatory
      Authorities   157
   Exposure Management   162
   Synthetic Instruments   162
   Liquidity   162
Pricing and Valuing Swaps   162
   Pricing an At-Market Swap   163
      Illustration 8–4: Pricing an Interest
         Rate Swap   164
   Swap Pricing Conventions   167
   Valuing a Swap (Marking the Swap
      to Market)   167
      Illustration 8–5: Valuing an Interest
         Rate Swap   168

9   Applications of Swaps   170

Using Swaps to Manage Interest
   Rate Risk   171
Using Swaps to Manage Foreign Exchange
   Rate Risk   173
Using Swaps to Manage
   Commodity-Price Risk   174
Using Swaps to Manage Equity
   Price Risk   176
Using Swaps to Reduce
   Transaction Costs   177
*Authored Box: Using Swaps
   at McDonald's
   Carleton Pearl, McDonald's
   Corporation   178*
Using Swaps to Increase Debt Capacity
   (or Gain Access to
   Debt Markets)   181
   Illustration 9–1: Mexicana
      de Cobre   182
Using Swaps to Create
   Synthetic Instruments   184
*Authored Box: Using Interest Rate Swaps
   to Synthesize a Long-Dated Foreign
   Exchange Forward
   Jacques Tierney   185*

10   A Primer on Options   190

The Option Contract   190
   The Contracting Parties   190
   The Right to Buy or to Sell   190
   The Specified Asset   191
   The Specified Price and Date   191
The Graphics of Options   191
      Illustration 10–1: Reading
         the Options Quotes   192
Option Valuation   195
   Put-Call Parity   195
   Bounding the Value of the Option   197
   A Simplified Approach to
      Option Valuation   201
      Illustration 10–2: A Realistic
         Approach?   201
      Illustration 10–3: Calculating
         the Hedge Ratio   203
      Illustration 10–4: An Option Payoff
         Diagram   204
*Authored Box: Risk Neutral Valuation
   Greg Hayt, CIBC World Markets   210*
A Note on American Options   214
   American Calls   215
   American Puts   216

11   First-Generation Options   218

The Black-Scholes Option
   Pricing Model   219
      ASIDE: A Continuous Ito Process   220
      ASIDE: Ito's Lemma   221
      ASIDE: Differential Equations   224
The Analytical Models   227
   Generalizations of the
      Black-Scholes Model   227
      ASIDE: Interpreting the Black-Scholes
         Formula   228
   Extensions to the Black-Scholes
      Model   230
      Options on Futures   230
      Options on Currencies   231
      Compound Options   232

Path-Dependent Options 232
American-Style Options 232
The Numerical Models 233
The Binomial Models 233
The Finite Difference Methodology 235
Monte Carlo Simulations 235
ASIDE: Evolution of Models to Value
Interest Rate Options 236
The Analytic Approximation Models 238
The Family Tree 238
ASIDE: Precursors to the
Black-Scholes Model 238

12 Applications of Options 241

Activity Levels in the Option Markets 242
Exchange-Traded Options 242
Over-the-Counter Options 242
Using Options to Manage Interest
Rate Risk 244
*Authored Box: To Hedge or Not to
Hedge—Part 2
Ira G. Kawaller, Chicago Mercantile
Exchange 246*
ASIDE: Hartmarx Corporation 249
Using Options to Manage Foreign Exchange
Rate Risk 250
Illustration 12–1: Constructing a
Currency Hedge 251
Using Options to Manage
Commodity-Price Risk 253
Using Options to Manage Equity
Price Risk 257
ASIDE: A Note on U.S. Tax
Law Changes 260
Using Options to Increase
Debt Capacity 261
Using Options as a Competitive Tool 263

13 Second-Generation Options 266

Path-Dependent Options 267
Mean-Dependent Options 267
Average Price 267

Average Strike 269
Cumulative 270
Extremum-Dependent Options 270
Barrier Options 270
Knock-Out Options
Illustration 13–1: Using
Knock-Out Caps 272
Capped Options 273
Lookback Options 274
Ladder Options 274
Shout Options 275
Illustration 13–2: Using a Ladder
Option to Hedge FX Risk 276
Illustration 13–3: Using a Shout
Option to Hedge FX Risk 277
Valuing Path-Dependent
Options 277
Analytic Method 277
Analytic Approximation
Method 277
Binomial Model (Lattice)
Method 278
Monte Carlo Simulation 278
Multifactor Options 278
Rainbow Options 279
"Better-of" Options 279
Outperformance Options 279
Max/Min Options 280
Quanto Options 280
Basket Options 282
Exchange-Traded Multifactor
Options 283
Pricing and Risk Management
for Multifactor Options 283
Time-Dependent Options 283
Chooser Options 283
Forward Start Options 284
Illustration 13–4: A Periodic
Cap 284
Cliquet Options 284
Single-Payoff Options 285
Binary Options 285
Contingent Premium Options 286

14 Engineering "New" Risk Management Products 288

Combining Building Blocks to Produce
 "New" Instruments 288
 Combining Forwards with Swaps 288
 Combining Options with Forwards 290
 ASIDE: Why Break Forwards? 291
 Combining Options with Swaps 294
 Combining Options with
 Other Options 296
Restructuring the Building Blocks to
 Produce "New" Instruments 298
 Restructured Swaps 298
 Delayed Reset Swaps 298
 Diff Swaps 299
 Illustration: A Delayed LIBOR
 Reset Swap 300
 Option on Forwards or Futures or Swaps
 or Other Options 303
 Options on Futures 303
 Options on Swaps: Swaptions 304
 Options on Options: Compound
 Options 305
 Restructured Options 306
Applying the Building Blocks to New
 Underlying Markets to Produce
 "New" Instruments 306
 Exchange-Traded Products 307
 Catastrophe Insurance Futures
 and Options 307
 Futures and Options on Commodity
 Indexes 307
 Futures and Options on Financial
 Instruments of Emerging
 Economies 307
 Electricity Futures 308
 New OTC Swaps and Options 309
 Commodity Derivatives 309
 Electricity Derivatives 310
 Real Estate Swaps 311
 Derivatives on Emerging Country
 Debt 311
 Credit Derivatives 312
 Forward Agreements 312

Total Return Swaps 313
Credit Swaps 313
Evolution of the Market 314
How Prevalent Are Credit
 Derivatives? 316

15 Hybrid Securities 319

The Evolution of Hybrid Securities 320
 A Taxonomy of Hybrid Securities 320
 Hybrids Composed of Debt
 and Derivatives 321
*Authored Box: Decomposing Hybrids
 to Assess Value
 Walter D. Hosp, Ciba Specialty
 Chemicals 322*
 Debt Plus Forward Contract 324
 Dual-Currency Bond 324
 Petrobonds 324
 Debt Plus Swap 325
 Inverse Floating-Rate Note 325
 Adjustable-Rate Convertible
 Notes 326
 Debt Plus One Option 326
 Bonds with Equity Warrants 327
 Convertible Bonds and Exchangeable
 Bonds 328
 Bonds with Indexed Principal 328
 Principal Indexed to Commodity
 Prices 328
 Principal Indexed to Exchange
 Rates 330
 Principal Indexed to Interest
 Rates 330
 Principal Indexed to Equity
 Indexes 330
 Bonds with Options on Issuer's
 Creditworthiness or Shareholder/
 Manager Behavior 331
 Puttable, Callable, Extendable
 Debt 331
 Convertible Debt 331
 LYON 332
*Authored Box: The End of the LYON
 Tyrone Po 333*

Explicit Options on Issuer's
Creditworthiness 332
Bonds with Options on
Catastrophes 335
Debt Plus a Package of Options 338
Commodity Interest-Indexed
Bonds 338
Bonds with Interest Payments
Determined by Equity Returns 340
Bonds with Packages of Interest
Rate Options 340
Floored Floating-Rate
Bonds 340
Step-Up Bonds 340
Index-Amortizing Notes 341
Range Notes 341
Inflation-Rate Interest-Indexed
Bonds 343
Hybrids Composed of Equity and
Derivatives 343
Equity Plus Swap 343
Equity Plus an Option 344
Convertible Preferred 344
Options on Equity or
Equity Indexes 344
Hybrids Designed to Decompose Equity
Claims 344
ASIDE: Index Participations 346
Authored Box: Observations on the
Shad-Johnson Accord
and SEC-CFTC Jurisdictional
Disputes, Kenneth Lehn, University
of Pittsburgh 347
Options on a Commodity 350
Options on Managerial Behavior 350
Options on the Outcome
of Litigation 351
Why Hybrids? Part 1: The Economic
Rationale for Issuing a
Hybrid Security 351
To Provide Investors
with a "Play" 351
To "Arbitrage" Tax and/or Regulatory
Authorities 352

To Align Interests of Shareholders and
Bondholders 353
Why Hybrids? Part 2: Investor Strategies
for Using Hybrids 354
Using Hybrids to Enhance Yield 355
Using Hybrids to Enhance Yield
by Reducing Transaction Costs 355
Using Hybrids to Enhance Yield
by Taking a View 355
Using Hybrids to Control Risk 356

16 The Dealer's Perspective 360

Who are the Dealers? 360
The Functions of a Dealer 366
The Trend Toward Integrated
Risk Management 367
Integrating Different Market
Risks 367
Integrating Market, Credit, and
Operational Risks 367

**17 Measuring and Managing
Default Risk 370**

ASIDE: The Basle Accord 371
Using the "Building Blocks" to Examine
Default Risk 372
ASIDE: Approach of the Basle
Committee on Banking
Supervision 374
Exposure 375
Current and Potential Exposures 376
Exposure over the Life of the
Transaction 378
The Amortization Effect 378
The Diffusion Effect 379
Combining the Amortization and
Diffusion Effects 381
Maximum versus Expected
Exposures 383
Maximum Exposure 383
Expected Exposure 385
Measuring the Exposure for an Individual
Transaction 385

The Worst-Case Approach   386
The Simulation Approach   387
Measuring the Exposure for a Portfolio
    of Transactions   388
    General Portfolio Effects   388
        ASIDE: Probability of Default:
        Swap versus Loan   388
    The Effect of Netting   389
        Netting by Novation   389
        Closeout Netting   389
        Cross-Product Netting   389
Measuring the Probability
    of Default   390
*Authored Box: International Bank
    Insolvencies and the Enforceability
    of Multibranch Master Netting
    Agreements
    Dan Cunningham, Cravath Swaine
    and Moore   391*
Methods for Reducing Credit
    Risk   395
    Termination Provisions   395
    Collateral   395
    Coupon Resets   397
    Assignments and Pair-Offs   398
Evidence on Defaults for the Risk Manage-
    ment Instruments   398
Settlement Risk   399
*Authored Box: Settlement Risks
    for OTC Derivatives
    Ronald D. Watson, The Bear Stearns
    Companies, Inc.   400*

**18   Managing Price Risk in a Portfolio
of Derivatives   405**

Measuring Price Risk—
    "Fraternity Row"   405
Delta   405
Gamma   406
Vega   408
*Authored Box: The Curse of
    Negative Convexity*

*Kosrow Dehnad, Chase
    Manhattan Bank   409*
Managing the Price Risk in a
    Simplified Warehouse   411
    Delta-Hedging a Warehouse   411
        Delta-Hedging a Swap   412
        Delta-Hedging a Cap   416
        Delta-Hedging a Warehouse   418
    Hedging the Warehouse against Risk
        Other Than Delta   419
        Hedging the Warehouse against Term
            Structure Twists   420
        Hedging Gamma and Vega   422
        Hedging the Warehouse
            against Jumps   422
Implementing the Hedge   424
Hedging Beyond Delta-Gamma-Vega   426
*Authored Box: The Market Risk Manage-
    ment Process
    Peter D. Hancock, J. P. Morgan   427*

19   Risk Governance   433

ASIDE: The Role of the Board of Direc-
    tors in Risk Governance   434
Precursors to VAR   435
    Interest Rate Sensitivity Measures   435
        Maturity Gap   435
        Value of an "01" and Duration   435
        Convexity   436
    Option-Based Sensitivity Measures   436
    Weaknesses of Traditional
        Measures   438
Value-at-Risk—A Summary Measure
    of Market Risk   438
    The VAR Concept   438
    Calculating VAR   440
        Historical Simulation Method   440
            Illustration 19–1: Obtaining a
                Historical Simulation
                VAR   442
        Monte Carlo Simulation
            Method   446

Illustration 19–2: Obtaining
A Monte Carlo Simulation
VAR   447
Analytic Variance-Covariance
Method   449
ASIDE: Analytic Variance-
Covariance—General Frame-
work   451
Illustration 19–3: Obtaining an
Analytic Variance-Covariance
VAR   452
Authored Box: "Diversified" versus
"Undiversified" VARs
Ziad Zakharia, CIBC
World Markets   462
Comparison of Calculated VARs   464
Comparison of VARs Generated
by Different Methods   464
Comparison of VARs Generated
by Same Method   469
Choosing Among the
Methods   471
Authored Box: The Tradeoff: Accuracy
vs. Computational Time
Matthew Pritsker, Federal
Reserve Bank   472
The Users   475
Derivatives Dealers and Other
Financial Institutions   476
End-users—Institutional
Investors   477
End-users—Nonfinancial
Corporations   477
Authored Box: Using Derivatives
at British Petroleum
R. K. Hinkley, British Petroleum   477
ASIDE: VAR: In Their
Own Words   482
Regulators—Bank and Securities
Firms Regulators   483
ASIDE: The Basle Internal
Models Approach   483
Regulators—Securities and
Exchange Commissions   484

Implementing VAR—Parameter
Selection   484
Time Horizon   484
ASIDE: Using the Square Root
of Time to Scale Up
One-Day VARs   485
Confidence Level   486
Variance-Covariance Data   486
Implementing VAR—Beyond a Single
VAR Number   487
Sensitivity Analysis   487
Scenario Analysis   487
Stress Testing   488
Back Testing   488

**20   Risk Management and the Value
of a Nonfinancial Firm   492**

Tactical Risk Management   492
Using Risk Management to Reduce
Funding Costs by Acting on
a View   492
Authored Box: Do Corporations Have a
Duty to Hedge?
Daniel P. Cunningham, Cravath,
Swaine & Moore   493
Using Risk Management to Reduce
Funding Costs by "Arbitraging"
the Markets   498
Authored Box: Do Forward Rates Predict
Future Interest Rates?
Greg Hayt, CIBC World
Market   499
Using Risk Management to Reduce Fund-
ing Costs by Reducing Transaction
Costs   500
Using Risk Management to Reduce
Funding Costs by Selling
Options   500
Strategic Risk Management   501
Theory 1—Risk Management Can
Add Value by Decreasing
Taxes   503

Illustration 20–1: Reducing Taxes
with Risk Management   504
Theory 2—Risk Management Can Add
Value by Decreasing Costs of
Financial Distress   505
Illustration 20–2: The Impact of Finan-
cial Risk on Sales: The Case
of Wang   507
Theory 3—Risk Management Can
Add Value by Facilitating
Optimal Investment   507
Illustration 20–3: The Impact of
Volatility on Debt
Capacity   509
Illustration 20–4: Cutting Rate Risk on
Buyout Debt   509
Illustration 20–5: Controlling Underin-
vestment with Hedging   510
Illustration 20–6: The Impact of
Earnings Volatility on Investment—
The Case of Merck   513
Evidence   513

**21   Measuring a Nonfinancial
Firm's Exposure to Financial
Price Risk   518**

Financial Price Risk Reflected in the Firm's
Financial Statements   518
*Authored Box: Risk Management
at British Petroleum
R. K. Hinkley, British
Petroleum   519*
The Balance Sheet   520
Statement of Consolidated Income
and Statement of Changes
in Financial Position   522
Illustration 21–1: Looking for Financial
Price Risk in the Firm's
Balance Sheet   523
The Letter to the Shareholders in the
Annual Report   526
Illustration 21–2: Looking for
Financial Price Risk in the Firm's

Statement of Consolidated
Income   527
Illustration 21–3: Looking for Financial
Price Risk in the Firm's Statement
of Changes in Financial
Position   529
External Measures of Financial
Price Risk   531
Illustration 21–4: Looking for Financial
Price Risk in the Letter to the
Shareholders   532
Box: Duration in the Context of a
Factor Model   534
Internal Measures of Financial
Price Risk   536
Statistical Analysis of Revenues
and Expenses   536
Simulation Analyses—Cash Flow
Sensitivity
VAR Doesn't Fit Many
Nonfinancial Firms   537
The Logic of the Cash Flow
Sensitivity Approach   537
Defining Exposures   539
Box: Framing Exposures   540
Simulating Financial Prices   541
Illustration 21–5: Cash Flow
Sensitivity for a Hypothetical
Manufacturing Firm   544

**22   Implementing a Risk
Management Program   550**

Lessons Learned from the Events
of 1994   550
Losses by Industrial Corporations   550
Codelco   550
Gibson Greetings   550
Box: Leveraged Swaps   551
Procter & Gamble   552
Mead   552
Air Products   552
Federal Paper   552
Caterpillar   552

Lessons Learned 552
  Rule 1: Make Sure You Know How
    Much Is at Risk 553
  Rule 2: Make Sure That Everyone Is
    on the Same Page 553
Designing Effective Policies
  and Procedures 553
Goals for Risk Management 554
Identify and Quantify
  Exposures 557
Define a Risk Management
  Philosophy 558
  "One-Off" or "Integrated"
    Risk Management? 558
    Integrating the Management of
      Different Market Risks 558
    Integrating the Management of
      Market and Property/
      Casualty Risk 558
    Integrating the Management
      of Market Risk throughout
      the Firm 559
    Implementation 559
  Derivatives versus
    "Natural" Hedges 559
    Box: Arguments against Managing
      FX Risk by Matching
      Currencies 560
  Passive versus Active Risk
    Management 560
    Box: "Active" Hedging 560
  Which Instruments? For What
    Purposes? By Whom? In
    What Amounts? 561
Authored Box: Hedging Interest Rate
* Risk without Using Up*
* Bank Lines*
* Roger Burge, Eurotunnel 562*
Counterparties: Who? How
  Much Exposure? 565
  Box: Calculating Credit
    Exposures 566
Evaluate and Control 569
The Role of the Board of Directors 569

Responsibility 1—Approval
  of Policies 569
  Box-G-30 Recommendation 1 570
Responsibility 2—Ensuring
  Capability 570
Responsibility 3—Evaluate
  Performance 570
Responsibility 4—Maintain
  Oversight 571
Some Items for a "Directors'
  Checklist" 573

**23 Uses of Risk Management Products
by Banks and Other Financial
Institutions 576**

Asset-Liability Management 576
  Measuring the Institution's Exposure
    to Interest Rate Risk 577
    Cash Flow Exposures—
      Maturity Gap 577
    Illustration 23–1: Using Financial
      Statement Data to Quantify the Im-
      pact of Interest Rate Changes
      on a Bank's Net Interest Income:
      The "Gap" Methodology 577
    Value Exposures—Duration
      and Convexity 579
      Illustration 23–2: Using Market Data
        to Quantify the Impact
        of Interest Rate Changes
        on the Value of a Bank's Portfolio
        or Equity 581
  Managing Cash Flow Risk 584
    Rate Mismatches 584
    Maturity Mismatches 585
  Managing Value Risk 585
    Changing the Duration of
      the Portfolio 585
      Illustration 23–3: Using an Interest
        Rate Swap to Change the Dura-
        tion of a Portfolio 586
    Changing the Convexity of
      the Portfolio 587

Hedging Callable Bonds   587
Hedging Mortgages or
    Mortgage-Backed Securities   588
The Impact on the Financial
    Institution   589
The Investment Portfolio   589
The Credit Portfolio   591
Applying Modern Portfolio Theory to the
    Loan Book   591
    ASIDE: CreditMetrics   592
Using Credit Derivatives to Restructure
    the Loan Book   597

**24   Uses of Risk Management Products
by Institutional Investors   599**

*Authored Box: Integrating Risk Management
    and Strategy
    Lisa K. Polsky, Morgan Stanley   605*
Using Derivatives in Portfolio
    Construction   608
Using Derivatives in Strategic
    Asset Allocation   608
Using Derivatives for Portfolio
    Rebalancing   608
    ASIDE: Using Derivatives to Re-
        balance a Portfolio   609
Using Derivatives for Alpha
    Transport   610
    ASIDE: Alpha   610
Using Derivatives to Satisfy
    Constraints   611
*Authored Box: Using Derivatives
    to Optimize a Portfolio
    Claude R. Lamoureaux and
    Robert G. Bertram,
    Ontario Teachers' Pension Plan   612*
Using Derivatives in Tactical or Insured
    Asset Allocation   614
    Tactical Asset Allocation   614
    Insured Asset Allocation
        (a.k.a. *Portfolio Insurance*)   614
        ASIDE: Using Derivatives in In-
            sured Asset Allocation   616

Using Derivatives to Reduce the Riskiness
    of the Portfolio   617
Using Derivatives to Reduce Interest
    Rate Risk   617
    Protecting Future Cash
        Flows   618
    Protecting the Value of a
        Bond   618
    Asset-Liability Management   619
Using Derivatives to Reduce Foreign
    Exchange Rate Risk   619
*Authored Box: Should FX Be Treated
    as an Asset Class?
    Ronald G. Layard-Liesching,
    Pareto Partners   620*
    Illustration 24–1: Using Derivatives to
        Hedge Currency Risk   622
Using Derivatives to Reduce Asset Price
    Risk—Equity Price Risk   622
Using Derivatives to Increase the Expected
    Return of the Portfolio   626
By Reducing Transaction Costs   626
By Exploiting Mispricing,
    i.e., Arbitrage   628
        ASIDE: Using Derivatives to Ex-
            ploit Mispricing   629
By Accessing Otherwise Unavailable
    Assets   630
By Using Derivatives to Implementing a
    View More Effectively   630
Concluding Remarks   634
    Controls   634
    Obligations?   636
*Authored Box: A Fiduciary Duty to Use
    Derivatives?
    George Crawford,
    Stanford Law School   637*

References   644

Index   654

1

THE EVOLUTION OF RISK MANAGEMENT PRODUCTS*

Unpredictable movements in exchange rates, interest rates, and commodity prices not only can affect a firm's reported quarterly earnings but even may determine whether a firm survives. Over the past two decades, firms have been increasingly challenged by such financial price risks. It's no longer enough to be the firm with the most advanced production technology, the cheapest labor supply, or the best marketing team; price volatility can put even well-run firms out of business.

Changes in exchange rates can create strong new competitors. Similarly, fluctuations in commodity prices can drive input prices to the point that substitute products—products made from different inputs—become more affordable to end consumers. Changes in interest rates can put pressure on the firm's costs: firms whose sales are hurt by higher interest rates may find themselves in financial distress as sales plummet and borrowing costs skyrocket.

Not surprisingly, the financial markets have responded to increasing price volatility. A range of financial instruments and strategies that can be used to manage the resulting exposures to financial price risk have evolved over the past 20 years.

At one level, financial instruments now exist that permit the direct transfer of financial price risk to a third party more willing to accept that risk. For example, with the development of foreign exchange futures contracts, a U.S. exporter can transfer its foreign exchange risk to a firm with the opposite exposure or to a firm in the business of managing foreign exchange risk, leaving the exporter free to focus on its core business.

At another level, the financial markets have evolved to the point that financial instruments can be combined with a debt issue to unbundle financial price risk from the other risks inherent in the process of raising capital. For example, by

---

*This chapter is based on Rawls and Smithson (1989).

coupling their bond issues with swaps, issuing firms are able to separate interest rate risk from traditional credit risk.[1]

The World Becomes a Riskier Place

There is general agreement that the financial environment is riskier today than it was in the past. Figure 1–1 provides some dramatic evidence of the change in the form of what must be regarded as long price series, the retail price index for England from 1666 to the mid-1980s. From the 17th century until the late 20th century, the price level in England was essentially stable. Prices did go up during wartime; the data series reflects conflicts like the one the British had with "that French person" in the early 19th century, but prices fell to prewar levels once the conflict ended.

In marked contrast, the price history for the second half of the 20th century indicates that the financial environment has changed. For the first time, prices have gone up—and stayed up. This phenomenon is evident not only for the United Kingdom; a similar pattern of price-level behavior exists for the United States, albeit, as our British colleagues point out, with fewer data points. (See Figure 1–2.) In fact, during this period of general uncertainty, the developed economies generally have begun to experience unexpected price changes—primarily increases.

In short, financial markets have been confronted by increased price uncertainty. Growing uncertainty about inflation has been quickly followed by uncertainty about foreign exchange rates, interest rates, and commodity prices.

FIGURE 1–1   Retail Price Index for England from the 17th to the 20th Century (1850 = 100)

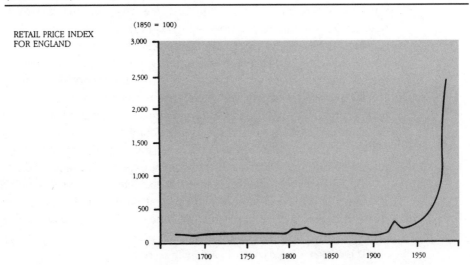

RETAIL PRICE INDEX
FOR ENGLAND

FIGURE 1-2　U.S. Price Index, 1800–1996

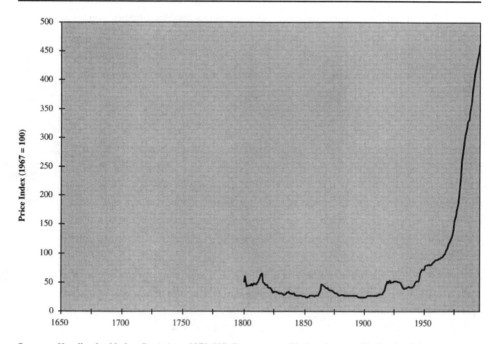

SOURCE: *Handbook of Labor Statistics—1973,* US. Department of Labor, Bureau of Labor Statistics.

Volatility of Foreign Exchange Rates

Figure 1–3 shows monthly percentage changes in the U.S. dollar-deutsche mark exchange rate since 1960. This figure clearly indicates that the foreign exchange market has become riskier. What is equally evident is the reason for the increased volatility of foreign exchange rates in the early 1970s: the breakdown of the Bretton Woods system of fixed exchange rates.[2]

Under the fixed exchange rate system of Bretton Woods, importers knew what they would pay for goods in their domestic currency, and exporters knew how much they would receive in their local currency. If the importer could sell at a profit to the consumer, and the exporter's costs were below the export price, then gains from trade were had by all.

With the breakdown of Bretton Woods, the rules have changed. Both sides to the transaction now face exchange rate risk. Each firm wants to transact in its own currency to prevent being "whipsawed" by the market. Importers' profit margins can, and often have, evaporated if their currency weakens sharply and the imported goods are priced in the exporter's currency.

FIGURE 1–3   Percent Change in U.S. Dollar-Deutsche Mark Exchange Rate (Month End)

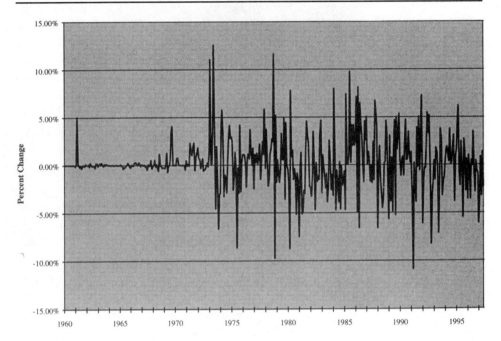

SOURCE: CIBC Economics Division.

Volatility of Interest Rates

Surprisingly, the increased volatility evident in the foreign exchange market did not spill over into the U.S. domestic money market at first. Indeed, compared with the early 1970s, interest rates actually became more stable immediately after the collapse of the Bretton Woods accord. As shown in Figure 1–4, interest rate volatility[3] declined during the period 1977–79, even though interest rates were rising in response to the inflation rate.

However, as illustrated in Figure 1–4, uncertainty hit U.S. interest rates with a vengeance in the early 1980s. On October 6, 1979, newly appointed Federal Reserve Board Chairman Paul Volcker abandoned the Fed practice of targeting interest rates and began to target money supply growth instead. As a consequence, interest rates became extremely volatile.

Volatility of Commodity Prices

In Figure 1–5, we have illustrated the volatility in the price of the benchmark crude oil—West Texas Intermediate (WTI)—between 1960 and 1996. Prior to 1973,

FIGURE 1–4   First Difference in Five-Year U.S. Treasury Rate (Month End)

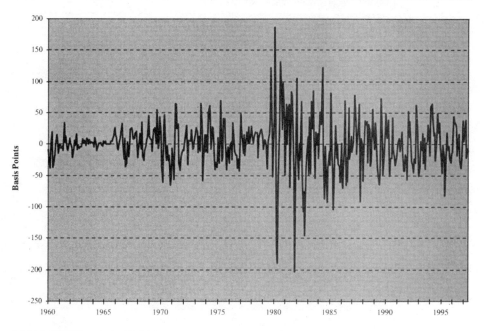

SOURCE: CIBC Economics Division.

there was no change in the price. And even during the 1970s and early 1980s, the changes in the price of WTI were episodic—the spike in 1973 reflects the effect of the oil embargo; the smaller set of spikes in 1979–80 reflects the effects of the Iran-Iraq war. The increase in general volatility in the mid-1980s coincides with the deregulation of oil prices in the United States. The most recent spike (in 1990) reflects the effect of the invasion of Kuwait by Iraq.

Of the commodities, the graph for U.S. oil prices is the most extreme—from *no* volatility to a volatility that is higher than that for foreign exchange or interest rates. But the same kind of behavior can be observed for the basic commodities in general. The volatility of commodity prices increased in the 1970s and 1980s.

The Impact of Increased Financial Price Risk on Firms

Over the past eight years, we have talked to hundreds of managers about the way that they view their firms' exposures to financial price risk. We have heard about several very different kinds of risk.

FIGURE 1–5   **Percentage Change in Price of West Texas Intermediate Crude Oil (Posted Prices, Beginning of Month)**

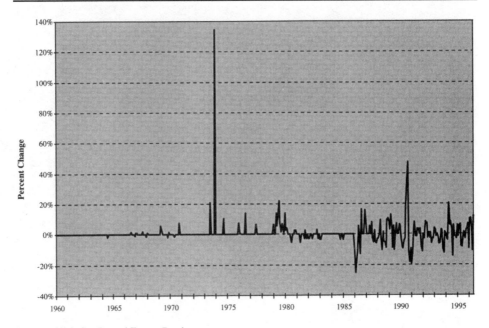

SOURCE: Oil & Gas Journal Energy Database.

Virtually every firm considers accounting-based exposures—those exposures that would be reflected directly in the firm's financial statements. Within these accounting-based exposures, *transaction exposures* receive the most attention. A transaction exposure exists when a change in one of the financial prices will change the amount of a receipt or an expense. Obviously, the amount of a transaction—a receipt or an expense—would be determined by price per unit and the number of units sold or purchased:

$$\text{Receipt or expense} = P \times Q \qquad (1\text{--}1)$$

Transaction exposures focus on only the direct effect of a price change—the impact of price changes on quantity is ignored.

Traditionally, the accounting profession has focused only on those transaction exposures where the transaction is a "firm commitment." However, a number of firms have transactions that, while not committed, are predictable with a high degree of certainty—for example, a firm that has been doing business through its subsidiary in Germany for the past 20 years knows with a great deal of certainty how many deutsche marks it will receive in each of the four quarters of next year. The

Financial Accounting Standards Board recognizes this as well and is considering the degree to which it would be willing to permit hedge accounting for "forecasted transactions."

Moving beyond the strict accounting-based exposures, some firms have begun to consider their *economic exposures*—also referred to as *competitive exposures.* In the context of Equation 1–1, changes in foreign exchange rates or interest rates or commodity prices will change the firm's receipts or expenditures not only because of the direct price change but also because the price change will change the amount that the firm sells or buys. This view of financial price risk recognizes changes in foreign exchange rates, interest rates, or commodity prices on the firm's sales and market share and then on the firm's net profits (net cash flows).

Whether the exposure is accounting-based or economic, changes in foreign exchange rates, interest rates, or commodity prices can change the real cash flows of the firm. The increased volatility in financial prices evident in the 1970s has led more firms to recognize their exposures to financial price risk.

Unfortunately, other firms have been forced to recognize their exposures the hard way: exposures to financial prices have caused them financial difficulties or, in some cases, put them out of business.

Exchange Rate Risk

In the context of foreign exchange rate risk, transaction exposures have received the lion's share of attention. A transaction exposure will often lead to trouble when there is a mismatch in revenues and expenses. A classic example—the one cited by almost every risk management marketer we have ever met—is Laker Airlines:

Illustration 1–1

Laker Airlines an FX Risk*

In the late 1970s, Laker Airlines had a problem, but it was a problem we all might like to have—there were more British vacationers lining up for Laker's flights than he had seats to fill. (At the time, the U.S. dollar was weak, so a U.S. vacation was a bargain). Freddie Laker solved the problem by buying five more DC-10s, financing them in U.S. dollars.

Laker Airlines' revenues were primarily in pounds—from those British vacationers— but the payments for the new DC-10s were in dollars. The result for Laker Airlines was a mismatch on revenues and expenses.

Laker Airlines an FX Risk continued

In 1981, the U.S. dollar strengthened, and the FX transaction exposure became evident as Laker's expenses increased. With the stronger dollar, Laker had to pay more pounds to make the payments on the debt. While not the only factor, this FX transaction exposure contributed in sending Laker into bankruptcy.[†]

*This illustration was taken from a story in *Business Week* (1982) and from Millman (1988).

[†]And we haven't told you all the story. Laker Airlines also had an economic exposure. With the stronger dollar, U.S. vacations were no longer the "bargain" they had been in the late 1970s, so at the same time Laker's expenses were increasing, revenues were declining.

Foreign exchange transaction exposures would be reflected in the firm's income statement. (We will look at some of the ways in which exposures are reflected in accounting data in Chapter 20.) A parallel exposure—one that also focuses only on the direct effects of a price change—that would be reflected in the firm's balance sheet is referred to as a *translation exposure*. A translation exposure reflects the change in the value of the firm as foreign assets are converted to home currency. Most of the firms we have talked with make a point of noting that they do not manage translation exposures.[4]

The evidence indicates very clearly that changes in foreign exchange rates can have a significant negative impact on a firm's ability to compete. Another classic illustration—indeed, the companion piece to the Laker Airlines story in the risk management marketer's litany of horror stories—is the Caterpillar story:

Illustration 1–2

Caterpillar's FX Whammy*

Throughout the early 1980s, Caterpillar cited the strong dollar as the primary cause of its difficulties. As the 1982 annual report put it,

> The strong dollar is a prime factor in Caterpillar's reduced sales and earnings. . . .

As the dollar strengthened relative to the yen, the price of Caterpillar equipment rose relative to Komatsu equipment, giving Komatsu a competitive advantage on Caterpillar.

*This illustration was adapted from Hutchins (1986).

And versions of the Caterpillar story continue to be repeated. In the early 1990s, competitive exposures related to the yen–dollar exchange rate were again in the news, only the competitive exposure was the other way around. By 1995, the trend in the yen-dollar exchange rate had reversed yet again. And we were back to stories about U.S. firms reporting difficulties.

Illustration 1–3

A Summer of Discontent for Japanese Manufacturers

Beginning in 1985, the U.S. dollar began a long slide. As the following figure illustrates, the value of the dollar (i.e., yen per dollar) fell almost continually for a decade.

Japanese Yen–U.S. Dollar Exchange Rate—January 1984–May 1995
(Yen per dollar at beginning of month)

SOURCE: Datastream.

By early 1993, the dollar had fallen to the 113–114 yen per dollar range. And as was reported by the *New York Times,* the weakening dollar was beginning to hurt Japanese firms that export to the United States. The *Times* noted that Japanese manufacturers would have to "take stern measures to reduce their costs and to improve their efficiency." Singled out was Toyota Motor Corporation.

A Summer of Discontent for Japanese Manufacturers continued

The New York Times

Rising Yen Rings Alarms in Tokyo

By JAMES STERNGOLD

Special to The New York Times

TOKYO, April 6 — For most of the last two months, the Japanese yen has been edging up in value to its strongest level of the postwar era, sending waves of anxiety through the Government and the business world.

The dollar fell to 113.40 yen at one point here on Friday, closing at 114. Some experts say it could plummet soon to 100 yen, less than half its value a decade ago.

Slight Gain in New York

On Monday, the dollar slipped to 113.70 in New York, its third consecutive postwar low. Today, the dollar recovered a bit, rising to 113.85 yen in New York. [Page D18.]

The dollar's steep drop has set off alarms here, with some experts arguing that the rising yen threatens the Japanese economy's fragile recovery and could undermine markets from Tokyo to Wall Street. But after a month of fretting, others are concluding that the stronger yen could ultimately prove an economic boon, giving Japanese consumers price breaks from cheaper imports they have long been denied.

Japan's soaring trade surplus and a sharp decline in the country's overseas investments are believed to be

A weak dollar is having a big impact on Japanese business.

among the reasons for the yen's strength. The dollar has lost around 8 percent of its value against the yen this year, and that decline is already having a big impact on corporate policies.

The Toyota Motor Corporation is said to be preparing to slice some $700 million from its production costs in the next few months; the Sharp Corporation has said it will move all its personal computer production out of Japan to lower costs, and the Daiei Corporation, a leading retailer, has said that for the first time it will substitute less expensive imported suits from China for some Japanese made suits.

The yen's rise comes as a harsh blow to Japanese exporters in particular, because Japanese goods are becoming more expensive for Americans and other foreigners. But it helps American companies, which is why the Clinton Administration has

largely supported the movement.

Less demand for Japanese goods is expected to force manufacturers to take stern measures to reduce their costs and to improve their efficiency, difficult steps at a time when profits have been battered by an economic slowdown. The Industrial Bank of Japan has estimated that the stronger yen could reduce economic growth as much as half a percentage point this year.

The uncertainty over exchange-rate movements also disrupts Japanese investment plans overseas. Some experts worry that the unease could encourage a flight of Japanese capital from America back to Japan. The value of American securities has already dropped sharply in terms of the yen, in many instances below what the investors paid for them.

'One Big Risk'

"The one big risk is a chain reaction of fear if Japanese investors decide they have to get out of dollar assets," Richard Koo, a senior economist at the Nomura Research Institute, said. "At these exchange rates, all the dollar-denominated paper they own is under water, and there is already some inclination to sell now before the exchange rate gets worse. That could become scary."

Japanese Government officials had clearly supported the yen's apprecia-

Copyright © 1993 by the New York Times Company. Reprinted by permission.

The *Asian Wall Street Journal* reported that Japanese manufacturers had large foreign exchange "bets" on the table. They were not hedging their foreign exchange exposure, expecting—betting—that the dollar would recover.

THE ASIAN WALL STREET JOURNAL.

    WEDNESDAY, JUNE 9, 1993, PAGE 9

MONEY AND INVESTING

Most Japanese Firms Hold Off Hedging Their Currency Needs

By July 1993, Japanese exports of automobiles were 14 percent below the level of a year before. And the *Wall Street Journal* was reporting that Standard & Poor's was considering a downgrade for Toyota, Nissan, and Honda. As the *Journal* noted, "Japan's economic slump and the yen's strengthening against the dollar . . . have hurt the companies' profits, leading

Interest Rate Risk

Transaction exposures are normally associated with foreign exchange rate risk. However, changes in interest rates can also have the same kind of impact on accounting statement income. While changes in interest rates could impact either receipts or expenses, most firms focus on interest expense. Perhaps the most widely cited example of interest rate transaction exposures—the interest rate counterpart to the Laker Airlines and Caterpillar stories—is the experience of the U.S. savings and loan association industry (S&Ls).

And changes in interest rates can also result in economic exposures. In contrast to interest rate transaction exposures, where we focus on the firm's expenses, interest rate economic exposures are somewhat more likely to be observed on receipts— changes in interest rates can change the quantities that the firm sells.[5]

Commodity-Price Risk

Our experience has been that firms are more likely to distinguish between *transaction* and *economic* exposures for foreign exchange rates and interest rates than for commodity prices.[6] Despite this hazy characterization, firms can be confronted with exposures to commodity prices. Such exposures moved from being possible in theory to being a reality with the spike in oil prices during the Iraq–Kuwait

Illustration 1–4

Time To Blame FX?*

The U.S. dollar reached a low of 80.63 yen per dollar in April 1995 and then began a strengthening that continued through the summer of 1997 (when this edition was being assembled).

Japanese Yen–U.S. Dollar Exchange Rate—January 1995–August 1997
(Yen per dollar at beginning of month)

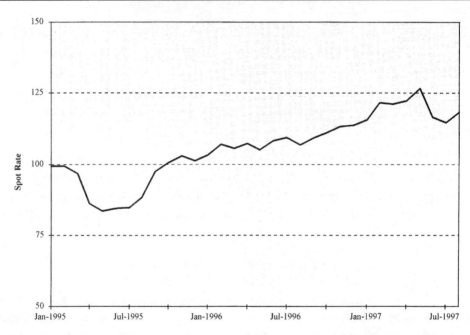

SOURCE: Datastream.

Not surprisingly, the "FX Whammy" we described in Illustration 1–2 reappeared for U.S. firms.

The pharmaceutical industry, an industry whose home-currency earnings are particularly sensitive to exchange rates, began to make statements similar to those made by Caterpillar in the early 1980s. Bristol-Myers Squibb noted to its shareholders that the growth of the U.S. dollar value of its sales had been adversely impacted by the strengthening dollar: "Sales for the quarter grew 10% (12%

excluding the unfavorable effect of foreign exchange). . . ." Eli Lilly went a little further to note that the strengthening dollar had a competitive impact, as well as a translation effect: "International pharmaceutical sales decreased 5% with volume growth of 6% being offset by an 8% unfavorable exchange rate comparison and a 3% reduction in selling price."[†]

The president of General Motors Corporation's North American Operations declared that the only cloud on the horizon for U.S. automakers was "the growing undervaluation of the Japanese yen." Indeed, Honda and Toyota were posting record sales in the United States.

However, in other U.S. industries, the complaints about the exchange rate were muted.

The impact of the strengthening dollar on many American firms had been cushioned by the productivity gains in the industry and by the fact that U.S. firms had moved operations offshore.

---

[*]This illustration is based on an article of the same name authored by Joseph Neu in the April 28, 1997, issue of *International Treasurer* and on "Who's Afraid of the Dollar?" *Business Week,* February 24, 1997.

[†]Notably absent from this list is Merck. As we will note several times in this text, Merck has undertaken a program of financial price risk management to avoid the impact of foreign exchange movements on its cash flows.

Illustration 1–5

From Money Machines to Money Pits: U.S. S&Ls

In the 1970s, S&Ls looked like money machines. The U.S. yield curve was upward sloping—and had been for as long as most of the S&L bankers could remember. In such an environment, S&Ls could earn a steady profit by making long-term fixed-rate mortgage loans and financing these assets by taking in short-term passbook deposits. Looking at the income statement, the S&Ls' receipts would be insensitive to interest rate changes, but changes in the short-term interest rate would have a direct effect on expenses—increases in rates would lead to increases in expenses. The S&Ls had a significant interest rate transaction exposure. But in the 1970s, the market was going their way and the big interest rate bet was paying off for the S&Ls.

In the 1980s the market turned against the S&Ls. The yield curve inverted—short-term interest rates rose dramatically—and S&Ls changed from money machines to money pits. The short-term rates the S&Ls had to pay on their passbook deposits exceeded the fixed rate they were receiving on their loans to homeowners.

Illustration 1–6

Inherent Exposures to Interest Rates:
Residential Construction

The firms that construct residential real estate and the firms that supply materials and fixtures to these construction firms are inherently exposed to interest rate risk—regardless of the manner in which the firms are financed. One of the primary determinants of the demand for housing is the level of interest rates. When interest rates are high, the demand for housing declines (and may decline dramatically). Consequently, the net incomes reported by the construction firms and their suppliers will move inversely with interest rates.

The *New York Times* provided a concrete example of this situation when it reported on the problems that the USG Corporation—the big Chicago-based maker of gypsum wall-

board—faced in 1991.* In 1991, U.S. interest rates were high and the real estate market was depressed. Consequently, the demand for USG's main product, Sheetrock, had tumbled.

And it wasn't enough that USG's revenues were low. In 1988, USG had beat back a hostile takeover by taking on increased debt. Therefore, high interest rates meant not only that revenues were decreased, but also that the interest expense on the floating-rate portion of USG's debt increased. As the *Times* put it, USG was choking on its borrowings.

---

*"USG's Struggle to Buy Time," by Eric N. Berg, *The New York Times* (Market Place column), March 20, 1991.

conflict in 1990. These transaction exposures to oil prices appeared in the firms' income statements via increased receipts for producer firms or increased expenses for the firms that use oil.

Illustration 1–7

A Gulf War Casualty: Continental Airlines*

On August 2, 1990, Iraq invaded Kuwait. By October, the price of jet fuel had more than doubled from its preinvasion level, and Continental Airlines was certainly feeling the pinch. Continental's fuel costs in October

were $81 million higher than they had been in June. This extra fuel expense hit Continental particularly hard because it was also servicing an extremely high debt load. (Continental's debt/capital ratio was almost twice

---

A Gulf War Casualty: Continental Airlines continued

the industry average.) On October 24 Continental announced a management shakeup and plans to sell some of its jets and routes to stem the red ink but said that it had "no intention of filing for bankruptcy protection."[†]

While fuel costs moderated a little in November, they were still 80 percent higher than the preinvasion levels.

On December 3, 1990, Continental Airlines visited the U.S. Bankruptcy Court—for a second time[‡]—filing for Chapter 11 protection from its creditors. Continental Airlines emerged from Chapter 11 protection in April 1993. Press reports suggested that Continental had taken pains not to make the same mistake again. Oil prices moved up again in 1996; this time Continental Airlines was "applauded for successfully hedging against soaring jet fuel costs."[‡] By hedging its fuel costs, Continental

Airlines was able to remain profitable even when the price of one its major inputs rose dramatically.

Reprinted by permission of *The Wall Street Journal* © 1990 Dow Jones & Company, Inc. All Rights Reserved Worldwide.

*This illustration is based on a story that appeared in *The New York Times:* "Continental Bankruptcy Study Seen," October 24, 1990, and two stories in *The Wall Street Journal:* "Troubled Continental Plans Asset Sales," October 24, 1990, and "Debt-Burdened Continental Air, Citing Rising Fuel Costs, Files Under Chapter 11," December 4, 1990.

[†]*The New York Times,* Wednesday, October 24, 1990.

[‡]Continental Airlines had sought protection from its creditors in September 1983.

[‡]Reuters, January 21, 1997.

The Forecasters Flunk

So far, we have told you two facts: First, in the 1970s and 1980s, financial prices became more volatile. Second, this increased financial price volatility has had a detrimental impact on a number of firms.

It is not surprising that senior management at a number of firms decided to solve the problem by getting better forecasts for the various financial prices. While we weren't privy to the meetings, we believe that the decision at many U.S. multinationals must have gone something like:

> If the deutsche mark–U.S. dollar exchange rate is more volatile, and if increases (or decreases) in this rate could have a significant impact on the viability of my firm, then I need to get more accurate forecasts about the DM–USD exchange rate.

However, as the following set of clippings from the mid-1980s demonstrated, this was easier said than done.

The Forecasters Flunk

Poor predictions give once prestigious pundits a dismal reputation

"I'm thinking of quitting and becoming a hockey goalie"   TIME, August 27, 1984

THE WALL STREET JOURNAL, TUESDAY, OCTOBER 16, 1984

Maybe Economists Should Be a Little Less Positive

BY DOUGLAS L. BENDT AND CAROLYNE LOCHHEAD

THE ECONOMIST'S NEW CLOTHES

Economic forecasters have fallen into disrepute because they keep trying to do the impossible.

■ Economists and economics have taken a lot of heat recently. What sensible business men have long suspected is now obvious: the economist has no clothes

In trying to predict the future values for foreign exchange rates, interest rates, and commodity prices, the forecasters flunked. The mid-1980s was a particularly active period of "economist bashing," but pointing out the errors in economists' forecasts is a pastime that continues.

Nonetheless, we do not find this lack of success in forecasting exchange rates, interest rates, and commodity prices to be at all surprising. The markets for these financial prices are all markets that would be characterized as *efficient markets.* An efficient market is a market characterized by:

A homogeneous product.

Liquid primary and secondary markets (i.e., a large number of market participants and the ability of the participants to enter and exit the market freely).

The ability to contract for current delivery or for delivery at some date in the future.

Low transactions (e.g., contracting) costs.

In an efficient market, the price of the commodity or asset reflects all currently available public information. In such an environment, price *changes* will be random. And if price changes are random, there is no way to accurately forecast prices. To see how this works, let's look at a market that has the characteristics of an efficient market.

As Illustration 1–8 indicates, you are unlikely to be successful trying to outpredict an efficient market. In an efficient market, the best forecast of the price in the future is the price today.

> In an efficient market, the price of the commodity or asset reflects all currently available public information. In such a market, price changes are random, so the best forecast of the future price is the current market price.

Illustration 1–8

Making Millions Trading Wheat Futures

A recent addition to the American scene (and one we have seen nowhere else in the world) is The Weather Channel—a 24-hour cable channel devoted entirely to weather reports. Basic economics tells us that the market price of wheat must be determined by the demand for and supply of wheat. And since the supply of wheat is in large part determined by weather conditions, shouldn't we be able to use those weather forecasts from The Weather Channel to make money?

More specifically, let's devise a trading strategy: If The Weather Channel forecasts bad weather (e.g., hail in Kansas), we will contract to buy wheat in the future at the price prevailing today. Then, when the bad weather conditions reduce the supply of wheat, the price of wheat will consequently rise. And (here comes the good part) when our contract matures, we will accept delivery of the wheat at the low price we contracted for today and immediately sell it at a higher price.

How much money would you expect to make on this strategy? (If you said anything greater than zero, write us, because we have some land deals to offer you.) The problem with this simple trading strategy is that it is based on available public information, while today's wheat price already reflects all of the available public information. As soon as any new information relevant to wheat is available, it will be reflected in wheat prices. What then will change the price of wheat? It follows from everything we have said so far that wheat prices will change when the available information changes.

The upshot is that if we want to be able to predict wheat prices, we need to be able to predict the new information *before it is available*. And if new information is really "new," it must be random. So predicting wheat prices would require us to predict a random variable.

There are people who have made a million in the futures market. But with the strategy we proposed above—one with trades based on available public information—the one who is making the millions is the broker executing the trades. In trying to predict the market, the forecasters flunked.

The very things that economists are usually called on to predict are the prices of assets or commodities traded in markets that are very efficient—the money markets (interest rates), foreign exchange markets (foreign exchange rates), and commodity markets (the prices of gold, copper, wheat, and so on). Therefore, it is not very surprising that economists have not done very well at forecasting these prices.

Note, however, that our illustration does not mean that it is impossible to make money in an efficient market. (Indeed, in our example our broker did make money.[7]) However, our example implies that one way to make money is to be the first one to get the information—to get the weather forecast. Such a line of reasoning might lead you to suspect that maybe it is the weather forecasters who are making the killings in the commodity markets. This line of reasoning caused the following headline from the *Wall Street Journal* to jump off the page at us.*

Some Meteorologists Reap Windfall from Crop Futures Markets

Since forecasting did not solve the problem of financial price risk, the firms that were confronted with financial price risk turned to methods of transferring the risk, the topic we explore next.

The Markets' Response: Tools to Manage Financial Price Risk

Exchange Rate Risk Management Products

Foreign exchange forward contracts have been available for decades. But not surprisingly, it was only in the early 1970s that this financial instrument came into its own. In Chapters 2 and 4 we will demonstrate that a forward contract involves the extension of credit. Consequently, by the 1970s the forward foreign exchange market had become primarily an interbank market, and for this reason, many firms confronted with foreign exchange risk were unable to take advantage of the forward market.

As illustrated in Figure 1–6, the financial market responded to the need for greater access to the forward market by creating a range of risk management instruments. The first to appear was futures contracts on foreign exchange. In May 1972, the International Monetary Market of the Chicago Mercantile Exchange (CME) began trading futures contracts on the British pound, Canadian dollar, deutsche mark, Japanese yen, Swiss franc, and French franc.[8]

Currency swaps were next to appear. In Chapter 8, we will note that precursors to swaps, such as back-to-back and parallel loans, had been used since the onset of volatility in foreign exchange rates. However, the World Bank–IBM swap of August 1981 is generally regarded as the public introduction of currency swaps.

Option contracts on foreign exchange followed closely on the heels of swaps. In December 1982, the Philadelphia Stock Exchange introduced an option contract on the British pound, which was followed by options on the Canadian dollar, deutsche mark, Japanese yen, and Swiss franc in January and February 1983.[9]

The Chicago Mercantile Exchange followed with the introduction of options on foreign exchange futures in these currencies:

---

*From the Tuesday, July 13, 1993 "Money & Investing" column, *The Wall Street Journal.* Reprinted by permission of *The Wall Street Journal* © 1993 Dow Jones & Company, Inc. All Rights Reserved Worldwide.

FIGURE 1-6   Evolution of Exchange Rate Risk Management Tools

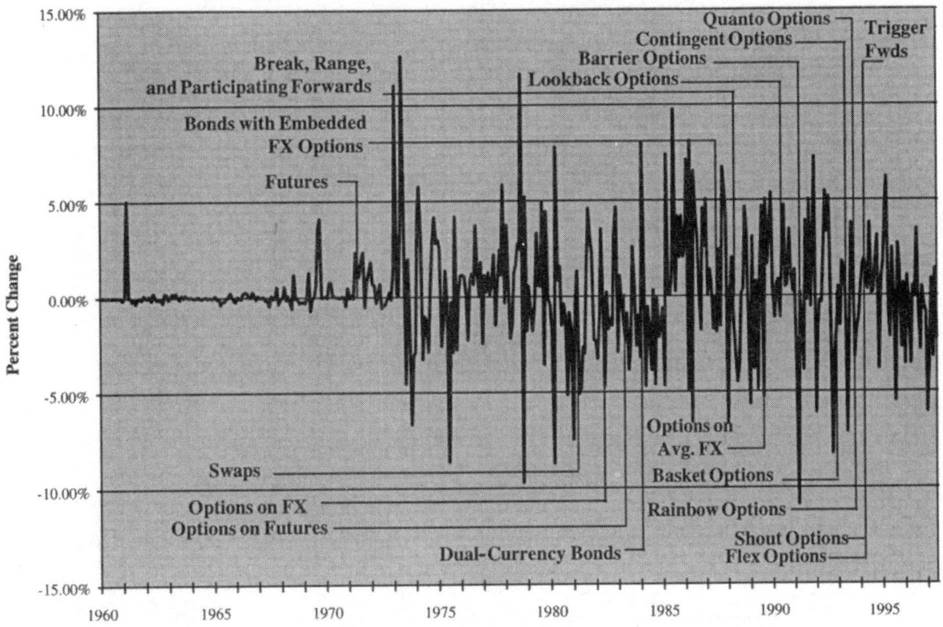

Percent change in U.S. dollar—
Deutsche mark exchange rate (month-end).

Deutsche mark and French francs, January 1984;
British pound and Swiss franc, February 1985;
Brazilian real, November 1985;
Japanese yen, March 1986; and
Canadian dollar, June 1986.[10]

Commercial banks responded by offering their clients over-the-counter foreign exchange options. As we will describe in Chapter 15, the banks also created forward foreign exchange contracts with optionlike characteristics. Break forwards, range forwards, and participating forwards had all entered the market lexicon by 1987.

Once the market had developed the basic building blocks—forwards, futures, swaps, and options—the next step was to introduce combinations of the building blocks and more complex forms of the basic instruments.

In Chapters 13 and 14 we will examine the evolution of more complex forms of the instruments. In Figure 1-6, we have illustrated the appearance of path-dependent options—options on average exchange rates, lookback options, barrier options, and contingent options—and multifactor options—rainbow options, quanto options, and basket options—in the 1990s.

In addition to the financial instruments themselves, rising foreign exchange rate volatility spawned a number of the "hybrid securities." We will discuss these in Chapter 15. Hybrid securities can be viewed as a combination of a standard debt instrument and one or more of the financial instruments. In Figure 1–6 we note the introduction of dual-currency bonds[11] in 1984 and bonds with embedded foreign exchange options in 1987.

Interest Rate Risk Management Products

As uncertainty about interest rates increased in the 1970s, financial institutions became less willing to make long-term rate commitments. Instead, lenders turned to floating-rate loans, which first appeared after the period of rising rates and volatility in 1973–74 and had become widely used by the 1980s.

Floating-rate loans helped banks and S&Ls manage their exposure to interest rate movements, but only by passing the interest rate risk to the borrower.[12] Better tools for managing interest rate risk were required, and as indicated in Figure 1–7, they were not long in coming.

In contrast to the foreign exchange market, there had been no long-established forward market for interest rates. Consequently, financial futures were the first fi-

FIGURE 1–7   Evolution of Interest Rate Risk Management Tools

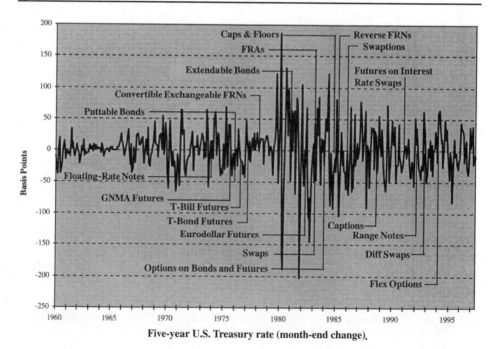

Five-year U.S. Treasury rate (month-end change).

nancial instrument designed to help firms manage their interest rate risk. The progression of futures contracts on U.S. dollar interest rates introduced on the Chicago Board of Trade (CBOT) and the Chicago Mercantile Exchange is presented below:

First Day Trading	Underlying Asset	Exchange
October 1975	GNMA	CBOT
January 1976	U.S. T-bills	CME
August 1977	U.S. T-bonds	CBOT
December 1981	Eurodollar	CME
May 1982	T-notes	CBOT

Although the futures exchanges had established a large lead in the field of interest rate risk management products, banks responded to the demand for these products in the 1980s. Interest rate swaps came first, in 1982. Then in early 1983 banks provided the missing forward market for interest rates with the introduction of forward-rate agreements (FRAs).

As was the pattern in the foreign exchange markets, the introduction of options followed quickly. Option contracts on the U.S. Treasury bonds and notes appeared on the Chicago Board Options Exchange (CBOE). Options on futures on the underlying asset were introduced on both the CBOT and the CME:

First Day Trading	Underlying Asset	Exchange
October 1982	T-bond futures	CBOT
October 1982	T-bond	CBOE
March 1985	Eurodollar futures	CME
May 1985	T-note futures	CBOT
July 1985	T-notes	CBOE
April 1986	T-bill futures	CME

And again as in the case of foreign exchange, banks responded to the exchanges by introducing interest rate options in over-the-counter form: caps, floors, and collars began to appear in 1983. As we will describe in Chapter 14, caps, floors, and collars are combinations of individual interest rate options. In other words, a two-year cap on three-month LIBOR is made up of seven options on three-month LIBOR, one with a maturity of three months, one with a maturity of six months, and so on until the final option, which has a maturity of 21 months.

As was the case with foreign exchange risk management products, we also saw the introduction of *hybrid securities,* debt with embedded interest rate risk management derivatives. In Figure 1–7, we note a few of the hybrids we will examine in Chapter 15: puttable bonds in 1976, convertible/exchangeable floating-rate notes in 1985, extendable bonds in 1982, and inverse floating-rate notes in 1986.

Most recently, we have seen the introduction of combinations and more complex forms of the basic interest rate risk management products: swaptions (an option on a swap), captions (an option on an interest rate cap), futures on interest rate swaps, and diff swaps (swaps on the differential between two interest rates). These instruments will be described in Chapter 14.

Commodity-Price Risk Management Products

As they did with foreign exchange and interest rates, financial markets responded to the increased commodity-price risk with new instruments. The evolution of financial instruments to manage petroleum price risk is traced in Figure 1–8.

Given the preponderance of long-term contracting in the oil industry, forward contracts per se had never been a significant feature of the petroleum market. But as oil prices became more volatile, futures contracts were not long in appearing. Heating oil futures appeared on the New York Mercantile Exchange (NYMEX) in November 1978, and futures on West Texas Intermediate (WTI) crude oil appeared there in March 1983.

And as with all the other risk management markets we have observed, options followed quickly. Options on WTI crude oil futures were introduced in November 1986, and options on heating oil futures followed in June 1987.

FIGURE 1–8   Evolution of Petroleum Price Risk Management Tools

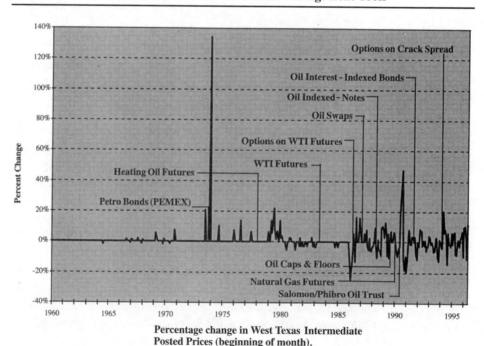

Percentage change in West Texas Intermediate
Posted Prices (beginning of month).

Commercial banks began providing commodity-price risk management products in 1986, when the Chase Manhattan Bank arranged the first oil swap. However, in 1987, the Commodity Futures Trading Commission (CFTC) challenged the legality of bank activity in this market in the United States.[13] Not surprisingly, the CFTC action had a "chilling effect on new product development"[14] and led to the business moving overseas. It was not until 1993 that the CFTC passed rules that provided comfort to this market and product development began again in earnest.

Hybrid securities involving commodities have also evolved. The earliest petroleum hybrid was the so-called Petrobonds issued by Pemex in 1973. As we will describe in Chapter 15, these Petrobonds can be viewed as straight debt plus a long-dated forward contract on oil. With its June 1986 issue of oil-indexed notes, Standard Oil made the first inroad into bonds with embedded oil warrants. And bonds with interest payments indexed to the price of petroleum products appeared in 1991.[15]

Recently, new futures contracts and new products have appeared. We have seen the addition of a futures contract on natural gas, now listed on the NYMEX. And we witnessed the development of investment products based on petroleum prices—e.g., the Salomon/Phibro Oil Trust.

How Much Is Really New?

So far in this chapter, we have traced the evolution in the 1970s and 1980s of financial structures that have come to be called innovations in the capital markets. Forward-rate agreements; futures contracts on foreign exchange rates, interest rates, metals, and petroleum; currency, interest rate, and commodity swaps; options on foreign exchange rates, interest rates, and petroleum; and hybrid securities—all these represent innovations in the sense that they provide firms with the ability to deal with an increasingly risky financial environment.

But it is misleading to think of these financial instruments as recent discoveries. If anything, these risk management instruments have been *rediscovered* in the 1970s and 1980s.

For example, while futures contracts have been traded since 1865 on the Chicago Board of Trade, futures contracts are actually much older.[16] Historians suggest that futures contracts first appeared in Japan in the 1600s. The feudal lords of Japan used a market they called *cho-ai-mai*—rice trade on book—to manage the volatility in rice prices caused by weather, warfare, and other sources.[17] Formal futures markets also appeared in Europe—in the Netherlands—during the 1600s. Among the most notable of these early futures contracts were the tulip futures that developed during the height of the Dutch "tulipmania" in 1636.[18]

7 PER CENT COTTON LOAN
OF THE
Confederate States of America,
FOR 3 MILLIONS STERLING OR 75 MILLIONS FRANCS.

Series A   № 1347

£1,000   **F25,000**

40,000 lbs. COTTON

THE CONFEDERATE STATES OF AMERICA are indebted to the Holder of this Bond in the Sum of ONE THOUSAND POUNDS Sterling, with Interest at the rate of Seven per Cent. per Annum, payable on the First Day of March and the First Day of September in each Year, in Paris, London, Amsterdam, or Frankfort °/M against delivery of the corresponding Coupon, until redemption of the Principal.

THIS BOND forms part of an issue of Seventy-five Millions of Francs, equal to Three Million Pounds Sterling, with Coupons attached till first September, 1883, inclusive, and redeemable at par in the course of twenty years by means of half-yearly drawings, the first of which takes place first March, 1864, the last first September, 1883.

At each drawing, one-fortieth part of the amount unredeemed by Cotton as indicated below is to be drawn; and all Bonds then drawn will be repaid at the option of the holder, in Paris, London, Amsterdam, or Frankfort °/M.

The Holder of the Bond, however, will have the option of converting the same at its nominal amount into Cotton, at the rate of sixpence sterling per pound—say 40,000 lbs. of Cotton in exchange for a Bond of £1000—at any time not later than six months after the ratification of a Treaty of Peace between the present belligerents. Notice of the intention of converting Bonds into Cotton to be given to the representatives of the Government in Paris or London, and sixty days after such notice the Cotton will be delivered, if peace, at the ports of Charleston, Savannah, Mobile, or New Orleans; if war, at a point in the interior within 10 miles of a railroad or stream navigable to the ocean. The delivery will be made free of all charges and duties, except the existing export duty of one-eighth of a cent per pound. The quality of the Cotton to be the standard of New Orleans middling. If any Cotton is of superior or inferior quality, the difference in value shall be settled by two Brokers, one to be appointed by the Government, the other by the Bondholder: whenever these two Brokers cannot agree on the value, an Umpire is to be chosen, whose decision shall be final.

The said issue and the above conditions are authorised by an Act of Congress, approved 29th January, 1863, a certified copy of which is deposited with Messrs. FRESHFIELDS & NEWMAN, in London, the Solicitors to the Contractors, and the faith of the Confederate States is pledged accordingly.

In Witness whereof, the Agent for the Loan of the Confederate States in Paris, duly authorised, has set his hand, and affixed the Seal of the Treasury Department, in Paris, the first day of June, in the year of Our Lord One Thousand Eight Hundred and Sixty-three.

LES ÉTATS CONFÉDÉRÉS D'AMÉRIQUE doivent au Porteur de cette Obligation la somme de MILLE LIVRES STERLING ou VINGT-CINQ MILLE FRANCS, portant intérêt à raison de Sept pour Cent l'an, payable le premier Mars et le premier Septembre de chaque année à Paris, Londres, Amsterdam et Francfort s/M, contre le Coupon respectif jusqu'à remboursement du Capital.

CETTE OBLIGATION fait partie d'une émission de Soixante-et-Quinze Millions de Francs, égale à Trois Millions de Livres Sterling, avec Coupons jusqu'au premier Septembre 1883 inclus, et remboursable au pair dans l'espace de vingt années moyennant des tirages semestriels, dont le premier aura lieu le premier Mars 1864, et le dernier le premier Septembre 1883.

Chaque tirage comprendra la quarantième partie du capital non-remboursé selon le mode indiqué ci-après, et chaque Obligation sortie sera remboursée au choix du Porteur à Paris, Londres, Amsterdam et Francfort s/M.

Le Porteur de l'Obligation aura le droit de réclamer le remboursement du montant nominal en Coton, au prix de sixpence sterling par livre de Coton, soit 40,000 livres par Obligation de £1000 (Frs. 25,000), et ceci, en tout temps, jusqu'aux six mois qui suivront la ratification d'un Traité de Paix entre les belligérants. La déclaration de convertir l'Obligation en Coton devra être faite aux représentants du Gouvernement à Paris ou à Londres, et soixante jours après le Coton sera délivré, en cas de paix, dans les ports de Charleston, Savannah, Mobile ou de la Nouvelle-Orléans, et, en cas de guerre, dans l'intérieur du pays, à une distance de dix milles au plus d'un chemin de fer ou d'une rivière navigable jusqu'à la mer. La livraison sera faite libre de tous frais et impôts, à l'exception du droit d'exportation actuellement en vigueur de ⅛ cent américain par livre. La qualité du Coton devra être le type de "New Orleans middling." Si tout ou partie du Coton est de qualité supérieure ou inférieure, la différence en valeur sera réglée par deux Courtiers, l'un désigné par le Gouvernement et l'autre par le Porteur de l'Obligation. Dans le cas où ces deux Courtiers ne pourraient s'accorder, un Arbitre sera choisi et sa décision sera définitive.

Ladite émission et les conditions ci-dessus indiquées sont autorisées par un Acte du Congrès approuvé le 29 Janvier 1863, dont une copie légalisée est déposée chez Messrs. FRESHFIELDS & NEWMAN, à Londres, Solicitors des Contractants: en conséquence les États Confédérés sont engagés.

En Foi de quoi, l'Agent pour l'Emprunt des États Confédérés à Paris, dûment autorisé, a signé et apposé le Sceau du Trésor à Paris, le premier Juin l'an mil huit cent soixante-et-trois.

Émile Erlanger
CONTRACTORS.

G. T. McRae
AGENT FOR THE LOAN.

(*Countersigned.*)

J. Henry Schroder
AGENTS TO THE CONTRACTORS IN LONDON.

John Riddell
COMMISSIONER.

ON 1st SEPTEMBER, 1883, a further Sum of £35 will be paid by Messrs. J. HENRY SCHRÖDER & Co., London; or Frs. 875 by Messrs. EMILE ERLANGER & Co., Paris; or the equivalents at the Exchange of the day by Mr. RAPHAEL ERLANGER, Frankfort o/M, and Messrs. B. H. SCHRÖDER & Co., Amsterdam; together with the principal Sum of £1000, or Frs. 25,000, on surrender of this BOND and WARRANT.

This is a facsimile of a bond issued in 1863 by the Confederate States of America.

The forward contract is even older. Historians suggest that forward contracts were first used by Flemish traders who gathered for trade fairs on land held by the counts of Champagne. At these medieval trade fairs, a document called a letter *de faire*—a forward contract specifying delivery at a later date—made its appearance in the 12th century.[19]

Of the financial instruments, options were the last to appear and therefore seem to be the most innovative. But options, too, are not new. As early as the 17th century, options on a number of commodities were being traded in Amsterdam.[20]

Even the hybrid securities are not new. In other periods of uncertainty, similar securities have appeared. Since we are Southerners, we would conclude by reminding you of the "cotton bonds" issued by the Confederate States of America.

In 1863, the Confederacy issued a 20-year bond denominated not in Confederate dollars but in French francs and pounds sterling. The most interesting feature of this bond, however, was its convertibility (at the option of the bondholder) into cotton.[21] In the parlance of today's investment banker, the Confederate States of America issued a dual-currency, cotton-indexed bond.

Concluding Remarks

The financial environment of the 1970s stimulated demand for new financial instruments, and the changes that resulted are important in understanding today's financial markets. The financial environment is the key determinant of the kinds of instruments that will be successful in the marketplace. In short, financial innovation is a demand-driven phenomenon.

If the financial environment is stable, the market will use simple instruments. In the late 1800s, for example, the financial instrument of choice was the consol, a bond with a fixed interest rate but no maturity; it lasted forever. Investors were quite happy to hold infinite-lived British government bonds because British sovereign credit was good and expected inflation was nil. Confidence in price-level stability led to a stable interest rate environment and therefore to long-lived bonds.

But in financial environments fraught with uncertainty, we can expect a proliferation of new risk management instruments and hybrid securities. Uncertainty, though disruptive and rife with problems, has stimulated much valuable financial innovation. Through this process of innovation, financial intermediaries can expand their activities by offering customers products to manage risk, or even the ability to turn such risk into an advantage. Moreover, through innovation, financial institutions can better evaluate and manage their own portfolios. Because price uncertainty cannot be eliminated, the clear trend now is to manage risk actively rather than to try to predict price movements.

Notes

1. This decoupling of interest rate risk and credit risk is stressed in Arak, Estrella, Goodman, and Silver (1988).

2. A description of the Bretton Woods system and its effect on prices is contained in Putman and Wilford (1986).

3. For exposition, Figure 1–4 provides the monthly first difference in the rate rather than percentage change or some other measure more closely related to volatility.

4. As we will note when we discuss the evolution of swaps in Chapter 8, U.S. firms were a lot more interested in translation exposures in the 1970s—before Accounting Statement FAS 8 was replaced by FAS 52. Under FAS 8, changes in the value of the asset induced by changes in foreign exchange rates would be reflected in the firm's income. Hence translation exposures would result in volatile income.

5. In the context of traditional economics, an economic exposure to interest rates would result if the firm produces a good that is interest elastic.

6. Whether the cause of this difference or not, it may be useful to note that while almost all of the firms we have talked to manage their exposures to interest rates and foreign exchange rates in the treasury, exposures to commodity prices are likely to be managed in other parts of the firm—for example, a purchasing department.

7. The function of a dealer (a broker) is to bring together buyers and sellers. For doing so, the dealer is rewarded with the bid-ask spread. As we will discuss throughout this book, in the risk management markets, dealers receive a bid-ask spread for facilitating the transaction. The dealer's task is then to manage the risks so that, at the maturity of the transaction, the dealer has retained as much of this spread as possible.

8. CME futures contracts on other currencies followed: Brazilian Real, November 1985; European Currency Unit, January 1986; Australian Dollar, January 1987; Mexican Peso, April 1995; and New Zealand Dollar and South African Rand, May 1997. The Mexican Peso was originally listed in May 1972, but was delisted due to banking problems. The Peso was subsequently relisted in 1995. The European Currency Unit was delisted in September 1987. The exchange is planning to relist futures with revised specifications in preparation for the Economic Monetary Unit.

9. Option contracts on the French franc began trading in 1984, followed by the ECU in 1986 and Australian dollar in 1987.

10. CME options on futures on other currencies followed: Australian Dollar, January 1988; Mexican Peso, April 1995; and New Zealand Dollar and South African Rand, May 1997.

11. In Chapter 15 we will demonstrate that a dual-currency bond can be viewed as a combination of a standard bond and a long-dated foreign exchange forward contract.

12. While floating-rate loans dealt with the immediate problem of interest rate risk, they did not turn out to be the panacea some expected. By passing the market risk to the borrower, floating-rate loans increased the default risk of the borrower.

13. Commodity Futures Trading Commission (1987).

14. Response of the SEC to the CFTC, August 19, 1988, p. 6.

15. The behavior of the price of metals differs from that of foreign exchange, interest rates, and oil prices in that the price volatility of metals increased in the 1950s as well as in the 1970s. Given what we have seen so far, then, it should come as no surprise that a forward contract on zinc was introduced on the London Metal Exchange (LME) in 1953. (Forward contracts on copper had been traded on the LME since 1883.) With the increase in volatility in the 1970s, forward contracts began trading on the LME on aluminum in 1978 and nickel in 1979.

    Futures contracts appeared later on the Commodity Exchange (Comex)—on copper in July 1983 and on aluminum in December 1983. An option on copper futures began trading on the Comex in April 1986.

    Hybrids that modify the timing of the options embedded in the bond have also begun to appear. Magma Copper Company's November 1988 Copper Interest-Indexed Senior Subordinated Notes, for example, were a 10-year issue paying a quarterly interest payment that varied with the prevailing price of copper.

16. The Board of Trade opened in 1842, but in its early years forward rather than futures contracts were traded, according to the Chicago Board of Trade (1988).

17. Teweles and Jones (1987).

18. Gorber (1986).

19. Teweles and Jones (1987).

20. International Chamber of Commerce (1986).

21. At a set rate of sixpence sterling per pound of cotton.

2 AN OVERVIEW OF THE RISK MANAGEMENT PROCESS

A Building-Block Approach to Forwards, Futures, Swaps, Options, and Hybrid Securities*

An Overview of the Risk Management Products

The increased economic uncertainty first evident in the 1970s has altered the way financial markets function. As foreign exchange rates, interest rates, and commodity prices have become more volatile, corporations have discovered that their value is subject to various financial price risks in addition to the risk inherent in their core business.

To illustrate the effect of changes in a given financial price on the value of a firm, we use the concept of a *risk profile*. Figure 2–1 presents a case in which an unexpected increase in financial price P (that is, the T-bill rate, the price of oil, or the dollar price of a yen) decreases the value of the firm (V). In Figure 2–1, the difference between the actual price and the expected price is shown as ΔP, while ΔV measures the resulting change in the value of the firm. Had ΔP remained small, as it did before the 1970s, the indexed changes in firm value would have been correspondingly small. But for many companies, the increased volatility of exchange rates, interest rates, and commodity prices (large ΔPs) in the 1970s and 1980s has been a major cause of sharp fluctuations in share prices (large ΔVs). With this greater potential for large swings in value, companies have begun exploring new methods for dealing with financial risks.

Confronted with the increased volatility of financial prices, companies found that the first and most obvious approach was to try to forecast future prices more accurately. If changes in exchange rates, interest rates, and commodity prices could be predicted with confidence, companies could avoid unexpected swings in value.

---

*This chapter is adapted from Smithson (1987).

FIGURE 2–1   A Risk Profile Relating the Expected Change in Firm Value (ΔV) to Unexpected Changes in a Financial Price (ΔP)

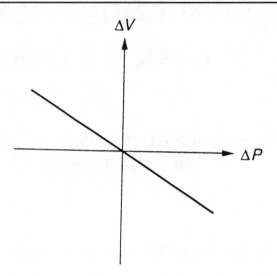

In the context of Figure 2–1, if the actual price could be completely anticipated, ΔP would equal zero and the value of the firm thus would be unchanged. However, economists were generally unsuccessful in predicting changes in interest rates, foreign exchange rates, and commodity prices.

This shouldn't be surprising; attempts to outpredict markets as efficient as the financial markets are unlikely to succeed. Because forecasting cannot be relied on to eliminate risk, the remaining alternative is to *manage* the risks. Financial risk management can be accomplished by using on-balance-sheet transactions. For example, a company can manage a foreign exchange exposure resulting from foreign competition by borrowing in the competitors' currency or by moving production abroad. But such on-balance-sheet methods can be costly and, as firms like Caterpillar have discovered, inflexible.[1]

Alternatively, financial risks can be managed with the use of off-balance-sheet instruments: forwards, futures, swaps, and options. When you first begin to examine these financial instruments, you are confronted by what seems an insurmountable barrier to entry: participants in the various markets and the trade publications seem to possess specialized expertise applicable in only one market to the exclusion of all the others. Adding to the complexities of the individual markets themselves is a welter of jargon—*ticks, collars, strike prices, straddles,* and so forth. Indeed, it appears to the novice like a Wall Street version of the Tower of Babel, with each group of market specialists speaking a different language.

In marked contrast to this specialist approach, this text presents a generalist approach. We treat forwards, futures, swaps, and options not as four unique instruments but rather as four closely related instruments to deal with a single problem—managing financial risk. Indeed, we are going to show how the off-balance-sheet instruments are like those plastic building blocks children snap together: you can build the instruments from one another (or combine the basic instruments into larger creations).

Forward Contracts

Of the four instruments we consider in this text, the forward contract is the oldest and, perhaps for this reason, the most straightforward. A forward contract obligates its owner to buy a given asset on a specified date at a price (known as the contract or forward price) specified at the origination of the contract. If, at maturity, the actual price is higher than the exercise price, the contract owner makes a profit; if the price is lower, the owner suffers a loss.

In Figure 2–2, the payoff from buying a forward contract is superimposed on the original risk profile. If the actual price at contract maturity is higher than the expected price, the firm's inherent risk will lead to a decline in the value of the firm, but this decline will be offset by the profit on the forward contract. Hence, for the risk profile illustrated, this forward contract provides a perfect hedge. (If the risk profile were sloped positively instead of negatively, this risk would be managed by selling instead of buying a forward contract.)

FIGURE 2–2   Payoff Profile for Forward Contracts

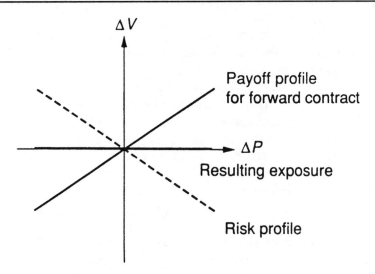

In addition to its payoff profile, two features of a forward contract should be noted. First, the default (or credit) risk of the contract is two-sided. The contract owner either receives or makes a payment, depending on the price movement of the underlying asset. Second, the value of the forward contract is conveyed only at the contract's maturity; no payment is made either at origination or during the term of the contract.

Futures Contracts

Although futures contracts on commodities have been traded on organized exchanges since the 1860s, financial futures are relatively new, dating from the introduction of foreign currency futures in 1972. The basic form of the futures contract is identical to that of the forward contract: a futures contract obligates its owner to purchase a specified asset at a specified exercise price on the contract maturity date. Thus, the payoff profile for the purchaser of a forward contract as presented in Figure 2–2 could illustrate equally well the payoff to the holder of a futures contract.

Like the forward contract, the futures contract also has two-sided risk. But in marked contrast to forwards, futures markets use two devices that virtually eliminate credit risk. First, instead of conveying the value of a contract through a single payment at maturity, changes in the value of a futures contract are conveyed at the end of the day in which they are realized. Look again at Figure 2–2. Suppose that on the day after origination the financial price rises and, consequently, the contract has a positive value. In the case of a forward contract, this value change would not be received until contract maturity. With a futures contract, this change in value is received at the end of the day. In the language of the futures markets, the futures contract is *cash-settled,* or *marked-to-market,* daily.

Because the performance period of a futures contract is reduced by marking-to-market, the risk of default declines accordingly. Indeed, since the value of the futures contract is paid or received at the end of each day, it is not hard to see why Fischer Black likened a futures contract to "a series of forward contracts. Each day, yesterday's contract is settled, and today's contract is written."[2] That is, a futures contract is like a sequence of forwards in which the "forward" contract written on day 0 is settled on day 1 and is replaced, in effect, with a new "forward" contract written reflecting the new day-1 expectations. This new contract is then itself settled on day 2 and replaced, and so on until the day the contract ends.

The second feature of futures contracts that reduces default risk is the requirement that all market participants—sellers and buyers alike[3]—post a performance bond called *margin.* If your futures contract increases in value during the trading day, this gain is added to your margin account at the day's end. Conversely, if your contract loses value, this loss is deducted. And if your margin account balance falls below some agreed-upon minimum, you are required to post an additional bond—

your margin account must be replenished or your position will be closed out.[4] Because this process generally closes any position before the margin account is depleted, performance risk is materially reduced.[5]

Note that the exchange itself limits the default risk exposure of its customers. Yet while daily settlement and the requirement of a bond reduce default risk, the existence of an exchange (or clearinghouse) primarily transforms risk. More specifically, the exchange deals with the two-sided risk inherent in forwards and futures by serving as the counterparty to all transactions. If you wish to buy or sell a futures contract, you buy from or sell to the exchange. Hence, you need only evaluate the credit risk of the exchange, not the credit risk of some specific counterparty.

From the point of view of the market, the exchange does not reduce default risk; the expected default rate is not affected by the existence of the exchange. However, the existence of the exchange can alter the default risk faced by an individual market participant. If you buy a futures contract from a specific individual, the default risk you face is determined by the default rate of that specific counterparty. If instead you buy the same futures contract through an exchange, your default risk depends not just on the default rate of your counterparty but on the rate of the entire market. Moreover, to the extent that the exchange is capitalized by equity from its members, the default risk you face is reduced further because you have a claim not against some specific counterparty but rather against the exchange. Therefore, when you trade through the exchange, you are in a sense purchasing an insurance policy from the exchange.

The primary economic function of the exchange is to reduce the costs of transacting in futures contracts. The anonymous trades made possible through the exchange, together with the homogeneous nature of the futures contracts— standardized assets, exercise dates (four per year), and contract sizes—enable the futures market to become relatively liquid. However, as was made clear by recent experience of the London Metal Exchange, the exchange structure, marking-to-market, and margin accounts do not eliminate default risk. In November 1985, the "tin cartel" defaulted on contracts for tin delivery on the London Metal Exchange, thereby making the exchange liable for the loss.[6]

In sum, a futures contract is much like a portfolio of forward contracts. At the close of business each day, in effect, the existing forwardlike contract is settled and a new one is written.[7] This daily settlement feature combined with the margin requirement allows futures contracts to reduce substantially the credit risk inherent in forwards.

Swap Contracts[8]

Because they were publicly introduced only in 1981, swaps are commonly portrayed as one of the latest financing innovations. But as we hope to be able to convince you, a swap contract is in essence nothing more complicated than a portfolio of forward contracts. We will also demonstrate that the credit risk attending swaps is somewhat less than that of a forward contract with the same maturity but greater than that of a comparable futures contract.

As implied by its name, a swap contract obligates two parties to exchange, or swap, some specified cash flows at specified intervals. The most common form is the *interest rate swap,* in which the cash flows are determined by two different interest rates.

Panel (*a*) of Figure 2–3 illustrates an interest rate swap from the perspective of a party who is paying out a series of cash flows determined by a fixed interest rate ($\bar{R}_T$) and receiving a series of cash flows determined by a floating interest rate ($\tilde{R}$).[9]

Panel (*b*) of Figure 2–3 demonstrates that this swap contract can be decomposed into a portfolio of forward contracts. At each settlement date, the party to this swap has an implicit forward contract on interest rates: the party illustrated is obligated to sell a fixed-rate cash flow for an amount specified at the origination of the contract. Also in this sense, a swap contract is like a portfolio of forward contracts.

In terms of our earlier discussion, this means that the solid line in Figure 2–2 also represents the payoff from a swap contract. Specifically, the solid line in Figure

FIGURE 2–3   (*a*) An Interest Rate Swap   (*b*) An Interest Rate Swap as a Portfolio of Forward Contracts

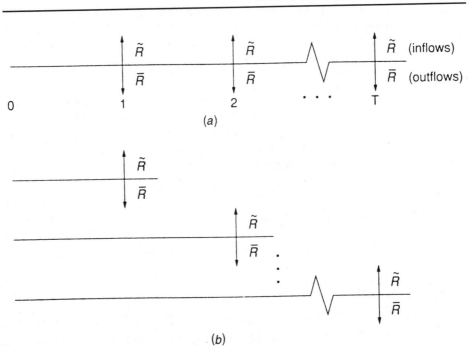

2–2 illustrates a swap contract in which the party receives cash flows determined by P (say, the U.S. Treasury bond rate) and makes payments determined by another price—say, London InterBank Offer Rate (LIBOR). Thus, in terms of their ability to manage risk, forwards, futures, and swaps all function in the same way.

But similar payoff profiles notwithstanding, the instruments differ with respect to their default risk. As we know, the performance period of a forward is equal to its maturity; because no performance bond is required, a forward contract is a pure credit instrument. Futures reduce the performance period (to one day) as well as requiring a bond, thus virtually eliminating credit risk. Swap contracts typically use only one of these mechanisms to reduce credit risk; they reduce the performance period.[10] This point becomes evident in Figure 2–3. Although the maturity of the contract is T periods, the performance period is generally not T periods long but is instead a single period. Thus, given a swap and a forward contract of roughly the same maturity, the swap is likely to impose far less credit risk on the counterparties to the contract than the forward. This credit risk difference between swaps and forwards is analogous to that between an amortized loan and a zero-coupon bond.

At each settlement date throughout a swap contract, the changes in value are transferred between the counterparties. To illustrate this in terms of Figure 2–3, suppose that interest rates rise on the day after origination. The value of the swap contract illustrated has risen. This value change will be conveyed to the contract owner not at maturity (as would be the case with a forward contract) nor at the end of that day (as would be the case with a futures contract). Instead, at the first settlement date, part of the value change is conveyed in the form of the "difference check" paid by one party to the other. To repeat, then, the performance period is reduced from that of a forward, albeit not to so short a period as that of a futures contract.[11] (Keep in mind that we are comparing instruments with the same maturities.)

At this point let us stop to summarize the two major points made thus far. First, a swap contract, like a futures contract, is like a portfolio of forward contracts. Therefore, the basic payoff profiles for each of these three instruments are similar. Second, the primary differences among forwards, futures, and swaps are the settlement features of the contracts and amount of default risk these instruments impose on counterparties to the contracts. Forwards and futures represent the extremes, with a swap being the intermediate case.

It is important to note that swaps do impose some credit risk. For this reason it is not surprising that commercial banks have become increasingly active in a market that was initiated, for the most part, by investment banks. The sharp difference of opinion that has arisen between commercial and investment banks over the "most advisable" evolutionary path for the swap market to follow is also understandable. Because investment banks are not in the business of extending credit, they would much prefer swaps to become more like futures—that is, exchange-traded instruments with bonded contract performance. Commercial banks, by contrast, have a comparative advantage in credit extension and thus stand to bene-fit if swaps remain credit instruments. Accordingly, they would prefer the credit risk to be managed by imposing capital requirements on the financial institutions arranging the swaps.

Option Contracts

As we have seen, the owner of a forward, futures, or swap contract has an *obligation* to perform. In contrast, an option gives its owner a *right,* not an obligation. An option giving its owner the right to buy an asset—a call option—is provided in Fig-ure 2–4. (Here, once again, the financial price P could be an interest rate, a foreign exchange rate, the price of a commodity, or the price of some other financial asset.) The owner of the contract illustrated has the right to purchase the asset at a speci-fied future date at a price agreed upon today. Consequently if P rises, the value of the option also goes up. But the value of the option remains unchanged (at zero) if P declines because the option contract owner is not obligated to purchase the asset if P moves to an unfavorable price.[12]

The payoff profile for the owner of the call option is repeated in panel (*a*) of Figure 2–5. In this case, the contract owner has bought the right to buy the asset at a specified price—the exercise (strike) price. (In Figures 2–4 and 2–5, the exercise price is implicitly equal to the expected price.)

FIGURE 2–4   The Payoff Profile of a Call Option

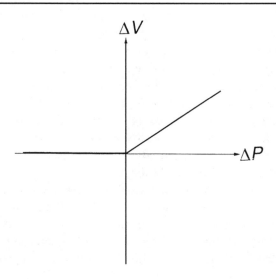

FIGURE 2-5   Payoff Profiles of Puts and Calls

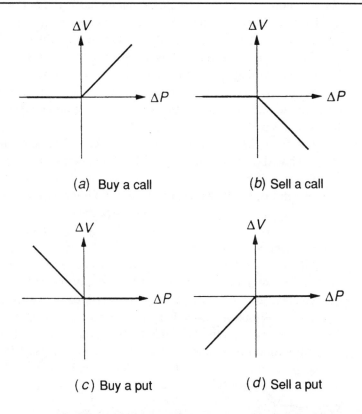

(*a*) Buy a call   (*b*) Sell a call

(*c*) Buy a put   (*d*) Sell a put

The payoff profile for the party who sold the call option (also known as the call writer) is shown in panel (*b*). Note that in contrast to the buyer of the option, the seller of the call option has the *obligation* to perform. For example, if the owner of the option elects to exercise his or her option to buy the asset, the seller of the option is obligated to sell the asset.

Aside from the option to buy an asset, there is also the option to sell an asset at a specified price, known as a *put* option. The payoff to the buyer of a put is illustrated in panel (*c*) of Figure 2–5, and the payoff for the seller of the put is shown in panel (*d*).

In many instances, jargon does more to confuse than to make clear, and this is particularly true in the buy-sell, call-put jargon of options. Suppose you were exposed to rising interest rates—that is, an increase in interest rates reduced your wealth. As illustrated by the left side of Figure 2–6, you could eliminate the downside exposure by buying a call on the interest rate (that is, you could buy an interest rate cap). Expressed in terms of bond prices, however, the proper strategy for hedging the same exposure would be to buy a put on bonds. As Figures 2–6 illustrates, a call on interest rates is equivalent to a put on bonds. The same thing occurs, moreover, in the foreign exchange market; a put on DM/$ is equivalent to a call on $/DM. (There have been times when two persons arguing about whether something was a put or a call were, in fact, both right.)

To this point, we have considered only the payoffs for the option contracts. Figures 2–4 through 2–6 assume in effect that option premiums are neither paid by the buyer nor received by the seller. By making this assumption, we have side-stepped the thorniest issues, the valuation of option contracts. We now turn to option valuation.

The breakthrough in option-pricing theory came with the work of Fischer Black and Myron Scholes in 1973. Conveniently for our purposes, Black and Scholes took what might be described as a building-block approach to the valuation of options. Look again at the call option illustrated in Figure 2–4. For increases in the financial price, the payoff profile for the option is that of a forward contract. For decreases in the price, the value of the option is constant, like that of a riskless security such as a Treasury bill.

The work of Black and Scholes demonstrates that a call option could be replicated by a continuously adjusting (dynamic) portfolio of two securities: (1) forward contracts on the underlying asset and (2) riskless securities. As the financial price rises, the call-option-equivalent portfolio contains an increasing proportion of forward contracts on the asset. Conversely, the replicating portfolio contains a decreasing proportion of the asset as the price of the asset falls. Because this replicating portfolio is effectively a synthetic call option, arbitrage activity should

---

FIGURE 2–6   Hedging Exposures with Options

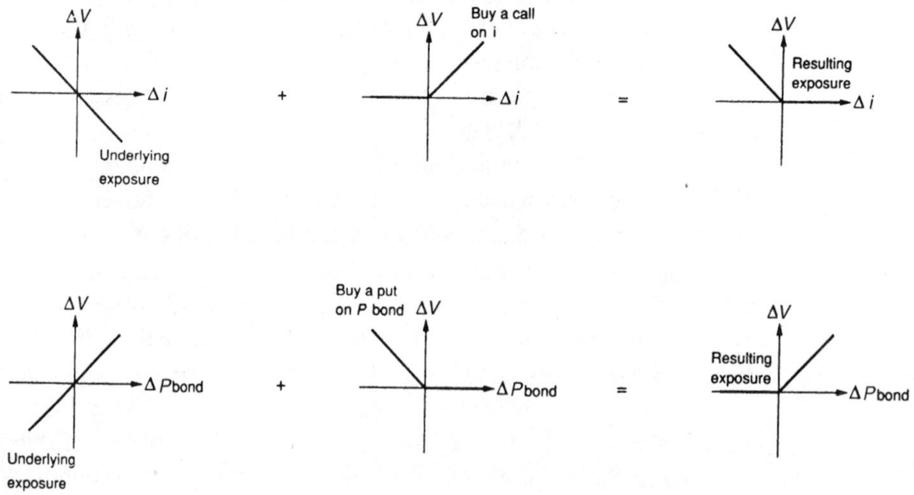

ensure that its value closely approximates the market price of an exchange-traded call option. In this sense, the value of a call option—thus the premium that would be charged its buyer—is determined by the value of its option-equivalent portfolio.

Panel (*a*) of Figure 2–7 illustrates the payoff profile for a call option that includes the premium. This figure (and all of the option figures thus far) illustrates an *at-the-money option,* an option for which the exercise price is the prevailing expected price. As panels (*a*) and (*b*) of Figure 2–7 illustrate, an at-the-money option is paid for by sacrificing a significant amount of the firm's potential gains. However, the price of a call option falls as the exercise price increases relative to the prevailing price of the asset. This means that an option buyer who is willing to accept larger potential losses in return for paying a lower option premium should consider using an out-of-the-money option.

FIGURE 2–7 (*a*), (*b*) **"At-the-Money" Option** (*c*), (*d*) **"Out-of-the-Money" Option**

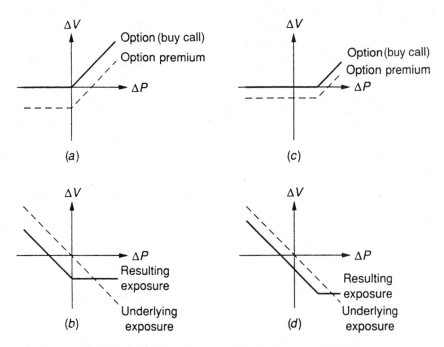

(*a*) The payoff profit for buying an at-the-money call option.
  The dashed line reflects the premium.
(*b*) The resulting exposure from buying the at-the-money option.
(*c*) The payoff profit for buying an out-of-the-money call option.
(*d*) The resulting exposure from buying the out-of-the-money option.

An out-of-the-money call option, illustrated in panel (*c*) of Figure 2–7, provides less downside protection than other instruments, but the option premium is significantly less. The lesson here is that option buyers can alter their payoff profiles simply by changing the exercise price.

For the purposes of this discussion, however, the most important feature of options is that they are not as different from other financial instruments as they might first seem. Options do have a payoff profile that differs significantly from that of forward contracts (or futures or swaps). But option payoff profiles can be duplicated by a dynamically adjusted combination of forwards and risk-free securities. Thus, we find that options have more in common with the other instruments than is immediately apparent. Futures and swaps, as we saw earlier, are in essence nothing more than particular portfolios of forward contracts; options, as we have just seen, are very much akin to portfolios of forward contracts and risk-free securities.

This point is reinforced if we consider ways that options can be combined. Consider a portfolio constructed by buying a call and selling a put with the same exercise price and maturity. As the top row of Figure 2–8 illustrates, the resulting portfolio (long a call, short a put) has a payoff profile equivalent to that of buying a forward contract on the asset. Similarly, the bottom row of Figure 2–8 illustrates that a portfolio constructed by selling a call and buying a put (short a call, long a put) is equivalent to selling a forward contract. The relation illustrated in Figure

FIGURE 2–8 Put-Call Parity

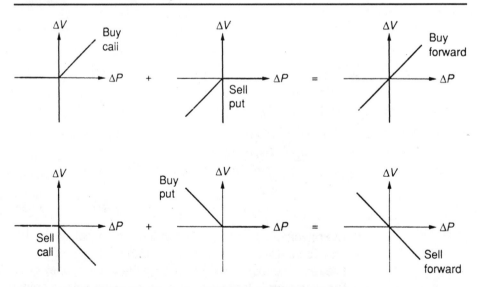

Same strike price and maturity is equivalent to the payoffs to buying a forward.
Selling a call and buying a put are equivalent to selling a forward.

2–8 is known more formally as put-call parity. The special import of this relation, at least in this context, is the building-block construction it makes possible: two options can be "snapped together" to yield the payoff profile for a forward contract.

At the beginning of this section, then, it seemed that options would be very different from forwards, futures, and swaps; in many ways they are. But we discovered two building-block relations between options and the other three instruments:

1. Options can be replicated by "snapping together" a forward, futures, or swap contract with a position in risk-free securities.
2. Calls and puts can be "snapped together" to become forwards.

The Box of Financial Building Blocks

Forwards, futures, swaps, and options—to the novice, they all look so different. And if you read the trade publications or talk to the participants in the four markets, the apparent differences among the instruments are likely to seem even more pronounced. It looks as if the only way to deal with the financial instruments is to pick one and then become a specialist in that market, to the exclusion of the others.

However, it turns out that forwards, futures, swaps, and options are more like building blocks—to be linked together into complex creations—and less like stand-alone, individual constructions. To understand the off-balance-sheet instruments, you don't need a lot of market-specific knowledge; you just need to know how the instruments can be linked to one another. As we have seen: (1) futures are built by snapping together a package of forwards; (2) swaps are similarly built by snapping together a package of forwards; (3) options can be built by snapping together a forward with a riskless security; and (4) options can be snapped together to yield forward contracts, or forwards can be snapped apart to yield a package of options.

Figure 2–9 characterizes each of the four instruments we have been discussing according to the shapes of their payoff profiles. It also reminds us of the put-call parity relation between options and forwards, futures, or swaps. In so doing, Figure 2–9 in effect provides the instruction manual for our box of financial building blocks. A quick look shows that though there can be many pieces in the box, there are only six basic shapes with which to concern yourself. The straight pieces come in three colors; we know we can obtain a forward payoff profile either with forwards (the red ones), futures (the yellow ones), or swaps (the blue ones). The kinked pieces are all the same color (white) because options can be combined to replicate a forward, a future, or a swap.

In forthcoming chapters, we examine the individual risk management instruments in detail. Chapters 4 and 5 deal with forwards. Chapters 6 and 7 describe futures. Swaps are discussed in Chapters 8 and 9, and Chapters 10–13 cover options.

FIGURE 2–9   **The Financial Building Blocks**

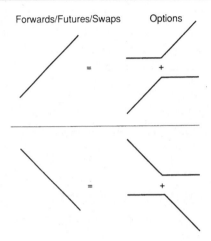

We do want you to have some detailed information about how each of the instruments, as well as the market within which it is traded, works. But in the chapters to come, we don't want you to lose sight of the building-block nature of these financial instruments. Indeed, we follow these chapters about the individual building blocks with two chapters (Chapters 14 and 15) that could best be described as a blueprint for constructing complicated financial instruments (the so-called hybrid securities) building block by building block.

Notes

1. See "Caterpillar's Triple Whammy," *Fortune,* October 27, 1986.
2. See Black (1976).
3. Keep in mind that if you buy a futures contract, you are taking a long position in the underlying asset—i.e., the value of the futures position appreciates with increases in the value of the asset. Conversely, selling a futures contract is equivalent to taking a short position.
4. When the contract is originated on the U.S. exchanges, an "initial margin" is required. Subsequently, the margin account balance must remain above the "maintenance margin." If the margin account balance falls below the maintenance level, the balance must be restored to the initial level.

5. Note that this discussion has ignored daily limits. If there are daily limits on the movement of futures prices, large changes in expectations about the underlying asset can effectively close the market. (The market opens, immediately moves the limit, and then is effectively closed until the next day.) Hence, there could exist an instance in which the broker desires to close out a customer's position but is not able to do so immediately because the market is experiencing limit moves. In such a case, the statement that performance risk is "eliminated" is too strong.
6. A description of this situation is contained in "Tin Crisis in London Roils Metal Exchange," *The Wall Street Journal,* November 13, 1985.

7. A futures contract is *similar* to a portfolio of forward contracts; however, a futures contract and a portfolio of forward contracts become identical only if interest rates are *deterministic*—that is, known with certainty in advance. See Jarrow and Oldfield (1981) and Cox, Ingersoll, and Ross (1981).

8. This section is based on Smith, Smithson, and Wakeman (1986).

9. Specifically, the interest rate swap cash flows are determined as follows: the two parties agree to some notional principal, P. (The principal is notional in the sense that it is only used to determine the magnitude of cash flows; it is not paid or received by either party.) At each settlement date, $1, 2, \ldots, T$, the party illustrated makes a payment $\bar{R}_T = \bar{r}_T P$, where $\bar{r}_T$ is the T-period fixed rate that existed at origination. At each settlement, the party illustrated receives $\tilde{R} = \tilde{r} P$, where $\tilde{r}$ is the floating rate for that period—that is, at settlement date 2, the interest rate used is the one-period rate in effect at period 1.

10. There are instances in which a bond has been posted in the form of collateral. As should be evident, in this case the swap becomes more like a futures contract.

11. We will show in Chapter 8 that unlike futures for which all of any change in contract value is paid or received at the daily settlements, swap contracts convey only part of the total value change at the periodic settlements.

12. For continuity, we continue to use the ΔV, ΔP convention in figures. To compare these figures with those found in most texts, treat ΔV as deviations from zero ($\Delta V = V - 0$) and remember that ΔP measures deviations from expected price ($\Delta P = P - P^e$).

3

IMPACT OF THE INTRODUCTION OF THE RISK MANAGEMENT PRODUCTS

In Chapter 1, we stressed that increased volatility in foreign exchange, interest rates, and commodity prices *led* to the development of the financial price risk management products. Such an argument requires us to say something about the *consequences* of the development of the financial price risk management products.

In this chapter, we will first examine the impact of the introduction of the risk management products on the markets for the underlying assets. Given our arguments in Chapter 1, we begin by looking at what happens to volatility of the financial prices once the financial risk management products appear; and we also look at the impact on adjustment speed, the bid-ask spread, and trading volume for the underlying assets. We will then look at the impact of the introduction of the risk management products on the economy as a whole.

We will return to the question of the impact of the introduction of the risk management products in Chapters 20 and 23, where we will look at the impact of the use of the risk management products on the industrial corporations and financial institutions that use them.

The Impact of Risk Management on the Markets for the Underlying Assets[1]

In marked contrast to the paucity of evidence on the impact of risk management on the performance of individual firms, we have a wealth of empirical evidence on the impact of derivatives on the markets for the underlying assets. For exposition, we will survey the evidence about the impact of the introduction of financial derivatives on the markets for the underlying assets as it relates to:

- The volatility of the underlying financial price.
- The speed of adjustment in the underlying markets.
- The bid-ask spreads in the underlying markets.
- Trading volume for the underlying asset.

The Impact on Price Volatility

> Futures and options are the tail wagging the dog. They have also escalated the leverage and volatility of the markets to precipitous, unacceptable levels.

> John Shad, former chairman,
> Securities and Exchange Commission

John Shad aptly summarizes the view that the introduction of derivatives has led to an increase in the volatility of underlying assets.[2] This view was widely voiced in the wake of the October 1987 stock market crash.

A more moderate position holds that there is no reason for the introduction of derivatives to have any effect on the volatility of underlying assets. Futures and options are created assets (for every long there is a corresponding short). Thus, the introduction of these contracts would have no predictable effect on trading in the underlying security.

A more radical counterargument suggests that with the introduction of derivatives, the volatility of an underlying asset should fall, not rise. After all, the newly created trading opportunity in this derivative security should increase market liquidity for an underlying asset.

The debate about the impact of the introduction of derivatives on the volatility of the price of the underlying asset has been going on for more than 20 years with no clear winner. The increased-volatility side gained credibility when this argument became a primary justification for a 1977 moratorium on expansion in options trading. (This argument also provided an interesting juxtaposition when, in 1983, the Golden Nugget—an enterprise apparently in favor of risk—argued in court that the introduction of options contracts on its shares should be prohibited because the options made buying its shares a more risky proposition.[3]

However, as summarized in Table 3–1, the empirical evidence fails to support the increased-volatility story. Indeed, the evidence supports the contention that the introduction of derivatives actually reduces the volatility in the underlying markets.

The futures market has been studied intensively. With the possible exception of the S&P 500 Equity Index, data on the behavior of the market before and after the introduction of futures contracts overwhelmingly support the contention that the introduction of derivatives decreases rather than increases the volatility in the underlying markets.

TABLE 3–1   **The Impact of the Introduction of Derivatives on the Volatility of the Price of the Underlying Asset**

Study: Asset Examined	*Change in Volatility*
Futures on Agricultural Commodities	
Working (1960): Onions	Decreased
Gray (1963): Onions	Decreased
Powers (1970): Pork bellies and cattle	Decreased
Taylor-Leuthold (1974): Cattle	Decreased
Cox (1976)	Decreased
Futures on U.S. Treasury Securities	
Dale-Workman (1981): Treasury bills	No change
Bortz (1984): Treasury bonds	Decreased
Simpson-Ireland (1985): Treasury bills	No change
Edwards (1988): Treasury bills	Decreased
Futures on GNMAs	
Froewiss (1978)	Decreased
Figlewski (1981)	Increased
Simpson-Ireland (1982)	No change
Corgel-Gay (1984)	Decreased
Moriarty-Tosini (1985)	No change
Futures on S&P 500 Index	
Santoni (1987)	No change
Stoll-Whaley (1987)	
Harris (1989)	Increased
Edwards (1988)	Decreased
Damodaran (1990)	Increased
Options on Shares	
Trennepohl-Dukes (1979)	Decreased
Hayes-Tennenbaum (1979)	Decreased
Klemkosky/Mannes (1980)	Decreased
Witeside-Duke-Dunnes (1983)	Decreased
Ma-Rao (1986, 1988)	Decreased
Bansai-Pruitt-Wei (1989)	Decreased
Conrad (1989)	Decreased
Skinner (1989)	Decreased
Damodaran-Lim (1991)	Decreased

And the recent evidence from examination of the impact of the listing of options contracts on individual shares is perhaps even more compelling. Douglas Skinner (1989) examines the volatility of share returns before and after the listing of options by observing a sample of 304 new listings of options (Chicago Board Options Exchange and the American Stock Exchange) between April 1973 and December 1986. He documents a decline in return volatility of between 10 and 20 percent following the listing of exchange-traded options on common stock. Jennifer

Less Is Brewing in Witching Hours

John Rozario

There once was a time when the triple-witching hour would inspire fear in even the most seasoned market professionals. The large price swings that occurred during triple-witching were much anticipated and discussed by the media. These occurrences were often used as "evidence" to hold index-linked derivatives trading responsible for making the market more volatile.

The second edition of this book contained a box with the same title as this one which indicated that those large price swings may be disappearing.[1] We wanted to see what more recent data suggested.

What Is the Triple-Witching Hour?

On the third Fridays of March, June, September, and December three types of derivative contracts expire—stock index options, stock index futures, and options on stock index futures. The maturities of all three used to occur at the close of the market. As a result there would be frenetic trading during the last hour of trading on those Fridays, usually accompanied by large price movements in the market.

Arbitrage-related program trading is an integral part of triple expirations. One form of arbitrage is to be long or short index futures and hold the opposite position in the underlying stocks. The arbitrageurs either close out or roll over their positions on expiration day.

What Has Happened to the Volatility Associated with Triple-Witching Sessions?

In a study[2] that looks at data from 1983–86, Edwards observed that the volatility of stock returns was higher on average for futures' expiration days than for non-expiration days. This effect was magnified in the last hour of trading. A similar result was obtained in a study[3] done by Stoll and Whaley that looked at futures' expiration days from 1983–85. They found that in the last hour of trading, volume and volatility were higher.

In 1987, the Chicago exchanges moved the expiration of S&P 500 options and futures from closing prices to opening prices. Options on the S&P 100 and on individual stocks still expire at closing prices. This gives specialists more time to match buy and sell orders and spreads trading across the entire day instead of concentrating it in the final hour.

A follow-up study[4] done by Stoll and Whaley to examine the effect of the above change concluded that expiration effects are economically small and "the market appears to have adjusted reasonably well to expirations of index futures and options."

In an extensive study[5] that looks at daily volatility measures from 1983 through 1997, Schwert found "no reliable evidence of an increase in volatility on the days when futures and options expire."

In his study, Schwert found strong evidence of increased volumes on expiration days. The buying and selling related to the arbitrage trading noted above contribute to significant increases in trading volumes during triple-witching sessions. For example the December 19, 1997 triple-witching session witnessed a volume of 793 million shares traded on the NYSE.[6] However, despite the huge volume, the NYSE composite slipped by less than 1%.

There are several explanations put forth on why expiration-related volatility has diminished. The one most often cited is linked to the change in the settlement of index-linked contracts from the close of trading to the open of trading on expiration days. Another possible contributor is the dissemination of information prior to the start of trading on an expiration day of order imbalances resulting from the unwinding of arbitrage. This information attracts traders on the opposite side and helps contribute to price stability. Also, in April 1992, the NYSE implemented a rule prohibiting traders from canceling market-on-close orders after 3:45 p.m. on expiration days. In September 1993, the NYSE ruled that market-on-close orders on expiration days could not be canceled at all. Prior to these regulations, traders could place large market-on-close orders for a particular stock, but not necessarily follow through. This would attract other participants thereby creating an order imbalance.

Whatever the reason, the message here is that even though triple-witching is still frequently mentioned, the volatility that it is supposed to conjure up remains conspicuously absent.

John Rozario is an Executive Director of CIBC Oppenheimer Corp. where he focuses on teaching and the development of courses on options, equity derivatives, credit derivatives, and value at risk for the School of Financial Products. John Rozario holds an M.B.A. degree in finance from the Wharton School at the University of Pennsylvania. He received a B.S.E. degree in Computer Science and Engineering from the University of Pennsylvania, and a B.S. degree in Physics and Math from the University of Bombay.

[1] Allen R. Myerson, "Less Is Brewing in Witching Hours," *The New York Times,* March 23, 1993.
[2] Franklin R. Edwards, "Does Futures Trading Increase Stock Volatility?" *Financial Analysts' Journal,* 44 (January–February 1988) 63–69; Franklin R. Edwards, "Futures Trading and Cash Market Volatility: Stock Index and Interest Rate Futures," *Journal of Futures Markets,* 8 (1988) 421–439.
[3] Hans R. Stoll and Robert E. Whaley, "Program Trading and Expiration-Day Effects," *Financial Analysts' Journal,* 43 (March–April 1987) 16–28.
[4] Hans R. Stoll and Robert E. Whaley, "Expiration-Day Effects: What Has Changed?" *Financial Analysts' Journal,* 47 (1991) 58–72.
[5] G. William Schwert, "Stock Market Volatility: Ten Years After the Crash," *Brookings-Wharton Papers on Financial Services,* October 1997.
[6] This volume was only exceeded once earlier on Tuesday, October 28, 1997 when 1.2 billion shares were traded on the NYSE.

Conrad (1989) reports similar results for option listings on the CBOE and AMEX from 1973 to 1980. Eighty-six of the 96 in her sample exhibited a decrease in share-price volatility with the introduction of an options contract. These results are reinforced by Aswath Damodaran and J. Lim (1991), who found a larger decrease in volatility following option listings than did previous studies. For a sample of 200 listings between 1973 and 1983, they reported a decline of 20 percent in volatility of both raw returns and excess returns.

FIGURE 3–1 **Evolution of Exchange Rate Risk Management Tools**

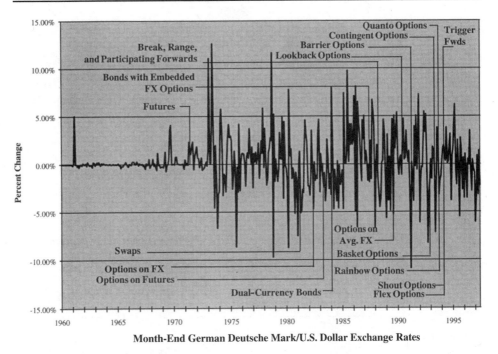

Month-End German Deutsche Mark/U.S. Dollar Exchange Rates

If the statistical evidence is so overwhelming, why do knowledgeable individuals like John Shad argue that the introduction of futures and options increased volatility? One answer may be that this is yet another instance in which cause and effect have been confused. There is no question that volatility and derivatives appear together; in Figure 3–1, we repeat a figure we showed you in Chapter 1. Some observers look at this pattern and conclude that the introduction of the derivative was responsible for the increased volatility:

$$\text{Derivatives} \rightarrow \text{volatility}$$

However, as we have noted throughout this book, risk management using derivative securities is a valuable activity only if prices in the cash market are volatile.

Responding to demand, the exchanges are more likely to list futures and options contracts on an asset when the underlying price becomes more volatile:

Volatility → derivatives

Consequently, the introduction of derivatives tends to coincide with increased volatility. But the empirical evidence we have summarized clearly indicates that volatility is the impetus for the introduction of derivatives, not the result.

Another answer is that observers may be confusing volatility with speed of adjustment. So let's look at the evidence on the impact of derivatives on speed of adjustment in the underlying markets.

The Impact on Adjustment Speed

The impact of the introduction of derivatives on the speed of price adjustment has been examined primarily in the context of options. The available evidence, summarized in Table 3–2, suggests that the derivatives may well increase the speed with which the market incorporates information and adjusts prices.

TABLE 3–2   The Impact of the Introduction of Derivatives on the Speed of Price Adjustment

Study (Sample Size—Period)	*Finding*
Jennings-Stark (1986) 180 stocks—1981–82	Prices of optioned stocks adjust *more quickly* to earnings reports
Skinner (1990) 214 stocks—1973–86	Reaction to earnings reports is smaller after listing of options
Damodaran-Lim (1991) 200 stocks—1973–85	Prices adjust *more quickly* to information after options are listed

Robert Jennings and Laura Stark (1981) examine the behavior of 180 stocks during the period 1981–82 and find that the prices of stocks that have traded options adjust *more quickly* to new information (specifically, earnings reports) than nonoptioned stocks of comparable size. Douglas Skinner (1990) considers 214 stocks for the period 1973–86 and finds that after options were listed, the reaction to earnings reports was smaller than it was without options. This evidence implies that some of the information content of the announcement already has been reflected in the share price and is consistent with the view that the option increases the incentive to invest in information about the firm. The Damodaran and Lim research we noted earlier also finds that share prices adjust *more quickly* to information after options are listed on a stock.

The Impact on the Bid-Ask Spread

Theory suggests that the introduction of derivative contracts should cause the bid-ask spread for the underlying asset to decline. There are two components of the bid-ask spread. One is the inventory component discussed by Demsetz (1968). The higher the cost of the inventory required to supply liquidity to the market, the higher the bid-ask spread. The introduction of derivatives, especially options, reduces this inventory cost by reducing the volatility of the underlying asset price and by increasing the volume of trading. The second component of the spread comes from the information disparity among traders. The larger the disparity within a market, the greater the spread. When it is available, the more informed traders tend to exploit their information in the options market. This translates informed traders' private information into prices that are publicly observable, thereby reducing the information disparity in the underlying market.

As was the case with speed of adjustment, the studies that have examined the impact on the bid-ask spread have focused on the listing of new options contracts on individual shares. The results of these studies are summarized in Table 3–3.

TABLE 3–3 The Impact of the Introduction of Derivatives on the Bid-Ask Spread in the Underlying Market

Study	Sample Size	Period	Effect on Bid-Ask Spread
Neal (1987)	16	1985–86	Decreases
Fedenia-Grammatikos (1992)	419	1970–88	NYSE: Decreases OTC: Increases
Damodaran-Lim (1991)	200	1973–86	Decreases

Robert Neal (1987) examines the behavior of 16 shares during the period 1985–86 and finds that the bid-ask spreads are *lower* for those shares that have listed options. Mark Fedenia and Theocharry Grammatikos (1992) use a much larger sample of 419 firms over the period 1970–88 and find that the average bid-ask spreads *decrease* after the listing of options for the 341 New York Stock Exchange–traded stocks. However, the bid-ask spreads increase for the 78 stocks in the sample that are traded over-the-counter. For their sample of 200 stocks, Damodaran and Lim conclude that the bid-ask spreads *decline* after the listing of options.[4]

The Impact on Trading Volume of the Underlying Assets

Theory suggests that trading volume on the underlying asset should increase when derivatives are introduced. As noted above, the introduction of derivatives can reduce the bid-ask spread in the underlying asset market. This reduction in transaction costs increases volume. Moreover, the derivatives market and the underlying asset market develop an important symbiotic relation. Shocks to either market are transmitted to the other by arbitrageurs exploiting any discrepancy in pricing between the markets.

The studies that have looked at the effects on trading volume when options are listed on the shares are summarized in Table 3–4. Unlike Tables 3–1, 3–2, and 3–3, this table reflects mixed conclusions.

TABLE 3–4   The Impact of the Introduction of Derivatives on Trading Volume in the Underlying Market

			Effect on Trading Volume	
Study	*Sample Size*	*Period*	*Raw*	*Market Adjusted*
Skinner (1989)	304	1973–86	Increase	
Damodaran-Lim (1991)	200	1973–86	Increase	No change
Bansal-Pruitt-Wei (1989)	175	1973–78		Increase
		1979–86		No change

In his examination of 304 shares, Skinner finds that there is an *increase* in the raw trading volume after the listing of options. For their sample of 200 shares, Damodaran and Lim report a similar increase in raw trading volume but find no significant change in market-adjusted trading volume. Vipul Bansal, Stephen Pruitt, and John Wei (1989) cast further light on this issue by categorizing option listings by time period. They find in their sample of 175 stocks over the period 1973–86 that the trading volume adjusted for the changes in the overall market *increases* after option listings prior to 1979 but not thereafter.

Summary

The empirical evidence discussed above on the impact of the introduction of derivatives on the markets for the underlying assets is summarized in Table 3–5. This evidence supports the following conclusions:

- With the possible exception of stock index futures, the introduction of derivatives has reduced price volatility in the underlying market.
- The introduction of derivatives enriches the information set and increases the speed with which prices adjust to information.
- The introduction of derivatives has decreased bid-ask spreads in the underlying market.
- The introduction of derivatives has had little effect on market-adjusted trading volume in the underlying market.

TABLE 3–5   The Impact of the Introduction of Derivatives on the Markets for the Underlying Assets: Summary

	Options on Individual Shares	Futures on		
		Commodities	Fixed Income Assets	S&P 500 Index
Volatility of the price of the underlying asset	−	−	− or no change	?
Speed of price adjustment for the underlying asset	+			
Bid-ask spread for the underlying asset	−			
Trading volume for the underlying asset	?			

The Impact of Risk Management on the Economy

In examining the remarkable growth of the derivative securities market, most financial economists conclude that the social benefits of financial innovation far outweigh the costs. Perhaps the principal benefit from the many securities innovations over the last two decades has been an improvement in the allocation of risk within the financial system. Derivatives have dramatically reduced the cost of transferring risks to those market participants who have a comparative advantage in bearing them. As Merton Miller (1992) says, "Efficient risk sharing is what much of the futures and options revolution has been all about."

Derivatives markets provide corporations the ability to hedge against currency, interest rate, and commodity-price risks far more quickly and cheaply than was possible before. For example, consider the developments in the mortgage market. Historically, a local institution originated, owned, and serviced the loan. Now investment bankers pool and repackage individual mortgages into securities and sell them in a national market. Local financial institutions more narrowly focus on origination and servicing, activities in which they are more likely to have a comparative advantage. The extraordinary growth of this as well as other forms of asset securitization has been made possible in part by the financial futures markets used to hedge the investment banker's exposures. And the bottom line is that this activity has resulted in substantial economic savings for consumers.[5]

These financial innovations—futures, swaps, and securitization—have permitted massive transfers of interest rate risk from local financial institutions to well-diversified institutional investors. This transfer has not only lowered mortgage rates for home buyers; it also should help protect the financial system from another disaster like the one experienced by the savings and loan industry.

We believe that it is critical to understand that even though one party's gain is another's loss in a derivatives market, the use of derivatives can create value. The more efficient risk sharing afforded by derivatives can reduce total risk for all market participants. For example, consider an oil company. Obviously, its profitability will be affected by market oil prices. Historically, to help manage this risk, the firm might diversify its activities by also operating a chemical subsidiary. But the skills required to run an oil company efficiently are not necessarily the same skills required in a chemical firm. And this diversified firm may well face difficult compromises in establishing its financing, dividend, or human relations policies. With access to a well-functioning oil derivatives market, the firms can split. Each can choose policies more customized for its needs, and both companies can hedge by exchanging their oil price exposures in the derivatives market.

Over the past two decades, derivatives have expanded the technology available to firms and individuals to manage risk. They have reduced the costs of managing exposures, thereby increasing liquidity and efficiency. While providing precise estimates of these benefits may be difficult, the continued growth of these markets suggests they are substantial.

The Impact of the Derivative Markets on Each Other

So far, we have seen strong evidence that the introduction of derivatives has had a beneficial impact on the markets for the underlying assets. While more *ad hoc,* the available evidence also suggests that the introduction of derivatives has had a beneficial impact on the macroeconomy.

However, there are those who continue to be concerned about the impact of the OTC derivative market on the exchange-traded derivatives. This was highlighted during the 1997 debate about an amendment to the Commodity Exchange Act (CEA) that would lead to a less-regulated "professional market" within the exchanges. In their testimony to Congress, the exchanges argued that volume in the OTC derivatives was increasing at the expense of the exchanges. A story that ran in the *Wall Street Journal* was particularly vivid:

> The volume numbers paint a grim picture for the exchanges. Once the center of the derivatives industry, the $16.3 billion market for exchange-traded futures is one-fourth the size of the freewheeling over-the-counter derivatives market, which consists primarily of private transactions between brokers, dealers and banks. And that less regulated, more customized OTC market is growing 10 times as fast, according to research by the Chicago exchanges. The CME, for years the second-largest futures exchange, has slipped to third behind the London Financial Futures and Options Exchange. The CME's foreign-currency volume dropped 24% during the past two years, while over-the-counter volume increased 43%. Without passage of the professional-markets legislation, "we'll lose our entire marketplace," says John F. Sandner, CME chairman.[6]

The dire prediction of the CME chairman was reiterated by Patrick Arbor, chairman of the Chicago Board of Trade: "Regulatory arbitrage is driving our business away, and if we don't provide a regulatory environment that fosters our ability to innovate, our markets will disappear."[7] And if simply looking at volume, you can see why the chairmen of the CBOT and CME were concerned. Figure 3–2 uses data from the BIS *67th Annual Report* to summarize the growth in notional principal outstanding in the OTC and exchange-traded markets between 1990 and 1996. Both markets are still growing, but the rate of growth of the OTC instruments has outstripped that of the exchange-traded instruments.

FIGURE 3–2   Growth in the OTC and Exchange-Traded Derivatives Markets

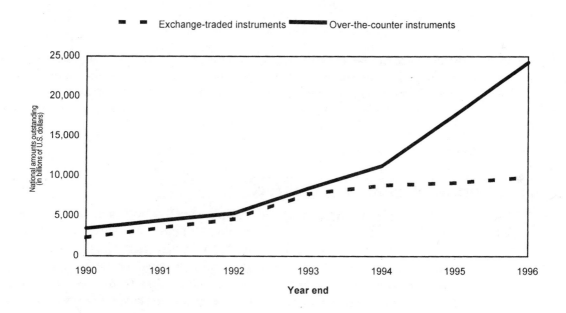

Notes

1. This section is based on Smith and Smithson (1989) and Damodaran and Subrahmanyam (1992).
2. *The Wall Street Journal,* January 15, 1988.
3. *The Wall Street Journal,* November 1, 1983.
4. The enhanced information provided by the option may also impact on the price of the underlying asset. Using a sample of 300 option listings during the period 1973–1986, DeTemple and Jorion (1990) found a significant increase in the price of the underlying stock around the listing date of the option—0.6 percent on the listing day and 2.9 percent in the two weeks surrounding the listing date. DeTemple and Jorion found a negative price effect associated with option delistings.
5. See Todd (1997).
6. Lucchetti (1997).
7. Reynolds (1997).

4 | FORWARD CONTRACTS

As indicated in Chapter 2, the forward contract is a fundamental building block for derivative instruments. It is the basis for the risk management instruments, both conceptually and in their use in the financial markets. (This becomes more evident when we look at the techniques dealers use to hedge their derivative portfolios in Chapter 18.)

The Structure of a Forward Contract

Of the financial derivatives, forward contracts are the most familiar, appearing in transactions as common as buying a puppy: "I'll pay you $X for that puppy with the spot on its right leg when it is weaned." A forward contract is a contract made today for the delivery of an asset in the future. *The buyer of the forward contract agrees to pay a specified amount at a specified date in the future to receive a specified amount of a currency, amount of a commodity, or coupon payment from the counterparty.* The specified future price (or rate) is referred to as the *contract* (or *forward*) *price.* The most notable forward market is the foreign exchange forward market, in which current volume is in excess of two thirds of a trillion dollars per day.[1] Forward contracts may require delivery of something physical, as in the case of the puppy or with most foreign exchange forwards. However, forward contracts can also be *cash-settled,* requiring only the exchange of the difference between the contract price and the spot price prevailing at the future date.

Figure 4–1 helps make this definition of a forward contract more concrete. Panel (*a*) illustrates a foreign exchange forward in which a party has agreed to pay, at time *T*, $Y to receive £X. Panel (*b*) illustrates a commodity forward contract in

FIGURE 4–1   Some Illustrative Forward Contracts

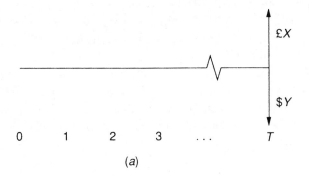

(a)

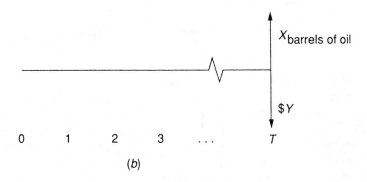

(b)

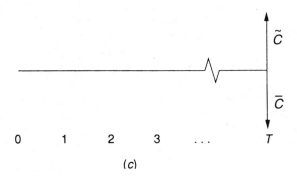

(c)

which a party has agreed to pay $Y to receive X barrels of oil at time T. Panel (c) illustrates a forward contract on interest rates, referred to in the market as a *forward-rate agreement (FRA)*. The parties to the contract have agreed on some *notional principal;* the party illustrated has agreed to pay a fixed-rate coupon on this notional principal, $\overline{C}$, at time T, in return for receiving a floating-rate coupon, $\tilde{C}$ (such as a six-month LIBOR).

At contract origination, the expected net present value of an *at-market* forward contract is zero. In an at-market forward, the contract price is set at the expected future price (the *forward price*); neither the buyer nor the seller of the forward will obtain value unless the exchange rate, commodity price, or interest rate differs from expectations.

Aside

Notional Principal

Many risk management products (including forward-rate agreements and cash-settled forwards on commodities) specify a notional principal for the contract. The principal is notional in the sense that it is not paid or received at contract maturity but is instead used only to calculate the cash flows paid and received. An example may help to clarify this point:

Suppose you enter into an FRA to receive floating/pay fixed with the following terms:

Maturity: 1 year

Notional principal: $1 million

Floating rate: one-year U.S. Treasury rate

Fixed rate (specified at contract origination): 5 percent

At contract maturity—in one year—the payment due to you is determined by the then current one-year Treasury rate and the notional principal of the contract. Suppose that one year from now the one-year Treasury rate is 6 percent; the payment due to you is

$$(0.06) \times \$1,000,000 = \$60,000$$

The payment you are required to make is determined by the fixed rate specified in the contract and the notional principal of the contract:

$$(0.05) \times \$1,000,000 = \$50,000$$

Since FRAs are cash-settled, only the net payment is made. You receive a check for $10,000.

The payoff profile for forward contract positions is illustrated in Figure 4–2. Panel (a) provides the payoff profile for the buyer of the forward contract (the party who is long in the forward contract). At contract maturity, the buyer of the forward contract is obligated to buy the asset at the contract price agreed to at contract origination, P_0^F. If the spot price at maturity, P_T, exceeds the contract price, the forward contract owner will be able to buy the asset at the lower exercise price and sell at the higher spot price, making a profit of $P_T - P_0^F$ per unit. Hence, the profit for the owner of the forward contract is

$$\text{Profit} = (P_T - P_0^F) \text{ (number of units contracted).} \qquad (4\text{--}1)$$

Conversely, the seller of the forward contract profits when the spot price at maturity is less than the exercise price; the seller of the forward can buy at the cheaper spot price and sell at the higher exercise price. Hence the profit for the seller of the forward contract is

$$\text{Profit} = (P_0^F - P_T) \text{ (number of units contracted).} \qquad (4\text{--}2)$$

Since the net present value at origination of the at-market forward contract is zero, why do parties enter into forward contracts? The contract must certainly have value for both the buyer and the seller of the contract; otherwise they would not transact. This value might exist because one party expects the future spot price to be different from the forward price—the prevailing view of the market. Or the forward contract may be used to create a synthetic asset. (We will return to this topic in Chapter 14.)

FIGURE 4–2   The Payoff for Forward Contract Positions

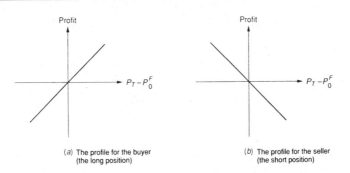

(*a*) The profile for the buyer
(the long position)

(*b*) The profile for the seller
(the short position)

A Framework for Forward Pricing

At origination of the forward contract, the counterparties agree on the price to be paid for the underlying asset at contract maturity.[2] How does that forward price get determined?

Forward Prices Must Reflect Costs and Benefits

Rather than starting with foreign exchange or interest rates, let's begin by considering a forward contract to purchase the *Mona Lisa*.[3] Suppose that you owned the *Mona Lisa* and had offered the painting for sale.

If delivery was to be immediate, the sales price—the spot price of the Mona Lisa—would be determined by the counterparties' assessment of the *Mona Lisa's* current market value.

But suppose that a potential buyer of the painting wanted to defer delivery of the painting for one year. The spot price of the *Mona Lisa* would have to be adjusted to reflect both the costs and the benefits of deferring the sale.

As the owner of the painting, you would incur some costs from the one-year deferral. Primary among these is an opportunity cost. If the sale were to occur today, you could take the proceeds of the sale and invest it in risk-free securities; so one cost of the one-year deferral is the interest that is forgone. In addition, you, the owner of the painting, will have some direct expenditures associated with storage and insurance.

However, as the owner of the painting, you would also gain some benefits in deferring the sale for one year. You could have a "showing" of the painting and charge admission. These admission receipts would represent income generation by the painting. (Note the similarity between the admission receipts for the painting and the coupon or dividend income generated by more traditional financial instruments.) And as the owner of the painting, you might also derive value simply by having the painting in your home so that you could look at it whenever you wanted, without having to leave your house. (Note the similarity between this and the "convenience yield" for commodities like oil.)

Incorporating the costs and benefits of deferring the sale, we could express the forward price of the *Mona Lisa* as[4]

$$\text{Forward price} = \text{spot price} + FV(\text{cost}) - FV(\text{benefits}) \qquad (4\text{--}3)$$

where *FV*( ) refers to the future value of costs and benefits.

Forward Prices Must Be Arbitrage-Free

Let's apply this framework we have developed to price a one-year forward contract on gold. The buyer of a gold forward agrees to pay a specified price in exchange for a specified quantity of gold at contract maturity—one year from today.

Let's suppose that the current spot gold price is $325 per ounce. On the cost side, let's use a one-year risk-free interest rate of 6 percent; but let's assume that someone will be willing to store and insure the gold for us for free.[5] On the benefit side, let's assume a gold interest rate of 2 percent—i.e., if I loan out gold, the interest rate I will earn is 2 percent per year. Given this information, the one-year forward price can be calculated as

$$\text{One-year forward price} = \$325 + (\$325 * 0.06) - (\$325 * 0.02)$$
$$= \$325 + \$19.50 - 6.50$$
$$= \$338$$

Some readers will be surprised to see that *expectations* about the future price of gold play no role in the determination of the forward price.[6] Instead of the expectations of either the buyer or the seller, what is important is that the forward price is a "no-arbitrage" price. To see what this means, let's consider what happens if the dealer sets a forward price different from $338.

Contract Prices above $338 Permit Arbitrage.   Suppose that the dealer quotes a forward price of $360—higher than the implied forward price calculated above. With such a price, you and I can make money at the dealer's expense. Today, you and I will:

Sell gold forward at $360	
Borrow $325 at 6%	$325
Purchase gold in the spot market at $325	($325)
Lend out the gold at 2%	

So today our transactions exactly offset. When the gold forward matures in one year, you and I will:

Pay back loan and accrued interest—325 × (1.06)	($344.50)
Receive accrued interest on gold on deposit	6.50
Deliver gold for $360	$360.00

Having repaid the loan, received the proceeds from lending the gold for one year, and delivered the gold, you and I will be left with a net profit of $22.

Contract Prices Below $338 Permit Arbitrage.   Suppose instead that the dealer quotes a forward price of $316—lower than the implied forward price calculated above. With such a price, you and I can again make money at the dealer's expense. Today, we will:

Buy gold forward at $316	
Borrow gold at 2%	
Sell gold in the spot market at $325	$325
Deposit $325 at 6%	($325)

So today our transactions exactly offset. When the gold forward matures in one year, we will:

Accept delivery of gold for $316	($316.00)
Return borrowed gold and pay accrued interest	(6.50)
Receive deposit and accrued interest	$344.50

Having accepted delivery of the gold, returned the borrowed gold, and received the proceeds from the one-year deposit, you and I will be left with a net profit of $22.[7]

Forward Contracts and Default

So far we have ignored default and transactions costs. However, the forward contract exhibits both performance risk and transactions costs. Since transactions costs for a forward contract are usually small,[8] we concentrate on performance risk.

Forward contracts are by nature credit instruments. Consider an FX forward contract in which you contract to deliver a specified number of deutsche marks one year in the future for a specified number of dollars. Suppose that this contract implies a forward rate of 3.0 DM/$ (the dollar price of a DM is $0.33). If, at contract maturity, the exchange rate has risen to 4 DM per dollar (the price of a DM has fallen to $0.08), you are now richer. You can buy the DM for $0.25 and then sell them for $0.33, a profit of 8 cents per DM. Conversely, your counterparty—the party who agreed to buy the DM—is now poorer by the same amount. Suppose the buyer of the forward contract—the loser on this contract—decides to abrogate the contract. You are out a sum of money, just as would be the case if your counterparty reneged on a loan. In this sense, a forward contract is a credit instrument.

The fact that forward contracts entail credit risk is important in determining who gets access to the forwards markets. Individuals, institutions, corporations, and governments that have access to credit lines are able to use forward contracts. Those for whom the costs of creating credit lines are high relative to the benefits of using the forward contract do not participate in the markets. Realistically, then, the forward market is less appropriate for the individual, the sole proprietorship, or the small corporation. It is a market for large corporations, governments, and other institutions—both financial and nonfinancial—that have access to credit lines as a daily part of their business.

Foreign Exchange Forwards

Foreign exchange forwards are traded in most major currencies, with bid-ask spreads quoted in standard maturities of 1, 2, 3, 6, 9, and 12 months.[9] Moreover, for the major currencies—sterling, yen, or deutsche mark—quotes for four months, five months, or other intervals are also available. On a negotiated basis, forwards are available in major currencies for "odd dates" (also referred to as "broken dates") as well. The extent to which a currency forward is available depends on whether exchange controls exist, the depth of alternative markets, and a country's monetary policy. Because of regulatory differences among domestic markets, the reference market used to price a forward (set a forward rate for a currency) is usually the Euromarket.

The forward foreign exchange markets—like the spot FX markets—are liquid and efficient and are used by sophisticated participants. The behavior of these markets will therefore be largely regulated by the legal contract under which they operate and the enforceability of that contract.

The Contract

Since forward contracts entail performance risk, the foreign exchange forward contract is written to address that risk, making the FX forward contract similar to that for a loan or a line of credit. The contract defines responsibility in payment once the contract matures, ensuring that nonperformance is equivalent to not making a payment on a loan.

After the two parties agree on the forward price for the future exchange of the underlying currencies, the parties specify other terms of the contract: the amount of one currency to be exchanged for a stated amount of the other, as well as the date and location of the exchange.

If the contract is to be cash-settled, it specifies the spot rate at the maturity date as the average of the bid-ask prices quoted by a specified bank for the spot purchase and spot sale, respectively, of the contract currency in exchange for U.S. dollars at a prescribed location (usually New York, London, or Tokyo) at a prescribed time (usually 11:00 A.M. local time).

Forward contracting requires the counterparties to agree on the forward price and settlement date and to exchange written confirmations. The settlement date of a forward contract is the date at which a contract is actually payable. For example, if on March 1 we agree to a three-month forward, the maturity date would be June 3, with the settlement date two days later.[10] These dates, as well as the date of origination of the contract, are stipulated in a confirmation telex exchanged between the contracting parties. As in a loan agreement, if one party is late in delivery of funds on contract settlement, penalty interest is incurred on the outstanding balance.

Not surprisingly, most forward contract documentation involves credit issues; pricing and settlement issues are a minority. Events of default receive particular attention, thereby underscoring the credit nature of the contract.

For a forward contract, the maturity date is the only relevant date in calculating the amount one party will owe the other on settlement date. That is, the legal agreement stipulates that the settlement flows are based only on the deviation in contract price from the spot price *on the maturity date.* According to the contract (though not necessarily from the contractors' perspectives), the time path that the foreign exchange rate follows between the origination date and the maturity date (when the settlement payment is calculated) is of no consequence.

The Forward Foreign Exchange Rate

The pricing of a foreign exchange forward contract is equivalent to determining the *forward foreign exchange rate.* In a sense, the forward rate is the wholesale price for the forward contract. To this, the dealer adds the bid-ask spread, which will be discussed in the next section.

Since the expected net present value of an at-market forward contract must be zero at origination, the easiest way to obtain the forward foreign exchange rate is to determine the exchange rate that guarantees that the net present value of the contract is zero. This relation is called *interest rate parity;* the technique used to do this is called *covered-interest arbitrage.*

Panel (*a*) of Figure 4–3 illustrates the cash flows for a forward foreign exchange contract for the party who has agreed to *buy* deutsche marks forward (or, conversely, *sell* dollars forward). The party illustrated must pay, at period *T*, a set number of dollars in return for a set number of deutsche marks. Panel (*b*) illustrates

FIGURE 4–3   A Forward Contract as a Pair of Loans

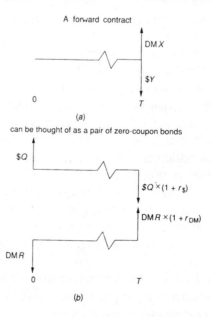

A forward contract

(*a*)

can be thought of as a pair of zero-coupon bonds

(*b*)

that the cash flows in panel (*a*) could be replicated with a pair of zero-coupon loans (or notes). At contract origination (time zero), the party illustrated borrows Q dollars and simultaneously lends the equivalent amount in deutsche marks, R. That is, given the spot exchange rate between dollars and deutsche marks at time zero, S_0, Q dollars is equivalent to R deutsche marks—R DM = $\$Q \times S_0$. At maturity—at time T—the party illustrated will have to pay back $Q \times (1 + r_\$)$ dollars, where $r_\$$ is the U.S. dollar interest rate for maturity T, and will receive $R \times (1 + r_{DM})$ deutsche marks, where r_{DM} is the T-period rate for a deutsche mark borrowing. If the two cash flows diagrams illustrated in panel (*b*) were added together to obtain a single cash flow diagram, the result would be the forward contract illustrated in panel (*a*), where

$$X \text{ DM} = R (1 + r_{DM}) \text{ DM} \qquad \text{and} \qquad \$Y = \$Q (1 + r_\$) \qquad (4\text{–}4)$$

Consequently, a forward contract for foreign exchange can be priced as if it were a pair of zero-coupon loans—the bullet repayments plus interest are netted against the future spot foreign exchange rate on the maturity date. Thus, from a purely mechanical pricing basis, the spot rate at origination, S_0, times the amount of the domestic currency, $\$Q$, fixes the amount of foreign currency to be lent. And with knowledge of the two relevant interest rates $r_\$$ and r_{DM}, the amounts of the two cash flows to be exchanged at T are determined.

Therefore, the forward foreign exchange rate at contract origination, F_0, can be obtained by dividing the cash flows at T by one another:

$$F_0 = \frac{R \times (1 + r_{DM})}{Q \times (1 + r_\$)} \qquad (4\text{–}5)$$

And since R deutsche marks equals $\$Q$ times the spot exchange rate at contract origination, $R = Q \times S_0$, it follows that the forward rate is

$$F_0 = S_0 \left[\frac{1 + r_{DM}}{1 + r_\$} \right] \qquad (4\text{–}6)$$

Generalizing, we can express the forward exchange rate for currencies 1 and 2 at time t as

$$F_t = S_t \frac{(1 + r_2)}{(1 + r_1)} \qquad (4\text{–}7)$$

where the forward and the spot are defined at time t as the number of units of Country 2's currency per units of Country 1's currency. [For example, if Country 2 is Germany and Country 1 is the United States, $F(t)$ and $S(t)$ are defined in deutsche marks per dollar.]

Alternatively, Equation 4–7 can be written in the form often referred to as interest rate parity:

$$F_t/S_t = (1 + r_2)/(1 + r_1) \qquad (4\text{–}8)$$

That is, the ratio of forward rate to the spot is a reflection of the relation between the interest rates in the two countries.

If the interest rate in Country 2 is higher than in Country 1, then the forward rate is greater than the spot—or Country 2's currency is weaker in the forward market than Country 1's. Returning to dollars and deutsche marks, if the dollar interest rate is lower than the DM interest rate, the forward DM/$ rate is greater than the spot; an alternative way of saying the same thing is that the dollar would be selling at a *premium* to the deutsche mark (or that DM is selling at a *discount* to today's spot rate).

Aside

Interest Rate Parity

The simplest way to illustrate the interest rate parity relation is to visualize the relation between currencies today and currencies in the future as a "box." In the following diagram we have continued using U.S. dollars and deutsche marks.

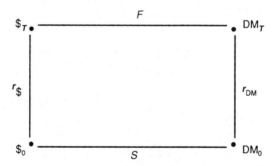

Dollars today ($\$_0$) are represented in the lower-left corner of the box; DM today are represented at the lower right. At the upper-left corner are future dollars ($\$_T$) and at the upper-right corner are future deutsche marks (DM_T).

Four markets link these magnitudes:

1. Dollars today ($\$_0$) and dollars in the future ($\$_T$) are related by the U.S. credit market, which determines the domestic interest rate ($r_\$$).

Interest Rate Parity continued

2. German credit markets link deutsche marks today (DM_0) with future deutsche marks (DM_T), through the interest rate in Germany (r_{DM}).
3. Dollars today and DM today are linked by the spot currency market (S).
4. Future DM and future dollars are linked through the forward/futures market (F).

We can get from future dollars to future DM via the forward currency market—across the top of the box. But we can also get from future dollars to future DM by going around the box the other way:

1. Borrow dollars today in the U.S. credit market.
2. Trade the current dollars received for current DM in the spot FX market.
3. Lend the DM today in the German credit market for future DM.

Since the same result can be achieved in two ways, arbitrage forces the U.S. dollar price for DM in the future to be the same, regardless of the way we "move around the box." Therefore, the spot FX, forward FX, and credit market prices must be mutually consistent. The forward foreign exchange rate must be related to the spot rate via the domestic and foreign interest rates.

Illustration 4–1

Pricing an FX Forward Contract

On August 25, 1997, foreign exchange and interest rates were as follows:

Spot DM per dollars	1.8175
U.S. interest rate (one year)	0.060000
DM interest rate (one year)	0.036150

Using Equation 4–7, we find that the one-year forward rate is

$$F = 1.8175 \times \left(\frac{1 + 0.036150}{1 + 0.060000} \right)$$

$$= 1.7766$$

In the foreign exchange market, the difference between the spot rate and the forward rate is called the *premium* if the difference is positive or the *discount* if negative. In our example, the premium is 0.0409.

Bid-Ask Spreads

In the preceding forward-rate calculations, we used what market participants normally refer to as *mid-rates*—the midpoint of the bid-ask spread. If buyers and sellers of FX forwards were to contract with each other directly, without having a dealer as an intermediary, the transactions would occur at this mid-rate. However, if a dealer is to provide immediacy—provide liquidity until the other side of the trade arrives—the dealer must earn a spread to cover the costs of creating the forward contract.

Since forwards are credit instruments, the dealers in the forward foreign exchange market are typically banks. The dealer (market maker) will quote one price to the buyer of FX forwards and another price to the seller. In the spot and forward foreign exchange markets, prices are usually quoted in units of foreign currency per dollar.[11] Prices are quoted at the fourth decimal point for currencies such as deutsche marks, sterling, and Canadian dollars, and to the first or second decimal place for currencies such as the Japanese yen and Italian lira (e.g., the lira was trading at 1771.9 per dollar on August 25, 1997. The bid-ask spread on the major currencies in the spot market is very small. For example, on spot deutsche marks, the bid-ask spread is usually as low as 5 to 10 "pips," a pip being 1/10,000 of a DM. (On August 25, 1997, deutsche marks were quoted at DM/$ 1.8172/77—i.e., DM/$ 1.8172 bid, 1.8177 offered.)

The interest rate markets (the money markets) also operate on this bid-offer concept.[12] For example, on August 25, 1997, at 10:30 A.M. EST, the bid-ask range for the 12-month Eurodollar deposit rate was 0.059375–0.060625 and that for the Euro-deutsche mark deposit rate was 0.035600–0.036700. Given this information, we can look again at the forward rate and the forward premium described in the previous example. But this time the exercise takes on a new twist: instead of mid-rates, we can calculate the relevant bid-ask forward rates.

Illustration 4–2

Pricing an FX Forward Contract Again

On August 25, 1997, the relevant bid-ask spreads were:

Spot FX: DM per dollar   1.8172 / 1.8177

U.S. interest rate (one-year)   0.059375 − 0.060625

DM interest rate (one-year)   0.035600 − 0.036700

Utilizing Equation 4–7, we can calculate a bid-ask spread for the forward rate. To obtain the 12-month bid rate for the forward, we divide $(1 + r_{DM}$ bid) by $(1 + r_\$$ ask) and then

Pricing an FX Forward Contract Again continued

multiply by spot bid. The reverse is done to obtain the forward ask rate:

Forward rate: 1.7743–1.7788

To understand the logic of this, let's construct the rate at which the dealer will buy DM in the future—the bid side on the forward rate. An alternative to buying the forward contract would be to borrow dollars, buy DM spot, and then invest the purchased DM for one year. Consequently, the relevant spot FX rate is the buy rate today—the bid spot rate—as our base. Since the dealer would be investing DM, the relevant interest rate is the deposit rate: the bid rate. Conversely, since the dealer would be borrowing dollars, he or she would have to pay the borrowing rate—the ask rate. In our example the premium is 0.0429–0.0389.

Notice that the premium is quoted with the higher number first. Usually the foreign exchange forward market quotes the spot and then the forward premium or discount. If the currency is at a premium to the dollar as in this case (if DM interest rates are lower), then the higher figure is quoted first, which indicates that the numbers are added to the spot bid-ask spread.

Forward-Rate Agreements

Forward-rate agreements (FRAs) exist in various currencies, but the largest markets are in U.S. dollars, pounds sterling, deutsche marks, Swiss francs, and Japanese yen. While the market is global, much of the business is done in London. Within the sterling and dollar markets, dealers will offer two-way quotes, with a bid-offer spread. This is, of course, similar to any actively traded securities market, and it closely parallels the forward foreign exchange market.

The Contract

Since a forward-rate agreement is a forward contract on interest rates and not a forward commitment to make a loan or take a deposit, the agreements underscore the notional-principal nature of the FRA—neither party has a commitment to lend or to borrow the contract amount. Furthermore, FRA contracts generally contain a "normal banking practice" clause that commits the parties to specific performance. If a party fails to perform, this clause makes the outstanding net cash value of the contract subject to the same conditions that would apply in the case of nonperformance on a loan. Such a clause highlights the fact that an FRA, like a foreign exchange forward, is a credit instrument: no value is conveyed at origin or over the life of the contract; all value is conveyed at maturity.

The Forward Interest Rate

In the previous discussion we took as given the contract rate—the forward interest rate. The fact is, however, that the forward interest rate, like the forward foreign exchange rate, can be derived from an arbitrage condition. To do so we will begin with an example and then generalize the arguments.

Illustration 4–3

Deriving a Forward Rate

Suppose you have $100 to invest for two years. Should you invest for one year, then reinvest the proceeds for another year, or should you invest for two years? Is there any difference?

Suppose that one-year investments are yielding approximately 4 percent and two-year investments are yielding approximately 5 percent. Is the fact that the two-year rate exceeds the one-year rate sufficient information for you to make your decision?

No. To compare the two investments, you need to know not only the rates for one and two years but also the rate you would be able to invest for one year in one year's time—the *forward* rate.

In the same way that the foreign exchange forward rate must be that which eliminates arbitrage profit in the spot foreign exchange market and the interest rate markets for the currencies involved, the forward interest rate for one year in one year, $_{12}R_{24}$, must eliminate any potential arbitrage over time in a particular interest rate market. Borrowing (lending) for one year and then rolling the borrowing (lending) over for a second year,

$$[\$100 (1 + 0.04)] \times [1 + {}_{12}R_{24}]$$

must be equivalent to the borrowing (lending) for two years.

$$\$100 [1 + 0.05]^2$$

Using this arbitrage relation,

$$[1 + {}_{12}R_{24}] = \frac{\$100[1 + 0.05]^2}{\$100[1 + 0.04]}$$

So the one-year forward rate in one year must be 6.01 percent.*

The decision to invest in one year and then reinvest for the second year versus investing for the full two years can now be made. On the basis of the forward-rate calculation, the market's "expectation" for the one-year rate in one year is 6.01 percent. If you expect the one-year rate in one year to be higher than 6.01 percent, then invest for one year, planning to reinvest for a second year at the end of the first year. If, however, you expect the one-year rate in one year to be below 6.01 percent, the most appropriate strategy is to invest for two years today.

---

*Alternatively, we can look at the future values of the two strategies. If you invest for one year and roll over at the end of the first year, the future value is

$$FV = (1.04) \times 100 \times (1.0601) = 110.25$$

If you invest for two years, the future value is

$$FV = (1.05)^2 \times 100 = 110.25$$

The future value is the same from both strategies. Of course, if it were not, the forward rate we calculated would not be the arbitrage rate, and one strategy would dominate the other.

To generalize the formula for one-year investments, we recognize that the forward rate is implicit in the yield curve itself. For example, for the one-year rate one year from today ($t = 0$), we solve the equation;[13]

$$(1 + {}_0R_1)(1 + {}_1R_2) = (1 + {}_0R_2)^2 \qquad (4\text{--}9)$$

where

$\quad {}_0R_1 =$ the one-year interest rate today

$\quad {}_0R_2 =$ the two-year interest rate today

$\quad {}_1R_2 =$ the forward interest rate for one year in one year
$\quad \quad$ (i.e., the rate between years 1 and 2)

In general, the forward rate from year j to year k is given by ${}_jR_k$ in

$$(1 + {}_0R_j)^j (1 + {}_jR_k)^{k-j} = (1 + {}_0R_k)^k \qquad (4\text{--}10)$$

For periods less than one year, the equation must be modified. If we want to know the forward rate from month j to month k and if the interest rates are quoted as *simple rates,* we solve for ${}_jR_k$:

$$[1 + (j/12)\, {}_0R_j]\, [1 + ((k - j)/12)\, {}_jR_k] = [1 + (k/12){}_0R_k] \qquad (4\text{--}11)$$

If, however, the interest rates are quoted as compound rates, the appropriate formula is[14]

$$(1 + {}_0R_j)^{j/12} (1 + {}_jR_k)^{(k-j)/12} = (1 + {}_0R_k)^{k/12}$$

Bid-Ask Spreads

In the same way that foreign exchange forwards evolved from parallel borrowing and depositing, FRAs evolved from *forward-forward contracts.* A forward-forward is an obligation in which one financial institution agrees to deposit money at another institution at a specified future date, at a specified interest rate (set at contract origination). Since physical deposits are to be made, the credit risk is obvious. The FRA evolved to separate the deposit risk from the interest rate risk. With an FRA, only the net interest flows need be exchanged, so the credit risk is reduced.

The language of the FRA market reflects this evolution; in the forward-forward market, the bid-offer spread is a deposit versus borrowing spread. Consequently, on a Reuters screen the FRA rate might be quoted, say, $3\frac{3}{4} - 3\frac{5}{8}$ (i.e., you can *borrow* at $3\frac{3}{4}$ or *deposit* at $3\frac{5}{8}$). Of course, since FRAs are cash-settled forwards, there is no actual borrowing or deposit as would be the case with forward-forward contracts.

As with foreign exchange forwards, bid-ask spread for an FRA is united by the actual cost associated with the physical depositing and borrowing that could occur instead of using the FRA. Indeed, since neither deposits nor borrowings occur, the bid-offer spread is more narrow for FRAs than for actual borrowings and deposits because the credit risk of the transaction has been reduced significantly. (There is, as pointed out earlier, still residual credit risk similar to that inherent in a forward foreign-exchange-rate contract.)

Figure 4–4 provides some insight into the bid-offer spreads for FRAs by reproducing a broker screen in Reuters. This screen presents quotes for three- and six-month UK sterling FRAs commencing in one month, two months, three months, . . . and 18 months; for three-month FRAs, a contract commencing in twenty-one months is also quoted. The jargon used in this market—3 × 6 for an FRA from month 3 to month 6 (a three-month rate in three months) and 5 × 11 for an FRA from month 5 to month 11 (a six-month rate in five months)—is a holdover from the forward-forward contract. The second and third columns provide the bid and offer prices for the FRAs, the fourth column indicates which broker (or bank) provided the respective quote, the fifth column indicates where the quote provider is located, and the sixth column indicates the time the quote was provided.

FIGURE 4–4   Prices in the Forward-Rate Agreement Market, Quoted on August 25, 1997

	GBP			*DEALING*	
1 × 4	7.31	7.35	TULLETTS	LON	20:02
2 × 5	7.28	7.33	HARLOWBUTLER	LON	01:28
3 × 6	7.35	7.40	HARLOWBUTLER	LON	01:28
4 × 7	7.39	7.44	HARLOWBUTLER	LON	01:28
5 × 8	7.40	7.45	HARLOWBUTLER	LON	01:28
6 × 9	7.41	7.46	HARLOWBUTLER	LON	01:28
7 × 10	7.42	7.47	HARLOWBUTLER	LON	01:29
8 × 11	7.41	7.46	HARLOWBUTLER	LON	01:29
9 × 12	7.40	7.45	HARLOWBUTLER	LON	01:28
12 × 15	7.34	7.39	HARLOWBUTLER	LON	01:28
15 × 18	7.31	7.31	TRADITION	LDN	07:41
18 × 21	7.04	7.07	TRADITION	LDN	04:00
21 × 24	7.45	7.45	TRADITION	LDN	07:41
1 × 7	7.38	7.43	HARLOWBUTLER	LON	01:28
2 × 8	7.42	7.47	HARLOWBUTLER	LON	01:28
3 × 9	7.46	7.51	HARLOWBUTLER	LON	01:28
4 × 10	7.47	7.52	HARLOWBUTLER	LON	01:28
5 × 11	7.47	7.52	HARLOWBUTLER	LON	01:28
6 × 12	7.47	7.52	HARLOWBUTLER	LON	01:28
7 × 13	7.54	7.56	TRADITION	LDN	12:53
8 × 14	7.51	7.53	TRADITION	LDN	12:39
9 × 15	7.52	7.54	TRADITION	LDN	12:34
12 × 18	7.37	7.42	HARLOWBUTLER	LON	01:28
18 × 24	7.33	7.38	HARLOWBUTLER	LON	01:28

SOURCE: Reprinted by permission of Reuters.

Risk Management in Practice

Pricing an FRA

George François

On August 25, 1997, XYZ Corporation anticipated that on November 28 of that year it would borrow $1 million for three months for which it would pay an interest rate determined by the then current U.S. dollar three-month LIBOR rate. (The liability would mature on February 27, 1998.)

XYZ wanted to transact an FRA to hedge the resulting exposure to the three-month U.S. dollar LIBOR rate in three months. The appropriate forward contract to hedge this exposure is a 3×6 FRA.

The following term sheet contains all of the data for the FRA . . . except the fixed rate (i.e., the contract rate).

Notional amount	USD 1 million
Transaction date	August 25, 1997
Effective date	August 27, 1997
Maturity date	November 28, 1997
Fixed payer	XYZ Corporation
Floating payer	ABC Bank
Fixed rate	———
Floating rate	Three-month USD LIBOR
Rollover convention	Modified following

The fixed rate for the 3×6 FRA would be the three-month forward, three-month interest rate. The price of the FRA is the rate that eliminates arbitrage in the interest rate market. For the 3×6 FRA, the no-arbitrage condition equates two six-month *investment* strategies: (1) an outright six-month investment and (2) two successive three-month investments (one at the spot three-month interest rate and the second at the three-month forward, three-month rate). Hence, the three-month forward, three-month rate, $_3R_6$, can be calculated as[†]

$$_3R_6 = [(1 + {_0R_6} * act/360) / (1 + {_0R_3} * act/360) - 1] * 360/act$$

where $_0R_3$ is the spot three-month LIBID (London Interbank Bid Rate), $_0R_6$ is the spot six-month LIBID, and act/360 is the day-count calculation methodology

Pricing an FRA continued

which counts the actual number of days in a holding period divided by a 360-day calendar year.[‡] On August 27, U.S. dollar interest rates were:

Term	Bid	Ask
3-month	5.5625%	5.6875%
6-month	5.6875%	5.8125%

So the fixed rate for the FRA was 5.7966%:

$$_3R_6 = [(1 + 0.056875 * 184/360) / (1 + 0.055625 * 93/360) - 1] * 4$$

$$= 0.057966$$

If, on November 28, 1997, U.S. dollar three-month LIBOR is above 5.7966%, XYZ Corporation will incur an increase in interest expense on its floating-rate liability, but will receive a net payment on its FRA position. Conversely, if the rate is below 5.7966%, XYZ will have a lower interest expense but a net payment on its FRA position.

George François is an Executive Director at CIBC Oppenheimer Corp. and faculty member within the *School of Financial Products*. Prior to joining CIBC World Markets in 1996, Mr. François worked at the International Swaps and Derivatives Association (ISDA) where he was primarily responsible for conducting the association's market survey, and developing specialized surveys of derivatives industry defaults and portfolio replacement values. Mr. François holds an M.B.A. in Finance from Fordham University.

[†]The no-arbitrage condition looks at investments which can be made at the relevant bid rates. Deposits (investments) can be made at a dealer's bid rate while loans can be obtained at the offer rate.

[‡]FRAs are quoted on a simple interest basis and day-count corresponding to the underlying interest rate. For example, USD LIBOR is quoted on an actual/360 day count.

Notes

1. In "Central Bank Survey of Foreign Exchange Activity in April 1995," the Bank for International Settlements reported that outright forward foreign exchange volume (net of all double counting) was $670 billion per day. (Daily spot FX volume was $520 billion.)

2. In most forwards, settlement occurs two business days after contract maturity.

3. This example is adapted from Kenneth R. French (1988), "Pricing Financial Futures Contracts," *Financial Markets and Portfolio Management*.

4. We got to Equation (4–3) by thinking about what the seller will want to charge; but we can also get there by thinking about the amount the buyer will pay. In an efficient market, market forces will prevent potential buyers of assets from avoiding the costs of

owning an asset by negotiating a forward sale. Stated another way, the costs of owning the asset should not be avoidable by purchasing a forward contract. In fact, if it were possible to avoid these costs, there would be an increase in demand for forward contracts which would drive up its price. Similarly, if there are benefits from owning the asset, forward purchasers should not be able to capture these benefits of ownership while avoiding the costs.

5. This somewhat surprising assumption is actually very close to the truth. If I owned a substantial amount of gold, I would have no trouble finding depositories that would store it for me for "free." Why? While the gold is in their vaults, they would be lending out my gold—in much the same way that my stockbroker lends out equity that I have left with him.

6. However, remember that expectations of the future gold price are incorporated in the current spot price of gold.

7. This arbitrage argument works for assets held as investments such as gold or silver for which short selling is feasible. For assets that are not held as investments and have consumption value, short selling may not be possible to execute the arbitrage strategy.

8. Transaction costs are small as a percentage of the forward contract size typically observed in the market. The cost of transacting has a high fixed-cost component, with very little marginal costs. Thus a $10,000 and a $10 million forward foreign exchange contract would have nearly the same transactions cost.

9. Longer-dated contracts do exist, in which case the bid-ask spreads are subject to negotiation.

10. Spot currency transactions are not actually dealt two days forward (with the exception of Canadian $/USD), and forwards are always quoted from spot. Thus, a March 1 spot quote is for March 3, so a three-month forward would be March 3 to June 3.

11. The exceptions to this rule are the pound sterling and the ECU, which are usually quoted as dollars per unit of sterling or ECU.

12. In this case we refer to the Euro markets; that is, the Eurodollar and Euro-deutsche mark markets.

13. The general formula simplifies the calculation of time factors. In practice, calculation of a time factor varies according to the respective interest rate market. For example, forward rates calculated based on U.S. dollar LIBOR follow an actual/360 day-count methodology.

14. The formula expressed here assumes annual compounding.

5

APPLICATIONS OF FORWARDS*

Forward contracts exist because they permit firms (as well as governments and some individuals) to separate financial price risk from the underlying business activity and transfer that price risk to another party. Forwards foster creativity. The creation of liquid forward foreign exchange markets, in various currencies, allows investors to develop customized investment strategies and firms to manage unavoidable business risks. In this chapter we will provide a few illustrations to show how forwards can be packaged to address the demands of financial institutions, industrial corporations, and portfolio managers.

The Markets

In Chapter 4 we concentrated on the forward markets for foreign exchange and interest rates (FX forwards and FRAs), but forward markets also exist for commodities—gold, oil, and so forth. Some of these forward contracts have joined FX forwards and FRAs as part of the standard trading operations of large financial institutions.[1] Other forward contracts are traded outside traditional interbank markets. For example, forward contracts on North Sea crude oil (Brent) and forward contracts on primary metals are traded on the London Metal Exchange.

Foreign Exchange Forwards

In the foreign exchange market, volume figures compiled by the Bank for International Settlements (Table 5–1) indicated that, by 1995, daily volume for forward

---

*This chapter was originally drafted by D. Sykes Wilford.

foreign exchange contracts was $670 billion, about 56 percent of total volume in the foreign exchange market.[2] Trading continues to be dominated by DM/$, £/$, and yen/$, followed by SF/$ and various nondollar to nondollar deals.

TABLE 5–1 Global Foreign Exchange Market Turnover in April 1995 Daily Averages in Billions of U.S. Dollars

Category	Amount	Percentage Share
Estimated global turnover	1,190	100
Spot transactions	520	44
Outright forwards and foreign exchange swaps	670	56
Memorandum item	70	
Futures and options*		

*Currency futures, OTC currency options, and exchange-traded currency options only. OTC options adjusted for local and cross-border double-counting; exchange-traded options and futures not adjusted for double-counting; including estimated gaps in reporting.

Major dealing centers can be divided by time zones.

Far East	Middle East	Europe	Americas
Tokyo	Bahrain	London	New York
Hong Kong		Paris	Chicago
Singapore		Zurich	Toronto
Sydney		Geneva	San Francisco
		Frankfurt	

Other centers, though on smaller scales, include Brussels, Luxembourg, Madrid, Milan, Amsterdam, Munich, Hamburg, Kuwait, Kuala Lumpur, Los Angeles, Montréal, and Johannesburg.

Many currencies can be dealt either directly or indirectly in the FX forward markets. These foreign currencies are currently traded:

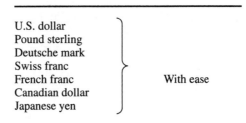

U.S. dollar
Pound sterling
Deutsche mark
Swiss franc
French franc
Canadian dollar
Japanese yen

With ease

Danish krone
Dutch guilder
Irish punt
Italian lira
Finnish mark
Belgian franc
Spanish peseta
Austrian schilling
Australian dollar
Singapore dollar
Hong Kong dollar   Less liquid but
Kuwait dinar   quotes are
New Zealand dollar   readily available
Malaysian ringit
South African rand
Portuguese escudo
Thai baht
Saudi riyal
Swedish krone
Norwegian krone
ECU
SDR

FRAs

The FRA market is also growing. Annual turnover in 1988 was estimated to be $300 to $500 billion, up from only $50 billion in 1985. Growth has been primarily in the interbank market, where FRAs are used as an effective tool for asset and liability management. But FRAs are becoming more widely used by corporate treasurers to manage interest rate risk. Though less than 10 percent of all FRA transactions now involve nonfinancial corporations, that percentage is expected to rise to 20 percent as the market becomes more developed.

Average sizes of forward-rate-agreement transactions are about $100 to $200 million. The most liquid markets are in dollars and sterling, but deutsche marks are becoming more important; they threaten to overtake the leaders as the most traded currency.[3]

Most trading continues to be done in London, with over 150 traders said to be trading FRAs. Considering the close relation between FRAs and interest rate swaps, which we described in Chapter 2, one might expect New York to dominate trading, at least in dollar FRAs, but this has not happened. Indeed, as with the forward foreign exchange market, London continues to dominate trading. Markets for both FRAs and FX forwards tend to be more liquid with finer bid-ask spreads in London trading hours.

The Trading Rooms

Foreign Exchange Forward Trading

FX forwards are normally traded in conjunction with the spot foreign exchange desk and the deposit desk. As shown in illustration 5–1, this practice allows the risk to be broken apart and reassembled into different forms.

In this example, the trader used the "typical" way of synthetically creating a hedge for the forward position. There are others. For example, the trader could have closed the spot leg and left open the deposit by putting the dollars in an overnight account or, if it were more convenient, used a 3-month deposit with a 3- versus 12-month FRA. (Indeed, because of volatility of the spot rates, most traders are likely to close the spot leg first, then worry about the other prices of the transaction.)

What is important to remember is that FX forwards, deposits, and FRAs can be put together to create alternative ways to close or open positions. Traders must open and close legs in the most cost-efficient way in order to maximize the return on their positions.

Illustration 5–1

Laying off an FX Forward

George Brown trades FX forwards at the London branch of XYZ Bank of Hong Kong. He makes a market in DM/$ forwards and is responsible for managing the risk of his position. Available to him on the trading room floor are the related markets: spot foreign exchange, Eurodeposits, FRAs, and all the rest.

On July 5, 1988, he receives a call from BHZ Co. of Birmingham, a firm he has talked to on a regular basis for several years. BHZ sells products it buys from a U.S. manufacturer in Germany. BHZ is long deutsche marks and short dollars.

BHZ: George, how's the dollar?

George: DM/$1.6800–1.6810, with the deutsche mark trading lower [weaker] in active trading.

BHZ: I am worried about a commitment we have in 12 months. If we get a bounce [if the deutsche mark gets stronger], let's cover for 50 dollars [$50 million] for 12 months outright.

George: Okay, the premium now for 12 months is 355/345, so the 12-month forward should be at DM/$1.6445–1.6465.

BHZ: Call me back in about an hour.

One hour and 20 minutes later and spot has moved against BHZ. The DM has weakened further and is now trading at

DM/$1.6900/10 spot. George calls BHZ with the bad news.

BHZ: Hello, George? Okay! That's awful.

George: No sign of intervention in Frankfurt but the SNB [Swiss National Bank] has done a FX swap for $120 million against Swissie for three months.

BHZ: What's an FX swap?

George: This is a forward outright with a spot transaction. It's designed to push interest rate differentials and soak up francs simultaneously. The Swiss are trying to break the strength in the dollar. Odds are the Bundesbank will be in later, but I'm not sure the Fed is committed. We'll have to watch when New York opens.

BHZ: Okay, call me if the Fed comes in by 3:00 P.M.

George calls BHZ at 4:00 P.M.

George: BHZ? Okay, the Fed's in and the spot has retreated to DM/$1.6795–1.6805. I think you should cover now.

BHZ: Okay, I'll cover; I want to buy dollars, 12 months forward for a size equal to $50 million.

George: Fine, done at DM/$1.6460 for $50 million.

How then does George lay off this position? He may be lucky enough to find someone who will sell $50 million in 12 months at his ask price (DM/$1.6440), giving him a profit of $100,000.

However, if George can't find that forward seller of dollars, he can lay off the position in the cash markets. In July 1988, the 12-month deposit rate for dollars was 8 percent, so Equation 4-6 and the techniques in the example of pages 62–64 indicate that the "no-arbitrage" DM borrowing rate would be 5.78 percent. For the forward contract he just concluded with BHZ, George knows that in 12 months, he will receive DM/82.3 million and will have to pay $50 million. If he borrows DM/77,803,000 at 5.78 percent, converts the DM into $46,297,500 at today's spot rate (1.6805), and then deposits the dollars at 8.00 percent, George would just break even:

Today	In 12 Months
Borrow DM/77,803,000	Owe DM/82,300,000
Convert the borrowed DM at spot rate of 1.6805→$46,297,500	
Deposit $46,297,500	Deposit worth $50,000,000

However, George wants to do better than just break even. It might be the case that the DM money market trader at XYZ Bank of Hong Kong is particularly aggressive and is willing to lend at an attractive rate.* If, for instance, the DM money market desk is willing to lend him DM for 12 months at 10 basis points below the market rate (at 5.68 percent) George can earn a profit of $43,800.

Laying off an FX Forward continued

	Today	In 12 Months

	Borrow DM/77,876,600
	  Convert the borrowed DM at spot
	  rate of 1.6805→$46,341,300
		Owe DM/82,300,000

	Deposit of $46,297,500	Deposit worth $50,000,000
	Profit of $43,800	

---

*A real-life George may have had access to an aggressive DM lending rate because the bank had unmatched DM yield-curve positions being managed in its Frankfurt office.

FRA Trading

Like foreign exchange forward trading, FRA trading is driven by arbitrage—in this case, the arbitrage of taking and placing deposits for mismatched dates. Consequently, the FRA is a vehicle that permits the user to move up and down the yield curve, leaving the balance sheet intact.

Trading FRAs is best illustrated by another example. (See Illustration 5–2.) This time we will begin with a user of FRAs and then turn our user into a trader.

Illustration 5–2

Using FRAs for Asset-Liability Management

MidWest Banc, a U.S. regional bank, has $5 billion in assets. MidWest deals with small corporations and, as the premier consumer bank in its market, directly with the public.

MidWest Banc has just formed a syndication with the New York branch of a Swiss bank and a major U.S. investment bank. In this syndication MidWest Banc agreed to provide $200 million on a two-year fixed-rate basis.

MidWest's Asset and Liability Management Committee (ALCO) has been convened to discuss the bank's increased exposure to interest rates. Before the transaction, the bank's asset and liability positions were matched with respect to maturity. MidWest has increased its assets by $200 million. This increase is currently being funded on an overnight basis in the Fed funds market. To replace the Fed funds borrowing, MidWest expects that it can increase its placings of six-month CDs with the state pension fund.* The ALCO decides to issue the CDs—MidWest's cheapest form of funding. However, funding the two-year syndication with six-month CDs leaves MidWest with a maturity mismatch.

Three months later the ALCO meets again: the CDs will be rolled over in another three months; the loans have one year and nine months to go, but the bank's management is worried that interest rates will rise. Indeed, MidWest's management is extremely concerned about a spike in rates just when Mid-West will need to issue the new CDs. The managers of MidWest tell their treasurer to "get them through" the upcoming refunding.

The treasurer has a dilemma. Does she issue new CDs now and seek out additional assets? Does she issue new CDs now and place the proceeds in the Euromarket for three months? In either of these cases the treasurer would "blow up" (increase) MidWest's balance sheet by an extra $200 million for three months. Given capital-adequacy ratios,† the treasurer decides instead to manage Mid-West's exposure off-balance-sheet.

She calls MidWest's interbank contact at DDF Bank in New York. After a short discussion, she decides to leave MidWest's position funded on a six-month basis but to use an FRA to lock in the bank's borrowing costs in three months' time. On the Reuters screen, three-month versus nine-month FRAs are being quoted as 3.44–3.38. That is, the implied six-month rate three months from now is about 3.41. With a bid-offer spread of 3 basis points around the midpoint, MidWest's treasurer will lock in a rate of 3.44 percent.

Having learned about this technique of managing the bank's interest rate risk, the treasurer decides that FRAs can be a better way to manage interest rate risk than actually taking and placing funds. Consequently, she hires an FRA trader to manage MidWest's risk. The trader will work closely with MidWest's funding desk to shift MidWest's risk profile. The treasurer can now finance assets with the "cheapest" source of funds relative to the market (the CD, in this case) and use FRAs to restructure MidWest's interest rate risk, depending on asset maturity mixes. No longer does the treasurer have to be as active in all different instruments on the liability side—from Fed funds to bonds—merely to shift interest rate risk.

---

*The pension fund buys the CDs in $100,000 amounts, getting a FDIC-guaranteed instrument at a higher rate than other government paper.

†The additional $200 million would require that this U.S. bank add an additional $14.86 million to its capital.

In Illustration 5–2, Midwest Banc utilizes an FRA trader to manage the bank's own interest rate risk. In this case the trader is constantly adjusting the FRA book in response to the bank's funding position. The FRA trader will adjust bids and offers away from the midpoint, depending on the bank's inherent position as a taker or a placer of funds of various maturities. Open positions will be covered in the funding book and vice versa. So the FRA trader is an integral part of the bank's treasury operation.

However, FRAs need not be traded in conjunction with a natural position. While the trader can run an FRA book using only other FRAs to hedge risk, it is more likely that FRAs will be traded with other instruments—that is, by a swaps trader or a futures trader. FRA positions can be substituted (or hedged) in these other markets as well. As we will see in Chapter 18, integration of risk across markets and exploitation of natural positions are the keys to a company's success in FRA trades.

End Users

Managing Foreign Exchange Risk

A primary use of FX forwards is to hedge transactions exposures. The easiest way for us to describe the techniques and problems involved in this application is through an illustration.

While FX forwards have heretofore been used primarily by industrial corporations to hedge transaction exposures—FX positions they do not want—FX forwards can be and are used by portfolio managers to manage their exposures. Illustration 5–3 helps explain this point.

Illustration 5–3

Hedging Transaction Exposures

SSW of North America, Inc., a subsidiary of a major German firm, imports and distributes German-made SSW cars. SSW of North America entered the U.S. market in 1984 when the dollar averaged DM/2.84. At that exchange rate, SSW realized a 20 percent profit margin on each imported automobile it sold in the United States.

Recognizing that SSW was in the U.S. market for the long haul, the firm brought capital into the United States and converted it into dollars. It contracted to hire Americans and distribute its autos through American-owned-and-operated outlets, with the autos priced in U.S.

dollars. The key to its strategy was to sell *at least* 50,000 cars per year (a goal that seemed likely at 2.8 deutsche marks per dollar). If, however, SSW were to sell only 20,000 cars, it would suffer a loss (at the same price per car).

At the end of 1984, the U.S. dollar had strengthened to more than DM/3.0, so the dollar price of a German auto had fallen, and the profit outlook for SSW of North America was bright. Indeed, when the time came to import the cars for sale in 1985, the dollar was so strong against the DM that SSW would have a profit margin of 30 percent if it could achieve its sales goal of 50,000 units.

Hedging Transaction Exposures continued

To lock in this windfall, SSW's CEO instructed the treasurer of SSW to hedge all the foreign exchange risk for 1985. Aware of the well-functioning market for foreign exchange forward contracts, the treasurer turned to this instrument to accomplish his task. But how much should he hedge, and how?

Within SSW of North America, dollars were coming in on each car (with a 30- to 60-day delay), and DM were going out. The lag from importation to sales was fairly predictable. The treasurer—knowing with reasonable certainty how much SSW of North America would receive for each car, how many cars would be imported per month during the year, and the latest forward foreign exchange rates—called his banker.

After listening to the treasurer's request, the bank's account officer passed the treasurer on to the dealing desk, where the problems began. The traders seemed to be speaking another language. When the treasurer asked for a price for the forward contract on DM/USD, they responded with: "Ten dollars at big figure 80/90." The account officer translated: 10 dollars? (10 million dollars.) Big figure? (The closest pfennig.)

And there were more questions: Did the treasurer want to hedge the DM purchase price in dollars on a monthly basis, weekly basis, yearly average, or what? Would the DM import price vary over the year?

After resolving questions, the SSW treasurer elected to hedge DM/187,500,000 per month with the first settlement in three months. But how would the treasurer implement the hedge? He knew that the next month and each month thereafter, he would have to come up with DM/187.5 million. But how?

The account officer said, "It is obvious. SSW will have to enter into a set of 12 forward contracts. The first contract is for one month, the second is for two months, and soforth on out to 12 months. Each contract is for the present value of 187.5 million DM." Relieved, the treasurer of SSW instructed the account officer to implement the hedge.

The treasurer thought the plan was set, but the account officer called back to say the 8-, 10-, and 11-month forwards were not "standard"; they would be a little more difficult and therefore more expensive to do. The treasurer, having gone so far, said, "Okay do it."

A week later the treasurer thought he could return to his job of managing lines of credit and investing excess corporate cash and finally forget about foreign exchange exposure for a while. But the account officer called again. "Sorry, but you have not signed a master foreign exchange forward agreement, so the back office at the bank rejected the forward order you placed yesterday." Too tired and busy to start over, the treasurer said to send out the document and he would have SSW's lawyers go over it.

By January 1985, the lawyers had spent two weeks looking over the document. The treasurer signed it and placed the order for 12 forward contracts (adjusting for the time lost during the discussions).

Yet the process was still not quite over. The account officer called back to say that SSW of North America had a low credit rating; it would have to provide collateral. Getting angry, the treasurer pointed out that SSW's debt was guaranteed by its AAA-rated German parent. Realizing that SSW was ready

Hedging Transaction Exposures continued

to do business elsewhere and acknowledging the parent's guarantee, the account officer backtracked and approached the credit chain of the bank for a foreign exchange credit line for SSW of North America.

Finally, the order was placed and executed. SSW was set for the year. The treasurer could see the CEO and report that everything was okay.

In the meantime, the dollar had strengthened even more and the treasurer was looking like a genius for taking so long to put on the hedge, thereby increasing the firm's profit margin. The CEO was happy. But just before the treasurer left for vacation, the CEO showed up with questions: "Which way do you think the dollar will go from here? Shouldn't we take our profit now?"

Managing Interest Rate Risk

One of the most apparent and widely publicized examples of firms subject to interest rate risk is found in the experience of the U.S. savings and loan associations (S&Ls) during the late 1970s and early 1980s. Let's consider the asset and liability structure of a typical 1970s S&L. As illustrated in Figure 5–1, the S&Ls' liabilities were short-term deposits that would be repriced frequently—daily, monthly, or semiannually—while the S&Ls' assets were long-term mortgages. The difference between the interest paid on the government-insured, short-term deposit on the liability side and the interest earned on the more lucrative, long-term mortgage on the asset side was *net interest income* (*NII*). In the mid-1970s, short-term deposit rates were in the neighborhood of 6 percent, while long-term mortgage rates were in the neighborhood of 10 percent. On assets of $100 million, net interest income would be $4 million. This yield-curve spread, or gapping (owning a long-term asset funded with short-term borrowings), was typical for S&Ls. Indeed, the managers of S&Ls were, at the time, considered conservative bankers.

FIGURE 5–1 A Stylized Balance Sheet for an S&L in the Mid-1970s

Assets	Liabilities
Mortgages	Government-insured deposits
	Equity

However, when the yield curve started shifting in the very early 1980s, the position of the S&Ls changed dramatically. By 1982, long-term rates had risen 10 percent to about 11 percent, but average short-term deposit rates had made a dramatic leap: from 6 percent to 12 percent. Let's presume that the S&L stayed at the same size ($100 million) and that one fourth of its mortgage loans had matured and had been replaced with new mortgage loans at the new higher rates. Now interest earned was

$$10\% \times (\$75 \text{ million}) + 11\% \times (\$25 \text{ million}) = \$10.25 \text{ million}$$

However, the S&L was still supported by short-term deposits, so interest paid was

$$12\% \times (\$100 \text{ million}) = \$12 \text{ million}$$

Hence NII was a *negative* $1.75 million.

As a result of interest rate volatility, NII swung from a plus $4 million to a negative $1.75 million. If an instrument had been available to manage that interest rate risk, it would certainly have helped.[4] For the moment, let us assume that a market in interest rate forward contracts, such as forward-rate agreements (FRAs), had existed.

And instead of waiting around for the crash, let's suppose that in 1979 the manager of the S&L decided to use a forward-rate agreement to hedge interest rate risk. Given the balance sheet in Figure 5–1, the manager is aware of the need to adjust the S&L's cash flows to protect against a rise in the cost of funding in case short-term rates rise. Utilizing the forward market in interest rates, the manager can neutralize the costs of unanticipated changes in rates.

FIGURE 5–2   The Risk Profile for the S&L

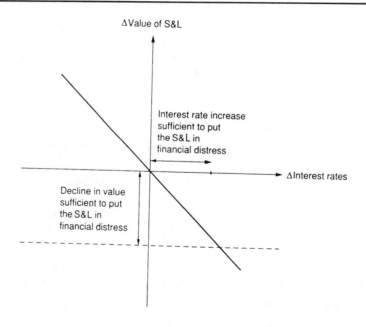

The risk profile for this S&L is illustrated in Figure 5–2: if interest rates rise, the firm could be forced into bankruptcy. Conversely, if rates fall, the S&L would make more profit. If rates remain as predicted by current forward rates, the expected profit is considered satisfactory. Consequently, the manager of the S&L decides to hedge, thereby neutralizing the effects of a volatile money market.

How do S&L managers create this hedge? They need the hedge to throw off a neutralizing cash flow with the same periodicity as the repricing of their liabilities, let's say every three months. To do so, they must construct a forward position such that if interest rates are greater than expected in the future, they will receive a payment, and if they are less they will make a payment. But they must construct the position such that the cash flows are thrown off every three months. Thus, they must construct a set of FRAs, one expiring every three months for the next, say, three years.

FIGURE 5–3   The Hedged S&L's Risk Profile

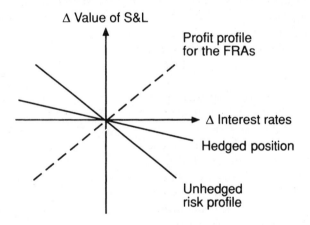

As illustrated in Figure 5–3, the FRAs offset the cash flows on the $100 million short-term deposits. Here, the manager chooses a partial hedge; the notional principal of each FRA is $80 million. The contract terms of the FRAs state that if a reference interest rate (say, three-month LIBOR) is above what is expected (the forward interest rate at contract origination), then the S&L receives the difference in interest rates times the $80 million notional principal. Of course, as with all forwards, the reverse would also hold true. The only problem with such a hedge is that FRAs, like all forwards, are credit instruments. And 12 of these forward contracts, the longest of which has a maturity of three years, could use up all of this S&L's credit lines. (A three-year FRA is fairly risky, and even in 1979, this S&L is likely not a AAA risk.)

Illustration 5–4

Using FRAs in an Insurance Company*

George Demitri is the asset manager for XYZ Insurance Company, which writes life insurance policies in California. As with any insurance company, the maturity profile of his portfolio is designed to match expected benefit payments (retirement and death). In general, these liabilities are of long maturity. In the main, the maturity of his assets is also long, except for one portion concentrated in T-bills.

But George has a problem. His boss is demanding higher yield on the short-term portfolio. George is told to increase yield—while maintaining liquidity. George knows that to maintain liquidity he must stay in short-dated U.S. Treasuries. (Liquidating a billion dollars of paper to get cash in an emergency—when an earthquake hits San Francisco—is not all that easy if it is tied up in mortgage-backed securities or Australian bonds.)

George notes that the yield curve is upward sloping, so instruments of longer duration increase his yield. Three-month rates are around 3 1/4 percent, and the five-year rate is over 6 percent. If only he could invest long term while at the same time maintaining liquidity, he could pick up yield. And he can. He can keep his short-term portfolio in place but use an FRA to "synthetically" construct a longer-term instrument.[†]

George decides to try to "extend the maturity" of $100 million in six-month Eurodeposits to three years. His six-month deposits are yielding 3.6 percent. George wants to lock in the premium of the three-year yield relative

to the 3.6 percent six-month yield. The way he will do this is with a series of FRAs.

Instead of starting at the beginning, let's look at the end. George wants to lock in a rate three years from now: in other words, in three years, he wants to pay six-month LIBOR and get some guaranteed rate. What is the six-month rate in three years?

While such a long forward interest rate—a six-month rate in three years—is not readily available on a Reuters screen, it can be calculated using the spot yield curve. The spot Eurodollar yield curve was as follows:

	Yield
6 month	3.60%
12 month	4.00
18 month	4.40
24 month	4.70
30 month	5.00
36 month	5.25
42 month	5.50

From this yield curve, George calculated the implied 6-month rate in 36 months, $_{36}R_{42}$:

$$(1 + {}_0R_{36})^3 (1 + {}_{36}R_{42})^{1/2} = (1 + {}_0R_{42})^{3.5}$$

$$(1.0525)^3 (1 + {}_{36}R_{42})^{1/2} = (1.055)^{3.5}$$

$$(1 + {}_{36}R_{42})^{1/2} = \frac{1.2061}{1.1659} = 1.0345$$

$$_{36}R_{42} = (1.0345)^2 - 1 = 7.01\%$$

George then calls his bankers and has them bid on that forward contract—in the jargon of the FRA market, a 36 × 42. With this FRA, George can lock in the premium implied in the yield curve for the six-month instrument he owns in three years. He could lock in a premium for the other four repricings in the same way.

Hence, George needs an FRA for each of the six-month periods, a strip of FRAs, one for each rollover date:

6 months vs. 12 months

12 months vs. 18 months

18 months vs. 24 months

24 months vs. 30 months

36 months vs. 42 months

In the same way that he has already calculated the forward six-month rate in three years, George must calculate the implied for-

ward rate for each period, package it, and get a bid on the "strip" of FRAs from his banks.[‡]

George can now report victory to his boss. With this strip of FRAs in place, he has locked in the higher yield without sacrificing liquidity.

---

[*]This example was created using interest rates that prevailed in the first quarter of 1993.

[†]Is this risky for XYZ Insurance Company? No. At present, the asset maturities are "too short" (because of the need to maintain liquidity) relative to the liabilities.

[‡]George, like you, is probably wondering if there is another contract that will accomplish the same trick: something that will look like a "strip" of FRAs, but will not entail signing so many contracts. The answer is swaps, an instrument we will discuss in Chapters 8 and 9.

In addition to financial institutions, insurance companies have significant interest rate exposures that could be managed through FRAs. Since an insurance company must have liquidity to meet claims as they occur, it will keep much of its assets in the form of short-term, highly liquid money market or Treasury instruments. However, the insurance company often finds that, in doing so, it has mismatched its assets and liabilities. By using FRAs, the institution can continue to hold the liquid assets it needs, while synthetically moving the payoffs to its asset portfolio further out the yield curve to better "duration-match" or "gap-match" its liability structure.

Suppose a bank wants to create assets. Instead of simply buying only floating-rate notes or floating-rate bonds to match its floating-rate funding, it might find it useful to have a "synthetically created" floating-rate instrument through a set of FRAs. The point is that the existence of the FRA allows institutions to change interest rate exposures without huge cost. And portfolio managers may wish to shorten the duration of their fixed-income portfolios; FRAs are one tool available for doing so.

Notes

1. Of particular interest are gold forwards, which are vehicles for institutions holding gold to create active returns on previously sterile (non-interest-bearing) assets.

2. An outright forward is the contract we have been discussing throughout Chapters 4 and 5. A foreign exchange swap, on the other hand, is the simultaneous execution of an outright forward and an offsetting spot transaction with the same counterparty. Thus, if the forward leg of the swap is the purchase of DM, the spot leg will be the sale of DM.

3. Estimates are from Dickens (1988) and Grindal (1988). Volume figures are estimates, and disputes about which currencies are most liquid abound. Indeed, one set of survey results found that sterling FRAs had 60 percent of the London market in 1987. Moreover, the domestic French franc market has developed considerable steam and provides an alternative to the MATIF for risk management.

4. Indeed, many managers used an instrument introduced during this period: financial futures, which we will discuss in Chapter 6.

6

FUTURES

The Futures Contract

As described in Chapter 2, a futures contract is a price-fixing mechanism that involves a legally binding commitment to buy or sell a specified quantity of a specified asset at a specified date in the future. Some futures contracts (notably agricultural futures) require physical delivery of the asset, so the buy-sell activities implied in the contracts are actually consummated. The price paid to take delivery or received to make delivery of a given asset on a given date is determined by the price at which that specific futures contract trades. Other futures contracts (notably stock index futures and Eurodollar futures) are cash-settled. In fact, few futures contracts are held to maturity and exercised; the majority of positions are closed through a reversing trade on the futures exchange.

Futures contracts are traded on organized exchanges; the oldest, the Chicago Board of Trade (CBOT), opened in 1842. The primary mechanism of futures trading is "open outcry" by buyers and sellers announcing their intentions in an open trading "pit."[1] Trading in futures contracts in the United States is regulated by the Commodity Futures Trading Commission (CFTC).

The range of available futures markets and contracts is extremely wide. In addition to the agricultural commodities for which the futures markets are best known—such as corn, oats, soybeans, pork bellies—futures contracts are traded on precious metals:

Gold	Platinum
Silver	Palladium

And on industrial commodities:

Aluminum	Copper
Lead	Nickel
Heating oil	Natural gas
Gasoline	Crude oil
Electricity	

Future contracts are also traded on a number of financial assets, including foreign exchange:

Swiss francs	Australian dollars
Deutsche marks	Canadian dollars
British pounds	Japanese yen
French francs	ECU
Mexican pesos	Brazilian real

And interest-bearing securities:

T-bills	T-notes and bonds
Gilts	Bank bills
Eurodollar deposits	German government bonds
Muni bond index	Federal funds
Euroyen deposits	Euromark deposits

And stock indexes:

S&P 500 Index	Value Line Index
Major Market Index	Institutional Index
NYSE Composite Index	Russell Indices
National OTC Index	Toronto Stock Exchange Index
Financial Times Index	Hang Seng Index
All Ordinaries Index	Barclays Index
Nikkei Index	

The first financial futures contracts, foreign currency futures, were introduced on the International Monetary Market of the Chicago Mercantile Exchange in 1972. Foreign currency futures were followed by GNMA futures in 1975, T-bill futures in 1976, T-bond futures in 1977, and so on. But as we have noted, futures contracts are not a recent development. As noted in Chapter 1, futures like contracts were traded as early as the 17th century in Japan. Futures first appeared on the Chicago Board of Trade in 1865 and have been traded ever since.[2] (When the CBOT opened in 1842, the contract it traded was the forward rather than futures contract.)

Forwards enabled the CBOT to permit farmers and millers to fix the price of grain, but it is not hard to imagine the kind of defaults that occurred. If the price of grain rose over the period covered by the forward contract, farmers had incentives to default; when the time came to deliver the grain, the miller would be left "waiting at the warehouse" (not a much better place to wait than at the altar), while the farmer sold grain for a better price elsewhere. Conversely, if the price of grain fell over the period of the contract, it would be the miller who had incentives to default and the farmer would be the one "waiting at the warehouse."[3] (Unfortunately, we can't show you examples of the complaint letters that were written, since the Great Chicago Fire of 1871 took care of the files.) The CBOT's response to the complaints—a switch from the forward to futures—better controlled these incentives and thereby reduced the likelihood of default.

Institutional Features That Reduce Credit Risk

The futures contract is like a forward contract in the sense that the futures contract is also a means of contracting in advance of delivery. With either of the contracts, we contract to buy or sell at a future date at a price agreed today.

However, as noted in Chapter 4, forward contracts have the significant limitation of being pure credit instruments. In a sense, a futures contract is designed to deal directly with the credit (default) risk problem; the futures contract is structured and traded so as to reduce substantially the credit risk borne by the contracting parties.

Moreover, the institutional features of the futures market are designed to provide a liquid secondary market. In the discussion to follow, we will highlight those institutional features of the futures contract that reduce the credit risk. In the final section of this chapter we look at those features of the contract itself, and of the market, that provide liquidity.

But first we consider the three institutional features of the contract and of the market that interact to lower the credit risk for a futures contract: *daily settlement, margin requirements,* and the *clearinghouse.* At the end of this section we will also consider another feature of some futures markets, *price limits,* to see its impact on the credit risk of a futures contract.

Daily Settlement

With a forward contract, the performance period is the same as the maturity of the contract:

> On July 1, Party A enters into a forward contract with Party B such that Party A agrees to purchase 125,000 deutsche marks on September 21 at a price of 61 cents per deutsche mark ($0.6100).
>
> On July 2, the market price of September 21 deutsche marks—that is, deutsche marks for delivery on September 21—rises to $0.6150.

Party A's position in the forward contract now has a positive value: Party A has the right to buy deutsche marks more cheaply than the prevailing market price. However, with this forward contract, Party A will not receive the value until contract maturity, in 82 days.

In the preceding example, Party A is exposed to the default risk of Party B (and vice versa). When the market price of the deutsche mark rises, Party B owes Party A, but this value will not be conveyed until contract maturity. Further, the risk of default increases as the performance period increases. For example, if the time to contract maturity in the preceding example were 120 days rather than 83 days, the risk of default would be greater. It follows then that reducing the performance period reduces the credit risk.

With a futures contract, the performance period is *one trading day*. Futures contracts are *marked-to-market* and *settled* at the end of every business day. To see the effect of daily resettlement, let's look at a simple example.

When the futures contract is marked-to-market and settled daily, the performance period is reduced to a single day. In Illustration 6–1, while the maturity of the contract is 83 days, the performance period is not 83 days but is instead one business day. With the reduced performance period, default risk declines accordingly.

Moreover, the illustration demonstrates a point we alluded to in Chapter 2: in effect, a futures contract is like a bundle of forward contracts. Each day the forward

---

Illustration 6–1

Implementing Daily Settlement

On July 1, Party A agrees to buy from Party B 125,000 deutsche marks for delivery on September 21 at a price of $0.6100 per deutsche mark.* At origination, both parties agree that $0.600 per deutsche mark is the prevailing price for September 21 deutsche marks, so the net present value of the contract is zero.

Suppose that on July 2, the price of September 21 deutsche marks rises to $0.6150 per deutsche mark. Such a rise is the result of changes in the demand for and supply of deutsche marks, both in the spot and futures market. However, for our purposes, let's simplify the situation and propose that a third party, C, enters the market demanding September 21 deutsche marks.

Since Party A has agreed to buy for $0.6100 per unit an asset that is now worth $0.6150 per unit, the value of Party A's position has risen. Marking the contract to market, Party A's contract now has a net present value of $625:

$$125,000 \ (\$0.6150 - 0.6100) = \$625$$

Conversely, the market value of the contract to Party B is a negative $625.

The contract is settled by Party B making a payment to Party A in the amount of $625. After the settlement, the net present value of the contract once again equals zero.

---

* Party A, by executing a "buy" trade, is "long" in the parlance of the futures market.

contract originated on the previous day is settled and replaced with a new contract with a delivery price equal to the settlement price for the previous day's contract.[4]

In this vein, the futures contract described in Illustration 6–1 can be viewed as follows: on July 1 a forward contract was purchased with a maturity of 83 days and a delivery price of $0.61 per deutsche mark. On July 2, the July 1 forward contract was settled at a price of $0.6150 per deutsche mark and was replaced with a new forward contract that has a maturity of 82 days and delivery price of $0.6150 per deutsche mark. Figure 6–1 depicts this view of a futures contract as a bundle of forward contracts.

Margin Requirements

Daily settlement reduces the performance period to one day, but for this one-day period the probability that the counterparty will default still exists. (In the context of our illustration, there is the possibility that on July 2 Party B would not make the necessary $625 payment.)

The surest way to deal with this interday credit risk is to require the contracting parties to post a *surety bond,* and that is precisely what is done. In the futures market, this bond is referred to as the *margin.* To buy or sell a futures contract, the individual must post a specified margin as bond to guarantee contract performance. The required margin is determined by the exchange itself for each contract.

FIGURE 6–1   A Futures Contract as a Bundle of Forward Contracts

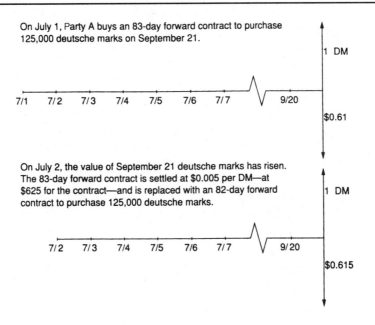

At the time the contract is bought or sold, the trader posts the *initial margin*. The initial margin varies with the type of futures contract; it should be no surprise that the initial margin is related to the maximum expected daily price change for the contract in question. That is, the amount of the surety bond required is generally enough to cover the largest changes in the value of the contract that have occurred historically.

The range of initial margin requirements is wide. It can be as little as 0.03 percent for Treasury bills (e.g., the initial margin on a futures contract to purchase $1 million is $270) or as much as 5 percent for the S&P Index contract.[5] Margin requirements change frequently and have been as high as 15 percent for the S&P Index contract. However, for most contracts, this initial margin is less than 5 percent.[6]

In U.S. futures markets, margin can be posted in the form of cash, a bank letter of credit, or Treasury instruments. If margin is posted in the form of securities, the customer continues to earn the interest accrued while the security acts as margin.

On each trading day, gains are credited or losses debited to customer's margin account—in cash—as the futures position increases or decreases in value. In the context of our example, on July 2, $625 would be transferred from Party B's margin account to Party A's margin account; this $625 is referred to as the *variation margin*. If, as a result of the value of the customer's position declining, the balance in the margin account declines below a specified level—referred to as the *maintenance margin*—the customer is required to replenish the margin, returning it to its initial level. If a customer's margin account falls below the maintenance level and is not replenished, the position is closed.[7] To see how this works in practice, let's return to our illustration.

As is indicated by Illustration 6–2, if the contract is marked-to-market daily, and if the initial and maintenance margins are set appropriately, the probability of loss from a default is quite low. However, with less than 100 percent margin, it is not eliminated. For example, on October 19 and 20, 1987, many futures positions were defaulted. Clearly, the margin levels were not set high enough to foreclose default, given this unprecedented change in prices.

The Clearinghouse

Although daily settlement and the margin requirement can reduce substantially default-induced losses in a futures contract, the costs associated with default are certainly not zero because two sources of costs resulting from credit risk remain.

First, as we have set up our illustration, Parties A and B would exchange funds directly with one another, so they would necessarily expend resources evaluating each other's credit risk. Thus, one remaining cost associated with default is the cost of evaluating the credit risk of the parties with whom you trade:

> Party A buys one September 21 futures contracts on 125,000 deutsche marks from Parties B and C and D. Party A would have to evaluate the credit risk of each of the three parties.

Illustration 6–2

Tracing Margin Balances

Suppose Parties A and B have agreed that the initial margin for a contract on 125,000 deutsche marks will be $2,025 and that the maintenance margin will be $2,000.*

On July 1, the futures contract between Party A and Party B is originated; both parties will be required to post the initial margin of $2,025.

On July 2, the price of September 21 deutsche marks rises from $0.6100 to $0.6150. Consequently, at the close of business on July 2, $625 will be transferred from the margin account of Party B to Party A. Party A now has a margin account balance of $2,650, but Party B has a margin account balance of only $1,400.

Since Party B's margin account is now below the maintenance margin, Party B will be requested to replenish the margin account, returning the balance to the initial margin. This means adding $625 to the margin account to restore the balance to $2,025.

If Party B replenishes the margin account, the contract continues. If, on July 3, the price of September 21 deutsche marks again rises, funds again will be transferred from Party B's margin account to Party A's account, and if the price increase is great enough, Party B may once again be required to add margin. (The reverse is true if the price of September 21 deutsche marks falls on July 3.)

If, however, Party B does not add the required $625 to the margin account, Party B's position is closed. Party B will no longer have the futures position and will be reimbursed the balance of $1,400 in the margin account. To continue to buy deutsche marks for a September 21 delivery, Party A must find another party to accept the sell position.†

---

*These were the actual margins for deutsche mark contracts on the International Monetary Market on February 17, 1993.

†In truth, Party A will not actually have to search for a counterparty. The clearinghouse performs this task.

Second, if a party with whom you trade defaults, you are protected against direct losses, but you are subject to an opportunity loss in the sense that the contract is closed. The remaining cost associated with credit risk is the cost of replacing a contract if your counterparty defaults:

> Party A has purchased September 21 futures contracts on deutsche marks from Parties B, C, and D. If the price of September 21 deutsche marks rises and Party C drops out (by not replenishing the margin account), Party A will not lose directly. However, Party A has to either search for a replacement counterparty or live with one less deutsche mark futures contract.

The clearinghouse handles these two problems by breaking apart and depersonalizing agreements. The clearinghouse does not take a position in any trade, but the clearinghouse interposes itself between all parties to every transaction. Hence, the equity of the clearinghouse provides an additional bond for the parties contracting for futures contracts through the clearinghouse.

The manner in which the clearinghouse functions is illustrated in Figure 6–2. Panel (*a*) illustrates the futures contract we have described so far: Party A agrees to buy 125,000 deutsche marks from Party B at a price of $0.6100 per deutsche mark. Panel (*b*) illustrates the same transaction, but with the clearinghouse interposed between the two parties: Party A agrees to buy 125,000 deutsche marks at $0.61 each from the clearinghouse. Party B agrees to sell 125,000 deutsche marks to the clearinghouse at $0.61 per DM. At this point, the *open interest* is 125,000 deutsche marks—or one contract.

Panel (*c*) illustrates what happens when the futures price of the DM rises and the contract is marked-to-market. Suppose that, as a result of changes in the demand for or supply of deutsche marks, the futures price of September 21 DM rises to $0.6150. This price change requires a payment of $0.0050 per DM ($0.0050 × 125,000 = $625) from Party B to the clearinghouse and the same payment from the clearinghouse to Party A.

Note that panel (*c*) again illustrates how a futures contract is like a bundle of forward contracts. On day 2, the 83-day forward contract is settled through a payment of $0.0050 per DM and is replaced with an 82-day forward contract with a price of $0.6150 per DM.

Panel (*c*) illustrates the marking-to-market. What if, as in our example, the marking-to-market requires that Party B replenish the margin account? If Party B returned the margin balance to the initial level, Figure 6–2 would reflect no change. However, if Party B failed to replenish the margin account, Party B's position would be closed.

Panel (*d*) of Figure 6–2 illustrates what happens when Party B fails to meet a margin call. When Party B is unable to restore the margin account to the initial level, the clearinghouse enters into a reversing trade with Party B—the clearinghouse contracts to sell 125,000 September 21 DM to Party B at a price of $0.6150 per DM—thereby netting out, or closing, the position.[8] However, Party A's position is still open; the clearinghouse is still obligated to deliver the September 21 DM. The clearinghouse covers this obligation by matching Party A with another contract, this one a contract to purchase September 21 DM from Party C at a price of $0.6150.

Panel (*e*) displays the effect of closing out Party B's contract. Note that the open interest is still only one contract.

Price Limits

In the aftermath of the "crash" of October 19, 1987, there has been considerable discussion of imposing price limits on financial futures contracts. More common for futures contracts on commodities than for financial futures, the concept of a price

FIGURE 6-2 Operation of the Clearinghouse

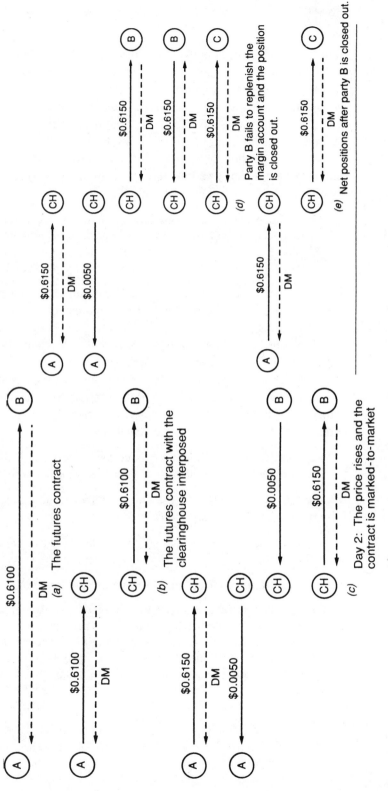

SOURCE: William F. Sharpe, *Investments*, 3e, © 1985, pp. 525–526. Adapted by permission of Prentice Hall, Inc., Englewood Cliffs, New Jersey. (*a*) The Futures Contract. (*b*) The Futures Contract with the Clearinghouse Interposed. (*c*) Day 2: The Price Rises and the Contract Is Marked-to-Market. (*d*) Party B Fails to Replenish the Margin Account, and the Position Is Closed Out. (*e*) Net Positions after Party B Is Closed Out.

limit has considerable intuitive appeal: with daily resettlement and the margin account mechanisms in place, the problem of default risk would arise only when the futures price moves "too much" in a single day. Therefore, to "solve" this problem, we institute a rule that says that price can move only so much in a single trading day.

More specifically, the rule is such that if the futures price for a specified contract moves the limit during a trading day, trading is then halted on that contract for the remainder of the day. This idea of a price limit is certainly appealing, but this kind of reasoning has a serious flaw. William Sharpe (1985) provided the best exposition of the fallacy in his story of a farmer:

> Tired of the violent fluctuations in temperature that occur from one day to the next in the American Great Plains (and the consequences on his crops), this farmer decided to "eliminate" this problem by having his thermometer altered so that it could move no more than five degrees in either direction from the previous day's reading.

The point of this anecdote is that price limits cannot eliminate volatility in futures prices any more than altering the thermometer can eliminate volatility in temperatures. Changing the thermometer does nothing to change climatic or meteorological conditions; price limits do nothing to change the underlying economic factors that lead to the volatility in futures prices.

However, it has been argued that price limits could reduce the credit risk problem to the extent that the price limit substitutes for margin.[9] The reasoning behind this argument is that price limits *could* reduce the amount of information available to the traders in the futures market. To see how this would work, let's return to our example:

> Suppose that on July 2, world economic conditions were altered such that the value of the dollar would decline dramatically relative to the deutsche mark.

If there are no price limits on the DM/$ futures contract, the futures prices could fully reflect the altered conditions:

> On July 2, the futures price of September 21 deutsche marks rose from $0.6100 to close at $0.6325.

With such a dramatic move, credit problems and "reneging" would be likely:

> Marking the contract to market, Party B owes $2,812.50 (and Party A is owed the same amount). However, Party B's margin account balance is only $2,025. Party B will face a margin call of $2,812.50 (to leave the margin account balance at $2,025).
>
> Given the $0.0225 one-day change in the price of a DM—a change of 3.6 percent in one day—Party B is unwilling to meet the margin call. Party B reneges on the futures contract. The contract will be closed out, but Party B's broker—or the clearinghouse[10]—will suffer a loss of $2,812.50 − $2,025 = $787.50.

Suppose, however, that a price limit were in effect for the DM/$ futures contract. Let's suppose that the daily price limit for the DM/$ futures had been set at $0.0100 per DM—in other words, if the price of DM rises or falls by as much as one cent, trading is suspended for that day. Such a rule would limit the amount that could be lost on a DM/$ futures contract to $1,250 per day:

> On July 2, the price of September 21 deutsche marks immediately begins to rise from $0.6100; with the price limit, it can rise no higher than $0.6200.
>
> Party B's contract must be marked-to-market at the end of the trading day. Consequently, Party B has lost $1,250, and his margin account balance has dropped below the maintenance margin to $775. Party B faces a margin call of $1,250.

With this limit on how much Party B could lose in a day, the ability of the futures market to convey information to the traders is reduced. Hence, the probability that the party will renege on the contract is altered:

> Party B knows that the $0.6200 is not an equilibrium price. Party B knows that the equilibrium price is higher than $0.6200 but not how much higher. If Party B thinks the equilibrium price is only a little above this level, say at $0.6210, Party B might be willing to meet the margin call of $1,250 to restore the position's margin account balance to $2,025.

The price limits might alter the amount of information available to the trader, but again the price limit does not alter the underlying economic conditions:

> On July 3, the market opens and immediately moves the limit: the price of September 21 deutsche marks rises to $0.6300 and trading is suspended.
>
> After losing another $1,250, Party B's margin account balance is down to $775. Again faced with a $1,250 margin call, Party B might make this margin call or might renege. Let's suppose the latter.
>
> On July 5, equilibrium is finally reached. The market opens and the price of September 21 deutsche marks immediately goes to its equilibrium price, $0.6325. Party B's broker closes the contract. The loss on the contract on July 5 is $312.50, which is subtracted from Party B's margin account, leaving a balance of $775 − $312.50 = $462.50, which is returned to Party B.

In the preceding example, the price limit reduced the credit risk to the broker and the exchange: without the pricing limit, the broker/exchange lost $787.50; with the price limit, the broker/exchange lost nothing. However, this change was solely the result of the customer's getting "tricked"; with the price limit in place, the customer's perception of what the equilibrium price would be was different from what the market-determined equilibrium price turned out to be. If the customer cannot be tricked, the effect disappears. The example implies that the futures price is the customer's only source of information. To the extent customers have alternative sources of information about the equilibrium price, the ability to trick them—the effectiveness of the price limit—declines. Thus, price limits are more frequently observed in agricultural futures markets, where there are few alternative sources of price information. Price limits are rarely observed in financial futures markets, where other related financial markets provide rich alternative sources of price information.

Institutional Features That Promote Liquidity

In addition to the three features that reduce default risk, two features of the futures contract and market enhance the liquidity of the market: *standardized contracts* and the *organized exchange*.

Standardized Contracts

For a market to be liquid, the commodity/asset being traded in the market must be homogeneous. To attain this homogeneity, contracts traded in the futures market are standardized. The contract specifies a standardized asset and a standardized maturity date.

> Consider again the deutsche mark futures contract. On the International Monetary Market (IMM) of the Chicago Mercantile Exchange (CME) the DM contract specifies a contract size of 125,000 deutsche marks with settlement occurring on the third Wednesdays of March, June, September, or December.

Moreover, in a futures contract, the mechanism for delivery is commonly standardized.[11] For example, on the IMM the T-bill future requires the delivery of T-bills with a total face value of $1 million and a time to maturity of 90 days at the expiration of the futures contract. The T-bond futures contract permits latitude with respect to the specific bonds to be delivered—the contract specifies the delivery of $100,000's worth of T-bonds that have at least 15 years remaining until maturity or to their first call date.[12]

Furthermore, the price of the futures contract is also standardized to the extent that the minimum price movement—the "tick size"—is also specified. For example, the tick size for the deutsche mark contract we have been following is $0.0001 per DM (or $12.50 per contract).

Organized Exchanges

To bring together buyers and sellers, the futures market is organized into exchanges, each exchange trading particular futures contracts. This is in marked contrast to a forward market, in which the contracts are negotiated on a one-off basis in a decentralized market.

Most futures exchanges are organized like the Chicago Board of Trade. Membership on the CBOT is by individuals and entitles members to the right to trade on the exchange and to have a voice in its operation. (While only individuals can be members, brokers like Merrill Lynch are permitted to trade on the exchange.) Memberships are traded like any other asset and can be purchased or leased from the current owner.

While the CBOT has at times been likened to a "club"—a nonprofit organization of its members—it is probably more fruitful to think of the futures exchanges as for-profit "partnerships." The members of these exchanges have strong individual incentives to form stringent rules for running the exchange that maximize the value of their memberships.[13] An anecdote might help to illustrate this point: when a trade is made in the "pit," there is always the possibility of an error. The buyer and the seller might write down different amounts or different prices, for instance. On the Chicago Mercantile Exchange and other exchanges, the rule for settling such errors is that if direct methods of correcting the error have been unsuccessful, the two parties split the loss. Traders will be unlikely to buy or sell contracts from a colleague with an unusually high error rate. Because the traders want to maximize their own profit, each has the incentive to maximize accuracy.

The upshot is that rules on the futures exchanges work to maximize the value of a membership on the exchange and simultaneously to maximize the liquidity on the exchange.

Futures Prices

At maturity, arbitrage between the underlying asset and futures markets forces the price of the futures and the cash price of the asset to be the same. Prior to maturity, the cash price and the futures price need not be the same. But because the futures price must converge to the cash price at maturity, we know some systematic relation between the two prices must exist. We examine this relation in the next section.

Futures Prices and the Cost of Carry

To examine the relation between cash and futures prices, let's look at some illustrative prices. Figure 6–3 provides data on the cash prices—the spot prices—of some grains and feeds on Monday, August 11, 1997. Figure 6–4 provides data on corresponding futures prices on the same day.

Look, for instance, at corn prices. The spot price of yellow corn is $2.74 per bushel in central Illinois. But the price of a futures contract on the Chicago Board of Trade that is deliverable in corn and will expire in 39 days—on September 19—is 249 cents ($2.49) per bushel.[14] And as Figure 6–4 indicates, the futures price of corn in December is higher than that in September; the futures price of corn in March 1998 is higher than that in December, and so on. Hence, the data on corn prices illustrate two frequently observed characteristics of futures prices: the futures price of a commodity or asset, F, is greater than the spot price, P,[15] and the futures price, F, rises as the time to maturity increases.[16]

These characteristics reflect the *cost of carry* for a futures contract and illustrate a critical arbitrage relation. To see how this works, an illustration is useful.

FIGURE 6–3   **Cash Prices**

Monday, August 11, 1997
(Closing Market Quotations)
GRAINS AND FEEDS

	Mon	Fri	Year Ago
Barley, top-quality Mpls., bu	uz	z	3.42½
Bran, wheat middlings, KC ton	u57-61	57-61	103.00
Corn, No. 2 yel. Cent. Ill. bu	bpu2.74	2.48	4.87½
Corn Gluten Feed,			
Midwest, ton	68-80	68-80	110.00
Cottonseed Meal,			
Clksdle, Miss. ton	170.00	175.00	190.00
Hominy Feed, Cent. Ill. ton	72.00	173.00	128.00
Meat-Bonemeal,			
50% pro. Ill. ton.	265-70	270.00	247.50
Oats, No. 2 milling, Mpls., bu	uz	1.88¼	z
Sorghum,			
(Milo) No. 2 Gulf cwt	u454-55	463-67	7.00½
Soybean Meal,			
Cent. Ill., rail, ton 44%	u252-62	256½-62	251.50
Soybean Meal,			
Cent. Ill., rail, ton 48%	u264-72	264½-68½	261.50
Soybeans,			
No. 1 yel Cent.-Ill. bu	bpu7.04	7.20½	8.19
Wheat,			
Spring 14%-pro Mpls. bu	u441-46	447¾-52¾	5.54¼
Wheat, No. 2 sft red, St.Lou. bu	bpu3.60	3.65	4.78½
Wheat, hard KC, bu	3.80½	3.84½	5.17½
Wheat,			
No. 1 sft wht, del Port Ore	u4.13	4.18	5.13

SOURCE: Reprinted by permission of *The Wall Street Journal*, © Dow Jones & Company, Inc. 1993. All Rights Reserved Worldwide.

Illustration 6–3 points out that the futures price must be related to the spot price through the *cost of carry, c,* for the futures contract in question. The illustration shows that, for commodity contracts, arbitrage guarantees that the futures price will be less than or equal to the spot price plus the cost of carry:

$$F < P + c \qquad\qquad 6\text{–}1$$

With respect to Equation 6–1, we saw in the illustration that if $F > P + c$, a trader could make a riskless profit by taking a long position in the asset and a short position in the futures contract. If $F < P + c$, the arbitrage strategy would be to buy the futures and sell the commodity short, but short sales of a physical commodity are difficult. (However, if one had a large inventory of wheat, the strategy could be accomplished by reducing inventory—selling wheat on the spot market—and buying futures.)

However, we are more concerned with futures on financial assets, and short selling *is* possible for financial assets. In this case, if $F < P + c$, a trader could make an arbitrage profit. Hence, with the financial futures, the principle of no arbitrage requires that Equation 6–1 be a strict equality:

$$F = P + c \qquad\qquad 6\text{–}2$$

FIGURE 6–4 Futures Prices

Monday, August 11, 1997

Open Interest Reflects Previous Trading Day.

GRAINS AND OILSEEDS

	Open	High	Low	Settle	Change	Lifetime High	Lifetime Low	Open Interest
CORN (CBT) 5,000 bu.; cents per bu.								
Sept	250½	250½	246	249¾	− 3¾	335	227½	50,291
Dec	253½	253¾	248½	253¼	− 3¾	310	227½	149,144
Mr98	260¾	262¾	257½	262¼	− 3½	305	236	34,041
May	265½	267	262	266¾	− 4	303	241¾	7,902
July	264	270¼	263½	269¾	− 3	315½	245	12,875
Sept	260	260	259	259½	− 2	270	244	1,497
Dec	260	262½	260	262½	− ¼	293	247	5,841

Est vol 54,000; vol Fri 50,206; open int 261,670, +1,439.

OATS (CBT) 5,000 bu.; cents per bu.								
Sept	163	163	159½	161¼	− 2	185	144	1,699
Dec	160	161	159	160½	− 2¼	183	143	5,658
Mr98	163¾	165	163½	164¾	− 2¾	174¾	148¼	779

Est vol 450; vol Fri 423; open int 8,232, −9.

SOYBEANS (CBT) 5,000 bu.; cents per bu.								
Aug	738¼	738¼	718	723¾	− 16	869½	663	7,546
Sept	661	661	642½	643	− 29½	803¾	605	16,038
Nov	628	628	609	610	− 27½	750	577	74,111
Ja98	628¼	630	614	614¼	− 28¼	752	583	15,860
Mar	629	631	623	625	− 25	749	593	5,685
May	650	650	629	631½	− 24¼	745	601	3,936
July	639	645	636½	637½	− 23½	751	611½	2,870
Nov	625	627	620½	620¾	− 9¼	702	597	849

Est vol 32,000; vol Fri 34,300; open int 126,922, −1,356.

SOYBEAN MEAL (CBT) 100 tons; $ per ton.								
Aug	254.50	254.50	246.10	250.00	− 4.40	283.80	203.50	9,816
Sept	227.50	227.50	222.40	223.10	− 6.60	262.50	201.50	21,866
Oct	210.00	210.50	206.50	206.80	− 8.40	240.00	193.00	15,170
Dec	206.50	206.50	201.00	201.20	− 8.80	234.00	186.00	39,673
Ja98	206.90	206.90	198.20	198.50	− 9.70	230.00	185.50	5,982
Mar	200.00	200.00	195.50	196.00	− 8.70	227.00	184.50	8,119
May	198.00	198.00	195.00	195.50	− 7.50	222.00	185.50	3,742
July	197.00	199.00	196.50	196.80	− 8.20	217.00	188.50	2,438

Est vol 12,000; vol Fri 14,914; open int 106,988, −204.

SOYBEAN OIL (CBT) 60,000 lbs.; cents per lb.								
Aug	21.60	21.60	21.25	21.60	− .17	28.90	21.25	1,031
Sept	21.65	21.70	21.30	21.68	− .21	28.45	21.30	20,987
Oct	21.76	21.90	21.55	21.89	− .16	27.70	21.55	15,912
Dec	22.00	22.17	21.72	22.11	− .25	27.50	21.72	44,088
Ja98	22.20	22.30	22.05	22.27	− .31	27.45	21.98	7,076
Mar	22.50	22.65	22.45	22.65	− .27	27.50	22.20	4,816
May	22.70	22.85	22.70	22.75	− .25	27.55	22.35	1,844
July	22.90	23.10	22.80	22.90	− .30	27.40	22.40	1,387

Est vol 7,000; vol Fri 7,908; open int 976-6, −1,107.

WHEAT (CBT) 5,000 bu.; cents per bu.								
Sept	366¾	367¼	362	363¾	− 3½	463	321	34,483
Dec	382	382½	378	378¾	− 5	473½	334¾	49,946
Mr98	390	392	387½	389½	− 3½	470	343¾	15,122
May	390½	392½	389	390¼	− 2¾	439½	345½	1,486
July	380½	385	379½	381½	− 1¼	425	333	4,808

Est vol 19,000; vol Fri 21,626; open int 105,868, +690.

WHEAT (KC) 5,000 bu., cents per bu.								
Sept	375	377½	374	376	− 4	498	325	27,813
Dec	389	391½	387½	389¾	− 3¾	498	340	21,235
Mr98	397	400	396	399	− 2½	491	350	6,818
May	393	396	393	395	− 1	450	350	1,343

Est vol 5,641; vol Fri 6,334; open int 56,965, −100.

WHEAT (MPLS) 5,000 bu.; cents per bu.								
Sept	393	398	393	396	− 1¾	479½	340	9,203
Dec	398	402¾	397	399¾	− 1	479	349	8,306
Mr98	404	408	402½	405	− ½	469	361	1,980
May	....	....	....	405	....	440	363	137

Est vol 2,660; vol Fri 3,579; open int 19,654, −132.

CANOLA (WPG) 20 metric tons; Can. $ per ton								
Aug	354.00	355.50	354.00	354.60	− 2.60	447.00	340.50	161
Sept	353.30	355.40	353.30	353.60	− 3.90	406.00	331.50	1,993
Nov	356.00	357.40	355.10	357.00	− 3.10	410.00	332.20	25,572
Ja98	360.50	361.80	360.40	361.40	− 3.70	393.70	337.00	2,447
Mar	362.50	362.50	361.60	361.60	− 3.70	389.00	339.00	466
May	....	....	....	365.50	− 3.00	371.00	341.00	170

Est vol 1,940; vol Fr 2,852; open int 30,809, +339.

WHEAT (WPG) 20 metric tons; Can. $ per ton.								
Oct	153.80	155.50	153.80	155.20	+ .40	171.50	147.40	4,332
Dec	154.50	155.00	154.50	155.00	+ .20	171.50	147.80	4,559
Mr98	156.30	156.30	156.30	156.30	....	172.00	150.00	1,667
May	....	....	....	156.50	− .10	169.50	152.50	670

Est vol 285; vol Fr 699; open int 11,228, −7.

BARLEY-WESTERN (WPG) 20 metric tons; Can. $ per ton								
Oct	130.00	133.20	130.00	132.10	+ 1.60	158.00	121.70	5,589
Dec	131.70	135.00	131.70	134.20	+ 1.80	143.00	123.50	4,566
Mr98	135.00	136.00	135.00	135.70	+ 2.00	141.20	126.30	422

Est vol 1,600; vol Fr 445; open int 10,582, +90.

Illustration 6–3*

Cash and Carry Limits on Wheat Futures Prices

Suppose the spot price of No. 2 Red Wheat in a Chicago warehouse is 300 cents per bushel, the yield on a one-month T-bill is 6 percent, and the cost of storing and insuring one bushel of wheat is 4 cents per month.

Given these data, what can be said about the price today for a one-month futures contract—that is, the price of a futures contract that has one month to maturity?

Instead of buying a futures contract on wheat, I could buy wheat today and store it for one month. In one month, that total cost of this transaction to me is the cost of using the money for one month (the forgone interest) and the cost of storing and insuring the wheat:

$$300.0[1 + (30/360)0.06] + 4.0 = 305.5$$

Hence, 305.5 cents per bushel is the maximum the one-month futures contract could cost. If the futures contract is priced at 306, I can sell futures contracts, buy wheat today, and store it for one month and make a riskless profit—an *arbitrage* profit.

———

*This illustration is adapted from Sharpe (1985).

In Figure 6–5 we provide data on financial futures for Monday, August 11, the same date that we used to illustrate futures prices for commodities. We also have annotated Eurodollar futures contracts data to show how they can be read.

The arbitrage underlying the cost-of-carry relation holds for financial assets as it does for commodities. The only difference is in the elements of the cost of carry. For commodities, the cost of carry includes the cost of storing and insuring the commodity. For financial assets, the cost of carry is limited to the *net* financing costs (coupon income minus financing costs). Put another way, the cost of carry is the difference between the opportunity cost of holding the asset (the short-term interest rate, the financing cost) and the yield earned from holding the financial asset (such as the coupon payments investors receive when holding bonds).

Equation 6–2 is useful for considering what is referred to as *basis* in a futures contract. Basis is defined as the difference between the futures price and the spot price:

$$\text{Basis} = F - P \qquad\qquad 6–3$$

From Equation 6–2 it follows that some movements in the basis for a particular asset are predictable movements, based on the cost of carry of the asset.

The first of these predictable movements is the convergence of the futures price to the price implied by the cost-of-carry relation. We must keep in mind that the cost-of-carry model is an equilibrium model. If the futures price strays from the price implied by Equation 6–2, the arbitrage forces we have described above act to bring the futures price back to that predicted by the cost-of-carry model; over the

FIGURE 6–5 Futures Prices

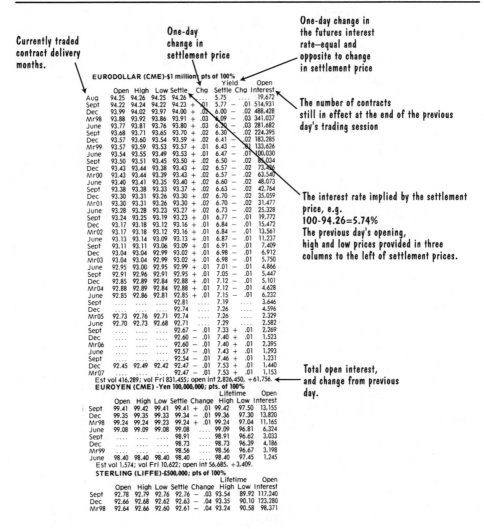

Currently traded contract delivery months.

One-day change in settlement price

One-day change in the futures interest rate—equal and opposite to change in settlement price

The number of contracts still in effect at the end of the previous day's trading session

The interest rate implied by the settlement price, e.g.
100−94.26=5.74%
The previous day's opening, high and low prices provided in three columns to the left of settlement prices.

Total open interest, and change from previous day.

EURODOLLAR (CME)-$1 million; pts of 100%

	Open	High	Low	Settle	Chg	Yield Settle	Chg	Open Interest
Aug	94.25	94.26	94.25	94.26	...	5.75	....	19,672
Sept	94.22	94.24	94.22	94.23	+ .01	5.77	− .01	514,931
Dec	93.99	94.02	93.97	94.00	+ .02	6.00	− .02	488,428
Mr98	93.88	93.92	93.86	93.91	+ .03	6.09	− .03	341,037
June	93.77	93.81	93.76	93.80	+ .03	6.20	− .03	281,682
Sept	93.68	93.71	93.65	93.70	+ .02	6.30	− .02	224,395
Dec	93.57	93.60	93.54	93.59	+ .02	6.41	− .02	183,285
Mr99	93.57	93.59	93.53	93.57	+ .01	6.43	− .01	133,626
June	93.54	93.55	93.49	93.53	+ .01	6.47	− .01	100,030
Sept	93.50	93.51	93.45	93.50	+ .02	6.50	− .02	85,034
Dec	93.43	93.44	93.38	93.43	+ .02	6.57	− .02	73,496
Mr00	93.43	93.44	93.39	93.43	+ .02	6.57	− .02	63,540
June	93.40	93.41	93.35	93.40	+ .02	6.60	− .02	48,073
Sept	93.38	93.38	93.33	93.37	+ .02	6.63	− .02	42,764
Dec	93.30	93.31	93.26	93.30	+ .02	6.70	− .02	35,059
Mr01	93.30	93.31	93.26	93.30	+ .02	6.70	− .02	31,477
June	93.28	93.28	93.23	93.27	+ .02	6.73	− .02	25,328
Sept	93.24	93.25	93.19	93.23	+ .01	6.77	− .01	19,772
Dec	93.17	93.18	93.12	93.16	+ .01	6.84	− .01	15,472
Mr02	93.17	93.18	93.12	93.16	+ .01	6.84	− .01	13,561
June	93.13	93.14	93.09	93.13	+ .01	6.87	− .01	11,237
Sept	93.11	93.11	93.06	93.09	+ .01	6.91	− .01	7,409
Dec	93.04	93.04	92.99	93.02	+ .01	6.98	− .01	6,912
Mr03	93.04	93.04	92.99	93.02	+ .01	6.98	− .01	5,750
June	92.95	93.00	92.95	92.99	+ .01	7.01	− .01	4,866
Sept	92.91	92.96	92.91	92.95	+ .01	7.05	− .01	5,447
Dec	92.85	92.89	92.84	92.88	+ .01	7.12	− .01	5,101
Mr04	92.88	92.89	92.84	92.88	+ .01	7.12	− .01	4,628
June	92.85	92.86	92.81	92.85	+ .01	7.15	− .01	6,232
Sept	....	....	....	92.81	....	7.19	....	3,646
Dec	....	....	....	92.74	....	7.26	....	4,596
Mr05	92.73	92.76	92.71	92.74	....	7.26	....	2,329
June	92.70	92.73	92.68	92.71	....	7.29	....	2,582
Sept	....	....	....	92.67	− .01	7.33	+ .01	2,269
Dec	....	....	....	92.60	− .01	7.40	+ .01	1,523
Mr06	....	....	....	92.60	− .01	7.40	+ .01	2,395
June	....	....	....	92.57	− .01	7.43	+ .01	1,293
Sept	....	....	....	92.54	− .01	7.46	+ .01	1,231
Dec	92.45	92.49	92.42	92.47	− .01	7.53	+ .01	1,440
Mr07	....	....	....	92.47	− .01	7.53	+ .01	1,153

Est vol 416,289; vol Fri 831,455; open int 2,826,450, +61,756.

EUROYEN (CME) -Yen 100,000,000; pts. of 100%

	Open	High	Low	Settle	Change	Lifetime High	Low	Open Interest
Sept	99.41	99.42	99.41	99.41	+ .01	99.42	97.50	13,155
Dec	99.35	99.35	99.33	99.34	− .01	99.36	97.30	13,820
Mr98	99.24	99.24	99.23	99.24	+ .01	99.24	97.04	11,165
June	99.08	99.09	99.08	99.08	....	99.09	96.81	6,324
Sept	....	....	....	98.91	....	98.91	96.62	3,033
Dec	....	....	....	98.73	....	98.73	96.39	4,186
Mr99	....	....	....	98.56	....	98.56	96.67	3,198
June	98.40	98.40	98.40	98.40	....	98.40	97.45	1,245

Est vol 1,574; vol Fri 10,622; open int 56,685, +3,409.

STERLING (LIFFE)-£500,000; pts of 100%

	Open	High	Low	Settle	Change	Lifetime High	Low	Open Interest
Sept	92.78	92.79	92.76	92.76	− .03	93.54	89.92	117,240
Dec	92.66	92.68	92.62	92.63	− .04	93.35	90.10	123,280
Mr98	92.64	92.66	92.60	92.61	− .04	93.24	90.58	98,371

life of the futures contract, futures prices will tend to converge toward that price implied by the cost-of-carry relation.

The second predictable movement is the convergence of the futures price to the cash price at expiration of the futures contract. As the time to delivery becomes shorter, the cost of carry declines. Storage and insurance costs are lower as there is less time to store the commodity, and the shorter the holding period, the smaller the opportunity cost for holding an asset. As specified by Equation 6–2, as the time to delivery becomes shorter and the cost of carry, *c*, becomes smaller, the futures price, *F*, converges to the cash price, *P*.

Futures Prices and Expected Future Spot Prices

So far, we have seen that the price today for a futures contract specifying delivery at period T is related to the *prevailing* spot price through the cost of carry. However, a more important question is how the price today for a futures contract specifying delivery at period T is related to the *expected* spot price at period T.

The expectations model proposes that the current futures price is equal to the market's expected value of the spot price at period T:

$$F_t = E(P_T) \qquad\qquad 6\text{--}4$$

If this expectations model is correct, a speculator can expect neither to win nor to lose from a position in the futures market; expected profits are zero:

$$E(\text{profit}) = E(P_T) - F_t = 0 \qquad\qquad 6\text{--}5$$

Put another way, if the expectations model is correct, the speculator can anticipate earning only the riskless rate of return. Illustration 6–4 explains this somewhat counterintuitive idea.

Illustration 6–4

Speculation and the Expectations Model

Suppose that, at time period 0, a speculator purchases a futures contract at a price of F_0 and posts 100 percent margin in the form of riskless securities. At contract maturity at time T, the value of the margin account will have grown to

$$F_0(1 + r_f)$$

where r_f is the risk-free rate of return for a period equal to that of the maturity of the futures contract. At maturity, the value of the futures contract itself will be

$$P_T - F_0$$

The actual return the speculator will earn is

$$r = \frac{(1 + r_f)F_0 + (P_T - F_0)}{F_0} - 1$$
$$= r_f + \frac{(P_T - F_0)}{F_0}$$

The expected return the speculator will earn is

$$E(r) = r_f + \frac{[E(P_T) - F_0]}{F_0}$$

Hence if the expectations model is correct, the expected return is

$$E(P_T) = F_0 \rightarrow E(r) = r_f$$

Proponents of the expectations model argue that, in a market with rational traders, the expectations model simply has to work. The argument behind this position goes something like this:

If most traders expect the spot price at maturity to be above the prevailing futures price, they will buy futures, thereby forcing up the futures price. Conversely, if these rational traders expected the spot price in the future to be below the current futures price, they sell futures, lowering the futures price. Hence, the only price that will give an equilibrium is for the futures price to equal the expected spot price at maturity.

Cost of Carry versus Expectations

So far, we have presented two views of the way in which futures prices are formed. Suppose the expected futures price does not change over the maturity of the futures contract; suppose price expectations are constant. The expectations model would yield a constant futures price, as illustrated by the horizontal line in Figure 6–6.

John Maynard Keynes (1930) was among the first to take exception to such a model. In his *Treatise on Money,* he looked at commodity futures and argued that futures provide a mechanism to transfer risk from the hedgers (the commodity producers who have natural long positions in the commodity) to speculators. To accomplish this transfer of risk, the equilibrium in the futures market would be such that hedgers would be (on net) short commodity futures contracts (to offset their natural long positions), while speculators would be long commodity futures contracts. Consequently, to get the speculators to buy the commodity futures contracts—to hold the long positions in futures—the expected rate of return for holding futures would have to exceed the risk-free rate. For the expected rate of return on the futures position to exceed the risk-free rate, the futures price would have to be

FIGURE 6–6 Futures Prices over Time with Constant Future Price Expectations

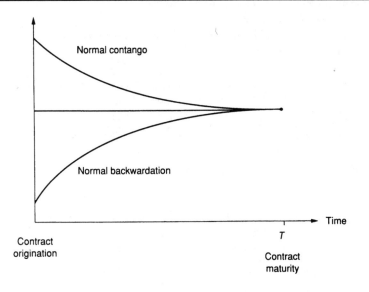

less than the expected spot price and rise as the contract maturity approaches. This relation, referred to by Keynes as *normal backwardation,* is illustrated as the rising line in Figure 6–6.

Conversely, if hedgers are the ones who were on net long futures contracts (that is, if hedgers are the users of the commodity), the speculators would have to be enticed to sell futures contracts. In this case the futures price would begin above the expected spot price and fall as contract maturity approaches. Referred to by Keynes as *normal contango,* this relation is illustrated by the falling line in Figure 6–6. Illustration 6–5 elaborates on both backwardation and contango.

Illustration 6–5

Backwardation and Contango in Bond Futures

Consider again construction of a synthetic futures position, this time a futures position on bonds: I borrow (at the short-term rate) and use the proceeds to purchase bonds (yielding the long-term rate).

The cost of this synthetic bond futures contract is the rate I have to pay on my short-term borrowing minus the rate I earn from the coupons I receive on the long-term bonds. And through arbitrage, the futures price in a standard futures contract must be equal to the cost of this synthetic futures.

If the yield curve is positively sloped, the cost of this synthetic futures is negative—the long-term yield I receive exceeds the short-term yield I pay. Hence, the expected return to the holder of the long futures position is positive. This is a case of *normal backwardation;* the futures price is less than the expected future spot price, and futures prices are lower for futures contracts whose delivery dates are further in the future. Look below at the prices of the Treasury bond futures traded on the Chicago Board of Trade on August 11, 1997. The further in the future is the delivery date, the lower the futures price is:

September	112–24
December	112–12
March '98	112–02
June '98	111–22
September '98	111–12
December '98	111–02

If the yield curve had been inverted—negatively sloped—the reverse would be true. The cost of the synthetic futures would have been positive, so bond futures prices would have exhibited *normal contango.*

Stephen Figlewski (1986) takes issue with Keynes; Figlewski holds that it is the cost-of-carry model, rather than the expectations model, that explains the manner in which futures prices are determined. He argues that the expectations model fails to take into account arbitrage. His reasoning can be paraphrased as follows:

If individuals are holding Treasury bonds that can be delivered against a Treasury bond futures contract, and if the futures price equals these individuals' expectations of the future spot price of Treasury bonds, arbitrage is possible. The bondholders sell futures against their cash positions, thereby eliminating all the risk in the positions but still earning the same return expected had the risky bond positions remained unhedged. This means that the expected returns the bondholders are earning exceed the risk-free rate; the bondholders earn a risk premium without bearing the risk.

Such a situation attracts other investors. As more people try to buy bonds and sell futures, the cash price is bid up and the futures price is bid down, until the cost-of-carry relation in Equation 6–2 is reestablished.

Figlewski's argument does not mean that the cost-of-carry relation ignores expectations. The market's expectation of the future spot price of the asset is reflected in the current spot price. In an efficient market—and everything we have seen suggests that these financial markets are efficient—the price today impounds all available information, including information about what the asset will be worth in the future. Following Figlewski (1986), "The point of the cost of carry model is that given the current cash price [which impounds a forecast for future spot prices], expectations about the cash price at expiration should not have any *independent* effect on futures prices."

Futures Prices and the Cost of Hedging: Basis

Given what we have said about hedging in general, it follows that as long as financial futures are priced according to the cost-of-carry relation, the total return to the holder of a fully hedged position should be the risk-free rate of return. The cash position in the underlying asset is a risky position, so the market return to holding this position would be made up of the risk-free rate of return plus a risk premium. By selling a futures contract against the underlying exposure, the hedger has transferred the riskiness of the asset to the buyer of the futures contract; the buyer of the futures contract should earn the risk premium. Hence, an individual who holds the asset and has hedged completely by selling a futures contract against the asset is left with the riskless rate of return.

The problem is that the underlying cash position may not be fully hedged; the return to the futures contract may not be exactly equal to the risk premium on the underlying asset. The hedger has a long position in the asset and a short position in the futures contract and has consequently invested in the difference between these two assets. Hence, the return to the hedged portfolio is determined by what happens to the difference between the spot and the futures prices, which is what we defined earlier as the *basis:*

$$\text{Basis} = F - P$$

The hedger, the person with the long position in the asset and the short position in the futures contract, profits if the basis gets smaller and loses if the basis gets larger. The reverse is true for the speculator.

Hence, the hedger has not eliminated all risk but has instead replaced price risk with basis risk. Hedgers use the futures market because basis risk is potentially more manageable than price risk. But managing the basis risk requires us first to understand the sources of this risk.

Basis risk goes to zero if the hedge is maintained until the maturity date of the futures contract. However, for shorter holding periods, basis risk results from unpredictable movements in the basis—unpredictable differences between the futures price and the spot price.[17] While these unpredictable movements in the basis arise from various sources, there are four primary sources of basis risk:

1. Changes in the convergence of the futures price to the cash price.
2. Changes in factors that affect the cost of carry.
3. Mismatches between the exposure being hedged and the futures contract being used as the hedge.
4. Random deviations from the cost-of-carry relation.

Changes in the Convergence of the Futures Price to the Cash Price.   Figure 6–7 depicts a "normal" pattern of convergence of the futures price to the cash price: Panel (*a*) illustrates the spot and futures price themselves; panel (*b*) illustrates the basis—the difference between these two prices. At contract maturity, the futures price and the cash price coincide, so for a hedge in which the futures contract is held to maturity, the return on the futures position will be equal to the return on the asset itself. However, if the futures position is unwound prior to contract maturity, the return from the futures position could be different from the return on the asset itself because of the basis risk. And as is obvious in Figure 6–7, the basis is in large part determined by the speed of and the path of convergence of the futures price to the spot price. Moreover, the convergence determines the behavior of the margin account. For the case illustrated, the futures price rises smoothly over time. Thus, there would be a gradual flow of margin from the account of the party who sold the futures contract to the account of the buyer of the futures contract.

Suppose the path of convergence was different from that in Figure 6–7. On one hand, if the futures price converged more rapidly than Figure 6–7 suggests, the basis would decline toward zero more quickly and would consequently be smaller at any point in time. In this case, the flow of margin from the futures seller to the futures buyer would occur more rapidly than indicated in Figure 6–7.[18]

Alternatively, consider the situation illustrated in Figure 6–8, in which the futures price overshoots its equilibrium. In this situation, the basis is negative for a

FIGURE 6–7 · Convergence of the Futures Price

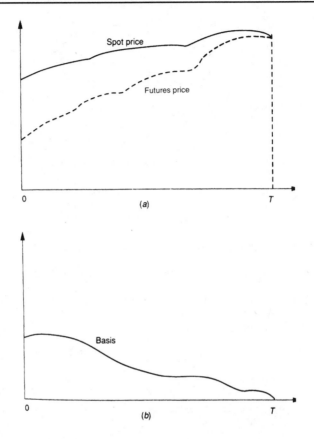

time. Also, margin first moves from the seller of the futures contract to the buyer, then from the buyer to the seller, then from the seller to the buyer.[19]

Changes in Factors That Affect the Cost of Carry. Clearly, as the cost of carry changes, the basis on a futures position changes. For commodity futures, the cost of carry includes storage and insurance costs; changes in either of these would cause the basis to change. However, the most significant determinant of the cost of carry is the interest rate. As the interest rate increases, the opportunity cost of holding the asset rises, so the cost of carry and, therefore, the basis rise.

Mismatches between the Exposure Being Hedged and the Futures Contract Being Used as the Hedge. So far, we have examined situations in which the exposure being hedged is the same as the futures contract, such as hedging an exposure to a

FIGURE 6–8   Convergence of the Futures Price

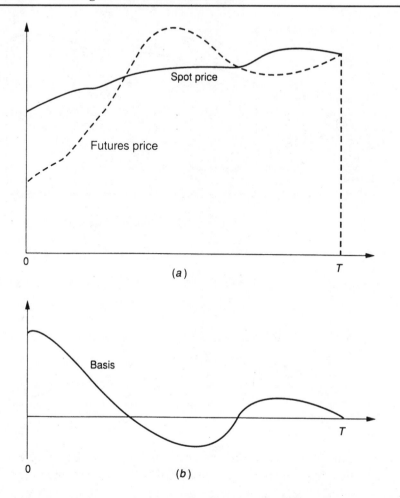

movement in the deutsche mark–dollar exchange rate with a deutsche mark futures contract or hedging an exposure to the U.S. Treasury bill interest rate with Treasury bill futures. However, in some situations the position being hedged is not the same as the deliverable for any futures contract, and the hedger will have to rely on a *cross-hedge*.[20] For example, a deutsche mark futures contract might be used as a cross-hedge for an exposure in Swedish krona,[21] or a Treasury bill futures contract might be used as a cross-hedge against an exposure to the U.S. commercial paper rate.

A cross-hedging situation entails an additional source of basis risk. Basis results not only from difference between the futures price and the prevailing spot price of the deliverable asset but also from differences between the spot prices of the deliverable asset and the exposure being hedged:

$$\text{Basis}_{\text{cross-hedge } x \text{ for } y} = (F_x - P_x) + (P_x - P_y)$$

For example, if I hedge an exposure to the U.S. commercial paper rate with a Treasury bill futures contract, basis could result either from differences in the futures and spot prices of Treasury bills or from differences in the spot Treasury bill and commercial paper interest rates. We can define the latter contribution to basis risk—differences in the spot Treasury bill and commercial paper interest rates—as the *cross-hedge basis*. In Chapter 7 we will look at how typical cross-hedge basis can be determined by the correlation between the spot price of the asset being hedged and the spot price of the deliverable in the futures contract being used as the hedge.

Figlewski (1986) has argued that there are three important factors responsible for variation in the basis for a cross-hedge:

1. *Maturity mismatch.* The maturity of the underlying instrument for the futures contract may be different from the maturity of the asset underlying the exposure. For example, an S&L facing exposure to 30-year mortgage interest rates can construct a hedge using Treasury bond futures, for which the underlying instrument has a maturity of 15 years.[22]

2. *Liquidity differences.* Suppose that the asset being hedged is traded in a market that is illiquid in comparison to the market for the deliverable asset in the futures contract. In such an instance, the price fluctuations for the asset being hedged would be likely to be large relative to the fluctuations in the price of the deliverable asset, implying that basis would increase. Hence, the basis is inversely related to the liquidity for the asset being hedged.

3. *Credit risk differences.* An example provided by Figlewski is the use of Treasury bond futures to hedge a portfolio of corporate bonds. Put another way, changes in the quality spread show up in the basis for a cross-hedge.

Random Deviations from the Cost-of-Carry Relation. This final source of basis risk is the catchall component. Day to day and minute to minute, the basis on a futures position will change for reasons not understood, but over longer periods this random, white-noise component of basis risk will cancel itself out.

Notes

1. This open outcry auction stands in marked contrast to the specialist system for trading equities.
2. Chicago Board of Trade (1988) presents a concise history of the futures markets in the United States.
3. The Chicago Board of Trade (1988) notes, "Many merchants were not fulfilling their forward commitments, causing bitter disputes between buyers and sellers."
4. This statement is adapted from Sharpe (1985). There are subtle, theoretical differences between a futures contract and a bundle of forward contracts, as French (1983) notes. However, as French concludes, the most important differences between forwards and futures lie in the structure of the contracts rather than the pricing.

5. Chicago Mercantile Exchange SPAN© Minimum Performance Bond Requirements, September 9, 1997.

6. The relatively small magnitude of the margin for futures contracts versus the margin requirement for stocks and the fact that initial margin for futures is set by the exchange rather than the Federal Reserve elicited considerable attention following the events of October 19, 1987. It should be noted, however, that the maintenance margin is set by the exchange in both cases. NYSE sets it maintenance margin for the entire exchange; thus, the margin for stocks should be related to the maximum price change for the most volatile stock on the exchange. The futures exchanges set the margin for each contract. Thus, since the volatility of the S&P Index is significantly less than that of individual stocks, the appropriate margin is correspondingly lower.

7. In the discussion so far, we have pretended that Party A contracts directly with Party B. However, in the futures markets, the parties are anonymous. The contracting process actually goes through a broker—a futures commission merchant—who then executes the trade on the futures exchange. Consequently, credit risk is further reduced by the fact that the broker endorses the contract, thereby accepting performance risk.

8. In the example at hand, the reversing trade locks in Party B's loss of $625 from July 1 to July 2, a loss that has already been paid from the margin account. The remainder of the margin account would be returned to Party B.

9. This discussion is adapted from Brennan (1986).

10. As Ira Kawaller points out, the loss would accrue to the clearing member before it accrued to the clearinghouse itself.

11. This delivery specification is particularly important for commodity futures. For example, in the case of wheat futures on the Chicago Board of Trade only certain kinds of wheat are acceptable for delivery (No. 2 Soft Red, No. 2 Hard Red Winter, No. 2 Dark Northern Spring, or No. 1 Northern Spring), and delivery may be accomplished only through warehouse receipts issued by warehouses approved by the exchange.

12. The deliverable bonds have a wide range of coupons and maturities. Consequently, there will be a range of prices for the deliverable bond; at any point in time there will be one bond that is cheapest to deliver.

To avoid problems with sellers of the futures contracts all wanting to deliver this one cheapest bond, and the consequent market corners or squeezes, the Chicago Board of Trade uses a conversion factor that adjusts the delivery values of the different bonds to reduce the effects of the differing coupons and maturities. The conversion factor is determined by the value of the specific deliverable bond having an X percent coupon and Y years to maturity relative to a "normal bond" having an 8 percent coupon and 20 years to maturity.

13. While the rules of operation are set by the exchange, they are subject to the approval of the Commodity Futures Trading Commission.

14. The expiration day for corn futures contracts is the seventh business day preceding the last business day of the delivery month.

15. In our corn example, this will be true even after we adjust for the transportation cost differential between St. Louis and Chicago.

16. In this we will ignore any seasonality like that evident in the futures price of oats.

17. Predictable movements in basis, like the convergence of the basis toward the cost of carry during the life of the futures contract and the convergence of the basis to zero at contract maturity, discussed earlier in this chapter, are incorporated into the expected return on the hedged position.

18. Regardless of the speed of convergence, the total amount of margin that moves from the seller of the contract to the buyer of the contract is the same; the only difference is in the timing of the cash flows. The slower the futures price converges to the spot price, the slower are the transfers of the margin. Consider an extreme situation in which the spot price moves as before, but the futures price does not move at all until just before maturity.

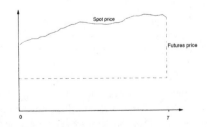

With the convergence as illustrated, no funds are transferred from the contract seller to the contract buyer until just before contract maturity. In such a case the futures contract behaves essentially like a forward contract.

19. However, since the starting and ending points for the futures price are the same, the undiscounted sum of margin payments that change hands remains the same.

20. In Chapter 7, we will spend considerable time examining the way a cross-hedge is constructed and managed.

21. This so-called proxy hedging was common in hedging European foreign exchange exposures until September 1992, when the relation between the deutsche mark and the other European currencies broke down.

22. As noted earlier, to be delivered against a T-bond futures contract the bond must have at least 15 years remaining to maturity.

7

APPLICATIONS OF FUTURES

As we noted in Chapter 1, futures contracts on financial assets are a recent addition to the financial engineer's tool box that appeared only with the introduction of foreign exchange futures in 1972. Nonetheless, financial futures have come to be widely used to hedge exposures to foreign exchange, interest rate, and commodity-price risk. An overview of the futures exchanges around the world and the types of contracts they trade is provided in Table 7–1.

To get an idea about the volumes being traded, Table 7–2 provides trading volumes for the U.S. exchanges for the various commodity groups.

To get a graphical perspective, Figure 7–1 illustrates the expanding use of futures by tracing the trading volume of some familiar futures contracts: the U.S. Treasury bond futures traded on the Chicago Board of Trade, the deutsche mark and Eurodollar futures traded on the Chicago Mercantile Exchange, and futures on crude oil traded on the New York Mercantile Exchange.

The logic of using futures to hedge an underlying exposure is apparent in Figure 7–2. If the firm has an inherent short position in a financial asset—if increases in the price of the asset will decrease the value of the firm—the hedge will be constructed by buying the appropriate number of the appropriate futures contracts for the appropriate expiration month. Combining the inherent position with the hedge, the exposure is neutralized. Ira Kawaller of the Chicago Mercantile Exchange provides an example.

For the firm with an inherent long position, the hedge is constructed by selling the appropriate number of the appropriate futures contract for the appropriate expiration month. The problem for the hedger is, of course, to determine those appropriates: the appropriate futures contract with the appropriate expiration month and the appropriate number of contracts. An example helps demonstrate how the hedger determines these *appropriates*. The following discussion concerns a firm

TABLE 7–1 International Futures Volumes, January–September 1997

Exchange	Volume	Underlying Asset			
		Interest Rates	Currencies	Equities	Commodities
Chicago Board of Trade	139,136,030	✓		✓	
London Intl. Financial Futures & Options Exch	129,113,530	✓		✓	✓
Chicago Mercantile Exch	117,401,038	✓	✓	✓	✓
New York Mercantile Exch	52,611,070				✓
Deutsche Terminborse	48,156,634	✓		✓	
Matif, Paris	43,373,303	✓		✓	✓
London Metal Exch	39,125,527				✓
Sydney Futures Exch	18,952,026	✓		✓	✓
Meff Renta FIJA, Spain	18,744,524	✓			
Tokyo International Financial Futures Exch	18,270,929	✓	✓		
SIMEX, Singapore	16,663,314	✓	✓	✓	✓
OM, Stockholm	11,104,818	✓		✓	
Internation Petroleum Exch, UK	10,545,272				✓
Hong Kong Futures Exch	4,739,062	✓	✓	✓	
Meff Renta Variable, Spain	4,029,805			✓	
Montreal Exch	3,817,777	✓			
Philadelphia Stock Exch	3,813,316		✓	✓	
American Stock Exch	3,134,803			✓	
SOFFEX, Switzerland	1,842,609	✓			
Austrian Futures & Options Exch	751,357	✓		✓	
Futop Clearing Centre, Denmark	449,168	✓		✓	

Volume = number of contracts traded during first three quarters of 1997
SOURCE: *Futures Industry Association, Monthly Volume Report*

TABLE 7–2 Trading Volumes on U.S. Futures Exchanges

Commodity Groups	1994	1995	1996	1997
Interest Rates	189.4	177.7	165.6	179.5
Agricultural Commodities	44.6	46.7	58.1	56.6
Energy Products	37.7	35.8	35.2	39.2
Foreign Currencies/Index	23.3	18.4	16.9	20.0
Equity Indices	12.2	15.5	16.7	17.1
Precious Metals	2.1	11.2	11.8	11.6
NonPrecious Metals	0.3	2.0	1.7	1.8
Others	324.4	0.4	0.6	0.8
TOTAL				

Volumes are for first three quarters of each year
SOURCE: *Futures Industry Association, Monthly Volume Report*

FIGURE 7–1   Yearly Contract Volumes

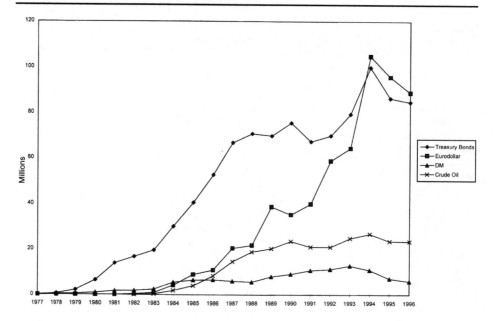

Risk Management in Practice

To Hedge or Not to Hedge*

Ira G. Kawaller

Edwin Charles, the treasurer of Benzoe Corp.,[†] plans to take down a $10 million loan within the next quarter. The loan rate will be set at the time of the takedown, at three-month LIBOR plus 100 basis points. This rate will be reset each quarter on balances remaining outstanding. Clearly, if interest rates rise before the takedown, Benzoe's interest expense will rise commensurately, but if rates fall, lower interest expenses will result. How can Edwin protect himself against the unknown at the lowest possible cost?

Strategy 1: Do nothing. This choice would be most appropriate if Edwin thinks that the likelihood that interest rates will rise is limited or negligible. He, of course, must be comfortable living with the consequences if his assessment turns out to be wrong.

Strategy 2: Lock in an interest rate today. This may be accomplished by selling Eurodollar futures contracts timed to expire at about the same time as the loan rate is to be set. Any expiration mismatch will foster some uncertainty or "basis risk," but less risk than the prevailing market interest rate exposure itself. The rate that Edwin can secure would be about 100 basis points above the rate implied by the futures contract (that is, 100 minus the futures price). The additional 100 basis points reflect the bank's spread over LIBOR.

Before the takedown, it is uncertain which strategy will generate the lower cost of funds. Each alternative hedge strategy should be assessed in light of its cost versus its potential benefits or consequences. For example, a consequence of using futures is forgoing the benefit of lower spot market interest rates.

Suppose, for example, that today three-month LIBOR is at 7 percent and that the Eurodollar futures contract is at 92.90 (in other words, at a rate of 7.10 percent). In the accompanying table, I consider two scenarios—one in which three-month LIBOR rises to 8 percent and the other in which three-month LIBOR falls to 6 percent.

Outcomes of Alternate Hedging Strategies

Hedge Strategies	1. Do Nothing	2. Sell Futures
Scenario I: Spot LIBOR Rises to 8 Percent		
Interest paid to bank (based on 9 percent interest)	$225,000	$225,000
P&L on hedge (10 contracts × price change of hedge vehicle)		22,500
Net interest	225,000	202,500
Effective rate	9 percent	8.10 percent
Scenario II: Spot LIBOR Falls to 6 Percent		
Interest paid to bank (based on 7 percent interest)	$175,000	$175,000
P&L on hedge (10 contract × price change of hedge vehicle)		(27,500)
Net interest	175,000	202,500
Effective rate	7 percent	8.10 percent

If Charles does nothing, the cost of funds will simply be equal to spot LIBOR plus 100 basis points—7 percent or 9 percent. If Charles sells futures, he locks in a rate of 100 basis points above the initial futures rate—8.10 percent.

When this was written, Ira G. Kawaller was vice president and director of the New York office for the Chicago Mercantile Exchange. He is now president of Kawaller & Co. After receiving a Ph.D. from Purdue University, he served at the Federal Reserve Board in Washington. He subsequently worked for the AT&T Company and J. Aron Company, Inc. Kawaller currently serves on the board of directors of the National Option and Futures Society and the board of advisors for the International Association of Financial Engineers. He is the author of *Financial Futures and Options*.

*This example was adapted from material in *Treasury and Risk Management* magazine, Fall 1991, and is reprinted with permission. © 1991 CFO Publishing Corp.

† The people and companies presented here are fictional.

FIGURE 7–2   The Logic of the Futures Hedge   (*a*) A Long Hedge   (*b*) A Short Hedge

If the firm has an inherent short
position

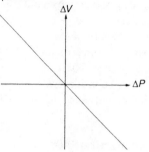

If the firm has an inherent long
position

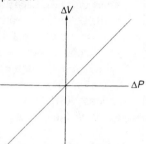

the hedge will be created by buying
the appropriate number of the
appropriate futures contract

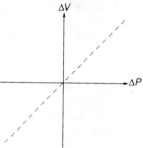

the hedge will be created by selling
the appropriate number of the
appropriate futures contract

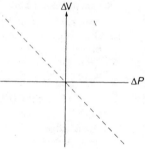

to neutralize the exposure.

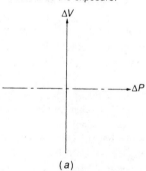

(*a*)

to neutralize the exposure.

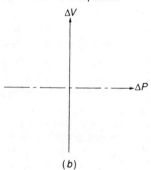

(*b*)

with an interest rate exposure, but the logic is the same for foreign exchange and commodity exposures.

Using Futures to Hedge an Underlying Exposure

To illustrate how a futures contract can be used as a hedge, it is probably best to begin with the simplest case.[1]

The construction of the hedge in Illustration 7–1 is simple because everything matched. The underlying exposure is to three-month LIBOR, the same as the deliverable for the futures contract. The end of the exposure matches exactly the delivery date for the futures contract. The magnitude of the exposure equals the amount of the futures contract.

Illustration 7–1

No Basis Risk

At the beginning of 1994, the treasurer of Ajax Enterprises knows that because of seasonal variations in sales and in the production of inventory for Christmas sales, the firm will require a three-month, $1 million bank loan on June 13. The treasurer knows that the contractual rate Ajax will have to pay on the loan will be the three-month Eurodollar rate (LIBOR) plus 1 percent. Hence, the treasurer is concerned about increases in three-month LIBOR, since every 1 percent (100 basis point) increase in LIBOR increases Ajax's borrowing costs by $2,500.

Using the Eurodollar futures contract traded on the Chicago Mercantile Exchange, the treasurer can achieve a perfect hedge. The treasurer can lock in the Eurodollar borrowing rate given by the implied forward LIBOR rate by selling one June Eurodollar futures contract.

Suppose that on January 2, the three-month LIBOR rate is 3.75 percent. Suppose further that the implied forward LIBOR rate from the June Eurodollar futures contract is 4.25 percent.* Given that Eurodollar futures are quoted as 100 minus the interest rate, this means that the price of the June Eurodollar futures contract on January 2 is

$$100 - 4.25 = 95.75$$

The treasurer of Ajax sells one June futures contract at 95.75 to lock in a three-month rate of 4.25 percent.

Suppose that the treasurer's fears are realized and that by the time he needs to borrow, the three-month LIBOR is up. While extreme, let's suppose that, precisely on June 13, the three-month LIBOR rate rises from 3.75 percent to 5.50 percent. This 175-basis-point increase in LIBOR means that Ajax's borrowing costs have increased by $1.75 \times \$2,500 = \$4,375$. Conversely, the increase in the interest rate means that Ajax has earned monies on the futures position that can be used to offset some of this increase in the borrowing cost. In 1994, June 13 will be the last day for trading and delivery of June Eurodollar futures contract. Thus, on June 13 as the futures contract expires, the futures rate and the spot rate must coincide, so the price of the June forward contract on June 13 must be

$$100 - 5.50 = 94.50$$

Hence, the price of the futures contract has declined by 1.25, or 125 "ticks." The price movement per tick is $25, so Ajax's profit on the futures contract is $125 \times \$25 = \$3,125$.

Combining the preceding, Ajax's net increase in its borrowing cost is $1,250,

$$\$4,375 - \$3,125 = \$1,250$$

which is equivalent to an increase in the three-month Eurodollar rate of 50 basis points. That is, the effect of the hedge is to lock in a three-month LIBOR rate of 4.25 percent, precisely the implied forward three-month LIBOR rate that existed when the hedge was established.

––––––––––

*These were the interest rates implied in the futures market as of April 1993.

Moreover, the price movement in Illustration 7–1 is such that no funds are transferred into or out of the margin account during the life of the contract. Consequently, Ajax neither earns additional interest income (in its margin account) nor forgoes interest on funds paid out of its margin account.

However, in the real world, the exposure being hedged typically does not match the characteristics of the futures contract exactly. Generally, the futures contract is liquidated before expiration, and as noted in Chapter 6, the convergence obtained in Ira Kawaller's example is not guaranteed. What is virtually assured is that price changes will not all occur on the final day of the futures contract. The remainder of this section demonstrates the impact these factors have on how the futures hedge would be constructed.

Mismatches on Maturities: Basis Risk

In Illustration 7–1, there is no basis risk; the period of the exposure matches precisely the period covered by the futures contract. Consequently, the futures price and the spot price are the same when the futures hedge is lifted. Were this not the case, basis risk would result.

The situation in Illustration 7–2 is typical; because of basis, the hedge can be more or less than 100 percent effective. Since the hedger can do nothing about the underlying causes of basis that we discussed in Chapter 6, the only other approach to try is to line up exposure dates—in the preceding example, loan pricing dates—with the maturity dates for the futures contract.

Illustration 7–2

Basis Risk

Suppose that Ajax would require the $1 million loan not on June 13 but on June 1, about two weeks before maturity for the futures contract. The treasurer of Ajax would still hedge the exposure by selling one June futures contract on January 2 at 95.75 in an attempt to lock in a three-month Eurodollar rate of 4.25 percent.

To keep the numbers simple, let's suppose that on June 1, three-month LIBOR rises to 5.50 percent (as it did on June 13 in the preceding example).* So, as before, the increased borrowing cost for Ajax will be $4,375. With this increase in the spot interest rate, the futures interest rate will also rise, so the price of the futures contract will fall. But since June 1 is not the expiration date for the contract, there is no guarantee that on June 1 the futures and spot rates will coincide. Let's suppose that they do not, and that on June 1 the futures price falls not to 94.50 but only to 94.75. The futures price has moved 100 ticks; Ajax's profit on the futures position is $100 \times \$25 = \$2,500$.

The result is that Ajax's net increase in its borrowing cost is

$$\$4,375 - \$2,500 = \$1,875$$

an amount equivalent to a 75-basis-point increase in the three-month LIBOR rate. Hence, the treasurer ends up not with the desired 4.25 percent rate but instead with a rate of 4.50 percent. The 25-basis-point difference is the result of the basis of 25 basis points that exists when the futures contract is closed.[†]

In this case, the basis goes against the treasurer, and the hedge is less than 100 percent effective. However, the basis could favor the hedger. If the price of the futures contract on June 1 were 94.25, the rate Ajax would end with would be 4 percent, and we would have said that the hedge was more than 100 percent effective.

---

*For now, we continue to suppose that the price change occurs only on June 1; LIBOR remains at 3.75 percent from January 2 to May 31, so the margin account is unaffected.

[†]When the futures contract is closed, the spot interest rate is 5.50 percent. The rate implied by the futures price is

$$100 - 94.75 = 5.25 \text{ percent}$$

Hence, the basis is 25 basis points.

Mismatches on Maturities: Strip and Rolling Hedges

So far, we have considered a single exposure in which the maturity for the exposure fits a single futures contract. However, a hedger might have more than one maturity to hedge.

The strategy in Illustration 7–3 works well as long as there is sufficient liquidity in the more distant futures contracts. However, if the more distant futures contracts do not have sufficient liquidity—or if the maturity of the exposure exceeds the term of the most distant traded futures contract—the hedger can resort to a rolling hedge. A rolling hedge can achieve the same result as the strip hedge.

While a rolling hedge can, in some instances, achieve the same results as a strip hedge (as in Illustration 7–4), in other instances a rolling hedge can also accomplish a hedge that was not possible with a strip hedge. By "stacking" the contracts, futures contracts can be used to hedge an exposure that extends beyond the end of the longest available contract. However, this stacking approach does have drawbacks.[2] First, more contracts must be bought and sold as the hedge is rolled forward, thereby increasing the transaction costs of the hedge. Second, the prices for futures contracts not yet traded are uncertain, creating an additional source of basis risk.

Mismatches in the Asset: Cross-Hedging

To this point, we have considered only cases in which the underlying exposure is to the same financial price that determines the price of the futures contract. In our examples so far, the firm is exposed to three-month LIBOR, precisely the same financial price that determines the price of the Eurodollar futures contract. Often, however, a traded futures contract does not match the hedger's exposure exactly. In such cases, the hedger must resort to a *cross-hedge*. This requires answering two questions: (1) What futures contract should be used to hedge the exposure? (2) How many contracts are required to hedge the exposure?

The short answer to the first question is simple. To establish the "best" cross-hedge, use the futures contract that is most closely correlated with the underlying exposure. To see how this works, let's look again at Ajax.

As Illustration 7–6A shows, the appropriate futures contract for instituting a cross-hedge is normally the futures contract that is most highly correlated with the underlying exposure. However, this simple decision rule may need to be modified if it leads to the selection of a futures contract that has insufficient liquidity. In an illiquid market, the bid-ask spreads will usually be large, leading to an increase in the all-in cost of the hedge. Moreover, if the futures contract is illiquid, a large order can have a discernible effect on the price. To the extent that the hedger's buy order triggers a price increase and sell order triggers a price decrease, the cost of

Illustration 7–3

A Strip Hedge

The treasurer of Beta Manufacturing also faces uncertainty about future borrowing costs. Like Ajax, Beta uses three-month borrowing for which it pays a rate linked to three-month LIBOR, but unlike Ajax, Beta borrows not simply once per year but rather throughout the year. On January 2, the treasurer of Beta expects the following borrowing pattern over 1994:

March 1	$15 million
June 1	45 million
September 1	20 million
December 1	10 million

To hedge the resulting exposure to the three-month Eurodollar rate, the treasurer of Beta would "sell a strip of futures." On January 2, she would sell 15 March Eurodollar futures contracts, 45 June contracts, 20 September contracts, and 10 December contracts.

On March 1, Beta would close out the hedge on its first borrowing by buying 15 March contracts. Likewise, on June 1, Beta would buy 45 June contracts; on September 1, Beta would buy 20 September contracts; and on December 1, Beta would buy 10 December contracts. As Illustration 7–2 showed, the effectiveness of the hedge would depend on the basis existing on the dates at which the contracts are closed.

Illustration 7–4

A Rolling Hedge

If the treasurer of Beta is concerned about the liquidity of more distant futures contracts, she can hedge the exposure to the three-month Eurodollar rate by rolling the hedge:

January 2	Sell 90 March Eurodollar contracts
March 1	Buy 90 March Eurodollar contracts
	Sell 75 June Eurodollar contracts
June 1	Buy 75 June Eurodollar contracts
	Sell 30 September Eurodollar contracts
September 1	Buy 30 September Eurodollar contracts
	Sell 10 December Eurodollar contracts
December 1	Buy 10 December Eurodollar contracts

By doing this, the treasurer takes advantage of the liquidity in nearby contracts.

Illustration 7–5

A Rolling Hedge Again

At the beginning of 1994, the treasurer of Beta continues to have the same expectations about borrowings in 1994:

March 1	$15 million
June 1	45 million
September 1	20 million
December 1	10 million

So on January 2, she implements the rolling hedge detailed in Illustration 7–4:

> January 2   Sell 90 March Eurodollar futures contracts

However, suppose that by March 1, the treasurer has developed her forecast for Beta's borrowing needs for March 1, 1995, as $20 million. To hedge this revised borrowing schedule, the transactions done by Beta on March 1 are as follows:

> March 1   Buy 90 March Eurodollar futures contracts
>
> Sell 95 June Eurodollar futures contracts

In Illustration 7–4, Beta's remaining planned borrowings total $75 million. Now, with an additional $20 million of borrowing forecast in March 1995, Beta's planned borrowings—the amount it wants to hedge—are $95 million, so Beta will sell 95 rather than 75 June futures contracts.

Continuing in the same manner, suppose that by June 1 the treasurer is forecasting borrowing $60 million for June 1, 1995. Hence:

> June 1   Buy 95 Eurodollar futures contracts
>
> Sell 110 September Eurodollar futures contracts

By buying the 95 June contracts, Beta is closing out the hedge for its June 1994 borrowing.* At the same time, it sells 110 contracts to hedge its September 1994 borrowing (20 contracts), its December 1994 borrowing (10 contracts), its March 1995 borrowing (20 contracts), and its June 1995 borrowing (60 contracts).

The treasurer can continue this system indefinitely. On September 1, she closes out the hedge for the September borrowing by buying the 110 September contracts and sells December '94, March '95, June '95, and September '95 contracts sufficient to hedge her anticipated borrowing needs in December 1994, March 1995, June 1995, and September 1995. On December 1, she buys December contracts to close out the hedge for the December borrowing and sells March '95, June '95, September '95, and December '95 contracts to hedge borrowing needs in March, June, September, and December 1995. On March 1, 1995. . . .

---

*The effectiveness of this strategy again depends on the basis between the spot three-month LIBOR rate and the implied rate from the futures price on June 1.

Illustration 7–6A

A Cross-Hedge: Selecting the Appropriate Futures Contract

At the beginning of 1994, the treasurer of Ajax Enterprises again expects Ajax will need to borrow on June 1. However, let's change the parameters of this expected borrowing. First, instead of $1 million, let's suppose the forecasted borrowing is $36 million. Second, instead of a three-month bank borrowing tied to LIBOR, let's suppose that the treasurer has decided to issue one-month commercial paper.

Nonetheless, the treasurer remains concerned about rising interest rates and wishes to hedge his interest rate exposure. But there is no futures contract in one-month commercial paper. To select the "best" contract to hedge the exposure to commercial paper rates, the treasurer looks at the correlations between the one-month commercial paper

(CP) rate and several interest rates for which there are traded futures contracts available.

Futures Contract	Interest Rate	Correlation with One-Month CP Rate*
U.S. T-bills	90-day T-bill rate	0.987
Eurodollars	90-day LIBOR	0.991
U.S. T-bonds	15-year T-bond rate	0.856

The high correlation between the 90-day LIBOR rate and the one-month commercial paper rate, shown below, leads the treasurer to select the Eurodollar contract as the most appropriate futures contract.

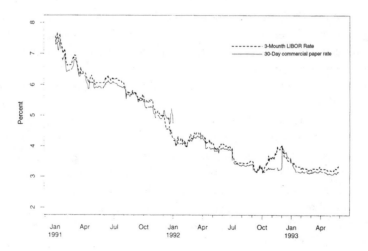

*The correlation coefficients displayed were calculated using data for the nearby futures con-tract for the period January 2, 1991, through May 28, 1993.

constructing a hedge increases. Consequently, concerns about the liquidity of a particular futures contract could result in the hedger's shifting to a contract that has higher liquidity but a lower correlation.

Once the appropriate futures contract is selected, the hedger must answer the second question: How many contracts are required to hedge the exposure? The answer is itself made up of two parts. The hedger must first consider the relation between movements in the underlying exposure and the price of the futures contract used in the hedge. Since the financial price used in the hedge is not the same as the financial price responsible for the firm's underlying exposure, there is no guarantee that there will be one-for-one movements in the two financial prices. The hedger must determine how these two prices move. For example, in the case of interest rate risk, if the rate in the hedge changes by X basis points, how much will the rate to which the firm is exposed change? While there are many ways to answer this question, the simplest and most straightforward is to use a linear regression. The analyst regresses the financial price to which the firm is exposed, $P_{exposure}$, on the financial price embedded in the futures contract being used as the hedge, $P_{futures}$,

$$P_{exposure} = a + bP_{futures}$$

Or in the case at hand in which the financial prices are interest rates, the regression equation would be

$$r_{exposure} = a + b(r_{futures})$$

where $r_{exposure}$ is the interest rate to which the firm is exposed, and $r_{futures}$ is the interest rate embedded in the futures contract. The estimate of b tells how the interest rate to which the firm is exposed moves in relation to the interest rate embedded in the futures contract. For example, if the estimate of b is 0.5, the rate to which the firm is exposed moves only half as much as the rate in the futures contract, so all other things equal, only half as many futures contracts are required to hedge the exposure. Conversely, if the estimate of b is 2, the rate to which the firm is exposed moves twice as much as the rate in the futures contract, and all other things equal, twice as many futures contracts are required to hedge the exposure.

In determining the number of futures contracts needed to hedge an exposure, the second thing the hedger must consider is the effect of a one-unit change in the financial price on the underlying exposure versus the effect of this one-unit change in the financial price on the value of the futures contract. For the case at hand, an increase in the interest rate need not have the same effect on the underlying exposure as it does on the value of the futures contract. If a given change in the interest rate has a larger impact on the underlying exposure than on the value of the futures contract, fewer futures contracts are required to hedge the position, and vice versa.

Illustration 7–6B

A Cross-Hedge: Selecting the Appropriate Number of Contracts, Part 1

The treasurer of Ajax has decided to hedge his June 1 exposure to the one-month commercial paper rate with June Eurodollar futures contracts, priced off three-month LIBOR. To determine how these two rates move in relation to one another, he uses monthly data for 1991–93 to estimate the relation.

$$r_{exposure} = a + b(r_{futures})$$

The estimate of b he obtains is 0.75. The treasurer, *considering only the relation between the one-month commercial paper rate and the three-month LIBOR rate,* knows that to hedge his \$36 million exposure, he must sell $36 \times 0.75 = 27$ June Eurodollar contracts.

Illustration 7–6C

A Cross-Hedge: Selecting the Appropriate Number of Contracts, Part 2

As we know, the treasurer of Ajax has decided to hedge a \$36 million June 1 one-month commercial paper borrowing with June Eurodollar futures—that is, with three-month LIBOR.

However, a one-basis-point movement in the interest rate does not have the same impact on a one-month borrowing as it does on the three-month futures contract. A one-basis-point movement changes the value of a one-month \$1 million borrowing by

$$\$1,000,000 \times 0.0001 \times 30/360 = \$8.33$$

But as we have already seen, a one-basis-point movement changes the value of the \$1 million futures contract by

$$\$1,000,000 \times 0.0001 \times 90/360 = \$25$$

The response of the futures contract is three times that of the underlying exposure, the one-month borrowing.

Hence, *considering only the difference in the way the borrowing and the futures contract respond to a given change in the interest rate,* the treasurer of Ajax knows that he requires only one third as many futures contracts to hedge the exposure; to hedge a \$36 million one-month exposure, he must sell 12 rather than 36 three-month futures contracts.

Putting the preceding together, the construction of a cross-hedge requires that the hedger do the following:

1. *Determine the appropriate futures contract to use as the hedge.* In general, the appropriate futures contract is the one that is most closely correlated with the underlying exposure. However, an alternate futures contract may be selected if there is insufficient liquidity in the preferred contract.

2. *Determine the appropriate number of futures contracts.* The appropriate number of futures contracts is determined by (a) the relation between movements in the underlying exposure and the price of the futures contract used in the hedge and (b) the effect of a one-unit change in the financial price on the underlying exposure versus the effect of this one-unit change in the financial price on the value of the futures contract.

To see how this is accomplished, let's put our example together in Illustration 7–6D.

Illustration 7–6D

A Cross-Hedge

At the beginning of 1994, the treasurer of Ajax Enterprises expects that it will be necessary for Ajax to borrow $36 million on June 1 by an issue of one-month commercial paper. Concerned about rising interest rates, the treasurer wishes to hedge his interest rate exposure. Since there is no futures contract in one-month commercial paper, he looks for the best contract to hedge the exposure by identifying the futures contract interest rate that has the highest correlation with the one-month commercial paper rate, which turns out to be three-month LIBOR. Hence the appropriate futures contract is the June Eurodollar futures contract.

To determine the appropriate number of June Eurodollar futures to hedge the $36 million one-month commercial paper exposure, the treasurer first uses monthly data for 1991–93 to estimate the relation

$$r_{exposure} = a + b(r_{futures})$$

The estimate of b he obtains is 0.75. Secondly, the treasurer notes that a one-basis-point movement changes the value of a one-month $1 million borrowing by $8.33, but a one-basis-point movement changes the value of the $1 million futures contract by $25. Hence, the response of the futures contract is three times that of the underlying exposure, the one-month borrowing. Putting this together, the number of contracts necessary to hedge the exposure is

$$36 \times 0.75 \times 0.33 = 9$$

Consequently, on January 2, the treasurer of Ajax sells nine June Eurodollar futures contracts.

Illustration 7–6E

The Results of the Cross-Hedge

Let's continue to suppose that on January 2 three-month LIBOR is 3.75 percent and the price of June Eurodollar futures is 95.75, implying a June futures LIBOR rate of 4.25 percent. Let's further suppose that on January 2 the spread between the spot LIBOR rate and the commercial paper rate is 60 basis points, so the one-month commercial paper rates 4.35 percent.

In preceding cases, Ajax hopes to lock in the futures rate of 4.25 percent, an increase in three-month LIBOR of 50 basis points. In Illustration 7–6B, the treasurer of Ajax estimates the relation between changes in three-month LIBOR and changes in the one-month commercial paper rate to be 0.75. So an expectation of a 50-basis-point increase in three-month LIBOR results in an expectation of a $0.75 \times 50 = 37.5$ basis-point increase in the one-month commercial paper rate. Hence, the one-month commercial paper rate Ajax is trying to lock in is 4.35 percent + 37.5 basis points = 4.725 percent.

As before, let's suppose that precisely on June 1 the three-month LIBOR rate rises to 5.50 percent* and the price of June futures falls to 94.75. As we saw in Illustration 7–2, Ajax's profit on each futures contract is $2,500, so the profit on the nine contracts is $22,500.

If the estimated relation between three-month LIBOR and one-month commercial paper holds, the 175-basis-point increase in three-month LIBOR (5.50 percent − 3.75 percent) should result in a $0.75 \times 175 = 131.25$ basis-point increase in the one-month

commercial paper rate. Hence the one-month rate the treasurer expects is 4.35 percent + 131.25 basis points = 5.6625 percent. However, let's suppose that on June 1 the one-month commercial paper rate rises to 5.75 percent. The increase in Ajax's borrowing costs resulting from the increase in the commercial paper rate is

$$\$36,000,000 \times (0.0575 - 0.0435) \times 30/360 = \$42,000$$

Combining the increase in the borrowing cost with the profit on the hedge position, Ajax's net increase in its borrowing cost is

$$\$42,000 - \$22,500 = \$19,500$$

An increase in the borrowing cost of $19,500 is equivalent to an increase in the one-month rate of 65 basis points. Hence Ajax's final one-month borrowing rate is 4.35 percent + 65 basis points = 5 percent.

The difference between this final rate Ajax pays on its borrowing, 5 percent, and the rate the treasurer tries to lock in, 4.725 percent, is 27.5 basis points. The difference is again the result of basis risk, but in this case there are two sources of the basis:

1. On June 1, the spot LIBOR rate of 5.50 percent differs from the LIBOR rate implied by the futures price, $100 - 94.75 = 5.25$ percent, by 25 basis points. Since the estimated relation between the three-month LIBOR rate and the one-month commercial paper rate is 0.75, the basis of 25 basis points for three-month LIBOR will translate to a basis

of $0.75 \times 25 = 18.75$ basis points for one-month commercial paper.

2. On June 1, the expected one-month commercial paper rate is 5.6625 percent, but the actual commercial paper rate is 5.75 percent. This difference results in a basis for the one-month commercial paper hedge of 5.75 percent − 5.6625 percent = 8.75 basis points.

Combining the two sources of basis,

$$18.75 + 8.75 = 27.5 \text{ basis points}$$

we obtain the total basis for this one-month commercial paper hedge.

----

*We are still presuming that the price change occurs only on June 1; from January 2 through May 31, LIBOR remains at 3.75 percent.

Once the cross-hedge is implemented, the degree to which it will actually hedge the underlying exposure is determined, as before, by the basis. However, in the case of the cross-hedge, the hedger is using a futures contract in financial price X to hedge an exposure to financial price Y, so there are two distinct sources of basis risk. First, the cross-hedge is subject to the normal basis; when the hedge is removed, the spot price for X need not be equal to the futures price of X.[3] The second source of basis risk is in deviations between the spot price of X and the spot price of Y.[4] To see how this occurs, let's examine how our cross-hedge worked.

Adjusting for the Margin Account: "Tailing" the Hedge

So far, in looking at the construction of a hedge we have considered only the gain or loss on the futures position at the end, when the hedge is removed. However, as you know from Chapter 6, profits and losses accrue to a futures contract over the life of the contract as funds are transferred into or out of the hedger's margin account. Since the funds in the margin account earn interest, funds that flow in early are more valuable than those that flow in later. (Conversely, the value of the hedger's position is higher if funds flow out of the margin account later rather than early.)

For purposes of illustration, suppose a firm sells a futures contract to hedge an underlying position. Gains on the hedge will be used to offset losses on the underlying position. Figure 7–3 illustrates the effect of the timing of cash flows and of the margin account. In all three panels, the gain to the hedger independent of the margin account is equal to the difference in the beginning and ending futures prices times the size of the futures contract $(F_0 - F_T)FC$. However, the accrued interest for the margin account is very different for the three cases

FIGURE 7–3   The Effect of the Timing of Cash Flows into the Margin Account

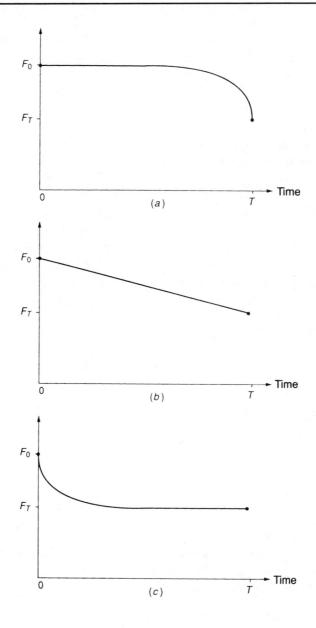

displayed in panels (*a*) through (*c*). First, compare panels (*a*) and (*b*). Panel (*a*) is much like the situation we have considered so far—the futures price remains constant until the end of the hedge period—while in panel (*b*) funds are flowing into the hedger's margin account smoothly over the duration of the hedge. In the situation illustrated by panel (*a*), there is essentially no interest earned, while for that illustrated by panel (*b*), the hedger earns interest on the increases in the margin account. Consequently, if the futures price behaves like panel (*b*) rather than panel (*a*), the number of futures contracts necessary to hedge a given position is smaller. And if futures prices behave like the situation illustrated in panel (*c*), the hedge position can be even smaller, since more of the funds flow in early during the hedge period.[5]

The upshot of all this is that the number of futures contracts needed to hedge an exposure must be adjusted for the effect of the daily resettlement of the margin account. Profits today are magnified by the interest earned if reinvested. This effect, if not accounted for properly, causes overhedging. Although the effect turns out to be small for short hedging periods and low interest rates, it can be corrected by a technique known in futures market jargon as "tailing" the hedge. The "tail" adjusts the number of futures contracts so that the *present value* of the hedge equals the underlying exposure. Hence, if ignoring the effect of daily resettlement of the margin account, the number of contracts to be sold to hedge a given exposure is N; then the "tailed" hedge is

$$Ne^{-rT}$$

where T is the maturity of the hedge and r is the appropriate riskless interest rate.

Illustration 7–7

A "Tailed" Hedge

Cassa Manufacturing, like Ajax, expects to have to issue one-month commercial paper in the future. However, Cassa expects to issue $400 million in 15 months.

The treasurer of Cassa wants to hedge this exposure using futures contracts. Using what we have seen in Illustration 7–6, it would appear that the appropriate futures contract is

the Eurodollar, and ignoring the effect of the margin account, the appropriate number of contracts to sell would be

$$400 \times 0.75 \times 0.33 = 100$$

However, if daily resettlement of the margin account is taken into account—if the hedge is "tailed"—the number of Eurodollar futures contract she should sell is

$$100e^{-rt}$$

where T is 15 months. If we suppose that the corresponding riskless interest rate is 8.2 percent, the treasurer of Cassa will sell 90 Eurodollar futures contracts,

$$100e^{-(0.082)(15/12)} = 90.25$$

Moreover, the hedger needs to monitor the rate at which funds are moving into or out of the margin account. If funds are flowing into or out of the margin account at a rate different from that expected when the hedge was established, the tailing factor for the hedge must be adjusted accordingly.

Finally, and most importantly, hedgers will have to monitor basis risk. After all, by using the futures contract, a hedger has accepted basis risk in place of price risk and should manage this basis risk as much as possible. Hence the hedge should be rebalanced occasionally if the relation between the prices of the assets being hedged and the assets underlying the futures contract changes. Change in the relation between the spot and futures prices also may require rebalancing the hedge.

The illustrations in this chapter rely on interest rate hedging to show how futures can be used. Futures, however, are equally well-suited to hedging commodity and foreign exchange exposures. Ira Kawaller demonstrates how a foreign exchange hedge works.

Risk Management in Practice

Waging War against Currency Exposure

Ira G. Kawaller

It was mid-December in 1990. An outbreak of hostilities between the United States and Iraq was imminent. As General Norman Schwartzkopf pondered ways to safeguard his troops, Treasurer Joanna Knobler pondered ways to safeguard the Trilobyte Corporation from potential swings in foreign exchange rates.

The computer manufacturer had just scored a tandem success. Aggressive bargaining clinched a deal to secure computer boards from Japan at a particularly attractive price of ¥125 million. Another campaign won a large contract to supply a German wholesaler with computers for DM1.25 million.

But if the coalition forces attacked Iraq, the gains Trilobyte had made could be wiped out by movements in foreign exchange rates. Knobler sought a way to safeguard Trilobyte's exposure to the wild currency swings that would inevitably accompany an army's march into the desert.

Because of the difference in timing between Trilobyte's needing to buy the ¥125 million in March and receiving the DM1.25 million in late May, Knobler found the uncertainty meant too much risk. Trilobyte would be vulnerable if the dollar weakened against the yen before March 1991 or if it strengthened against the deutsche mark before late May.

If the dollar behaved as it had during periods of international tension, it would weaken on the outbreak of war, which would drive up Trilobyte's cost of buying yen. If fighting was prolonged, the company's German deal would benefit from a weakened dollar. But what if the war was over quickly and the dollar soared?

Knobler decided to hedge her bets, as well as her exposure. She hedged all of Trilobyte's yen requirements. But because the deutsche mark deal would be more profitable if the dollar weakened, she hedged only 50 percent of that exposure up front. If the dollar dropped significantly, she could lock in the other half of the deutsche mark exposure at lower levels. On the other hand, if she saw signs of a longer-term strengthening of the dollar, she would move quickly to hedge the rest of the deutsche mark exposure.

- On December 14, 1990, she bought 10 yen futures contracts for March delivery—each contract covered ¥12.5 million for coverage of the ¥125 million exposure.
- She also sold short five June deutsche mark futures contracts, each for DM125,000 to cover half her exposure on the German contract.

On January 17, the Middle East battle began. Knobler took the opportunity to capture some of the consequent weakness in the value of the dollar by short selling another five deutsche mark futures contracts worth DM625,000, locking in a more favorable exchange rate.

The hedge positions and the results on May 20 are summarized in the following table.

The Yen Hedge

Dec 14	Bought 10 March ¥ Futures at $0.(00)7508/¥
March 18	Cover 10 March ¥ Futures at $0.(00)7225/¥
	Buy ¥125 million at 138.4 = $903,114

Waging War against Currency Exposure continued

Effective Rate for Yen:

$$\frac{\dfrac{¥125 \text{ million}}{¥138.41/\$} - 10[(7225 - 7508) \times \$12.50]}{¥125 \text{ million}} = \$0.(00)7508 \text{ or } ¥133.19/\$$$

Effective cost of ¥ 125 million at 133.19 = \$938,509
Opportunity cost of yen hedge = \$ 35,395*
Commissions would bring the rate to \$0.(00)7509 or \$0.(00)7510

*Knobler would have done better by not hedging the yen.

The Deutsche Mark Hedge

Dec 14	Sold 5 June DM futures at \$0.6671/DM
Jan 17	Sold 5 June DM futures at \$0.6712/DM
May 20	Cover 10 June DM at 0.5762/DM
	Sell DM1.25 million at DM1.7325/\$

Effective Rate for Deutsche Mark:

$$\frac{\dfrac{DM1.25 \text{ million}}{DM1.7325} + 5[(6671 - 5762) + (6712 - 5762)] \times \$12.50}{DM1.25 \text{ million}} = \$0.6702/DM \text{ or } DM1.4922/\$$$

Sale of DM1.25 million at 1.7325 = \$721,500
Sale of DM1.25 million at hedge rate 1.4922 = \$837,689
Benefit of deutsche mark hedge: \$116,189*
Commissions bring the effective rate to \$0.6700 or 0.6701/DM.

*Knobler's deutsche mark hedge worked out well, saving her \$116,189.

As it happened, Knobler's yen exposure coincided with the quarterly delivery cycle of currency futures traded on the International Monetary Market of the Chicago Mercantile Exchange. But for the deutsche marks, the nearest she could get to her May 20 date was the June contract, scheduled to expire three weeks later.

Although Knobler wanted to lock in a DM-USD exchange rate for May 20, the nearest futures contracts she could use actually reflected the forward rate for June 20, four weeks later. A firm hedging with futures contracts can be assured of realizing the futures rate only if the hedge is held to the futures expiration date, as was the case with the yen hedge but not with the deutsche mark hedge. By unwinding the hedge before expiration, the

Waging War against Currency Exposure continued

nonconvergence of spot and futures prices upon hedge liquidation results in an exchange rate that generally conforms to the desired forward date (May 20 here), as opposed to the futures value date (June 20). Knobler could have locked in the exact dates by hedging in the interbank market. But she might have less flexibility to adjust the hedge and—as a smaller company—would have to pay retail prices for her foreign exchange cover. In contrast, futures markets essentially offer wholesale prices to all customers; no one gets preferential treatment.

The amount of risk a treasurer is willing to take determines how much exposure to offset at any time. Thus, futures can be progressively applied or selectively unwound as rates swing to and fro. Knobler set criteria beforehand, based on her expectation of the future. She didn't, therefore, chase the market with hedges to cover every short-term trend in rates.

Adjustable hedges with trigger points take a great deal more self-discipline and confidence to manage than a "fire and forget" application of futures. The initial decision to hedge is critical: treasurers should understand from the beginning exactly what they hope to achieve. If the goal is to eliminate risk by locking in a currency rate, a hedge will do that—even if in hindsight it would have been more profitable not to hedge the risk. It's worth remembering that the maximum exposure occurs when people have no hedge at all.

Ira G. Kawaller's biography appears earlier in this chapter. This example was adapted from material in *Treasury and Risk Management* magazine, Fall 1992, and is reprinted with permission. © 1992 CFO Publishing Corp.

Managing a Futures Hedge

Once the hedge has been established, it is essential that it be monitored. As observers of the futures market note, placing a hedge and then forgetting it amounts to imprudent hedging.[6]

Margin calls and the daily marking-to-market demand a hedger's attention. In many cases, the funds required to meet the margin calls must be obtained from sources other than the underlying position itself. For this reason, a successful hedging program must include a source of these funds. Clearly, hedgers do not want to have too small a source of funds to meet margin calls; if the funds are not available, the hedge will be closed. But hedgers do not want to keep too large a pool of liquid funds available for meeting margin calls, since they forgo interest that could otherwise be earned.[7]

Notes

1. This case and some of those that follow have been adapted from *Using Interest Rate Futures and Options*, a publication of the Chicago Mercantile Exchange.
2. Drabenstott and McDonley (1984).
3. Again, the spot price and futures prices are guaranteed to be equal only at expiration of the futures contract.
4. As Ira Kawaller points out, this second source of risk is the risk that the *ex post* relation between X and Y (the parameter b in our equation) turns out to be equal to the *ex ante* estimate of the relation from the regression equation.
5. For purposes of illustration, we have presumed that funds flow in only one direction during the duration of a hedge. This is certainly not necessary. As illustrated below, funds could first flow out of the margin account from period 0 to period t_1, then flow into the margin account from period t_1 to t_2, and then flow out of the margin account again from period t_2 to T.

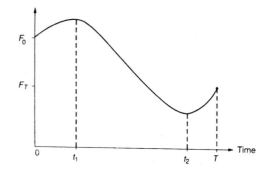

6. Drabenstott and McDonley (1984).
7. Figlewski (1986, Chapter 8) provides a method for determining the optimal pool of liquid funds available to meet margin calls.

8

SWAPS*

Swaps are the newest of the risk management products. When we traced the evolution of such products in Chapter 1, we noted that forwards were used at least as early as the 12th century, that futures existed as early as the 16th century, and that option contracts were used as early as the 17th century. However, the origins of the swap are generally dated from the public announcement of the currency swap between IBM and the World Bank in 1981.

The swap market has grown dramatically since 1981. This dramatic growth, however, is one of the few aspects of the swap market upon which market participants agree. The market's rapid growth contributed to much confusion, misinformation, and folklore about the hows and whys of swaps.

In this chapter, we hope to clear up some of this confusion. We describe how the swap contract first appeared and how it evolved over time. We examine the development and subsequent growth of the swap market and discuss how swaps are priced and valued.

Evolution of the Swap Contract

When swaps were introduced in the 1980s, the conventional wisdom was that swaps somehow "appeared"—as if by magic—in the markets. (Indeed, we have often said that it sounded as if swaps were something handed down on stone tablets

---

*I am particularly indebted to Clifford W. Smith, Jr., and Lee MacDonald Wakeman for the development of our discussion of swaps. Much of the material is taken from three papers we co-authored: Smith, Smithson, and Wakeman (1986), (1987), and (1988).

on some mountain top.) The truth is swaps did not just appear; they evolved from existing financial products. And from these first swaps—which now seem simple in retrospect—increasingly complex swap structures have evolved.

From Parallel Loans to Currency Swaps

As we described in Chapter 1, the breakdown of the Bretton Woods accord in 1973 brought increased foreign exchange risk to multinational companies. With elimination of fixed exchange rates, the volatility of foreign exchange rates increased dramatically. Coupled with the prevailing accounting treatment of foreign-denominated assets and liabilities (Statement 8), the increase in foreign exchange volatility produced massive swings in reported earnings.

In some instances, changes in exchange rates had a greater impact on the reported earnings of the firm than did changes resulting from operations. For firms with significant overseas operations, the effects of financial changes were swamping the effects of real changes.

For example, if the pound became more valuable (in other words, if the dollar price of a pound rose), the dollar value of the assets held by a UK subsidiary of a U.S. firm would rise; its U.S. parent would be better off, and vice versa. (See Figure 8–1.)

FIGURE 8–1   Risk Profile for a U.S. Company with a UK Subsidiary

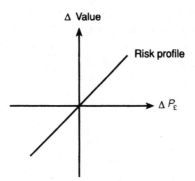

If a U.S. parent has assets in the United Kingdom, it faces risks resulting from movements in the price of the pound. If the dollar price of a pound ($P_{\pounds}$) rises, the value of the assets in the United Kingdom rises. This increases the value of the U.S. parent through the increased reported earnings.

Before the introduction of currency swaps, these foreign exchange exposures could have been hedged using *parallel loan agreements* (also known as back-to-back loans).

Parallel loan structure worked and became popular with many U.S. firms as a means of hedging the currency exposures created by U.S. accounting practices. However, the use of parallel loans involves two major problems:

1. *Default risk.* The loans are independent instruments, so default by one party does not release the counterparty from contractually obligated payments.

2. *Balance sheet impact.* If the balance sheets of the parent and its subsidiary must be consolidated, the parallel loans inflate the balance sheet, which can lead to problems with financial covenants. Although the two loans effectively cancel each other out, they remain on the balance sheets for accounting and regulatory purposes.

Illustration 8–1

Hedging a U.S. Parent/UK Subsidiary with a Parallel Loan

The U.S. company and its UK subsidiary would be matched with a UK company that had a U.S. subsidiary. The U.S. company would make a dollar-denominated loan to the U.S. subsidiary of the UK company. Simultaneously, the UK company would make a pound-denominated loan of equal current value to the UK subsidiary of the U.S. firm.*

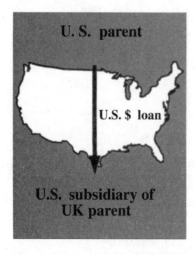

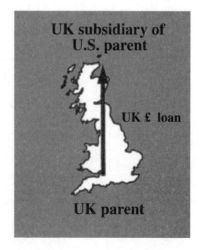

Hedging a U.S. Parent/UK Subsidiary with a Parallel Loan continued

The loans have parallel interest and principal repayment schedules, as illustrated by the following.

Cash Flows from a Parallel Loan Agreement

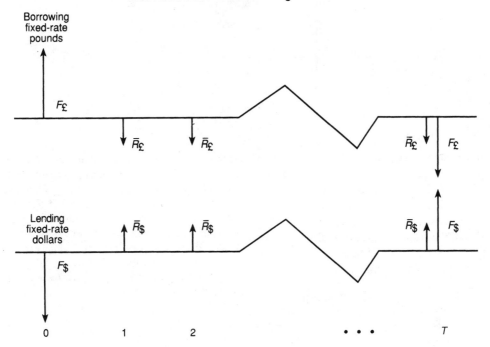

In this figure, inflows are denoted by upward arrows and outflows by downward arrows. The magnitude of the cash flow is indicated by the arrow's length.

At time 0, the U.S. firm, through its UK subsidiary, borrows pounds ($F_£$) at the prevailing T-period pound rate. At the same time, the U.S. firm makes a loan to the U.S. subsidiary of the UK firm—at the prevailing T-period dollar rate—in an amount in dollars that is equivalent (at the current exchange rate) to the sterling principal it borrowed ($F_\$$).

During the term of the loan, the U.S. firm makes interest payments in pounds ($R_£$) to the UK firm, which in turn makes interest payments in dollars ($R_\$$) to the U.S. firm. At maturity (time T) the two firms make their final interest payments and return the principals; the U.S. firm returns pounds and the UK firm returns dollars.

As illustrated on page 144, this parallel loan structure would hedge the U.S. parent's exposure to dollar–pound movements.

Hedging a U.S. Parent/UK Subsidiary with a Parallel Loan continued

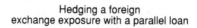

Hedging a foreign
exchange exposure with a parallel loan

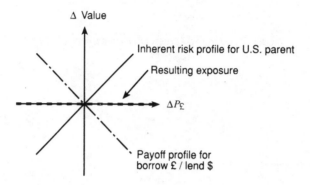

If the value of the pound rises (falls), the U.S. parent would suffer a loss (profit) on the parallel loan. Hence, the change in the value of the parallel loan would offset the firm's inherent position. If the U.S. parent matched the size of the parallel loan to the size of the inherent exposure, its U.S. dollar, UK pound exposure could be eliminated.

———————

*The motivation for the U.S. firm to enter into this parallel loan agreement would have been to reduce the volatility of reported income (under SFAS 8). The UK firm would have been attracted to this transaction because the British government had (as had other governments) imposed controls on capital movements, in effect taxing the export of capital. These capital controls would have made it difficult for the UK parent to fund expansions in its U.S. subsidiary. By entering into the parallel loan agreement, the UK parent would have been able to bypass the capital controls and provide funds to its U.S. subsidiary.

Default risk can be managed by establishing cross-default provisions between the two loans, or the problem can be handled by combining the two independent instruments into a single instrument. Put another way, we can "staple the two contracts together." As a result, the two sets of cash flows for a parallel loan become the single set of cash flows illustrated in Figure 8–2. The resulting instrument is a *currency swap.*

As Figure 8–2 indicates, the counterparties to the swap contract have agreed to exchange, or swap, cash flows. To determine the magnitude of the cash flows, the counterparties define some *notional principal.* The principal is "notional" in the sense that neither party owes it to the other—as would be the case in a loan.

FIGURE 8-2   Making a Parallel Loan Agreement into a Single Instrument: Creating a Currency Swap

---

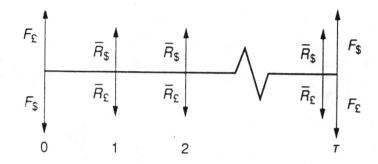

The party illustrated in Figure 8–2 agrees to pay a series of cash flows based on the notional principal of the swap (in sterling) and the fixed sterling interest rate that is appropriate for the maturity of the swap:

$$\bar{R}_\pounds = (\bar{r}_\pounds)\,(NP_\pounds)$$

This party receives a series of cash flows determined by the U.S. dollar notional principal of the swap and a fixed U.S. dollar interest rate that is appropriate for the maturity of the swap:

$$\bar{R}_\$ = (\bar{r}_\$)\,(NP_\$)$$

The counterparty takes the reverse position.

By combining the parallel loans into a single legal document called a swap, the default risk has been reduced substantially. Default risk can be reduced further by *netting* the payments: at each of the *settlement dates* 1,2, . . . ,*T*, it is not necessary for the party illustrated in Figure 8–2 to pay $\bar{R}_\pounds$ and receive $\bar{R}_\$$. Instead, the two parties can exchange a *difference check*. If the value of sterling rises, the party illustrated in Figure 8–2 pays a difference check to the counterparty; if the value of sterling falls, the party illustrated in Figure 8–2 receives a difference check.

The second problem with parallel loans, their impact on balance sheets, disappears when the parallel loans are stapled together to form the currency swap: current accounting and regulatory practices treat swaps as off-balance-sheet instruments. So the swap will not inflate the firm's balance sheet.

From Currency Swaps to Interest Rate, Commodity, and Equity Swaps

From the currency swap evolved other kinds of swaps. As we have seen, the currency swap involves the exchange of fixed-rate cash flows in one currency for fixed-rate cash flows in another. As shown in Figure 8–3, replacing one of the

---

Aside

Currency Swaps versus FX Swaps

If swaps were not confusing enough, it turns out that the name "swap" is used to describe two different transactions in the foreign exchange market. One is the "currency swap" defined above; the other is the "FX swap" familiar to traders in the foreign exchange spot and forward markets.

An FX swap involves the simultaneous sale and purchase of FX forward contracts of different maturities. For example, suppose a firm currently will receive yen in 60 days but will not have to make a corresponding yen payment for 90 days. The firm might then do an FX swap where it sells a 60-day forward contract on yen and simultaneously buys a 90-day forward on yen.

In Chapter 2 we stressed that swaps—currency swaps—can be viewed as a portfolio of forward contracts with different maturities but, within the portfolio, all either long or short. As you can see from the preceding, the FX swap can also be viewed as a package of forward contracts with different maturities, one long and the other short.

fixed-rate cash flows with a floating-rate cash flow is a simple matter. The resulting instrument is a cross-currency swap.

A special case of a cross-currency swap occurs when the two currencies are the same. This special case, an *interest rate swap,* is illustrated in Figure 8–4. As with currency swaps, initial principal exchange is not necessary in an interest rate swap. However, in contrast to standard currency swaps, interest rate swaps do *not* require

---

FIGURE 8–3   Currency Swap Converted to a Cross-Currency Swap

---

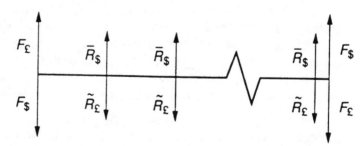

A swap of a fixed-rate cash flow ($\bar{R}_\$$) in one currency for a floating-rate cash flow ($\tilde{R}_£$) in another currency is called a cross-currency swap.

FIGURE 8–4   Cross-Currency Swap Converted to an Interest Rate Swap

---

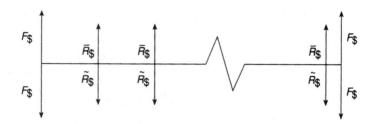

If all the cash flows in the cross-currency swap are paid in
the same currency, the result is an interest rate swap.

the reexchange of principal at maturity, because all the principal amounts of an interest rate swap are expressed in the same currency units. Therefore, we can illustrate the interest rate swap as in Figure 8–5.

In an interest rate swap, the cash flows are determined by one fixed interest rate and one floating interest rate (both in the same currency). In a *basis swap,* both interest rates are floating (again, both are in the same currency). Thus, the basis swap permits a borrower (or investor) to exchange a stream of payments determined by one floating interest rate for a payment stream determined by another floating interest rate. For example, a basis swap would permit firms to convert from six-month LIBOR to one-month U.S. commercial paper rates.

Figure 8–6 illustrates such a swap. As this figure suggests, a basis swap is equivalent to a combination of two simple interest rate swaps. The flows are converted from floating to fixed, and then converted from fixed to floating (but on a different basis).

FIGURE 8–5   An Interest Rate Swap: Cash Flows for a Floating-Rate Payer

---

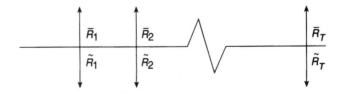

The counterparty illustrated receives a series of cash
flows determined by the *T*-period fixed interest rate
($\bar{R}t$) at origination, in return paying a series of cash
flows ($\tilde{R}t$) determined by the relevant floating interest
rate, reset at the beginning of every period.

FIGURE 8–6   A Basis Swap: LIBOR to U.S. Commercial Paper

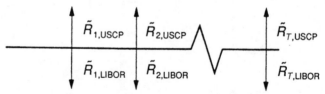

The party illustrated receives semiannual cash flows based on the compounded one-month U.S. commercial paper rates, while paying cash flows determined by six-month LIBOR rates.

Swaps that are defined in prices other than interest rates and foreign exchange rates also have appeared. Once a principal amount is determined and that principal is contractually converted to a flow, any set of prices can be used to calculate the cash flows.

In 1986, the first *oil swap* was transacted. As in the other swaps we have described, the parties agree on a notional principal, but in this case the notional principal is expressed in barrels of oil rather than in dollars. Then in a manner analogous to the fixed and floating payments in an interest rate swap, regular settlements are made on the basis of fixed and floating oil prices. Figure 8–7 illustrates the cash flows for a party who receives cash flows based on a fixed price per barrel and pays cash flows determined by the floating (spot) price of oil. In contrast to currency and interest rate swaps, the floating price used in an oil swap is not normally a single spot price but rather the average price of oil over a specified period.

FIGURE 8–7   An Oil Swap

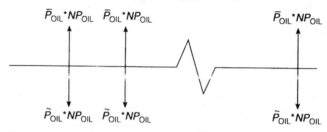

The party illustrated receives a cash flow based on an oil price which is fixed at origination ($\bar{P}_{OIL}$) and pays a cash flow based on the average spot price over the period ($\tilde{P}_{OIL}$). The notional principal (NP_{OIL}) is expressed in barrels of oil.

While the cash flows are expressed in terms of oil, no physical quantities of oil need be involved. At the settlement date, the difference check paid or received simply reflects the price of oil. If oil prices have risen since contract origination, the party illustrated in Figure 8–7 pays a net difference check; if oil prices have fallen, this party receives the check.

Note also that the oil swap, like all other swaps, can be decomposed into long and short positions in loans (that is, lending and borrowing). For example, the oil swap illustrated in Figure 8–7 can be decomposed into lending with standard fixed-rate coupon payments and simultaneously borrowing the same amount where the coupon payments are expressed in terms of barrels of oil.

As Chapter 1 noted, the early development of the commodity swap market was chilled by regulatory action by the Commodity Futures Trading Commission. However, since the CFTC established "safe harbors" for commodity swaps, the market for OTC derivatives on commodities has developed rapidly.

The next type of swap to appear was the *equity index swap*. In an equity index swap, the parties pay and receive on the basis of the rate of return on a specified equity index. Figure 8–8 illustrates cash flows for an equity index swap for the counterparty who receives cash flows based on the rate of return on the Tokyo Stock Price Index (TOPIX) and makes payments determined by U.S. dollar LIBOR. However, equity index swaps can be structured so that the party makes payments on the basis of one equity index (such as the S&P 500) and receives payments on the basis of another. Recently, *single equity swaps* have begun to appear. In this structure, one side of the cash flows would be determined by the rate of return for a single equity rather than an equity index. And additional types of swaps continue to appear. In Chapter 14, we will describe "credit swaps."

FIGURE 8–8   An Equity Index Swap

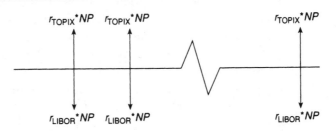

At settlement t ($t = 1, 2 \ldots, T$), the party receives a cash flow determined by the rate of return on the TOPIX between $t - 1$ and t (minus or plus a spread) and pays a cash flow determined by U.S. LIBOR (minus) or plus a spread)

Development of the Swap Market

The historical development of the swap market is evident both in the evolution of the products and in changes in the market's participants. Both tell the same story. We first examine the products.

Currency swaps, as we noted, came first. The earliest swaps were done on a one-off basis, which involved a search for matching counterparties, matching not only in the currencies but also in the principal amounts and timing desired. These early swaps were custom-tailored products. Because the deals were all one-off, they involved a lot of work by the financial institution arranging the swap. But (and this point is crucial) they involved virtually no direct exposure for the broker. In the language of the market participants, the early swaps required "creative problem solving" rather than capital commitment from the intermediary.

As interest rate swaps emerged, the movement toward a more standardized product began. There were fewer areas in which counterparties might not match with the U.S. dollar interest rate swaps than had been the case for currency swaps. The product had become more homogeneous, and so the demand for one-off deals declined. Instead of looking for one exactly matching counterparty, the intermediary could look for a number of counterparties that together matched the notional principal.

With the move toward homogeneity and the reduced reliance on an identifiable counterparty, markets for swaps—in particular, interest rate swaps—began to look more and more like markets for commodities. Increased competition forced down the spreads. And with the increased competition, an extensive search for a counterparty or group of counterparties was unprofitable for the intermediary. Instead, the intermediaries began to accept swap contracts without having a matching counterparty. Intermediaries took the interest rate risk into their own books and hedged the residual risk with interest rate futures or U.S. Treasuries. (We will return to this idea in Chapter 18 when we describe the way a dealer hedges a portfolio of derivative transactions.)

Thus, the evolution of the products offered in the swap market paralleled that of most markets. Swaps evolved from a customized, client-specific product into a standardized product. With the customized product, the role of the intermediary had been one of problem solving. As the product became more standardized, the role of the intermediary changed considerably, with less emphasis on arranging the deal and more on transactional efficiency and capital commitment.

Among participants in the swap market, the dominant intermediaries in the early stage of development were investment banks. As the market evolved, the entrants into this market were more highly capitalized firms, in particular commercial banks. The evolution of the role of the intermediary mirrors the change in the products. In the early stages the emphasis was on the intermediary's arranging the transaction rather than accepting risk from the transaction; investment banks were the natural intermediaries. But as swaps became more standardized, it became essential for the intermediary to be willing to accept a potential transaction into its books. Hence, commercial banks, with their greater capitalization and comparative advantage in managing high-volume, standardized transactions, became a more significant factor.

Standardization has been in large part behind the growth in swaps. One market observer put it well by noting that "swaps have become a high-volume, lower margin business, rather than the personalized, corporate financial deal of the past."[1]

The growth of the swap market also has corresponded to the expanding liquidity available through the secondary market. Swap positions can be traded (that is, the swap contract can be assigned to a third party), and this market is growing. However, much of the secondary market in swaps involves the reversing (unwinding) of a position. The simplest way to unwind a swap involves the cancellation of the agreement, with a final difference check determined by the remaining value of the contract. Alternatively, the swap could be unwound by writing a *mirror swap* to cancel the original. Most market observers indicate that the secondary market is sufficiently deep to decrease risks in the primary market, particularly for short-term swaps.

Growth of the Swap Market

In the early stages of the development of the swap market, analysts ascribed the growth to some kind of "arbitrage opportunity" through swaps. Robin Leigh-Pemberton, then a governor of the Bank of England, articulated this view when he argued that swaps enabled borrowers to "arbitrage" the credit markets, allowing "a good credit rating in one part of the currency/maturity matrix to be translated into relatively cheap borrowing in another."[2]

An example of this "credit arbitrage" that was widely cited in the 1980s is the case of an interest rate swap between an AAA-rated borrower and a borrower with a BBB rating.[3] As illustrated in Table 8–1, a borrower rated AAA would be expected to be able to borrow more cheaply than one rated BBB in either fixed or floating. However, note in Table 8–2 that the credit spread between the AAA and the BBB is higher for fixed than for floating.

TABLE 8–1 Illustrative Borrowing Costs for AAA and BBB Borrowers

	AAA	*BBB*
Borrow fixed	10.8%	12.0%
Borrow floating	LIBOR + 1/4%	LIBOR + 3/4%

TABLE 8–2   Illustrative Credit Spreads

BBB—AAA Borrowing Rates

Fixed	12.0% − 10.8%	= 120 basis points
Floating	(LIBOR + 3/4%) − (LIBOR + 1/4%) =	50 basis points

The assertion is that the swap "arbitrages the credit spread differential" of 120 − 50 = 70 basis points. As illustrated in Table 8–3, suppose the AAA borrows fixed and the BBB borrows floating. Then, if the two firms enter into an interest rate swap, both firms can end up with lower borrowing costs. Indeed, in the preceding case where there was no financial intermediary, the firms ended up splitting the credit-spread differential.

This illustration is entirely consistent with the available data:

1. There exist quality differentials between fixed and floating borrowing, referred to as the *quality spread,* and these quality spreads are generally observed to increase with maturity.[4]

2. The fixed-rate payer in a swap is generally the less creditworthy party.

3. Firms have been able to lower their nominal funding costs by using swaps in conjunction with these quality spreads.

However, it is less clear that this kind of evidence has anything to do with classic financial arbitrage. First, financial arbitrage should lead to decreasing, not increasing, swap volumes. As the quality spread is arbitraged, the rate differences would be eliminated, and this rationale for interest rate swaps should disappear. Second, this simplistic "credit arbitrage" story ignores the underlying reason for the quality spread.

TABLE 8–3   The "Savings" from a Swap

	AAA	*BBB*
AAA borrows fixed	(10.8%)	
BBB borrows floating		(LIBOR + 3/4%)
AAA receives	10.9%	
Pays floating	(LIBOR)	
BBB receives floating		LIBOR
Pays fixed		(10.9%)
All-in cost of funding	LIBOR − 1/10%	11.65%
Savings	0.35%	0.35%

Comparative Advantage

In the 1980s, we heard many market participants assert that quality spreads result from firms having a "comparative advantage" in one of the credit markets. According to this view, the AAA-rated company borrows in the fixed-rate market where it has a comparative advantage. The BBB-rated company borrows in the floating-rate market where it has a comparative advantage. Then the firms use an interest rate swap to exploit their comparative advantages and produce interest rate savings.

While this comparative-advantage argument is appealing, it neglects arbitrage. With no barriers to capital flows, the comparative-advantage argument from elementary trade theory cannot hold. Arbitrage eliminates any comparative advantage. Given the weakness in this comparative-advantage rationale, several alternative explanations have been proposed.

Aside

Comparative Advantage

International trade theory relies on the concept of comparative advantage to explain why countries trade. As you should remember from your economics courses, this concept was based on *factor immobility:* the United States has a comparative advantage in wheat because the United States has wheat-producing acreage not available in Japan. If land could be moved—if land in Kansas could be relocated outside Tokyo—the comparative advantage would disappear.

For the concept of comparative advantage to make sense as a rationale for swaps, immobility would have to be a characteristic of the financial markets. It is not. Integrated capital markets provide the BBB access to fixed-rate markets, either directly or indirectly by AAA-rated firms borrowing fixed and re-lending to BBB-rated firms.

Underpriced Credit Risk (Risk Shifting)

Some have suggested that the quality spread results from the difference in pricing credit risk in the market for fixed-rate funding and in the market for floating-rate funding. Specifically, analysts have argued that credit risk is underpriced in floating-rate loans.[5] Underpriced credit risk for floating-rate loans would certainly explain the growth of the interest rate swap market; the gain from the swap would be at the expense of the party who is underpricing credit risk in the floating-rate debt market. But the expansion of the swap market effectively increases the demand for floating-rate debt by lower-rated companies and the demand for fixed-rate debt by higher-rated companies, thereby eliminating the supposed differential pricing. So like the comparative-advantage argument, this rationale is self-defeating; it does not explain the continuing growth of the swap market.

Along a similar line, Jan Loeys (1985) has suggested that the quality spread is the result of the shifting of risk from the lenders to the shareholders. To the extent that lenders have the right to refuse to roll over debt, more default risk is shifted from the lender to the shareholders as the maturity of the debt decreases. With this explanation, the "gains" from a swap would instead be transfers from the shareholders of the lower-rated firm to the shareholders of the higher-rated firm.

Differential Cash Flow Packages

The differences in nominal (stated) borrowing cost obtained through a swap can also be explained by considering options available to the borrower. Most fixed-rate debt includes a prepayment option. If interest rates decline, the borrower can put the loan back to the lender and obtain lower-cost financing by paying the prepayment fee and the origination fees on the new financing. Indeed, in standard corporate bond issues, this is simply the *call provision.*

In contrast, interest rate swaps contain no such prepayment option. According to the master agreement developed by the International Swaps and Derivatives Association, early termination of a swap agreement requires that the remaining contract be marked-to-market and paid in full.

Hence, the positions of the firm that has borrowed fixed directly and the one that has borrowed floating and swapped to fixed are quite different. The former owns a put option on interest rates; the latter does not.

Illustration 8–2

Embedded Interest Rate Options

Consider the BBB-rated firm described above. It can obtain fixed-rate funding in two ways. It can either:

1. borrow fixed directly at 12 percent, or
2. borrow floating and swap to fixed at 11.65 percent.

If capital markets are efficient, and the available evidence says they are, the fact that 1 costs more than 2 implies that 1 has something 2 does not. Included in that something may well be the right to repay the loan early. When would the firm want to exercise this right? Clearly the firm would want to exercise the right if rates fall.

If rates fall, the firm could pay off this loan and refinance at the lower rate; the further rates fall, the more valuable this right becomes.

Embedded Interest Rate Options continued

The illustration of the value of the right to repay early is the payoff profile for owning an interest rate option, specifically a put option on interest rates. Hence it is not surprising that 1 costs more than 2, since 1 contains an option that 2 lacks.

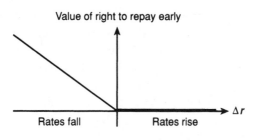

In this context, the transaction between the AAA-rated firm and the firm rated BBB looks less like financial arbitrage and more like an option transaction. The BBB-rated firm can borrow at a fixed rate more cheaply by swapping from floating because the borrow-floating/swap-to-fixed alternative does not include the interest rate option contained in the borrow-fixed alternative. The BBB firm in effect has sold an interest rate option. The funding cost "savings" obtained by the BBB firm (as well as the cost savings gained by the AAA firm) simply reflect the premium on this option.

More generally, for the differences in cash flows in Table 8–3 to represent arbitrage opportunities, the resulting cash flow characteristics must be equivalent. Here, this is not the case. Since the BBB company borrowed short term, the credit risk premium on the loan varies over the life of the swap; it is not fixed as it is with the long-term borrowing. (To fix the credit spread, one would have to examine a swap plus a floating-rate loan of the same term with the fixed-rate borrowing.)

Information Asymmetries

Why does a firm choose to issue short-term floating-rate debt and then swap this floating-rate payment into a fixed-rate payment rather than one of the alternatives: keeping the short-term debt unswapped, issuing long-term fixed-rate debt, or issuing long-term floating-rate debt? Marcelle Arak, Arturo Estrella, Laurie Goodman, and Andrew Silver (1988) have argued that the "issue short-term/swap-to-fixed" combination would be preferred if the firm is in one of these circumstances:

- The firm has information causing it to expect that its own credit spread will be lower than the market expects in the future.
- The firm is less risk-averse than the market to changes in its credit spread.
- It expects higher risk-free interest rates than does the market.
- It is more risk-averse to changes in the risk-free rate than is the market.

For example, suppose the firm desired fixed-rate funding for a project but the company had inside information indicating that its credit rating would improve in the future. By issuing short-term debt, the firm would be able to exploit its information asymmetry, and by swapping the debt into fixed rate, the firm would be able to eliminate its exposure to interest rate risk.

As Arak et al. point out, firms that are pessimistic about future risk-free rates but optimistic about their own credit standings are drawn to the swaps market; they issue short-term debt to take advantage of the information asymmetry and then swap the debt to a fixed rate to protect the firm against future interest rate increases. The expected savings will be divided between this firm and the counterparty based on the prevailing demand and supply conditions.

Tax and Regulatory Arbitrage

In contrast to the classic arbitrage considered above (in which the firm would earn a riskless profit by exploiting pricing differences for the same instrument), tax and regulatory arbitrage enables the firm to earn a risk-free profit by exploiting differences in tax and/or regulatory environments.

A firm issuing dollar-denominated fixed-rate bonds in the U.S. capital markets must comply with the requirements of the U.S. Securities and Exchange Commission. In the less-regulated Eurobond market, the costs of issue could be considerably lower—as much as 80 basis points less (Loeys, 1985). However, not all firms have direct access to the Eurobond market. The swap contract gives firms access to the Eurobond market and enables more of them to take advantage of this regulatory arbitrage.

Moreover, firms that issue in the U.S. capital markets, as well as the security purchasers, generally face the provisions of the U.S. tax code. The introduction of the swap market has allowed an "unbundling," in effect, of currency and interest rate exposure from the tax rules in some very creative ways. For example, with the introduction of swaps, a U.S. firm could issue a yen-denominated debt in the Eurobond market, structure the issue to receive favorable tax treatment under the Japanese tax code, avoid much of the U.S. securities regulation, and yet still manage the firm's currency exposure by swapping the transaction back into dollars. Unlike the classic financial arbitrage described above, there is no reason for opportunities for tax or regulatory arbitrage to disappear (barring changes, of course, in the various tax and regulatory codes).

To illustrate the manner in which tax and regulatory arbitrage induces swaps, consider the way one U.S. firm used swaps to exploit special tax and regulatory conditions in Japan. (See Illustration 8–3.)

Illustration 8–3

Arbitraging Japan's Tax and Regulatory Authorities

In 1984, *Business Week* reported that U.S. firms had discovered a way to make "free money."* As it turns out, this "free money" was being given away by the Japanese tax authorities. In 1984, zero-coupon bonds received particularly favorable tax treatment in Japan. The income earned from holding the zero-coupon bond (the difference between the face value of the bond and the price at which the bond was purchased) was treated as a capital gain; since capital gains were untaxed, the effect was to make the interest income on the zero-coupon bond nontaxable for the Japanese investor. The result was that a zero-coupon bond sold to Japanese investors would carry a below-market interest rate.

In contrast, the U.S. tax authorities regarded zeros as they did any other debt instrument. Any U.S. firm issuing such a bond was permitted to deduct the imputed interest payments from income, thereby maintaining its tax shield.

Hence, a tax-arbitrage opportunity arose. The two tax authorities treated the same instrument differently. Not surprisingly, a number of U.S. firms—Exxon and General Mills among them—issued zero-coupon yen bonds, illustrated below.

Zero-coupon yen bond

The U.S. firm issuing the zero-coupon bond was no doubt pleased with the savings it achieved in interest expense. However, most U.S. issuers were much less pleased with the yen exposure that came with this yen zero.

Therefore, the assignment to the merchant/investment bank was relatively straight-forward: eliminate the yen exposure while keeping as much of the savings in interest expense as possible.

As should be clear, the exposure profile for this U.S. issuer of a zero-coupon yen bond is as illustrated below. Such an exposure could be managed through a forward yen–dollar contract. But the maturity of these bonds, 5 to 10 years, eliminated forward contracts as a possibility, since the bid-offer spread on a 10-year forward contract was unacceptably high.

Futures contracts were also eliminated as a means of managing this exposure, since 5- and 10-year futures contracts were not available. (Five- and 10-year strips of futures are still not available. The longest available futures contract on foreign exchange is about 12 months.)

Hence, the best available financial instrument for neutralizing this yen exposure was (and still is) a swap. To minimize the cost of the swap—the bid-offer spread—we would want to use a standard, at-market-rate currency swap. However, when we combine such a currency swap with our zero-coupon bond, we see in the following that our task is

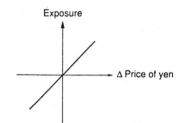

not yet complete; there are still some yen cash flows.

The remaining yen cash flows could be eliminated by adding a simple loan with a sinking fund. As the bottom figure illustrates, the amortizing yen loan would eliminate the remaining yen cash flows, and the U.S. issuer would end up with a set of cash flows identical to those for a dollar bond with below-market coupons.

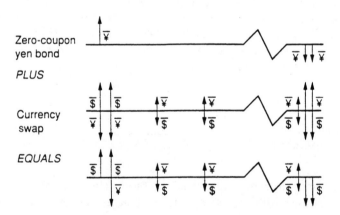

However, it turned out that there was a way to structure the package that would result in a still lower realized interest rate for the U.S. issuer. In addition to the tax arbitrage, a regulatory arbitrage was available: the Ministry of Finance limited the amount a Japanese pension fund could invest in non-yen-denominated bonds issued by foreign corporations to at

Arbitraging Japan's Tax and Regulatory Authorities continued

most 10 percent of its portfolio. However, the Ministry of Finance ruled that dual-currency bonds qualified as a yen issue for purposes of the 10 percent rule, even though the dual-currency bond has embedded within it a dollar-denominated zero. By issuing the dual-currency bond, the U.S. firm was able to capitalize on the desire of Japanese pension funds to diversify their portfolios internationally, while at the same time adhering to the regulations imposed by the Ministry of Finance.

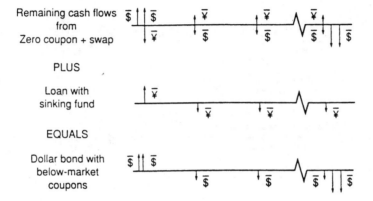

Therefore, the remaining yen cash flows from the yen zero would be absorbed not by the amortizing loan but rather by the combination of a dual-currency bond and a spot currency transaction, as illustrated below. Moreover, this figure illustrates that the resulting cash flows are like those for a deep-discount dollar bond with below-market coupons.

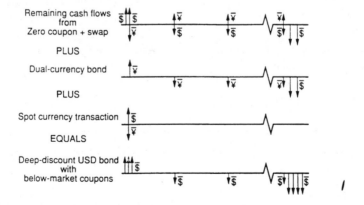

Arbitraging Japan's Tax and Regulatory Authorities continued

The U.S. firm will:

(1) Issue a zero-coupon yen bond in the amount of X yen

(2) Issue a dual-currency bond for 2X yen

(3) Enter into a currency swap with a principal of 2X yen

(4) Use a spot currency transaction to convert X yen to dollars

To end up with a set of cash flows that are like a deep-discount dollar bond with below-market coupons

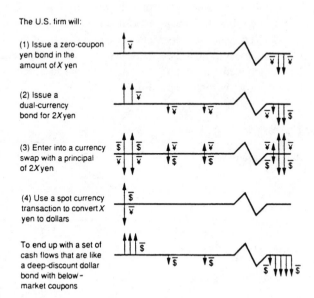

The entire process can be summarized as follows: the U.S. firm will:

1. issue a zero-coupon yen bond in the amount of X yen,

2. issue a dual-currency bond in the amount of 2X yen,

3. enter into a currency swap with a principal of 2X yen, and

4. use a spot currency transaction to convert X yen to dollars.

The result of these transactions is a set of cash flows that are like a deep-discount dollar bond with below-market coupons.

The chief financial officer of this firm is happy because the firm obtains below-market funding. The merchant/investment banker is happy because the bank earns a nice fee. And the *Wall Street Journal* and *Financial Times* are both happy because the papers receive the advertising revenue for running the three tombstones.

Business Week (1984).

Arbitraging Japan's Tax and Regulatory Authorities continued

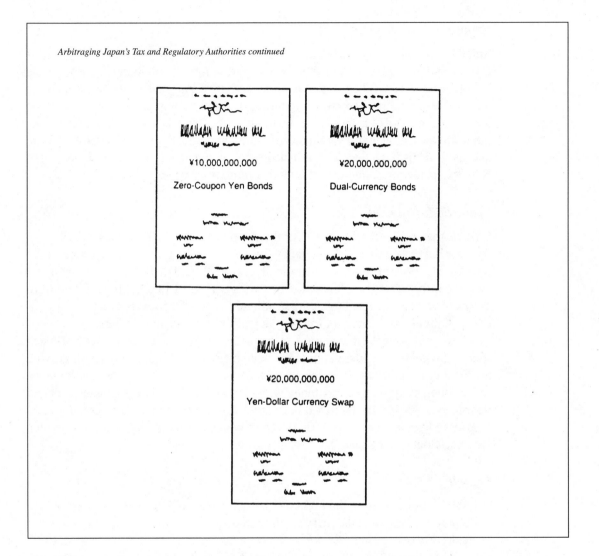

The arbitrage opportunity in the preceding example disappeared when the Japanese tax authorities changed their ruling on yen zeros. However, other tax and regulatory opportunities have been available, and some still are. For example, in many European countries the purchasers of a zero-coupon bond do not escape taxes (as was the case in our example), but the tax is deferred until the maturity of the bond, and the tax rate paid is the lower capital gains rate. Sometimes there are also regulatory barriers limiting entry of potential issuers and thereby reducing the cost of borrowing in that market.

Exposure Management

Since swaps can be used to manage a corporation's exposure to interest rate, foreign exchange, and commodity-price risk, part of the growth in interest rate swaps simply reflects general corporate hedging activities. As we demonstrated in Chapter 3, corresponding to the growth in the swaps market, market data suggest that the use of the other off-balance-sheet hedging instruments is also increasing. So another way of asking why swaps have grown so dramatically is to consider why more and more firms have decided to manage their exposures to financial prices—that is, to exchange rates, interest rates, and commodity prices.

Synthetic Instruments

Still another reason for the growth of the swap market is the usefulness of swaps in the creation of "synthetic" financial instruments. For example, consider long-dated interest rate forward contracts, historically a very illiquid market. Since interest rate swaps can be viewed as portfolios of forward interest rate contracts, long-term swaps have been stripped to create synthetic long-dated forwards and thereby increase liquidity in the market for long-dated forward-rate agreements.

Less obvious is the manner in which currency and interest rate swaps have been used to fill gaps in the international financial markets. In Chapter 9, we will provide an illustration of the way in which swaps have been used to create other instruments.

Further, swaps can be combined with existing products to create new financial instruments. As will be described in Chapter 15, the combination of a conventional fixed-rate loan and an interest rate swap in which the party pays fixed results in a "reverse-floating-rate loan."

Liquidity

A final factor explaining the observed growth in this market is the substantial reduction in bid-ask spreads. In 1982, the bid-ask spread for interest rate swaps exceeded 200 basis points. As we will note later in this chapter, in August 1997, the bid-ask spread for a three-year interest rate swap in the interbank market was less than one basis point. Even a 10-year swap had a bid-ask spread less than one basis point. Thus, the dramatic increase in volume has been accompanied by an equally dramatic increase in the liquidity of the swaps market.

Pricing and Valuing Swaps

We have demonstrated that a swap can be decomposed into either a portfolio of loans or a portfolio of forward contracts. In Chapter 17, we will make use of the concept of a swap as a portfolio of forwards to gain insights into the default risk of a swap. Here we use the concept of a swap as a portfolio of loans to provide insights into the pricing of a swap.

Pricing an At-Market Swap

Figure 8–9 again illustrates the equivalence between an interest rate swap and a pair of loans. The implication of this figure is that if you can value (price) loans, you should be able to value (price) a swap contract. Put another way, if you know the mechanics of pricing loans, you should be able to determine the appropriate fixed rate in the swap illustrated in Figure 8–9. And that is indeed the case.

The loans are both zero-expected net present value (NPV) projects.[6] Consequently, since the swap is nothing more than a long and a short position in loans, the expected NPV of the swap must also be zero; if you can determine the actual or expected floating-rate payments at time periods $1, 2, \ldots, T$ and if you know the term structure of interest rates, you can set the NPV of the swap equal to zero and solve for the fixed rate. Perhaps the best way to explain this is to go directly to an example. (See Illustration 8–4.)

As our example illustrates, pricing an interest rate swap requires that the cash flows be identified and then discounted by the zero-coupon—spot—interest rate.

To obtain the expected cash flows for the floating payments, it is necessary to obtain the forward interest rates from the forward yield curve. And finally, in the

---

FIGURE 8–9   Decomposition of an Interest Rate Swap into a Portfolio of Loans

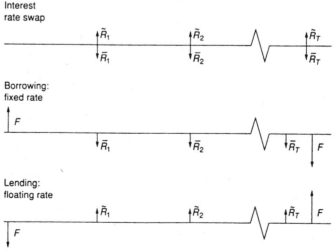

The cash flows from an interest rate swap where the party pays fixed is equivalent to the cash flows of a portfolio of two loan contracts, where borrowing is at a T-period fixed rate ($\bar{R}_t$), lending is at a floating rate ($\tilde{R}_t$), and F is the face value of the loan.

Illustration 8–4

Pricing an Interest Rate Swap

Galactic Industries (GI) wishes to enter into a swap in which GI will pay cash flows based on a floating rate and receive cash flows based on a fixed rate. In the jargon of the swap market, Galactic—the floating-rate payer—is referred to as the seller of the swap (or as short the swap).

Market convention is to quote the terms of interest rate swaps as the floating-rate index (normally LIBOR) flat against some fixed rate; Galactic will pay cash flows based on the floating rate flat and will receive cash flows based on a fixed rate of X percent. The question is, "What is the appropriate fixed rate; what is X?"

To keep our calculations at a minimum, suppose GI requested a quote from the Dead Solid Perfect Bank (DSPB) on the following simple swap:

From these terms, we know what Galactic will pay: at the six-month settlement, GI pays a "coupon" determined by the six-month LIBOR rate in effect at contract origination. At the 12-month settlement, GI's "coupon" payment is determined by the six-month LIBOR rate prevailing at month 6. What is missing is the fixed interest rate that will determine the payments Galactic will receive from DSPB.

Suppose that the LIBOR yield curve—the spot yield curve—prevailing at origination of this swap is the simplified yield curve shown below:

Notional principal amount	$100
Maturity	One year
Floating index	Six-month LIBOR
Fixed coupon	____ %
Payment frequency	Semiannual
Day count	30/360*

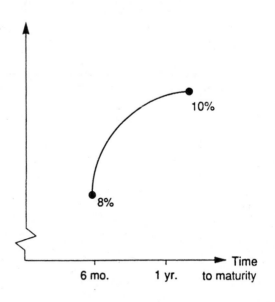

Pricing an Interest Rate Swap continued

To determine the appropriate fixed rate, the managers of DSPB must consider the contractual/expected cash flows from this swap:

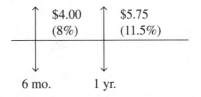

6 mo.   1 yr.

The first floating-rate inflow—$\tilde{R}_1$—is the easy one. The floating-rate cash flow DSPB will receive at the first settlement date is determined by the six-month rate in effect at contract origination, 8 percent. Hence at the six-month settlement, DSPB expects to receive

$$\tilde{R}_1 = \$100\ [(180/360)0.08]$$
$$= \$100\ (1/2)\ 0.08 = \$4.00$$

Note that in this calculation and all that will follow, we use the bond method for calculating interest payments.[†]

To obtain the expected floating-rate inflow at the one-year settlement, we need to know the six-month rate in six months. This rate, the rate from $t = 6$ months to $t = 1$ year, is the *forward rate*. Arbitrage guarantees that[‡]

$$(1 + {}_0R_{12}) = [1 + (1/2){}_0R_6] \times [1 + (1/2){}_6R_{12}]$$

where ${}_0R_{12}$ and ${}_0R_6$ are, respectively, the current one-year (12-month) and six-month *zero* (spot) rates. Using this arbitrage condition, the six-month and one-year rates of 8 percent and 10 percent, respectively, require that the forward rate ${}_6R_{12}$—that is, the six-month rate in six months—be 11.5 percent. Therefore,

$$\tilde{R}_2 = \$100 \times (1/2) \times 0.115 = \$5.75$$

Hence, the contractual/expected floating-rate inflows to DSPB are as illustrated below:

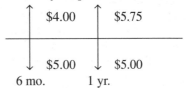

6 mo.   1 yr.

What DSPB needs to determine is the outflows, the appropriate fixed-rate payments. At origination, the expected net present value of this at-market swap is zero. That is,

$$\frac{(\$4.00 - \bar{R}_1)}{[1 + (1/2)0.08]} + \frac{(\$5.75 - \bar{R}_2)}{(1.10)} = 0$$

where $\bar{R}_1 = \bar{R}_2$. Solving this equation, $\bar{R}_1 = \bar{R}_2 = \$4.85$. Hence, the appropriate fixed rate is 9.70 percent.

At first blush, if you look at the term structure of interest rates, it might seem that the appropriate fixed, one-year interest rate would be 10 percent, so the fixed-rate out-flows would be

$$\bar{R}_1 = \bar{R}_2 = \$100(1/2)0.10 = \$5.00$$

However, if $\bar{R}_1 = \bar{R}_2 = \$5.00$:

$$
\begin{array}{c}
\uparrow \quad \$4.00 \qquad \uparrow \quad \$5.75 \\
\hline
\downarrow \quad \$5.00 \qquad \downarrow \quad \$5.00 \\
\text{6 mo.} \qquad\quad \text{1 yr.}
\end{array}
$$

The present value of the swap to DSPB would be negative,

$$\frac{-1.00}{1 + 1/2(0.08)} + \frac{0.75}{1.10} = -0.28$$

Pricing an Interest Rate Swap continued

The problem is that 10 percent is a zero-coupon rate. As should be clear from Figure 8–9, $\bar{R}$ is associated with a coupon-bearing instrument (loan). What we need is the market coupon-interest rate, the *par* rate. The par rate is that coupon rate that would have the bond trade at par. In our case that means the compounded annualized par rate r_{1yr} is given by

$$100 = \frac{(1/2)(\bar{r})100}{[1 + (1/2)0.08]} + \frac{(1/2)(\bar{r})100}{(1.10)} + \frac{100}{(1.10)}$$

Solving the preceding equation, the one-year par rate, r_{1yr}, is 9.70 percent, precisely the rate we solved for earlier.

Hence, in the case of this simple, at-market swap, the appropriate fixed rate is the one-year par rate, 9.70 percent. The terms of this swap can now be completed:

Notional principal amount	$100
Maturity	One year
Floating index	Six-month LIBOR
Fixed coupon	9.70%
Payment frequency	Semiannual
Day count	30/360

The expected cash flows for DSPB are as illustrated below.

$4.00 (8%) $5.75 (11.5%)
$4.85 (9.7%) $4.85 (9.7%)
6 mo.   1 yr.

*We use this 30/360 convention for convenience in our example. In truth, the day count convention for LIBOR is actual/360, as are commercial paper and banker's acceptances.

†For maturities less than one year, prevailing market practice is to quote interest rates such that compounding is already embedded in the quoted rate. If the annualized six-month rate is 8 percent, the amount that will be received at the end of six months on an investment of $100 can be calculated simply as

($100) × (180/360) × 0.08 = $4.00

where the convention is that compounding occurs annually but the periodicity of the rate is monthly.

In contrast, the convention used by most finance textbooks is to treat the interest rate as *subject to compounding*. The most common method of compounding is *discrete compounding*. Using this method, if the annualized six-month rate is 8 percent, the amount that will be received at the end of six months on the $100 investment is

($100) × (1.08)$^{180/360}$ − $100 = $3.92

where the periodicity is again monthly, but the rate is now compounded monthly. Put another way, to yield the $4 at the end of six months, the stated interest rate using the method of discrete monthly compounding would be 8.16 percent:

($100) × (1.0816)$^{180/360}$ − $100 = $4.00

While the different conventions are sometimes confusing, they cause no problem as long as the user is sure which convention is being used.

‡In the preceding footnote, we noted the various ways interest rates can be quoted and the coupons calculated. Had the interest rates been quoted subject to monthly compounding, the arbitrage condition would have had to take the compounding into consideration. If we denote the annualized rate subject to compounding as i, the arbitrage condition would become

$$(1 + {}_0i_{12}) = (1 + {}_0i_6)^{1/2}(1 + {}_6i_{12})^{1/2}$$

case of this simple at-market swap, the appropriate fixed rate was simply the par rate. Hence, to price an interest rate swap, we ended up using three yield curves: the zero-coupon yield curve, the forward yield curve, and the par yield curve.

Swap Pricing Conventions

The swap described in Illustration 8–4 and illustrated in Figure 8–9 is referred to (almost condescendingly) as a *plain vanilla* interest rate swap. For this simple, one-year swap, we ended up with a quote of

Six-month LIBOR (the spot rate)

against

One-year par rate

The market convention has come to be to price these plain vanilla swaps as LIBOR *flat* (i.e., no spread) against the U.S. Treasury [par] rate *plus* a spread. An illustration of market-style quotations for such a swap is provided in Figure 8–10.

As Figure 8–10 indicates, on Monday, August 25, 1997, the market was pricing a three-year interest rate swap such that:

If you want to receive the fixed rate, you will pay LIBOR and receive the three-year Treasury par rate + 28.5 basis points.

If you want to pay the fixed rate, you will receive LIBOR and pay the three-year Treasury par rate + 29.3 basis points.

The difference between the receive Treasuries and pay Treasuries—approximately one basis point—was the bid-ask spread.

Valuing a Swap (Marking the Swap to Market)

This market convention of LIBOR versus Treasuries + spread works well if all you want to do is price at-market swaps at origination. However, this par-rate convention does not work well if you want to value a swap after origination or if you want to value (price) an off-market swap.

FIGURE 8–10   U.S. Dollar Interest Rate Swap Quotes: Treasury–LIBOR

USD	TREASURY SPREADS			DEALING		
2Y	25	35	CITIBANK	TOK	20:52
3Y	28.5	29.3	TRADITION	LDN	09:44
4Y	31.0	32.0	TRADITION	LDN	09:44
5Y	28	38	CITIBANK	TOK	20:52
7Y	33	43	CITIBANK	TOK	20:52
10Y	37.8	38.3	TRADITION	LDN	10:24

SOURCE: Reuters Datafeed Service (August 25, 1997).

After origination, the only way to value a swap is to employ the zero-coupon yield curve. Once the swap has been contracted, its value depends on what happens to the market price on which the swap is based. The value of a dollar-sterling currency swap to the party paying dollars rises (falls) as the value of sterling rises (falls). The value of a commodity swap varies with the market price of the commodity. And as we illustrate in the continuation of our example, the value of an interest rate swap depends on what happens to market interest rates.

Illustration 8–5

Valuing an Interest Rate Swap

Galactic Industries and the Dead Solid Perfect Bank contracted to the interest rate swap outlined in the preceding example on the afternoon of July 23.

On the morning of July 24, the LIBOR yield curve (zero-coupon curve) shifts up by 1 percent as illustrated below.

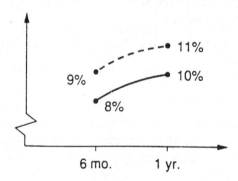

The terms of the swap contract specify that DSPB will pay at an annual rate of 9.70 percent. DSPB's first floating-rate receipt was determined at origination, so the $4 DSPB will receive in six months is also unchanged. For this one-year swap, the only cash flow that will be changed is the expected floating-rate inflow at one year. With the new term structure the forward rate $_6R_{12}$ is 12.4 percent,

$$(1 + 0.11) = [1 + (1/2)0.09] \times [1 + (1/2)_6R_{12}]$$

so the expected floating-rate inflow in one year is

$$\tilde{R}_2 = \$100 \times (1/2) \times 0.124 = \$6.22$$

and DSPB's expected cash flows are as illustrated below:

$$
\begin{array}{ccc}
\uparrow \ \$4.00 & \uparrow \ \$6.22 \\
(8\%) & (12.4\%) \\
\hline
\downarrow \ \$4.85 & \downarrow \ \$4.85 \\
(9.7\%) & (9.7\%) \\
\text{6 mo.} & \text{1 yr.}
\end{array}
$$

Calculating DSPB's expected net cash inflows,

$$\frac{\text{6 mo.}}{-\$0.85} + \frac{\text{1 yr.}}{\$1.37}$$

and discounting these expected net cash inflows by the corresponding zero rates from the *current* zero-coupon yield curve,

$$\frac{\text{6 mo.}}{9\%} + \frac{\text{1 yr.}}{11\%}$$

the value of the swap to DSPB has risen from zero at origination to 42 cents,

$$\frac{-\$0.85}{[1 + (1/2)0.09]} + \frac{\$1.37}{(1.11)} = \$0.42$$

In the following example, we *marked the swap to market.* And if we calculate the value of the swap for different shifts in the yield curve, we can obtain a payoff profile for the swap. For example, if we look at the value of the following swap for shifts in the Treasury zero curve of $+2$ percent, $+3$ percent, -1 percent, -2 percent, and -3 percent, the average change in the value of the swap contract per 1 percent change in the yield curve—(Δ value of swap)/Δr—is 42 cents. We can sketch the payoff profile for this swap as in Figure 8–11.[7]

The lesson in all this is simple. To price an at-market interest rate swap, you can use the par yield curve. But to value a swap after origination, it is necessary to use the zero-coupon yield curve, not the par yield curve.

FIGURE 8–11   Value of Swap to DSPB

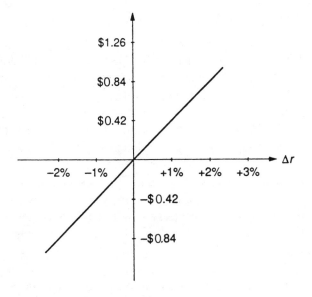

Notes

1. Schuyler (1985).
2. Stevenson (1987).
3. The specific example we use was adapted from a 1985 Bankers Trust Company brochure. However, the arguments in this example were used widely in the swap market in the 1980s.
4. For a discussion of the quality spread in the context of swaps, see Wall and Pringle (1988, 1989).
5. For example, Ramaswamy and Sundaresan (1986) look at the market for floating-rate loans and argue

that the default premiums for floating-rate loans are lower than would be predicted.
6. We presume here again that the capital markets are efficient.
7. Although the value of a swap does exhibit some nonlinearity with respect to interest rates, we continue to use a linear approximation. In Chapter 18, we will consider the nonlinearity—also known as convexity or "gamma"—inherent in a swap.

CHAPTER

9

APPLICATIONS OF SWAPS

The end users of swaps (as well as the other OTC derivatives) include industrial corporations, financial institutions, governments, and institutional investors. Firms use swaps to modify the nature of either balance sheet items or cash flows (income or expenses).

Swaps have been used widely to change the nature of assets and liabilities which appear on the firm's balance sheet. When end users employ swaps to modify their debt, they normally are trying to match the interest sensitivity of their assets, reduce their funding costs, or increase their debt capacity. When end users employ swaps to modify assets, they are usually trying to enhance yield, as well as to protect the portfolio from interest rate and equity price risk. On both the asset and liability sides, end users make use of swaps to create synthetic instruments.

Swaps are also widely used to modify the exposure of the firm's cash flows to volatility in foreign exchange rates, interest rates, and/or commodity prices. In some cases, the hedge is a hedge on income (e.g., some firms hedge the foreign exchange exposure of the income they earn in other countries and remit to the parent). In other cases, the hedge is a hedge on cost (e.g., cruise ship operators or transportation companies may hedge their exposure to fuel prices). In still other cases, the hedge is more macro, involving both revenues and expenses. Perhaps the most straightforward example of a macro hedge is the asset-liability management done by financial institutions in which they hedge net interest income (or the value of the equity) against changes in interest rates.

Using Swaps to Manage Interest Rate Risk

The available evidence indicates that management of interest rate risk is the most common use for swaps. Table 9–1 traces the growth of the interest rate swap market. The market for interest rate swaps is far and away the largest of the swap markets—and, furthermore, is the largest of the OTC derivative markets.

TABLE 9–1   Interest Rate Swaps Outstanding

	1988	1989	1990	1991	1992	1993	1994	1995	1996
Number of contracts	49,560	75,223	102,349	127,690	151,545	236,126	248,798	347,966	513,735
Notional principal (U.S.$billion)	1,010	1,539	2,311	3,065	3,850	6,178	8,816	12,811	19,171

*Outstandings as of December 31, 1996
SOURCE: *International Swaps and Derivatives Association (ISDA).*

The general perception of market participants is that interest rate swaps have been used most extensively to hedge liabilities—the firm's debt. In particular, interest rate swaps have been widely used to convert floating-rate debt to "synthetic" fixed-rate debt.[1] Figure 9–1 illustrates how an interest rate swap allows a firm with a floating-rate liability to create debt that is effectively fixed at an 8.00 percent rate. XYZ Company has a $10 million bank loan that has a floating rate of interest priced at LIBOR + 1 percent. To create a synthetic fixed rate, XYZ enters into a swap with a notional amount that matches that of the loan. The floating-rate payments received by XYZ should largely offset the interest payments required on the loan. However, the difference between these floating payments needs to be added to the swap's fixed rate to determine the net fixed cost to the borrower. Most of the difference between these floating-rate payments will be attributable to the credit spread on the loan (1.00 percent or 100 basis points, in the example). However, it is also possible for differences to arise in other ways. "Basis risk" is used sometimes to refer to differences that result should the rate-setting mechanisms on both transactions not be identical. Furthermore, while in this example we are able to simply add the credit swap to the fixed rate to determine all-in cost, in practice additional calculations may be required to make all the rates comparable if different payment frequencies (quarterly, semiannual) or day-count conventions (actual days/360, 30/360) are utilized.

FIGURE 9–1   Using an Interest Rate Swap to Create Synthetic Fixed-Rate Debt

---

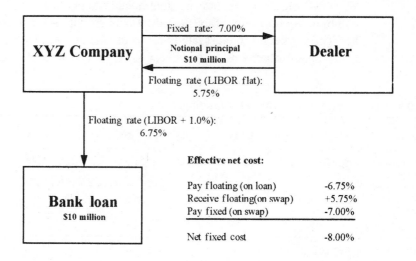

However, swaps are not used exclusively for liabilities. Swaps can be used to manage the interest rate risk associated with the value of a firm's assets. And corporate treasurers are increasingly taking account of the interest rate sensitivity of both assets and liabilities in designing hedges. Interest rate swaps can be used to adjust the average maturity or interest rate sensitivity of a company's debt portfolio so that it more closely matches the interest rate sensitivity of the asset side of the balance sheet. This reduces the exposure of the company's net worth or market value to interest rate risk.

The trade press has reported that Kraft, the U.S.-based food company owned by Philip Morris Companies, takes an active approach to interest rate risk management.[2]

> Kraft's debt grew from $600,000 in 1985 to $1.6 billion in 1987, making interest rate risk a serious concern to management. Viewing its balance sheet as a portfolio, Kraft's treasury assigned a duration to all its assets and liabilities. Given its estimate of asset duration, Kraft used interest rate swaps to adjust the duration of its debt to keep the balance sheet hedged.

Increasingly, banks, insurance companies, and large investors are using interest rate swaps to reduce the interest rate risk inherent in their portfolios. Most institutional investors have a mismatch between the duration of their assets and liabilities. Consider, for instance, an investor who holds short-term liabilities and long-term assets. The investor could swap out some portion of the cash flows based on its long-term assets at a fixed rate and receive a short-term floating rate. This would offset losses if short-term rates were to rise relative to long-term rates.

Using Swaps to Manage Foreign Exchange Rate Risk

Table 9–2 traces the growth of the currency swap market. The evidence we have seen suggests that the dominant use of currency swaps is to modify the nature of a debt issue. A firm will borrow in one currency and use a swap to transform the cash flows to another currency.

Currency swaps have been used to hedge the firm's foreign exchange rate risk—primarily transaction exposures. For example, a U.S. manufacturing firm might contract to provide product to a distributor in Germany at a fixed deutsche mark price. As long as the deutsche mark value of the dollar remains stable or declines, the U.S. manufacturing firm is happy. (If the DM value of the dollar declines, the same number of DM received by the U.S. firm will be converted into more U.S. dollars.) The worry is, of course, that the value of the dollar will rise. To protect against adverse foreign exchange rate movements, the U.S. manufacturing firm could enter into a currency swap in which it pays a fixed deutsche mark cash flow and receives a fixed U.S. dollar cash flow from its counterparty. The swap contract changes the deutsche mark receipts into dollar receipts—thereby eliminating the foreign exchange exposure.

Governmental entities, including national governments, local governments, state-owned or -sponsored entities, and supranationals, use derivatives for much the same reasons as nonfinancial corporations. They use derivatives in financing activities, to diversify their sources of funds and to achieve cost savings through the issuance of structured securities. Derivatives are also used for debt management purposes, especially by those governments borrowing in many different currencies. A case in point is Finland:[3]

> Finland is a highly rated sovereign and an active borrower in the international capital markets. The government of Finland, through the Ministry of Finance, actively used swaps to lower its effective cost of debt, to manage the currency composition of its foreign liabilities and to hedge its foreign exchange risks. During the period 1987 to 1990,

TABLE 9–2 Currency Swaps Outstanding

	1988	1989	1990	1991	1992	1993	1994	1995	1996
Number of contracts	10,271	15,285	22,717	31,035	32,841	32,606	28,729	30,842	43,156
Notional principal (U.S.$billion)	317	435	578	807	860	900	915	1,197	1,560

*Outstandings as of December 31, 1996
SOURCE: *International Swaps and Derivatives Association (ISDA).*

Finland entered into approximately 50 swaps with a notional principal equivalent to U.S. $50–200 million at a time. Roughly 30% of the government's total outstanding foreign debt was swapped, with most swaps being related to newly issued debt. Swaps were used in 1990 to achieve funding costs of 30–50 basis points below LIBOR. They were also used to configure the currency composition of Finland's foreign liabilities in the direction of its official currency basket. The Finnish mark was pegged to the value of the currency basket. The Ministry used currency swaps to access the lowest-cost off-shore debt markets and then translated the currency composition of the debt portfolio to the desired mix. Substantial changes in the debt composition were achieved through swaps. For example, although the actual share of the Japanese yen in the external debt was 23% in 1989, currency swaps were used to reduce the effective share to 12% in 1989 and 5% in 1990.

Using Swaps to Manage Commodity Price Risk

Few surveys have been conducted regarding activity in the commodity swap market. Nevertheless, a comparison of ISDA and BIS surveys indicates that commodity-price risk management has seen substantial increases in volume in recent years. Table 9–3 summarizes the results of the first and only commodity survey conducted by ISDA in 1992 and the results of a 1995 BIS survey. In 1992 ISDA estimated a commodity derivative notional principal of $30 billion ($18 billion for commodity

TABLE 9–3   Commodity Derivative Market Growth, 1992–95
Notional Principal Billions of U.S. Dollars

	1992 ISDA Survey			1995 BIS Report*	
	Between Dealers	*With End Users*	*Total*	*Between Dealers*	*With End Users*
Commodity swaps					
Energy	$5	$10	$15		
Metals	—	3	3		
Subtotal	5	13	18		
Commodity options					
Energy	$2	$ 3	$ 5		
Metals	2	5	7		
Subtotal	4	8	12		
Total notional principal	**$9**	**$21**	**$30**	**$71**	**$245**

*BIS notional principals are "reported" amounts. BIS also calculated "estimated gaps in reporting" to capture instances of less than full coverage in some reporting countries. For commodity transactions this gap amounted to $32 billion to arrive at an estimated market size of $350 billion.
SOURCE: International Swaps and Derivatives Association and Bank for International Settlements.

swaps; $12 billion for commodity options). ISDA's survey also indicated that energy underlyings (such as oil and natural gas) dominated the swap market while activity in metals underlying options dominated the options market. A 1995 BIS report does not break out the same level of detail that the ISDA survey provided. But it does demonstrate that commodity derivative growth has been strong. The central bank survey conducted by BIS estimated that the notional amount of commodity derivatives in March 1995 stood at $350 billion.

As noted at the outset of this chapter, the most common type of commodity swap is one indexed to energy prices. A firm that is a user of energy—a chemical manufacturer or a utility firm or an airline—face two types of risk. First, the energy user is exposed to delivery risk—the firm must be sure that it will receive the oil or natural gas or jet fuel when and where it needs it. In order to assure itself of a reliable supply of the commodity, the energy user might enter into a long-term agreement with an energy producer, calling for the delivery of a specified amount of the product at a specified date but with the price determined by the spot market. The second risk—price risk—is not mitigated by the long-term agreement. To eliminate this remaining price risk, the energy user could enter into an energy swap in which the energy user will pay cash flows determined by a fixed energy price and will receive cash flows determined by the spot price of the energy product.

Firms also use swaps to hedge commodity exposures other than energy.

FMC is a diversified manufacturer of everything from chemicals and defense equipment to food, petroleum, and material handling equipment. It sells in 85 countries and manufactures in 14 of them. Sales in 1989 totaled $3.5 billion.

By entering into a long-term contract with the U.S. Army to build the Bradley Fighting Vehicle at an essentially fixed price, FMC accepted long-term exposures to the price of metals.[4] Traditionally, metals purchasers had relied on forward contracts to hedge their exposures; but FMC discovered that, because the credit risk for swaps is smaller than that for forwards, long-term hedges using swaps were cheaper than long-term hedges composed of forward contracts. Consequently, FMC turned increasingly to commodity swaps to hedge its exposure to metal price volatility—by 1991, 30 percent of FMC metals hedges were commodity swaps.

Following the run-up in oil prices that resulted from the invasion of Kuwait by Iraq in 1990, some governmental entities have turned to commodity derivatives to manage oil price risk.[5] By mid-1991, numerous municipal governments and authorities, including Atlanta, Boston, San Francisco, and Washington, D.C., were using derivatives to lock in fuel costs as a way of controlling their energy budgets. For example, the Metropolitan Atlanta Rapid Transit Authority (MARTA) entered into a one-year commodity swap in May 1991 to lock in a fuel price for its budget. The swap contract guaranteed MARTA a price of 53.3 cents per gallon for No. 2 heating oil on 9 million gallons of fuel purchased during the 1991–92 fiscal year.

The transaction is estimated to have saved MARTA more than $1.5 million over actual market prices.

Using Swaps to Manage Equity Price Risk

The results of ISDA's only equity survey, conducted in 1992, indicated a market size of approximately $76 billion (ISDA's results are summarized in Table 9–4.) An indication of the growth in this market since 1992 is found in the BIS's 1995 survey of derivative market activity. In its study, BIS estimated that global outstandings amounted to $630 billion.[6] About two thirds of the reported outstandings (i.e., $373 billion) were conducted with end users; the remaining third consisted of interdealer transactions.

Figure 9–2 outlines a simple equity swap example. An end user desires to protect a stock portfolio, which is highly correlated with the S&P 500, from downside market risk for a specified period of time. To hedge its position, the end user enters into a swap in which it exchanges its S&P return for floating payments based on LIBOR. It is important to note that because equity returns can be either positive or negative, the cash flow of the equity leg can go in either direc-

TABLE 9–4   Equity Swaps and Options—1992 Notional Principal in Billions of U.S. Dollars

	Between Dealers	*With End Users*	*Total*
Equity Swaps—Indexes by Country			
Japan	$ 3	$ 3	$ 6
United States	1	1	2
Other	—	1	1
Baskets and individual stocks	—	1	1
Subtotal	4	6	10
Equity Options—Indexes by Country			
Japan	$11	$ 9	$20
United States	3	8	11
United Kingdom	6	5	11
Germany	4	2	6
France	3	2	5
Other	2	2	4
Baskets	—	2	2
Individual stocks	1	6	7
Subtotal	30	36	66
Total	**$34**	**$42**	**$76**

SOURCE: International Swaps and Derivatives Association.

FIGURE 9–2   Using an Equity Swap to Convert an Equity Return into a Synthetic Fixed-Income Return

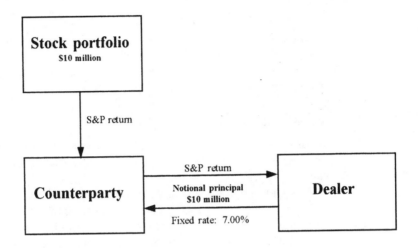

tion. In this illustration, the end user would make S&P appreciation payments but would actually receive S&P depreciation from the dealer (in addition to the LIBOR-based payment). Thus, by entering into an equity swap, the end user is able to replicate the sale of the stock portfolio and the investment of the proceeds into cash instruments that pay LIBOR. While equity swaps are often structured utilizing indexes such as the S&P 500, the London Financial Times Index, or the Nikkei, it is also possible to construct swaps in which the equity leg is based upon a single stock.

Using Swaps to Reduce Transaction Costs

Avoiding transaction costs may become one of the most important uses of swaps as markets get more efficient. Transaction costs include not only the bid-ask spread, but also such things as the costs of acquiring information and liquidity costs.

Swaps may help end users in highly regulated markets avoid some business costs. In such markets, substituting swaps for on-balance-sheet instruments may reduce associated costs to the firm, such as capital requirements.

For an international corporation, borrowing needs in a particular country or countries may be too small to be funded cost-effectively through the local capital markets. The firm may find it cost-effective, however, to borrow more than needed in its own capital markets and swap excess debt into the other needed currencies.

Using Swaps at McDonald's Corporation

Carleton Pearl

As a global company, McDonald's has financing needs that carry multiple risks in the foreign exchange and interest rate arenas. Swaps are some of the tools used to manage these debt portfolio risks and to implement our financing strategies.

Interest Rate Swaps

We use interest rate swaps to manage the interest rate exposures of our portfolio. As of mid-1993, the swap portfolio included 45 interest rate swaps in eight currencies.

As a general rule, because of the long-term nature of our business assets and our desire to lock in occupancy costs, our debt portfolio consists primarily of long-term fixed-rate debt. Depending on our upcoming funding needs and our view of interest rate trends, the overall percentage of consolidated fixed-rate debt generally ranges from 60 to 80 percent.

We use interest rate swaps in three ways—to change the mix of our fixed- and floating-rate debt, to position the company for an expected change in interest rate levels, and to adjust the average maturity of the portfolio.

In July 1993, we secured historically low fixed-rate U.S. dollar funding when we issued $200 million of 40-year bonds domestically. So as not to sacrifice the entire benefit of low U.S. floating rates over the near term, we swapped $100 million of it into five-year floating-rate debt and the second $100 million into seven-year floating-rate debt. The swaps reduce the interest cost on the bond by an average of over 200 basis points.

Internationally, we have also reduced our interest costs by positioning our portfolio for expected changes in interest rates.

In September 1992, for example, we felt that UK interest rates were going to be declining. In four transactions, we swapped 60 million of fixed-rate pound sterling liabilities into three- and five-year floating-rate liabilities on which we receive about 9 percent fixed. Interest rates have declined and we are currently paying about 6 percent floating after having paid over 9 percent on the initial three- or six-month terms. The fixed rates we are receiving average more than 2 percent above current market rates, which, of course, means that the debt could be refixed at 2 percent below its original fixed rate.

Because of its huge size, the swap market is flexible, readily accessible, efficient, and cost-effective—much more so than alternatives for managing our interest rate risks, and that's important because views on interest rates and the needs of the company can change.

We can choose the effective date for a swap, which can be two days from transaction or farther into the future on a forward start basis. We can also easily initiate and close out positions, and prompt execution permits us to lock in the terms of the deal immediately. The alternative method for adjusting out fixed- to floating-rate debt is to issue new floating-rate debt and use the proceeds to call or repurchase one of our fixed-rate bonds or to purchase fixed-rate government securities; however, these alternatives are much more costly and time-consuming, and impractical in many instances.

Currency Swaps

The advantages of interest rate swaps carry over into currency swaps, which we use to manage the currency mix of our debt portfolio. As of mid-1993, we had 51 currency swaps in our portfolio, denominated in 12 different currencies.

In line with our overall financing philosophy, currency swaps create foreign currency liabilities and cash outflows that match assets and cash inflows in those currencies. Currencies received in swap transactions of McDonald's are often onlent to foreign subsidiaries.

The subsidiary balance sheet reflects an intercompany liability in a currency that matches the land, buildings, and equipment on the asset side. The subsidiary income statement reflects interest expense in the same currency as revenues generated from product sales and license fees.

McDonald's, as a borrower of foreign currency in the swap and as lender of the same currency to the international market, also has a matched asset and liability and a matched stream of interest income and interest expense.

In addition to this hedging of intercompany loans, the matching of foreign currency liabilities and cash flows helps us to manage the parent company's exposures that arise from its international investments. The parent company balance sheet reflects a liability in a currency that matches the international investment, and its income statement reflects interest payments in the same currency as cash receipts, such as royalties and dividends, generated by that investment.

Ideally, we would like to create foreign currency obligations by borrowing the needed currencies in the domestic or Euro public markets, or the private placement or loan markets of specialized investors or banks. However, in terms of timing, amounts and terms needed, flexibility, and cost-effective pricing, what we want is not always what is available.

The swap market is often the only source of long-term fixed-rate foreign currency for certain of our international markets, whose borrowing needs are just too small to be funded through the capital markets. Local bank lines are most likely available, but they are generally more expensive by at least 150 basis points.

Here are some examples of small borrowings that could not have been done in the capital markets.

In June, 1992, we swapped $16 million of commercial paper into 100 million Danish kroner and repaid more expensive local Danish bank lines. The swap market's ready access permitted us to complete the deal just before the Danish vote on the Maastricht treaty and to avoid the interest rate increase that occurred after the vote. Even if size was not an issue, a bond or any long-term borrowing in Danish kroner would have been difficult if not impossible at that time.

In June 1993, we swapped $40 million of commercial paper into 5 billion Spanish pesetas and repaid more expensive local Spanish bank lines. The flexibility of the swap market afforded us the chance to do half the deal just prior to Spanish parliamentary elections as a hedge against possible interest rate increases, and to do the other half after the elections had passed and interest rates had actually fallen.

Up until recent months, the swap market has provided foreign currencies at more cost-effective terms than the public debt markets. For most of the past year or two, our debt market interest rates have been higher than those of the swap market by at least 20 to 40 basis points.

During 1992 and the first two quarters of 1993, McDonald's converted $950 million into nine foreign currencies through 30 swaps. The 20–40 basis-point benefit in pricing means $1.9 to $3.8 million in annual interest savings.

In some instances, currency swaps help us achieve economies of scale by deriving more than one currency from an attractively priced larger borrowing.

In July 1991, McDonald's borrowed 50 million deutsche marks for five years through a private placement and onlent 30 million of the total to our German subsidiary, where more expensive local bank lines were repaid. The remaining 20 million deutsche marks were not needed in Germany and were swapped into fixed-rate Swiss francs for use in our Swiss operation—pricing on the swap was 180 basis points better than local fixed-rate funding available to Switzerland.

In other instances, currency swaps help us capitalize on arbitrage between the debt and swap markets, which can exist because of the different basis for pricing in each.

In February 1990, we issued a 100-million New Zealand dollar bond at attractive rates. Twenty-five million New Zealand dollars were onlent to our New Zealand subsidiary to repay more expensive local bank lines and 50 million New Zealand dollars were ultimately swapped into U.S. dollars. Because of the arbitrage, we were able to get 11 basis points below our commercial paper cost. The remaining 25 million New Zealand dollars were simply converted to U.S. dollars, creating a long-term hedge, and the proceeds were used to pay down outstanding commercial paper.

Since we first entered the swap market in 1983, the transactions have proven invaluable in allowing us to secure cost-effective financing in a timely fashion and to properly manage the foreign exchange and interest rate risks that naturally arise in our business. Swaps do carry risks that other financing alternatives do not, but the risks are certainly manageable and they are definitely outweighed by the benefits provided.

Using Swaps at McDonald's Corporation continued

Carleton Day Pearl is Senior Vice President and Treasurer for McDonald's Corporation. In addition to being a member of McDonald's management team, he was elected by shareholders to serve as an advisory director with McDonald's Board of Directors. Mr. Pearl joined McDonald's in 1978 as Director of International Finance. He was promoted to Assistant Vice President and Managing Director of International Finance in 1981, was promoted to Vice President in 1982, was named Treasurer in 1987, and was promoted to Senior Vice President in 1996. Prior to joining McDonald's, Mr. Pearl worked for Bankers Trust Company in New York where he held positions in both the domestic and international lending areas and was General Manager of Bankers Trust (International) Midwest Corporation, the Chicago Edge Act Corporation for Bankers Trust. Mr. Pearl is a Trustee of the Aon Funds; and, he sits on the Advisory Board of the School of Liberal Arts and Sciences at DePaul University in Chicago and the Council of Advisors of the Society of International Treasurers. A Colgate University graduate, Mr. Pearl received an M.B.A. in Finance and International Business from New York University.

Mr. Pearl thanks Frank Hankus, formerly the director of Financial Markets for McDonald's Corporation, for his assistance with this article.

Using Swaps to Increase Debt Capacity (or Gain Access to Debt Markets)

One of the primary themes of this book has been (and will continue to be) that, if used appropriately, swaps—and other financial derivatives—reduce the riskiness of a firm. And if a firm is less risky, it should be able to support more debt.

Greg Millman made this point more concretely when he reported that by stabilizing the company's net worth and keeping it from tripping technical default triggers, swaps and other hedging techniques have permitted companies like Kaiser Aluminum and Union Carbide to carry more debt.[7]

Indeed, at Kaiser, comprehensive financial price risk management was apparently one of the cornerstones of the firm's drive to stabilize performance and thereby sustain a heavy debt burden. Kaiser's lenders were well aware that Kaiser was subject to external price risks from energy and aluminum. By managing these financial price risks, Kaiser increased its debt capacity by removing volatility from its cost and revenue stream.

Turning the preceding argument the other way around: *the more financial price risk the firm faces, the less debt it can carry*. Taking this argument to its limit, there could be cases where the financial price risk is so great that the firm is effectively denied access to the debt markets. In such a case, swaps could be used to provide access to the debt markets. And this is precisely the point of the following example which demonstrates a highly innovative use of a commodity swap.

Mexicana de Cobre (Mexcobre) is the copper-exporting subsidiary of Grupo Mexico, a large Mexican mining group. In the late 1980s, Mexcobre would have been barred access to international capital markets because of credit risk concerns within the banking community. However, in 1989, Mexcobre was able to borrow $210 million for 38 months from a consortium of 10 banks, led by Paribas. Let's look at the way in which the Mexcobre loan was structured to minimize the political and commodity price risks inherent in the transaction.

Illustration 9–1

Mexicana de Cobre*

The 10 banks lent Mexcobre $210 million for 38 months at a fixed rate of 11.48 percent. This replaced borrowings from the Mexican government at 23 percent that Mexcobre had previously been paying.

To reduce political risk, a forward sale was incorporated into the transaction. A Belgian company, Sogem, agreed to buy from Mexcobre 3,700 tons of copper per month at the prevailing spot price for the copper—determined by the LME price of copper. The payments from Sogem went not to Mexcobre but instead into an escrow account in New York. Funds in the escrow account were then used to service the debt (and any residual was returned to Mexcobre).

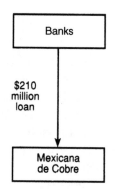

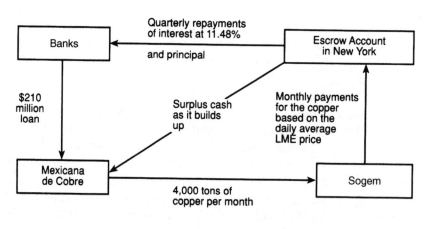

Mexicana de Cobre continued

While the New York escrow account dealt with the political risk, it did nothing about the copper price risk. Were the price of copper to fall, there could be a shortfall in the escrow account. To eliminate this price risk, Paribas arranged a copper swap *with the escrow account* in which the payments received based on a floating copper price were converted to payments based on a fixed price of copper.

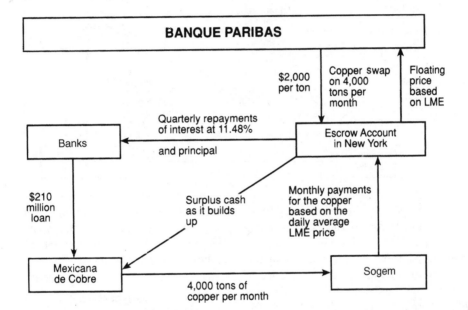

As a result of the swap, the payments into the escrow account were fixed at a level 10 percent above what was needed to service the bank debt.

There was a final step. The loan to Mexcobre was a fixed-rate loan; but the banks in the syndicate wanted a floating-rate asset. Paribas arranged another swap—this time an interest rate swap with the banks—to convert the cash flows from fixed rate to floating rate.

Mexicana de Cobre continued

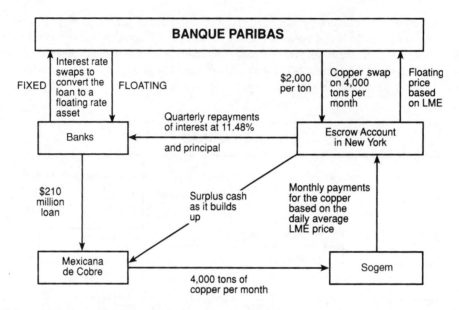

Mexcobre's net position is of owing fixed-rate payments on its debt and receiving fixed-rate payments for its copper, where the fixed-rate payments on its copper production are in excess of what it needs to service its debt. The end result was that Mexcobre was able to borrow a larger amount for a longer term than would otherwise have been the case. The deal, which was agreed to in July 1989, was the first voluntary foreign currency borrowing for a private-sector Mexican company since the debt crisis began in 1982. Without the copper swap, it is unlikely that money would have been lent.

———

*This discussion is based on Paul B. Spraos, "The Anatomy of a Copper Swap," *Corporate Risk Management,* and on "Mexcobre Loan Deal Repays Debt," *Corporate Finance,* August 1989.

Using Swaps to Create Synthetic Instruments

We have already seen that one of the most common uses of swaps is to transform one form of debt to another:

Floating-rate debt
plus
Pay-fixed/receive-floating interest rate swap
results in
Synthetic fixed-rate debt

In the same way, by combining a pay-floating swap with fixed-rate debt, a firm creates synthetic floating-rate debt.

Going a step further, as we will describe in Chapter 15, a pay-fixed swap can be combined with floating-rate debt to create an *inverse floating-rate note.*[8] An inverse floating-rate note pays a pre-specified (fixed) interest rate *minus* LIBOR, e.g., 8 percent − LIBOR might be the yield for a three-year inverse floater.

Synthesizing financial instruments—financial engineering—is a topic which more and more treasurers are becoming familiar with. (And a topic to which we will return in Chapters 14 and 15.) In this text, we will stress the simplicity—we talk a lot about assembling building blocks. However, as the following discussion illustrates, the people who actually put financial engineering to work at industrial corporations sometimes have to do a little more engineering to get the theory into practice.

Risk Management in Practice

Using Interest Rate Swaps to Synthesize a Long-Dated Foreign Exchange Forward

Jacques Tierny

In Chapter 4, the author showed how a foreign exchange forward could be created—read that *synthesized:*

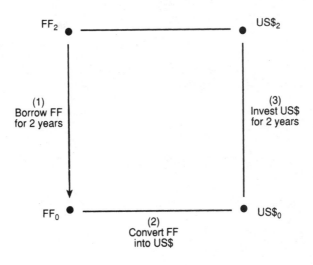

The preceding figure indicates that I could synthesize a two-year French franc–U.S. dollar forward by (1) borrowing French francs for two years, (2) converting the French francs I borrowed to U.S. dollars via a spot foreign exchange transaction, and (3) depositing the U.S. dollars for two years.

In this simple exposition, the author glosses over the fact that the two-year borrowing and two-year deposit necessary to synthesize the foreign exchange forward must be a zero-coupon deposit (e.g., certificate of deposit, or CD). However, we do not have ready access to zero-coupon borrowings. Instead we rely on LIBOR-based borrowings, loans on which we make annual interest payments.

So before I could actually synthesize that two-year French franc–U.S. dollar forward, I must first synthesize a two-year zero-coupon borrowing. Interest rate swaps permit me to do precisely that—I can use a combination of standard LIBOR borrowings and interest rate swaps to synthesize a zero-coupon borrowing.

At origination, I borrow P_0 for one year

P_0 $P_0(1+L_0)$

...and I also enter into a one-year interest rate swap

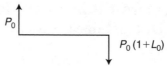

$(NP)_1 - L_0$
$(NP)_1 - F_1$

...and a two-year interest rate swap

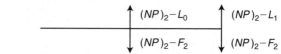

$(NP)_2 - L_0$ $(NP)_2 - L_1$
$(NP)_2 - F_2$ $(NP)_2 - F_2$

At the end of the first year, I "roll over" the loan

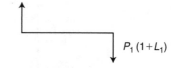

$P_1(1+L_1)$

If I select $P_0,$ $P_1,$ $(NP)_1,$ and $(NP)_2$ appropriately

P_0 100

The way that this is accomplished is illustrated in the accompanying figure: Initially, I need to do three transactions:

- I borrow P_0 for one year. At maturity of this transaction, I will owe $P_0 \times (1 + L_0)$ where L_0 is the one-year LIBOR rate known at the time I originate the set of transactions.
- I enter into a standard, one-year interest rate swap with a notional principal of $(NP)_1$ in which I receive an annual cash flow determined by one-year LIBOR and make an annual payment determined by the one-year swap rate, F_1 (which is specified at origination).
- I also enter into a standard, two-year interest swap with a notional principal of $(NP)_2$ in which I receive annual cash flows determined by one-year LIBOR and make annual payments determined by the two-year swap rate, F_2 (which is specified at origination).

At the end of the first year, I need to roll over the loan:

- I borrow P_1 for one year. At maturity of this transaction—at year 2—I will owe $P_1 \times (1 + L_1)$ where L_1 is the one-year LIBOR rate in one year—at the time I roll over the loan.

I have four parameters. Two are loan principals—the principal of the original loan, P_0, and the principal of the rollover, P_1. The other two are the notional principals of the swaps—the one-year swap, $(NP)_1$, and the two-year swap, $(NP)_2$. If I set these parameters "appropriately," I can end up with a (par) zero-coupon borrowing with a principal repayment of 100.

And it turns out that finding the "appropriate" values is not as hard as it might first appear.

Begin with the year 2 cash flows. The face value of the zero-coupon loan (FVZCL), 100, must be equal to the repayment of the rollover, $P_1 \times (1 + L_1)$, plus the fixed-rate payment on the two-year interest rate swap, $(NP)_2 \times F_2$, minus the floating-rate receipt on the two-year interest rate swap, $(NP)_2 \times L_1$.

$$\text{FVZCL} = 100 = P_1 \times (1 + L_1) + (NP)_2 \times F_2 - (NP)_2 \times L_1 \qquad 9\text{--}1$$

Moreover, I know that the face value of the zero-coupon loan is invariant to changes in LIBOR:

$$\frac{d(\text{FVZCL})}{dL_1} = P_1 - (NP)_2 = 0 \qquad 9\text{--}2$$

Using Equation 9–2 in Equation 9–1, we see that the unknown one-year LIBOR rate at year one drops out and we can solve for P_1 and $(NP)_2$.

$$P_1 = (NP)_2 = \frac{100}{1 + F_2} \qquad\qquad 9\text{–}3$$

Using these values, we iterate back to solve for P_0 and $(NP)_1$. As illustrated in the accompanying figure, the principal of the rollover, P_1, must be equal to the amount due from the original loan, $P_0 \times (1 + L_0)$, plus the fixed-rate payments on both the one- and two-year interest rate swaps, $(NP)_1 \times F_1 + (NP)_2 \times F_2$, minus the floating-rate receipts for the one- and two-year interest rate swaps, $(NP)_1 \times L_0 + (NP)_2 \times L_0$.

$$\begin{aligned} P_1 = P_0 \times (1 + L_0) + (NP)_1 \times F_1 + (NP)_2 \times F_2 \\ - (NP)_1 \times L_0 - (NP)_2 \times L_0 \end{aligned} \qquad 9\text{–}4$$

And similar to Equation 9–2 for the face value of the zero-coupon loan, the principal of this rollover loan is invariant to changes in the one-year LIBOR in effect when the transaction is begun.

$$\frac{dP_1}{dL_1} = P_0(NP)_1 - (NP)_2 = 0 \qquad\qquad 9\text{–}5$$

Since we already know P_1 and $(NP)_2$ and since L_0 is known, Equations 9–4 and 9–5 represent two equations with two unknowns; so we can solve for P_0 and $(NP)_1$.

Precisely the same method can be used to construct zero-coupon loans with maturities of three years or more.

Once the zero-coupon loan is synthesized, I can then create the synthetic foreign exchange forward.* But the question you may be asking yourself is, why? Why would a treasurer go to all of this trouble to synthesize FX forwards, since FX forwards are available in the market?

The answer is that the synthetic forwards can cost less. The bid-ask spread for long-dated FX forwards can be large. In contrast, the bid-ask spreads for LIBOR borrowings, for standard interest rate swaps, and for spot FX transactions are tiny. If I build my own FX forwards, I have found that I can cut by one half to two thirds the bid-ask spreads for long-dated FX forwards.

---

*To reduce the involvement of the company's balance sheet, the deposit and loan can be combined via the "FX swap" described in the first part of Chapter 8: In the spot market, I sell the U.S. dollar deposit against the French franc. Simultaneously, I buy it back in the one-year forward market.

Jacques Tierny is responsible for group treasury in a multinational company, a position he has held for the past 12 years. He manages the company's financial exposures and has centralized and netted the company's foreign exchange exposures. Moreover, he has put in place several arbitrage and opportunity-driven financing structures. Jacques Tierny is a graduate of H.E.C. in France.

Notes

1. Remember, however, that the synthetic fixed-rate debt is not precisely like the "normal" fixed-rate debt—e.g., the synthetic fixed-rate debt has no call provision.
2. "Kraft: The Well-Processed Spreadsheet," September 1990.
3. See Beidleman (1992).
4. This discussion is taken from "FMC Uses Metals Swaps to Lock in Margins" (January 1991).
5. This example is taken from the Group of Thirty, *Report of the Derivatives Study Group* (July 1993).
6. Specifically, the BIS survey noted $579 billion in reported outstandings and estimated that $51 bil-

lion may not have been captured by the central bank surveys.
7. Millman (1991).
8. We will show in Chapter 15 that an inverse floating-rate note is composed of a floating-rate note and an interest rate swap with a notional principal twice that of the original floating-rate note. The floating-rate note has a principal P and coupon payment R. If this *FRN* is combined with an interest rate swap with notional principal $2P$, the resulting coupon payment is $2R - R$—if interest rates rise, the coupon payment falls.

10 A PRIMER ON OPTIONS

In contrast to forward, futures, and swaps contracts, which impose *obligations* on the counterparties, an option contract conveys from one contracting party to another a *right*. Where a forward, futures, or swap contract *obliges* one party to buy a specified asset at a specified price on a specified date and *obliges* the other party to make the corresponding sale, an option gives its purchaser the *right* to buy or to sell a specified asset at a specified price on (or before) a specified date. To flesh out this definition, let's look more closely at the option contract and the contracting parties.

The Option Contract

The Contracting Parties

In an option contract, one party grants to the other the right to buy or to sell an asset. The party granting the right is referred to as the *option seller* (or the *option writer* or the *option maker*). The counterparty, the party purchasing the right, is referred to as the *option buyer.* Alternatively, the option buyer is said to be long the option position. It follows that the option seller is said to have a *short* position in the option.

The Right to Buy or to Sell

An option to buy an asset at a specified price is a *call* option on the asset. The call buyer has the *right* to purchase the asset. On the other side of the transaction, the call option seller has the *obligation* to sell. An option to sell an asset at a specified price is a *put* option on the asset. The put buyer has the *right* to sell; the put seller has the *obligation* to buy.

The Specified Asset

Options are available on a wide range of assets: equities, equity indices, interest rates (or bond prices), foreign exchange rates, and commodities. Since our objective is to provide a general understanding of how options work, we begin with those options about which the most has been written—options on shares of stock. In Chapter 12, we will expand the discussion to the other assets.

The Specified Price and Date

The price at which the option buyer can buy or sell the asset is called the *exercise* or *strike* price.

The final date on which the option owner can buy or sell the asset is known as the *expiration* or *maturity* date. An option that can be exercised only on the expiration date is referred to as a *European* option. An *American* option can be exercised on or before the expiration date.[1]

The Graphics of Options

As with the other financial derivatives, the simplest way to understand how options work is with a picture. Let's begin by considering the value at expiration of a European call option for a share of stock. For options, we use the following notation[2]:

$$S = \text{the share price, the price of the asset}$$

$$X = \text{the exercise price for the option}[3]$$

$$C = \text{the value of the call option}$$

$$P = \text{the value of the put option}$$

If, at expiration, the share price is less than the exercise price $(S < X)$, the option to purchase the asset for the exercise price is worthless $(C = 0)$. In this case, since the share could be purchased in the cash market for less than X, the right to buy it for X has no value. However, if the share price is greater than the exercise price at expiration of the option $(S > X)$, the value of the right to buy the share at the exercise price is equal to the difference between the share price and the exercise price $(C = S - X)$. If $S > X$ at expiration, the call owner could purchase the share for X and then sell it in the cash market at S, pocketing $S - X$ as profit. The value of a call option at expiration is summarized in the mathematical expression

$$C = \text{Max}[0, (S - X)] \qquad (10-1)$$

and is summarized graphically in Figure 10–1. As illustrated, if at expiration the share price is higher than the exercise price, the owner of the call option benefits at

Illustration 10–1

Reading the Options Quotes

We have reproduced a portion of the quotes on equity options as they appeared in the *Wall Street Journal* on Tuesday, August 12, 1997.

These quotes are for the close of business on the preceding trading day—in this case, on Monday, August 11.

C24 THE WALL STREET JOURNAL TUESDAY, AUGUST 12, 1997

LISTED OPTIONS QUOTATIONS

Monday, August 11, 1997

Composite volume and close for actively traded equity and LEAPS, or long-term options, with results for the corresponding put or call contract. Volume figures are unofficial. Open interest is total outstanding for all exchanges and reflects previous trading day. Close when possible is shown for the underlying stock on primary market. CB–Chicago Board Options Exchange. AM–American Stock Exchange. PB–Philadelphia Stock Exchange. PC–Pacific Stock Exchange. NY–New York Stock Exchange. XC–Composite. p–Put.

MOST ACTIVE CONTRACTS

SOURCE: Reprinted by permission of *The Wall Street Journal* © 1997 Dow Jones & Company, Inc. All Rights Reserved Worldwide.

Let's use British Telecom as an illustration. The name of the underlying equity (BritTel) is displayed in the first row of the first column. Columns 2 and 3 give you the exercise price and the maturity month of the option. The *Journal* indicates that while other options on British Telecom may be listed, trading activity on August 11 was focused on five options—three of the options have an exercise price of $60—an October call, an October put, and a January call. The remaining two options—an October call and an October put—both have an exercise price of $70.

Column 1 provides you with the closing price for the underlying share. Note that on August 11, British Telecom shares closed at 70 7/16; so the calls are all in-the-money calls.

Columns 4 through 7 display the volumes and last traded prices for the calls and puts, respectively. Look, for instance, at the October call struck at $60: 6,185 contracts were traded on August 11, the last of which was priced at 9 3/4. Only 53 contracts were traded on the October put struck at $60 which ended the day priced at 2 7/8.

FIGURE 10-1 The Value at Expiration of a European-Style Call Option
(*a*) The Payoff Profile for the Call Buyer (*b*) The Payoff Profile for the Call Seller

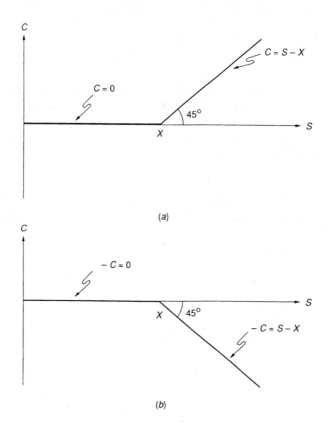

the expense of the seller of the call option: the payoff to the option owner is $S - X$; the payoff (expense) to the seller of the option (the option "writer") is the reverse, $X - S$. If, however, the share price at expiration is less than the exercise price, the call option is worthless; the payoff to both parties is zero.

Given the preceding development of the value of the call option, the valuation at expiration of a put option on a share of stock follows directly. The put option—the right to sell the share of stock at a price of X—is worthless ($P = 0$) when the price of the share in the asset market is greater than the exercise price ($S > X$). (Why exercise the option and sell the asset for a price of X when it could be sold in the cash market for more than that?) If, however, the price of the share at expiration is less than the exercise price, the right to sell the share at a price of X is valuable: the value of the option is the difference between the price the share can be sold at by exercising the option and the price it could be sold for in the asset market directly, $X - S$.[4] Hence the value of the put option at expiration can be summarized mathematically as

$$P = \text{Max}[0, (X - S)] \qquad (10\text{--}2)$$

or graphically as in Figure 10–2. As illustrated, value is conveyed from the seller of the put option to the buyer of the put option only if at expiration the price of the share in the asset market is less than the exercise price.

To the reader with any experience in markets, Figures 10–1 and 10–2 should provoke a question: Since the writer of the option can only lose, why would anyone write an option? Clearly the answer to this question is something not included in these payoff profiles—the *option premium*. At origination, the buyer of the option pays the option premium to the writer of the option. As illustrated in Figure 10–3

FIGURE 10–2   The Value at Expiration of a European-Style Put Option
(*a*) The Payoff Profile for the Put Buyer   (*b*) The Payoff Profile for the Put Seller

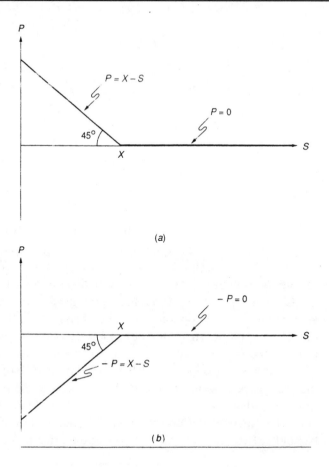

for the call option, the option premium shifts the payoff profile for the option buyer down and that for the option writer up. Precisely the same is true for the put option.

Hence, 'we know that both at origination and during the life of the option, the option has some value—the premium that would be required to purchase the option. But how can we determine this value? It is to this question we turn.

FIGURE 10–3   The Value at Expiration of a European-Style Call Option Including the Option Premium   (*a*) The Profit Profile for the Call Buyer   (*b*) The Profit Profile for the Call Seller

---

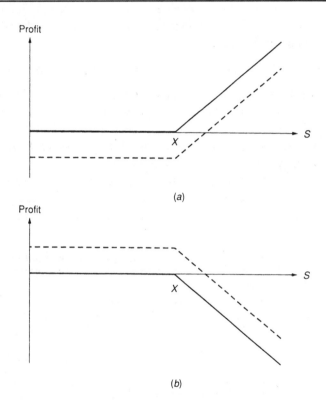

Option Valuation

Put-Call Parity

The preceding discussion suggests that we will have to derive two option premiums—the premium for calls and the premium for puts. Luckily, there is a relation between European puts and calls that requires us to derive only one of the premiums. If we know the premium for a call, we can solve for the premium for a put and vice versa. This useful relation is referred to as *put-call parity*.

To see how this relation works, consider two portfolios: Portfolio 1 is made up of a European call option on a share of stock and the discounted exercise price for this option. (Remember that the option can be exercised only at maturity—in T days.) Hence, today I don't need to hold the exercise price, X, but instead need to hold only the discounted value of the exercise price XD. The discount factor, D, is a function of the time to maturity, T, and the prevailing Treasury bill rate for that maturity, r.[5]

$$\text{Portfolio 1: } C + XD$$

The second portfolio is made up of a European put option on the share of stock that has the same exercise price and time to maturity as the call option in portfolio 1 and a share of the stock.

$$\text{Portfolio 2: } P + S$$

For these two portfolios, let's consider the values at the maturity of the options (and let's denote these expiration values using an asterisk). As Table 10–1 indicates, we must consider two cases. If the share price at expiration is less than (or equal to) the exercise price for the options ($S^* \le X$), the value of the call is zero but the value of the put is $X - S^*$. If, however, the share price at expiration is greater than the exercise price ($S^* > X$), the value of the put is zero but the value of the call is $S^* - X$. However, at expiration the two portfolios are guaranteed to have the same value: if $S^* \le X$, the value of each portfolio is X, and if $S^* > X$, the value is S^*.

TABLE 10–1   The Arbitrage Relations for Put-Call Parity

	$S^* \le X$	$S^* > X$
Portfolio 1: $V_1 = C + XD$	$0 + X$	$(S^* - X) + X$
Portfolio 2: $V_2 = P + S$	$(X - S^*) + S^*$	$0 + S^*$
	$V_1^* = V_2^*$	$V_1^* = V_2^*$

Since the value of the two portfolios is guaranteed to be the same at expiration, arbitrage guarantees that the two portfolios will have the same value at origination. Hence, it follows that

$$C + XD = P + S \tag{10–3}$$

or after rearranging some terms,

$$P = C - (S - XD) \tag{10–4}$$

That is, as long as I know the value of the call (the call premium), the value of the share, and the discounted value of the exercise price, I can solve for the value of the put.

However, $S - XD$ is the value of a forward contract on a share with an exercise price of X.[6] Hence, put-call parity is normally remembered as the relation among calls, puts, and forwards[7]:

- The combination of long a call and short a put is equivalent to being long a forward position,

$$C - P = F$$

- The combination of long a put and short a call is equivalent to being short a forward position,

$$P - C = -F$$

These relations are illustrated graphically in Figure 10–4.[8]

Bounding the Value of the Option[9]

Given the put-call parity, we need only to consider one type of European option; if we know the value of a European call, we can solve for the value of a European put and vice versa. Using T to denote the time remaining until expiration of the option, we know that for $T = 0$ (in other words, at expiration), the value of the call option is

$$C^* = \text{Max}[0, (S^* - X)] \qquad (10\text{–}5)$$

However, what is most important to the buyer and seller of the option is not how much the option will be worth in the future (at expiration) but how much the option is worth today.

Before we take up the explicit valuation of this call, let's build some intuition by looking at the bounds on the value of a call option.

To bound the value of an option, we rely on the fact that markets price assets so that no asset is "dominated."

> For asset A to "dominate" asset B over some period, the rate of return to A must be at least as great as the rate of return to B for all possible outcomes and the rate of return to A must be strictly greater than the rate of return to B for some outcomes.

In a well-functioning market, dominated securities will not exist or, at least, will not exist very long. Since no one would want to hold a dominated security, its price would be bid down until the domination is eliminated.

The *value of a call cannot be negative*. From the definition of a call option, exercise is voluntary. Since exercise will only be undertaken when in the best interests of the option holder:

$$C(S, T; X) \geq 0 \text{ [European call]} \qquad (10\text{–}6)$$

$$C_A(S, T; X) \geq 0 \text{ [American call]} \qquad (10\text{–}7)$$

FIGURE 10–4   Put-Call Parity Relations   *(a)* **Long a Call + Short a Put = Long a Forward**   *(b)* **Long a Put + Short a Call = Short a Forward**

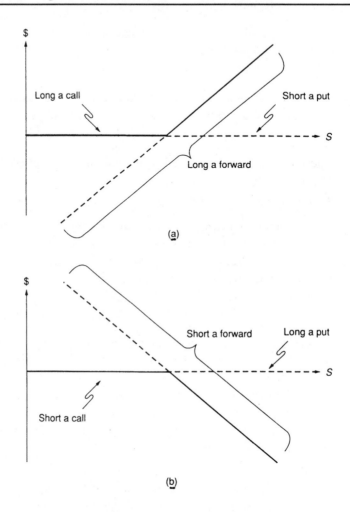

(a)

(b)

At any date prior to the maturity date, an American call must sell for at least the difference between the stock price and the exercise price. An American call can be exercised at any time before the expiration date; therefore:

$$C_A(S, T; X) \geq \text{Max}[O, S - X] \qquad (10\text{–}8)$$

If two call options differ only with respect to the expiration date, the one with the longer term to maturity, T_1, must sell for no less than that of the shorter term to maturity, T_2. At the expiration date of the shorter option, its price will be equal to the maximum of zero and the difference between the stock price and the exercise price (from Equation 10–5), and this is the minimum price of the longer option by Equation 10–8. Thus, to prevent dominance:

$$C(S, T_1; X) \geq C(S, T_2; X) \tag{10–9}$$

where $T_1 > T_2$.

If two call options differ only in exercise price, then the option with the lower exercise price must sell for a price that is no less than the option with the higher exercise price. This can be demonstrated by constructing and comparing the payoffs to two portfolios: portfolio A contains one European call with exercise price X_2, $C(S, T; X_2)$, and portfolio B contains one European call with exercise price X_1, $C(S, T; X_1)$ where $X_1 > X_2$. As illustrated in Table 10–2, if, at maturity, the stock price is above the lower exercise price, X_2, the terminal value of portfolio A, V_A^*, is greater than that of portfolio B, V_B^*. If the current prices of the two portfolios were equal, then the rate of return to portfolio A would exceed the rate of return for portfolio B whenever the stock price exceeded X_2 and portfolio B would be a dominated portfolio. Thus, if $X_1 > X_2$, the current price of portfolio A must be no less than the current price of portfolio B:

$$C(S, T; X_1) \leq C(S, T; X_2) \tag{10–10}$$

An American call must be priced no lower than an identical European call. Since an American call confers all the rights of the European call plus the privilege of early exercise, then

$$C_A(S, T; X) \geq C(S, T; X) \tag{10–11}$$

The value of the call option cannot exceed the value of the underlying stock. More specifically, the underlying stock is at least as valuable as a perpetual call ($T = \infty$) with a zero exercise price. From equations 10–8, 10–9, and 10–10, it follows that

$$S \geq C(S, \infty; 0) \geq C(S, T; X) \tag{10–12}$$

[S may exceed $C(S, \infty \, 0)$ because of dividends, voting rights, etc.].

TABLE 10–2   A Call with a Lower Exercise Price, X_2, Will Have Dollar Payoffs Greater Than or Equal to a Call with a Higher Exercise Price, X_1

		Stock Price at t^*		
Portfolio	*Current Value*	$S^* \leq X_2$	$X_2 < S^* \leq X_1$	$X_1 < S^*$
A	$c(S,T;X_2)$	0	$S^* - X_2$	$S^* - X_2$
B	$c(S,T;X_1)$	0	0	$S^* - X_1$
		$V_A^* = V_B^*$	$V_A^* > V_B^*$	$V_A^* > V_B^*$

**TABLE 10–3   A Call plus Discount Bonds with a Face Value of *X*
Yields a Terminal Value Greater Than or Equal to That of the
Respective Stock if the Stock Pays No Dividends**

		Stock Price at t^*	
Portfolio	*Current Value*	$S^* \le X$	$X < S^*$
A	$C(S,T;X) + XD(T)$	$0 + X$	$(S^* - X) + X$
B	S	S^*	S^*
		$V_A{}^* > V_B{}^*$	$V_A{}^* = V_B{}^*$

A call on a non-dividend-paying stock must sell for at least the stock price mi-nus the discounted exercise price. Let $D(T)$ be the discount factor for payments re-ceived T periods from now (alternatively, it is the price of a risk-free, pure discount bond that pays \$1 T years from now). Now consider two portfolios: portfolio A con-tains one European call, $c(S, T; X)$ and X bonds which have a current value of $XD(T)$; portfolio B contains the stock, S. Table 10–3 demonstrates that the terminal value of portfolio A, $V_A{}^*$, is not less than that for portfolio B, $V_B{}^*$. Therefore, the current value of portfolio A, $V_A{}^*$, must be greater than or equal to the current value of port-folio B to avoid dominance. This restriction can be rearranged to yield

$$C(S, T; X) \ge \text{Max}[0, S - XD(T)] \qquad (10\text{–}13)$$

Figure 10–5 summarizes the preceding boundary restrictions on the value of call options. Equation 10–6 requires that the value of the call be no less than zero; Equa-tion 10–12 requires that it be no greater than the stock price; and Equation 10–13 re-quires that it be no less than the stock price minus the discounted exercise price.

FIGURE 10–5   Bounds on the Price of a Call Option

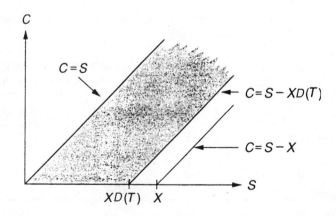

A Simplified Approach to Option Valuation

So far, we have specified the value of an option *at maturity*. However, the real question facing the buyer and the seller of the option is not the value at maturity but rather the value *today*. In the next chapter, we will examine the range of option-pricing models that have been developed to value different types of options on the various underlying assets. But first let's look at a simplified approach to option pricing provided by William F. Sharpe (1978) and expanded by John C. Cox, Stephen A. Ross, and Mark Rubinstein (1979). This approach is referred to as the *binomial option pricing model,* or—given its authors—the Cox, Ross, Rubinstein (C-R-R) approach. While the binomial pricing model is most widely used in the valuation of interest rate options, for simplicity we begin by looking at the pricing of a European option on a share of stock that pays no dividend. (We return to other applications of the binomial model in Chapter 13.)

In this simplified approach to option pricing, we are going to envision our continuous-process world as a series of snapshots. Let's suppose that today, on day 0, the price of a particular share of stock is $100. Let's suppose further that tomorrow it could rise or fall by 5 percent:

Day 0	*Day 1*	
100 ⟨	105	Up by 5 percent
	95	Down by 5 percent

Let's consider the value of a one-day call option on this share of stock. For simplicity, set the exercise price of this one-day call option at $100. The value of the call option *at maturity—at day 1—is as shown below:*

Illustration 10–2

A Realistic Approach?

At first blush, the preceding lattice looks too simplistic to have any connection to the real world. However, it is simple only because we have let the share price move only once per day. What if we let the share price move up or down by 5 percent every 12 hours?

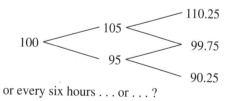

or every six hours . . . or . . . ?

If we make the intervals shorter, this simple binomial model becomes more realistic, in much the same way that a movie approximates continuous movements although it is a series of still pictures.

Share Price at Expiration	Value of Call at Expiration
$105	$5
95	0

However, if I am thinking about selling (or buying) this call option, I am not as interested in its value at maturity as I am in its value *today*. The approach we are going to follow is modeled on the approach of Fischer Black and Myron Scholes (1973): instead of trying to value the option separately, we will value the option by valuing an *arbitrage portfolio* that contains the option.

An arbitrage portfolio is one that earns a riskless return. Let's form such a portfolio out of the two risky assets—the share of stock and the call option on the share of the stock. That is, let's form a portfolio in which the gains made on one of the assets would be exactly offset by losses on the other. As the following table indicates, for the case in point, such a portfolio could be formed by creating a portfolio in which we are *long* one share of stock and *short* two call options:

S	C	2C	S-2C
105	5	10	95
95	0	0	95

As indicated, the value of this portfolio—S-$2C$—will be $95 regardless of the value of the share of stock. Hence, we have formed a portfolio that has no risk. (See illustration 10–3.)

In the remainder of this discussion, we will refer to the *hedge ratio* (Δ) as the *inverse* of the number of calls necessary to form the arbitrage portfolio,

$$\Delta = 1/N \tag{10–14}$$

Hence, for the case in point, the hedge ratio is $\Delta = 1/2$.

On day 0, the value of the share is $100; the value of the arbitrage portfolio, $S - 2C$, is $100 - 2C$, which reinforces the fact that the value of the call option on

---

Illustration 10–3

Calculating the Hedge Ratio

In the preceding, it was pretty easy to see that two calls would exactly hedge the movement in one share of stock.* However, we will need a more general rule when we encounter more complex situations. Not surprisingly, it's nothing more than a little algebra. For the case in point, we want to find the number of call options that will make the value of the portfolio when share price is 105,

$$105 - (N \times 5)$$

equal to the value of the portfolio when the share price is 95,

$$95 - (N \times 0)$$

Hence, if

$$105 - (N \times 5) = 95 - (N \times 0)$$

it follows that $N \times 5 = 10$; so $N = 2$.

Generalizing, let's define the share price if the price change is up as SU and the share price if the price change is down as SD. Likewise, define the value of the call option when the share price is up as CU and the value of the call when the share price is down as CD. Then the number of calls necessary to form the arbitrage portfolio (N) is

$$N = (SU - SD)/(CU - CD)$$

---

*The share price could change by $10; the value of the call could change by $5; so it would take two calls to cover the possible change in the value of the share.

---

day 0 is so far unknown. We do know, however, that on day 1, the value of the portfolio is 95. Hence, we know that

$$(100 - 2C)_{\text{day } 0} < (95)_{\text{day } 1}$$

To turn the preceding into an equality—and therefore to be able to solve for C, the value of the call option on day 0—it is necessary to discount day 1 values to day 0 values or to inflate day 0 values to day 1 values. The convention is to discount rather than to inflate; so we can express the present value of the $95 to be received in one day as

$$100 - 2C = 95/(1 + r)$$

where r is a one-day interest rate. Since the arbitrage portfolio is riskless, the interest rate used is the *risk-free interest rate.* Continuing our example, if the annualized one-day risk-free rate—the Treasury bill rate for one-day bills—is 7.5 percent, the rate for one day is $(1/365) \times 0.075 = 0.0002$, and the preceding equation becomes

$$100 - 2C = 95/(1.0002)$$

Illustration 10–4

An Option Payoff Diagram

The tree diagram in Figure 10–6 provides the value of the call of a particular share price on day 0—in this instance, a share price of $100. To transform this tree diagram to a more familiar option diagram, we need to think about the value of the call on day 0 for *various* share prices.

To accomplish this, we need the general expression for the value of this one-period call option as provided by Cox, Ross, and Rubinstein*:

$$C = \frac{\left\{\dfrac{(1 + r) - {}^{SD}/_S}{(SU - SD)/S}\right\}CU + \left\{\dfrac{{}^{SU}/_S - (1 + r)}{(SU - SD)/S}\right\}CD}{(1 + r)}$$

where *SU, SD, CU,* and *CD* are as defined earlier, and *S* is the initial stock price. Using this general equation, consider three cases†:

1. *If on day 0, the share price is less than or equal to X/(SU/S), the value of the call option is zero.* For the case in point, if the share price on day 0 is less than or equal to $100/(105/100) = 95.23$, the value of the call is zero.

2. *If on day 0, the share price is greater than or equal to X/(SD/S), the value of the call option is $S - X/(1 + r)$.* For the case in point, if the share price on day 0 is greater than or equal to $100/(95/100) = 105.26$, the value of the call is $S - 99.98$.

3. *If on day 0, the share price is greater than X/(SU/S), but less than X/(SD/S), the value of the call option is*

$$\left\{\frac{(1 + r) - {}^{SD}/_S}{(SU - SD)/S}\right\}\left\{\frac{SU - X}{(1 + r)}\right\}.$$

For the one-period option we have been looking at

Share Price on Day 0	Value of Call
101	3.04
100	2.51
99	1.98

An Option Payoff Diagram continued

The payoff diagram for the specific option we have been examining can then be drawn as follows:

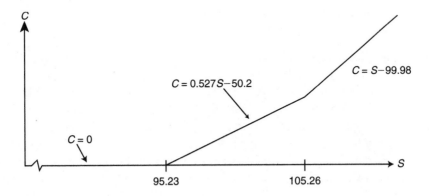

Or more generally, the payoff diagram for a one-period option can be illustrated as

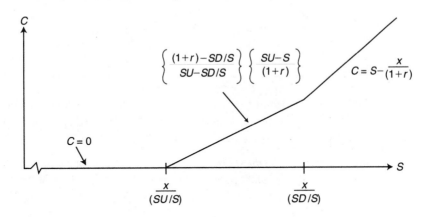

---

*Cox, Ross, and Rubinstein (1979).

†This material is taken from Cox and Rubinstein (1985).

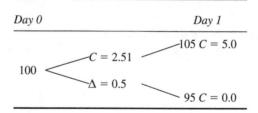

FIGURE 10–6   Valuing a One-Day Option

Hence, for our example, the value of the one-day call option on day 0 is $2.51. (See Figure 10–6.)

At this point some of you may be saying that this is all very well and good . . . but not very relevant since it is not very likely that we will encounter many one-day option contracts. So let's see what happens when we let the option run for two days.

Continuing to assume that the share price can move up or down by 5 percent every day, the distribution of share prices over the three days—and the resulting values of the call option—is as follows:

Day 0	*Day 1*	*Day 2*	
		110.25	$C = 10.25$
	105		
100		99.75	$C = 0$
	95		
		90.25	$C = 0$

If we want to derive the value of the call option at day 0, we first must determine the values of the option for the share prices that could exist on day 1 (that is, 95 and 105) and then use these values to determine what the option will be worth on day 0.

On day 1, if the value of the share is 105, the arbitrage portfolio would be $S - (1.025)C$. That is, the number of call options necessary to hedge one share of stock would be

$$N = (110.25 - 99.75)/(10.25 - 0)$$

$$= 10.50/10.25$$

$$= 1.025$$

(Alternatively, the hedge ratio is $1/N = 0.976$.) So

$$(105 - 1.025C)_{day\ 1} < (99.75)_{day\ 2}$$

Therefore,

$$(105 - 1.025C) = (99.75)/(1.0002)$$

so the value of the call would be $5.14.

On day 1, if the value of the share is 95, the value of the call would be zero, since the value of the call will be zero regardless of whether the value of the share rises to $99.75 or falls to $90.25.[10]

On day 0, the relevant lattice has become

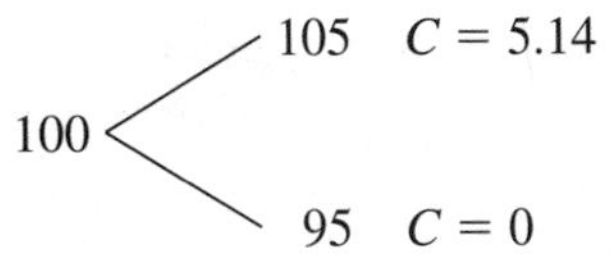

```
                    ╱ 105   C = 5.14
            100  ⟨
                    ╲ 95   C = 0
```

Hence, the number of call options necessary to hedge one share of stock is

$$N = (105 - 95)/(5.14 - 0)$$
$$= 10/5.14$$
$$= 1.95$$

(Or the hedge ratio is 0.514).) Thus, the arbitrage portfolio is $S - 1.95C$:

$$(100 - 1.95C)_{day\ 0} < (95)_{day\ 1}$$

Therefore, continuing to use 7.5 percent as the relevant annualized rate for a one-day Treasury bill,

$$(100 - 1.95C) = (95)/(1.0002)$$

so *the value of the call option would be 2.579—that is, $2.58.*

This valuation is summarized in Figure 10–7.

If we can value a two-day option, we can value a three-day or four-day or *n*-day option: the logic is exactly the same—we solve iteratively from expiration to time period 0; the only thing that changes is the size of the problem.

FIGURE 10–7   Valuing a Two-Day Option

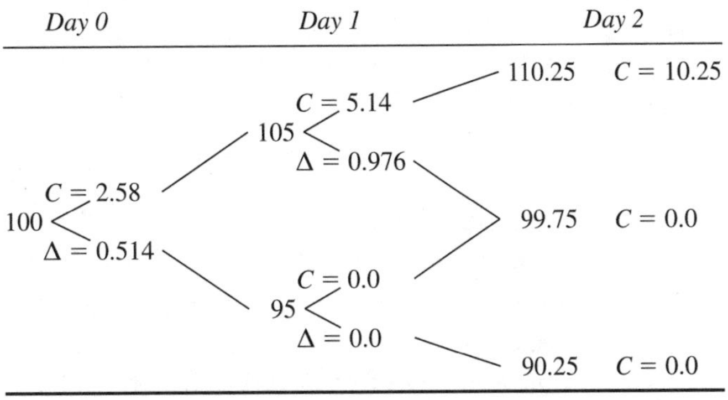

| *Day 0* | *Day 1* | *Day 2* |

$C = 2.58$

100 $\Delta = 0.514$

$C = 5.14$
105 $\Delta = 0.976$

$C = 0.0$
95 $\Delta = 0.0$

110.25 $C = 10.25$

99.75 $C = 0.0$

90.25 $C = 0.0$

The purpose of this pricing discussion is twofold. The first purpose is obvious: to demonstrate that the pricing of an option is not as difficult as it might otherwise seem. The second objective is much more subtle: to highlight the five variables that determine the value of an option. Look again at the examples. We employed the following five variables to value the option:

The prevailing share price, *S*. In our example the share price on day 0, the date of origination of the option contract, was $100.

The exercise price of the option, *X*. In our example we used $100 as the exercise price.

The time to expiration of the option, *T*. We considered both one day and two days.

The risk-free interest rate corresponding to the time remaining on the option, *r*. In our example, the annualized rate for a one-day T-bill was 7.5 percent; the one-day interest rate was 0.0002 percent.

The volatility in the share price, σ. In the context of the binomial pricing model we have been using, the value of the call option was determined in part by the magnitude of the movements in the share price. In our example, we used price movements of 5 percent up or down per day. This magnitude of the movements in the share price could be summarized by the variance in the distribution of share prices. (Normally the variance is denoted as σ^2—and the standard deviation as σ.)

Hence, we could write an implicit function for the value of a European-style call option on a share that pays no dividend as

$$C = C(\,S, X, T, r, \sigma) \tag{10–15}$$

The discussion also provides insight about the manner in which the option value changes as these five variables—determinants—change.

Increases in the share price increase the value of the call option. For example, if we increase the original share price by $10 in our example,

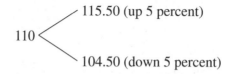

while leaving the exercise price at $100 and the other determinants un-changed, the value of the call option will rise from $2.51 to $10.02.

Increases in the exercise price decrease the value of the call option. If we increase the exercise price rise from $100 to $101, the value of the one-day call option would fall from $2.51 to $2.01.

Increases in the time to expiration increase the value of the call option.
As noted, increasing the time to maturity from one to two days increased the
value of the call option from $2.51 to $2.58.

**Increases in the risk-free interest rate increase the value of the call
option.** If the annualized rate on a one day T-bill rose from 7.5 percent
to 15 percent, the daily risk-free interest rate would rise from 0.0002
to 0.0004 and the value of the one-day call option would rise from $2.51
to $2.52.

**Increases in the volatility of share price increase the value of the call
option.** Suppose that instead of 5 percent up or down each day, share prices
could move up or down by 10 percent each day:

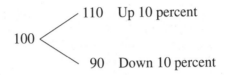

$$
100 \begin{cases} 110 & \text{Up 10 percent} \\ 90 & \text{Down 10 percent} \end{cases}
$$

With no other changes in the determinants of the option value, the value of
our one-day call option would rise from $2.51 to $5.01.

The preceding relations between the value of a European call option on a share that
pays no dividend and the five determinants can be summarized as

$$
\overset{+\ -\ +\,+\,+}{C = C(S, X, T, r, \sigma)} \tag{10–16}
$$

The definition of a put option makes it clear that the right to sell an asset at a
predetermined price X becomes more valuable as the market price of the asset (S)
falls or the exercise price (X) rises. Using the put-call parity relations defined in
Equation 10–4, the value of a European put can be expressed as

$$
\overset{+\ -\ +\,+\,+}{P = C(S, X, T, r, \sigma)} \overset{-\,-}{- S + XD(r, T)} \tag{10–17}
$$

From the put-call parity relation, the effect of both T and r on the value of a put
are more difficult to sign because both T and r increase the value of the call (C)
but decrease the discounted exercise price (XD); the offsetting effects may lead to
a net increase, a net decrease, or no change in the value of the put.[11] In the case of
the interest rate, increases in r will cause the discounted exercise price to fall
faster than the value of the call will be rising; so, an increase in the interest rate will
lead to a decrease in the value of the put. However, if T increases, no general relation exists about the relative speeds of the increase in the value of the call and the
decrease in the discounted exercise price; so, the relation between time to maturity
and the value of the put is indeterminant. Finally, since an increase in volatility (σ)

Risk-Neutral Valuation

Gregory Hayt

The pricing example presented in this chapter is based on a no arbitrage (or cost-of-carry) approach to valuation. A widely-used alternative approach is *risk neutral* valuation.

As its name implies, risk-neutral valuation involves pricing derivatives by assuming that all investors are risk-neutral. Although no one would argue that investors are actually risk-neutral, it turns out that for the special case of derivatives we can act as if they are and still get the correct answer. This simplification is one of the most powerful tools used by financial engineers to develop pricing models.

Can We Really Assume Risk Neutrality?

There are two important implications of the risk-neutrality assumption. First, investors focus only on the expected return of an investment and ignore its standard deviation, or riskiness. Since risk is ignored, there is no additional compensation demanded for owning risky securities rather than, say, a Treasury bill. If no compensation is required to bear risk, then all securities will be priced to have the same expected return—the risk-free rate. The second point is a consequence of the first. Since investors do not demand compensation for bearing risk, they will discount future cash flows at the risk-free rate. Thus, the price of any security (or derivative) in a risk-neutral world is its expected future cash flow, discounted at the risk-free rate.

The obvious question is, How can a technique that assumes risk neutrality provide correct prices in the real, "risk-averse," world in which we live? The answer depends on what is being priced. For the case of derivatives, risk-neutral pricing gives the correct answer because derivatives are priced by constructing arbitrage portfolios like the ones you have seen in this chapter. Arbitrage portfolios use existing securities, the prices of which are known, to replicate the cash flows of a given derivative and thus determine its value.

Recall the arbitrage portfolio for the one-day option priced in this chapter. By combining two call options with one share of stock, a riskless portfolio was created. Everyone, *regardless of individual risk preferences,* agrees on the value of the call because everyone can agree on the value of the riskless arbitrage portfolio. Its value depends only on the current stock price, the time, and the risk-free rate, all of which are observable.* Individuals who disagree on the likely future value of the stock, i.e., on its expected return, would still agree on the price of the call because the call is priced *relative* to the *known* values of the stock and arbitrage portfolio.

To be a bit more formal about it, the construction of the arbitrage portfolio conveniently eliminates the expected return of the stock (or other underlying security) from the calculation. The stock's true expected return depends on the risk preferences of investors, but since it has dropped out of the equation, we can safely assume *any* set of risk preferences we want. The obvious choice is the relatively simple world of risk-neutral preferences where the stock's expected return would be the risk-free rate. In general, whenever a derivative can be combined with the underlying asset to create an arbitrage portfolio, we can make the simplifying assumption that investors are risk-neutral.[†]

We can illustrate the application of risk-neutral valuation with a forward contract on a share of stock. If risk-neutral pricing really works, the answer obtained in a risk-neutral setting should be the same as the answer derived earlier in this book when no assumption of risk-neutrality was made.

Does the Risk-Neutral Approach Work? The Case of Pricing a Forward Contract

Let's value a forward contract on a share of stock using the assumption that investors are risk-neutral. The current value of the forward contract, which matures at time T, is denoted by f. The forward price is given by K, and the risk-free interest rate over the period is r. In a risk-neutral world, the value of the forward contract today must equal the present value of its expected future cash flows as given by the following equation:

$$f = \frac{\overline{E}[S_T - K]}{1 + r}$$

In the preceding equation, S_T is the value of the stock at maturity of the forward contract and $\overline{E}$ designates the expected payoff of the forward contract *when investors are risk-neutral*. The expectation can be computed by assuming the stock's value grows at the risk-free rate (its expected return in a risk-neutral world) from today to time T.

$$f = \frac{\overline{E}[S_T] - K}{1 + r} = \frac{S \times (1 + r) - K}{1 + r}$$

$$= S - \frac{K}{1 + r}$$

To verify that this expression is equivalent to the one derived for a forward contract in Chapter 4, remember that at origination the value of the contract, f, is zero. Therefore the forward price of the stock, K, would be $S*(1 + r)$ at origination. This is identical to the cost-of-carry model developed earlier in the book using an arbitrage portfolio.[‡]

Pricing an Option Contract Using Risk-Neutral Valuation

The development of the binomial option pricing model in this chapter hinged on the construction of an arbitrage portfolio. In order to construct the portfolio, it was necessary to know the stock's volatility (the range of up and down moves), but once constructed, the value of the call depended only on the current stock price, the time, and the risk-free interest rate. Since the stock's expected return does not enter the equation, risk-neutrality can be assumed.

With risk-neutral investors, the price of the option is given by its discounted expected value, as in the following equation.

$$C = \frac{1}{1 + r} \times \overline{E}[\max(S_T - X, 0)]$$

In keeping with the illustration in this chapter, C is the price of the European-style call, r is the risk free-interest rate, X is the strike price, and S_T is the value of the stock at expiration. $\overline{E}$ designates the expected value when investors are assumed to be risk-neutral—it is not the actual expected value of the underlying security. The option is more complicated than the forward, and in order to evaluate $\overline{E}$ the *risk-neutral probabilities* corresponding to the stock's possible values at time T are required. It will turn out that these probabilities are embedded in the prices of the traded instruments used in the arbitrage portfolio.

To see how this works, consider the general expression for the one-period binomial model given in Illustration 10–4. (Remember that this formula was derived without assuming anything about risk preferences.)

$$C = \frac{\left\{\frac{(1 + r) - \frac{SD}{S}}{\frac{(SU-SD)}{S}}\right\}CU + \left\{\frac{\frac{SU}{S} - (1 + r)}{\frac{(SU-SD)}{S}}\right\}CD}{(1 + r)}$$

In this expression, SU is the value of the stock given an up move, SD is the stock price given a down move, and CU and CD are the payoffs to the call option in an up and down move, respectively. Since this expression is crowded with terms, substitute the symbol p for the first term in brackets. Algebraic

Risk-Neutral Valuation continued

manipulation shows that the second term in brackets can be expressed as $(1 - p)$, resulting in the following simplified expression,

$$C = \frac{pCU + (1 - p)CD}{1 + r}$$

When written in this fashion, the value of the call option looks suspiciously like the expected payoff of the option at maturity, discounted at the risk-free rate. The preceding equation would correspond exactly to the general risk-neutral formula if p and $(1 - p)$ are the risk-neutral probabilities needed to evaluate $\bar{E}$.

To show that p and $(1 - p)$ are indeed the risk-neutral probabilities, calculate their values using the one-day option example from the text. In the text, $SU = 105$, $SD = 95$, $S = 100$, and $r = 0.0002$ (7.5 percent per annum divided by 365). From Equation 3a the expression for p is

$$p = \left\{ \frac{(1 + r) - SD/_S}{(SU-SD)/_S} \right\} = \left\{ \frac{(1 + 0.0002) - ^{95}/_{100}}{(105-96)/_{100}} \right\} = 0.502$$

The value of $(1 - p)$ is therefore 0.498. Now calculate the expected value of the stock and from that, the expected return.

$$\bar{E}[S] = 0.502 \times \$105 + 0.498 \times \$95 = \$100.02$$

Dividing the expected stock price by $100 and subtracting one shows that the expected return on the stock calculated with p and $(1 - p)$ is exactly the risk-free rate, 0.0002 (7.5 percent per annum), i.e., the return on the stock in a risk-neutral world. Similarly, using the values for p and $(1 - p)$ gives a value for the call of $2.51, the same as in the text. The binomial model is equivalent to assuming investors are risk-neutral and then calculating the risk-neutral expected payoff of the option discounted at the risk-free rate.

In the two-day example in the text, there are three possible outcomes for the stock. Solving for p and $(1 - p)$ at each node (they will be the same for all nodes in this type of tree) and calculating the stock's expected return will again show that the stock earns the risk-free rate over the two-day holding period.

Why Risk-Neutral Pricing Works

The risk-neutral technique works for derivatives because derivatives are priced in terms of other traded securities. Risk neutrality cannot be assumed for valuing, say, a share of stock because an arbitrage portfolio containing the stock and other traded securities cannot be constructed. The stock's price, therefore, depends on investors' risk preferences. It's not that derivatives' prices don't

---

Risk-Neutral Valuation continued

reflect risk preferences; it's just that these preferences are already incorporated into the prices of the underlying securities used in valuing the derivative.

Risk-neutral pricing will come up again in the discussion of the Black-Scholes model in Chapter 11. There it is shown that the risk-neutral methodology provides an alternative derivation of the famous Black-Scholes differential equation. The equivalence of risk-neutral pricing with the binomial or Black-Scholes model is important. Either technique will give the same answer, but it will often simplify the problem to frame it in risk-neutral terms.

Gregory Hayt is an executive director of CIBC Financial Products where he focuses on teaching and the development of curriculum for the CIBC World Markets School of Financial Products. Prior to joining CIBC, Mr. Hayt was a vice president at Chase Manhattan Bank, where he advised clients on a wide range of risk management issues, from financial modeling and exposure measurement to the design and implementation of risk management policies.

*The stock's volatility implicitly enters the equation since we need to know the "up" and "down" moves on the stock to calculate the correct number of calls to short.

†Technically, the underlying asset must be a traded security, i.e., one not held primarily for consumption. This complicates the application of risk-neutral techniques to, for instance, commodity options. A discussion of how to overcome these and other problems in risk neutral valuation can be found in Hull.

‡Other direct costs of carry such as physical storage or insurance can be included without changing the result that the risk-neutral approach and the cost-of-carry (no-arbitrage) approach give the same answer.

---

increases C but has no effect on S or XD, it follows that an increase in volatility will increase the value of the put option. These relations can be summarized as follows:

$$
\begin{array}{ccccc}
- & + & ? & - & + \\
\end{array}
$$
$$
P = P(S, X, T, r, \sigma) \tag{10–18}
$$

A Note on American Options

An American option gives its owner all the rights in a European option plus something extra: the American option also gives its owner the right to early exercise; the owner of the American option has the right to exercise the option before its maturity. It follows then that the value of the American option is always at least that of the European option. Whether or not the American option is worth more than the European option depends on whether or not the option would ever be exercised early.

Hence, the question of the value of an American option depends on yet another question: Will an American option ever be exercised early? And as with so many other things, the answer is "it depends."

American Calls

If the share of stock pays no dividend, it is never optimal to exercise the American call early. To understand why, suppose that at some time prior to expiration, the American call is in the money; that is, the prevailing share price (S) is greater than the exercise price for the call option (X). If the option is *exercised,* the owner will receive a gain equal to the difference between the prevailing share price and the exercise price for the option receipt from early exercise, $S - X$. However, if instead the owner of the option *sells* the option, the market value of the option will not be less than the difference between the prevailing share price and the *discounted exercise price;* so the receipt from the sale will not be smaller than $S - XD$. The strategies are detailed in Table 10–4.

As long as there is any time remaining to maturity of the option, $D < 1$, it follows that $(S - XD) > (S - X)$ and

$$S - XD + \text{Time value} > S - X \qquad (10\text{–}19)$$

Hence, for a non-dividend-paying stock, early exercise of an American call option will never occur. Therefore, in this case, the value of an American call option is identical to that for a European call option.

For an American call option on a dividend-paying share of stock, early exercise will be optimal if the dividend is sufficiently large, and if at all, early exercise will occur immediately before the stock goes ex-dividend. Since shares purchased on or after the ex-dividend day do not receive the next dividend, the share price will fall on the ex-dividend day by an amount approximately equal to the dividend. It is this drop in price that provides the incentive for early exercise of the American call option: if I exercise the option just before the ex-dividend date, I receive a dividend payment that I would not receive if I do not exercise the option. Hence, the issue is whether the amount I receive if I exercise the option,

$$S_x - X + \text{dividend}$$

(where S_x is the ex-dividend stock price) is greater or less than the value of the call option if I were to continue to hold it:

$$C(S_x, X, T)$$

TABLE 10–4 Strategies for Realizing an In-the-Money American Option

Strategy	Gain
Exercise the option early	$S - X$
Sell the option	$S - XD$ + time value

It follows that the American call would be exercised early if

$$\text{Dividend} > C(S_x, X, T) - (S_x - X) \tag{10--20}$$

And to value the American call, the value of this early exercise provision would have to be evaluated for each of the ex-dividend dates that occur during the life of the option. This early exercise provision of American calls is most valuable when the dividend is large, the time to maturity is short, and the call is significantly in the money.

American Puts

Early exercise of an American put option will be optimal if the price of the stock falls sufficiently below the exercise price. This rather complex concept is best explained with an example. Let's consider an American put option with these characteristics: $X = \$100$; $T = 1$ year; and $r = 20$ percent.

Suppose the price of the share has fallen to $10. If I exercise the option early, I will receive $X - S = \$100 - \$10 = \$90$ today. If I hold that $90 in a T-bill, I will have at maturity $\$90 \times (1.2) = \$108$. Instead, if I hold the option to maturity, the most the option will be worth is $100, and this only if the share price falls to zero. In this case, since $\$108 > \$100$, it is clear that the American put option will be exercised early.

If, however, the share price has fallen only to $20, the situation is more complex. If I exercise the option early, I will receive $80 today and will have $\$80 \times (1.2) = \$96$ at the end of one year. As before, the option could be worth at maturity as much as $100; it may not be optimal to exercise early. But the option is worth $100 only if the value of the share drops to zero. If instead the share price were $5 at expiration, the value of the option would be $95, and it would have been better to exercise the option early. Hence, in this case, it may or may not be optimal to exercise the American put option early, depending on the probability distribution of share prices.

The point of the preceding is that to determine the value of an American put option on a non-dividend-paying stock, it is necessary to determine whether it would be optimal to exercise the option early on any of the days prior to expiration. Since there exists no simple formula that provides the solution, this involves an iterative, numerical approximation problem—not unlike the binomial lattice we have just considered: we first check to see if early exercise could be optimal on the day prior to expiration, then on the day before that, then on the day before that, and so on.

Interestingly, while dividends make it more difficult to value American call options (because dividends make it possible that early exercise is optimal), the existence of dividends makes it easier to value American put options. As we have noted, American puts are exercised early only if there is a sufficiently large drop in the share price. And as indicated above, for non-dividend-paying stocks, we would have to check this relation for each trading day prior to expiration. However, for dividend-paying stocks, the predictable share price fall on an ex-dividend date makes the probability of optimal early exercise highest on ex-dividend dates. Hence, for American puts on dividend-paying stocks, the correct value can be closely approximated by considering early exercise only for the finite number of remaining ex-dividend dates.

Notes

1. Note that the terms *European* and *American* refer only to the style of the option—whether or not it can be exercised before the expiration date. The fact that an option is European or American says nothing about where the option is traded; e.g., options on individual shares traded on the Amsterdam Exchange are American, not European, options. In Chapter 13, we will describe other options with geographic names—"Asian" and "Bermuda" options.

2. To keep things simple, we ignore transaction costs and taxes.

3. In other sources, you may find the symbol K used to denote the exercise price.

4. Put another way, if $S < X$, the owner of the put option could purchase the share for S and sell it at X, thereby profiting in the amount of $X - S$.

5. If we employ discrete discounting, the discount factor is

$$D_{DISCRETE} = 1/(1 + r)^T$$

If we were to use continuous discounting, the discount factor would be

$$D_{CONTINUOUS} = e^{-rT}$$

In either case, increases in the time to maturity, T, or the interest rate, r, would decrease the discount factor, D.

6. Applying the logic of Chapter 4 since the forward contract calls for no payments prior to maturity, the price of a forward on a non-dividend-paying stock is simply the current stock price minus the discounted exercise price of the forward.

7. We have distinguished between forwards as commitments and options as rights, but now that we have derived put-call parity we can make the relation more precise. Because the forward can be decomposed into a long call and a short put, the forward is a package containing both a right if it matures in the money and a commitment if it matures out of the money.

8. In Figure 10–4 we do not illustrate the option premium. However, since the option premiums would cancel out, this exclusion does not affect the conclusions drawn from the figure.

9. The bounds for the value of an option were first discussed by Robert Merton (1973).

10. Put another way, since the number of shares necessary to hedge one share of stock is, in the limit, a positive infinity,

$$N = (99.75 - 90.25)/(0 - 0)$$

$$= 9.50/0 > \infty$$

the value of the call option must approach zero as a limit.

11. On first inspection of Equation 10–17, the reader might also think that the effects of changes in S and X on the value of a put are indeterminant:

$$\partial P/\partial S = \partial C/\partial S + (-1)$$

$$\partial P/\partial X = \partial C/\partial X + D(r, T)$$

However, a little more investigation clears up the confusion. Since the value of the call does not rise as rapidly as the share price, $\partial C/\partial S < 1$, so $\partial P/\partial S < 0$. And the change in the value of a call for a change in the exercise price, $\partial C/\partial X$, is smaller in magnitude than $D(r, T)$; so, higher exercise prices are associated with higher put prices—$\partial P/\partial X > 0$.

11 | FIRST-GENERATION OPTIONS*

> This chapter is the most analytical in this book. While we have attempted to hold the mathematics to a minimum, we recommend that readers who find themselves bogged down by the math skim this chapter and then move on to Chapter 12.

In 1973, Fischer Black and Myron Scholes published the first general equilibrium solution for the valuation of options. Recognizing that shares and calls could be combined to construct a riskless portfolio, they developed an analytical model that provides a no-arbitrage value for European-style call options on shares as a function of the share price, the exercise price of the option, the time to maturity of the option, the risk-free interest rate, and the variance of the stock price. As the benchmark around which trades could occur, the Black-Scholes model provided the breakthrough that permitted the rapid growth of the options market.

The Black-Scholes model is often regarded as either the *end* or the *beginning* of the story. In truth, it is *both*. It is the end of the story in the sense that it solved a problem that economists had wrestled with for at least three quarters of a century. It is the beginning of the story in the sense that it spawned a number of generalizations or extensions.

Indeed, it is most helpful to consider the Black-Scholes model in the context of a *family tree of option pricing models*. Using this family tree analogy, it is possible to identify three major *tribes* within the family of option pricing models: analytical, numerical, and analytic approximation.

---

*This chapter is based on "Wonderful Life" by Charles Smithson which appeared in *Risk* in 1991 and on "Option Pricing: A Review" by Clifford Smith, which appeared in the *Journal of Financial Economics* in 1976. The original "Wonderful Life" paper was followed by two updates that I wrote with Shang Song for *Risk* in 1995 (Smithson and Song, 1995a and 1995b). These updates covered the new option valuation models that appeared since the 1991 paper was published, and examined the way that the "family" of term structure models has intertwined with the interest rate option valuation family.

The Black-Scholes option pricing model is itself an analytical model. So, before we begin our examination of the "genealogy," let us take some time to examine the Black-Scholes model itself.

The Black-Scholes Option Pricing Model

The paradigm that makes the Black-Scholes model work is the concept of the *arbitrage portfolio*—you can combine options and shares to form a portfolio that is riskless. Black and Scholes were the first to note that a riskless hedge can be created out of positions in the option and shares of underlying stock. Because the hedge is (instantaneously) riskless, arbitrage ensures that the return to the hedge must be the riskless rate. By combining this equilibrium condition with the appropriate boundary conditions, Black and Scholes were able to derive a specific option pricing model.

The Black-Scholes model was developed to value European-style options on shares of stock. It is crucial to remember that the Black-Scholes model is based on a number of assumptions. These assumptions are summarized in Table 11–1.

Most of these assumptions are straightforward. However, the *continuous Ito process* probably needs a little explanation.

On the basis of the preceding definitions, Figure 11–1 provides an illustrative path of a random variable, S, which follows a continuous Ito process through time.

When we examined the simplified approach to option pricing in Chapter 10, we noted that the crucial concept is the hedge portfolio—the arbitrage portfolio—which is formed by combining both stock and call options. The value of the hedge portfolio, V_H, can be expressed as

$$V_H = Q_s S + Q_c C \tag{11-1}$$

where S is the price of a share of the stock, C is the price of a European call option to purchase one share of the stock, Q_s is the quantity of stock in the hedge, and Q_c is the quantity of call options in the hedge.

TABLE 11–1   Assumptions Embedded in the Black-Scholes Model

1. The share pays no dividends.
2. Transactions cost and taxes are zero.
3. Interest rates are constant.
4. There are no penalties for short sales of stock.
5. The market operates continuously, and the share prices follow a *continuous Ito process*.
6. The distribution of terminal stock prices (returns) is lognormal.

Aside

A Continuous Ito Process

In various mathematics texts, an Ito process is defined simply as "a Markov process in continuous time." For our purposes, a little more detail is in order.

A *Markov process* is one where the observation in time period t depends only on the preceding observation. For example, if the stock price follows a Markov process, the stock price S in period t could be defined as

$$S_t = X(S_{t-1}) + E_t$$

where X is a constant and E_t is a random error term.

A process is *continuous* if it can be drawn without picking the pen up from the paper.

FIGURE 11–1   A Continuous Ito Process

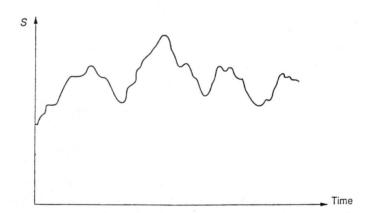

The change in the value of the hedge, the derivative of the value of the hedge, dV_H, is simply

$$dV_H = Q_s dS + Q_c dC \qquad (11\text{–}2)$$

Note in Equation 11–2 that, since the quantities of options and stock are given at a point in time, the change in the value of the hedge results simply from the change in the prices of the assets, dS and dC.

As noted in Table 11–1, the stock price is assumed to follow a continuous Ito process; so there exists a specific mathematical expression for dS. We know that the call price is a function of the stock price and the time remaining to expiration

---
Aside

Ito's Lemma

Ito's Lemma is a differentiation rule for random variables whose movement can be described as an Ito process. If stock price follows a simple Ito process, the returns to the stock can be represented by

$$\frac{dS}{S} = \mu dt + \sigma dZ$$

Where μ and σ are constants, dt is the change in time, and dZ is a normally distributed random variable with a mean of zero and a variance dt. Multiplying both sides of the equation by S, it follows that

$$dS = \mu S dt + \sigma S dZ$$

The expected value and variance of dS are

$$E[dS] = \mu S dt \qquad Var[dS] = \sigma^2 S^2 dt$$

As noted above, the value of a call option written on the stock is a function of the stock price and the time remaining to expiration of the option:

$$C = C(S, t)$$

What we want to know is the effect of incremental changes in S and t on the value of the call option, i.e., $C(S + \Delta S, t + \Delta t) - C(S, t)$. To obtain $C(S + \Delta S, t + \Delta t)$, we use a second-order Taylor series approximation:

$$C(S + \Delta S, t + \Delta t) = C(S, t) + \frac{\partial C}{\partial t} \Delta t$$

$$+ \frac{\partial C}{\partial S} \Delta S + \frac{1}{2} \frac{\partial^2 C}{\partial S^2} (\Delta S)^2$$

Then:

$$dC = C(S + \Delta S, t + \Delta t) - C(S, t)$$

$$= \frac{\partial C}{\partial t} \Delta t + \frac{\partial C}{\partial S} \Delta S + \frac{1}{2} \frac{\partial^2 C}{\partial S^2} (\Delta S)^2$$

and interpreting $(\Delta S)^2$ as the variance of dS:

$$dC = \frac{\partial C}{\partial S} dS + \left(\frac{\partial C}{\partial t} + \frac{1}{2} \frac{\partial^2 C}{\partial S^2} S^2 \sigma^2 \right) dt$$

---

of the option. What we need is a mathematical expression for dC. This is provided by *Ito's Lemma*. As indicated on this page, Ito's Lemma provides an expression for the differential of functions of variables that follow Ito processes.

A crucial insight of Ito's Lemma is that the change in the call price, dC, can be expressed as the sum of two terms, one related to the change in the stock price and the other related to the change in the time to maturity,

$$dC = \frac{\partial C}{\partial S} dS + \left(\frac{\partial C}{\partial t} + \frac{1}{2} \frac{\partial^2 C}{\partial S^2} S^2 \sigma^2 \right) dt \qquad (11\text{--}3)$$

It is helpful to look at this decomposition of the change in the call price graphically. Figure 11–2 illustrates the first term in Equation 11–3. For small changes in the stock price, dS, the associated change in the call price is given by the slope of the tangent, $\partial C / \partial S$, times the stock price change, dS. The second term in

FIGURE 11–2   **The Change in the Call Price, *dC*, from a Change in the Stock Price, *dS*, Is the Slope of the Tangent *∂C/∂S*, Times the Stock Price Change, *dS***

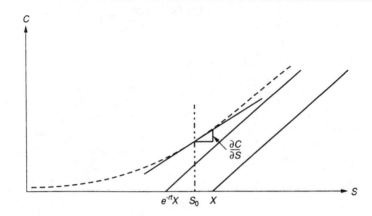

Equation 11–3, the component related to the change in the time to maturity, is illustrated in Figure 11–3. Given the prevailing stock price, S_0, a decrease in the time to maturity increases the present value of the exercise price. Thus, from Equation 11–3, decreasing the time remaining to maturity decreases the value of the call. Note that on the right-hand side of Equation 11–3 only the first term, $(\partial C/\partial S)dS$, is stochastic; the rest of the terms are deterministic.

If Equation 11–3 is substituted into Equation 11–2, we obtain the following expression for the change in the value of the hedge portfolio:

FIGURE 11–3   **The Change in the Value of the Call, *dC*, from a Change in the Time to Maturity, *dt*, Is the Shift in the Curve When the Present Value of the Exercise Price Changes from $e^{-rt}X$ to $e^{-rt'}X$**

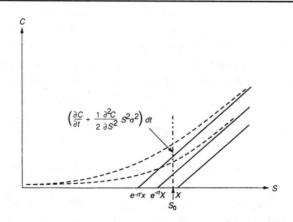

$$dV_H = Q_s dS + Q_c \left[\frac{\partial C}{\partial S} dS + \left(\frac{\partial C}{\partial t} + \frac{1}{2} \frac{\partial^2 C}{\partial S^2} S^2 \sigma^2 \right) dt \right] \qquad (11\text{-}4)$$

If the quantities of stock and of call options in the hedge portfolio are chosen so that Q_s/Q_c equals $-(\partial C/\partial S)$, the first two terms on the right-hand side of Equation 11–4 sum to zero. And since these are the only stochastic terms, it follows that if Q_s/Q_c is equal to $-(\partial C/\partial S)$, the change in the value of the hedge becomes deterministic—that is, the hedge portfolio becomes riskless.

What this means is that, with the appropriate long position in the stock and short position in the call, an increase in the price of the stock will be offset by the decrease in the value of the short position in the call, and vice versa.[1] This can be illustrated graphically by returning to Figures 11–2 and 11–3. By setting Q_s/Q_c equal to $-\partial C/\partial S$, the unanticipated change in the call price because of a stock price change (illustrated in Figure 11–2) is hedged by the stock price change itself so that the predictable change in the call price from the reduction in the time to maturity illustrated in Figure 11–3 is all that remains.

Hence, the insight provided by Black and Scholes is that if the quantities of the stock and of the call option in the hedge portfolio are continuously adjusted in the appropriate manner as asset prices change over time, then the return to the portfolio becomes riskless. Setting $Q_c = -1$ and $Q_s = (\partial C/\partial S)$ in Equation 11–4 yields

$$dV_H = -\left[\frac{\partial C}{\partial t} + \frac{1}{2} \frac{\partial^2 C}{\partial S^2} S^2 \sigma^2 \right] dt \qquad (11\text{-}5)$$

Therefore, mathematically we have eliminated all the stochastic terms (since dt is deterministic, dV_H is deterministic); so this hedge portfolio is riskless. Hence, the return to the hedge portfolio must equal the riskless rate

$$\frac{dV_H}{V_H} = (r)dt \qquad (11\text{-}6)$$

We are now ready to do some arithmetic to derive an explicit expression for the change in the call price. Imposing $Q_c = -1$ and $Q_s = (\partial C/\partial S)$ on Equation 11–1,

$$V_H = \left(\frac{\partial C}{\partial S} \right) S - C \qquad (11\text{-}7)$$

Then, using Equation 11–7 in Equation 11–6:

$$dV_H = r \frac{\partial C}{\partial S} S \, dt - (rC) \, dt \qquad (11\text{-}8)$$

And setting the right-hand sides of Equation 11–5 and Equation 11–8 equal to one another, we obtain

$$\frac{\partial C}{\partial t} = rC - r\frac{\partial C}{\partial S}\, S - \frac{1}{2}\frac{\partial^2 C}{\partial S^2}\,(S^2\sigma^2) \tag{11-9}$$

Thus, we are close to our objective: we want an expression for the value of the call. What we have in Equation 11–9 is an expression for the change in the value of the call over time—what mathematicians call a differential equation. What we need to do is get from the differential equation to an equation for the value of the call—that is, given the differential equation in Equation 11–9, we want to solve for the value of the call.

As noted in the following, to derive an expression for the call value we must have a boundary condition, something to tie down our expression for the change in call value. The required boundary condition for the solution of this differential equation is the condition we outlined in Chapter 10: at expiration of the option, the option value must equal the maximum of either the difference between the stock price and the exercise price, $S^* - X$, or zero,[2]

$$C^* = \text{Max}\,[S^* - X, 0] \tag{11-10}$$

Thus, the value of the call option will be obtained by solving Equation 11–9 subject to Equation 11–10.

Before proceeding, note that, whatever the form of the solution, it must be a function only of five variables—the stock price, S; the exercise price, X; the vari-

---

Aside

Differential Equations

A differential equation is simply an equation that contains derivatives. If there is a single independent variable, the derivatives are ordinary derivatives and the equation is an ordinary differential equation. For example an ordinary differential equation would be $dy/dx = 0.8$. If there are two or more independent variables, the derivatives are partial derivatives and the equation is called a partial differential equation. Note that Equation 11–9 is a partial differential equation because it involves both $\partial C/\partial S$ and $\partial C/\partial t$.

To provide some intuition, consider the simple ordinary differential equation above, $dy/dx = 0.8$. Since the differential equation is equal to a constant, 0.8, the equation is telling us that the slope of y plotted against x would be a constant 0.8. In other words, this differential equation implies that the function linking y and x is a straight line with a slope of 0.8. But there are an infinite number of straight lines with a slope of 0.8—which one is the correct one? To identify one line, we also need a "boundary condition," a fixed point to tie down the function. Hence, also knowing that if $x = 0$, $y = 2$ tells us that the unique solution we seek is $y = 2 + 0.8x$.

ance rate, σ^2; time, t; and the riskless interest rate, r—because these are the only variables that appear in the problem.

To obtain the solution to the differential equation Black and Scholes noted that Equation 11–9 could be transformed into an equation that is familiar to physicists— the *heat-exchange equation*. However, since we would anticipate that few of you are familiar with this particular equation, a more intuitive solution technique is likely to be more useful and informative.[3]

Note that when we described the equilibrium return to the hedge portfolio, the only assumption we made about the preferences of the market participants is that two assets that are perfect substitutes must earn the same rate of return—because the hedge portfolio has no risk, it must earn the riskless rate of return. Hence, since no assumptions involving the risk preferences of the economic agents have been made, the pricing model implied by Equation 11–9 must be invariant to risk preferences. It follows then that if we can find a solution to the problem for a particular preference structure, it must also be the solution to the differential equation for any other preference structure that permits a solution.

Therefore, to solve Equation 11–9, we choose the preference structure that simplifies the mathematics: we assume a preference structure in which all agents are risk-neutral. In a risk-neutral world, the expected rate of return on all assets would be equal. Hence, the current call price is the present value of the expected call price at expiration of the contract, $E[C^*]$ discounted at the marketwide discount rate, r. That is,

$$C = e^{-rT}E[C^*] \qquad (11-11)$$

where T is the amount of time remaining until expiration. If we assume further that the distribution of stock prices at any future date will be lognormal, Equation 11–11 can be expressed as

$$C = e^{-rT}\int_X^\infty (S^* - X)L'(S^*)dS^* \qquad (11-12)$$

where $L'(S^*)$ is the lognormal density function.

Equation 11–12 is integrated using a theorem developed by Cliff Smith (1976). The result of this integration is the Black-Scholes solution to the European call pricing problem:

$$C = S * N\left\{\frac{\ln(\frac{S}{X}) + (r + \frac{\sigma^2}{2})T}{\sigma\sqrt{T}}\right\} - e^{-rT}X * N\left\{\frac{\ln(\frac{S}{X}) + (r - \frac{\sigma^2}{2})T}{\sigma\sqrt{T}}\right\} \quad (11-13)$$

where $N\{\cdot\}$ is the cumulative normal distribution function.

As we would have anticipated given the results in Chapter 10, the Black-Scholes option pricing model involves only five variables,

$$\begin{array}{ccccc} + & - & + & + & + \end{array}$$
$$C = C(S, X, T, r, \sigma)$$

where the signs above the variables represent their partial derivatives. The partial effects again have intuitive interpretations.

- As the stock price increases, the expected payoff of the option increases.
- With a higher exercise price, the expected payoff decreases.
- With a longer time to maturity, the present value of the exercise payment is lower, thus increasing the value of the option.
- With a higher interest rate, the present value of the exercise payment is lower, thus increasing the value of the option.
- With a larger variance for the underlying stock price (or with a longer time to maturity), the probability of a large stock price change during the life of the option is greater. Since the call price cannot be negative, a larger range of possible stock prices increase the maximum value of the option without lowering the minimum value.

Figure 11–4 illustrates graphically the relation between the Black-Scholes valuation of the call and the stock price (holding the exercise price, time to maturity, variance rate, and the riskless rate constant).

Additional understanding of the Black-Scholes model is obtained by going a little deeper into the risk-neutral pricing.

FIGURE 11–4   Black-Scholes Call Option Price for Different Stock Prices, with a Given Exercise Price, Interest Rate, Variance Rate, and Time to Maturity

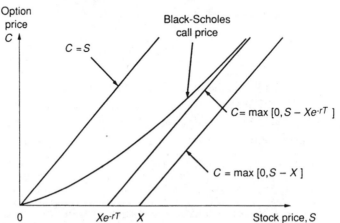

The Black-Scholes call option prices lie below the maximum possible value, $C = S$ (except where $S = 0$), and above the minimum value, $C = \max[0, S - X e^{-rT}]$. Note that the curve relating the Black-Scholes call price to the stock price asymptotically approaches the $C = \max[0, S - X e^{-rT}]$ line.

The Analytical Models

In the same way that we can distinguish among the analytical, numerical, and analytic approximation *tribes,* we can subdivide the analytical tribe itself into two distinct *lineages—generalizations* to the Black-Scholes model and *extensions* of the Black-Scholes model. In the discussion of these lines, we will, to as great an extent as possible, highlight the similarities and differences of the members of these lines by showing how they relate to the Black-Scholes model—that is, by showing how Equation 11–13 would be modified to obtain the option valuation model in question.

Generalizations of the Black-Scholes Model

As Table 11–1 highlights, the Black-Scholes model is based on a number of assumptions. The decade following the publication of the Black-Scholes model saw the development of models that relaxed the assumptions. The "genealogy" of this line of the analytical tribe is illustrated in Figure 11–5. In addition to the "genealogy," we can also summarize these models in the *generalization* line by relating the various members of this line to the assumption that was relaxed. Table 11–2 provides these relations.

In 1973, Robert Merton considered European-style options on dividend-paying shares. The inclusion of dividends changes the Black-Scholes formula as follows:

$$C = \left| S * N \left\{ \frac{\ln(\frac{S}{X}) + (r + \frac{\sigma^2}{2})T}{\sigma\sqrt{T}} \right\} - e^{-rT}X * N \left\{ \frac{\ln(\frac{S}{X}) + (r - \frac{\sigma^2}{2})T}{\sigma\sqrt{T}} \right\} \quad (11\text{–}14)$$

where δ is the constant dividend yield. As Equation 11–14 demonstrates, the dividend reduces the value of the share to the holder of the option by the present value of the forgone dividend and reduces the cost of holding a share by the dividend stream that would be received.

In 1976, Jonathan Ingersoll took Merton's inclusion of dividends one step further to consider a world where dividends are taxed at rate τ, while capital gains are untaxed.

$$C = \left| S * N \left\{ \frac{\ln(\frac{S}{X}) + (x + \frac{\sigma^2}{2})T}{\sigma\sqrt{T}} \right\} - e^{-xT}X * N \left\{ \frac{\ln(\frac{S}{X}) + (x - \frac{\sigma^2}{2})T}{\sigma\sqrt{T}} \right\} \quad (11\text{–}15)$$

Aside

Interpreting the Black-Scholes Formula

We can rewrite Equation 11–12 to express the value of the call in terms of conditional expected value,[4]

$$C = e^{-rT}E(S^* > X)\,\text{Prob}(S^* > X)$$
$$- e^{-rT}X\,\text{Prob}(S^* > X)$$

The first term is the product of

- discounted expected value of the stock at maturity, conditional on the stock price at maturity exceeding the exercise price and
- probability that, at maturity, the stock price is greater than the exercise price.

The second term is the product of

- discounted exercise price and
- probability that, at maturity, the stock price is greater than the exercise price.

The Black-Scholes value for a call option varies from zero (for way out-of-the-money calls) to the difference between the share price and the discounted exercise price (for way in-the-money calls). To see this, consider two extreme cases:

An extremely out-of-the-money call $(S^* << X)$: The ratio of stock price to exercise price is much less than 1—$S/X << 1$. The logarithm of that ratio is negative— $\ln(S/X) << 0$—so the area under a normal distribution from negative infinity to that point is very small, $N(\ln(S/X)) \to 0$. Therefore, the value of this extremely out-of-the-money call is approximately zero.

An extremely in-the-money call $(S^* >> X)$: The ratio of stock to exercise price is much greater than 1—$S/X >> 1$. The logarithm of that ratio is positive—$\ln(S/X) > 0$—so the area under a normal distribution from negative infinity to that point is close to 1— $N(\ln(S/X)) - 1$. Therefore, the value of this extremely in-the-money call is approximately $S - e^{-rT}X$.

In the 1973 paper in which he considered dividends, Robert Merton also considered variable interest rates, a generalization that alters the Black-Scholes formula to

$$C = S * N\left\{\frac{\ln\left(\frac{S}{X}\right) + \left(r + \frac{\sigma^2}{2}\right)T}{\sigma\sqrt{T}}\right\} - e^{-rT}X * N\left\{\frac{\ln\left(\frac{S}{X}\right) + \left(r - \frac{\sigma^2}{2}\right)T}{\sigma\sqrt{T}}\right\} \quad (11\text{–}16)$$

where the annotations indicate $-\ln B(T) + (\hat{\sigma}^2/2)T$ replacing $\left(r + \frac{\sigma^2}{2}\right)T$, $B(T)$ replacing e^{-rT}, $-\ln B(T) + (\hat{\sigma}^2/2)T$ replacing $\left(r - \frac{\sigma^2}{2}\right)T$, and $\hat{\sigma}$ replacing σ.

where $B(T)$ is the value of a default-risk-free discount bond with a maturity equal to the maturity of the option and $\hat{\sigma}$ is a variance measure that incorporates not only the variance of the stock but also the variance in the value of the discount bond (interest rate).

FIGURE 11–5 **The Analytical Models**

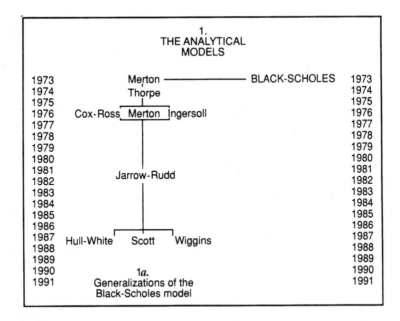

1.
THE ANALYTICAL
MODELS

1973	Merton ———————— BLACK-SCHOLES	1973
1974	Thorpe	1974
1975		1975
1976	Cox-Ross Merton Ingersoll	1976
1977		1977
1978		1978
1979		1979
1980		1980
1981		1981
1982	Jarrow-Rudd	1982
1983		1983
1984		1984
1985		1985
1986		1986
1987	Hull-White Scott Wiggins	1987
1988		1988
1989		1989
1990	1a.	1990
1991	Generalizations of the Black-Scholes model	1991

In the Black-Scholes model, prices follow a pure diffusion process—price moves continuously from one value to the next. The consequence of this pure diffusion process is that the terminal distribution of share prices is lognormal. The idea that prices do not move continuously but rather jump from one point to another was first suggested by John Cox and Stephen Ross in a 1975 University of Pennsylvania working paper—an idea subsequently expanded in the Cox-Ross-Rubinstein binomial model discussed in Chapter 10.

TABLE 11–2 **Models That Relaxed the Black-Scholes Assumptions**

Assumption	*Relaxed by*
No dividends	Merton (1973)
No taxes or transaction costs	Ingersoll (1976)
Constant interest rates	Merton (1973)
No penalties for short sales	Thorpe (1973)
Market operates continuously, and share price is continuous	Merton (1976) Cox-Ross (1976)
Terminal stock price (returns) distribution is lognormal	Jarrow-Rudd (1982)

Robert Merton (1976) went a step further by proposing the combination of a jump process and a diffusion process—after each jump, price again follows a diffusion process. If we constrain the jump process by assuming that the size of the jumps are distributed lognormally, this jump-diffusion model can be illustrated as a modification to the Black-Scholes formula[5]:

$$
C = \left(\sum_{n=0}^{\infty} \frac{e^{-\lambda(1+k)T}[\lambda(1+k)T]^n}{n!} \left[S*N\left\{ \frac{\ln(\frac{S}{X}) + (\hat{r} + \frac{\hat{\sigma}^2}{2})T}{\hat{\sigma}\sqrt{T}} \right\} - e^{-\hat{r}T}X*N\left\{ \frac{\ln(\frac{S}{X}) + (\hat{r} + \frac{\hat{\sigma}^2}{2})T}{\hat{\sigma}\sqrt{T}} \right\} \right] \right) \quad (11\text{--}17)
$$

where λ is the rate at which jumps occur, k is the average jump size as a proportional increase in the share price, $\hat{r}$ is $r - \lambda k + \{n[\ln(1 + k)]\}/T$ and $\hat{\sigma}^2$ is $\hat{\sigma}^2 + n\,\sigma_j^2/T$ with σ_j^2 being the variance in the distribution of jumps.

In 1982, Robert Jarrow and Andrew Rudd examined the case in which prices follow a diffusion process, but not necessarily a process that generates a lognormal distribution. They examined the effect on the valuation of an option as the variance, skewness, and kurtosis of the actual distribution differ from a lognormal distribution. In general, as the tails of the resulting distribution are "fatter" or "thinner" than those of the lognormal distribution, the Black-Scholes formula will undervalue or overvalue the option. Jarrow and Rudd provided an adjustment to the Black-Scholes model that takes into account the discrepancies between the moments of the lognormal distribution and the true distribution.

In 1987, all three of the dominant academic finance journals published papers that dealt with the same generalization of the Black-Scholes model. The option pricing models proposed by John Hull and Alan White, Louis Scott, and James Wiggins all allowed volatility to itself be a stochastic process.

Extensions to the Black-Scholes Model

As we noted at the outset, the Black-Scholes model was designed to value European-style options on individual shares of stock. Not surprisingly, subsequent research was aimed at valuing options on underlying assets other than stock and on valuing American-style options. The family tree of option valuation models, with the addition of this *extension* line of the analytical tribe, is illustrated in Figure 11–6.

Options on Futures.   In 1976, Fischer Black extended the model he developed with Myron Scholes to incorporate options on futures contracts:

FIGURE 11–6 Extensions to the Analytical Models

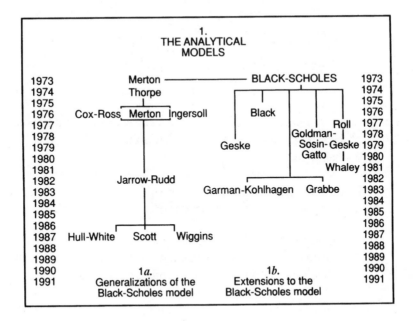

where F is the forward (futures) price.

Options on Currencies.   In 1983, Mark Garman and Steven Kohlhagen provided an analytic valuation model for European options on currencies using an approach similar to that used by Merton for European options on dividend-paying stocks:

$$C = S * N\left\{\frac{\ln(\frac{S}{X}) + (x + \frac{\sigma^2}{2})T}{\sigma\sqrt{T}}\right\} - e^{-xT}X * N\left\{\frac{\ln(\frac{S}{X}) + (x - \frac{\sigma^2}{2})T}{\sigma\sqrt{T}}\right\} \quad (11\text{–}19)$$

where r_D is the interest rate on the domestic currency and r_F is the interest rate on the foreign currency. Note that in Equation 11–19, the interest rate on the foreign currency has the same function as did the dividend rate on the share in Equation 11–14.

In the same year—indeed, in the same issue of the same journal—Orlin Grabbe provided an alternative specification for the value of European options on currencies using an approach similar to that used by Black for futures.

$$C = \$ * N \left\{ \frac{\ln\left(\frac{\$}{X}\right) + \left(x + \frac{\sigma_F^2}{2}\right)T}{\sigma_F \sqrt{T}} \right\} - X * N \left\{ \frac{\ln\left(\frac{\$}{X}\right) + \left(x - \frac{\sigma_F^2}{2}\right)T}{\sigma_F \sqrt{T}} \right\} \quad (11\text{--}20)$$

where $B(T)$ is the price of a *domestic* currency discount bond, F is the forward price of the foreign currency, and σ_F is determined by the variance of the forward foreign exchange rate.

Note that Equations 11–19 and 11–20 are mirror images of each other. Using interest rate parity, we can value an option either using the spot rate and the foreign interest rate (Garman-Kohlhagen) or using the forward rate (Grabbe).

Compound Options.   That an option on a firm's equity is actually a compound option was recognized by Black and Scholes. They noted that the equity for any firm that issues debt is like a call option on the value of the assets; so an option on equity is an option on an option on the value of the firm's assets. An analytic model for the valuation of compound options was provided by Robert Geske in 1979. Geske noted that the fundamental problem in using the Black-Scholes formula for the valuation of compound options is that Black-Scholes assumes that the variance is constant, while in the case of options on shares variance depends on the level of the share price (or more fundamentally on the value of the firm). When compared with the Black-Scholes model, the compound option model delivers higher values for deep out-of-the-money options and near-maturity options and lower values for deep in-the-money options.

Path-Dependent Options.   In 1979, Barry Goldman, Howard Sosin, and Mary Ann Gatto examined the pricing of a European call option in which the exercise price is the minimum price of the share over the life of the option—an option now referred to as a "lookback" option. We will return to this topic when we discuss "second-generation" options in Chapter 13, where we will examine a number of option pricing models developed to consider not only "lookback" options but also other options for which the path the price takes is important in valuation—options on the average price and barrier options ("up and in," "down and out," and the like). Many of the models used to value path-dependent options are regarded as proprietary, so there is less about these models in the public record.

American-Style Options.   The analytic valuation model for an American-style share option was developed by Richard Roll (1977), Robert Geske (1979b), and

Robert Whaley (1981). As illustrated by Equation 11–21, an analytic solution which provides for early exercise requires that the Black-Scholes formula be expanded to include not only the cumulative standard normal distribution $N\{.\}$, but also a cumulative bivariate normal distribution $M\{.,.,.\}$. Following John Hull,[6] the model developed by Roll, Geske, and Whaley can be written as

$$
\begin{aligned}
C = {} & S * N\left\{\frac{\ln(\frac{S}{X}) + (r + \frac{\sigma^2}{2})T_D}{\sigma\sqrt{T_D}}\right\} - e^{-rT}(X - D) * N\left\{\frac{\ln(\frac{S - e^{-rT_D}D}{X}) + (r - \frac{\sigma^2}{2})T_D}{\sigma\sqrt{T_D}}\right\} \\
& + M\left\{\frac{\ln(\frac{S - e^{-rT_D}D}{X}) + (r + \frac{\sigma^2}{2})T}{\sigma\sqrt{T}}, \frac{\ln(\frac{S - e^{-rT_D}D}{S}) + (r + \frac{\sigma^2}{2})T_D}{\sigma\sqrt{T_D}}, \sqrt{\frac{T_D}{T}}\right\} \\
& + XM\left\{\frac{\ln(\frac{S - e^{-rT_D}D}{X}) + (r - \frac{\sigma^2}{2})T}{\sigma\sqrt{T}}, \frac{\ln(\frac{S - e^{-rT_D}D}{S}) + (r - \frac{\sigma^2}{2})T_D}{\sigma\sqrt{T_D}}, \sqrt{\frac{T_D}{T}}\right\}
\end{aligned}
\tag{11-21}
$$

where D is the final dividend prior to option expiration, T_D is the time until the final dividend, and S is the solution to $C(S, T) = S + D - X$. Given the complexity of an analytic valuation, it is not surprising that most users turn to the binomial models and analytic approximation models (also discussed in this chapter) for valuation of American-style options.

This listing is by no means a complete catalogue of the analytical option pricing models that have been developed and are currently in use. Other examples include the model developed by William Margrabe in 1978, which values the option to exchange one asset for another, and the model developed by René Stulz in 1982 to value an option on the minimum or the maximum of two risky assets.

The Numerical Models

Within the tribe of the numerical models, there are three lineages. The best known is the binomial model line; the other two are the finite difference models and the Monte Carlo simulation models.

The Binomial Models

We introduced you to the binomial approach to option valuation in Chapter 10. This approach—also known as the *lattice approach*—was first suggested by William Sharpe in 1978. However, this methodology is normally associated with the paper John Cox, Stephen Ross, and Mark Rubinstein published in 1979.

As proposed by Cox-Ross-Rubinstein, this approach divides the time until option maturity into discrete intervals and presumes that, during each of these intervals, the price of the asset—for example, the stock price—follows a binomial process moving from its initial value, S, to Su (with probability p) or Sd (with probability $1 - p$). As illustrated in Figure 11–7, this process yields a "tree" (or lattice) of stock prices. Given this set of share prices, the call can be valued by working backwards from maturity. If we begin with one of the terminal share values, we can obtain the corresponding terminal value of a call option directly. Then, using Black and Scholes's insight that shares and calls can be combined to create a riskless portfolio, we can work our way back down the tree from time period T to time period $T - 1$, discounting portfolio values in period T to period $T - 1$ values using the risk-free interest rate. We continue the process from $T - 1$ to $T - 2$ and so on until we obtain the value of the call at contract origination.[7]

FIGURE 11–7   Lattice of Stock Prices

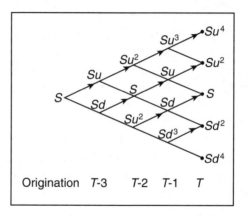

The power of the binomial model is that it can deal with a range of different assets or options or market conditions. Consequently, it has been widely used to value American-style options and to value more complex options.

One of the most widely discussed uses of the binomial option pricing model is in the valuation of interest rate options. Early on, either the Black-Scholes model or Black's futures model was used to value bond options. The users recognized that there are two problems with using these models: (1) the Black-Scholes and Black models assume that interest rates are constant, an assumption clearly at variance with pricing an option on bond prices; (2) the Black-Scholes and Black models assume that volatility is constant; but, for interest rates, volatility declines as maturity increases—as the bond approaches maturity, volatility tends toward zero.

The first binomial pricing model designed to deal with interest rate options was that proposed by Richard Rendleman and Brit Bartter in 1979. They use a single-parameter model to describe the term structure, a model that assumes that the risk-free rate grows at a constant rate and has a constant volatility.

Many of the interest rate option pricing models that followed Rendleman-Bartter could be solved via a binomial technique. But they aren't *really* binomial option pricing models; they are more term structure models applied to option pricing. It is hoped that this point will become more clear when we discuss the evolution of models to value interest rate options, a little later in this section.

The Finite Difference Methodology

This approach was first suggested by Eduardo Schwartz in 1977 and was extended by Georges Courtadon in 1982.

This methodology is based on finding a numerical solution to the differential equation that the option valuation must satisfy—that is, the differential equation is converted into a set of difference equations, and the difference equations are solved iteratively. However, it is probably useful to employ the insight provided by Michael Brennan and Eduardo Schwartz and think of this methodology as a *trinomial lattice* approach. In 1990, John Hull and Alan White provided a modification that ensures that the trinomial lattice methodology converges to the solution of the underlying differential equation.

Monte Carlo Simulations

The problem faced in option pricing is that the value of an option is determined by the *expected value* of the underlying asset at expiration of the option. So far, we have reviewed three different ways of dealing with this expected value: analytical models like the Black-Scholes model and the models that followed were based on specifying and solving a stochastic differential equation. The lattice models avoided the requirement to solve a stochastic differential equation by specifying a particular process for the underlying asset price (a binomial process) and then using an iterative approach to solve for the value of the option. The finite difference methodology involves replacing the differential equation with a series of difference equations.

In 1977, Phelim Boyle proposed a simulation methodology. This method uses the fact that the distribution of asset values at option expiration is determined by the process that generates future movements in the value of the asset. If this process can be specified, it can be simulated on a computer. Each time this simulation is done, a terminal asset value is generated. If this simulation process is done several times—make that several thousand times—the result is a distribution of terminal asset values from which one can directly extract the expected asset value at option expiration.

The finite difference method and the Monte Carlo simulation lines complete the numerical models *tribe*. The complete genealogy for this tribe is illustrated in Figure 11–8.

Aside

Evolution of Models to Value Interest Rate Options

As we noted, when OTC dealers first began making markets in interest rate options (primarily caps and floors), they used a Black-Scholes model to value the options. However, since the relevant underlying interest rate is a forward rate, not a spot rate, the dealers soon changed to a Black model.

However, the Black model still presumes that interest rates are fixed—a presumption at odds with the facts if one is valuing options on interest rates. This led some market makers to switch to binomial models like the Rendleman-Bartter model described earlier. But the problem was that such models considered a single stochastic interest rate, while in fact the forward rate is determined by the term structure, rather than a single interest rate.

In 1986, Thomas Ho and Sang-Bin Lee provided a model that considers changes in the whole term structure rather than just changes in an interest rate. The Ho-Lee option pricing model incorporated the term structure model developed by Cox, Ingersoll, and Ross (1985) which permits nonconstant volatilities and thereby processes like mean reversion.* In the Ho-Lee model each node of the lattice represents a set of discount bond prices and the tree is constructed so that it reflects bond prices observed in the market. However, like the Rendleman-Bartter model, it requires that all interest rates have the same volatility—all spot interest rates and all forward interest rates are equally variable.

The next step in the evolution was to incorporate volatility. The model proposed by Fischer Black, Emanuel Derman, and William Toy in 1990 expanded on the Ho-Lee model by specifying a time-varying structure for volatility—i.e., $\sigma(t)$. And since the Black-Derman-Toy model uses a declining volatility curve, it incorporates mean reversion. The model proposed by John Hull and Alan White (1990) permits the future volatilities of short rates to be set independently from those for long rates. The Hull-White model incorporates not only a time-varying structure for volatility—$\sigma(t)$—but also another time-varying function—$\varphi(t)$—which permits the future variability of short interest rates to be set independently of other data.

The most recent step in the evolutionary process is the model proposed by David Heath, Robert Jarrow, and Andrew Morton (1992). This model considers the stochastic behavior of the forward interest rate, rather than the spot rate as in the preceding models. Moreover, the Heath-Jarrow-Morton model is a generalization of the Ho-Lee, Black-Derman-Toy, and Hull-White models.

Black-Scholes (1973)

|

Cap and floor values determined by forward, rather than spot, rates

↓

Black (1976)

|

Incorporate variable, rather than fixed, interest rates

↓

Rendelman-Bartter (1979)

|

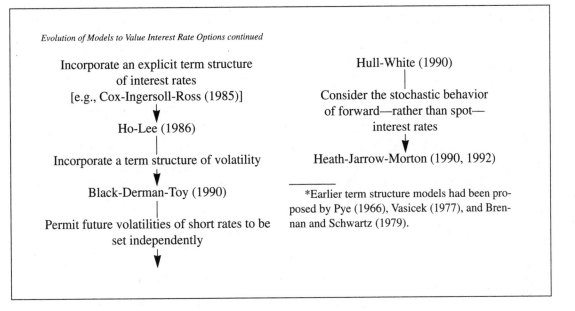

Evolution of Models to Value Interest Rate Options continued

Incorporate an explicit term structure
of interest rates
[e.g., Cox-Ingersoll-Ross (1985)]

↓

Ho-Lee (1986)

Incorporate a term structure of volatility

↓

Black-Derman-Toy (1990)

Permit future volatilities of short rates to be
set independently

↓

Hull-White (1990)

Consider the stochastic behavior
of forward—rather than spot—
interest rates

Heath-Jarrow-Morton (1990, 1992)

―――――――

*Earlier term structure models had been pro-
posed by Pye (1966), Vasicek (1977), and Brennan and Schwartz (1979).

FIGURE 11–8   The Numerical Models

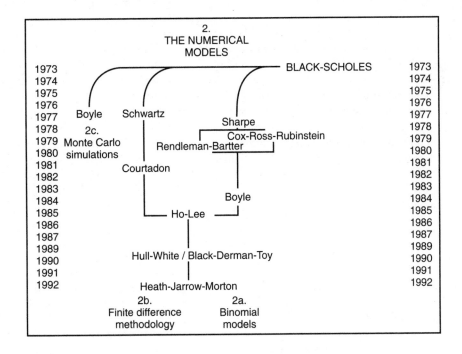

2.
THE NUMERICAL
MODELS

The Analytic Approximation Models

Stretching the analogy of a family tree one more time, we might say that this tribe represents a reunification of the other two tribes. The analytic approximation technique involves estimating the premium for early exercise (using a numerical technique) and then adding this premium to the price of a European option (obtained from an analytical model).

Lionel Macmillan originally suggested valuing options using a quadratic approximation approach in 1986. The approach was implemented by Giovanni Barone-Adesi and Robert Whaley in 1987. This approach has been used to value American calls and puts on stocks, stock indexes, currencies, and futures contracts.

The Family Tree

We have talked about a lot of option pricing models. However, there is yet one more group of models we should point out to you. As we alluded to as we began this chapter, there were some *precursors* to the Black-Scholes model.

Aside

Precursors to the Black-Scholes Model

The earliest attempt we know of to provide an analytical valuation for options was in Louis Bachelier's doctoral dissertation at the Sorbonne in 1900. Bachelier posited that share prices follow an arithmetic (rather than geometric) Brownian Motion process leading to a normal distribution of share returns. While Bachelier was on the right track, the process Bachelier used to generate share prices would permit both negative security prices and option prices that exceed the price of the underlying asset, the formulation required risk neutrality, and no time value of money was included.

Case Sprenkle (1964) dealt with two of the problems in Bachelier's formulation. He assumed that stock prices are lognormally distributed and allowed drift in the random walk (thereby ruling out negative security prices and permitting risk aversion). To give you some idea how close Sprenkle came, following is Sprenkle's model written as a modification of the Black-Scholes model:

$$C = e^{\rho T} S * N\left\{\frac{\ln(\frac{S}{X}) + (\rho + \frac{\sigma^2}{2})T}{\sigma\sqrt{T}}\right\} - (1 - z) e^{\rho T} X * N\left\{\frac{\ln(\frac{S}{X}) + (\rho - \frac{\sigma^2}{2})T}{\sigma\sqrt{T}}\right\}$$

Precursors to the Black-Scholes Model continued

where ρ is the average rate of growth of the share price and z is the degree of risk aversion.[8]

James Boness (1964) went a step beyond Sprenkle by including the time value of money—i.e., he discounted the expected terminal stock price back to the present using the expected rate of return to the stock.

Paul Samuelson (1965) extended Boness's model by permitting the option to have a different level of risk than does the stock. To show how close these precursors to Black-Scholes had come, we can write this specification as a modification of the Black-Scholes equation,

$$C \overset{e^{(\rho-\omega)T}}{=} S * N\left\{\frac{1(\frac{S}{X}) + (\overset{\rho}{*} + \frac{\sigma^2}{2})T}{\sigma\sqrt{T}}\right\} - e^{\overset{\omega}{-*T}}X * N\left\{\frac{\ln(\frac{S}{X}) + (\overset{\rho}{*} - \frac{\sigma^2}{2})T}{\sigma\sqrt{T}}\right\}$$

where ρ is the average rate of growth of the share price and w is the average rate of growth in the value of the call.

If we combine Figures 11–6 and 11–8 and then add the "genealogies" for the analytic approximation models and the precursors, we get the family tree illustrated in Figure 11–9. This family tree illustrates graphically what we said at the outset—the Black-Scholes model is both the beginning and the end of the story.

However, even this complex family tree is incomplete. We noted earlier that we did not include Margrabe's model for the valuation of the option to exchange one asset for another and Stulz's valuation model for an option on the minimum or the maximum of two risky assets. The 1990s have witnessed expansion in the use of these options—the so-called multifactor options. We will return to a consideration of these options in Chapter 13.

Notes

1. The riskless hedge could also be created with a short position in the stock and a long position in the call. Note that the above restriction is placed on the ratio Q_s/Q_c; it makes no difference which asset is short.
2. In general, for the solution of a partial differential equation (a differential equation that is a function of more than one variable) one boundary condition is required for each dimension. Equation 11–10 is the boundary condition in the time dimension. In the stock price dimension, the boundary condition is that the call price is zero if the stock price is zero. However, because it is explicitly assumed that the call price is lognormally distributed, the stock price cannot be zero, the boundary condition will never be binding, and therefore in this special case the boundary condition can be ignored.

FIGURE 11–9   **The Family Tree of Option Pricing Models**

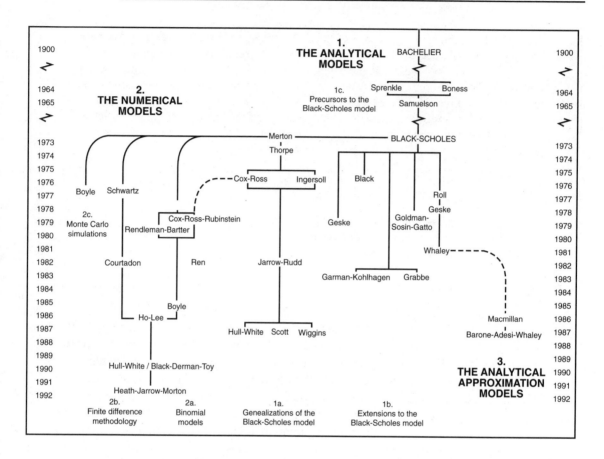

3. See Friedman (1975), especially page 148, for a mathematical proof of the solution technique.

4. As long as individuals are risk-neutral.

5. This description of the jump-diffusion model is adapted from Hull (1989) at pages 312–13 and 323–24.

6. Hull (1989), pp. 131–33.

7. The line I call "the binomial model line" can also include trinomial models. Phelim Boyle (1986) was the first to suggest replacing the binomial tree with a trinomial tree to obtain a more efficient valuation algorithm.

8. Indeed, Fischer Black mentioned that he and Myron Scholes used Sprenkle's paper to get the solution to their system of equations.

12

APPLICATIONS
OF OPTIONS

A firm may elect to purchase an option instead of using forwards, futures, or swaps for several reasons. First, the most that can ever be lost is the price paid for the option, but increases in the underlying financial price will be reflected in the value of the option. Consequently, many firms choose options because they wish to remain in a position to benefit if the financial price goes their way. Second, options are highly flexible tools for designing hedges or targeting investment objectives. With options, it is easy to buy the protection you need and sell off coverage you do not need. And because such tailored hedges can be constructed by combining relatively standardized products, the hedge usually can be reconfigured if information about the size or timing of the underlying exposure changes or if changes in the company's risk management policy require more or less coverage. Third, options can be purchased either on an exchange or over-the-counter, so the end user has considerable flexibility in the choice of marketplace.

Users sell options as well as purchase them. Selling calls generates a premium that can be kept in the event that the underlying instrument declines or remains unchanged. A firm might choose to sell a call option as an alternative to selling a forward contract or a futures or to entering into a swap. However, if I sell a call option, I face unlimited potential risk—in the same way as I do if I use forwards, futures, or swaps—but my gain is limited to the price received for the option—unlike forwards, futures, or swaps.

In this chapter, we examine several ways that options are being used. So far, we have seen how financial price risk can be managed using forwards, futures, or swaps. Options are another important weapon in the risk manager's arsenal. But unlike forwards, futures, or swaps, options provide the end user with protection against adverse movements in a financial price without forgoing completely the advantages from a favorable movement in the financial price.

Before we turn to the various ways that options are used to manage interest rate, foreign exchange rate, commodity price, and equity price risk, it might be useful to look at levels of activity in the options markets.

Activity Levels in the Option Markets

Exchange-Traded Options

Table 12–1 provides data on the volume of options traded on U.S. exchanges in 1995 and 1996.

TABLE 12–1   Trading Volume for Exchange-Traded Options in the United States

Commodity Group	1995	1996
Interest rates	3,683,086	3,702,403
Foreign currency/indexes	440,829	404,474
Energy products	627,063	698,111
Precious metals	3,201	8,765
Nonprecious metals	5,115	5,574
Total	4,759,294	4,819,327

SOURCE: Futures Industry Association.

In Chapter 7, we saw that the 1987 crash in the equity market caused a dramatic and long-lived decline in activity on futures on equity indexes in the United States. Figure 12–1 traces activity in options on equity indexes in the United States. There was a sharp decline in 1988. But the number of contracts traded exceeded the 1987 level in 1992 and has continued to increase.

Over-the-Counter Options

Volume data on OTC interest rate caps, floors, and combinations are provided in Table 12–2. As was the case with interest rate swaps, volumes continue to rise.

FIGURE 12–1   Exchange-Traded Equity Index Derivatives

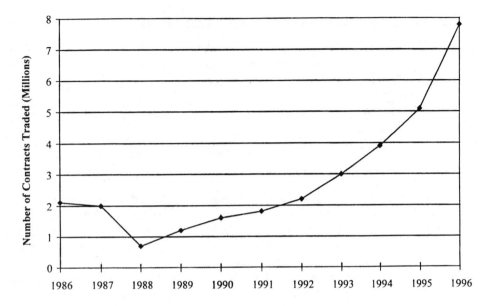

SOURCE: Futures Industry Association.

TABLE 12–2   Caps, Floors, and Specialized Combinations,* 1989–1995 (Notional Principal in Billions of U.S Dollars)

	1989	1990	1991	1992	1993	1994	1995	1H 1996†
Caps								
U.S. dollar	177	251	225	232	428	486	1,275	1,052
Non-U.S. dollar	77	68	92	105	214	320	731	1,140
Subtotal	253	319	317	337	642	806	2,006	2,192
Floors								
U.S. dollar	54	76	73	62	131	172	447	656
Non-U.S. dollar	32	34	56	76	157	179	335	428
Subtotal	86	110	129	138	288	351	782	1,084
Specialized Combinations								
U.S. dollar	35	33	13	14	43	38	84	100
Non-U.S. dollar	4	5	10	18	14	32	68	48
Subtotal	39	38	22	32	57	70	152	148
Total	**378**	**467**	**468**	**507**	**987**	**1,227**	**2,940**	

*"Specialized combinations" include collars, participations, and options on caps/floors.
†Outstandings as of June 30, 1996.
SOURCE: International Swaps and Derivatives Association and Bank for International Settlements.

Using Options to Manage Interest Rate Risk

A firm funded with floating-rate debt is usually concerned about the possibility of rising interest rates. To protect against this, the firm could buy a call option on the relevant interest rate—an *interest rate cap*.[1] If rates rise, gains on the cap would offset the increased costs of borrowing. If, instead, rates fall, the firm would still be able to take advantage of the lower borrowing costs. The price of this protection is the premium paid for the cap. Often, the choice between locking in a rate via a swap and "insuring" against future rate increases is made on the basis of the firm's view about the level of rates.[2]

> By 1989, Falcon Cable had grown to be the 15th largest multiple system cable operator, with 800,000 subscriptions serving 500 small to medium-sized communities. To continue its aggressive expansion, Falcon had expanded its borrowings—between 1989 and 1990, total borrowings increased 41 percent. Consequently, interest rate risk became an important concern.
>
> Falcon fixes a substantial portion of its debt through interest rate swaps. It manages its remaining interest rate risk with caps and collars.
>
> In 1990, the company evaluated the relative benefits of using swaps or caps to hedge $35 million of a $70 million variable-rate loan. At the time, the yield curve was positively sloped—three-year Treasury rates were 8.75 percent and five-year rates were 9.02 percent. A three-year swap would have left Falcon with a 12.60 percent fixed rate at a time when its borrowing rates were 11 percent.
>
> The company's view was that rates were relatively high. So Falcon chose to "insure against" further increases in interest rate risk with a cap—and pay the up-front premium—rather than to enter into a swap—and lock in what the firm viewed as a high fixed rate.

While most firms have a continuous interest rate exposure, some retailers have more seasonal borrowing needs. These firms go from net borrowers in the spring and summer to net investors after the peak Christmas selling season. An option strategy can be constructed that caps such a firm's short exposure in the spring and, if desired, puts a floor on the firm's long position in January. One of the most widely cited such transactions was the seasonal hedge constructed for L. L. Bean.[3]

> L. L. Bean, the clothing and outdoor equipment retailer based in Freeport, Maine, is a seasonal borrower. As do other retailers like Sears, F. W. Woolworth, and Mattel Toys, L. L. Bean relies on borrowings to expand inventories before the critical fourth quarter. Consequently, L. L. Bean faces the risk that interest rates will rise in spring or summer, when they need capital most.
>
> L. L. Bean constructed a three-year seasonal interest rate cap on its annual borrowing costs. The hedge was designed specifically to be seasonal because the company only wanted to hedge interest expense during its peak borrowing season—the summer, when it builds up inventory for the Christmas ordering season.

Interest rate floors—put options on interest rates—can be used to hedge natural long exposures to interest rates. A company that holds a floating-rate asset has just such an exposure to interest rates. If short-term rates fall, then the income received from this asset will also fall. As the following example illustrates, the company could hedge this exposure with an interest rate floor.[4]

> First Union Bank, a regional bank in the southeastern United States, uses derivatives to actively manage the interest rate risk inherent in its investments.
>
> In 1991, First Union bought a five-year interest rate floor giving it the right to receive 6.5 percent minus three-month LIBOR on a notional principal of $1 billion. First Union paid a $3 million premium for the floor. The floor protected the earnings on First Union Bank's assets from a decline in interest rates.
>
> By February 1992, in fact, interest rates had fallen so far that the value of First Union's floor was $30 million. The floor offset, in part, the reduced earnings on its investments over the life of the floor.

Caps and floors can be sold as well as purchased. Interest rate options might be sold and the premium received used to reduce the cost of funding the firm or to increase the yield on an investment.

For example, a firm with a floating-rate asset might choose to sell an interest rate cap to boost yield. The asset owner collects a premium from the sale of the cap, but in return effectively agrees to "cap" the interest rate it receives on the floating-rate asset. If the floating interest rate remains unchanged or falls, the premium received on the sale of the cap acts as a "supplement" to the asset owner's interest income. However, if the floating rate rises above the cap rate, the asset owner forgoes interest income that "might have been."

Resuming an example he began in Chapter 7, Ira Kawaller takes us through the process a treasurer might use to decide whether to hedge the interest rate risk of a prospective borrowing by selling a futures contract or buying an interest rate cap—or selling an interest rate floor.

Buying and selling caps and floors are the four basic hedging strategies for interest rate options. However, instead of using a single instrument, many firms use combinations of these to achieve specific hedging objectives.

Consider a firm using floating-rate lines of credit to fund operations. The firm might want to cap its exposure to higher rates but views the premium for the cap as "too expensive." By simultaneously selling a floor, the firm collects a premium to offset the cost of the cap.

As we will discuss in more detail in Chapter 14, such a combination of buying a cap and simultaneously selling a floor is called a *collar*. Collars effectively lock in a range for the firm's borrowing costs: the cap sets a maximum possible borrowing rate for the life of the contract, protecting the firm against higher interest rates, while the floor establishes a minimum rate for the firm's borrowing costs.[5]

Risk Management in Practice

To Hedge or Not to Hedge: Part 2

Ira G. Kawaller

In Chapter 7, I introduced Edwin Charles, treasurer of Benzoe Corp.,* who is planning to take down a $10 million loan within the next quarter. (The loan rate will be set at the time of the takedown, at three-month LIBOR plus 100 basis points.) In that earlier example, I considered two strategies:

Strategy 1: Do nothing.

Strategy 2: Lock in an interest rate today by selling Eurodollar futures contracts timed to expire at about the same time as the loan rate is to be set.

Edwin has a third course of action.

Strategy 3: Insure against rising rates.

Buying an interest rate cap or buying puts on Eurodollar futures will accomplish this end. Doing either involves an initial cash outlay, which will vary depending on the level of the cap rate (or strike price), the length of time for which the insurance is required, and the market's collective assessment of prospective volatility. But ultimately, if the market rate for LIBOR is higher than the cap rate (or the futures price is lower than the strike price of the put option), the final value of the cap will compensate for the market rate being higher than the ceiling rate. This strategy may sound like the most attractive one—until Edwin goes to write the check for the desired protection.

As before, the strategy that performs best depends on the state of the environment; each alternative hedge strategy should be assessed in light of its cost versus its potential benefits or consequences. Using futures means forgoing the benefit of lower spot market interest rates. The consequence of purchases of options is the forgone premium when interest rates decline.

To evaluate the three strategies, again consider the environment used in Chapter 7: suppose, for example, that today three-month LIBOR is at 7.00 percent and that the Eurodollar futures contract is currently priced at 92.90 (that is, at a rate of 7.10 percent). Now, suppose that the price of a put option on Eurodollar futures with a strike price of 93.00 (7.00 percent) is 0.40. The following table considers two scenarios—one in which three-month LIBOR rises to 8 percent and the other in which three-month LIBOR falls to 6 percent.

To Hedge or Not to Hedge: Part 2 continued

Hedge Strategies	1. Do Nothing	2. Sell Futures	3. Buy Puts
Scenario I: Spot LIBOR rises to 8.00%			
Interest paid to banker (based on 9.00%)	$225,000	$225,000	$225,000
P&L on hedge (10 contracts × price change of hedge vehicle)	NA	22,500	15,000
Net interest	225,000	202,500	210,000
Effective rate	9.00%	8.10%	8.40%
Scenario II: Spot LIBOR falls to 6.00%			
Interest paid to banker (based on 7.00%)	$175,000	$175,000	$175,000
P&L on hedge (10 contracts × price change of hedge vehicle)	NA	(27,500)	(10,000)
Net interest	175,000	202,500	185,000
Effective rate	7.00%	8.10%	7.40%

If Mr. Charles does nothing, the cost of funds will simply be equal to spot LIBOR plus 100 basis points—7.00 percent or 9.00 percent. If Mr. Charles sells futures, he locks in a rate of 100 basis points above the initial futures rate—8.10 percent. (Note again that this example assumes perfect convergence of spot and futures rates at the time the hedge is liquidated.) Buying puts guarantees a worst case of 8.40 percent in this example (100.00 percent − 93.00 percent + 1.00 percent + 0.40 percent), with the potential benefit of lower costs if interest rates decline.

Note, however, that Mr. Charles could create his own "middle ground" by combining bits and pieces of the different alternatives. Edwin could deal with the expense of buying insurance protection by "selling off" some of his potential benefits. For example, he could buy a cap that protects against LIBOR rising above, say, 7 percent and simultaneously sell a cap that protects against LIBOR rising above 8 percent. That is, once rates exceed the higher cap level (8 percent), Edwin is again exposed. By doing this combination, the receipts from selling the second cap offset the initial cost—at least partially—of the first cap.

Another common way of mitigating the expense of protection is to sell a floor against a cap. For example, buying a 7 percent cap and selling a 6 percent floor covers Edwin from the risk of rates rising above 7 percent but forces him to forgo the benefit if rates drop below 6 percent. His up-front cost would then be the cost of the cap minus the price of the floor.

To Hedge or Not to Hedge: Part 2 continued

So what should Edwin do? Strictly speaking, there isn't a "correct" choice, only reasonable actions. Frankly, any treasurer's decision will reflect his or her operating style and corporate investment policies. In a few instances, however, I would recommend the "do nothing" approach. Consistently taking this posture strikes me as shrinking from responsibility because it leaves a firm chronically exposed to interest rate risk. I don't think this approach is reasonable.

From the perspective of hedging with derivative instruments, at a minimum, I think Edwin should either use futures to lock in some portion of his interest rate exposure or buy puts—also on a fractional basis. The choice would largely depend on the implied volatility conditions for the put options at the time of hedging initiation. Most commercial bankers and any institutional broker could give Edwin a reading on the volatility conditions. With low implied volatilities, Edwin should probably opt for puts; with high implied volatilities, he might be better served by selling futures. In the midrange, he should think about buying puts and selling at least some alternative options. If he feels that interest rates probably won't rise very much, he should sell cheaper puts, such as a second cap with a higher ceiling rate than the original cap. If he thinks it more likely that interest rates will go up, he should sell calls.

---

*The people and companies presented here are fictional.

Ira G. Kawaller is vice president–director of the New York office for the Chicago Mercantile Exchange. After receiving a Ph.D. from Purdue University, Mr. Kawaller served at the Federal Reserve Board in Washington. He subsequently worked for the AT&T Company and J. Aron Company, Inc. Mr. Kawaller currently serves on the board of directors of the National Option & Futures Society and the board of advisors for the International Association of Financial Engineers. Mr. Kawaller is the author of *Financial Futures & Options* (Probus).

This example reprinted with permission from the Fall 1992 issue of *Treasury and Risk Management.* © 1992 CFO Publishing Corp.

Muzak, the well-known provider of office music, used a two-year collar when it refinanced term floating-rate debt in 1990. Muzak was looking for insurance against sharply higher rates. However, in order to reduce the cost of the interest rate cap, Muzak sold a floor at the same time. Muzak's interest costs can still vary through several hundred basis points up or down, but the firm is protected from catastrophic rate increases.

In Chapter 10 you saw that in-the-money options cost more than out-of-the-money options. In the OTC market, interest rate options can be bought or sold at any strike price. Because of this flexibility, a popular hedging strategy is to create a so-called zero-cost collar.

A zero-cost collar is created by varying the strike prices of the cap purchased and the floor sold so that the income received from the sale of the floor exactly matches the cost of the call. Zero-cost collars are popular because they provide the firm with interest rate protection at no out-of-pocket expense.

There may be instances in which relying on bank credit facilities is more cost-efficient than issuing equity capital or public debt. The availability of interest rate options makes it easier for firms to take advantage of bank debt when the form and structure of borrowing needs is of concern to the firm. Bank debt is most often floating-rate debt; but by utilizing zero-cost interest rate collars, the firm can effectively limit the maximum interest rate and cost of the debt.[6]

> Revolving credit lines are part of the everyday mix of funding sources for a corporation. These credit lines typically allow a corporation to borrow up to a fixed limit at a floating interest rate.
>
> In 1991, Applied Power, Inc., used its $200 million revolving credit facility to finance an acquisition, consolidate outstanding liabilities, and refinance existing long-term fixed-rate debt. Not wanting to remain exposed to floating interest rates, Applied Power then hedged its resulting exposure with zero-cost interest rate collars.
>
> Borrowings under the line of credit were priced at a floating rate equal to either the bank's reference rate or to LIBOR plus 1 percent. After drawing on its credit facility, Applied Power hedged $120 million of the debt with interest rate collars—it bought interest rate caps with an average cap rate of 9.5 percent and sold interest rate floors with an average floor rate of 7.75 percent. When it subsequently reduced its borrowings, Applied Power sold back some of its interest rate collars to keep its hedge in line with its falling debt level.

The decision whether to use a cap or collar often depends on prevailing market conditions as well as the company's specific hedging objectives. Caps—call options on forward interest rates—get more expensive as the yield curve steepens (that is, as the forward rates rise) and as the volatility of the underlying interest rate increases. Market conditions may lead the company to want to change the extent or structure of its hedge. The flexibility afforded by options gives the hedger the ability to modify an existing hedge with subsequent options trades. A company that originally purchased a cap for protection can create a collar by selling a floor sometime in the future when market conditions are more favorable.[7]

Aside

Hartmarx Corporation

Hartmarx Corporation is the nation's largest manufacturer and retailer of men's tailored clothing. The Chicago-based company manufactures some three million suits a year under such well-known lines as Hart Schaffner and Marx, Kuppenheimer, Pierre Cardin, and Austin Reed.

Hartmarx Corporation continued

In the late 1980s, Hartmarx began expanding operations through mergers and acquisitions and by opening new retail stores, financing new inventory with short-term borrowings. As a result, its bank loans rose from $57 million in 1987 to $267 million in 1989, leading Hartmarx to become concerned about its exposure to interest rate risk.

The company considered several options. It could, for instance, replace its current short-term debt with long-term borrowings. Alternatively, it could enter into a pay-fixed/receive-floating swap, effectively locking in a fixed rate. The third alternative was an interest rate cap or collar.

Several concerns entered into the decision about which was the best hedging strategy to pursue. First, both the long-term borrowing and the swap would lock the company into a long-term rate that the company believed to be unattractive. Second, the firm expected its borrowing needs to decline over time and did not want to lock itself into a long-term rate, only to later decide it had overborrowed. These factors led Hartmarx to conclude that a flexible hedging strategy, using caps, floors, and collars, was the most appropriate mechanism to serve its needs.

Early in 1989, Hartmarx bought a $50 million interest rate cap. This was meant to serve as a straightforward "insurance policy" in light of rising interest rates. By October 1989, the yield curve inverted—short-term rates were higher than long-term rates. Because of this, the price of interest rate floor contracts rose. Hartmarx was able to receive a higher premium for the sale of an interest rate floor than it would have received in the beginning of the year when it first established the hedge.

Having thus bought a cap and sold a floor—although at different times—Hartmarx had created a "costless" collar. Its borrowing costs were capped at the then-current rate of 8.75 percent, and an interest rate floor was established at 7.5 percent. As a result, Hartmarx had no upside exposure on the hedged amount and would benefit from any fall in rates down to 7.5 percent.

Hartmarx established five such collar transactions for a total hedge of $125 million, about half of its total short-term borrowings. Because of its advantageous timing, the 8.75 percent ceiling was about 125 basis points lower than it would have had to pay on a long-term borrowing.

Going the other way, a firm with a collar can buy back the floor to leave it with a cap only. It might decide to do this, for instance, if it wishes to regain the opportunity to benefit from subsequent declines in interest rates.

Using Options to Manage Foreign Exchange Rate Risk

Most corporate hedging of foreign exchange risk is of "firm commitments"—both the timing and the amount to be hedged are known. A company that contracts to deliver goods overseas on particular delivery dates for a specified amount of foreign

Illustration 12–1

Constructing a Currency Hedge*

Suppose that a U.S. food products firm contracted to sell DM19 million worth of goods to a German supermarket chain over the next year. Delivery of the goods and payment in deutsche marks will take place on the 15th of March, June, September, and December.

If the current exchange rate is $0.59 per DM, this firm knows it has roughly $2.8 million worth of receivables coming to it each quarter for the next year. If it does nothing and the mark weakens, then the revenue from the contract, once translated into dollars, may fall enough to make the deal unprofitable.

Consider the following three strategies:

1. The firm can buy at-the-money puts with a strike price of $0.59 per DM. This will hedge the firm completely, but is the most expensive hedge.

2. The firm can buy out-of-the-money puts—for example, with a strike price of $0.57 per DM. This will cost the company less, but will leave the company exposed to possible losses in the range of a dollar appreciation between $0.59 and $0.57 per DM.

3. The company could lock in a range over which the currency is allowed to fluctuate, but outside which the firm is fully hedged. For example, the firm could buy a put with a strike price of $0.58 and sell a call with a strike price of $0.60.†

Each quarter the company receives (DM19 million)/4—or DM4.75 million. Because the

identical transaction will take place four times on four distinct dates, let's examine how the company might manage the foreign exchange exposure of the first transaction. Subsequent transactions could be hedged identically or by another strategy.

The company could hedge by matching the amount of foreign currency it will receive with the size of the option contract. For instance, if the firm uses the currency option contract traded on the Philadelphia Stock Exchange that delivers into DM62,500, the hedge would be DM4.75 million/DM 62,500 = 76 contracts.

Strategy 1 involves purchasing 76 at-the-money put option contracts at the Philadelphia Stock Exchange with a strike price of $0.59. The cost of this option is, say, $0.0188 per unit of currency, making the total cost of the hedge

$$76 \times 0.0188 \times 62,500 = \$89,300$$

Strategy 2 involves purchasing 76 out-of-the-money puts with a strike price of $0.57. This option might cost roughly 0.0090 per unit of currency, so the total cost of the hedge would be

$$76 \times 0.0090 \times 62,500 = \$42,750$$

In strategy 3, we buy a somewhat out-of-the-money put with a strike price of $0.58 and sell an out-of-the-money call with a strike price of $0.60. The price of these options would be about 0.0135 and 0.0072 per unit of currency, respectively. So the total cost of the hedge is

---

Constructing a Currency Hedge* continued

Cost of put

$$76 \times 0.0135 \times 62{,}500 = \$64{,}125$$

Less price of call

$$76 \times 0.0072 \times 62{,}500 = \$34{,}200$$

Total cost of hedge $= \$29{,}925$

---

*This example was constructed by Gregory Greiff.

†As we will note in Chapter 14, such a structure is called a *range forward.*

---

currency is just such an example. If this company decides to hedge with options, it could use the strategies described above. There is no "right answer" as to which of these three strategies the company should choose to hedge. Each offers a different level of protection at a different cost.

Moreover, the company is not limited to just these three strategies. The company can choose any strike price it wants; each strike price offers the company a different level of protection at a different cost.

The company could also choose different combinations of options; for instance, the company could buy an at-the-money put and sell an out-of-the-money put. This would give the firm protection down to a certain level (the level at which the lower strike was sold), but no more, so if the currency went below the lower strike, the company would not be protected against further falls.

Another strategy is for the company to scale down its protection by buying options at different strike prices. For instance, instead of buying all 76 options at one strike price (at-the-money options), the firm could instead buy 19 puts with a strike price of $0.59, 19 puts with a strike price of $0.585, 19 puts with a strike price of $0.58, and 19 puts with a strike price of $0.575. This strategy would give a kind of "intermediate" protection when compared with the strategy of buying all at-the-money options versus all out-of-the-money options. The cost of the hedge would be intermediate too. (Note that the company could sell calls in much the same way in strategy 3; this would generate less revenue but more potential for upside gain than the strategy detailed above.)

The great advantage of options is that they allow this type of flexibility, giving the firm the opportunity to choose the level of protection it needs at a cost it is willing to pay.

So far, we have confined ourselves to hedging transaction exposures. As we noted in earlier chapters, foreign exchange risk often takes on strategic dimensions, impacting on the firm's ability to compete effectively with overseas rivals. Hence, the firm's risk management policies should be directly related to its sales and marketing policies.

Options give corporations the added flexibility to manage risk in a way that makes it easier to pursue broader strategic considerations.[8]

Applied Biosystems, a California-based manufacturer of instruments and chemicals for life sciences research, believes that pricing goods in local currency is part of keeping international customers satisfied. Applied Biosystems is rather unusual in that few companies of its size—annual sales totaled just $163.9 million in 1991—deal with management of foreign exchange risk in order to pursue this "dual-currency" pricing strategy. Central is the idea that providing stable, long-term pricing is key to keeping customers in highly competitive markets and to building shareholder value.

Initially, Applied Biosystem's foreign exchange risk management program was designed to protect its balance sheet, using forwards to lock in the dollar value of its receivables. As the company became more concerned about the strengthening dollar, however, it began to use options to hedge, and it began to revise its risk management policies. Risk management moved beyond hedging specific items related to the long-term delivery of product, either to or from the company, to a broader strategy of protecting operating margins. The company uses options to hedge projected sales volume, based on a long history of sales in these countries. The idea is to lock in a floor so that no matter how far the dollar strengthens, the company's operating margin was protected.

To do this, the company first determined its risk tolerance levels—that is, the point above which the dollar's strengthening would be unacceptable. Then the company purchased out-of-the-money options. Applied Biosystems considered anything beyond a 5 percent currency change to be detrimental to its operating margin. Thus, it purchased options that were 5 percent out-of-the-money. Purchasing out-of-the-money options also reduced its premium costs to no more than 0.5 percent of international sales.

Using Options to Manage Commodity-Price Risk

The concerns that motivate firms to manage interest rate and foreign exchange rate risk also exist for commodity-price exposures. Energy and metals represent some of the basic inputs to manufacturing and service industries. Uncertainties in the prices of these basic inputs can interfere with management's ability to price and market finished goods. Fluctuations in costs can also lead to undesirable fluctuations in a company's cash flow and profitability over time, which can in turn lead to additional problems, such as higher costs of credit.

Consider a company with a long-term contract to supply a finished product at a fixed price. Rising input costs would cut into the firm's margin. By locking in the cost of its production inputs, the firm is in a better position to protect this margin. If the firm could not lock in its costs in this way, it might be unwilling to enter into a long-term supply relationship. This could prevent the company from capturing profitable business if customers—who are also looking to fix their costs—prefer long-term arrangements to minimize their risks. Even if customers did not have such strong preferences, the willingness to enter into such a contract might prove to be a competitive advantage in competition with other firms.

Tour operators in the UK, who started hedging their exposures to fuel costs, are finding that they can use this situation to their advantage, both in marketing their services and in competing with other firms.[9]

> The negative publicity that resulted when tour operators imposed surcharges to cover unexpected increases in fuel prices (not to mention pressure from UK regulators) led some of Europe's largest airlines and tour operators to begin taking a more active approach to hedging their jet fuel exposure. Thomson, a tour operator and airline owner, offered its customers a no-surcharge guarantee on holidays booked for the next year. Thomson hedged its exposure through a series of jet fuel cap agreements covering its entire fuel requirement.
>
> International Leisure Group and Sitmar, a cruise company, also entered the oil derivatives market through a series of swaps and caps.

Many firms use options to lock in a margin between operating costs and selling prices. Small firms, or those in financial distress, may be required to hedge some or all of their exposures by their banks or other creditors. Decreasing the probability of bankruptcy and its incumbent costs increases the value of the firm. Thus, the firm that hedges away such exposures can be expected to have access to capital at lower costs. Even financially healthy firms can benefit in this way by hedging away unnecessary risks.

All of the option strategies available for hedging interest and foreign exchange rate risk apply equally well to hedging commodity-price risk. Firms might simply buy puts or calls, or they might use strategies involving combinations of options.[10] The firm might decide to "spread" options—for example, a firm might decide to buy a call option at one strike and then sell a call at a higher strike, a "call spread." Option spreads have several possible advantages:

1. Spreads allow the company to target a range for protection and to precisely tailor the hedge to the underlying exposure or to the company's expectations for movement in the underlying instrument.

2. Spreads allow the company to target the cost of protection. By selling off the right to profit from gains over favorable ranges of price movement, the company can reduce or eliminate the cost of protecting against unfavorable price movements.

3. Spreads allow the company to match its hedging needs with its outlook on the underlying volatility of the market.

Collars, especially zero-cost collars, are a popular strategy. Firms that use collars are often more concerned with reducing the uncertainty associated with volatility in the markets in which they buy and sell than with positioning themselves to take advantage of windfall gains in the event that market prices move favorably. As with any hedging decision, there is no "right answer" as to whether a firm should collar a risk rather than, say, cap it—that will depend on the firm's hedging objectives, market circumstances, and other considerations. But many firms find that collaring a risk enables the company to achieve other objectives laid out in a business plan.

The following two examples illustrate how firms use options for these kinds of business purposes. A firm can use options to keep on track with the objectives laid out in a business plan.[11]

> Qualex, the nation's largest photofinisher, recovers silver as a by-product of its photofinishing operations; more than 100,000 ounces of 99 percent pure silver are collected each month and sold to refiners at the spot market price. Because receipts from silver sales are credited to the firm's cost of goods sold, the company's gross profit is sensitive to fluctuations in silver prices. Qualex thus believes that fixing the price of silver is important to gain control over its business planning.
>
> Qualex uses commodity collars to set a lower limit on the revenue it will receive for its silver. The company originally intended to buy floors. However, since Qualex requires a floor level close to the prevailing market price (to meet its business plan), the premium for such a near-the-money floor was prohibitive. To reduce this cost, the company sold a ceiling at the same time it bought the floor. This means the firm would have to forgo potential windfall profits if silver prices ran up sharply; but the company's primary interest was in protecting its business plan, not speculating on the price of silver.
>
> Moreover, the collar was custom-tailored to meet the seasonal patterns in Qualex's recovery of silver. Because there are peak periods—after Christmas and the summer vacation season—the number of ounces specified in the collar agreement varies from month to month.

Alternatively, a firm can hedge with options to send a signal to prospective investors that it has costs under control.[12]

> The Paducah & Louisville (P&L) Railroad transports coal, chemicals, and aggregates, including stone and clay, on 300 miles of track in western Kentucky. The railroad uses approximately 500,000 gallons of fuel monthly. When the cost of diesel fuel averages around 50 cents a gallon, as it did prior to the invasion of Kuwait, diesel fuel expense makes up about 10 percent of most railroads' operating expenses. Severe cold weather can double fuel expense, as it did in December 1989, when a sudden cold snap boosted fuel oil prices to more than $1 a gallon.
>
> In August 1990, when P&L was preparing to talk to the investment community about plans to raise new equity capital through a public offering, it decided to hedge its exposure to oil price volatility. The Iraqi invasion of Kuwait had sent crude oil prices soaring, and the company wanted to assure public investors that it would not be vulnerable to further increases in diesel fuel prices.
>
> The company hedged its exposure by purchasing a cap on 250,000 gallons per month, about half its normal consumption (the rest of the company's exposure is protected by cost-escalation clauses in contracts with customers).[13] Before selecting a

commodity cap, P&L considered using a swap or collar. In the end, the company viewed the cap as cheap insurance; in addition, it feared that if it sold a floor or swapped into a fixed price, it might put the company at a competitive disadvantage if fuel costs dropped.

State and local governments face risks with respect to their costs and revenues just as much as corporations. Government entities, however, often have less flexibility to respond when they experience a shortfall in revenues or an increase in costs.

Legislatures are understandably reluctant to pass retroactive tax increases when revenues do not meet budgeted levels. Although some entities may go into deficit spending in such circumstances, many are restricted by constitutional or other legal prohibitions requiring a balanced budget.

Other governmental bodies, such as transit authorities, may not be able to raise fares to make up for unexpected cost increases. These agencies are generally charged with providing a long-term, stable price and have little or no room to adjust fares or prices in the short term.

Faced with risks on both the revenue and cost side and with restricted ability to respond by changing price or reducing output (such as temporarily reducing services, such as schools, police and fire protection, etc.), it would seem that governments and governmental agencies would be quite frequent users of risk management products. It turns out that this is not yet true.

Not unexpectedly, the biggest constraint to government use of hedging tools is also political: it is difficult to communicate to constituents the objective of even the most conservative hedging programs or to convince them that use of derivatives is not some kind of "gambling." Most private firms report that convincing a board of directors about the importance of a risk management program is an uphill climb. The task of communicating and informing the public at large—the ultimate board of directors in the political arena—is all the more difficult.

Nonetheless, a number of states and other governmental agencies are testing the waters in this area—cognizant of the advantages of improved planning at the budgeting stage that a sound risk management program can help provide. Massachusetts, New Mexico, New York, Ohio, and Oklahoma all have legislation pending that would allow them to manage their risks. Even the federal Department of Energy is considering using derivatives to manage the nation's strategic oil reserves. In addition, many transit authorities, which are large consumers of fuel, are using, or considering using, derivatives to manage their risks. The following example describes Texas's initial foray into using derivatives to manage the risk that revenues from a 4.6 percent severance tax on every barrel of oil produced will not meet budgeted levels because of fluctuations in the price of oil.[14]

In Texas, a plunge in the price of oil can lead to shortfalls in oil tax revenues, and thus can contribute to unexpected budget deficits and the political crises that accompany them (as it did in 1986–87). Thus, the state has begun to recognize its interests in protecting its income and in stabilizing revenues so as to make the budgeting process less uncertain.

Texas's limited hedging program involves purchasing out-of-the-money puts three months out. The state views this as cheap insurance. The state is also considering OTC alternatives such as swaps and collars.

One option strategy under study in 1992 was a "straddled zero-cost collar." A standard zero-cost collar combines a long out-of-the-money put with a short out-of-the-money call; so, if the price of oil were $22 per barrel, the state could buy a put with a strike price of $20 and sell a call with a strike price of $23.50; the cost of the call would offset the price of the put, and the state would have locked in a range at no out-of-pocket cost.

In a straddled zero-cost collar, the state buys a deep out-of-the-money call on top of the collar to allow it to participate if oil prices undergo a "Texas rally." So, for instance, it could buy a call with a strike price of $25, which would offset the lower $23.50 strike call if prices rise that high. In order to keep the hedge at zero out-of-pocket cost, the state must lower the strike price of the put it buys, say to $19. This would give the state a little less protection on the downside, but it could save it from the political risks if oil prices rise dramatically and the hedge prevents the state from enjoying the benefits.

States that are consumers of energy are also using derivatives to hedge their purchasing costs. States that are exclusively energy consuming, such as Delaware, and municipal transit authorities in Washington, D.C., and Pennsylvania, are already using energy derivatives to manage their budgets. Other states and transit authorities are considering following suit. In many cases, fuel is the single largest purchase made annually. Hedging these costs can aid substantially in the planning process.

Using Options to Manage Equity Price Risk

The obvious users of options to manage equity price risk are investors. However, corporations are also users of equity options.

An increasingly common use of equity options by corporations is as part of a stock repurchase program.[15] Once a firm has decided to repurchase stock, the question is the optimal repurchase technique; and recently many firms have focused significant attention on the sale of put options as an alternative to outright purchase of shares.[16] Indeed, according to James Angel, Gary Gastineau, and Clifford Weber, at least 10 percent of the public companies that repurchase their stock on the open market now sell puts on their shares as part of the repurchase program.

Figure 12–2 illustrates how sales of puts could be used in a share repurchase program. The firm has announced that it plans to repurchase shares at a price of 100; so, effectively the firm has a short position at 100. Suppose that the firm sells a put on its own shares with an exercise price of 95. The purchaser of the put has

---

FIGURE 12–2   Selling Equity Puts as Part of a Share Repurchase Program

---

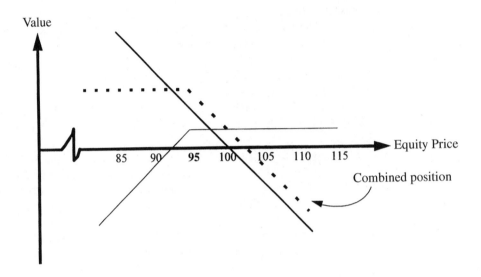

the right to sell the stock to the corporation at the exercise price. If the price of the stock is below 95 at expiration, the option will be exercised and the corporation will buy its stock back. If, however, the stock price rises, the premium earned from selling the put may leave scope for even more stock repurchases.[17]

One reason that corporations sell puts as part of a share repurchase program is because there may be an opportunity to sell puts for more than their fair value. If the market price for puts on the firm's shares reflects a higher level of volatility than management deems likely over the life of the put contract, then the put is "overpriced" and the firm has a possibility of profiting by selling the put.

And selling put options can also provide more flexibility in the timing of stock purchases. Rules of the SEC limit stock purchases by the issuer to 25 percent of the average daily trading volume of its stock.[18] However, selling a put counts against the daily stock volume on the day the put is sold, not on the day it is exercised. Suppose that the management of the firm knows that, at a specified period in the future, it will have the funds to repurchase some of its stock; and suppose further that the volume of trading on the firm's shares is currently high. The firm may want to take advantage of the high volume and sell puts today, with the expectation that cash will be available when the puts mature. In this case, the put represents a kind of "deferred purchase contract" that is designed to match opportunity (i.e., high stock volume) with later cash flow.

Corporations also use equity options as part of merger and acquisitions. The trade press outlined a "sell the asset, keep the risk" strategy employed by the Norwegian construction company Kvaerner to help pay down a debt facility it had used for its acquisition of Trafalgar House. Kvaerner decided to sell its 17 percent stake in the Bergesen shipping group, but was faced with two concerns. First, because the firm was bullish on Bergesen's share price, Kvaerner wanted to retain exposure to it. Second, the firm wanted to avoid the discount that a block trade would entail. To address these concerns, Kvaener turned to a derivatives solution. It sold its Bergesen shares, at their market price, to an investment bank releasing about $300 million in capital. In addition, the firm bought an American-style call option on Bergesen while also selling a put with the same maturity. The put was structured so that it could only be exercised during the period immediately before maturity, and it knocks out if the call is exercised. The precise terms of the transaction were not made public, but the transaction gave Kvaerner exposure to most of Bergesen's share price performance while passing on some of the equity risk to the bank. Furthermore, the proceeds from this deal, together with the sale of another of Kvaerner's cross-holdings, allowed it to repay it acquisition debt.[19]

Corporations use equity options as a way of "monetizing" equity positions. Many individuals and companies hold large equity stakes which they are unwilling to sell in the cash market. It might be the case that the shares are "restricted"—i.e., they cannot be sold for some period of time. Or it might be the case that the sale of shares may trigger taxes which the holder would prefer to defer.

As illustrated in Figure 12–3, the owner of the shares might purchase an equity collar and simultaneously take a loan (collateralized by a pledge of the stock). Since the pledged stock and the put serve as collateral that has a known minimum value at maturity, the dealer will lend a percentage of that amount today. The owner of the shares is able to obtain cash without physically selling shares.

Finally, corporations use equity options to help manage employee stock option programs. The firm could hedge the exposure from already granted and expected future employee stock options by buying call options on its own stock.

Investors use equity options to protect the value of their portfolio and to enhance the portfolio's yield.

As is illustrated in Figure 12–4, the investor could protect the value of the portfolio by purchasing a put. Or as illustrated in Figure 12–5, the investor might elect to use a collar to protect the portfolio.

FIGURE 12–3   "Monetizing" an Equity Position

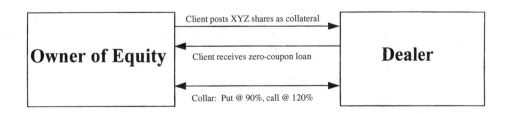

Aside

A Note on U.S. Tax Law Changes

The bull market in U.S. equities in the 1990s led to a substantial amount of monetization activity. This, in turn, led to increased scrutiny by the tax authorities. In the Taxpayer Relief Act of 1997, the U.S. Congress acted on some of the concerns regarding "constructive sales"—transactions that essentially eliminate economic ownership of assets while deferring taxes on gains. Specific techniques such as "short against the box," in which the owner of a stock sells borrowed shares of the same stock, and equity swaps were disallowed. And Congress empowered the Treasury to write regulations to expand the type of transactions to which these new rules apply, but directed that those regulations be applied only prospectively.*

---

*"The Taxpayer Relief Act of 1997," Arthur Anderson LLP, Office of Federal Tax Services, August 1997.

FIGURE 12–4   **Protecting the Portfolio by Buying Puts**

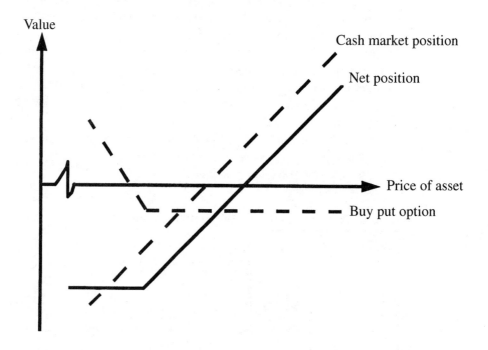

FIGURE 12–5   Protecting the Portfolio via a Collar

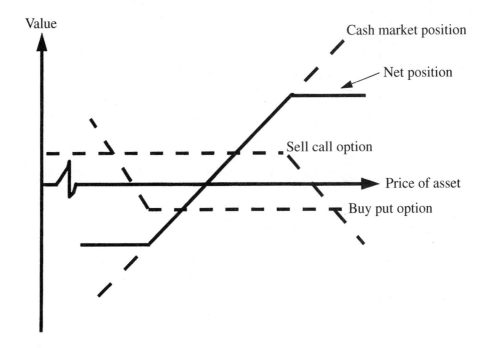

And investors could sell options to enhance yield of portfolio. Figure 12–6 illustrates a strategy where the investor is neither bullish nor bearish on the underlying assets; instead the investor believes that the assets will range trade. Consequently, based on this view, the investor might elect to sell out-of-the-money puts and calls with strikes set outside the perceived trading range.

Using Options to Increase Debt Capacity

In Chapter 15, we will spend some time talking about shareholder-bondholder conflicts that have the effect of reducing the amount of debt a firm can carry—or even limiting the firm's access to debt financing—due to the fact that potential bondholders are concerned that the equityholders of the firm will behave opportunistically. However, at this point it is useful to note that the use of options can manage some of these conflicts and thereby increase the debt capacity of the firm.

Potential bondholders could be concerned that the equityholders could dilute the bondholders' claims by increasing debt or adding debt senior to that held by

FIGURE 12–6   Selling Options to Enhance Yield

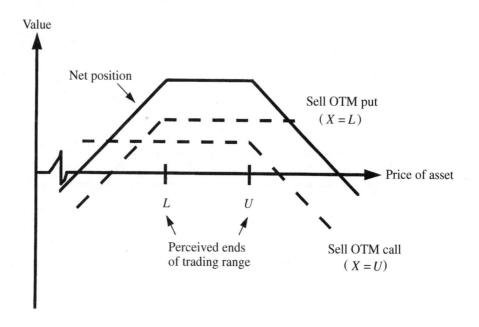

the bondholders in question. Giving bondholders the right to put the bonds back to the issuer—i.e., adding a put option—reduces this problem. If the shareholders attempt to dilute the bondholders' claim, the bondholders have the right to "cash in" their bonds. In this way, we might look at the put as a golden parachute for the bondholders.

Potential bondholders could be concerned that the equityholders could invest in more risky projects. Making the bonds convertible reduces the problem. If the shareholders attempt to expropriate value from the bondholders by investing the proceeds of the debt into more risky investment projects, the bondholders can exercise their option to convert the bonds to equity.

Potential bondholders could be concerned that if income is sufficiently volatile, the firm may pass up positive-NPV projects. Options can be embedded in the debt that will reduce the volatility of the firm's net income, thereby reducing the probability of default. An excellent example of such a construction is the debt issued by Magma Copper in 1988. Magma Copper decreased the volatility of income by attaching copper options to its debt; the result was that potential bondholders were willing to pay more for the bond.

Using Options as a Competitive Tool

When a firm makes an overseas bid, it is confronted with both a high degree of uncertainty about success and, most likely, a need to establish costs and revenues in local currency. The following example shows how a defense firm turned this problem into a competitive advantage by purchasing a cleverly designed over-the-counter option[20]:

> A U.S. defense manufacturer was submitting a bid to sell scientific equipment to a Scandinavian firm. A complicating factor was that payment was to be made in unequal disbursements at six irregularly spaced dates over two years.
>
> The principal competition was a French firm. The U.S. company was confident that it had the superior technology and lower cost. But it was concerned about presenting a bid denominated only in U.S. dollars, since the French firm's bid was in Norwegian kroner.
>
> The manufacturer turned to its bank, which provided a multiple option facility. This facility permitted the Scandinavian customer to choose to pay in U.S. dollars, deutsche marks, French francs, Finnish markka, or Norwegian kroner. The deal was structured so that the customer could choose its preferred currency of payment on each successive payment date.
>
> In essence, what the bank sold to the U.S. company was a two-year American-style call option on the dollar, with puts against each of the four nondollar currencies. The strike prices for the options were set at the spot levels of June 1990, when the deal was struck.[21] These strike levels give the Scandinavian customer a ceiling on the amount of foreign currency it will have to pay at any time, while guaranteeing that the U.S. firm will always receive the full dollar price.

> The first payment was for the amount of $2.5 million.
>
> Suppose that the dollar had weakened so that spot rates on the payment date were below the strike prices for the nondollar currencies and that the customer decided to make the first payment in deutsche marks, at a prevailing market rate of DM1.5/dollar. The customer pays 3.75 million deutsche marks to the U.S. company, which, in turn, sells the deutsche marks in the spot market and pockets the $2.5 million. In this case the U.S. company does not need to exercise its put.
>
> Suppose instead that the dollar had strengthened to, say, 2.0 marks per dollar. At the spot rate, the customer would pay DM5 million to cover its obligation. But with the option in place, it pays only the ceiling amount of DM4.25 million. The U.S. company, in turn, exercises its put at the strike price of DM1.7 to get the full $2.5 million.

The strike levels thus represent the worst-case scenarios for the customer. Over the life of the contract, the customer knows it will never be required to pay more than a specific maximum amount in any particular currency. Thus, this gives the customer the ability to directly compare these worst-case scenarios with the terms of any other competing offers denominated in the same foreign currency.

The total cost to the U.S. customer for this customized option was about $400,000; it was passed on to the customer in the total purchase price.[22] By offering its customer five different currencies in which to pay, the U.S. firm gave the customer the opportunity to reduce its costs by paying a lower price if one of the five currencies depreciated relative to the Norwegian kroner. Although this option may not have itself sealed the deal, it may have provided an edge over the French firm competing for the same contract with a deal that allowed payment in only one currency.

The versatility of options permits corporations to create or market products more finely attuned to the needs of particular buyers. Burns & McBride, a small, family-owned heating oil distributor in Wilmington, Delaware, recognized the interests and concerns of customers and responded through the use of options.[23]

> In 1990, Burns & McBride offered their customers protection from unexpected increases in heating oil prices during the winter months. The firm offered a guaranteed price, in effect, selling a call option on heating oil prices to their customers. The firm protects itself by hedging 60 percent of its fuel requirements with the heating oil futures (New York Mercantile Exchange). The firm buys over-the-counter call options to protect itself on the remaining 40 percent of its requirements. Out-of-the-money put options are also used to allow the firm to benefit from any sharp price drops.
>
> When they offered this price protection, Burns & McBride experienced a substantial increase in its customer base—even though the option premiums add several cents per gallon to the price charged to customers.

In this case Burns & McBride offered its customers something they probably could not get on their own—few residential customers buy enough heating oil to justify purchasing their own hedge. Burns & McBride was able to bring a kind of efficiency of scale by aggregating the collective hedging needs of many residential consumers.

More common are examples of financial firms using options to segment and target their customer base. Banks and insurance companies are familiar with options and so are able to design attractive products with embedded options.

One of the most widely cited such product was the S&P-indexed CD first introduced by the Chase Manhattan Bank in 1987. This FDIC-insured CD guaranteed the depositor the better of a fixed interest rate or a rate indexed to the performance of the S&P 500 Index. Decomposed, this product is simply a standard CD plus a call option on the S&P 500 Index. However, the package provided depositors with a lower-cost access than was available otherwise.

Banks and insurance companies have made use of options to craft financial products designed to appeal to different customer bases. These products could not be offered unless there were an underlying derivatives market in which the company could manage its risk. But with the strategic use of options to help tailor the company's menu of investment choices, customers are given a wider variety of products from which to choose. This extends the range of prospective customers to the firm and enables the firm to serve the needs of existing customers more fully.

Notes

1. Options on debt instruments can be based on different conventions: on *bond prices* or on the *interest rates* implied by the bond prices. A call on interest rates is the same thing as a put on bond prices. Thus, a cap could also be defined as a put on the price of the debt instrument. To avoid confusion, we will use the convention of discussing options on interest rates.

2. Adapted from "Falcon Cable Foils Risk" (1990).

3. This discussion is adapted from "Hedging Seasonal Borrowing" (1989).

4. This example is adapted from work by Robert Mackay, director, Center for Study of Futures and Options Market, Virginia Tech. The transaction was described in *United States Banker,* August 1992.

5. "How Muzak Stays in Tune with Interest Rates" (1990).

6. "Applied Power Hedges a Strategic Acquisition" (1991).

7. "Hartmarx Buttons Down an Interest Rate Collar" (1990).

8. "Biosystems Is Ready for the Dollar's Rebound" (1992).

9. "Chocks Away for New Market in Oil Hedging" (1988).

10. Some of these strategies, including the use of straddles and strangles, will be discussed in Chapter 14.

11. "Qualex Protects Its Silver Lining" (1990).

12. "The P&L Railroad Keeps Its Fuel Costs on Track" (1991).

13. The company faces some basis risk on the hedge because the reference price on the cap is tied to the price of heating oil rather than diesel fuel.

14. "Texas Parries" (1992).

15. This discussion of the use of equity puts in a share repurchase program is based on Angel, Gastineau, and Weber (1997).

16. However, because the holder of a put option is not obliged to sell the stock to the corporation if the stock is selling above the strike price of the option, selling puts is not a perfect substitute for outright repurchase of the stock.

17. Ty Po pointed out to me that this discussion presupposes that the firm will behave "mechanistically," when in fact many firms are more "opportunistic." As evidence, he noted that many firms end up buying back shares at a price substantially below the announced target price.

18. SEC Rule 10b-18.

19. "Risk Innovations: Latest Techniques for Better Hedging" (1997).

20. "Corporate Risk Management's 'Done Deals'" (1991).

21. The strike prices were 1.7 deutsche marks, 5.7 French francs, 6.5 Finnish markka, and 4.0 Norwegian kroner.

22. The currency that contributed the most to the price of the facility was the Norwegian kroner. On a larger deal, the thin market in kroner options and the high volatility of the currency would make inclusion prohibitively expensive. But this deal was small enough that the company wanted to include the kroner to increase the flexibility of the structure.

23. "Burns & McBride Hedges a White Christmas" (1990).

13 | SECOND-GENERATION OPTIONS*

The "second-generation" options—a.k.a. "exotic" options—include path-dependent, multifactor, time-dependent (chooser and forward start), and single-payout options (binary and contingent premium).

However, before we begin, there is another option that we have not yet mentioned that is sort of a second-generation option. In Chapter 10, we described two exercise styles: European-style options can be exercised only at maturity; American-style options can be exercised on *any* date on or prior to maturity of the option. A third exercise style permits the option to be exercised prior to expiration of the option, but only on *specific* dates—e.g., a one-year option might be able to be exercised on the final business days of each quarter, in addition to maturity. Such an option lies between the European and American styles in the sense that it has more exercise rights than a European-style option but fewer exercise rights than an American-style option. Since such options "lie between" European and American options, they came to be called *Bermuda options*.[1] Bermuda options are often found embedded in callable or puttable corporate bonds. For example, a corporation may issue a five-year callable bond with a refunding provision. This issue can be called at any coupon date (limited exercise dates) and replaced with a new issue at a lower rate. Not surprisingly, the price of a Bermuda option also lies between the prices of American and European options. Since the American option may be exercised at any time, it is more expensive than the Bermuda option. Similarly, the Bermuda

---

*This chapter is based on two articles that William Chan and I did for *Risk:* "Path-Dependency: Defining and Categorising Path-Dependent Options" (April 1997) and "Multifactor Options: Definitions and Categorisation" (May 1997).

option is more expensive than the European option since it can be exercised more frequently than the European option.

Path-Dependent Options

The terminal value of a standard European-style option depends only on the price of the underlying asset at expiry of the option—it does not matter how the price got there. In contrast, the value of a path-dependent option depends on the path that the price of the underlying asset follows during the life of the option. In keeping with our family tree concept, we can categorize path-dependent options as in Figure 13–1.

Note that binary options are not included as path-dependent options. In our review of the literature, we did not find unanimity on this point. While some authors include binary options as a form of path-dependent options, our perception was that the majority do not.

Mean-Dependent Options

Several members of the path-dependent option family use average prices over some period of the option's lifetime, rather than spot prices at expiry, in determining the final payout. These are called *mean-dependent options.*

Average Price.   The most widely observed of the mean-dependent options is the *average rate* (or *price*) *option,* also known as an *Asian option.* For an average rate option, the payout at expiry is based on the difference between the strike and the average spot rates observed over some designated period during the contract's life:

$$\text{Average rate call payout} = \max \left[S_{\text{AVG}} - X, 0 \right]$$

where S_{AVG} is the average price of the underlying. The number and timing of price observations is determined in advance and may start at the beginning or near the

FIGURE 13–1   Taxonomy of Path-Dependent Options

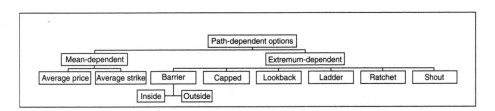

end of the life of the option. Observations may also be weighted in favor of prices observed on designated dates. There are two ways of calculating the average price for Asian options. An arithmetic average is a simple weighted average of prices:

$$A = \sum_{i=1} w_i S_i$$

where the weights w_i (in percentage) add up to one. The geometric average is based on the product of prices:

$$A = (\prod_i S_i)^{1/n}$$

where n is the total number of prices.[2]

As the volatility of an average price is always less than the volatility of the price series that makes up the average, the premium for an average price option is less than that of the corresponding standard option. Table 13–1 shows the reduction in

---

TABLE 13–1   The Price of a Six-Month At-the-Money Call Option on Equity: A Comparison of Various Option Types

Type of Call Option	Averaging Period	Barrier	Option Price
Standard European style			$12.87
Standard European style			$12.88
Average price	30 days		$12.03/$12.16
(geometric/arithmetic)	60 days		$11.23/$11.30
	180 days		$7.31/$7.13
Up and out		$160	$0.17
		$190	$4.46
Up and in		$190	$8.41
		$160	$12.70
Down and out		$130	$10.48
		$110	$12.83
Down and in		$110	$0.04
		$130	$2.39
Capped with the ceiling strike at $160			$5.64
Lookback			$23.12
Ladder with two rungs at $170 and $190			$14.58
Ratchet with the reset dates on 30, 60, 90, 120, and 150 days			$19.23
Shout			$16.69

NOTE: Spot price = $145; exercise price = $145; risk-free rate = 6%; dividend rate = 3%; volatility = 29.5%; maturity = six months. The averaging period is the number of days from expiry. Many of the options in this table were priced using Monis Software's Optimum: Exotics package.

price relative to a standard option for an arithmetic average price option over three different averaging periods. Not surprisingly, the longer the averaging period, the lower the price.

Multinational corporations are likely to view their exposures to foreign exchange rates over a set period—e.g., a quarter, the next six months, a year—rather than at a specific date in the future. Consequently, average rate options are becoming more widely used in the currency markets.

Average rate options are the norm in the energy markets (oil and refined products)[3] and base metals markets (aluminum, copper, nickel, and zinc). The following example shows how Phelps Dodge, the world's second largest copper producer, used "average cost" options to hedge the price of its principal product: copper cathode[4]:

> Phelps Dodge used options where the average spot price was defined as the 1991 annual average price. At a time when the spot price of copper was near $1.30 per pound, Phelps Dodge bought puts on 258 million pounds of copper cathode (about 25% of its expected 1991 mine production) at a strike price of $1 a pound and simultaneously sold calls on 86 million pounds at a strike price of $1.23 per pound to help finance the put purchase.[5]
>
> Phelps Dodge purchased out-of-the-money puts and sold in-the-money calls. By using in-the-money calls, the company was able to finance more out-of-money puts than it would have been able to using a more traditional out-of-money call in the collar. The company chose this combination because it was bullish on copper prices and so did not want to lock itself out of the opportunity to gain if copper prices rallied.[6]
>
> One-third of the resulting hedge was a collar (a result of the combination of the long put and short call); the other two-thirds was straightforward put protection. The total cost of this hedge was less than 10% of the margin on the firm's copper sales. Phelps Dodge's cost of copper at the time the hedge was implemented was about 60¢ per pound. In the worst case scenario of a selling price of $1 per pound, the firm's margin is 40¢; thus, the hedging strategy cost is only about 4¢ per pound.

While less common than in the foreign exchange and commodity markets, average rate options have also been observed in fixed-income and equity markets.

Average Strike.   These options are less common. In the average rate option, the spot price is the average of observed spot prices and the strike price is set at origination. For the *average strike option,* the spot price is the observed spot price at maturity and the strike price is the average of observed spot prices over a specified period. For example, the payout at expiry for an average strike call option is

$$\text{Average strike call payout} = \max[S - X_{AVG}, 0]$$

where the exercise price of the option, X_{AVG}, is the average price of the underlying asset. In contrast to the average rate option, whose payout depends on the relationship between an average of prices for the underlying and a strike rate specified at origination, the payout for the average strike depends on the relationship between the average of the underlying financial price and the spot price at expiry.

Cumulative.   Another path-dependent option which is based on average prices is the *cumulative option*. Perhaps the most widely used of this type is the cumulative interest rate cap. The cumulative interest rate cap pays off if interest rates have moved over the year in such a way that the firm's annual interest expense exceeds the specified cap level—i.e., if the average of the interest rates observed at the rollover dates for the firm's underlying financing exceeds some specified rate. This allows a treasurer to hedge interest rate expense against short-term changes in interest rates over a year.

Extremum-Dependent Options

Another class of path-dependent options depends on the "extreme" price—either up or down—attained by the underlying.

Barrier Options.   These exist in many forms. The most common require the user to specify a "trigger (barrier) price" in addition to the strike price and the maturity. Depending on the type of barrier option used, when the spot price of the underlying asset hits this trigger price, the option will either appear (be "knocked in") or disappear (be "knocked out").

Knock-out options are the most common type of barrier option. If the trigger price is above the spot price at origination, it is an "up-and-out" option. If the trigger price is below the spot price at origination, it is a "down-and-out" option.

The payoff of a knock-out is the same as a standard option unless the underlying price touches the trigger price. If, however, the underlying price touches the trigger price, the option disappears. As there are situations in which the option would disappear, the premium for the knock-out option is less than that of the standard option. The closer the trigger is set to the prevailing price, the greater the cost savings relative to the standard option, because it becomes less likely that the instrument will survive the daily price fluctuations.

Consider a call option on the Nikkei 225 stock price index. In the early 1990s, a fund manager might have found the premium on a standard six-month call on the Nikkei 225 to have been prohibitively expensive—the volatility was in excess of 30 percent. However, if the fund manager is relatively confident that the market is not ready for a market correction in the near term, she could purchase a six-month down-and-out call with a trigger set at 10 percent below the current at-the-money strike price.

Figure 13–2 illustrates possible outcomes based on alternative paths for the index over the six-month life of the option. If the index remains above the trigger price, the fund manager's returns on the knock-out will exceed those for purchas-

FIGURE 13–2 Payout of a Down-and-Out Call

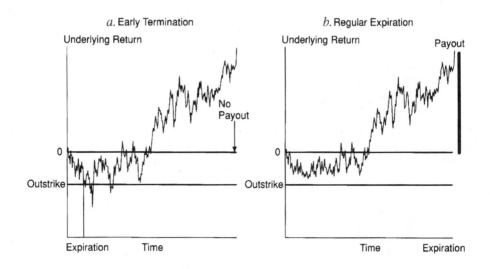

ing a standard call by the amount of the premium "savings." However, if the index dips below the trigger—even temporarily—the option disappears. After hitting the trigger, if the index subsequently rises, the fund manager will forgo all future profits because the knock-out option would no longer exist. The closer the trigger is set to the prevailing price, the greater the cost savings relative to the standard option but also the less likely that the instrument will survive the daily price fluctuations.

Some up-and-out puts have been used by multinational corporations to reduce the cost of hedging a foreign exchange exposure. However, the user must keep in mind that this strategy works only as long as the management of the firm is willing to forgo the hedge if the underlying value moves sufficiently in the firm's favor.

In Table 13–1, we calculate the price of an up-and-out call at two trigger prices. Both cost less than the standard European option. However, the price reduction is greatest for the option with the lower trigger (barrier). The lower costs of down-and-out calls and up-and-out puts may be viewed as the premium reduction that reflects the potential for the protection to disappear. The reduced cost of other forms of barrier options might better be viewed as reflecting the limited profit potential. Up-and-out calls and down-and-out puts are automatically exercised when the underlying financial price reaches the trigger price[7]; this serves to cap the gain on the option at a predetermined level.

Knock-in options are the form of the barrier option in which the option appears only when the trigger price is reached. Up-and-in calls and down-and-in puts are activated when the trigger is reached, producing a standard contract.

Illustration 13–1

Using Knock-Out Caps*

Early in 1995, it appeared that German monetary policy was at a crossroads. In May of 1995, market participants were being told that, over the next few weeks, short-term rates were likely to go up as down.

Caps were therefore back on the agenda—but not conventional caps, because the recent steepening in the yield curve had made these too expensive. Of much more interest was the "knock-out cap."

A popular structure was a five-year knock-out with a strike of 6 percent and a knock-out level of 9 percent. This works like a conventional cap, provided LIBOR sets below 9 percent. However, if on any fixing date LIBOR sets above 9 percent, then, for that period only, the cap knocks out. In May 1995, a conventional five-year 6 percent cap on three-month LIBOR cost 350 bp. A 6 percent knock-out which knocked out in a particular period if LIBOR was above 9 percent on the reset date cost only 210 bp—a saving of 40 percent over the conventional cap. The magnitude of the saving might seem surprising, since the knock-out level was so far from the existing level of three-month LIBOR (4.6 percent). The saving was the result of the steepness of the yield curve.

---

*This illustration is based on Esterle and Robb (1995).

For instance, the down-and-in S&P 500 put can be constructed to activate if the index falls by 10 percent over the contract life. Its holder enjoys portfolio protection if declines go beyond the trigger level, but not until that point.

The more common barrier options are those for which the same asset price serves as both the underlying price and the trigger price; these are called *inside* barriers. However, barrier options can be created where the asset price used for the trigger is different from the underlying price; these are called *outside* barriers. For example, suppose the payout of an option is a function of the U.S. dollar-Canadian dollar exchange rate (the underlying asset) but the price of gold triggers whether the option is knocked in or knocked out.[8]

Roll-up puts and roll-down calls start out looking like standard options, but if the underlying price moves to a prespecified level (the roll-up or roll-down strike), they change to a knock-out barrier form and the strike price is reset. In the case of the roll-up put, if the roll-up strike is breached, the standard put becomes an up-and-out put with the roll-up strike serving as the new, more favorable strike price. The trigger price for the up-and-out put will have been set in advance at a price above the roll-up strike. The roll-up put affords the manager a higher level of protection unless the trigger is reached, causing it to expire. This type of product may be used for hedging stocks or fixed-income portfolios when the manager anticipates a moderate short-term rise in value and wants to lock in or reset the put to incorporate the new market conditions. The price for a roll-up (-down) option is usually close to that for the corresponding standard option with the same original strike.

Double-barrier options,[9] variation on the barrier option, are double knock-outs, which can knock out at either of two points. A version that enjoyed some popularity in 1995 was dollar puts that knock out when the currency goes either lower or higher. (Note that if the put knocks out lower, it does it in-the-money.) Double knock-outs carry a much lower premium than a straight dollar put.

To make this more clear, let's consider an example. In the summer of 1995 DM/US$ was trading at a spot level of DM/$1.4050. An end user who wants to buy a dollar put at DM/$1.4000 could have reduced the premium by adding a standard knock-out at DM/$1.4850. However, to cut the premium even further, the user could have agreed to an additional lower trigger level of DM/$1.3250. The addition of the lower barrier means that the user would be exposed—reexposed—should the dollar fall through the lower barrier level. The user is compensated for the additional risk with a lower premium:

Option Structure	Premium
Standard 1.4000 dollar put	2.78%
Single knock-out: 1.4000 dollar put with barrier set at 1.4850	2.65%
Double knock-out: 1.4000 dollar put with barriers set at 1.4850 and 1.3250	0.43%

Although the double knock-out is most common, there can be variants where one of the barriers may be a knock-in and the other a knock-out or both barriers are knock-ins. The payoff can be either the exercise of the standard option or a cash payout. It is also possible to create double barriers on different underlyings—e.g., the upper range could be set on the U.S. dollar against the yen and the lower range might be set on the dollar against the deutsche mark.

Capped Options. *Capped options* may be thought of as a variant of up-and-out calls and down-and-out puts. An American-style capped call option looks like a vertical call spread—long a call at a lower strike price and short a call at a higher strike price. If the underlying price reaches the upper strike, the American-style capped option is automatically exercised for its intrinsic value (upper strike minus lower strike). If the underlying never touches the upper strike, the option will pay out the greater of zero or the difference between the spot and the lower strike price.

Lookback Options.   *Lookback options* are path-dependent options that allow the holder to exercise the option against the most favorable price of the underlying asset that has occurred during the contract's life. For example, if I hold a lookback call option on an equity index, the value of my call at expiry is the difference between the terminal price at expiry and the lowest price the equity index reached during the life of the contract:

$$\text{Lookback call payout} = \max [S_T - S_{LOW}, 0]$$

The lookback option can be used for any financial asset, but so far it has been applied primarily to foreign exchange and equities.

The value of the lookback option at expiry will be greater than or equal to that of a standard American- or European-style option, so it will have a higher premium at the outset. The higher the underlying volatility, the more valuable the lookback feature and hence the greater the difference in premium between the lookback and the standard contract. As shown in Table 13–1, the price of the lookback call in our example is more than twice the price of the standard European-style call.

Ladder Options.[10]   A *ladder option* is a special type of path-dependent option whose strike price is periodically reset (automatically) when the price of the underlying asset passes through prespecified price levels—i.e., when the price of the underlying asset rises/falls enough to hit a "rung." The purchaser may specify one or more rungs when the option is initiated.

For example, consider a ladder call on an asset with an initial strike price of $100 and ladder reset levels set at $5 intervals. If the price rises above $105, the strike price is automatically reset to $105, thereby locking in the $5 price appreciation. More generally, we have written the at-expiration payoff to standard call option as

$$\text{MAX} [0, S - X]$$

where S is the price of the underlying asset at option expiry and X is the strike price of the option agreed at the time of entry into the option. The at-expiration payoff to the ladder call option can be expressed

$$\text{MAX} [0, (S - X), \text{MAX} \{(L_i - X), 0\}]$$

where L_i = the ith ladder achieved over the life of the option.

Figure 13–3 illustrates different possible payoffs with a ladder option. The diagram shows three possible asset price paths (A, B, and C) and two ladder steps ($L1$ and $L2$). The payoffs under this scenario are:

- Path A: Payoff equal to final asset price less the strike price.
- Path B: Payoff equal to $L2$ less the strike price.
- Path C: Payoff equal to $L1$ less the strike price.

FIGURE 13–3   Payoffs for a Ladder Option

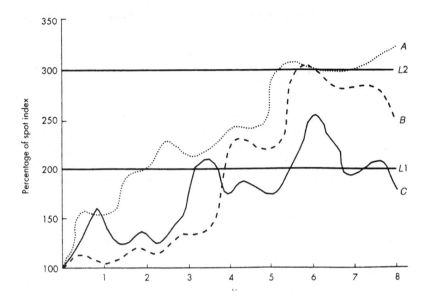

Shout Options.   A shout option is a variation of the ladder option; in a ladder option the rungs are agreed to in advance; in the shout option the owner must decide when to specify a rung to be activated.

At any time before expiry, the owner of a shout option can contact the seller of the option and lock in ("shout") the intrinsic value of the option (the difference between the exercise price of the option and the spot price at the time the shout was made), while retaining further potential to benefit from favorable moves. On the day the option expires, the payout to the buyer will be the greater of the intrinsic value locked in by the shout and the intrinsic value at maturity. Typically, a shout option gives its owner only one opportunity to shout, although it could be structured to give the right to shout more than once.

The at-expiration payoff for a shout option is

$$\text{Call: MAX } [0, S - X, \text{SHOUT} - X]$$

$$\text{Put: MAX } [0, X - S, X - \text{SHOUT}]$$

where SHOUT is the asset price "shouted" by the option owner.

The shout option combines features of the ladder and lookback options. Figure 13–4 provides a comparison of the payoff to a shout option with that for lookback and ladder options.

Illustration 13–2

Using a Ladder Option to Hedge FX Risk

Satyajit Das (1995b) provided an example of the way that a U.S. manufacturer who imports raw materials from Canada (priced in Canadian dollars) might use a ladder option.

Suppose that the current is US$1 = C$1.34. The importer is concerned about a strengthening U.S. dollar; but the U.S. importer expects the U.S. dollar to weaken to C$1.30 or even C$1.29. In this case, the importer might well decide to purchase a European-style, one-month ladder option with ladder levels of C$1.30 and C$1.29.

Suppose that at maturity the U.S. dollar was weaker than at origination—US$1 = C$1.32. The payoff from the option will depend on the path the exchange rate took over the one-month life of the option. Following are some illustrative payoffs:

If C$1.32 was the weakest that the U.S. dollar got over the option life, the option expires out-of-the-money and the option premium paid is not recovered.

If the U.S. dollar got as low as C$1.295 during the month, the ladder level of C$1.30 would have been breached and the net payment to the importer is

$$1.32 - \text{MIN} [1.32, 1.30]$$
$$- \text{premium} = 1.32 - 1.30 - \text{premium}$$

If the U.S. dollar got as low as C$1.285 during the month, the ladder level of C$1.29 would also have been breached and the net payment to the importer is

$$1.32 - \text{MIN} [1.32, 1.30, 1.29]$$
$$- \text{premium} = 1.32 - 1.29 - \text{premium}$$

FIGURE 13–4   **Comparison of the Payoffs for a Shout Option with That for Lookback and Ladder Options**

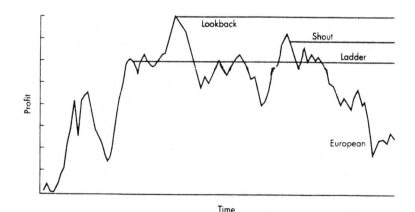

Illustration 13–3

Using a Shout Option to Hedge FX Risk

Think again about Satyajit Das's U.S. importer of materials from Canada. Instead of a ladder option, suppose the importer purchased a European-style shout option.

As before, at the time of the purchase, the prevailing exchange rate was US$1 = C$1.34. Suppose that, one week later, the U.S. dollar has weakened to C$1.30; but the importer now believes that the U.S. dollar is unlikely to weaken further, and so he "shouts" at the prevailing exchange rate.

Suppose that the importer called the market correctly, and in the remaining three weeks, the U.S. dollar regained a little of its loss against the Canadian dollar, ending the month at US$1 = C$1.32. In this case the net payment to the importer is

$$1.32 - 1.30 - \text{premium}$$

However, suppose that the importer had misjudged the market and the U.S. dollar continued to weaken, ending the month at C$1.28. In this case, the net payment to the importer is

$$1.34 - 1.28 - \text{premium}$$

A shout option is more expensive than a standard European-style option because one can lock in gains before expiry. A shout option will be more expensive than a ladder option as the rungs can be chosen by the optionholder during the lifetime of the option rather than being set on the initial deal date. The greater the number of shout opportunities, the higher the price of the shout option. (Note that the price of a shout option will eventually converge with the price of a lookback option as the number of shout opportunities increases.)

Valuing Path-Dependent Options

In general, there are four ways to value path-dependent options:

Analytic Method.   The derivative is valued by solving the differential equation that the derivative's price satisfies. The differential equation can be solved by converting it into a finite difference equation and solving it numerically or by applying the technique of *risk-neutral valuation*. This technique relies on one key property of the Black-Scholes differential equation: the option's price is not affected by the risk preferences of investors.[11]

Analytic Approximation Method.   Some options cannot be valued by the analytical method, e.g., arithmetic Asians, ladders, ratchets, and shouts. In these cases, an approximation is possible. In 1991, Stuart Turnbull and Lee Wakeman applied the analytic technique to value options on arithmetic averages. They provided an accurate and fast analytical approximation in which they calculated the first two moments of the probability distribution of the arithmetic average and then assumed that the distribution of the arithmetic average was lognormal with those first two moments.

Binomial Model (Lattice) Method.   This technique is one of the most versatile in valuing derivative securities. It is a discrete version of the continuous Black-Scholes model. The binomial model assumes that at each point the asset price faces an independent decision whether to rise or to fall. The value of the option is solved by working backward from the expiry until time 0 based on a risk-neutral world.

Monte Carlo Simulation.   A computer program is used to simulate the random evolution of the asset price through time and the corresponding option payouts. Over a large number of iterations, the estimated fair value of the option can then be determined by averaging out all the possible payouts.

Multifactor Options

In contrast to standard options and path-dependent options, the values of which are determined by the behavior of a single financial price, the value of a multifactor option is determined by the behavior of two or more financial prices and by the correlation between these financial prices.

Continuing our taxonomy, in Figure 13–5, we subdivide the multifactor options into three groups: rainbow, quanto, and basket options. The rainbow and quanto groups can be further subdivided based on the payout structure of the option.

FIGURE 13–5   Taxonomy of Multifactor Options

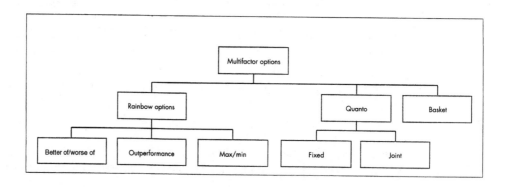

Rainbow Options

The value of a rainbow option is determined by the performance of two or more underlying assets. Such an option based on *n* underlying assets is referred to as an *n*-color rainbow option; e.g., one based on two underlying assets is referred to as a *two-color rainbow.* We are aware of three different payout structures for rainbow options.

Better-of/worse-of options. *Better-of* options have been used widely in the equity markets, allowing investors to obtain the return associated with the better performing of some number of equity indexes. For example, an investor might be debating between holding a position in the German equity index—the Deutsche Aktienindex (DAX)—and holding a position in UK equities—the Financial Times Stock Exchange Index (FTSE). The investor could buy a better-of option that would pay according to the better performing of the DAX or FTSE index. If, at maturity, the FTSE had increased by 13 percent and the DAX had decreased by 6 percent, the holder of the rainbow option would receive a return based on the 13 percent increase in the FTSE. If both indexes had declined, the holder would pay the performance of the asset with the smaller decrease in value.

While better-of options usually involve assets from the same asset class, they can involve assets from different asset classes. A popular combination in the early 1990s was a better-of option based on the performance of a stock market index and a bond market index. An investor who is unsure whether to invest in stocks or bonds could buy a better-of option that, over its time period, has a payout determined by the better performance of stocks or bonds. If, at expiry, the stock market had increased by 10 percent while the bond market had increased by 5 percent, the payout to the holder of the better-of option would be based on the 10 percent performance of the equity index.

The payout for a better-of option could just as easily be determined by the worse performing of two assets. The payout of an *n*-color better-of rainbow option is

$$\text{Max} \ (S_1, S_2, S_3, \ldots, S_n)$$

and the payout of the worse-of option is

$$\text{Min} \ (S_1, S_2, S_3, \ldots, S_n)$$

where S_i is either the price level or the percentage change in asset *i*.

Outperformance Option. Another form of payout for rainbow options is based on the difference in the performance of two assets. For example, an investor holding a position in the DAX could protect against the DAX underperforming the FTSE by purchasing a rainbow outperformance option that would pay out according to the difference in returns of the two indexes—but only if the FTSE outperformed the

DAX. If the FTSE increased by 13 percent and the DAX increased by 6 percent, the holder would receive a return based on the 7 percent difference in the returns. Similarly, if the FTSE increased by 13 percent and the DAX decreased by 6 percent, the holder would receive a return based on the 19 percent spread between the returns. But if the FTSE underperformed the DAX, the payout is zero. When the outperformance option is held with a cash position in the DAX index, the investor ends up with an outperformance position on the total return of the DAX versus the FTSE.

The payout of an outperformance option[12] is

$$\text{Max}\,(S_2 - S_1, 0)$$

where S_1 and S_2 are either the price level or the percentage change.

Max/Min Option.   This form of rainbow option depends on the maximum or minimum of two or more assets, e.g., shares. The payout of a max call option is

$$\text{Max}\,[\max\,(S_1 - X_1, S_2 - X_2, \ldots, S_n - X_n), 0]$$

and the min call option is

$$\text{Max}\,[\min\,(S_1 - X_1, S_2 - X_2, \ldots, S_n - X_n), 0]$$

where S_i is the price level and X_i is the strike level for asset i.

The max/min option payout is similar to that of better-of/worse-of options when the strikes X_1 through X_n are set to zero. Table 13–2 shows the price comparison among various two-color rainbow options.

Quanto Options

Quanto options eliminate the exchange rate risk inherent when buying an asset denominated in a currency other than the purchaser's home currency. The easiest way to explain a quanto option is via an example. Suppose a U.S. investor buys a

---

TABLE 13–2   The Price of a Six-Month At-the-Money Two-Color Rainbow Option on Equities

Type of Option	Option Price ($)
Better of/worse of	60.89/49.11
Outperformance	10.89
Maximum/minimum call	7.03/1.94

NOTE: Spot price 1 = $50; spot price 2 = $60; volatility 1 = 29%; volatility 2 = 33%; correlation = 48% risk-free rate = 5%; dividend yield 1 = 6%; dividend yield 2 = 7%; maturity = six months.

European-style option giving him the right to buy a deutsche mark–denominated asset (e.g., the DAX). At maturity, the dollar value of this option depends on the spot dollar-deutsche mark exchange rate at option maturity (FX_T) and the value of the deutsche mark–denominated asset (S_{DM}):

$$FX_T \times \max (0, S_{DM} - X)$$

Alternatively, the U.S. investor might want an option which eliminates the foreign exchange rate risk. This is done by fixing the exchange rate on the date when the option is purchased (FX_0).[13] At maturity, the dollar value of such an option would be

$$FX_0 \times \max (0, S_{DM} - X)$$

With the quanto, the investor does not gain (lose) from an appreciation (depreciation) of the deutsche mark. However, the writer of the option is confronted with a new exposure not present in the standard deutsche mark–denominated call: the option seller has taken on exposure to the deutsche mark on an uncertain amount—$\max (0, S_{DM} - X)$.

To hedge this risk, the option writer must consider the correlation between the value of the underlying asset and the foreign exchange rate.

There is an alternative form of quanto options called a *joint* quanto. In this case, the value of the option depends on the spot dollar–deutsche mark exchange rate at option maturity (FX_T) relative to a guaranteed level of the exchange rate ($FX_{GUARANTEED}$). At maturity, the dollar value of such an option would be

$$\max (FX_T, FX_{GUARANTEED}) \times \max (0, S_{DM} - X)$$

Table 13–3 shows a price comparison of a standard option and the two quanto options.

TABLE 13–3 The Price of a Six-Month At-the-Money Option on Foreign Equity

Type of Call Option	Option Price ($)
Standard European style	2.644
Quanto	2.708
Joint quanto	2.828

NOTE: Spot price of equity = DM50; strike price of equity = DM50; domestic interest rate = 5%; dividend yield of share = 6%; volatility of share = 29%; initial foreign exchange rate = 1.5; guaranteed foreign exchange rate = 1.5; volatility of foreign exchange rate = 20%; foreign interest rate = 6%; correlation = 10%; maturity = six months.

Basket Options

A basket option pays out on the basis of the aggregate value of a specified "basket" of financial assets, rather than on the value of the individual assets. It is an application of portfolio theory—as long as the financial prices that make up the basket are less than perfectly positively correlated, the option on the basket will be less expensive than buying individual options on each of the assets. At maturity, the value of a basket call option is

$$\text{Max }(\Sigma \alpha_i S_i - X_{\text{BASKET}})$$

where the α_i is the percentage of asset i in the basket, S_i is the price of asset i, and X_{BASKET} is the strike price defined in terms of the aggregate value of the basket.

Basket options are often used for foreign exchange. For example, a U.S. firm that exports goods to Germany and Japan might want protection against the dollar rising relative to the deutsche mark and the yen. It could buy separate put options on both the deutsche mark and the yen, or it could buy a basket option on the pair of currencies. Since the deutsche mark and yen are not perfectly correlated, the basket option will be cheaper than the corresponding basket of two options. This is essentially the same as creating an index on which to base the option and has the same effect of lowering the volatility.

But basket options are also used for other assets. Table 13–4 shows how the cost of buying a basket option on two equities would be less expensive than buying the individual option.

TABLE 13–4   Pricing a Six-Month At-the-Money Call Option on Equities

Asset 1		Asset 2	
Spot price	$50	Spot price	$60
Volatility	29%	Volatility	33%
Dividend yield	6%	Dividend yield	7%

Correlation = 48%
Risk-free rate = 5%

Basket of options

Call option on asset 1: X = $50, premium = 3.91 ⎫
Call option on asset 2: X = $60, premium = 5.33 ⎬ Premium 9.24

Option on a basket

Call option on basket: X = $110
                    Volatility = 26.69% ⎬ Premium = 6.84

NOTE: The options in this table were priced using Monis Software's Optimum:Exotics package.

Exchange-Traded Multifactor Options

Almost all multifactor options are found in the over-the-counter market. We are aware of only one multifactor option traded on an exchange: in 1994, the New York Mercantile Exchange listed a rainbow spread option—an option on the "crack" spread (Chan and Turner, 1994). The payout for these American-style options is determined by the spread between the price of crude oil and the price of a refined product. NYMEX listed two crack spread option contracts, one for the spread between heating oil and crude oil prices and the other for the spread of the unleaded gasoline price over the price of crude oil. Both options contracts were quoted in terms of the price of one barrel of the refined product less the price of one barrel of crude oil. In 1996, the volume of the unleaded gasoline–crude oil crack spread option was 31,743 contracts; the volume in the heating oil–crude oil crack spread option was 45,920 contracts.

Pricing and Risk Management for Multifactor Options

Multifactor options are priced using the same techniques used in pricing path-dependent options. In general, there are four ways to value multifactor options: the analytic method, the analytic approximation method, binomial models, and Monte Carlo simulations. Researchers have provided analytic (closed-form) solutions for two-color rainbows, including better-of/worse-of, outperformance (Margrabe, 1988), max/min (Stulz, 1982; Johnson, 1987), and quanto options (Reiner, 1992). However, no closed-form solutions for basket options are currently known. In the case of basket options, the difficulty is that the sum of lognormal variables is no longer lognormal, so the usual techniques break down.[14] One can numerically solve the basket option by solving a partial differential equation subject to final and boundary conditions (Wilmot, Dewynne, and Howison, 1994). And an analytical approximation for the price of the basket option has been proposed (Huynh, 1994).

When a dealer offers multifactor options, she is exposed to an additional source of risk—correlation risk. When pricing the multifactor option, the dealer makes an assumption about the correlation between the asset prices.[15] The dealer would like to hedge the resulting correlation risk, i.e., that the actual correlation is different from the assumed. However, the ability of the dealer to hedge correlation risk is limited by the availability of spread or quanto options.

Time-Dependent Options

Chooser Options[16]

The owner of a chooser option (also called a *pay-now–choose-later option*) has the right to choose between receiving a standard call option or a standard put option at a specified date in the future.

Illustration 13–4

A Periodic Cap

Ravi Dattatreya and Kensuke Hotta (1994) provided an illustration of a one-year periodic cap on three-month LIBOR. The exercise rates for each of the caplets—with maturities of three, six, and nine months—were specified to be the previous three-month LIBOR plus 50 basis points.

At origination: Three-month LIBOR was 3.5 percent; so the exercise rate for the caplet that matures in three months was set at 3.5 + 0.5 = 4.0 percent.

At month 3: LIBOR was 3.75 percent. The first caplet expires out-of-the-money.

The exercise rate for the second caplet was set at 3.75 + 0.5 = 4.25 percent.

At month 6: LIBOR was 4.3 percent. The second caplet expires in-the-money by five basis points, and the end user receives a payment. The exercise rate for the third caplet was set at 4.3 + 0.5 = 4.8 percent.

At month 9: LIBOR was 4.0 percent. The third caplet expires out-of-the-money.

Forward Start Options

The purchaser of a forward start option pays premium *today* for an option that starts in the future, with the exercise price set equal to the spot price of the underlying asset on the agreed-upon start date. Such options have appeared in the interest rate markets as "periodic caps and floors." In a standard cap, the exercise rate for each "caplet" is specified at origination; in a periodic cap, the exercise rate for each caplet could be set as a spread over the then prevailing LIBOR.

Cliquet Options

A *cliquet option* (also known as a ratchet option) is a strip of forward starting options.[17] The purchaser of the cliquet option selects reset dates over the life of the option. At the reset date, the strike is reset at-the-money, thereby locking in the gains to that reset date.

$$\text{MAX} \{ 0, \text{Max} [S(t_0), S(t_1), S(t_2), \ldots, S(t_n)] - S(t_0)\}$$

where t_0 is the date on which the cliquet is originated and $t_1, t_2, \ldots, t_n$ are the selected reset dates.

Single-Payout Options

Binary Options

Once the strike price is reached, the payoff for a standard rises continuously with the price of the underlying. In contrast, the payoff for a binary option is discontinuous. As illustrated in Figure 13–6, a binary option pays a *fixed* amount if the strike price is reached. The payoff amount of a binary option is a predetermined fixed amount that is not related to the amount by which the underlying financial price is above or below the strike.

Like standard options, binary options can be either calls or puts. A binary call option would pay a predetermined amount if the underlying financial price closed above a certain level, while a binary put would pay a predetermined amount if the underlying closed below a certain level. For example, a binary call option on the value of XYZ shares with a payoff of $5 and a strike price of $80 would pay $5 if XYZ closed above $80 at expiration. If the price of XYZ shares was below $80 at expiration, the holder would receive nothing.

So far, we have described binary options that resemble standard, European-style options: *all-or-nothing options* pay off if the price of the underlying is above (for a call) or below (for a put) the strike price *at expiration.* However, binary options can be path-dependent: one-touch options pay off if the price of the underlying reaches a specified trigger price at any time during the life of the option.

The price of a binary option depends on two factors: (1) the likelihood that the underlying will touch (in the case of a one-touch option) or close above or below (in the case of an all-or-nothing option) a certain price and (2) the present value of the payoff amount.

FIGURE 13–6 A Binary Option

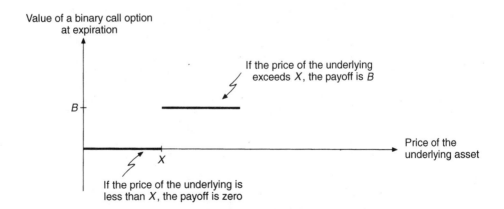

Contingent Premium Option

In a contingent premium option—sometimes referred to simply as a contingent option—the premium is set at contract origination but is paid only if the contract expires in-the-money. If the option is out-of-the-money at expiration, the seller receives nothing. And since there will be cases in which the option seller receives no premium, the contingent premium is substantially higher than that of a standard option.[18]

Figure 13–7 provides a comparison of the at-expiration payoff for at-the-money options—one a contingent premium option and the other a standard option. At expiration, if the price of the underlying asset has declined, the purchaser of the contingent premium option pays nothing. If, however, the price of the underlying asset has remained constant or increased, the contingent premium option is automatically exercised and the holder receives the difference between the spot and strike prices, less the larger premium amount. Obviously, it takes a much larger movement in the index to recover the contingent premium, but the benefit is that no up-front premium is paid.

A contingent premium option could be constructed as the sum of a long standard option and a short binary option with the same strike.

The trade press suggests that contingent premium options have been used in the equity, foreign exchange, and interest rate markets as a form of "disaster insurance" in periods of high volatility. For example, the uncertainty about the cross-rates in the ERM during the early 1990s induced some fund managers who desired protection against massive devaluations to use contingent premium puts to provide "disaster insurance" with no premium outlay if the unfavorable movement failed to materialize.[19]

FIGURE 13–7   **Payoff of a Contingent Premium and Standard Call Option**

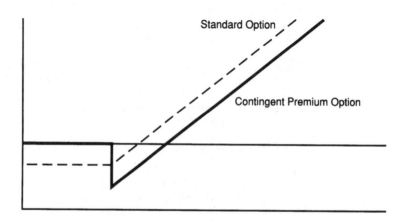

Notes

1. Bermuda options are also referred to as *mid-Atlantic, quasi-American,* or *limited exercise options.*

2. The most important difference between options based on arithmetic and geometric averages is the pricing methodology. When the underlying asset price is lognormally distributed, the geometric average is also lognormally distributed so a closed-form (Black-Scholes type) pricing model is possible. In contrast, the arithmetic average is not lognormally distributed even if its underlying is.

3. Average price options are also used in the natural gas market, but the average price is calculated only on the last three trading days.

4. "Hedging during Market Backwardation" (1991).

5. These are average prices. Phelps Dodge actually entered into several transactions with different financial institutions at different times and using different strike prices.

6. At the time these transactions were done, the copper market was in "backwardation"—futures prices were lower than spot market prices. Normally, futures prices are above spot prices, reflecting such factors as storage fees and carrying costs. When the futures price falls below the cash price, it indicates either a short-term supply squeeze or bearish expectations from the market.

7. The profit on exercise can be transferred immediately or deferred until the standard expiration date. These options are widely available in the OTC market. And in 1991, the Chicago Board Options Exchange (CBOE) listed *CAPS*—an exchange-traded form of up-and-out and down-and-out options—on the S&P 100 and S&P 500 indexes.

8. In principle, outside barrier options belong to the multifactor class of second-generation options, since the correlation between the spot price and the barrier price is necessary to value the options. We will consider the impact of correlation in the next section of this chapter.

9. This discussion is based on Thompson (1995).

10. Our discussion of "ladder" and "shout" options is adapted from Das (1995b).

11. An excellent discussion of this and other techniques is contained in Hull (1997).

12. Outperformance options are sometimes referred to as "spread" options, but there is a difference. In contrast to the payout for the outperformance option where the strike is generally zero, the payout structure of a spread option is Max $[S_2 - S_1 - X, 0]$.

13. In the jargon of quanto options, this type of option is called a *fixed* or *true* quanto; the standard option structure in which the value is converted at the at-maturity exchange rate is sometimes referred to as a *flexo* quanto.

14. Remember that the same kind of situation arises in arithmetic average price options, where the average of the asset prices is no longer lognormal even though the underlying itself is lognormal.

15. Statisticians refer to the concept of correlation when they discuss the joint behavior of variables, such as exchange rates or commodity prices, subject to random fluctuations. Correlation is expressed as a number between $+1$ and -1. A correlation of $+1$ means that the financial prices are perfectly correlated; i.e., they move in the same direction to the same degree. A correlation of -1 means that they are perfectly negatively correlated; i.e., the prices move in the opposite direction to the same degree. Zero implies that the financial prices are uncorrelated; i.e., their movements are unrelated.

16. Our discussion of chooser and forward start options is adapted from Dattatreya and Hotta (1994).

17. This discussion is adapted from Howard (1995).

18. In the November 1991 issue of *Risk,* Jim Durrant, head of research for Paribas Capital Markets, was quoted as saying that the premium for a contingent premium option was typically twice that for a standard European-style option. Armand Tatevossian, a vice president in the New Products unit of Fuji Capital Markets Corporation, was quoted as specifying the same price relation in the September 24, 1992, issue of *Derivatives Week.* More generally, the premium for a contingent premium option is approximated by the standard option premium divided by its delta.

19. "Buy Now, Pay Later," (1991).

14 ENGINEERING "NEW" RISK MANAGEMENT PRODUCTS*

Over the past several years, the term *financial engineering* has come into the vocabulary of the financial markets. In addition to the building blocks—forwards, futures, swaps, and options—the dealers of the financial derivatives have engineered a dazzling array of tools for managing financial risks. To the casual observer of the markets for financial derivatives, it often seems that the dealers are constantly developing *new* instruments. However, many of the structured products are not really new.

In this chapter, we will show you how the "new" products are created by (1) combining the existing instruments, (2) restructuring the existing instruments, or (3) applying the existing instruments to new underlying markets.

Combining Building Blocks to Produce "New" Instruments

In Chapter 2, we introduced our "building-block" theme, identifying forwards, futures, swaps, and options as the risk management building blocks. In subsequent chapters, we have shown how the individual risk management building blocks can be used. One way—in many respects the simplest way—that new risk management products are engineered is by combining two or more of the building blocks to construct a customized product.

Combining Forwards with Swaps

Combining a forward and a swap into a single instrument—specifically, offering a forward contract on a swap—results in an instrument normally referred to as a *forward* or *delayed-start swap*. (See Figure 14–1.)

FIGURE 14–1   Creating a Forward Swap

Pay fixed, receive floating for periods 1 through T

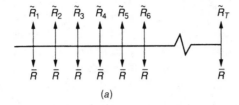

(a)

Plus   Pay floating, receive fixed for periods 1 through 4

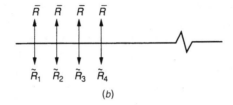

(b)

Equals   A four-period forward contract on a pay fixed, receive floating swap

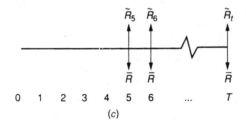

(c)

Although the swap payments do not begin until the specified future date, the forward swap is identical to a regular swap once the start date is reached. A forward swap is often used by a treasurer who expects to issue floating-rate debt in the future and wants to lock in existing rates. For example, if XYZ Corporation intends to issue floating-rate notes in nine months but wants to lock in today's fixed rate, it can enter into a nine-month forward swap, with the notional principal and maturity of the swap set equal to that of the expected debt offering. In nine months, the payments on the swap will begin: XYZ will pay a fixed rate, which was known at origination of the forward swap, and will receive cash flows based on LIBOR (which XYZ will in turn use to make payments on the floating-rate debt).

Combining Options with Forwards

The forward-swap combination eliminates the potential for unfavorable outcomes but also eliminates potential favorable outcomes. The combination of options with forward contracts allows managers to hedge against potential unfavorable situations while participating in gains if rates move in the user's favor.

The most common forward-option combinations are referred to as types of forwards—*break, range,* and *participating forwards.* While not limited to FX, these constructions have been more common in the foreign exchange markets.

In Figure 14–2, we have illustrated a situation in which the contract rate of a standard sterling forward contract is $1.50. Alternatively, the risk manager can buy a break forward contract that is constructed with a contract rate of $1.55 and that permits the holder to break—unwind—the forward contract at a price of $1.50.

FIGURE 14–2   Break Forward

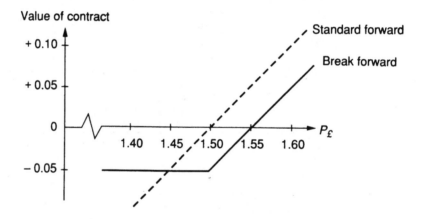

Note that the payoff of this modified forward is equivalent to a long call on sterling—the right to buy sterling at a price of $1.50. If the dollar value of sterling rises, at expiration the manager will earn the then prevailing spot price minus $1.55. On the other hand, if the value of sterling declines, the holder of the break forward will unwind the contract at $1.50. The $0.05 difference in the contract rates for the standard forward contract versus the break forward represents the implicit premium paid for the option structure.

A range forward takes the forward and option combination one step further, adding a second option position. As we saw in Chapter 12, a common option strategy involves the sale of a put in order to fund the call option premium. Figure 14–3 provides an example of a range forward: The standard forward contract has a contract rate of $1.50. In Figure 14–3, the premium for a put option on sterling with an

---
Aside

Why Break Forwards?

At this point, many of you ought to be wondering why break forwards ever appeared. After all, a break forward is simply an option with a different way of expressing the premium. The reason lies in the accounting treatment of the two building blocks. Under FASB Statement No. 52, forward foreign exchange contracts would be eligible for hedge accounting treatment—gains or losses in the forward could be deferred until the hedged transaction was recognized. However, options that were sold would have to be marked-to-market. In the late 1980s and early 1990s, break forwards (and other "complex forwards") were accounted for as forwards rather than as options. This practice was discontinued in March 1992 when the staff of the Securities and Exchange Commission objected to this practice.

---

exercise price of $1.56 is equal to the premium for a call with an exercise price of $1.43. A range forward contract would allow the holder of the contract to purchase sterling at $1.50 at maturity while allowing him to unwind the contract if sterling falls below $1.43. But it also allows the seller of the range forward the right to unwind the contract if sterling rises beyond $1.56.[1] In this range forward, the implicit premium for the right to unwind the forward contract is covered by the short put position so that the risk manager has eliminated the out-of-pocket cost for the option construction.[2]

FIGURE 14–3   Range Forward

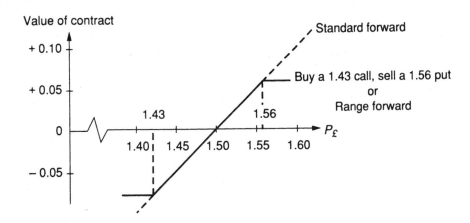

With the break forward, the option premium is reflected in an "off-market" contract rate for the forward contract; the range forward reduces—or eliminates—the premium by having the holder of the complex forward position sell an option to finance the one he wants to purchase. A *participating forward* (or *participation*) eliminates the up-front premium in a different manner.

As is illustrated in panel (*a*) of Figure 14–4, buying an out-of-the-money call can provide a floor on the financial price risk. The cost of the "insurance" is the option premium. In the range forward, the option premium for the purchased call would be offset by the option premium for selling an out-of-the-money put. However, the risk manager need not sell an out-of-the money put. Another alternative is to sell a put at the same strike as the desired call. This put would be in-the-money; and as panel (*b*) of Figure 14–4 illustrates, the premium for this in-the-money put would exceed the premium for the out-of-the-money call. So instead of selling a put with the same notional value as the call, the risk manager would only have to sell a fraction of the put to finance the cost of the call. In panel (*b*) of Figure 14–4 we illustrate a situation in which the risk manager would have to sell in-the-money puts for only 1/2 of the notional principal of the forward. Panel (*c*) of Figure 14–4 illustrates the complete construction: no up-front premium is paid—the contract rate for the participating forward is the same as that for a standard forward. As panel (*d*) illustrates, the protection is paid for only if the final asset price is below the strike price *X*. As the final asset price declines, the cost of the protection increases. The provider of the floor is paid with a portion of the potential profits—the seller of this structure "participates" in upside gains.

The break, range, and participating forwards can be viewed as combinations of forwards and standard options. A *trigger forward* can be viewed as the combination of a forward and a barrier option. In a trigger forward, the user enters into an outright forward at a rate significantly more attractive than the prevailing market rate. However, if the spot exchange rate hits a predetermined trigger level, the structure knocks out. For example, if the outright forward rate for USD/Italian lira (ITL) was 1,668, a trigger forward could be constructed so that the user could sell USD against ITL at 1,710 in nine months' time unless a USD/ITL rate of 1,450 is hit during the nine-month period. If 1,450 trades, the whole structure knocks out.

If the USD appreciates against ITL, the user is obliged to sell USD at 1,710.

If the USD depreciates against ITL but does not reach 1,450, the customer can sell USD at 1,710.

If the USD depreciates against ITL and reaches 1,450, the structure knocks out.

An *at-maturity trigger forward* is similar to the trigger forward but less risky in the sense that it only knocks out if the spot exchange rate is below a specified rate

FIGURE 14–4 Participating Forward

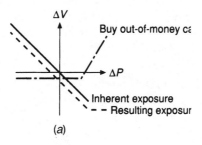

(a)

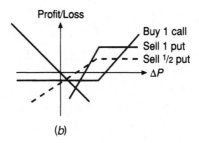

(b)

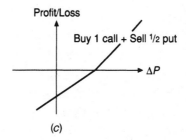

(c)

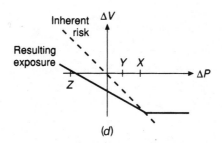

(d)

on the day of maturity. Because of this, the knock-out level is closer to the current spot rate than with the trigger forward. Continuing the example, with an outright forward USD/ITL rate of 1,668, an at-maturity trigger forward could be constructed with the new nine-month forward rate at 1,710 and the knock-out at 1,510.

> If the USD appreciates against ITL, the customer is obliged to sell USD at 1,710.
>
> If the USD depreciates against ITL but the spot is above 1,510 *at maturity,* the customer can sell USD at 1,710.
>
> If the USD depreciates against ITL and spot is at or below 1,510 *at maturity,* the structure is knocked out.

The trigger forward has a better-than-market forward rate because the user is selling an option. A *double trigger forward* provides the user with a better forward rate than in the standard trigger forward, because the user sells an additional option. This structure is easiest to explain via an example. Suppose the outright forward rate for the USD/Japanese yen (JPY) exchange rate was 97.50. A nine-month double trigger forward structure could be constructed with a forward rate of 105.00 (rather than 97.50). This structure would knock out at 90.00. And if USD/JPY trades at 111, a USD call is knocked in.

> If spot remains between 90.00 and 105.00, the user sells USDs at 105.00 on expiry date.
>
> If spot trades 90.00 at any time, the structure is knocked out.
>
> If, at maturity, spot is above 105.00 but not at 111.00, the user sells USDs at the prevailing market rate on expiry.
>
> If spot trades at 111.00, the dealer selling the structure can buy USDs from the user of this structure at 105.00.

Combining Options with Swaps

Cancelable swaps—also referred to as *collapsible swaps*—embed an interest rate option in the swap contract.[3] The firm enters into a swap but has the right to cancel the transaction. For example, the treasurer, if receiving LIBOR in the swap, would like to cancel the swap if interest rates decline; a cancelable swap gives the treasurer that right—that option. The treasurer pays for the option to cancel by paying a fixed rate on the swap that is higher than prevailing fixed rates.

In a cancelable swap, changes in interest rates trigger a change in the *nature* of interest payments or receipts—e.g., if the interest rate falls, the treasurer has the right to switch from paying a fixed-rate coupon to paying a floating-rate coupon. In an *index amortizing swap*—also referred to as an *indexed principal swap*—

changes in interest rates trigger a change in the *level* of the underlying notional principal on which interest rate–determined flows are paid or received.

For example, in an index amortizing swap, the fixed-rate payer has the right—the option—to amortize the notional principal of the swap if interest rates fall. This is implemented by having the notional principal of the swap tied to the future movement of an interest rate—usually LIBOR. The notional principal will decline according to a preestablished schedule if rates decline.[4] To pay for the embedded interest rate option in an indexed-principal swap, the fixed rate paid is higher than the rate for a standard swap.

Index amortizing swaps have been used primarily by financial institutions (and we will return to examine some of the applications of this structured product in Chapter 23). Index amortizing swaps could be used to express a view on the future path of interest rates—e.g., if I expect a period of low-rate volatility, I might enter into an index amortizing swap as a fixed-rate receiver, locking in a higher-than-market fixed rate. However, the principal advantage of an index amortizing swap is that it exhibits positive convexity.[5] Such an instrument can be used to mitigate the negative convexity exhibited by many mortgage-backed securities—e.g., pools of mortgages characterized by high prepayment when interest rates decline.

Both the cancelable and the index amortizing swaps were combinations of swaps with standard options. The *semifixed swap* is the combination of a swap with a binary option. As illustrated in Figure 14–5, a semifixed interest rate swap has two fixed rates—one below and the other above the current market swap rate. The trigger which will determine which rate applies could be the current interest rate.

For example, in May 1993, three-month LIBOR was 3.25 percent and the three-year swap rate was 4.65 percent. Suppose a treasurer believed that three-month LIBOR would stay below 6.0 percent for the next three years. By acting on that view, the treasurer could have reduced the swap rate by 50 basis points via a semifixed swap structured so that the firm will pay 4.15 percent as long as three-month LIBOR remains at or below 6 percent; but if three-month LIBOR is above

FIGURE 14–5   Semifixed Swap

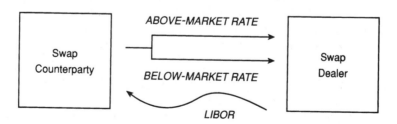

6 percent, the firm would pay 7.15 percent. And these rates are entirely adjustable. The treasurer might want to save more than 50 basis points—the lower rate to be below 4.15 percent. To obtain this larger saving from the prevailing swap rate, she would have to agree to either a higher upper rate (higher than 7.15 percent) or a lower exercise price for the binary option (lower than 6 percent).

The trigger for the semifixed swap need not be an interest rate; it could as easily be another financial price. Indeed, a firm that relies heavily on oil or oil products as inputs might wish to enter into a semifixed swap with oil prices as the trigger—if the price of oil is high, the oil user pays a below-market interest rate; if the price of oil is low, the oil user pays an above-market interest rate.

Combining Options with Other Options

In the same way we can create new payoff profiles by combining options with forwards and swaps, we can create still more new payoff profiles by combining options with other options. One big difference is that option combinations generally have more colorful names—like straddles, strangles, butterflies—than do the combinations of options with forwards and swaps. Figure 14–6 illustrates some of these combinations.

Straddles and strangles are option strategies that allow the buyer of the combination to make money when the price of the underlying asset moves—regardless of whether the price increases or decreases. Hence, in these strategies, the buyer of the combination is in essence "buying volatility" and the seller of the combination is "selling volatility."

A long straddle position is created by buying a call and a put with the same strike price (as well as the same time to expiration). If the stock price increases, the call ends in-the-money; if the stock price decreases, the put ends in-the-money. This strategy can be quite expensive because the buyer must pay premiums for the two options; but if the underlying financial price is volatile enough, the call or the put will finish in-the-money by enough to offset the cost of the two options. Panel (*a*) of Figure 14–6 shows the payout of a long straddle.

A strangle is similar to the straddle, but the call and the put are both purchased out-of-the-money. In comparison to the straddle, this substantially reduces the cost of the strategy, but the holder can lose both premiums if the underlying closes between the two strikes; the break-even price move for a strangle is higher than that for the straddle. Panel (*b*) of Figure 14–6 shows the payout of the long strangle.

Straddles and strangles involve combinations of two options; a butterfly involves the combination of four options. Panel (*c*) of Figure 14–6 shows the pay-off of the long butterfly constructed by buying a call with a strike at *X*, buying a put with a strike of *Y*, and selling both a call and a put at strike *Z*. However, there are three other ways that this butterfly could be constructed:

1. Buy a call at strike X, sell two calls at strike Z, and buy a call at strike Y.
2. Buy a put at strike X, sell two puts at strike Z, and buy a put at strike Y.
3. Buy a put at strike X, sell a put and a call at strike Z, and buy a call at strike Y.

In contrast to straddles and strangles, which pay off when the underlying financial price changes, butterflies are used when the underlying asset is expected to stay within a certain range.

FIGURE 14–6 Combinations of Options

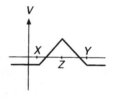

(a) Straddle

(b) Strangle

(c) Butterfly

And this list by no means exhausts the possibilities of option combinations—or the colorful names for these combinations. For example, in the same way that a straddle can change into a strangle by moving the strike prices apart, a butterfly can change into a "condor."

Restructuring the Building Blocks to Produce "New" Instruments

Instead of creating "new" instruments via the combination of standard building blocks, we have also seen "new" instruments created by *restructuring* the standard building blocks. In some instances, it is difficult to differentiate between combinations and restructurings.

> Should a participating forward be viewed as a combination of options or a restructured forward?

And while some of this restructuring has dealt with swaps—notable "delayed-reset" swaps—most of the focus of the restructuring has been on options.

Restructured Swaps

Delayed Reset Swaps.   As we saw in Chapter 8, in a standard swap, the floating-rate payment made at one settlement is determined by the floating rate that was in effect when the last settlement was made. A *delayed-reset swap*—also referred to as an *in-arrears* or *back-end-set swap*—restructures the cash flows such that the floating-rate payment is determined by the floating rate in effect at the settlement date.

Figure 14–7 illustrates the cash flow differences between the standard and delayed-reset structures for a swap where the floating rate is six-month LIBOR. For the standard swap, the floating-rate payment at the first settlement date—month 6—is determined by six-month LIBOR at origination; the payment at the second settlement date—month 12—is determined by six-month LIBOR at month 6, and so on. The delayed-reset swap advances the date for computing the floating-rate cash flows by six months. The first payment, made at month 6, is determined by the six-month LIBOR rate in effect at month 6; the second floating-rate payment, made at month 12, is determined by the six-month LIBOR rate in effect at month 12.[6]

With a standard swap both parties know the amount of the floating-rate payment six months in advance. With the delayed-reset swap neither party knows for certain what the floating-rate payment will be until the payment is due.

In Chapter 8 we showed you how the forward rates determine the fixed rate in a standard swap. The fixed rate in a delayed-reset swap is determined in the same way; but the relevant forward rates are one period further out for a delayed-reset

FIGURE 14–7   A Restructured Swap

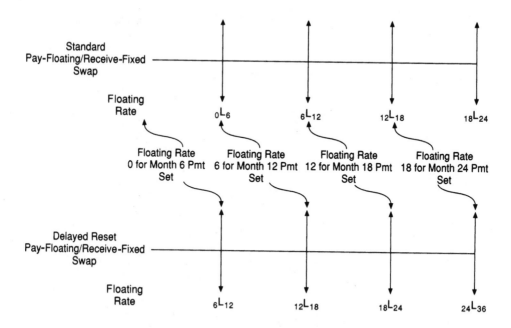

swap. Hence, the difference between the fixed rate in a standard swap and delayed-reset swap is as a result of the difference in the forward rates.

If the yield curve is upward sloping, the fixed rate for a delayed-reset swap is higher than that for a standard swap—because the forward rates used to price the delayed-reset swap will be higher. And the more steeply upward sloping the yield curve is, the higher the fixed rate in a delayed-reset swap relative to that in a standard swap. Consequently, when the yield curve is steeply upward sloping, pay-floating/receive-fixed delayed-reset swaps are particularly attractive because the fixed rate is so high.

However, there is no "free lunch" here. The counterparties who enter into these trades are implicitly taking a view that the future spot rates will be lower than the rates implied by the forward yield curve.

Diff Swaps.   *Differential ("diff") swaps*—a.k.a. *cross-indexed* or *quanto swaps*—are swaps that permit users to take advantage of differences between rates in different markets, without exposing themselves to foreign exchange rate risk. Perhaps an example might be the most effective way to introduce this structure.[7]

As illustrated in Figure 14–8, in the spring of 1992, U.S. dollar interest rates were significantly lower than German interest rates—six-month USD LIBOR was 4.25 percent, while six-month DM LIBOR was 9.63 percent. Moreover, the

---

Illustration 14–1

A Delayed LIBOR Reset Swap

In Chapter 8 we considered a one-year inter-est rate swap between Galactic Industries and the Dead Solid Perfect Bank when the spot LIBOR yield curve is as follows:

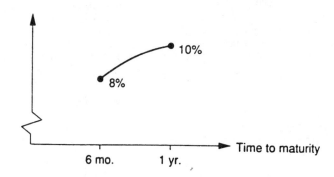

We saw in Chapter 8 that for a standard (plain vanilla) swap, the fixed rate Galactic would receive was 9.70 percent. Let's change our swap between Galactic Industries and the Dead Solid Perfect Bank to a delayed LIBOR reset swap. With this structure, at origination, the rate DSPB *expects* to receive at month 6 is not the six-month spot rate at origination, 8 percent, but is instead the forward rate—the six-month rate in six months—11.5 percent. Hence:

$$\tilde{R}_1 = \$100 \, (1/2)0.115 = \$5.75$$

Likewise, in an in-arrears swap the rate DSPB expects to receive at month 6 is not the six-month rate in six months but the six-month rate in *12 months*. Let's suppose this forward rate is 13 percent and

$$\tilde{R}_2 = \$100 \, (1/2)0.13 = \$6.50$$

DSPB's expected outflows are as illus-trated below.

To determine the appropriate fixed rate for DSPB to pay, we know that the expected net present value of the swap at origination must be zero, so

$$\frac{5.75 - \bar{R}}{1 + \frac{1}{2}(0.08)} + \frac{6.50 - \bar{R}}{1.10} = 0$$

Solving the preceding equation, $\bar{R} = \$6.11$. Hence in the case of this off-market swap, the appropriate fixed rate for Galactic to re-ceive is 12.22 percent, not the par rate of 9.70 percent.

FIGURE 14–8   Implied Forward Six-Month LIBOR Rates (Semiannual, Actual/360 Basis)

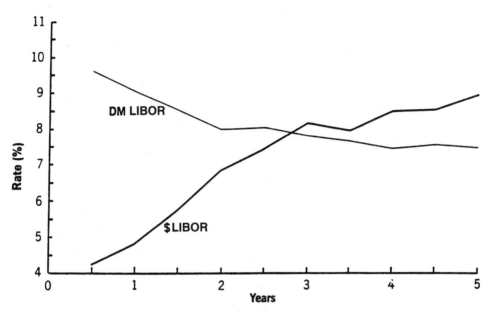

SOURCE: William Falloon, "Curves and the Fuller Figure," *Risk* 5, no. 5 (May 1992).

U.S. yield curve was steeply upward sloping while the German yield curve was inverted. A common diff swap structure required the holder to pay cash flows determined by six-month USD LIBOR and a USD notional principal and receive cash flows determined by six-month DM LIBOR *but a USD notional principal.*

	Receive	Pay
Diff swap	$r_{6mUSDLIBOR}*NP_{USD}$	$r_{6mDMLIBOR}*NP_{USD}$

This swap is portrayed graphically in Figure 14–9. The parties entering into such a swap were implicitly taking the position that U.S. rates would not rise as rapidly as implied by the forward yield curve and/or that German rates would not fall as rapidly as implied by the forward yield curve.

FIGURE 14–9   A Diff Swap

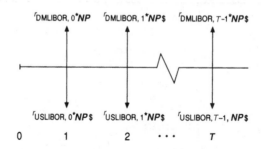

At period t ($t = 1, 2,..., T$) the party receives
(pays a cash flow determined by the *difference*
in the *nominal* DM and US LIBOR rates in effect at
period t-1. That is, the payment is
$$(^{r}\text{DMLIBOR, } t\text{-1} - {}^{r}\text{USLIBOR, } T\text{-1})^*NP\$$$
If the payment is positive (negative), the party
illustrated receives (makes) a payment.

A diff swap looks deceptively similar to the other structures. When we first heard about diff swaps, it seemed like a diff swap "should be" made up of some combination of interest rate and currency coupon swaps:

Interest rate swap—USD		$r_{\text{6mUSDLIBOR}}{}^*NP_{\text{USD}}$
$r_{\text{FIXED}}{}^*NP_{\text{USD}}$		
Interest rate swap—DM	$r_{\text{6mDMLIBOR}}{}^*NP_{\text{DM}}$	$r_{\text{FIXED}}{}^*NP_{\text{DM}}$
Currency coupon swap	$r_{\text{6mUSDLIBOR}}{}^*NP_{\text{USD}}$	$r_{\text{6mDMLIBOR}}{}^*NP_{\text{DM}}$

But regardless of how you combine these swap structures, USD notional principals will always be associated with USD interest rates. It is impossible to put together the preceding swaps to end up with a USD notional principal multiplied by a DM interest rate.

In order to hedge or deconstruct a differential swap, it is necessary for the seller of the differential swap to hedge USD-denominated DM interest rate risk using DM-denominated instruments. Although the prevailing exchange rate will determine the initial quantum of the hedge, ongoing changes in the exchange rates will vary the size of the hedge required. In order to calculate the cost associated with this hedge rebalancing, the seller of the differential swap must make assumptions about the correlation—covariance—between DM LIBOR and $/DM exchange rate.

$$\text{Cov}\,(r_{6mDMLIBOR}, S_{\$/DM})$$

And if the dealer overestimates this covariance, she will lose money. It follows then that, for the dealer, the diff swaps must be managed like the multifactor options we examined in Chapter 13—i.e., rainbow, quanto, and basket options.

Options on Forwards, Futures, Swaps, and Other Options

Options on Futures.   In our description of the evolution of the risk management products in Chapter 1, we noted that options on futures contracts on financial prices first appeared in the early 1980s. Options on futures trade on most of the major futures exchanges in the world and are available on a wide range of financial prices—commodity prices, foreign exchange rates, and interest rates.

Given the relations we have established between futures and forwards and futures and swaps, you probably suspect that the introduction of options on forwards and options on swaps would have followed close on the heels of the options on futures. However, options on forwards—in particular, options on forward rate agreements—and options on swaps—referred to as swaptions—appeared only at the end of the 1980s.

Options on Swaps: Swaptions.   The holder of a swaption has the right to enter into an interest rate swap in the future.[8] Swaptions can be European style, meaning that the holder of the swaption can enter into the swap only on a specified date (the expiration date of the swaption); or they can be American style, meaning that the holder of the swaption can enter into the swap at any time prior to the expiration date of the swaption. Instead of using the jargon of puts and calls, the swaption market refers to *payer swaptions*, which give the holders the right to enter into a swap in which they will pay the fixed rate, and *receiver swaptions*, which give the right to enter into a swap to receive the fixed rate.

The buyer of a "payer swaption" holds the functional equivalent of a call option on interest rates—the buyer will exercise the right to enter into a pay-fixed swap if the floating rate rises. Conversely, the buyer of a "receiver swaption" holds the equivalent of a put option on interest rates—the buyer benefits from a drop in interest rates by exercising into a receive-fixed swap if the floating rate declines.

For swaptions, corporate hedgers may opt for physical settlement: the parties actually enter into the swap agreement upon exercise. However, in order to minimize the credit risk associated with a swaption, the market is increasingly moving toward cash settlement: at exercise, the underlying swap is marked-to-market and the value is conveyed to the owner of the swaption in cash.

Most swaptions permit the buyer of the swaption to specify the settlement dates for the underlying swap when the swaption is exercised rather than upon origination of the swaption. Therefore, to avoid nonstandard coupon exchange dates, these swaptions tend to be European style.[9]

As illustrated in Table 14–1, since introduction in the late 1980s, the swaption market has grown dramatically—even faster than the market for the underlying interest rate swaps. While the U.S. dollar–based contracts still account for the majority of deals outstanding, swaptions in other currencies, particularly the deutsche mark, are rapidly outstripping the volume in U.S. dollar–denominated swaptions.

TABLE 14–1   Swaptions Outstanding (Notational Principal in Billions of U.S. Dollars)

	1989	*1990*	*1991*	*1992*	*1993*	*1994*	*1995*
U.S. dollars	51	63	57	31	129	159	393
Other currencies	21	31	52	96	282	187	371
Total	72	94	109	127	411	346	764

SOURCE: International Swaps and Derivatives Association, Inc.

The swaption market got a "kick start" early on when many firms realized that swaptions could be used to "monetize" the value of the interest rate option embedded in the call provision of bonds issued in the U.S. capital market. A case in point is Ford Motor Credit Corporation.[10]

> Ford Motor Credit Corporation issued 10-year fixed-rate notes callable after five years. Since FMCC had the option to call the notes, they had a put option on interest rates. The firm then entered into a standard "pay-floating/receive-fixed" interest rate swap, turning the fixed-rate liability into a floating-rate liability. However, at the same time, FMCC also sold through its underwriter the right to terminate the swap after five years; that is, FMCC sold a swaption. In effect, the buyer of the swaption purchased the right to pay floating and receive the fixed rate specified today for years 5 through 10. Clearly, this right is valuable (would be exercised) only if rates fall; that is, the buyer of this swaption has bought the put option on interest rates that Ford Motor Credit owned as a result of the call provision on its notes. According to *Investment Dealers' Digest,* this structure "was rumored to have cut Ford's borrowing costs by roughly 20 basis points." Put another way, the put option on interest rates sold by Ford had a value equivalent to 20 basis points on the $250 million borrowing.

Deals like the preceding worked because the swaption market valued the embedded interest rate options higher than the bond investor. Issuers could lower financing costs by "selling the call" to the swaption dealer, earning an up-front premium. If interest rates rise, the swaption expires worthless and the issuer need not call the bonds—the issuer continues to pay the fixed rate obtained at issue.

However, if interest rates fall sufficiently, the purchaser of the swaption will exercise: the purchaser of the swaption will elect to receive the fixed rate and pay the now lower floating rate for the maturity of the swap contract. This will likely require the issuer to call the bonds, but the benefit of the lower interest rate goes to the purchaser of the swaption rather than the issuer.[11]

For this "monetizing calls" strategy to work, the swaption dealer must place a higher value on the interest rate options than do the purchasers of the callable bonds (the sellers of the interest rate options to the bond issuer). The available evidence suggests that the difference between these values narrowed dramatically during the early 1990s. As you would expect, access to this market increased the efficiency of the pricing and reduced the impetus for corporations to sell swaptions.

Instead, corporations are increasingly purchasing swaptions as components of their interest rate risk management. Long swaption positions can be employed to hedge an anticipated or uncertain exposure. For example, a corporation bidding on a project may want to take advantage of current low financing rates without being locked into a long-term swap if the transaction is not executed. A long payer swaption position enables the corporation the opportunity to pay the fixed and receive the floating rates if interest rates rise prior to expiration.

Note, however, that instead of the swaption, an interest rate cap could be used to hedge a potential future liability. In order to have equivalent terms, the cap would be structured as a series of calls that cover the life of the swaption plus the life of the underlying swap. The cap offers multiple settlement dates and thus multiple opportunities to gain from favorable rate movements. Therefore, the premium on a swaption is less than that of a comparable cap; this provides greater leverage and requires less capital tied up in the hedge during the period of uncertainty.[12]

Options on Options: Compound Options.   An option that gives its purchaser the right to buy a specified option at some time in the future for a premium that is specified today is one member of the family of compound options we introduced in Chapter 11. In Chapter 11, we concentrated on the pricing difficulties encountered by the dealer—the price of an option on an option depends not only on the volatility of the underlying asset but also on the volatility of the value of an option. Here we will concentrate on the user's perspective, noting that options on options can make sense to an end user because it is cheaper to purchase an option of an option than to purchase the option itself.

The first time we encountered applications of compound options was in the foreign exchange markets—options on foreign exchange options. An engineering or construction firm that was bidding on a project in a foreign country faced a dilemma. If it won the contract, it would have a foreign exchange exposure that it would want to cover—and the cost of that cover needed to be included in the bid. However, knowing that it might not be awarded the contract, the firm did not want to be locked into a forward contract, nor did it want to pay a large premium for an option it might not need. The option on an option worked for this firm. If it won the contract, the firm would exercise its right to purchase an option—at a price specified at the time it made its bid. If it lost the contract, the "insurance premium" was as small as possible.

In addition to foreign exchange, compound options have been used in both the interest rate and equity markets. Indeed, to date, the widest acceptance of compound options many well be in the interest rate markets: options on caps and floors, or *captions* and *floortions*.[13]

A caption gives its holder the right to buy a specified cap at a specific price on (or if the caption is American-style, before) a given date. The captions contract specifies not only the cap rate and the maturity for the underlying cap but also the premium that will be paid for the cap if the caption is exercised—the strike price for the caption—and the time to expiration for the caption.[14]

For example, consider a two-year cap that currently has a premium of 100 basis points. An at-the-money six-month caption—an option to purchase the cap in six months for 100 basis points—could currently be purchased for 10 basis points. If, at the caption's expiration, the cap has a value of 125 basis points, the holder of the caption exercised the option to buy the cap for 100 basis points. A caption will increase the current premium of the cap—the total cost to the buyer is 110 basis points (the premium for the underlying cap plus the cost of the caption); however, it will lock in the ability to hedge at a later date.

Restructured Options

So far, in this section, we have been considering "standard" options. In a real sense, the second-generation options we described in Chapter 13 could be considered to be structured products created by restructuring the cash flows from an option.

And these second-generation options can be restructured further to yield other structured products. For example, a *basket-digital option* is a combination of a binary option and a basket option.[15] This structured product combines the diversification found in a basket option with the "either-or" profile of a digital option. The idea is that a basket digital with an either-or payout profile will be attractive to an investor who has a view only on whether or not a price level is broken, rather than on how far prices would rise above the strike level.

Applying the Building Blocks to New Underlying Markets to Produce "New" Instruments

In some instances, financial engineering has led to the development of products that are nothing more than the standard building blocks applied to new underlying markets. Derivative exchanges are always looking for ways to develop standardized contracts based on previously untapped underlying markets. OTC dealers are always anxious to write or buy derivatives on any underlying index or security that will solve customers' risk management problems. This section explores these new derivative markets, both on and off the exchange floors.

Exchange-Traded Products

Several new or proposed exchange-traded futures and options products represent the use of existing building blocks for new underlying markets.

Catastrophe Insurance Futures and Options.   Three of the contracts traded on the Chicago Board of Trade (CBOT) are based on property/casualty insurance claims for the United States and for two regions of the United States—the East and Midwest. Each contract represents the ratio of quarterly catastrophe losses to earned premiums as tracked by a loss index provided by the Insurance Services Office (ISO). The eastern contract essentially monitors hurricanes, while the midwestern contract focuses on tornadoes. The catastrophe contracts are geared toward both insurance companies wishing to hedge the risk of a catastrophe and speculators willing to bet that a catastrophe will not occur. The CBOT began trading the eastern and national contracts in 1992; the midwestern contract began in May 1993.

In 1995, the CBOT added nine new catastrophe insurance option contracts. In contrast to existing contracts which are based on loss ratios (i.e., claims), the new contracts are based on indexes of catastrophe loss estimates. Estimates are provided by Property Claim Services covering the United States and eight regions—California, Florida, Texas, the West, the Northeast, the Southeast, the East, and the Midwest.

Futures and Options on Commodity Indexes.   The Chicago Mercantile Exchange listed futures and options on the Goldman Sachs Commodity Index in mid-1992. These products allow trading in a liquid group of nonfinancial commodities with a single trade. The GSCI is a market value-weighted index that represents the sum of each commodity's U.S. dollar value of world production. The index includes grains and oil seeds, livestock, metals, energy, and food and fiber. The underlying futures contracts for each of these commodities are used to determine the dollar value of world production. This index is unique because it is the first derivative product that is based on an index of futures prices.

Futures and Options on Financial Instruments of Emerging Economies.   In 1995 the Chicago Mercantile Exchange voted to create its first new division in 13 years. The Growth and Emerging Markets (GEM) Division will allow its members to trade *futures and options based on financial instruments in emerging economies.* The new division will have 50 full seats that will be offered to the public at $30,000 apiece, with an additional 417 full memberships being added over a five-year period. Also in 1995, the New York Cotton Exchange listed futures on Latin American Brady bonds and introduced options on its FINEX exchange in early November. The cash-settled contracts are based on a weighted average of Brady bonds of Mexico, Argentina, Brazil, and Venezuela.

Electricity Futures.   Once a textbook example of a "natural monopoly," the market for electricity is changing. The changes are the result of both improved power generation and transmission technology and the deregulation of energy markets. Deregulation in the wholesale markets has occurred or is imminent in Norway, Sweden, the United States, the United Kingdom, Finland, Australia, New Zealand, and Canada.

Futures contracts on electricity have been introduced or announced in the United States, Norway, Sweden, Finland, Australia, and New Zealand. The contracts in the United States and Scandinavia are summarized in Table 14–2.

TABLE 14–2   Exchange-Traded Electricity Derivatives

Country	Exchange	Contracts	Delivery
United States	New York Mercantile Exchange	California-Oregon Border (COB) futures/options	Physical
United States	New York Mercantile Exchange	Palo Verde futures/options	Physical
Norway/ Sweden	Nordic Electricity Exchange	Daily, weekly, monthly futures	Physical
Finland	El-Ex Electricity Exchange	Spot (hourly), weekly, seasonal	Physical

Figure 14–10 tracks the volumes for the two U.S. futures contracts from the time they were introduced in March 1996 through June 1997. Market observers suggest that two factors inhibit trading. First, the slow pace of retail deregulation in California means that local utilities are still able to pass on costs to consumers; so hedging is not yet crucial. Second, the segmentation of electricity distribution into loosely interconnected regional power grids means that prices and volatility vary substantially across the United States; so hedging of electricity bought outside the delivery points, for example with Nymex futures in the Pennsylvania–Maryland–New Jersey region, is impractical—the basis risk is too high.[16] Instead, hedges are done bilaterally or through large brokers and power marketers with the experience to structure and price customized transactions tied to the local market.

**FIGURE 14–10   Nymex Electricity Futures Contracts Volume:
March 1996—June 1997**

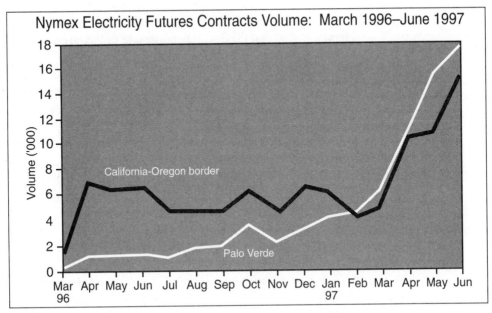

Nymex Electricity Futures Contracts Volume: March 1996–June 1997

SOURCE: Risk.

New OTC Swaps and Options

Commodity Derivatives.   The OTC market has also witnessed a movement toward the application of existing derivative structures to new underlying markets.
One important recent development has been the over-the-counter market for commodity derivatives such as swaps, caps, and floors on commodities ranging from
orange juice to electricity. Listed commodities futures and futures options offer
physical settlement, standardized terms, and generally liquid and transparent markets. In contrast, the OTC products have expanded the number of tools available
for hedging risk by offering longer maturities, greater position size, cash settlement, and overall better customized payoffs.

Volatilities in natural gas and electricity and soft commodities markets, such as
orange juice, coffee, cotton, and wheat, created interest in hedging price risk using
the OTC swap market. To date, maturities have usually been limited to less than
five years. These deals are primarily driven by the producers in the energy market
and users in the soft commodities markets. Where a natural two-sided market does
not appear, the dealer lays off risk in the listed markets if sufficient liquidity is
available. While it is difficult to measure the impact of the OTC market on the listed

market, exchange volume provides some indication—e.g., the volume of natural gas futures traded on NYMEX more than tripled in 1991, in large part due to the growth of the OTC business.

Electricity Derivatives.   Two reasons lead observers to expect electricity derivatives—exchange-traded and OTC—to become one of the largest of the derivatives markets. First, the physical market for electricity is one of the world's largest—in the United States alone, annual electricity sales exceed $200–250 billion. Second, electricity prices exhibit the high-volatility characteristic of successful derivatives markets—in the United States, futures volatility ranges between 25 and 50 percent, while spot market volatility regularly exceeds 100 percent.

The growth of the electricity derivatives market has been impeded by a lack of price transparency. The market tends to be based on physical delivery of power and privately negotiated transactions. As countries deregulate, the price transparency issue is being resolved through development of spot market price indexes—like the ones published by Dow Jones in the United States—screen-based broker markets and futures markets.[17]

Another block to the rapid growth of electricity derivatives is the simple fact that electricity is not readily storable. Existing financial and commodity derivatives are priced according to the "cost of carry" model described in Chapter 6. That model is of little use in the electricity market. Forwards are not linked to the spot market by cash and carry arbitrage trades but are driven by the pricing models and demand forecasts of individual market participants. Except for the thinly traded futures markets, these prices are not observable by third parties, and forward price curves are therefore difficult to come by.

Power marketers and brokers are offering a wide range of derivative strategies built on the standard building blocks of forwards, swaps, and options. Two classes of transactions receiving attention are the "spark" spreads and so-called integrated hedges.

The spark spread is the spread between natural gas and electricity prices. Spark spread trades can be physical or purely financial. In the physical market, they involve the purchase of gas, its transmission to a particular generator, and the final sale or consumption of the electricity produced. A key input to the pricing of the spread is the efficiency with which the gas is converted to electricity—the "heat rate." Assuming a heat rate of 10,000 BTU/KWh, the spark spread would equal the electricity price minus 10 times the natural gas price (using NYMEX contracts). Where forward markets exist, such as at COB, the purely financial version of the spread can be executed.

Integrated strategies look much like structured transactions in traditional derivatives, in which payments for one product are linked to the price of a second. For example, an aluminum smelter might structure its electricity purchases so that the price it pays for electricity varies with the wholesale price of aluminum. Option contracts may have the strike price linked to a multiple of the price of natural gas.

Real Estate Swaps. Early in 1993, Morgan Stanley executed what is believed to be the first *real estate swap* deal, done for a U.S. fund manager. The deal was a two-part, five-year, $20 million swap in which the fund, with sizable real estate holdings, pays a floating rate based on the level of the Frank Russell National Council of Real Estate Investment Fiduciaries (NCREIF) Index. The fund paid the dealer a floating LIBOR-based rate but also swapped out of LIBOR into the return on an index of foreign stocks. Thus, the fund was able to shift its exposure from real estate to foreign equities without having to liquidate its position in the cash markets. Interested parties continued to extol the advantages of real estate derivatives, arguing that real estate derivatives would allow property companies to hedge their risks and to "monetize" positions by selling options on real estate and that real estate derivatives would increase liquidity in real estate by permitting investors to participate in the property market without property management. However, as late as 1997, there was almost no volume. In a survey conducted by builder Jones Lang Wootton, more than 50 percent of the respondents said they would be interested in participating in real estate derivatives once the market is established; but less than 10 percent of respondents said they had already traded in the real estate derivatives market.[18] The proponents of real estate derivatives blame the failure to evolve on the absence of a suitable real estate index. Real estate indexes are available only in the United States and the United Kingdom; but the two indexes currently in use in the United Kingdom are unsuitable as a basis for trading, because they are based on valuations, rather than transactions.

Derivatives on Emerging Country Debt. Derivatives on the debt of less developed countries (in Latin America, Eastern Europe, and Asia) appeared in the early 1990s. While forwards were traded, the most common transactions were options on the debt—e.g., a put option on a Venezuelan Brady bond. While the underlying cash market remains small relative to other, more established markets, high volatility in the prices of these securities stimulated demand for hedging by the purchasers of the underlying debt,[19] as well as some speculative activity. The market downturn in late 1991, coupled with historic lows in U.S. interest rates, fueled the growth of trading of forwards and options on LDC debt. As one example of their usage, suppose a U.S. fund manager desires a higher yield than U.S. instruments are carrying. He may move from U.S. bonds into Mexican or Venezuelan Brady bonds and purchase insurance in the form of short-term put options. Currently, only the largest dealers are participating in LDC debt derivative market-making; but this market is likely to develop as cash market trading grows. Perhaps the most important thing about this market is that it was one of the precursors to the development of ***credit derivatives,*** the topic we turn to next.

Credit Derivatives.[20]   Derivative contracts on default risk are not new; options that pay in the event of default by a particular credit have been around for more than 20 years—in the form of bond insurance.[21] Other "traditional" credit derivatives— letters of credit (options on the creditworthiness of a borrower) and revolving credits (options on the borrower's credit spread)—have been around even longer. However, the over-the-counter credit derivatives are relatively new, dating from 1991.

Three credit derivative "building blocks" exist—forward contracts (forward agreements or default-contingent forwards), swaps (total return swaps), and options (credit swaps). (There is, as yet, no futures contract.) While more complicated trades are being done, by and large they are constructed from these building blocks.

Forward Agreements.   Credit forwards are the simplest of the credit derivatives, but they were not the first structure to appear. As with interest rate derivatives, the swap and option structures came first. A *forward agreement* is a forward contract on the *reference asset*[22] that commits the buyer to purchase the specified bond or loan at a specified future date at a price specified at contract origination. Figure 14–11 illustrates the cash flows for a forward agreement.[23]

FIGURE 14–11   Cash Flows for a Forward Agreement

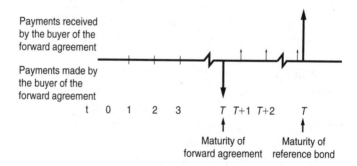

In a forward agreement like that illustrated in Figure 14–8, default risk is borne by the buyer. If a credit event[24] occurs, the transaction is marked-to-market and unwound.

A variation on the standard forward is the *default-contingent forward.* In this structure the seller of the forward bears the default risk on the underlying bond or loan from origination to the maturity of the forward contract, at which time the bond (and the credit risk) is transferred to the buyer of the forward contract.

Total Return Swaps. The most widely used of the swap structures is a *total return swap*. The terms of a total return swap are illustrated in Figure 14–12.

FIGURE 14–12   Total Return Swap

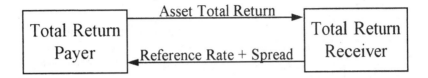

The cash flows for the total return receiver are illustrated in Figure 14–13. At origination ($t = 0$), the counterparties define the reference asset and determine its initial value (P_0); they also agree on the reference rate.[25] At the settlement dates ($0 < t < T$), the asset receiver receives the cash flows (CF) generated by the reference asset and pays an amount determined by the reference rate (RR). At maturity ($t = T$), the counterparties revalue the reference asset (P_T). If the reference asset has appreciated, the asset receiver receives a payment of $P_T - P_0$; if the reference asset has declined in value, the asset receiver makes a payment of $P_0 - P_T$.[26]

FIGURE 14–13   Cash Flows for a Total Return Swap

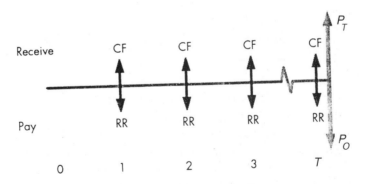

In a total return swap, the total return receiver bears the default risk. Put another way, the total return receiver is "synthetically" long the underlying bond or loan, with all the market *and* credit risk that goes with it; the total return payer is synthetically short the underlying security or portfolio.

Credit Swaps. The most widely used of the option structures is a *credit swap*. The buyer of a credit swap pays a premium (either lump sum or periodic) to the seller, who then assumes the default risk for the reference asset. If there is a credit event during the term of the option, the seller pays the buyer a default payment.[27] The cash flows for a credit swap are illustrated in Figure 14–14.

FIGURE 14–14   Credit Swaps

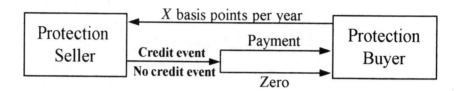

The market has also developed *spread options,* options on the spread between the yield of the reference asset and a base security such as a U.S. Treasury with the same maturity. Figure 14–15 illustrates a spread option. At origination the parties agree on a strike spread with the payout at maturity being a function of the actual spread versus the strike multiplied by a duration factor.

FIGURE 14–15   Spread Options

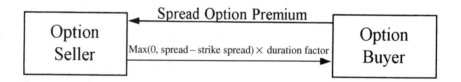

Evolution of the Market.   Although credit derivatives are very new instruments, they are already in their third "incarnation."

The first incarnation could be regarded as defensive, in the sense that they evolved from the need of financial institutions to manage their own illiquid credit concentrations.[28] Dealers had some success using default puts to hedge their credit exposures, but interest in these structures was limited elsewhere because counterparties were unfamiliar with them.

Efforts to turn this one-sided market into a two-sided market spawned the second incarnation of credit derivatives. Existing derivatives techniques were applied to emerging market debt and to corporate bonds and syndicated bank loans. In this phase of investor-driven trades, the credit derivatives market was still a "cash and carry" market. Dealers would hold the underlying instruments—corporate bonds or syndicated loans—on their balance sheets and sell customized exposures to investors via total return swaps and structured notes. Investors were attracted to these new structures for a number of reasons:

- Credit derivatives gave investors access to new asset classes. For example, investors are not capable of providing the servicing that goes with bank loans; therefore they have been precluded from investing directly in loans. Credit derivatives overcome this obstacle by passing the return on a loan to the investor while the back-office processing is handled by a bank. In a similar vein, by selling the total return on a loan or bond, an investor can effectively go short in a market where physical short sales are difficult if not impossible.

- Like derivatives on interest rates, currencies, equities, and commodities, credit derivatives can reduce transaction costs.

- Credit derivatives permit some investors to leverage positions on bonds or loans.

- The pricing of credit derivative structures was often attractive due to disparities in the way credit was priced in the bond, loan, and equity markets. (As the credit derivatives markets develop, these disparities can be expected to disappear and credit risk will be priced uniformly across an issuer's obligations.)

- Credit derivatives allowed bond investors to express specific views about credit without necessarily having to accept the interest rate risk associated with holding a firm's debt. Although bond managers are trained to evaluate credit risk, the primary source of volatility in the bond market is interest rate risk.[29] Since credit derivatives allow credit exposure to be isolated from interest rate exposure, bond managers can express the views they are trained to express.

- Credit derivatives made it possible to create synthetic assets that meet a specific set of investment criteria. An example suggested by Allen Wheat (1995) is an investor who views Argentinian debt as an attractive investment but is subject to two constraints: (1) the principal must be protected and (2) maximum maturity is 10 years. Argentina Brady bonds satisfy the first constraint as their principal is guaranteed—but their maturity is 30 years. Credit derivatives can be used to create a 10-year structure based on the Argentina Brady bonds.

As credit derivatives have moved into their third incarnation, several factors coincided to make this market look more like other derivatives markets. As a result of efforts to educate counterparties and develop investor interest in these products, there is more two-way business. Dealers have begun to "warehouse" trades and cross-hedge, managing risk on a portfolio basis in the same way that an interest rate derivatives book is managed. Brokers have entered the market, and the International Swaps and Derivatives Association (ISDA) has responded to the increased activity by developing standard documentation for credit derivatives.

How Prevalent Are Credit Derivatives?   In May 1996, we informally polled the six major dealers of the products for their best guess about the total volume of credit derivatives transactions executed to that date. The resulting estimates of cumulative notional principal by type of derivative and underlying credit are provided in Table 14–3.

TABLE 14–3   Estimates of the Size of the Credit Derivatives Market Obtained from an Informal Survey in May 1996

	Corporate Bonds	Corporate Loans	Emerging-Market Sovereign Bonds	Total
Forward agreements	100	0	250	350
Total return swaps	2,500	5,000	5,000	12,500
Price-spread options	250	50	7,500	7,800
Default puts	5,000	500	5,000	10,500
Correlation products	2,000	0	0	2,000
Notes	500	500	5,000	6,000
Total	10,350	6,050	22,750	39,150

In November 1996 the British Bankers Association conducted a survey of the London credit derivatives market. A total of 15 institutions participated in the survey. Five institutions, referred to in the survey as "leading houses," claimed notional outstanding of £1–5 billion. Seven firms classified themselves as having less than £100 million notional outstanding, with the rest falling somewhere in between. The survey results presented in Table 14–4 are based on the responses from the "leading houses."

TABLE 14–4   BBA Credit Derivatives Report: Estimated Size of the Credit Derivatives Market in London

	Year		
	1996	1998	2000
Average (mode)	**$20 bn**	**$40 bn**	**$100 bn**
High	$75 bn	$300 bn	$1,200 bn
Low	$15 bn	$40 bn	$40 bn

SOURCE: Survey of the London Market, November 1996.

Notes

1. The numbers in Figure 14–3 are only for purposes of illustration. To determine the exercise prices at which the values of the puts and calls are equal, one would have to use an option-pricing model.

2. In options terminology, the combination of a long call and short put with an underlying position is known as a *collar.*

3. In fact, the option embedded is actually a "swaption"—a structure we will discuss in the next section of this chapter.

4. Most indexed-principal swaps have a "lockout period" at the beginning of the swap during which no amortization will occur. After the lockout period, if rates decline, the fixed-rate payer in effect exercises the option to reduce or cancel a portion of the remaining term of the swap.

5. Specifically, the fixed-rate pay side of an indexed-principal swap has positive convexity.

6. Actually, the rate is set some number of days prior to the settlement date.

7. This example is adapted from "Curves and the Fuller Figure," *Risk,* May 1992.

8. Note that this is different from the payoff of the forward swap. The forward swap parties are *obligated* to enter the swap at the specified future date, while the swaption holder has the *right* to enter the swap on the future date. No "premium" is paid by the forward swap purchaser.

9. Reportedly, 90 percent of swaption transactions are European style. The remaining 10 percent that have American-style exercise are mostly reversible contracts—swaptions whose underlying swap terms are set at the inception of the contract. "Behind the Mirror" (1989).

10. This illustration is adapted from "First Boston Snares Ford Credit with Swaption-Linked Deal," *Investment Dealers' Digest,* January 16, 1989, pp. 42–43.

11. Once the swaption is exercised, the issuer of the bond must begin paying the holder of the swaption a fixed-rate "coupon." Consequently, the bonds will likely be called and the debt refinanced on a floating-rate basis, so the floating rate that the bond issuer will receive on the swap can flow through to the holders of the bonds. After all this, the net effect is that the issuer of the bond is still paying a fixed rate—only now the fixed-rate payment is going to

the holder of the swaption rather than the holders of the bonds.

12. For a more detailed discussion of the relative premiums, see Rombach (1991).

13. To show you the extent to which the jargon goes, there are some who speak of "collartions."

14. The tenor of the caption is generally less than that of the cap.

15. See Yang and Zhang (1995).

16. In the summer of 1997, Nymex was expecting to launch a new futures contract with a delivery point on the East Coast of the United States during the first half of 1998.

17. In Australia, the Sydney Futures Exchange proposed a standardized, screen-based market for trading derivatives linked to transactions in New South Wales, one of two states with a wholesale power market. The United Kingdom has a standardized forward-swap contract, the electricity forward agreement. However, trading levels are low because of uncertainty about regulation of electricity prices.

18. See Lane (1994). The London Futures and Options Exchange introduced four property futures contracts based on commercial property, commercial rents, residential property, and mortgage interest rates in May 1991, but was forced to delist them in October of the same year because of a lack of liquidity. Similarly, so-called PINC and SAPCO property contracts introduced by corporates failed to get off the ground.

19. The purchaser of the debt instrument from a developing country might buy "insurance" to put a floor on the value of the bond by buying a put on the bond.

20. This section is based on two articles that originally appeared in *Risk:* "Credit Derivatives: What Are These Youthful Instruments and Why Are They Used?" with Hal Holappa, December 1995, and "Credit Derivatives (2): A Look at the Market, Its Evolution and Current Size" with Hal Holappa and Shaun Rai, June 1996.

21. Das (1995) notes that AMBAC has been insuring municipal bonds since 1971.

22. The reference asset could be (1) an actively traded corporate or sovereign bond or a portfolio of these bonds or (2) a widely syndicated loan or portfolio of loans.

23. In Figure 14–11, the forward contract is based on the *price* of the reference asset, but it could instead be

based on the reference asset's *spread* over a benchmark asset (usually, a treasury security).

24. A credit event could be (1) bankruptcy or insolvency or payment default, (2) a stipulated price decline for the reference asset, or (3) a rating downgrade for the reference asset.

25. The reference rate is an agreed fixed or floating interest rate, e.g., three-month LIBOR.

26. As with forward agreements, total return swaps can be based on *spread,* rather than *price.* At maturity, the asset receiver pays the difference in the spread of the reference asset over a treasury security of comparable maturity at origination and at maturity.

27. The default payment could be (1) par-post default price of the reference asset as determined by a dealer

poll, (2) a fixed amount or a fixed percentage of the notional amount of the transaction, or (3) payment of par by the seller in exchange for physical delivery of the defaulted reference asset.

28. As a result of running a swaps book—as well as more traditional activities such as lending to corporations or purchasing receivables—banks end up with concentrations of credit risk.

29. In Chapter 59 of his *Handbook of Fixed-Income Securities,* Frank Fabozzi notes that interest rate fluctuations account for about 90 percent of the risk of corporate bonds in the United States. Fabozzi, Frank J., and T. Dessa Fabozzi (1991). *The Handbook of Fixed-Income Securities,* 3rd ed. New York: McGraw-Hill.

15 | HYBRID SECURITIES*

> Twenty-five years ago it was comparatively easy to acquire a sound knowledge of the general investment field . . . [but now] the different types of securities have multiplied in number to an almost unlimited extent.

The preceding quote aptly summarizes the way that many (if not most) of us feel about the dizzying array of securities available in the market today. But even though the sentiment is contemporary, the quote is not—this observation was made by John Moody in 1910.[1]

One of the forces that has contributed to the almost unlimited breadth of securities is the continuing evolution of *hybrid securities*. While the term *hybrid* is more commonly associated with agricultural commodities like corn or wheat, *hybrid* may also be used to describe a hybrid security. In the same way that a hybrid corn variety is created by combining two types of corn, a hybrid security is created by combining two types of securities: typically a standard debt or equity security and an OTC derivative—a forward contract, a swap, or an option.

Hybrid securities are not new. Convertible bonds—formed by adding equity options to standard debt—were first issued by the Erie Railroad in the 1850s; the combination of bonds and equity warrants first appeared in 1911 (issued by

---

*This chapter has its roots in a paper with Donald H. Chew, Jr., "The Uses of Hybrid Debt in Managing Corporate Risk," which appeared in the *Journal of Applied Corporate Finance* (Winter 1992). The chapter that appeared in the second edition of this book was expanded and updated for presentation at the joint SAAJ - AIMR seminar held in Tokyo on March 11, 1996. I am indebted to John Finnerty (who created much of the literature on hybrid securities) and Gary Gastineau (who is currently creating the newest of these hybrid securities at the American Stock Exchange) for their comments and suggestions on this chapter.

American Light & Power).[2] Even hybrids created by adding commodity derivatives to debt are not new. In 1863, the Confederate States of America issued a 20-year bond (denominated in French francs and pounds sterling) that was convertible into cotton. This *cotton-indexed bond* can be viewed as a combination of a standard bond and an option on cotton. By the 1920s, commodity-linked hybrids were a feature of the U.S. capital markets. A case in point is the gold-indexed bond issued by Irving Fisher's Rand Kardex Corporation in 1925, in which the principal repayment of the bond was tied directly to gold prices. The firm's funding costs could be lowered significantly by furnishing a scarce security desired by investors—in this case, a long-dated forward on gold prices.[3]

The Evolution of Hybrid Securities

While not new, the range of hybrid securities increased dramatically over the last two-and-a-half decades. Figure 15–1 traces the development of "modern" hybrid securities that began in 1973, when PEMEX, the state-owned Mexican oil producer, issued bonds that incorporated a *forward contract* on a commodity (in this case, oil). In 1980, Sunshine Mining Co. went a step further by issuing bonds incorporating a commodity *option* (on silver). In 1988, Magma Copper made yet another advance by issuing a bond giving investors a *series of commodity options* (on copper)—in effect, one for every coupon payment.

Other new hybrids had their payoffs tied to interest rates, foreign exchange rates, and the behavior of the stock market. In 1981, Oppenheimer & Co. issued a security whose principal repayment is indexed to the volume of trading on the New York Stock Exchange. Notes indexed to the value of equity indexes appeared in 1986; and inflation-indexed notes (tied to the Consumer Price Index—CPI) were introduced in 1988.

Hybrids with payoffs that, like those of convertibles, are tied to company-specific performance also emerged in the 1980s. For example, the rating-sensitive notes issued by Manufacturers Hanover in 1988 provide for increased payments to investors if Mannie Hannie's creditworthiness declines. And the LYON* pioneered and underwritten by Merrill Lynch in 1985 grants investors not only the option to convert the debt into equity but also the right to "put" the security back to the firm.

A Taxonomy of Hybrid Securities

Since a hybrid security is the combination of a standard debt or equity security and a derivative—a forward contract, a swap, or an option—even seemingly complex hybrids should be able to be decomposed into these simpler, more understandable

---

*LYON is a registered service mark of Merrill Lynch & Co., Inc.

FIGURE 15–1 **Evolution of Hybrid Securities**

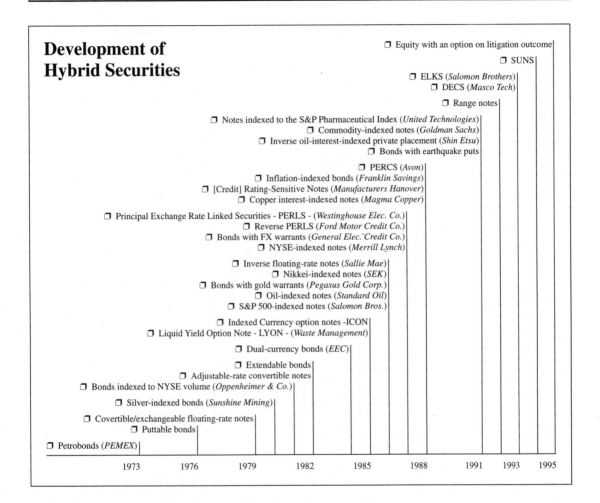

Development of Hybrid Securities

❒ Equity with an option on litigation outcome|

❒ SUNS|

❒ ELKS (*Salomon Brothers*)|
❒ DECS (*Masco Tech*)|

❒ Range notes|

❒ Notes indexed to the S&P Pharmaceutical Index (*United Technologies*)|
❒ Commodity-indexed notes (*Goldman Sachs*)|
❒ Inverse oil-interest-indexed private placement (*Shin Etsu*)|
❒ Bonds with earthquake puts|

❒ PERCS (*Avon*)|
❒ Inflation-indexed bonds (*Franklin Savings*)|
❒ [Credit] Rating-Sensitive Notes (*Manufacturers Hanover*)|
❒ Copper interest-indexed notes (*Magma Copper*)|

❒ Principal Exchange Rate Linked Securities - PERLS - (*Westinghouse Elec. Co.*)|
❒ Reverse PERLS (*Ford Motor Credit Co.*)|
❒ Bonds with FX warrants (*General Elec. Credit Co.*)|
❒ NYSE-indexed notes (*Merrill Lynch*)|

❒ Inverse floating-rate notes (*Sallie Mae*)|
❒ Nikkei-indexed notes (*SEK*)|
❒ Bonds with gold warrants (*Pegasus Gold Corp.*)|
❒ Oil-indexed notes (*Standard Oil*)|
❒ S&P 500-indexed notes (*Salomon Bros.*)|

❒ Indexed Currency option notes -ICON|
❒ Liquid Yield Option Note - LYON - (*Waste Management*)|

❒ Dual-currency bonds (*EEC*)|

❒ Extendable bonds|
❒ Adjustable-rate convertible notes|
❒ Bonds indexed to NYSE volume (*Oppenheimer & Co.*)|

❒ Silver-indexed bonds (*Sunshine Mining*)|

❒ Covertible/exchangeable floating-rate notes|
❒ Puttable bonds|

❒ Petrobonds (*PEMEX*)|

| 1973 | 1976 | 1979 | 1982 | 1985 | 1988 | 1991 | 1993 | 1995 |

building blocks. This decomposition is not unique. Indeed, many corporate treasuries decompose structures into their components—into their building blocks—to evaluate the structure.

To examine how hybrids are constructed, we look first at hybrids constructed by adding derivatives to debt. We then consider hybrids constructed by adding derivatives to equity.

Hybrids Composed of Debt and Derivatives

It turns out that "standard debt" isn't all that standard; there are various types, reflecting the various ways in which the coupon and principal are paid. In addition to

Risk Management in Practice

Decomposing Hybrids to Assess Value

Walter D. Hosp

As a corporate finance manager in a large multinational organization, I spend much of my time evaluating the merits of various financial proposals. All such proposals have pricing elements, which also require evaluation. The simple question, "Are we receiving full value?" is usually asked several times throughout the decision-making process. My challenge has often been to deliver proposals for approval and to demonstrate why they are cost-effective. I have found the technique of decomposition to be very useful in meeting this challenge.

Decomposition is a term I use to describe the process in which a risk identified by a company is examined and unbundled into components. An example would be the purchase of computer equipment. Aside from the risk of loss or theft, there is also the risk of obsolescence. Property insurance can diversify or eliminate the risk of loss or theft but not the risk of obsolescence. However, leasing instead of purchasing the equipment can allow for the transference of this risk. By decomposing the risks associated with the purchase of computer equipment, separate solutions to each risk component can be found to address the total risk of purchasing this equipment.

How, then, can decomposition be used to show the cost-effectiveness of a given financial proposal? Two specific examples, the pricing of a convertible bond and the pricing of underwriting fees, should demonstrate the value of this technique.

A bond that is convertible into a set amount of equity shares is a hybrid instrument with two pricing components. The first component is a straight debt piece; the second component is a call option on the equity (it is a call option because the holder has the right, but not the obligation, to buy the equity shares through conversion at a set price over a predetermined time period). These two components can be valued separately and added together to verify the price of the convertible bond. If the sum of the parts is greater than the whole, then cost-effective pricing has been achieved. If the reverse is true, then a corporate issuer must have some other overriding reason for issuing a convertible bond. At the very least, the cost of this overriding reason is quantified. Because the synthetic alternative to the convertible bond exists, a direct check of the pricing can be achieved with nearly identical terms and timing.

Decomposing Hybrids to Assess Value continued

This method is more precise than comparing to a similar, recently issued convertible bond.

In a similar fashion, underwriting fees can be broken down into two components. The first component is the service of selling a security. The advice of traders and the use of the distribution network of the investment bank are all part of this component. The second component is the pricing risk associated with underwriting securities. This is the risk that the price of the security will move lower before the investment bank can sell off the position it takes from underwriting. This is a short-term risk usually lasting from only several hours to a week. Noteworthy is the fact that there is upside potential as well as downside risk to the underwriter's position.

The two components of the underwriter's fee can now be priced separately. Most investment banks will readily quote a transaction under an "agented basis" versus a "fully underwritten" transaction. Under an agented arrangement no price guarantee is made to the issuer, and the security is sold on a "best efforts" basis. This pricing for the service of selling the security can be readily compared to other agented transactions of similar size and complexity. The underwriting risk can be synthetically priced by looking at the price of an interest rate hedge for a bond offering or the price of a short-dated put option for an equity offering. Again, if the sum of the pricing of the two components exceeds the full underwriting commission, then cost-effective pricing exists. If not, then the issuer has reason to negotiate further on pricing or accept only an agented transaction and obtain downside price protection elsewhere, if desired.

These are only two examples using the technique of decomposition to establish cost-effective pricing. Used creatively, the technique can at least serve as a verification of the pricing of some financial proposals. At best, it can offer different and more cost-effective alternatives.

Walter D. Hosp is the chief financial officer of Ciba Specialty Chemicals Corporation in North America. He was formerly vice president and treasurer of Ciba-Geigy Corporation. He holds M.B.A. and B.S. degrees from New York University.

traditional fixed-rate coupons, debt can be structured to pay floating-rate coupons or no coupon at all (zero-coupon debt).[4] The principal can be either amortized over the term of the debt or repaid at maturity (a coupon repaid at maturity is known as a *bullet*). These types of debt have been combined with forwards, swaps, and options to create a range of hybrid debt securities.

PHILIP MORRIS CREDIT CORPORATION

Dual Currency Bonds Due 1993
U.S. $ 57,810,000

Interest Payable in SFr. at 7¼%
on the Aggregate Subscription price of
SFr. 123,000,000

Debt Plus a Forward Contract

Dual-Currency Bond (1984).   The combination of a fixed-rate, bullet-repayment bond and a long-dated forward contract on foreign exchange yields a dual-currency bond. As illustrated below, such a bond was issued by Philip Morris Credit in 1985.

Figure 15–2 illustrates the decomposition of a dual-currency bond like the one issued by Philip Morris Credit in which the coupon payments are made in Swiss francs, while the principal is repaid in U.S. dollars.

A variant of the dual-currency structure is the *Principal Exchange Rate Linked Security (PERLS)*. In 1987, Westinghouse Electric Company issued a PERLS, wherein the bondholder received at maturity the U.S. dollar value of 70.13 million New Zealand dollars. The issuer's motive in this case was likely to reduce its funding costs by taking advantage of an unusual investor demand for long-dated currency forwards. Earlier in the same year, and presumably with similar motive, Ford Motor Credit Company issued *Reverse PERLS*. In that case, the principal repayment varied inversely with the value of the yen.[5]

Petrobonds (1973).   The bonds issued by PEMEX in 1973 were very similar to dual-currency bonds, except that the principal was indexed to oil prices, rather than the price of some foreign exchange. Hence the petrobonds could be viewed as the combination of straight debt and a forward contract on crude oil.

FIGURE 15–2   A Dual-Currency Bond

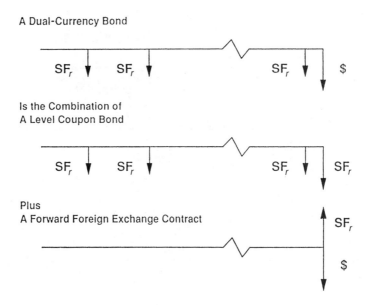

Debt Plus Swap

Inverse Floating-Rate Notes (1986).   When they were first issued in the public debt market, these hybrids were referred to as "yield-curve notes." The first of these was issued by the Student Loan Marketing Association (SallieMae).

As illustrated in Figure 15–3, an inverse floating-rate note is composed of a floating-rate, bullet-repay note and an interest rate swap. Begin with a floating-rate note (FRN) with principal P and coupon payment of $\tilde{R}$. If this FRN is combined with an interest rate swap with notional principal P, the resulting coupon payment is the fixed coupon $\bar{R}$, so we would have constructed a synthetic fixed-rate note. However, to construct a reverse floater, this FRN is combined with an interest rate swap with notional principal of $2P$, so the resulting coupon payment is $2\bar{R} - \tilde{R}$— if interest rates rise, the coupon payment falls.

An inverse floater could also be called a *dual-index note* or a *leveraged note.* Dual-index notes have coupon rates that are determined by the difference between two market indexes, typically the constant-maturity treasury rate (CMT) and LIBOR. Leveraged notes pay investors according to a formula that is based upon a multiple of the increase or decrease in a specified index, such as LIBOR, the CMT rate, or the prime rate. For example, the coupon might be $1.5 \times$ 10-year CMT + 150 basis points. The leveraging multiplier (1.5) causes the coupon to magnify movements in market yields. A *deleveraged note* would involve a multiplier less than 1.

$150,000,000

SallieMae

Student Loan Marketing Association

Yield Curve Notes due 1990

Interest on the Yield Curve Notes Due 1990 will accrue from April 11, 1986 and is payable
semi-annually in arrears on each April 11 and October 11, commensing October 11,
1986, at a rate for the Initial Interest Period of 3.50% per annum and thereafter at
a floating rate of 15.10% per annum minus the arithmetic mean of the London
interbank offered rates for six month Eurodollar deposits ("LIBOR")
prevailing two Business Days before the beginning of each Interest
Period. Interest will be computed on the basis of a 365 or 366 day
year, as the case may be, and the actual number of days in the
applicable Interest Period.

Copies of the Offering Circular may be obtained in any State from the undersigned
in compliance with the securities laws of such State.

MORGAN STANLEY & CO.
Incorporated

April 7, 1986

Adjustable-Rate Convertible Notes (1982). As Figure 15–4 illustrates, an adjustable-rate convertible note can be viewed as the combination of a convertible floating-rate note with coupon payment $\tilde{R}$ and a swap wherein the bondholder pays $\tilde{R}$ and receives a rate tied to the dividend rate on the firm's common stock.

Debt Plus One Option. There exists a wide range of hybrid securities that can be decomposed into a debt security and an option. For exposition, these hybrids have been divided into four types: (1) bonds with equity warrants, (2) convertible bonds, (3) bonds that have their principal indexed to a financial price, and (4) bonds with options on the issuer's creditworthiness or on shareholder behavior.

FIGURE 15–3   An Inverse Floating-Rate Note

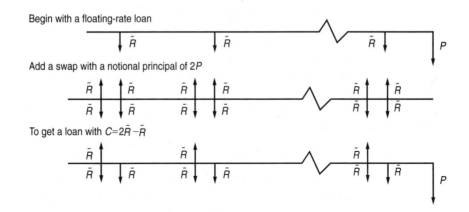

FIGURE 15–4   An Adjustable-Rate Convertible Note

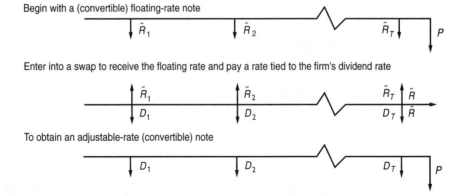

1. Bonds with Equity Warrants.   As noted earlier, bonds with equity warrants are common in the U.S. capital market. The equity option that makes up the warrant can be American or European. Moreover, the equity option can be "detachable," permitting it to be traded independently, or "nondetachable."

Warrants now have been used wherein the options are on commodities or foreign exchange. In 1986, Pegasus Gold Corporation, a Canadian gold mining firm, issued a Eurobond with detachable gold warrants. In 1987, General Electric Credit Corporation made a public offering made up of debt and yen-US$ currency exchange warrants.[6]

2. Convertible Bonds and Exchangeable Bonds.   Like the bonds with warrants described above, convertible bonds are made up of bonds and equity options, but with one important difference. The bondholder can exercise the option embodied in a warrant and still keep the underlying bond; to exercise the option in a convertible bond, the bond must be surrendered.

Corporations have raised money by tapping the equity stakes they hold in other companies and issuing exchangeable bonds, which the holder can convert into that particular pool of stock. Pennzoil used such a format in 1993 to monetize its holdings of Chevron stock. In a different variation, in 1994, Atlantic Richfield announced notes that would be convertible, at Arco's option, into shares of Lyondell Petrochemical, of which Arco owned 49.9 percent.

3. Bonds with Indexed Principal.   Constructions similar to convertibles—hybrid bonds that enable the bondholder to receive either the value of the bond or the value of the option, but not both—have appeared where the underlying asset is a commodity or some amount of a foreign currency or another bond or an equity index, rather than shares of a particular stock.

Principal Indexed to Commodity Prices.   The silver-indexed bonds issued by Sunshine Mining in 1980 are generally perceived as the first of the modern commodity-indexed bonds. As described in the following excerpt from the prospectus, the promised principal repayment for the Sunshine Mining bonds was linked to the price of silver.

PROSCPECTUS　　　　$25,000,000
Sunshine Mining Company
8 1/2% Silver Indexed Bonds Due April 15, 1995
Interest payable April 15 and October 15

Each $1,000 Face Amount bond shall be payable at maturity or redemption at the greater of $1,000 or the Market Price of 50 Ounces of Silver ("Indexed Principal Amount"). If the Indexed Principal Amount is greater that $1,000, the Company may at its option deliver Silver to holders electing to accept such delivery in satisfaction of the Indexed Principal amount. As of the close of trading on April 9, 1980, the Spot Settlement Price of Silver on the Commodity Exchange, Inc. in New York was $16.00 per Ounce and, accordingly, at such price 50 Ounces of Silver would be valued at $800.

Figure 15–5 demonstrates that the holder of this hybrid holds a position that is equivalent to the combination of a long position on a fixed-rate, bullet-repayment bond and a long position on a European option on silver.[7]

It was, however, the oil-indexed notes issued by Standard Oil that led to heightened interest in hybrid securities, particularly by regulators.[8] As noted in the fol-

FIGURE 15–5   **Silver-Indexed Bond**

A standard fixed-rate bond

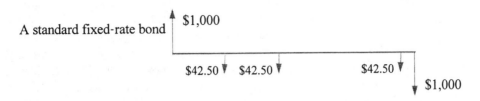

Plus:

A 15-year call option on 50 ounces of silver with a strike price of $20

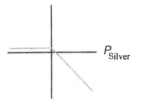

lowing tombstone advertisement, oil-indexed notes with maturities of 1990 and 1992 were issued in 1986. In the case of the notes due in 1990, at maturity the holder of the note would receive $1,000 plus the excess of the (per barrel) crude oil price over $25 multiplied by 170 barrels.

This announcement is neither an offer to sell nor a solicitation of offers to buy any of these securities. The offering is made only by the Prospectus and the related Prospectus Supplement.

NEW ISSUE   June 23, 1986

The Standard Oil Company

37,500 Oil Indexed Units

Consisting of

$300,000,000   6.30% Debentures Due 2001

$37,500,000 Oil Indexed Notes Due 1990

$37,500,000 Oil Indexed Notes Due 1992

The Debentures and Notes are being offered in Units, each of which consists of eight Debentures of $1,000 principal amount each, one Oil Indexed Note Due 1990 and one Oil Indexed Note Due 1992 of $1,000 principal amount each. The Debentures and Notes will be issued only in registered form and will not be separately transferable until after July 31, 1986, or such earlier date as may be determined by the Underwriters with the concurrence of the Company.

Price $7,976 Per Unit

plus accrued interest on the Debentures from July 1, 1986

Figure 15–6 illustrates that this hybrid issued by Standard Oil can be decomposed as the combination of a zero-coupon bond and a European-style option on oil with the same maturity.[9]

The next step in the evolution was a hybrid security with its principal linked to a portfolio of commodities, rather than a single commodity. In 1991, Goldman Sachs offered three-year zero-coupon notes with the return linked to the performance of the Goldman Sachs Commodity Index (GSCI). The GSCI tracks a basket of 18 commodities, including oil, gold, aluminum, copper, grains, coffee, sugar, cotton, and livestock.[10]

Principal Indexed to Exchange Rates.   When this structure appeared with an embedded foreign currency option, the hybrid was called an *Indexed Currency Option Note* (or ICON). This security, which was first underwritten by First Boston in 1985, combines a fixed-rate, bullet-repayment bond and a European option on foreign exchange.[11]

Principal Indexed to Interest Rates.   In the same way that the bondholder can have an option to exchange the underlying bond for a commodity or a specified amount of a foreign currency, hybrid securities have been marketed in which the bondholder has an option to exchange the bond for another bond. Floating-rate notes that give the holder the right to convert to (exchange for) a specified fixed-rate bond appeared in 1979. Extendable bonds, bonds that give the holder the right to exchange the underlying bond for a bond of longer maturity, appeared in 1982.

Principal Indexed to Equity Indexes.   1986 witnessed the introduction of bonds with the principal indexed to an equity index, either the Nikkei or the S&P 500. In this case, the principal repayment is linked to the value of an equity

---

FIGURE 15–6   Oil-Indexed Note

Begin with a zero-coupon note

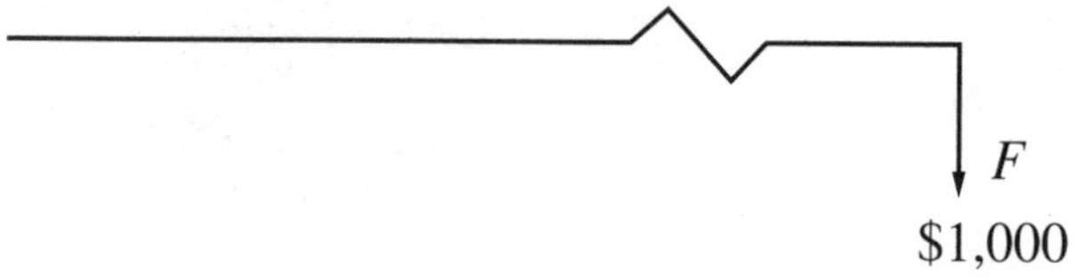

F
$1,000

Add a four-year option on 170 barrels of oil
with strike price = $25

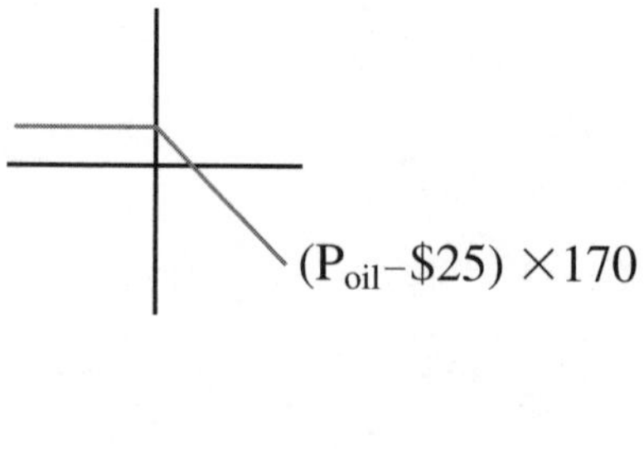

$(P_{oil} - \$25) \times 170$

index rather than to the value of an individual equity. The equity index–linked hybrid introduced by Salomon Brothers—*S&P 500 Index Subordinated Notes (SPINs)**—can be viewed as the combination of a fixed-rate, bullet-repay bond and a call option on the S&P 500 Index.[12] A similar construction introduced by Goldman Sachs & Co.—*Stock Index Growth Notes (SIGNs)*—can be viewed as the combination of a zero-coupon bond and a call option on the S&P 500 Index.[13] Subsequently, bonds appeared with the principal repayment indexed to other equity indexes (such as the NYSE Index) and subsets of indexes (such as the zero-coupon bond indexed to the S&P Pharmaceutical Index that United Technologies issued in 1991).

4. Bonds with Options on Issuer's Creditworthiness or Shareholder/Manager Behavior

Puttable, Callable, Extendable Debt. Extendable debt, as we have explained, is the combination of debt and an interest rate option (a put option on interest rates held by the bondholder).[14] Callable and puttable bonds can also be described as debt plus interest rate options in which puttable bonds (introduced to the market in 1976) contain call options on interest rates held by the bondholder and callable bonds contain put options on interest rates held by the issuing firm.

However, these debt structures also contain embedded options on the credit spread of the issuer. With puttable and extendable debt, the bondholder holds the option. If the credit spread of the issuer increases, the right to put the bond to the issuer has value. If the credit spread of the issuer decreases, the right to extend the maturity of the bond (at the old credit spread) has value. With callable debt, the issuer holds the option. If the issuing firm's credit spread declines, the right to call the bonds (and reissue at a lower credit spread) has value.

Convertible Debt. As we have noted, convertible bonds contain embedded equity options—a standard bond plus a call option on the value of the issuing firm's equity. But this right to convert to equity also can be viewed as an option held by the bondholder on the behavior of the firm's shareholders. If the shareholders behave opportunistically so as to transfer value from bondholders to shareholders, the right to become a shareholder becomes valuable.

Earlier, we used the term *exchangeable* to refer to a bond that can be exchanged for a different bond from the same company. *Exchangeable debt* also refers to a form of convertible debt in which the debt is exchanged for equity of a company different from the one that issued the debt. Brad Barber (1993) notes that exchangeable debt has been offered since the early 1970s and, by the 1980s, accounted for 6 percent of all equity-linked debt.

---

*SPINs and S&P 500 Index Subordinated Notes are service marks of Salomon Brothers Inc.

LYON.   While a number of bonds are puttable or convertible, the Liquid Yield Option Note (LYON) introduced by Merrill Lynch in 1985 is perhaps the best example of a hybrid security designed to deal with this potential for opportunistic behavior on the part of the shareholders or managers. The first of these hybrids was issued by Waste Management, Inc.

PROSPECTUS

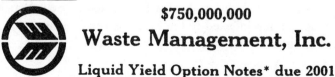

$750,000,000

Waste Management, Inc.

Liquid Yield Option Notes* due 2001
(Zero Coupon—Subordinated)

The issue price of each Liquid Yield Option Note* ("LYON") will be $250 (25% of principal amount) and there will not be any periodic payments of interest. The LYONs are subordinated to all existing and future Senior Debt and will mature on January 21, 2001. The LYONs are convertible at the option of the holder at any time, unless previously redeemed, into Common Stock, $1.00 par value, of the Company at the conversion rate of 4.36 shares per LYON. The conversion rate is not adjusted for accrued original issue discount but is subject to adjustment under certain conditions. On April 11, 1985, the last reported sale price of the Common Stock on the New York Stock Exchange—Composite Tape was $52¼ per share.

Each LYON will be purchased by the Company at the option of the holder on June 30, 1988 and on each June 30 thereafter at various purchase prices as set forth in this Prospectus. See "Description of LYONs— Purchase of the LYONs at the Option of the Holder".

Prior to June 30, 1987, the LYONs are redeemable at the option of the Company only under certain circumstances. The LYONs are redeemable at any time on or after June 30, 1987 prior to maturity. Redemption prices vary and are set forth elsewhere in this Prospectus. See "Description of LYONs— Redemption of LYONs at the Option of the Company".

*Trademark of Merrill Lynch Capital Markets

The LYONs are offered by the Underwriter subject to prior sale, when, as and if delivered to and accepted by the Underwriter and subject to its right to withdraw, cancel or modify such offer and to reject orders in whole or in part. It is expected that the LYONs will be ready for delivery in New York, New York on or about April 22, 1985.

Merrill Lynch Capital Markets

The date of this Prospectus is April 12, 1985.

As described by McConnell and Schwartz (1986) and illustrated in Figure 15–7, the LYON is a puttable, callable, convertible, zero-coupon bond.

LYONs were met with a warm reception by the market when they were introduced in 1985. But what has happened since then? In the following, Ty Po describes recent evidence about the issuance of LYONs.

Explicit Options on the Issuer's Creditworthiness.   In 1988 Manufacturers Hanover issued floating-rate, rating-sensitive notes in which Manufacturers Hanover agreed to pay a spread above LIBOR that varied with the corporation's senior debt rating. For every step that Mannie Hannie's credit rating decreased,[15] the investors would receive an additional 1/16 in yield. Therefore, if Manufacturers Hanover became less creditworthy, the bondholders would automatically receive a higher yield.

FIGURE 15–7 A LYON: A Puttable, Callable, Convertible, Zero-Coupon Bond

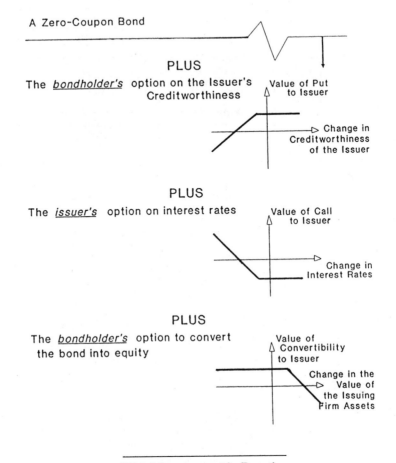

A Zero-Coupon Bond

PLUS

The *bondholder's* option on the Issuer's Creditworthiness

Value of Put to Issuer

Change in Creditworthiness of the Issuer

PLUS

The *issuer's* option on interest rates

Value of Call to Issuer

Change in Interest Rates

PLUS

The *bondholder's* option to convert the bond into equity

Value of Convertibility to Issuer

Change in the Value of the Issuing Firm Assets

Risk Management in Practice

End of the LYON

Tyrone Po

Merrill Lynch's Liquid Yield Option Notes (LYONs) proved to be highly successful with issuers as well as retail investors. Since the first transaction in 1985, in excess of $52 billion (face value) has been issued in approximately 75 separate issues.

End of the LYON continued

As the following chart illustrates, LYONs reached a peak in terms of the number of issues in 1993 when $8 billion were sold. Since then, the number of issues and the amount raised has fallen considerably. In addition, while LYONs were originally designed as a retail product, the market now seems dominated by 144a transactions. What caused LYONs to diminish in popularity?

No Longer Roaring: The Decline in LYON Issuance

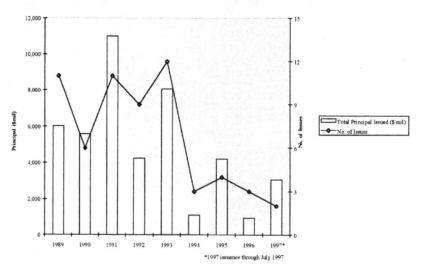

*1997 issuance through July 1997

SOURCE: Securities Data Corp.

There are several factors which may have resulted in LYONs becoming less appealing. First, interest rates fell, causing many LYONs to be called. In 1991, Merrill Lynch itself called a LYON which it had issued in 1986. The call resulted in an uproar from investors, who complained that LYONs were marketed as a good "long-term investment" and that they had been led to believe that a call was unlikely. Most issuers chose to exercise their options, so that by the end of 1993, relatively few old LYONs were still outstanding.

Second, the rise in the number of calls led to longer no-call periods. At first, LYONs typically were issued with two-year no-call periods (unless the stock price traded above a specified level for some length of time). In 1992, after Merrill called its LYONs, most new issues had a four-year no-call period. In 1993, as more old LYONs were called, a five-year no-call feature became predominate on new transactions, and in some instances since (e.g., Roche

End of the LYON continued

Holdings due 2010), the no-call period has been as long as eight years. While the longer no-call period may have satisfied investor demands, it may have dampened issuer enthusiasm.

A third factor leading to the decline of LYONs has been the creation of other equity-linked products which have offered issuers and investors more choices. Later in this chapter, you will hear about PERCS (Preferred Equity Redemption Cumulative Stock), ELKS (Equity-Linked Securities), and other similar structures.

Tyrone Po is a managing director at the Chase Manhattan Bank. He works in Structured Finance Services, which is a part of Chase's Global Trust Services group. His current responsibilities include strategy analysis and planning as well as product development. His background also includes substantial experience in derivatives and corporate finance.

While this idea is attractive, there is an obvious flaw. If the option becomes valuable, the optionholder must look for payment to the entity whose creditworthiness has declined. A hybrid that avoided this problem was the syndication developed in 1990 by the Chase Manhattan Bank for Sonatrach, the state hydrocarbons company of Algeria. If oil prices decline, the creditworthiness of Sonatrach declines, so the syndicate banks would like to have a higher return. However, if oil prices decline, Sonatrach will have less money to pay out, so a structure like the Mannie Hannie Rating Sensitive Note would not work. Instead, as Figure 15–8 illustrates, the transaction was structured so that Chase accepted two-year call options on oil from Sonatrach and then transformed the two-year calls into seven-year calls and puts that are passed on to the syndicate members. The calls Chase received from Sonatrach have desirable credit characteristics; Chase will look to Sonatrach for payment only if the oil price is high; and if the price of oil is high, Sonatrach has the money. If the price of oil declines, the members of the syndicate receive a higher yield; this increase comes from Chase, not from Sonatrach.

5. Bonds with Options on Catastrophes.   The need for an alternative to reinsurance, coupled with the need for additional capital, has led insurance companies to consider derivatives embedded in debt securities—*catastrophe bonds.*

Traditionally, insurance companies manage their exposure to catastrophes through the use of reinsurance. While reinsurance is similar in appearance to a derivative contract, there are some important differences: First, there exists the expectation that there will be a long-term relationship between the buyer and seller

FIGURE 15–8   Sonatrach Hybrid

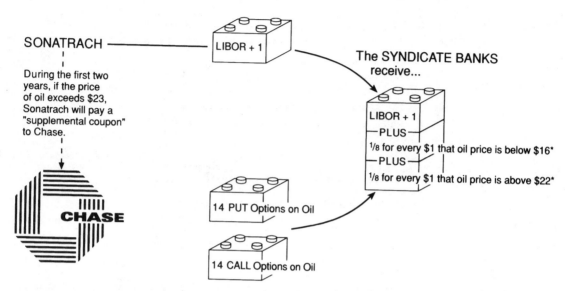

*In the first year, the syndicate receives additional interest of the price if oil falls outside the range of $16–$22. In year 2, the range widens to $15–$23, then to $14–$24 in year 3, and to $13–$25 in years 4 through 7.

of the reinsurance, allowing the reinsurance seller to recover losses over time. Second, there exists positive correlation between the timing of a claim under the reinsurance contract and the deterioration of the credit quality of a reinsurer who will be expected to pay the claim.[16]

Writing in *Global Finance,* Ellen Leander (1996) argued that the underwriting capacity of U.S. insurance companies is only $195 billion. Adding $30 billion in international reinsurance capacity and $10 billion in capacity at Lloyds, the total insurance capacity for the United States would be $235 billion. Since $75 billion of that is already "spoken for" as the estimated present value of environmental liabilities, there is only some $160 billion in insurance capacity for the $7 trillion U.S. economy and $15 trillion in U.S. real estate. A single large natural catastrophe could wipe out all of that—as a case in point, the damage estimate for the Kobe earthquake was $100 billion.

Since in some cases these catastrophe bonds would be an alternative to traditional reinsurance—meaning that insurance companies would be purchasers as well as sellers of these bonds—there was an important regulatory concern. For an investment-grade bond, insurance companies need to hold assets equal to only 0.3 percent of their purchases—$30,000 against a $10 million investment. But an insurance company would have to hold 100 times that amount on an equity investment—$3 million against a $10 million equity investment. In June 1997, the National Association of Insurance Commissioners, which oversees the investment activities of insurers, indicated that it will classify any such catastrophe-risk schemes as bonds, rather than equity investments.[17]

Hurricane Bonds. In June 1997, Residential Reinsurance issued $477 million *hurricane-linked private placement* to fund catastrophe reinsurance for United Services Automobile Association (USAA), the fourth-largest home-owner insurer in the United States. The reinsurance would be triggered if a category three, four, or five hurricane hits one of 20 states or the District of Columbia within 12 months after the issue and causes more than $1 billion of claims against USAA. Residential Reinsurance would pay for USAA's losses between $1 billion and $1.5 billion, with the bond investors sharing proportionately in 80 percent of this $500 million. The private placement, managed by Merrill Lynch, Goldman Sachs, and Lehman Brothers, consisted of two tranches. As is described below, one of the tranches has guaranteed principal, while the other does not.

	Tranche 1 *$164 million* *LIBOR plus 2.73%*	*Tranche 2* *$313.18 million* *LIBOR plus 5.76%*
Claims less than $1 billion	100% of principal returned at maturity	100% of principal returned at maturity
Claims $1 billion to $1.5 billion	11% to 42% of principal returned at maturity Balance of principal returned 10 years later	20 to 80% of principal returned at maturity Balance of principal is not returned
Claims more than $1.5 billion	Principal returned 10 years later	No principal is returned

Demand for the issue was high. *Risk* reported that the size of the issue was initially planned to be only $100 million[18]; and the *New York Times* reported that the $477 million issue was oversubscribed by $500 million.[19]

Earthquake Bonds. In July 1997, Swiss Reinsurance Company issued a two-year $137 million *earthquake-linked private placement.* This security, linked to California earthquake risk, was the first earthquake bond with an investment-grade tranche.[20] Lead-managed by Credit Suisse First Boston, the private placement was offered in three tranches.

The first tranche received a preliminary Baa3 rating from Moody's, because it provided protection for at least 40 percent of the principal—remaining principal redemptions are reduced in increments of roughly 20 percent as losses from a single California earthquake cross thresholds of $18.5 billion, $21 billion, and

$24 billion.[21] Prior to issue, the first tranche's coupon was expected to be three-month U.S. dollar LIBOR plus 220–250 basis points.

The second tranche had similar triggers, but offered no principal protection. It was expected to yield LIBOR plus roughly 300 basis points. The final tranche—also without principal protection—will be triggered at a lower threshold of $12 billion and was expected to yield LIBOR plus about 600 points. Because they offered no principal protection, the second and third tranches received below-investment-grade ratings.

Debt Plus a Package of Options.   The debt-plus-option hybrids considered so far are all combinations of debt with a single option. Hybrids have also appeared that are made up of debt and a package of options with various maturities—typically with the maturities of the options matching the coupon dates of the underlying bond. In the following, we will describe four hybrid structures that incorporate packages of options: (1) commodity interest-indexed bonds, (2) bonds with interest determined by equity returns, (3) packages of interest rate options, and (4) inflation-rate interest-indexed bonds.

1. Commodity Interest-Indexed Bonds.   The Magma Copper Company 1988 Copper Interest-Indexed Senior Subordinated Notes were the first of the bonds to have interest payments indexed to a commodity price.

As is illustrated in Figure 15–9, this 10-year debenture has embedded in it 40 option positions on the price of copper—one with maturity three months, one with maturity six months, and so on, the last being one with maturity 10 years.[22] The re-

---

This announcement appears as a matter of record only.

COPPER COMPANY

$503,000,000

Recapitalization

$200,000,000 Bank Term Loan and Revolving Credit

$210,000,000 Copper Interest-Indexed
                      Senior Subordinated Notes

December 1988

FIGURE 15–9 Magma Copper's Senior Subordinated Notes

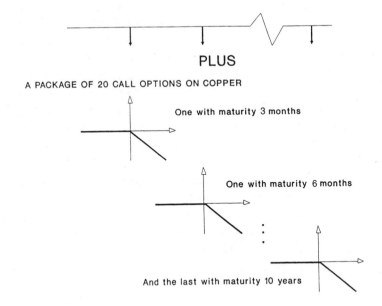

sult of these option positions is that the quarterly interest payment is determined by the prevailing price of copper:

Average Copper Price	Indexed Interest Rate
$2.00 or above	21 percent
1.80	20
1.60	19
1.40	18
1.30	17
1.20	16
1.10	15
1.00	14
0.90	13
0.80 or below	12

A structure that was similar but had the coupons linked to the price of natural gas was issued by Presidio Oil Company in 1989.[23] And in 1991, VAW Australia used a bond with a similar structure—but this time tied to the price of aluminum—to finance the expansion of its aluminum smelter north of Sydney.[24]

While the examples cited have all been firms that have a direct exposure to the price of the commodity, the same kind of structure can also be used by firms that have an inverse exposure to the price of the commodity. In 1991 Sin Etsu, a Japanese chemical manufacturer—a commodity user, rather than a commodity producer—issued a private placement in which the coupon floated *inversely* with the price of oil.

In March 1994, Merrill Lynch listed debt securities tied to the movement of Amex's Oil Index[25]—*Stock Market Annual Reset Term (SMART) Notes.* Interest will be based on the principal amount ($1,000) times the average percent change in Amex's Oil Index between 258.61 and the average value determined at the end of 1994, times a participation rate of 85 percent. A new index base level will be determined each year. Investors will receive a minimum annual payment of $20 per each $1,000 principal amount, regardless of the index level each year. The notes cannot be redeemed prior to maturity.

2. Bonds with Interest Payments Determined by Equity Returns.   In April 1994, the American Stock Exchange introduced a structure in which interest payments would be determined by changes in equity values. Lehman Brothers' Global Telecommunications *Stock Upside Note Securities (SUNS)** will pay interest at a rate determined by a percentage change in the Global Telecommunications Basket, a group of 24 stocks or American Depository Receipts (ADRs) of companies in 17 countries. On April 10 of each year and at stated maturity, investors will be entitled to receive an interest payment based on the annual appreciation, if any, in excess of 5 percent in the value of the basket during the immediate preceding year. At maturity, investors will receive the principal amount.

3. Bonds with Packages of Interest Rate Options

Floored Floating-Rate Bonds.   The combination of a standard floating-rate bond and a package of European put options on the index interest rate (with the maturities of the put options set to match the coupon reset dates) results in a floating-rate bond that has a minimum interest rate. However, the cost of this minimum rate protection is the premium that must be paid for the put options. And there could clearly be times when the premiums would be "too expensive." This cost can be reduced by replacing the European options with Asian interest rate options. Instead of paying off if the interest falls below a specified rate, the average rate options would pay off if the interest rate falls below the average rate over a specified period prior to the reset date. The resulting security has a floor, but the level of the floor depends on the path interest rates have followed. Such a structure is referred to as a *path-dependent floater.*

Step-Up Bonds.   Step-up bonds initially pay the investor an above-market yield for a short noncall period and then, *if not called,* "step up" to a higher coupon

---

*SUNS is a service mark of Lehman Brothers Inc.

rate. If the bond is not called, the stepped-up coupon would be below then current market rates (if not, the bond would have been called). The investor initially receives a higher yield because of having implicitly sold a call option.

Index Amortizing Notes. Index amortizing notes (IANs) repay principal according to a predetermined amortization schedule that is linked to the level of a specific index (usually LIBOR). As market interest rates increase (or prepayment rates decrease), the maturity of an IAN extends, similar to that of a collateralized mortgage obligation.

An index amortizing note is constructed by combining a standard amortizing bond with an index amortizing swap. In an *index amortizing swap,* changes in interest rates trigger a change in the *level* of the underlying notional principal on which interest rate–determined flows are paid or received. In an index amortizing swap, the fixed-rate payer has the right to amortize the notional principal of the swap if interest rates fall. This is implemented by having the notional principal of the swap tied to the future movement of an interest rate—usually LIBOR. The notional principal will decline according to a preestablished schedule if rates decline.[26] To pay for the embedded interest rate option in an indexed-principal swap, the fixed rate paid is higher than the rate for a standard swap.

Range Notes (a.k.a. *Corridor* or *Accrual Notes*). Range notes were designed to allow an investor to profit from a very specific view—i.e., that the interest rate will stay within a narrow band. As long as the interest rate stays within a specified range, interest accrues at an above-market rate; if, however, the interest rate moves outside the range, no interest accrues. As the OCC noted in its *July Advisory Letter,* range notes were often structured to reflect an investor's view that is contrary to the "rate forecast" embedded in the yield curve.

A range note is a combination of standard debt and a package of binary options. In a range note, the purchaser has *sold* a package of binary options. The way a range note behaves is probably best seen via an example.

Aside

John Finnerty (1994) examined some of the range note issues that were sold publicly in the Euromarket in 1994. Among the range notes he examined was a $100 million two-year range note issued by Norddeutsche LB London that promised to pay 3-month LIBOR plus 100 basis points, with interest accruing only on days when three-month LIBOR was between 3 percent and 4 percent in the first six months, 3.125 percent and 4.75 percent in the next six months, 3.25 percent and 5.5 percent in the third six months, and 3.5 percent and 6 percent in the last six months. On days when three-month LIBOR lies outside these boundaries, no interest would accrue on the note.

For simplicity, let's use a 360-day year convention; so each semiannual period would contain 180 days. Within each of the six-month periods, the purchaser of the range note has sold 260 binary options on three-month LIBOR—130 calls and 130 puts.

Exercise Prices

During the first six months, the exercise price on the call is 4 percent and the exercise price on the put is 3 percent.

During the second six months, the exercise price on the call is 4.75 percent and the exercise price on the put is 3.125 percent.

During the third six months, the exercise price on the call is 5.5 percent and the exercise price on the put is 3.25 percent.

During the fourth six months, the exercise price on the call is 6 percent

and the exercise price on the put is 3.5 percent.

Maturity

On the first day of each semiannual period one call and one put expire. The second call-put combination expires on the second day of the six-month period; and so on.

On any day, if three-month LIBOR is high enough that the call is exercised, the purchaser of the range note—the seller of the binary option—effectively pays to the buyer of the binary call

$$\frac{(3\text{-month LIBOR} + 100 \text{ basis points})}{360} \times \$100 \text{ million}$$

Likewise, on any day, if three-month LIBOR is low enough that the binary put is exercised, the purchaser of the range note effectively pays the buyer of the put the same amount.

It is clear that the spread on the range note—the 100 basis points in the case of the Norddeutsche LB London issue—is determined by the premium for the binary options the purchaser of the range note has sold.

Given the behavior of interest rates in 1994, most of the original range notes "busted" through their ranges and paid no interest after March. Consequently, range notes were singled out by regulators as "inappropriate investments" for banks and mutual funds. One of the SEC's concerns was that the notes did not "reset to pay" and thus violated certain provisions of the legislation that determines what investments mutual funds can purchase. As a result, one-month reset structures appeared.[27]

While the first range notes were tied to U.S. dollar interest rates, range notes have subsequently been issued with the boundaries of the range linked to other interest rates, foreign exchange rates, or differences between rates. A number of French franc range notes were issued in 1994—e.g., a one-year note issued by Societe Generale Acceptance, with the payout based on three-month PIBOR. Similar deals were also issued in deutsche marks for investors confident that rates would fall slowly. And in March 1994, Societe Generale launched what it called the *Boost (Banking on Overall Stability)* product. This range product appeared as exchange-traded instruments based on French Oat (Obligations Assimilables du Trésor) bond yields, German bond yields, and the dollar-deutsche mark and deutsche mark-French franc exchange rates. For each day that the price stays in the "stability band"—range—specified, the value of the Boost increased (by Ffr1 in the case of a Boost priced in francs). The Boost is a knock-out structure; when the underlying breaks the range, the holder of the Boost receives all the capital accrued to that date.[28]

4. Inflation-Rate Interest-Indexed Bonds.

In 1988 the Franklin Savings Association issued notes called *Real Yield Securities (REALS),* in which the investors received interest payments calculated as the sum of 3 percent and the rate of inflation as measured by the change in the Consumer Price Index. Hence this hybrid could be viewed as the combination of a fixed-rate, bullet-repayment bond plus a package of options on the CPI inflation rate, with the maturities of the options coinciding with the quarterly coupon payment dates.

The U.S. Treasury first issued inflation-indexed notes in 1997. Ten-year notes were auctioned in January 1997 and again in April of that year (a total of $15 billion). In July, the U.S. Treasury issued five-year inflation-indexed notes. While the promised yield was higher than had been expected, demand for the securities was strong—the auction drew bids totaling $24.5 billion (more than three times the amount offered).

Hybrids Composed of Equity and Derivatives

While we identified five forms of standard debt, standard equity comes in only two forms, common and preferred.

Equity Plus Swap. *Adjustable-rate preferred stock,* introduced to the market in 1982, paid a dividend that was adjusted quarterly to reflect changes in short-term interest rates. Looking at the "building blocks," adjustable-rate preferred stock can be viewed as the reverse of the adjustable rate convertible note described earlier. In the same way that we viewed an adjustable-rate note as the combination of a floating-rate note and a swap in which the bondholder pays a floating rate and receives a rate tied to the firm's dividend rate, adjustable-rate preferred stock can be viewed as the combination of standard, fixed-dividend-rate preferred stock and a swap in which the preferred equityholder pays a rate tied to the fixed dividend rate on the firm's preferred stock and receives a floating rate.[29]

Equity Plus an Option

Convertible Preferred.   As described by Bergsman (1994), Occidental Petroleum provided a new twist on "converts" in 1994 with an issue of 11.4 million shares of convertible preferred stock. The preferred shares are convertible into Oxy common shares, but the conversion value is indexed not to Oxy's share price, but rather to the stock price of Canadian Occidental Petroleum, of which Occidental owns 30 percent. Why base the convertible on Canadian Occidental's share price instead of Occidental Petroleum itself? Convertible preferred can be viewed as the combination of standard preferred and an embedded call option. To extract the most value from the issue (whether in an increased price or in reduced preferred dividends), Occidental wants to make the call as attractive—as valuable—as possible. Canadian Occidental's stock is more volatile than Occidental's.[30] Moreover, the dividend yield on Canadian Occidental is 1.3 percent, compared with 5.6 percent for Occidental itself. (Increases in volatility of the price of the underlying equity and decreases in the dividend yield both increase the value of a call option on equity.)

Options on Equity or Equity Indexes

Hybrids Designed to Decompose Equity Claims.[31] In the early 1980s, hybrid securities appeared that enabled investors to separately trade the dividend and capital gains components of equity. Shares of a particular firm were tendered into an investment trust, and the trust was then bifurcated into two hybrid securities: *PRIME (Prescribed Right to Income and Maximum Equity)* paid to their holders all the dividend income and, at maturity (the termination date) of the trust, the value of the underlying share up to a predetermined price (the termination claim).[32] *SCORE (Special Claim on Residual Equity)* paid to their holders the value of the underlying share above the termination claim. As illustrated in Figure 15–10, the PRIME can be viewed as the functional equivalent of being long the share (including the dividend) and short a call on that share, while the SCORE is the functional equivalent of being long a call on the share.[33]

The developer of this structure, A. Joseph Debe, filed *Americus Trusts* with the SEC in January 1984; but it was not until 1985 that the first Americus Trust (on Exxon) was listed (on the American Stock Exchange).[34]

Americus Trust–like structures appeared in other markets.[35] And a number of variants on the Americus Trust were attempted. Some of these variants made it to the market; others did not.

One of those that did not make it to the market was *unbundled stock units (USU)*. As described by Finnerty (1992), unbundled stock units were designed to divide the returns from an individual equity into three components: (1) a 30-year "base-yield" bond that would pay interest equal to the dividend rate for the issuer's common stock, (2) a preferred share that would pay dividends equal to the excess,

FIGURE 15–10   Decomposition of a Share of Common Stock into a PRIME and a SCORE

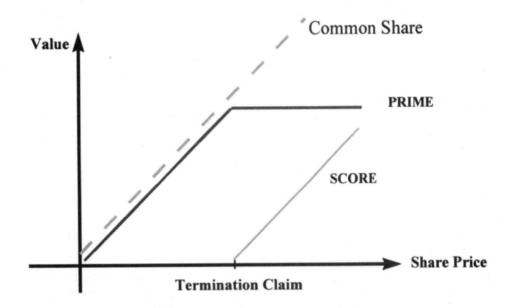

if any, above the "base rate," and (3) a 30-year warrant that would pay the excess, if any, of the issuer's share price above the redemption value of the base-yield bond.[36] Shearson Lehman Brothers announced forthcoming USUs—on American Express, Dow Chemical, Pfizer, and Sara Lee—in November 1988; despite heavy marketing, the offering was canceled in the spring of 1989.

In October 1990, the Chicago Board Options Exchange (CBOE) listed *Long-term Equity AnticiPation Securities* (*LEAPS*). LEAPS were subsequently listed on the American, Philadelphia, and Pacific Stock Exchanges. Like SCOREs, the LEAPS were long-dated options—one, two, or three years. But in contrast to SCOREs, LEAPS were issued on equity indexes, as well as individual shares, and were listed in put form, as well as calls.

An idea that made it to the market but failed to survive was the *SuperTrust*. Introduced by Leland-O'Brien-Rubinstein (LOR),[37] instead of holding an individual equity, the trust would hold a portfolio made up of the S&P 500 portfolio and a portfolio of Treasury bills. LOR trust was be composed of two *SuperUnits* securities: (1) Index SuperUnits which would be redeemable for shares of an S&P 500 Index mutual fund and (2) Money Market SuperUnits which would be redeemable for shares of a mutual fund holding short-term U.S. Treasury securities. Against this portfolio the trust sold four *SuperShares:* (1) Priority SuperShares—holders receive all dividends plus the value of the S&P 500 portfolio to a specified level,

(2) Appreciation SuperShares—holders receive the value of the S&P 500 portfolio above a specified level (a call option on the S&P 500 Index), (3) Protection Super-Shares—holders receive the value of any decline in the value of the S&P portfolio below a specified level (a put option on the S&P 500 Index), and (4) Money Market Income SuperShares—holders receive the interest from the Treasury bills plus the value of the Treasury bills after the Protection SuperShares have been paid.

In November 1992, SuperUnits were listed on the American Stock Exchange; at the same time, the four SuperShares were listed on the Chicago Board Options Exchange. The initial SuperUnits had a maturity of three years; at the end of the three years, the SuperUnits and SuperShares were redeemed and the project discontinued.

Aside

Index Participations

While the SuperTrust itself was discontinued, part of the structure has lived on. In January 1993, the American Stock Exchange listed *Standard & Poor's Depositor Receipts* (*SPDRs*, "spiders"). Like the Index Super-Units, SPDRs are exchange-traded claims on an S&P 500 portfolio. However, the SPDRs represent interests in a long-term unit investment trust that holds a portfolio that "tracks" the price performance and dividend yield of the S&P 500 Index.

And the idea expanded from "spiders" to "webs." Created by Morgan Stanley, *World Equity Benchmark Shares (WEBS)* are based on the same idea as the SPDRs, except that the WEBS are claims on non-U.S. equity portfolios. In 1996, AMEX began trading WEBS on equity indexes for 17 countries: Australia, Austria, Belgium, Canada, France, Germany, Hong Kong, Italy, Japan, Malaysia, Mexico, Netherlands, Singapore, Spain, Sweden, Switzerland, and the United Kingdom.

But the idea of trading a derivative security that tracks an index had occurred earlier. As Ken Lehn points out, index participations were first introduced in 1989, but they ran into a regulatory firestorm.

Regulation in Canada was more accommodating to innovation in this area. Consequently, in 1990, the Toronto Stock Exchange (TSE) introduced the Toronto 35 Index Participation Units (TIPs)—index participations on the TSE 35. According to Kirzner (1995), from an initial offering of C$248 million, the market for TIPs now represents about C$925 million in value, with TIPs trading averaging about 230,000 units per day.

Observations on the Shad-Johnson Accord and SEC-CFTC Jurisdictional Disputes

Kenneth Lehn

The dramatic growth in the market for derivatives and hybrid financial products (which combine attributes of derivatives and securities) in the 1980s revealed great inadequacies in the structure of U.S. financial regulation. Concurrent with the growth in these markets, the Securities and Exchange Commission (SEC) and the Commodity Futures Trading Commission (CFTC) engaged in a costly turf battle over which agency should be the dominant regulator of these new evolving markets.

Jurisdictional disputes between the two agencies have been common ever since the CFTC's inception in 1975. In the 1974 amendments to the Commodity Exchange Act (CEA), which created the CFTC, Congress gave the CFTC exclusive jurisdiction over financial products that have elements of a futures contract. The SEC and CFTC soon were embroiled in a controversy over the regulation of Ginnie Mae options. Were these products futures or were they securities? By the early 1980s, there was great uncertainty about which agency had regulatory authority over options generally and stock index futures.

In 1982 the chairmen of the SEC and CFTC (John Shad and Phillip Johnson, respectively) negotiated the Shad-Johnson agreement, which attempted to resolve this jurisdictional dispute. Under Shad-Johnson, the SEC has exclusive jurisdiction over options on securities and stock index options, and the CFTC has exclusive jurisdiction over all futures contracts (including stock index futures) and all options on futures (including options on stock index futures).

In some respects, the Shad-Johnson agreement has served investors well. Perhaps most importantly, this agreement saved stock index futures from excessive regulation by the SEC. As the SEC revealed after the 1987 stock market crash and the 1989 mini-crash, it has unwarranted hostility toward stock index futures. Undoubtedly, the SEC would have overregulated the stock index futures market and reduced the efficiency of this product as a risk management tool if Shad-Johnson had given the SEC jurisdiction over stock index futures.

Although the Shad-Johnson agreement sensibly divided jurisdiction over well-defined futures, options, and securities, it did not anticipate the proliferation of hybrid financial products that has occurred since 1982. As a result, it did not establish a framework for allocating jurisdiction over hybrids between the two agencies. This has resulted in substantial costs as the SEC and CFTC continue to engage in jurisdictional disputes over hybrids.

The most glaring illustration of the costs associated with these jurisdictional battles concerns the SEC's approval of a new product, index participations (IPs), in 1989. IPs are financial instruments that are priced off an index of stocks, such as Standard & Poor's (S&P) 500. IPs have features of both futures contracts (holders can cash out on a quarterly basis at prices equal to the index values on these settlement dates) and securities (they pay dividends and have indefinite lives). In 1989, the SEC approved proposals from the Philadelphia Stock Exchange, American Stock Exchange, and Chicago Board Options Exchange to trade IPs. Literally within hours, futures exchanges sued the SEC on grounds that these products were futures contracts that, under the CEA, only the CFTC could regulate.

Later in 1989, Judge Easterbrook of the U.S. Seventh Circuit Court of Appeals ruled in favor of the futures exchanges and ordered that trading in IPs be ceased until the CFTC approved the trading of this product on registered futures exchanges. Judge Easterbrook acknowledged that IPs had features of both futures and securities and equated the court's task to deciding "whether tetrahedrons belong in square or round holes." However, the exclusivity clause of the CEA compelled the court to rule as it did, and it resulted in the cessation of trading of a product for which there was demand.

A more sensible alternative to Shad-Johnson would be to allow any product that has elements of a security to trade on a securities exchange and any product that has elements of a futures contract to trade on a futures exchange. This would enable any exchange to register new hybrid products either as securities, subject to SEC regulation, or as futures, subject to CFTC regulation. This rule would create healthy competition between the two agencies, as exchanges would opt in to whichever body of regulation is most suitable for the trading of these products. This would remove existing, anticompetitive, regulatory impediments to the development on new hybrid instruments that serve the interests of both investors and issuers.

Kenneth Lehn is professor of business administration in the Katz Graduate School of Business Administration at the University of Pittsburgh. Previously, he served as chief economist at the U.S. Securities and Exchange Commission (1987–1991). Professor Lehn has published extensively, not only in the leading academic journals (*Journal of Financial Economics, Journal of Finance, Journal of Political Economy,* and *Journal of Law and Economics*), but also in more popular publications (*Wall Street Journal* and *National Law Journal*). He is the editor of *Modernizing U.S. Securities Regulation: Economic and Legal Perspectives.* Professor Lehn received his Ph.D. in economics from Washington University in 1981.

Embedding a Derivative in an Equity Security. So far in this section, we have looked at equity hybrids that synthetically decompose equity claims into option positions. Alternatively, equity hybrids have been created by inserting an equity option into a security. The idea is not new; bonds with equity warrants fit in this category, as do convertible bonds. But the implementations have become more innovative.

Preference Equity Redemption Cumulative Stock (PERCS) was invented by Morgan Stanley.[38] The first PERCS issue by Avon in 1988[39] was followed with issues by nonfinancial corporations including General Motors, Kmart, Sears, and Texas Instruments; Citicorp was the first bank to issue PERCS.[40] As described by Chen, Kensinger, and Pu (1994), PERCS is preferred stock that pays an above-market dividend. In return for the higher dividend, the PERCS investor grants to the issuer the right to convert the preferred stock to common equity at a predetermined price.[41] The conversion price, called the *cap,* is initially 30–45 percent above the common price. If the conversion takes place at maturity of the PERCS,[42] shares of PERCS are converted to shares of common stock on a one-for-one basis. If, however, the share price rises and the issuer mandates conversion prior to maturity, shares of PERCS are converted to fractional shares of common stock, based on the cap price. Hence, as is illustrated in Figure 15–11, a position in a PERCS is equivalent to a long position in the common equity itself and a short position in a call on the equity. Figure 15–11 illustrates the similarity between PERCS and the PRIMEs described earlier.

Chen and Chen (1995) described two variants of PERCS that appeared in 1993. One variant is *Equity-Linked Securities (ELKS).* Salomon Brothers issued the first ELKS in which the return was tied to the performance of Digital Equipment Corporation's common stock (although Digital Equipment Corporation was not

FIGURE 15-11   PERCS—Equivalent to Writing Covered Call Options

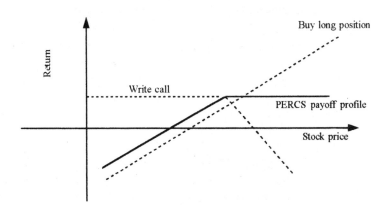

involved in the offering).[43] Like the original PERCS, the payoff for an ELKS issue is essentially that of a covered call: in the original offering, the amount that each ELKS would pay at maturity was the lessor of (1) 135 percent of the issue price, i.e., $50.625, or (2) the average closing price for Digital Equipment Corporation common stock for the 10 trading days immediately prior to expiration of the ELKS. The difference between the ELKS and the original PERCS is that while the value of the PERCS is tied to the value of the issuing firm's share, the value of the ELKS is tied to the value of some other firm's equity.[44]

The other variant of PERCS, *Dividend Enhanced Convertible Stock (DECS)*, was first issued by Masco Tech in July 1993. PERCS can be viewed as equivalent to covered call writing. An investment in DECS can be viewed as equivalent to purchasing a bull-call spread—see Figure 15–12.

FIGURE 15–12   DECS—Equivalent to Purchasing a Bull-Call Spread

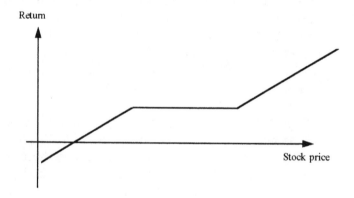

Option on a Commodity.   St. Goar (1994) described how, in 1994, Freeport-McMoRan financed expansion of its operating subsidiary's project in Indonesia by issuing $95 million worth of preferred stock with a dividend payout pegged to the price of silver. Metals-denominated financings are typically arranged as gold- or silver-backed loans from commercial banks. By issuing preferred stock, Freeport-McMoRan has fewer restrictive covenants than with a loan. Moreover, by issuing preferred stock, Freeport-McMoRan also gets a tax benefit. Because the company lends the preferred offering's proceeds to its Indonesian subsidiary, the dividend payments are tax-deductible, under local tax law.

Option on Managerial Behavior.   In November 1984 Arley Merchandise Corporation issued stock. As described by Andrew Chen and John Kensinger (1988), the investor buys a hybrid made up of a share of common stock and a right that entitles the investor to claim more stock if the market price of the stock is below a stated level at a predetermined date. At the predetermined date, if the market price of the share is above the guaranteed floor price, nothing happens; if the market price of the share is below the guaranteed floor price, the issuing firm must make up the difference in value by giving the investor additional common shares. This hybrid can be viewed as an equity security plus an equity-settled put option on the value of the equity; as Chen and Kensinger point out, this hybrid is comparable to a convertible bond.

Option on the Outcome of Litigation. In 1995, California Federal Bank disclosed plans to issue a security that would give its shareholders 25 percent of any cash award it might receive in its pending lawsuit against the federal government. California Federal filed a registration statement with the Federal Office of Thrift Supervision to issue 5.1 million "certificates of participation" without charge to its 49 million shareholders, entitling them to receive a 25 percent share of California Federal's potential legal winnings. In its 1992 suit, California Federal contended that the government reneged on a contract that underpinned its takeover of six failing savings and loans. California Federal's suit, and others like it, contends that when Congress approved bailout legislation in 1989, it broke a contract that had allowed savings and loans 40 years to classify as capital an intangible asset known as goodwill. The 1989 legislation forced savings and loans to write off goodwill faster and depleted the capital cushion of many institutions. (In testimony to a Senate subcommittee hearing, the chairman of the Federal Deposit Insurance Corporation estimated that the potential payout from these suits could be $4.9 billion or more.)

Why Hybrids? Part 1: The Economic Rationale for Issuing a Hybrid Security

Once we observe that hybrid securities can be decomposed into simpler building blocks, we must ask why firms issue these hybrids securities instead of the simpler individual components. The answer lies in the following three rationales.[45]

To Provide Investors with a "Play"

The most straightforward reason for issuing a hybrid is to provide investors with a means of taking a position on a financial price. If the issuer provides a "play" not available otherwise, the investor will be willing to pay a premium, thereby reducing the issuer's cost of funding.

The play can be in the form of a forward contract. Perhaps the best example of such is dual-currency bonds. Dual-currency bonds provide investors with foreign exchange forward contracts that have much longer maturities than those available in the standard market—that is, the forward contract embedded in dual-currency bonds normally has a maturity of 10 years, while the liquidity in the standard foreign exchange forward market declines for maturities in excess of one year and falls dramatically for maturities beyond five years.

However, the play has more commonly been in the form of an option embedded in the bond, generally an option of longer maturity than those available in the standard option market. Examples include PEMEX's petrobonds, Sunshine Mining's silver-indexed bonds, Standard Oil's oil-indexed notes, Salomon Brothers' market-indexed notes, and the gold warrants issued by Pegasus Gold Corporation.

To "Arbitrage" Tax and/or Regulatory Authorities

Hybrid securities have been used to take advantage of asymmetries in the tax treatment across national boundaries and in regulations in different markets. A classic example is the case we described in Chapter 10:

> There was a tax arbitrage opportunity: Japanese tax authorities ruled that the income earned from holding a zero-coupon bond would be treated as a capital gain, and since capital gains were untaxed, the interest income on zero-coupon bonds would not be taxed for Japanese investors. In contrast, U.S. tax authorities permitted any U.S. firm issuing a zero-coupon bond to deduct imputed interest payments from income.
>
> Moreover, there was regulatory arbitrage that would allow the issuing firms to eliminate some of the resultant exposure to yen, while obtaining a still lower realized interest rate: the Ministry of Finance (MoF) limited the amount a Japanese pension fund could invest in non-yen-dominated bonds issued by foreign corporations to at most 10 percent of their portfolio, but MoF ruled that dual-currency bonds qualified as a yen issue.

Hence, U.S. firms would (1) issue a zero-coupon yen bond, (2) issue a dual-currency bond, and (3) hedge the remaining yen exposure with a currency swap. The result was a set of cash flows that are like that of a deep discount dollar bond with below-market coupons.

Another example of how asymmetries in tax regulations influence the construction of hybrids is found in PERCS. As we noted earlier, theory suggests that a position in a PERCS should be equivalent to a long position in the common equity itself and a short position in a call on the equity. However, when Chen, Kensinger, and Pu (1994) examined the available data, they found that PERCS has been "overpriced" when compared with the combination of long the equity and short a call on the equity.[46] Chen, Kensinger, and Pu attributed the "overpricing" to two things. First, the transaction cost for the single PERCS security *may* be lower than the sum of the transaction costs for buying the equity position and selling a call on the equity. Second, PERCS is tax-advantaged: the premium due to the investor for selling the call is conveyed in the form of higher dividends. To the extent that PERCS is held by U.S. corporations, 70 percent of the "option premium in the form of dividend income" is excluded from corporate income tax.

Hybrids have also been constructed to create "tax-deductible equity." Perhaps the most thinly disguised attempt to issue tax-deductible equity was the *adjustable-rate convertible debt* introduced in 1982. Such convertibles paid a coupon determined by the dividend rate on the firm's common stock; moreover, the debt could be converted to common stock at the current price at any time (in other words, there was no conversion premium). Not surprisingly, once the IRS ruled that this was equity for tax purposes, this structure disappeared.

On a less ambitious level, hybrids have been developed that reduce the combined tax liabilities of the issuers and investors. As a case in point, a number of issuers took advantage of the treatment of zero-coupon instruments by U.S. tax authorities: the issuer could deduct the deferred interest payments from current income, thus reducing potential liquidity problems faced by firms in the near term. Merrill Lynch's LYON is one hybrid structure that provides this benefit.[47]

To Align Interests of Shareholders and Bondholders

Michael Jensen and William Meckling (1976) bring into focus the impact of conflicts between shareholders and bondholders (as well as managers, workers, suppliers, and customers) on the behavior of the firm. Clifford Smith and Jerry Warner (1979) highlight the sources of shareholder-bondholder conflict, suggesting that potential bondholders are concerned that shareholders will behave opportunistically:

1. *Shareholders could dilute the bondholders' claims by increasing debt or adding debt senior to that held by the bondholders in question.* In the practitioners' jargon, this is referred to as *event risk;* academics refer to this as the *claims-dilution problem.*

2. *Shareholders could invest in more risky projects.* This is referred to as *asset substitution.*

3. *If income is sufficiently volatile, the firm may pass up positive-NPV projects.* In periods in which the firm has less income, the firm may be induced to pass up otherwise profitable projects.[48] (Academics refer to this as the *underinvestment problem.*)

Hybrid securities provide ways of dealing with these concerns.

Making the bond puttable reduces the claim-dilution problem. If the shareholders attempt to dilute the bondholders' claim, the bondholders have the right to "cash in" the bond. In this way, we might look at the put as a "golden parachute" for the bondholders.

Making the bond convertible reduces the asset-substitution problem. If the shareholders attempt to expropriate value from the bondholders by investing the proceeds of the debt into more risky investment projects, the bondholders can elect to become shareholders.[49]

A puttable and convertible structure, like Merrill Lynch's LYON, would therefore be attractive in situations in which shareholder-bondholder conflict is likely, such as when the issuing firm requires substantial capital investment and has available to it a wide range of alternative investment projects (with varying degrees of risk). Interestingly, the LYON structure was used early on in this context to fund firms that faced acute asset-substitution problems; Waste Management and Turner Communications are two examples.

The puttable and convertible features of a LYON make it attractive to the retail investor. However, it turned out that another feature of the LYON, the call feature, was less popular with investors.

Hybrids can be structured to reduce the volatility in the underlying net income of the firm, thereby reducing the probability of default compared with straight debt. Examples of hybrid issues that have decreased the volatility of income include Magma Copper's Copper interest-indexed notes, Presido's natural gas interest-indexed notes, and Franklin Savings' CPI-indexed bonds. The inverse floating-rate note could effectively reduce the volatility of net income for firms that are adversely affected by interest rate increases—for instance, firms that supply materials for new home construction.

As an alternative to reducing the probability of default, the conflict between shareholders and bondholders could be diminished by compensating the bondholders if the issuing firm becomes more risky. Manufacturers Hanover's rating-sensitive notes were meant to address this problem.

Why Hybrids?—Part 2: Investor Strategies for Using Hybrids

The impression I intended to convey with Figure 15–1 is that, since 1973, a large number of hybrids have been structured and issued. Obviously, for these structures to have been issued, some investors had to have purchased them; so Figure 15–1 should also convey the impression that hybrids have been increasingly accepted by investors.

The growing acceptance of hybrids by investors is highlighted by the fact that, in 1993 and into the beginning of 1994, sales of hybrid securities (structured notes) boomed. Many dealers claimed that they experienced fivefold increases over the 1992 level. *Euromoney* suggested that, in 1993, some $60–$70 billion of structured notes were issued—a substantial percentage of the medium-term-note market.

Why are investors using hybrids? As with all investment questions, the answer to this one can be found by looking at the way that hybrids can impact the yield or riskiness of the portfolio.

Using Hybrids to Enhance Yield

The primary reason that the structured-note market boomed in 1993 was because U.S. dollar interest rates were so low in 1993 and into 1994. The rates available in 1993 meant that investors were replacing maturing assets which had been yielding 8 percent with new securities which were offering something like 4 percent. Investors wanted to "enhance yield." There are several ways that investors used hybrids to enhance yield.

Using Hybrids to Enhance Yield by Reducing Transaction Costs.   As noted above, some hybrid securities "arbitraged" taxes or regulations; so from the perspective of the issuers and investors, the hybrid generated savings in the form of reduced taxes or reduced regulatory costs. On a less ambitious level, if a hybrid bundles together several securities, the underwriting fee for the hybrid could be lower than the sum of the underwriting fees for the unbundled securities. Regardless of the source of the cost savings, the hybrid security would be attractive to investors because it provided a means of obtaining an asset more cheaply than in the cash market or via a stand-alone derivative transaction.

Taking the cost-reduction argument to its limit, some hybrid securities were designed to provide investors with investments that were not otherwise available—rather than simply more expensive. Indeed, some of the commodity-linked hybrids were designed to satisfy investor demand.[50] For example, in the 1980s, some investors wanted longer-term options on gold. Such an option was simply not available as a stand-alone derivative; so bonds with gold warrants were issued to satisfy this demand.

Using Hybrids to Enhance Yield by Taking a View.   When confronted by low yields in 1993, investors recognized that if they wanted to increase yield, they had to either move down the credit spectrum or accept more market risk. Many chose the latter route.

One way that an investor can take a view is a directional play. Of the directional plays, the most naive is a bet about the future *level* of rates. In 1992 and 1993, investors who expected U.S. dollar interest rates to remain low—or decline even further—could implement their view by purchasing an inverse floater. Rather than trying to predict the level of rates, a more subtle directional play is one in which the investor expresses a view about whether rates will rise as fast as is implied by the yield curve. The steep yield curve that existed in the United States in 1992 led a number of investors to predict that rates would not rise as fast as that steep yield curve "predicted."

Instead of directional plays, investors often take a position about volatility. For example, an index amortizing note could be used to express a view about volatility—e.g., if I expect a period of low-rate volatility, I could purchase an index amortizing note, expecting to receive a higher-than-market fixed rate. It was views about volatility that led a number of investors to turn to range notes in 1992 and 1993.

Using Hybrids to Control Risk

Hybrid securities can also be used to control the riskiness of a portfolio. In the simplest case, investors can use hybrids to obtain exposures that will—via traditional portfolio theory—result in lower variance for the portfolio.

Or hybrids can be purchased with the intention of changing the portfolio's duration (delta) or convexity (gamma) or changing the portfolio's exposure to volatility changes (vega). In the preceding section, we noted that index amortizing notes could be used to take a view on rate volatility. However, since an index amortizing note exhibits positive convexity,[51] it can be used to mitigate the negative convexity exhibited by many mortgage-backed securities—e.g., pools of mortgages characterized by high prepayment when interest rates decline.

Notes

1. John Moody was the founder of Moody's Investors Services. Peter Tufano (1989a) drew my attention to this quote.
2. The dates for the first issuance of convertible debt and debt with warrants are taken from Tufano (1989a).
3. This innovation was imitated by a number of other U.S. companies during the 1920s, but like so many of the financial innovations of the 1920s, that wave of hybrid debt financing was ended in the United States with the regulatory reaction of the 1930s. Specifically, the "gold clause" virtually eliminated indexed debt by prohibiting "a lender to require of a borrower a different quantity or number of dollars from that loaned." And it was not until Congress passed the Helms Amendment in 1977 that the legal basis for commodity-indexed debt was restored. (See McCulloch, 1980).
4. Tufano (1989) notes that floating-rate debt appeared in 1974 and zero-coupon debt in 1981.
5. See Capatides (1988).
6. The notes and warrants were offered simultaneously, but they were sold separately, with the warrants trading on the AMEX.
7. When this chapter was written during the summer of 1997—with silver trading at about $5 per ounce—the

exercise price of $20 per ounce might seem bizarre. However, between October 1979 and January 1980 the price of silver actually averaged $26 per ounce.
8. See Jordan, Mackay, and Moriarty (1990).
9. While this option appears to be European style, its payoff was actually determined by the average price of oil over a specified period, making it an average-rate option (an "Asian" option).
10. According to the *Wall Street Journal* ("Goldman Sachs Offers a First: Inflation Friendly Notes," October 25, 1991), unlike the commodity indexes published by the Commodity Research Bureau and Dow Jones, the GSCI reflects not only the changes in the prices of the commodities but also a "yield" component that is derived from the "roll yield" that is earned as long as the forward curve is in "contango" (i.e., as long as prices for futures contracts maturing further in the future are higher than those maturing sooner).
11. Finnerty (1992) notes that ICONs "were introduced and disappeared quickly."
12. SPINs were examined in detail by K. C. Chen and R. S. Sears (1990). The first SPIN (September 1, 1986) was a four-year bond, with a 2 percent coupon (payable 1 percent every six months). At matu-

rity, the holder received (1) the principal amount of $1,000 per bond plus accrued interest and (2) the excess (if any) of the S&P 500 Index value over the initial (exercise) value of the index multiplied by a predetermined "multiplier." Chen and Sears found that the market prices supported the theoretical equivalence: the available data indicated that the price differences between the SPIN and the "long a bond plus long a call on the S&P" were very small.

13. SIGNs are discussed at length in Finnerty (1993).

14. John Finnerty reminded me that the quoting conventions regarding interest rate options often cause confusion. In the exchange-traded option markets, the convention is to quote calls and puts on the price of some fixed-income security; in the OTC option markets, the convention is to quote calls and puts on an interest rate. Consequently what is a call in the exchange-traded market would be a put in the OTC market, and vice versa. In this chapter, I will use the OTC convention and refer to calls and puts on *interest rates*.

15. The note specified that the lower of S&P or Moody's rating would be used.

16. Moreover, the small number of investment-grade reinsurers prevents diversification of this credit risk.

17. Gutscher (1997a, 1997b).

18. Nusbaum (1997).

19. USAA attempted to issue a similar structure in 1996, but that deal attracted little investor interest. Several reasons were given for the success of the 1997 structure. In addition to the facts that the pricing on the 1997 issue was more attractive and that investors were more familiar with the structure, the 1997 structure was a private placement (rather than a public offering) and the 1997 issue contained a "principal-protected" class not present in the 1996 issue.

20. Apparently, it was not the first earthquake bond. It has been reported that in 1990 a European entity used a seven-year, US$50 million private placement to borrow money from Japanese insurance companies—by making the debt puttable at par in the event of a Richter scale 7 or greater earthquake within 100 kilometers of four key city halls in Japan. Interestingly, the Kobe earthquake qualified the bonds for early redemption; but the reports suggest that none of the bonds were have been put back—apparently because the Japanese insurers had a strong cash posi-

tion and because there was a lack of attractive reinvestment alternatives. (See Bankers Trust Insurance Merchant Bank, 1995.)

21. Although the guaranteed principal protection in the investment-grade tranche is low, Moody's was comfortable with the structure because of the high initial loss threshold and incremental nature of the triggers. One insurance specialist noted that claims structures have changed since the January 1994 Northridge earthquake, which cost the insurance industry $12.5 billion. To reach losses of $18 billion today, an earthquake would need to be nearly three times stronger than Northridge. (See Belcher, 1997.)

22. In effect, the owner of the note is long a call option with an exercise price of $0.80 and is short a call with an exercise price of $2.

23. It was Forest Oil Company that first considered issuing the natural gas–linked debt. However, Forest Oil subsequently felt sure that certain natural gas prices were about to rise, which would make the *ex post* price of the natural gas–linked debt too great. It turned out that Forest Oil made a large bet that went against the firm; natural gas prices fell, and Forest Oil was forced to restructure the standard debt it had issued (*Wall Street Journal*, May 7, 1991).

24. As reported in the June 1992 issue of *Risk*, VAW Australia used a five-year US$31 million facility that had interest payments indexed to the average LME price of aluminum. As the price of aluminum rises, the interest rate VAW Australia pays rises.

25. The Amex's Oil Index includes 15 actively traded oil stocks: Amerada Hess Corporation; Amoco Corporation; Atlantic Richfield Company; British Petroleum Company p.l.c.; Chevron Corporation; E. I. duPont de Nemours and Company; Exxon Corporation; Kerr-McGee Corporation; Mobil Corporation; Occidental Petroleum Corporation; Oryx Energy Company; Phillips Petroleum Co.; Sun Company, Inc.; Texaco Inc.; and Unocal Corporation.

26. Most indexed principal swaps have a "lockout period" at the beginning of the swap during which no amortization will occur. After the lockout period, if rates decline, the fixed-rate payer in effect exercises the option to reduce or cancel a portion of the notional principal over the remaining term of the swap.

27. See "US Derivatives: Range Notes with 1-Month Resets Said to Sell Well" (1994).

28. See "Home in the Range" (1994).

29. Michael Alderson and Don Fraser (1993) argue that adjustable-rate preferred stock failed to flourish because the value was too volatile—the dividend rate did not change as rapidly as did the interest rate to which it was tied, and the dividend rate did not change to reflect changes in the creditworthiness of the issuing firm. They point out that adjustable-rate preferred stock gave way to a second-generation hybrid—auction-rate preferred stock.

    In the same vein, Finnerty (1992) noted that adjustable-rate preferred could trade at substantial premiums or discounts to par. To keep the price of the adjustable-rate preferred near par, another second-generation product was devised—*convertible adjustable preferred stock (CAPS)*. To the adjustable-rate preferred structure, CAPS adds an option: at each dividend payment date, the security would be convertible into enough shares to make the security worth its par value.

30. One source of this volatility is Canadian Occidental's 52 percent interest in a major oil field in the Republic of Yemen.

31. Much of the information in this section is taken from Harty (1995). Harty, Emmett J., "Americus Trust's PRIMEs, and SCOREs: Precursors to LEAPS, PERCS, ELKS, YEELDS, CHIPS, and SuperTrust, in *The Handbook of Equity Derivatives,* Jack Clark Francis, William W. Toy, and J. Gregg Whittaker, eds. (1995). Burr Ridge, IL: Irwin Professional Publishing.

32. The termination date was approximately five years; the termination claim was set approximately 25 percent above the share's closing price the day before the offering.

33. Harty notes that since it could not be exercised until the termination date, the SCORE would normally be considered a European-style option; but he goes on to suggest that since a SCORE could be "exercised" by submitting the SCORE along with a PRIME to the trustee and obtaining a share of the stock in return, a SCORE could be viewed as an American-style option with a variable strike price (equal to the value of the PRIME).

34. Prior to the listing of the Americus Trusts, Kidder Peabody created an Americus Trust–like structure for AT&T.

35. In 1986, the Amsterdam Stock Exchange listed a *SCORE*-like structure (called a *FALCON*) on shares of Royal Dutch Petroleum Company. In 1992, RBC Dominion Securities created an Americus Trust–like structure for the Bank of Montreal, in which the two hybrid securities were called PEACs (Payment Enhanced Capital securities) and SPECs (Special Equity Claim securities), instead of PRIMEs and SCOREs.

36. Harty (1995) noted an important difference between the Americus Trust PRIMEs and SCOREs and the USUs: Both would decompose equity returns; but the USUs would have had the effect of changing equity into debt—with the consequent impact on the tax liabilities of the potential issuers of USUs.

37. LOR note that the idea for the SuperTrust had been proposed originally by Nils Hakansson (1976).

38. Merrill Lynch underwrites a similar security knows as Mandatory Conversion Premium Dividend Preferred Stock.

39. Stovall (1991) asserts that the public issues were preceded by a privately placed American Express PERCS with Warren Buffett.

40. Because PERCS is mandatorily convertible into common stock, the rating agencies grade PERCS as full-credit equity; so the PERCS issued by Citicorp was treated as Tier 1 capital by the Federal Reserve.

41. Shares of the underlying stock are held in trust (known as depository shares), and the PERCS shares are sold from the trust.

42. Stovall (1991) notes that most PERCS have a maturity of three years.

43. Chen and Chen (1995) noted that several ELKS-like securities have been offered: YEELDS (Yield Enhanced Equity Linked Debt Securities) by Lehman Brothers, CHIPS (Common-Linked Higher Income Participation Securities) by Bear Stearns, and PERQS (Performance Equity-Linked Redemption Quarterly-Pay Security) by Morgan Stanley. Whittaker and Kim (1995) described S. G. Warburg's ELKS-like security which they call SHIELDS.

44. In addition, since the value setting for the ELKS is done not on a single date, but rather as the average over the final 10 days of the security's life, the option in an ELKS could be considered to be an average-rate option (an Asian-style option), rather than a European-style option as in the case of a PERCS. (However, this distinction may be, as Gary Gastineau pointed out, "a triumph of form over substance.")

45. In addition, some hybrids were issued to obtain accrual accounting treatment for a derivative structure

that would otherwise be marked-to-market. For more on this rationale, see Singleton (1991).

46. Since data on options that have the same maturity as PERCS are not generally available, Chen, Kensinger, and Pu used data on LEAPs (Long-term Equity AnticiPation securities).

47. John Finnerty (1992) noted that the ability to use straight-line amortization for the original issue discount was eliminated in 1982 by the Tax Equity and Fiscal Responsibility Act (TEFRA). When interest rates rose dramatically in 1981 and 1982, there was a flood of zero-coupon issues. Subsequent to TEFRA, most of the zero-coupon issues are convertible.

48. In addition to the three sources of shareholder-bondholder conflict we consider here, Smith and Warner identify a fourth source of conflict, dividend payout. This source of conflict is normally dealt with through debt covenants.

49. See Brennan and Schwartz (1981).

50. Commodities are particularly interesting in this context. Empirically, the return on commodities has been low; but there exists some evidence that commodity returns are negatively correlated with fixed-income returns. Consequently, portfolio optimization would lead investors to consider including commodities. The low returns for commodities in the cash market might lead the investors to opt for an option on the commodity, rather than hold the commodity itself.

51. Specifically, the fixed-rate-pay side of an indexed principal swap has positive convexity.

16

THE DEALER'S PERSPECTIVE

Derivatives have proved to be profitable products for the dealers. The derivatives business generates profits in and of itself. For example, Union Bank of Switzerland (UBS) notes that the derivatives business "is at the very upper end in terms of the return on equity that one has in a bank."[1] Moreover, derivatives are also useful in the dealer's own core activities: underwriting, trading, asset management, and asset-liability management.

Who Are the Dealers?

Dealing in OTC derivatives has tended to concentrate among principals possessing not only the requisite technology and know-how but also ample capital and credit experience. To give you some idea who the dealers are, we have provided in Table 16–1 a ranking of the largest 100 derivatives dealers. The data are based on the latest disclosures during the 12 months ended March 31, 1997. As you can see from the table, the largest dealers tend to be commercial banks, but the list also contains investment banks, securities firms, and insurance companies. Moreover, these rankings are by no means static. Only six firms maintained the same ranking as in 1995; and 16 firms not ranked in the top 100 in 1995 did so in 1997.

The top derivatives dealers are from the United States, Europe, Canada, Asia, and Australia. In terms of market share, U.S. firms account for a significant portion of the activity. Overall, industry activity tends to be concentrated among the largest dealers. The top 10 dealers accounted for 34 percent of the derivatives reported in the 1997 survey compared with 31 percent in 1995. And given the consolidation in the financial services industry in 1997, we would expect this to

TABLE 16–1   Largest 100 Derivatives Dealers

Rank			
1997	*1995*	*Firm*	*Total Derivatives (Millions of US$)**
1	(1)	Chase Manhattan	6,555,634
2	(3)	J.P. Morgan	5,277,239
3	(5)	Swiss Bank Corporation	3,402,240
4	(4)	Societe Generale	3,180,767
5	(18)	Deutsche Bank	2,952,656
6	(22)	NatWest Bank	2,895,873
7	—	Bank of Tokyo-Mitsubishi	2,836,469
8	(2)	Citicorp	2,702,090
9	(14)	Credit Suisse	2,602,912
10	(9)	Compagnie Financiere de Paribas	2,390,962
11	(16)	Salomon	2,358,500
12	(25)	Merrill Lynch	2,260,000
13	(17)	Barclays	2,235,503
14	(19)	Banque Nationale de Paris	2,218,958
15	(7)	Fuji Bank	2,023,274
16	(11)	Union Bank of Switzerland	1,976,110
17	(6)	Bankers Trust	1,966,252
18	(8)	Industrial Bank of Japan	1,804,671
19	(26)	Sanwa Bank	1,756,059
20	(31)	Goldman Sachs	1,744,831
21	(20)	BankAmerica	1,693,453
22	(10)	Sumitomo Bank	1,676,791
23	(28)	Lloyds TSB	1,658,811
24	(24)	Dai-Ichi Kangyo Bank	1,553,303
25	(13)	HSBC Holdings	1,528,784
26	(29)	Lehman Brothers	1,516,822
27	—	Credit Suisse Financial Products	1,441,421
28	(23)	Sakura Bank	1,427,745
29	(42)	NationsBank	1,416,214
30	(34)	Morgan Stanley	1,317,000
31	(36)	ABN-Amro	1,207,926
32	(30)	Credit Lyonnais	1,207,090
33	(33)	Tokai Bank	1,123,992
34	—	Credit Agricole Indosuez	1,123,753
35	(38)	First Chicago NBD	1,102,122
36	(50)	Commerzbank	1,093,175
37	(39)	Canadian Imperial Bank of Commerce	1,058,011
38	(45)	Dresdner Bank	901,098
39	(37)	Royal Bank of Canada	872,978
40	(63)	Caisse des Depots	763,722
41	(32)	Long-Term Credit Bank	709,507
42	(64)	Den Danske Bank	655,345
43	(61)	Svenska Handelsbanken	636,016
44	(51)	American International Group	623,950
45	(65)	Bayerishe Verinsbank	622,322

TABLE 16–1   *Continued*

Rank		Firm	Total Derivatives (Millions of US$)*
1997	*1995*		
46	(48)	Skandinaviska Enskilda Banken	605,824
47	(53)	Bank of Nova Scotia	599,277
48	(40)	Nomura Securities	544,867
49	(57)	Union Europeene de CIC	540,486
50	(52)	Credit Commercial de France	509,653
51	(49)	Bank of Montreal	495,076
52	(58)	Rabobank	491,337
53	(62)	General Re Corporation	483,918
54	(60)	Australia and New Zealand Bank	471,537
55	(55)	Westdeutsche Landesbank	465,946
56	(47)	Mitsubishi Trust & Banking	438,828
57	(93)	Bankgesellschaft Berlin	416,879
58	(54)	Toronto-Dominion Bank	416,274
59	(66)	Istituto Bancario San Paolo di Torino	415,913
60	(71)	Kredietbank	411,085
61	—	Merita Group	404,277
62	(72)	Unibank	402,831
63	(69)	Standard Chartered	391,158
64	(46)	Westpac	362,493
65	(41)	Sumitomo Trust & Banking	359,795
66	(67)	Republic New York	344,346
67	(70)	ING Group	340,547
68	(73)	Bank Brussels Lambert	328,985
69	(68)	Royal Bank of Scotland	321,160
70	(59)	National Australia Bank	303,717
71	—	Norinchukin Bank	300,857
72	(85)	Santander	286,738
73	(96)	Bear Stearns	282,300
74	(87)	DG Bank	276,414
75	—	Yasuda Trust & Banking	265,592
76	(77)	Generale Bank	262,030
77	(88)	Banca Commerciale Italiana	250,210
78	(80)	Swedbank	249,869
79	(84)	Bayerische Hypotheken-und Wechsel Bank	244,632
80	(76)	Bayerische Landesbank	241,933
81	—	Mitsui Trust & Banking	241,098
82	—	Dexia	235,883
83	(79)	Commonwealth Bank of Australia	219,234
84	(78)	Abbey National	218,957
85	(74)	Banco Central Hispanoamericano	216,158
86	—	CPR	183,807
87	(75)	Nordbanken	181,565
88	(81)	Banco Bilbao Vizcaya	180,670
89	—	Banque Populaire	175,591
90	—	Bank of New York	174,129
91	—	Landesbank Hessen-Thuringen	171,699
92	(89)	BHF-Bank	163,879

TABLE 16–1 *Continued*

Rank			
1997	*1995*	*Firm*	*Total Derivatives (Millions of US$)**
93	(100)	Credit National BFCE	161,951
94	(94)	Credito Italiano	161,325
95	—	Banque Paribas Belgique	160,560
96	(99)	Schroders	157,941
97	—	Postipankki	157,322
98	(44)	Hambros Bank	156,921
99	—	Bank Austria	154,215
100	—	Union Bank of Norway	144,442

Data are from the *Swaps Monitor* biennial survey of dealer annual reports (November 24, 1997).
*The data reflect holdings of exchange-traded and OTC derivatives for trading and asset-liability management purposes and include interest rate, currency, equity, commodity, and other derivatives.

continue as major dealers acquire smaller-niche players to broaden their product and service capabilities.

The credit standing of the dealer is very important. (In Chapter 22, we will provide data indicating that to be a successful dealer, the dealer must have a minimum of a single-A rating; and many transactions require the dealer to be rated double A.) Because of the importance of credit, several dealers have created special-purpose, credit-enhanced derivatives product companies—*special purpose vehicles* (SPVs). The SPVs are known by a number of names. Some refer to them as *derivative product companies* (DPCs). Standard & Poor's describes them as *bankruptcy-remote* subsidiaries. And, since in almost all of the cases to date, the SPVs have been rated AAA, they are also referred to as *AAA subsidiaries*.

The stand-alone, separately capitalized SPVs created to the middle of 1997 are displayed in Table 16–2.

Two credit-enhancement structures are used for the stand-alone, separately capitalized SPVs—*continuation structures* and *termination structures*.[2]

The *continuation structure* was pioneered by Merrill Lynch in November 1991 (MLDP). In January 1994, Lehman Brothers extended the Merrill Lynch structure: Lehman Brothers Financial Products (LBFP) keeps the basic continuation model but adds a contingency manager who steps in to run the book in the event of problems at the parent. Like MLDP, each transaction entered into between LBFP and a counterparty is offset with an equal and opposite trade with Lehman Brothers' swaps operation. LBFP then effectively takes back the market risk from the swap and hedges it in the conventional way with government bonds, futures, and over-the-counter instruments. The overall risk that LBFP carries, therefore, is greatly reduced. If the parent falls into difficulty and LBFP is cut loose, the contingency manager, an AAA-rated European bank, will inherit a book of swaps with the market risk fully hedged.

TABLE 16–2   AAA-Rated Derivative Product Subsidiaries

	Date of Rating	*Sponsor*	*Structure*	*Initial Capital*
Merrill Lynch Derivative Products	11/91	Merrill Lynch	Continuation	$350m
Goldman Sachs Financial Products International	3/92	Goldman Sachs	Cash flow/runoff	$70m
Swapco	3/93	Salomon Brothers	Termination	$175m
Paribus Derives Garantis	12/93	Banque Paribas	Termination	Ffr800m
Morgan Stanley Derivative Products	1/94	Morgan Stanley	Termination	$150m
Lehman Brothers Financial Products	4/94	Lehman Brothers	Continuation	$200m
Westpac Derivative Products	5/94	Westpac	Termination	$200m
Credit Lyonnais New York Program	2/95	Credit Lyonnais	Termination	$200m
Tokai Derivative Products	2/95	Tokai	Continuation	£100m
Sumitomo Bank Capital Market Derivative Products	5/95	Sumitomo Bank	Continuation	$300m
BT Credit Plus	2/96	Bankers Trust	Termination	$100,*
Sakura Prime Financial Program	8/96	Sakura Global Capital Inc.	Termination	†
Nationsbank Financial Products	9/96	NationsBank N.A.	Continuation	$300mm‡
Bear Stearns Financial Products	10/96	Bear Stearns	Continuation	$150mm#
Trading & Risk Management	10/96	Bear Stearns	Termination	

SOURCE: Moody's Investors Service and Standard & Poor's.

*$75mm in collateral pledged by BT Co. and a $25mm policy from Financial Security Assurance Inc. (FSA).

†Termination payments to counterparties supported by an unlimited insurance policy from Capital Markets Assurance Corp. (CMAC).

‡Initial capital includes $100mm in equity and $200mm in subordinated debt.

§Contingent manager must maintain a minimum long-term rating of A3.

#Bear Stearns Financial Products and Trading & Risk Management are supported by a single pool of $150 million in capital, collateral, and counterparty receivables.

The *termination structure* was invented by Salomon Brothers. Rather than appointing a contingency manager in the event of parental difficulty, all contracts terminate within days at midmarket price.

As John Behof (1993) pointed out, the use of SPVs to reduce the credit risk in a derivatives transaction is analogous to more traditional asset securitization, in which a separate structure (e.g., a trust) is set up to isolate the assets being securitized from other risks. In the case of the SPVs, a separate organization is established to isolate the derivatives transactions from the risks in the overall firm.

Common features in the AAA-rated SPVs include:

Nonconsolidation. The SPV is structured to be legally separate from the parent. Consequently, if the parent were to experience bankruptcy, the assets of the SPV would not be consolidated with those of the parent.

Capitalization. The SPVs are overcapitalized in order that the excess capital provide a "cushion" against default. The rating agencies tend to require that the capital of the AAA subsidiary be able to withstand the most extreme stress scenario. GSFPI was capitalized by a portfolio of in-the-money Nikkei Index options and warrants valued at 9.3 billion Japanese yen. MLDPI was capitalized by $300 million in common stock sold to the parent and by a $50 million preferred stock offering sold to a third party. Swapco was initially capitalized with $175 million but is required to maintain additional capital if the size or composition of the derivatives portfolio increases the risk of the SPV.

Operating guidelines. In order to maintain the AAA rating, the behavior of the SPV is prescribed by certain parameters and guidelines within which the SPV's transactions must be conducted. These guidelines prescribe acceptable counterparties: MLDPI was initially permitted to enter into transactions with only AA or better counterparties.[3] Swapco will have to maintain more capital if it deals with lower-rated credits. The guidelines also limit the SPV's exposure to individual counterparties and its aggregate exposure to classes of counterparties (e.g., by credit rating or by country of origin of counterparty) to specified dollar (or percent of capital) limits.

Matching and affiliate transactions. Since the AAA subsidiary is set up to provide counterparties with more comfort on default, the SPV is required to take actions to limit its market risk—i.e., the SPV is restricted from taking unmatched positions. In the case of MLDPI and Swapco this is accomplished by requiring that the SPV enter into a "mirror" transaction with the parent every time it enters into a transaction with a third party. By passing the interest rate or foreign exchange rate on to its parent, the SPV will not be directly exposed to fluctuations in financial prices. To maintain the credit rating, the SPV's transactions with the parent are collateralized (on a net basis).

The Functions of a Dealer[4]

A derivatives dealer is a classic intermediary. The dealer provides over-the-counter risk management products to the end users. As financial intermediaries, banks have traditionally offered foreign exchange and interest rate management products to their customers. By tailoring derivative products to their customers' needs, the dealers are able to provide more flexibility than that offered by exchange-traded derivatives, especially for hedging longer-term exposures.

By providing OTC derivatives to end users, the dealers expose themselves to a number of risks[5]:

- *Credit risk.* The risk that the end user (the dealer's counterparty) defaults.
- *Market (or price) risk.* The risk that unhedged inventories of OTC products decline in value substantially.
- *Operating risk.* The possibility that internal controls over trading activity may prove inadequate.

And the dealers also accept legal risk—i.e., the possibility that contracts are not enforced by the courts.

The dealers have not always accepted all of these risks. In the days of the first currency and interest rate swaps, investment banks, commercial banks, merchant banks, and independent broker-dealers acted mainly as intermediaries for their corporate clients by finding counterparties with offsetting requirements in terms of notional amount, currencies, type of interest to be paid, and maturity. Acting as agent or broker for a fee, the institutions arranging the swaps took no principal position in the transactions and, hence, were exposed to neither credit nor market risk.

But most financial institutions discovered that they could expand their business by offering themselves as counterparties (or principals). Transactions designed to meet a given customer's requirements were immediately matched by entering into an offsetting transaction such as a "matched swap." Because each pair of transactions was dealt with separately and discretely, the dealer's book of business was relatively simple to monitor and manage. This new role, however, required a commitment of capital since dealers now faced credit risk and some limited market risk.

The next step in the evolution of dealer activities was the "warehousing" of derivatives transactions. In this phase of development, dealers would temporarily hedge a swap—typically with a cash security or futures position—until a matched transaction could be found to replace the temporary hedge. This advance in risk management practice increased the ability of dealers to accommodate customer needs.

Today, major dealers have moved from the warehouse approach to a "portfolio" approach in which the dealer simply takes the customer's transaction into its portfolio (or "book") of derivatives and manages the residual risk of its overall position.

As we will illustrate in Chapter 18, each transaction is broken down by the warehouse manager into its component cash flows to yield a measure of its net, or *residual,* exposures arising from all its positions. The residual exposures can then be hedged by entering into other OTC transactions, taking positions in the cash market, or using exchange-traded instruments. By thus improving their ability to monitor and manage the various components of their own market risk, this shift by dealers to a portfolio approach has significantly increased their ability to provide their customers with a broad and continually expanding range of transactions. In a business that has become increasingly competitive, moreover, dealers also earn increasingly higher returns for the financial engineering that goes into developing the highly customized and structured transactions. (For an account of the most recent "structured" transactions, see Chapters 13, 14, and 15.)

In the process of providing products for end users, dealers also provide liquidity by quoting bid and offer prices. To supply the immediacy demanded by end users, dealers either use their own inventory, or establish new positions and manage the resulting risk. They are compensated by the bid-ask spread. In addition, some dealers take market risk positions with the expectation of profiting from anticipated movements in prices or rates. Some dealers also provide an arbitrage function, identifying and exploiting anomalies between derivatives and underlying cash market instruments, thereby enhancing market liquidity and pricing efficiency.

The Trend toward Integrated Risk Measure[6]

"Integrated risk management" is the phrase of the day in the financial community; but in practice the phrase means different things to different firms. There are two ways in which dealers are attempting to integrate their measurement and management of risk.

Integrating Different Market Risks

Dealers are working to integrate the management of interest rate, foreign exchange rate, commodity price, and equity price risks in a portfolio. We know from recent surveys that 46 percent of large dealers disclose value-at-risk (VAR) statistics.[7] Since VAR calculations are predicated on a portfolio approach, it follows that dealers are using this approach to measure and disclose risk. However, we do not know the extent to which dealers manage their risk on a portfolio basis.

Integrating Market, Credit, and Operational Risks

Financial product dealers (and financial institutions in general) face risk other than market risk. For example, the U.S. Office of the Comptroller of the Currency lists nine sources of risk—credit, interest rate, liquidity, price, foreign exchange, transaction, compliance, strategic and reputation. Dealers are working to aggregate these risks under three major headings—market, credit, and operational—and then integrating their management.

The rationale for the integration of market and credit risk is straightforward. The magnitude of market risk faced by the firm is determined by the composition of the portfolio and the distribution of the market factors relevant to that portfolio (i.e., level, volatility, and correlation). In the broadest sense, credit risk is determined by the institution's exposure (net of recovery) and probability of default. Since an institution's exposure can be measured in much the same way as market risk, it follows that credit risk is determined by the composition of the portfolio and the distribution of market factors relevant for that portfolio.[8] Hence, the determinants of market risk are a subset of those for credit risk:

Determinants of Market Risk	*Determinants of Credit Risk*
Portfolio composition	Portfolio composition
Distribution of market factors	Distribution of market factors
	Recovery
	Probability of default

The argument for integrating the management of operational risk and market and credit risk is less straightforward. In a general sense, operational risk can be expressed as

$$\text{Operational risk} = f(\text{transaction processing, liquidity management, organizational structure, personnel, compliance})$$

where the determinants are the necessary components for operating a financial enterprise, each of which is an aggregation of several other variables.[9] The arguments for integrating management of operational risk with that of market and credit risk are based on a commonality of technique, rather than on a mathematical basis; i.e., the techniques that firms are using to manage market and credit risk can be used to manage operational risk.[10]

There is little information on how far financial institutions have integrated the management of market, credit, and operational risk. However, some insight can be gained from the work of the Wharton Financial Institutions Center. During the 1995–96 academic year, the center, led by Anthony Santomero, conducted on-site visits with commercial, investment, and universal banks to "review and evaluate the risk management systems and the process of risk evaluation . . . in place." The report on this research project (Santomero, 1997) notes that "at the organizational level, overall risk management is being centralized," with the objective being "to empower one individual or group with the responsibility to evaluate overall firm-level risk and determine the best interest of the bank as a whole."

However, the study also makes it clear that while financial institutions are moving in the direction of integrated risk management, they have not yet reached the goal. At the time of the visits, the risk management process was driven by independent analyses of different types of risk and "the analytical approaches that are subsumed in each of these analyses are complex, difficult and not easily communicated to non-specialists." Most importantly for us, the study considered the question: "How are banks selecting appropriate levels for each risk and [selecting] or at least articulating an appropriate level of risk for the organization as a whole?" According to the report, "the simple answer is: 'not very well' . . . senior management often is presented with a myriad of reports on individual exposures" and "the risks are not dimensioned in similar ways."

Notes

1. "UBS Profiting from Derivatives," *American Banker*, December 15, 1992.
2. Bennett (1994).
3. However, in May of 1993, Moody's relaxed the rule to permit MLDP to deal with single-A counterparties.
4. This section draws heavily on the Report of the Global Derivatives Project sponsored by the Group of Thirty, July 1993.
5. It is important to note that these risks are not unique to derivatives. These risks are the same risks that financial institutions face with their "traditional" products.
6. This section is based on one of the articles I wrote in the "Class Notes" series for *Risk* (March 1997), "Firm-Wide Risk Management: How Firms Are Integrating Risk Management," *Risk*, March 1997.
7. Basle Committee on Banking Supervision and the Technical Committee of the International Organization of Securities Commissions, *Survey of Disclosures about Trading and Derivatives Activities of Banks and Securities Firms,* November 1996.
8. For a discussion of the relation between credit risk and market risk, see Mark (1997).
9. For example, transaction processing problems can arise because of human error, technology failure, incorrect models, mark-to-market valuation errors, security problems, or disasters. Organizational structure issues include incentive compensation and the ethical standards implicit in the culture of the organization. Personnel risk, e.g., fraud or the lack of adequate skills in employees, includes not only hiring practices but also training and retention.
10. One approach is to calculate an "operational VAR." This involves the compilation of a loss-event database with each loss being attributed to one of the operational risk factors. A probability distribution of losses due to this factor is constructed. A firm can then estimate, with a specified degree of confidence, a maximum loss that it would be exposed to due to this operational risk factor.

17 MEASURING AND MANAGING DEFAULT RISK

The magnitude of the default risk[1] inherent in an OTC derivatives transaction has been—and remains—a source of concern for both market participants and the regulatory authorities. The U.S. Federal Reserve had begun to view the credit risks from intermediating OTC derivatives as "a significant element of the risk profiles of . . . the large multinational banking organizations that act as intermediaries between end users of these contracts."[2]

The bankruptcy of Drexel Burnham Lambert and the failure of the Bank of New England and Barings led the users of risk management products to attempt to do more of their derivative transactions with AAA and AA financial institutions. The bankruptcies of nonfinancial entities—notably Olympia & York—highlighted to intermediaries of the risk management products the importance of performing careful credit analyses. And when the UK House of Lords ruled that the UK local authorities of Hammersmith & Fulham could walk away from derivative transactions they had entered into, the market realized that failure to perform can be the result of reasons other than a financial inability to pay.

Concern about credit risk led to the development of risk-based capital adequacy standards for the derivatives transactions intermediated by commercial banks. The requirements were established in July 1988 by the Basle Committee on Banking Supervision—that is, representatives of the central banks of Belgium, Canada, France, Germany, Italy, Japan, the Netherlands, Sweden, United Kingdom, the United States (the Group of Ten countries) plus Switzerland and Luxembourg. These requirements—commonly referred to as the Basle Accord—came into full force at the end of 1992.

Market participants differentiate between the credit risk that exists prior to contract settlement—"presettlement" risk—and the credit risk that exists when the

The Basle Accord

The objective of the accord was to establish minimum capital standards to protect the banking system against the *credit risk* inherent in a derivatives transaction. In the accord, the exposure of the bank to a derivatives transaction was related to the more familiar exposure in a loan through the *credit equivalent exposure:*

Credit equivalent exposure = current exposure + potential exposure
= Max (MTM, 0) + ("Add-on" factor) × (notional principal)

The accord provided a 2 × 2 matrix of "add-on" factors:

Residual Maturity	Interest Rate	Exchange Rate
One year or less	0.0%	1.0%
One year or greater	0.5%	5.0%

This original credit risk accord has been amended in 1994 and 1995.

1994 Amendments

In April 1993, the Basle Committee on Banking Supervision issued a consultative proposal: *The Supervisory Recognition of Netting for Capital Adequacy Purposes.* This proposal recommended the recognition of netting for current but not potential exposure.

In its December 1993 response to the Basle Committee, ISDA argued that netting has an effect not only on current but also on potential exposure and that the effect on potential exposure should be recognized. Staying within the framework of the original accord, ISDA recommended that the add-on factors could be revised to reflect the impact of netting. ISDA argued that the relation between the add-on for netted transactions (A_{net}) and the add-on that had been used previously (A_{gross}) should be

$$A_{net} = NGR \times A_{gross}$$

where *NGR* is the ratio of net replacement cost to gross replacement cost for transactions which can be legally netted. Generalizing, the relation between the net and gross add-on could be expressed as

$$A_{net} = [(1 - a) + (a \times NGR)] \times A_{gross}$$

In the context of this generalized relation, ISDA's December 1993 proposal was that the *NGR* "weight" be set at 1.

In July 1994, the Basle Committee issued *Amendment to the 1988 Capital Accord for Bilateral Netting.* This amendment did two things. First, it laid out the ground rules for netting to be permitted. Second, the 1994 amendment recognized that netting could have an impact on potential exposure. In the context of the generalized expression introduced above,

$$A_{net} = [(1 - a) + (a \times NGR)] \times A_{gross}$$

The Basle Accord continued

Basle's proposal was that the *NGR* "weight" be set at 0.5.

1995 Amendments

In April 1995, the Basle Committee on Banking Supervision issued *Basle Capital Accord: Treatment of Potential Exposure for Off-Balance-Sheet Items.* This document formally recognized the effect of netting on potential exposure.

In terms of the generalized expression,

$$A_{net} = [(1 - a) + (a \times NGR)] \times A_{gross}$$

the Basle Committee set the *NGR* weight at 0.6.

The April 1995 document also included an expanded matrix of add-on factors. As is illustrated below, the new add-on matrix added one new row and three new columns:

Expanded Add-On Matrix
(The original 2×2 matrix is indicated by boldface type.)

Residual Maturity	*Interest Rate*	*Exchange Rate and Gold*	*Equity*	*Precious Metals Except Gold*	*Other Commodities*
One year or less	**0.0%**	**1.0%**	6.0%	7.0%	10.0%
Over one year to five years	**0.5%**	**5.0%**	8.0%	7.0%	12.0%
Over five years	1.5%	7.5%	10.0%	8.0%	15.0%

contract matures or reaches a settlement date and the counterparties would be required to pass payments to each other—"settlement" risk. Since presettlement risk is by far the larger of the two, most of this chapter will focus on presettlement risk. We will, however, return to the issue of settlement risk at the end of the chapter.

Using the "Building Blocks" to Examine Default Risk

When the "building-block" approach was introduced in Chapter 2, we began with forwards and moved toward options. To develop some insight about the default risk associated with derivatives, we can again use the building blocks. But since the determinants of default risk are most apparent for options, we begin at the other end this time.[3]

Default risk for an option is one-sided. There is no duty to perform on which the option buyer could default; once the premium payment is made, the buyer only receives payments. It is the option seller who has the obligation to perform. Two circumstances are necessary for the seller of the option to default.

First, the option must be in-the-money. Unless the option is in-the-money, the seller of the option will not be required to perform.

Second, for default to occur, the seller of the option must be released from contractual obligations by a court. The most likely circumstance—and the one that we will focus on here—is bankruptcy of the option seller.

Indeed, the default risk of this option can itself be viewed as an option. However, the value of this "default-risk option" depends on two uncertain values—the underlying financial price on which the option is written and the value of the other assets of the seller of the option. Consequently, the option to default is a compound option.[4] And if we look at the option to default as a compound option, the probability-weighted loss that could result from a distress-induced default on an option contract is determined by three things:

The value of the option, itself determined by the relation between the exercise price and the prevailing spot price, the volatility of the underlying financial price, and the time to maturity.

The credit standing of the seller of the option, determined by the critical change in the value of the other assets necessary to put the option seller into distress as well as the volatility of these other assets.

The correlation between the underlying financial price and the value of the option seller's other assets, which depends on whether the option sold is a call or a put.

As we saw in Chapter 10, selling a forward is equivalent to buying a put and selling a call. Conversely, buying a forward is equivalent to selling a put and buying a call. This equivalence has direct implications for the default risk for a forward contract.

First, evaluation of the default risk for a forward contract must involve valuation of the same default-risk "option" as with options themselves. To evaluate the default risk for a forward, it is necessary to consider the embedded "short" option positions.

Second, the default risk of a forward contract is associated with both the buyer and seller of the forward. The seller of the forward has sold a call; the buyer of the forward has likewise sold a put.

Since a swap can be viewed as a package of forward contracts, default risk for a swap is again a compound option. However, it is a more complex compound option than for options or forwards. Under "full two-way" payment, default on a swap would oblige immediate cash settlement of the contract. A swap counterparty can only default once. Therefore, there could exist an "optimal default strategy" that would depend on the joint distribution of the counterparty's asset values and the underlying asset price *at each settlement date.* Although this default option is dramatically more complex than for calls and forwards because of the multiple settlement dates, the variables that determine its value are the same.

The compound option framework is useful in developing an understanding of the default-risk problem, and we believe that this path is one that will be followed in the future. However, this approach will be quite demanding, both computationally and with respect to data collection and management.

Thus, both market participants and regulators have employed the simplifying approximation that the financial price underlying the derivative transaction and the counterparty's other assets *are uncorrelated.* With this simplifying approximation in place, any measure of risk based on the potential default-induced loss to the intermediary must be a function of three determinants:

1. *Exposure*—the amount at risk.
2. *Recovery*—the amount that would be recovered in event of default.
3. *Probability of default*—the likelihood of a loss.

Using a simple mathematical expression, we can denote potential default-induced loss as

Potential default-induced loss = (exposure − recovery) × (probability of default)

It is with the exposure generated by and the probability of default for risk management transactions that most of this chapter will deal. We will, however, also consider some of the techniques used to measure credit risk, methods for reducing credit risk, and some evidence on the default history to date for risk management instruments.

Aside

The Approach of the Basle Committee on Banking Supervision

The approach we will describe in this chapter mirrors that which the Basle Committee on Banking Supervision used in developing the capital adequacy guidelines. They considered an exposure measure weighted by the probability of default, one that "applies credit conversion factors to the face value, or notional principal, amounts of off-balance sheet exposures and then assigns the resulting credit equivalent amounts to the appropriate risk category in a manner generally similar to balance sheet assets."* To make this cryptic description more clear, the following flow chart describes the manner in which the process is accomplished.†

The Approach of the Basle Committee on Banking Supervision continued

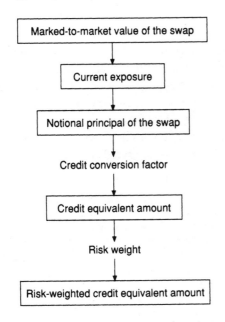

Next, the current exposure is combined with the *notional principal amount* of the swap and a *credit conversion factor* to define the *credit equivalent amount* for the swap:

$$\begin{aligned} &\text{Current exposure} \\ +\ &\text{notional principal of swap} \\ \times\ &\text{credit conversion factor} \\ =\ &\text{credit equivalent amount} \end{aligned}$$

This is equivalent to the "exposure" described above.

Then, to get from this "exposure" measure to some measure of potential default-induced loss, the credit equivalent amount is multiplied by a *risk weight* to yield a *risk-weighted credit equivalent amount:*

$$\begin{aligned} &\text{Credit equivalent amount} \times \text{risk weight} \\ =\ &\text{risk-weighted credit equivalent amount} \end{aligned}$$

The process begins with the *marked-to-market value of the risk management product.* From this measure, the *current exposure* of the financial institution to default on the swap is defined as the positive portion of the marked-to-market value:

$$\begin{aligned} \text{Max [0, marked-to-market value]} \\ = \text{current exposure} \end{aligned}$$

Federal Reserve System Capital Maintenance: Revisions to Capital Adequacy Guidelines, 12 CFR Part 225, Appendix A (Regulation Y), January 24, 1988, pp. 61–62.

†This process is taken from the January 24, 1988, Federal Reserve System publication, pp. 103–06.

Exposure

When dealing with credit risk, banks are used to dealing with loans. The exposure to the bank on a loan is straightforward: The amount of money the bank has at risk is the amount that "walked out of the bank" less any principal repayments that have occurred. However, things are not quite so simple for the risk management products[5]: At any point in time, the bank is exposed not only for the *current value of the derivative* but also for *potential changes in value*. Also, the calculation of the exposure must take into consideration the fact that the *exposure will change over the life of the transaction.* Moreover, the bank must consider two exposure measures— *maximum* and *expected.*

Current and Potential Exposures

As an example of a risk management transaction, consider an interest rate swap. In Figure 17–1, we have illustrated how the value of the swap changes as the underlying interest rate changes. Panel (*a*) illustrates the value profile for the fixed-rate payer: if interest rates rise, the expected present value of the inflows becomes larger than that for the outflows and the value of the swap becomes positive; but if rates fall, the value of the swap to this fixed-rate payer becomes negative. Panel (*b*) illustrates the reverse, the value of a swap to the party receiving fixed and paying floating.

FIGURE 17–1   Marking a Swap Contract to Market (*a*) The value of a swap in which the party illustrated pays fixed, receives floating   (*b*) The value of a swap in which the party illustrated pays floating, receives fixed.

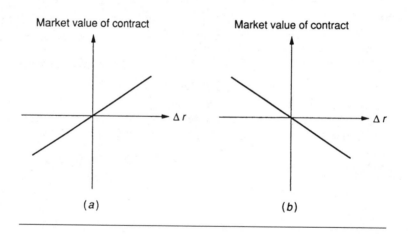

Market value of contract

Market value of contract

(*a*)

(*b*)

The current replacement cost of a swap—the current exposure of the swap—is obtained directly from the market value of the swap contract. In panel (*a*) of Figure 17–1, if rates have fallen since origination, there will be no loss if the counterparty defaults; if rates have fallen, the fixed-rate payer is making payments to the counterparty. For the fixed-rate payer, a default-induced loss will occur only if rates rise.

Hence, for this individual transaction, the current cost of replacing the counterparty in a swap contract is given by the positive segment of the market value profile for the swap contract. This is illustrated in Figure 17–2.

Albeit an essential element, market value—current replacement costs—alone does not accurately portray the credit risk faced. As noted by the Board of Gover-

FIGURE 17-2 **Current Replacement Cost** (*a*) **The current cost of replacing a float-ing cash flow** (*b*) **The current cost of replacing a fixed cash flow.**

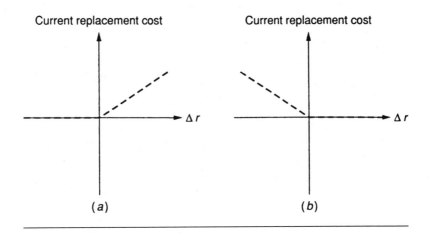

(*a*) (*b*)

nors of the Federal Reserve System and the Bank of England (1987), "The cost to a banking organization of a counterparty default . . . is the cost of replacing the cash flows specified by the contract"—the *total* exposure characterized by the Fed as the sum of the current replacement cost and "a measure of the potential future credit exposure that may arise from further movements over the remaining life of the instrument."

Put another way, the current replacement cost indicates the cost of replacing the swap counterparty if the counterparty defaults *today*. However, the counterparty may default not today but rather at some date in the future, at which time the interest rate may be different from that today. For example, consider default by a floating-rate payer.

Panel (*a*) of Figure 17-2 is reproduced as Figure 17-3. Suppose that the current interest rates are lower than those that prevailed at contract origination, $\Delta r_t < 0$—a situation illustrated by point A in Figure 17-3. In this case, the *current* replacement cost is zero. However, since the issue is the magnitude of the total exposure to loss today of default that may occur in the future, we need to know the current replacement cost *plus* the potential credit exposure illustrated by point B in Figure 17-3.

What determines this potential credit exposure? In the context of Figure 17-3, the exposure to default-induced loss depends on potential interest rate movements. For a default-induced loss to occur, the interest rate at some future default date must exceed the rate which prevailed at contract origination (r_0). Clearly, the likelihood of this increase in rates occurring depends on the volatility of interest rates, σ_r, and on the remaining life of the contract, T. And since the exposure is the result of lost

FIGURE 17–3   Potential Credit Exposure

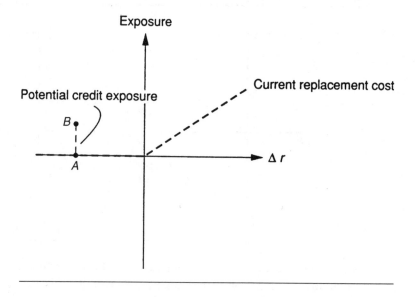

cash flows *in some future periods,* we also require a discount factor $D = D(r,T)$ where r is the relevant discount rate and T is the time remaining to contract maturity.

Exposure over the Life of the Transaction

For some traditional bank products, the bank's exposure to the borrower is constant throughout the life of the transaction. If the bank makes a zero-coupon loan, the principal exposure—the amount of money that left the bank at origination—is unchanged during the life of the transaction.[6] However, other products are structured so that the amortization effect reduces the bank's exposure over time. In the case of an amortizing loan, the bank's exposure to the borrower declines dramatically over time as principal is repaid. The exposure on a loan that pays regular interest payments but returns all the principal at maturity (a "bullet"-repayment loan) declines over time, but not nearly as dramatically as the amortizing structure.

The credit exposure generated by intermediating risk management instruments also varies over the life of the transaction. As will be described below, there are two reasons for this changing exposure. One is the familiar amortization effect; the other is much less familiar.

The Amortization Effect.   In the same way that the bank's exposure declines as principal is repaid or coupons paid, the bank's exposure to some derivative transactions also declines as the time remaining to contract maturity declines. Figure 17–4

FIGURE 17–4   The Amortization Effect

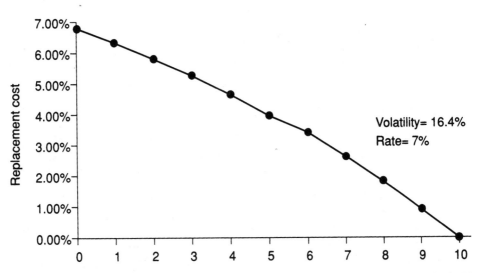

Source: This figure is adapted from a presentation made to the Bank for International Settlements by Denise M. Boutross, executive vice-president, DKB Financial Products, Inc., on January 21, 1993.

demonstrates that the amortization effect for a 10-year interest rate swap is like that for an amortizing loan: At time 0—origination—the bank is exposed for 10 years, 20 settlements. (In the case of an amortizing loan, at month 0, the bank is exposed for the entire principal.) Over time, settlement payments are made and the bank's exposure declines. (In the case of an amortizing loan, over time, principal is repaid and the bank's exposure declines toward zero.)

The Diffusion Effect.   Unlike a traditional bank product, where the bank's concern is about principal exposure, the bank's exposure to its counterparty for a risk management product is also influenced by the degree to which the underlying price can differ from the price that existed at contract origination. This effect is referred to as *the diffusion effect.*

As we described earlier, volatility deals with the amount the financial price can change in a single period. In panel (*a*) of Figure 17–5, we use the now-familiar lattice diagram to illustrate this concept: in a single period, the financial price could move up from P_0 to P_0*u or down to P_0*d. The volatility for this binomial process is a function of the initial price and the size of the up-and-down movements.[7]

Diffusion deals with the amount the financial price can change over a number of periods. Panel (*b*) of Figure 17–5 presumes the same volatility as panel (*a*) but illustrates that, over three periods, the financial price could be as high as P_0*u^3 or as low as P_0*d^3.

FIGURE 17–5 Volatility and Diffusion

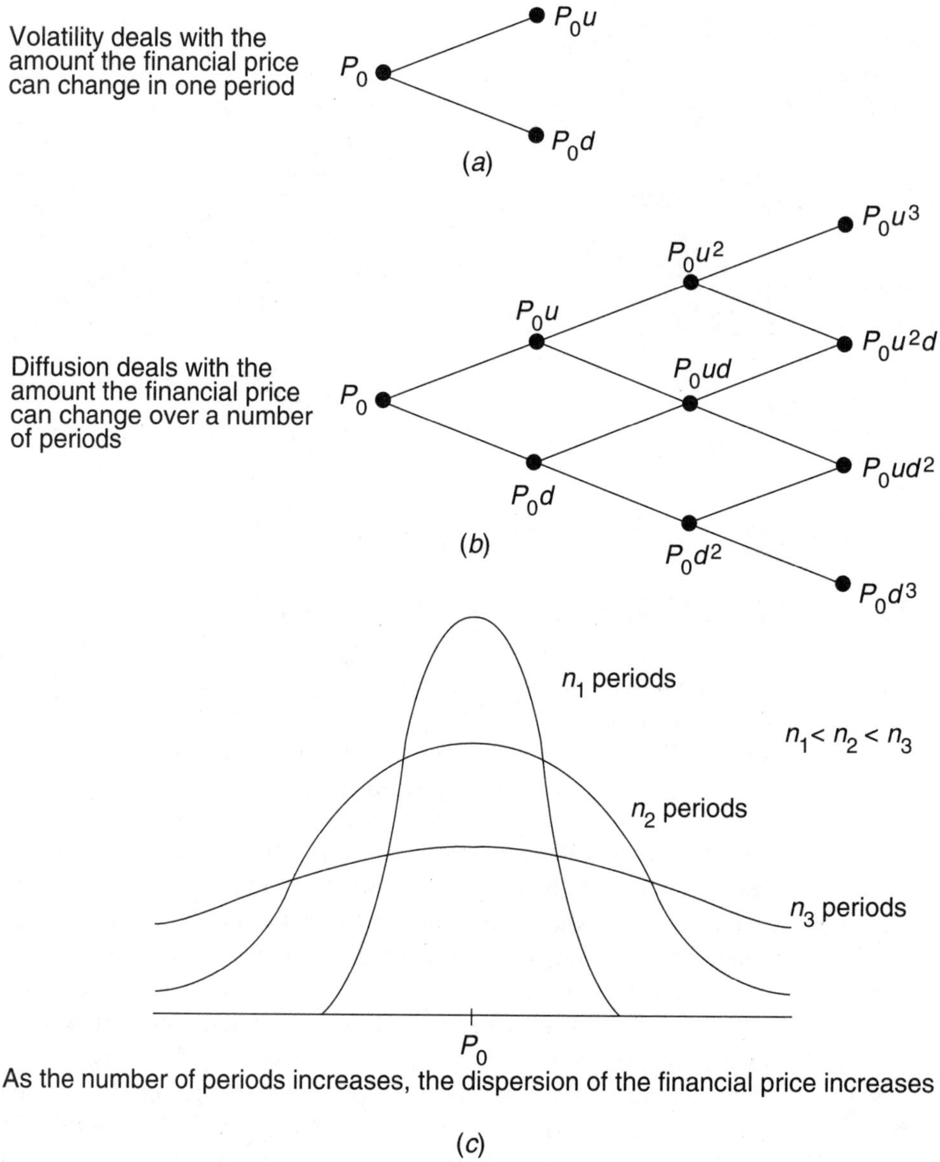

Volatility deals with the amount the financial price can change in one period

P_0 → P_0u

P_0 → P_0d

(a)

Diffusion deals with the amount the financial price can change over a number of periods

P_0 — P_0u — P_0u^2 — P_0u^3

P_0ud — P_0u^2d

P_0d — P_0d^2 — P_0ud^2

P_0d^3

(b)

n_1 periods

$n_1 < n_2 < n_3$

n_2 periods

n_3 periods

P_0

As the number of periods increases, the dispersion of the financial price increases

(c)

The diffusion process illustrated in panel (*b*) will generate a set of distributions for the underlying financial price. Panel (*c*) of Figure 17–5 illustrates how, as time elapses, the diffusion processes causes the dispersion of prices to increase. As more time elapses, increasingly high (low) prices will be feasible.

This probability distribution for prices provides a framework for the bank to evaluate its potential exposure. If the bank is receiving the financial price, the potential exposure becomes greater when more time to maturity remains. Figure 17–6 illustrates the effect that diffusion will have on the bank's exposure to its counterparty: With more time remaining until contract expiration, the bank's potential exposure increases—that is, the possible deviation in the financial price from its level at origination increases.[8]

Combining the Amortization and Diffusion Effects

For an interest rate swap, if we combine the amortization effect (Figure 17–4) and the diffusion effect (Figure 17–6), we obtain the familiar "humped" exposure profile illustrated in panel (*a*) of Figure 17–7. The rising portion of the profile indicates that the diffusion effect dominates early in the life of the swap; the falling section indicates that at some point in the swap's life, the diffusion effect is swamped by the amortization effect as the time to maturity gets short and there are fewer settlements outstanding.[9]

FIGURE 17–6   The Diffusion Effect

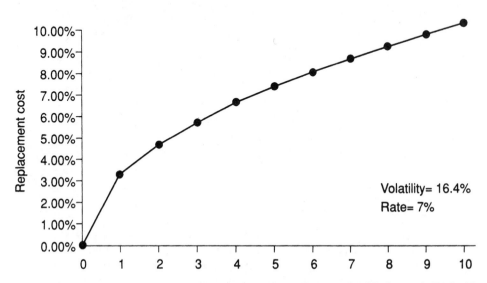

SOURCE: This figure is adapted from a presentation made to the Bank for International Settlements by Denise M. Boutross, executive vice-president, DKB Financial Products, Inc., on January 21, 1993.

FIGURE 17–7   Combining the Amortization and Diffusion Effects

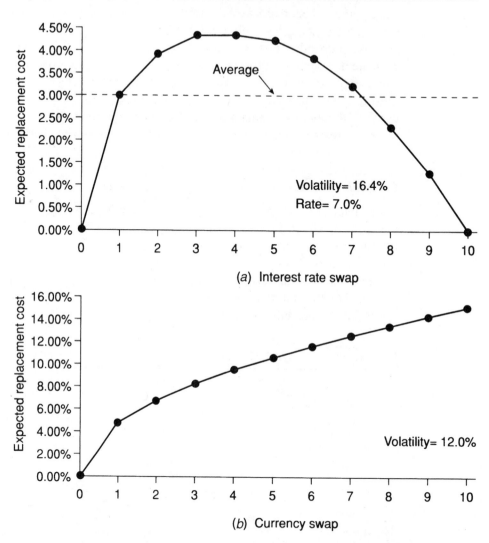

SOURCE: This set of figures is adapted from a presentation made to the Bank for International Settlements by Denise M. Boutross, executive vice-president, DKB Financial Products, Inc., on January 21, 1993.

While standard interest rate swaps and other derivative transactions that have periodic payments and no final exchange of principal have the humpbacked exposure profile, panel (*b*) of Figure 17–7 illustrates that the exposure profile for a cross-currency swap rises over time. Since the bank is exposed to the principal reexchange at maturity, the amortization effect from the periodic settlements is swamped by the effect of diffusion on the principal reexchange.

Maximum versus Expected Exposures

In the process of developing the capital adequacy standards, the U.S. Federal Reserve System and the Bank of England noted that when the swap counterparties evaluate their exposures, they should be asking about *two* exposure measures[10]:

1. What is my *maximum exposure* if my counterparty to this contract defaults?
2. What additional exposure do I accept by entering into this contract—that is, what is the *expected exposure* generated by this contract?

Note that in the case of a loan contract, the same number—the loan principal—answers both questions. Consequently, since commercial banks have become the dominant intermediaries for swaps and since commercial banks are used to dealing with the credit risk of loans, the two-question aspect of this issue has become veiled.

Maximum Exposure. The maximum credit exposure[11] should reflect the greatest amount that the intermediary could lose were the counterparty to default. This measure is most widely used in the credit allocation function for the financial institution intermediating the transaction—to determine how much to allocate for the risk management transaction against general counterparty lines of credit.

A measure of the maximum exposure is also crucial for the credit risk control function. Maximum exposure sets some "alarm level." If the current exposure (the mark-to-market exposure) ever exceeds the exposure that was defined as the maximum when the contract was originated, "the alarm goes off." Once the alarm sounds, the duty of management is to determine whether the alarm was set off because of (1) a random draw from the interest rate distribution or (2) a change in the structure of interest rates. If the alarm rang because of (1), no response is necessary—all we know is that an unlikely event occurred. If, however, the alarm rang because of (2), the policies with respect to the next swap transaction must be reexamined.

In practice, determination of the maximum exposure for a risk management product is difficult because financial prices are stochastic. Since there is a distribution for the underlying financial price, there likewise exists a distribution for the market value of a the risk management instrument. Consequently, there can be no true *maximum* exposure for the risk management transaction. Hence, when measuring the maximum exposure for a risk management transaction, the intermediary must define some value that will be the maximum exposure with some specified probability.

To illustrate this, Figure 17–8 expands the exposure profiles presented in Figure 17–7 to provide maximum exposure profiles with confidence levels of 90 percent and 95 percent for an interest rate swap [panel (*a*)] and a cross-currency swap [panel (*b*)].

In the context of Figure 17–8, a measure of the maximum exposure could be defined as the peak exposures attained by the maximum exposure profiles. Note that these peaks are relatively small percentages of the notional principal of the transaction.

FIGURE 17-8   Maximum and Expected Exposures

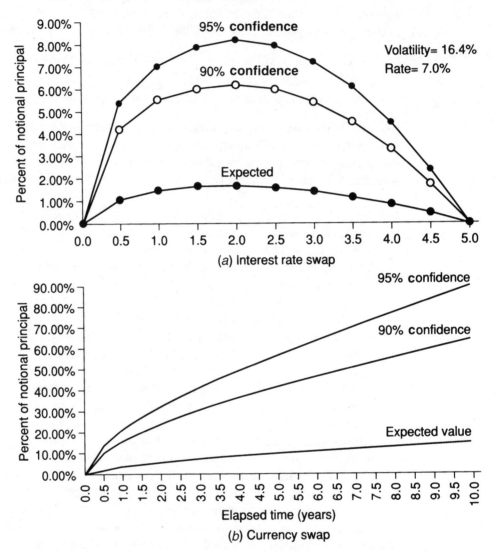

SOURCE: This set of figures is adapted from a presentation made to the Bank for International Settlements by Denise M. Boutross, executive vice-president, DKB Financial Products, Inc., on January 21, 1993.

Expected Exposure. The expected exposure for a risk management instrument would reflect the likely future overall exposure of the intermediary's derivatives portfolio that would result from intermediating this additional transaction.

Expected exposure gives the intermediary an *ex ante* measure of how much, on average, it could expect to lose if the counterparty were to default. Hence, this exposure measure is the one the banking regulators have focused on in determining how much capital a bank should be required to hold against derivative transactions.

Within the firm intermediating the risk management transaction, expected exposure is used both to price and to evaluate the profitability of a transaction. Expected exposure is used to determine the appropriate credit margin to include in the pricing of a risk management transaction. Expected exposure is also the appropriate exposure to use in the denominator when evaluating the rate of return for the risk management transaction.

As its name implies, an expected exposure recognizes the probability distributions for the underlying financial prices (and the value of the risk management instrument). However, in comparison to maximum exposures that look at the exposure that will be exceeded only 1 percent or 5 percent or 10 percent of the time, the expected exposure uses the mean value. The relation between expected exposures and maximum exposures is illustrated in Figure 17–8.

Measuring the Exposure for an Individual Transaction

When we illustrated current and potential exposure in Figure 17–3, the resulting figure was an option payoff diagram. Indeed, since default occurs only if it is in the counterparty's interest, default must be viewed in an option-theoretic framework.[12] Moreover, when we discussed potential exposures, we noted that five parameters go into the determination of the exposure to default-induced losses for the interest rate swap: the interest rate at the evaluation date, r_t; the interest rate at origination, r_0; the volatility of interest rates, σ_r; the discount rate, r; and the time remaining to contract maturity, T. Not surprisingly, these parameters are the same ones that are needed to value an option—in this case a call option. An option pricing approach would result in a credit exposure profile like that illustrated in Figure 17–9.[13] For an "in-the-money" swap (one where the market value of the swap is positive due to an increase in rates), the current replacement cost rises as the swap moves further and further into-the-money; but at the same time, the potential credit exposure declines as time value decreases.

However, we are not aware of dealers who measure their exposures using an explicit option valuation approach. Early on, dealers used a "scenario" approach in which they calculated a "worst-case" exposure. More recently, dealers have moved to a simulation approach.

FIGURE 17–9   Credit Equivalent Exposure as an Option

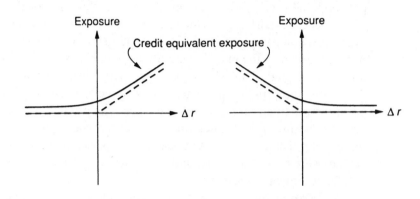

The "Worst-Case" Approach

Early measures of the credit risk for swaps and the other risk management products were based on "worst-case" assumptions about market risk and default. As Mark Ferron and George Handjinicolaou (1987) described the process, the bank would make conservative high and low projections for the future level of replacement interest rates and then use these extreme cases to calculate the maximum cost of replacing all cash flows associated with a single swap. The worst-case procedures we have heard market participants describe provide overly conservative assessments of swap risk by assuming the worst outcome for the dealer from *both* the diffusion and amortization processes. That is, they calculate the exposure by assuming that the underlying financial price moves immediately to the extreme value and that default occurs immediately after inception of the contract (so the dealer will lose all future payments).

We illustrate this in Table 17–1 by providing worst-case measures for two transactions:

> *Transaction 1*—a five-year, $10 million interest rate swap in which this counterparty is paying fixed at 8.18 percent (semiannual) and receiving six-month dollar LIBOR.
>
> *Transaction 2*—a five-year, $10 million currency swap in which this counterparty is paying fixed deutsche mark at 6 percent (semiannual) and receiving fixed dollar at 6.55 percent (semiannual).

We calculated the exposure displayed in Table 17–1 by assuming that, immediately after inception of the transaction, all of the underlying financial price shifted two

TABLE 17–1 Comparison of Exposure Measures for Individual Transactions

	Scenario Approach, Worst Case	*Simulation Approach*
Interest rate swap	953,766	536,558
Currency swap	3,361,009	1,748,674

standard deviations (corresponding to a 98 percent one-tail confidence level) in the direction that would maximize the value of the transaction.

The Simulation Approach

Most dealers now use Monte Carlo simulations to provide exposure measures that accurately reflect both the amortization and diffusion effects. Such a simulation process could be thought of as following six steps:

1. *Specify the manner in which the underlying financial price behaves.* For example, the most common assumption is that interest rates follow a lognormal probability distribution.
2. *Specify the initial value for the financial price.*
3. *Specify the volatility of the financial price.*
4. Use 1, 2, and 3 to simulate a number of *paths (as few as 1,000, as many as 10,000) that the financial price could take over the life of the risk management transaction.*
5. For each of the simulated financial price paths, calculate the corresponding value of the risk management product at specified intervals over its lifetime.
6. *Combine the individual estimates of the value of the transaction to obtain probability distributions for exposure at specified intervals.*

In Table 17–1 we have provided illustrative simulation measures for the interest rate swap and currency swap described above. We assumed that dollar and deutsche mark interest rates and the deutsche mark-dollar exchange rate were distributed lognormally. We estimated the variances of the distributions using data from the preceding 100 days. We simulated 500 random changes in the spot foreign exchange rate and the yield curves (assuming parallel shifts) at half-yearly intervals up to five years. At each six-month point, we calculated the market value of the swaps (assuming they had aged accordingly), setting any negative values to zero, and, from the 500 values, identified the 98th percentile value. The values reported in Table 17–1 are the "expected maximum" over the life of the transaction, i.e., the average of the ten 98th percentile values.

Measuring the Exposure for a Portfolio of Transactions

So far, we have considered the exposure of a bank were it to intermediate a *single* derivative transaction. However, most market participants (notably, financial intermediaries) hold large portfolios of risk management products.

General Portfolio Effects

As with loans, portfolio effects exist such that the exposure of the sum is less than the sum of the individual exposures. But default on derivatives transactions should be more idiosyncratic than would be default on a loan. And because default on derivatives is more idiosyncratic, the portfolio effect should be more pronounced for derivatives than for loans.

Aside

Probability of Default: Swap versus Loan

Unfortunately, the similarity between loans and swaps that was so useful in examining the evolution and pricing of swaps in Chapter 10 proves counterproductive when we look at credit risk. We believe that there are three primary differences between the default implications of loans versus those of swaps.

First, the principal in a swap is not at risk; as we have described, the principal in a swap is only notional. In contrast, a significant component of the credit risk of a loan has to do with the potential failure to repay the principal.

Second, for a swap, the periodic net cash flows to be paid or received (that is, at settlement dates) are proportional to the difference in rates (for example, in an interest rate swap, I pay or receive on the basis of the difference between a fixed interest rate and a floating rate). In a loan, the periodic cash flows to be paid or received (that is, at the coupon payment dates) are determined by the level of rates (for example, with a floating-rate loan, I pay or receive on the basis of the level of a floating interest rate). Hence, the periodic cash flows from a swap must be smaller than those from a comparable loan.

The third difference is that default on swaps requires that *two* conditions exist simultaneously while default on a loan requires only *one*. Default on a loan requires only that the firm be in financial distress. Default on a swap requires both that the party to the swap be in financial distress and that the remaining value of the contract to that party be negative. Hence, the probability of default on a swap is a joint probability: the probability of the value of the swap being negative and the probability of the party being in financial distress. Therefore, this joint probability (on a swap) will be less than would be the simple probability (on a loan).

The Effect of Netting

For an individual transaction, the current cost of replacing the counterparty in a risk management contract is given by the positive segment of the market value profile for the contract. However, for a portfolio of transactions, if the bank could net its exposures, the bank's exposure resulting from a positive-valued transaction could be offset by a transaction that has a negative mark-to-market value.

For OTC derivatives, netting is currently accomplished on a bilateral basis—positive mark-to-market values on transactions for one counterparty could be offset by negative mark-to-market values for the same counterparty. However, multilateral netting—offsetting positive mark-to-market values on transactions with one counterparty with negative mark-to-market values for transactions with another counterparty through a clearinghouse—is being discussed.

Confining ourselves to bilateral netting, a spectrum of netting arrangements could be used:

Netting by Novation. The two counterparties agree that *matched* pairs of transactions—transactions that are based on the same underlying financial price and have the same settlement date—will be deemed terminated and replaced by a single transaction requiring a payment equal to the difference between the novated transactions. In essence, the counterparties agree to maintain a running balance. Netting by novation is common in foreign exchange spot and forward transactions in which counterparties (typically banks) are likely to have a large number of offsetting payments due in the same currency on the same value date; but it is less common for derivatives.[14]

Closeout Netting. This form of netting becomes operative only in the event of default (or a triggering event such as a downgrade). For a specific product (such as interest rate swaps), the positive contract values for a particular counterparty are netted against the negative contract values. Closeout netting has become the standard (indeed, one credit officer indicated that the exception is not to have it). For example, the current ISDA master agreement specifies that if a default occurs, all transactions covered by the master will be terminated, and the values of the various transactions will be netted to a single number.

Cross-Product Netting. Bilateral netting is increasingly being extended to net across products: the bank could reduce its current exposure by offsetting positive mark-to-market values for the counterparty's interest rate swap positions with foreign exchange positions for the same counterparty that have negative mark-to-market value.

Given the impact of netting on the exposure, it is not surprising that the firms that intermediate the derivative products have been in favor of netting. The problem has been the legal enforceability of netting agreements. Because of the impact netting would have on exposures, the impetus is to recognize netting more widely.[15] As we noted earlier, the Basle Accord was amended in 1994 and 1995 to recognize the effects of netting.

Measuring the Probability of Default

As we alluded to in the beginning of this chapter, the probability of default for an individual risk management transaction is determined by four general factors. The first two of these are familiar to those who are used to evaluating the credit risk inherent in traditional bank products:

1. Creditworthiness of the counterparty: The more creditworthy (higher rated) the counterparty, the lower the probability of default.
2. Maturity of the transaction: The longer the maturity of the transaction, the more likely it is that the firm's credit quality will deteriorate, so the higher the probability of default is.

However, the last two factors require us to step away from our simplifying assumption that the correlation between the underlying price and the counterparty's assets is zero. The third determinant of the probability of default for a risk management transaction deals with the use to which the transaction is put:

3. The counterparty's inherent exposure to movements in the financial price on which the swap is based.

Whether or not the firm is using the transaction as a hedge for its underlying exposure to interest rates, exchange rates, or commodity prices has a potentially significant effect on the probability of default. A derivative transaction used as a hedge has a lower probability of default. Although for more creditworthy counterparties the financial institution is less concerned with the counterparty's core business exposure, for lower-rated counterparties it is clearly in the financial institution's interest to understand the customer's exposure.

The fourth is a characteristic of most derivative transactions.

4. Volatility of the underlying financial price: The more volatile the underlying financial price, the more likely it is that there will be a price movement sufficiently large to put the counterparty into financial distress.

Firms that intermediate risk management products have all developed systems (with varying degrees of sophistication) that reflect the probability of default arising from factors 1, 2, and 4. Many firms use a set of matrices—one for each product—to assign required credit premiums, which rise as the maturity of the transaction rises or the credit rating of the counterparty declines. Such a set of matrices is illustrated in Figure 17–10.

International Bank Insolvencies and the Enforceability of Multibranch Master Netting Agreements

Daniel P. Cunningham

A concern for international bank regulators is the oversight of banks that transact business through branches or agencies in other jurisdictions. A home country regulator may find significant discrepancies between its approach to bank regulation and those of regulators in other countries in which the parent bank operates branches or agencies. This conflict can be especially acute in the case of a bank insolvency involving branches and agencies in multiple jurisdictions.

While some European bank regulators have adopted a unified approach to cross-border banking insolvencies, U.S. regulators tend to view U.S. branches and agencies of foreign banks as distinct entities, subject to an insolvency proceeding independent from a proceeding in the home country. For example, New York State banking law dictates a "ring-fencing" approach to international bank insolvencies. Assets of a New York branch or agency in liquidation are first used to satisfy the creditors of the New York branch or agency; any remaining assets are then transferred to the banking authority of the country in which the bank's principal office is located.

Since different regulators would attempt to distribute the same pool of assets, this approach invites conflict. For example, when they attempted to ring-fence the assets of the New York agency of the Bank of Credit and Commerce International (BCCI) during the global liquidation of that bank, New York Banking Department regulators clashed with banking regulators from England, Luxembourg, and other jurisdictions.

Though local creditors of a foreign bank branch or agency may applaud ring-fencing (because their claims are more likely to be satisfied than if they are forced to seek satisfaction in a foreign liquidation proceeding), this policy could frustrate the intention of parties who have entered into derivatives transactions documented under master agreements that include multibranch netting arrangements. A multibranch master netting agreement permits a party to make or receive payments or deliveries under derivatives transactions that are documented ("booked") through any eligible branch or agency. A bank that enters into a multibranch master agreement expects that amounts owed to counterparties or due to it from counterparties will be netted across all branches and

International Bank Insolvencies and the Enforceability of Multibranch Master Netting Agreements continued

agencies of the bank. A liquidator applying a ring-fencing approach to a multi-branch master agreement would be forced to set aside the explicit terms of the agreement and instead focus on the amounts owed under only the transactions booked through the local branch or agency.

Despite great gains that have been made toward global recognition of the enforceability of bilateral netting agreements in OTC derivatives transactions, enforceability issues regarding multibranch netting agreements have not received sufficient attention. Nevertheless, the enforceability risk may concern many participants in derivatives transactions. A study of global derivatives practices by the Group of Thirty indicates that multibranch master agreements have been used with some degree of frequency.

The New York Banking Department's experiences in the BCCI case led to amendment of the New York banking law in August 1993. The amendments were intended to enhance the ability of the superintendent of banks to deal with foreign regulators, while retaining the ring-fencing to derivatives transactions, termed "qualified financial contracts." However, the final version of the amendment abandoned the ring-fencing approach for qualified financial contracts and adopted an approach that enforces multibranch netting agreements. Under the amended version of the New York banking law, qualified financial contracts are not automatically terminated upon the superintendent's taking possession of an insolvent New York branch or agency, and the superintendent shall not assume or repudiate qualified financial contracts documented under a multibranch netting agreement. Instead, the home country banking regulator of the foreign bank may assume or repudiate multibranch master agreements, and counterparties will be allowed to terminate such agreements in accordance with their terms.

Upon any repudiation or termination, netting of amounts owed under a qualified financial contract shall be calculated on both a global and New York–only basis. The global net amount is the amount owed by or to the foreign banking corporation as a whole if *all* transactions subject to the multibranch netting agreement are considered. The New York or local net amount is the amount owed by or to a foreign banking corporation after netting *only* the transactions entered into by the New York branch or agency. The superintendent shall only be liable to pay the *lesser of* the global net amount and the local net amount. Any amount due to a counterparty after payment of a local net amount can still be collected from the home office. Likewise, when a counterparty owes a net amount pursuant to a repudiated or terminated qualified financial contract, the superintendent of an insolvent New York branch or agency may demand from the counterparty a payment of the *lesser of* these two net amounts.

In addition to enhancing the enforceability of multibranch master netting agreements, the amendment also enforces collateral arrangements securing net amounts due under multibranch master agreements. Upon a termination or repudiation, collateral of an insolvent branch or agency properly held by a counterparty may be applied against any outstanding claims under a multibranch master agreement, up to the global net amount owed by the bank. Such collateral therefore will not be considered an asset of the branch or agency subject to return to the branch or agency upon the taking of possession by the superintendent.

This amendment to New York banking law is an important first step toward a unified approach to international bank regulation. A multilateral regulatory treatment of qualified financial contracts during bank insolvencies would provide greater legal certainty for parties to multibranch master agreements and reduce systemic risk for all participants in derivatives transactions. Other jurisdictions (especially other major financial centers) should follow New York's lead and where necessary adopt similar laws to fully address the global concerns raised by the risk of global banking insolvencies.

Daniel P. Cunningham is a partner of the law firm of Cravath, Swaine & Moore. His corporate finance practice includes derivative instruments, mergers and acquisitions, and receivables finance.

Mr. Cunningham serves as outside counsel to the International Swaps and Derivatives Association (ISDA). In that capacity, he has participated in the preparation of standard master agreements for derivative transactions and has served as legal coordinator for the preparation of memoranda under the laws of 34 jurisdictions, examining the status of the 1987 and 1992 ISDA master agreements with counterparties that have become insolvent under the laws of those nations.

Mr. Cunningham was a member of the Group of Thirty Derivatives Project Working Group.

Mr. Cunningham received a BA degree from Princeton University in 1971. In 1975 he graduated from Harvard Law School.

FIGURE 17–10 **Matrices for Assigning Credit Premiums**

Maturity of Transaction	AAA			AA			A		
	IRS	*CS*	*Caps*	*IRS*	*CS*	*Caps*	*IRS*	*CS*	*Caps*
2	XXX	XXX	XXX	XXX	XXX	XXX	XXX	XXX	XXX
3	XXX	XXX	XXX	XXX	XXX	XXX	XXX	XXX	XXX
4	XXX	XXX	XXX	XXX	XXX	XXX	XXX	XXX	XXX
5	XXX	XXX	XXX	XXX	XXX	XXX	XXX	XXX	XXX
7	XXX	XXX	XXX	XXX	XXX	XXX	XXX	XXX	XXX
10	XXX	XXX	XXX	XXX	XXX	XXX	XXX	XXX	XXX

For interest rate swaps, the shape of the term structure can also have an impact on the probability of default. If the term structure is upward sloping (as it has been during most of the history of the interest rate swap market), the probability of default is reduced if the counterparty pays fixed and receives floating. To show how this can occur, in Figure 17–11 we have illustrated the relation between the fixed-rate and floating-rate payments for a three-year interest rate swap. Since the term structure is upward sloping, the expectation is that the party paying fixed and receiving floating will pay difference checks early in the term of the swap:

| Settlement 1: | Pay R_{36} | Receive r_6 |
| Settlement 2: | Pay R_{36} | Receive $_6r_{12}$ |

and receive net payments in later periods:

Settlement 3:	Pay R_{36}	Receive $_{12}r_{18}$
Settlement 4:	Pay R_{36}	Receive $_{18}r_{24}$
Settlement 5:	Pay R_{36}	Receive $_{24}r_{30}$
Settlement 6:	Pay R_{36}	Receive $_{30}r_{36}$

Thus, the credit risk of the fixed-rate payer is less than would be the case if the term structure were flat. An overview of the market for interest rate swaps indicates that

FIGURE 17–11   Relation between Fixed-Rate and Floating-Rate Payments

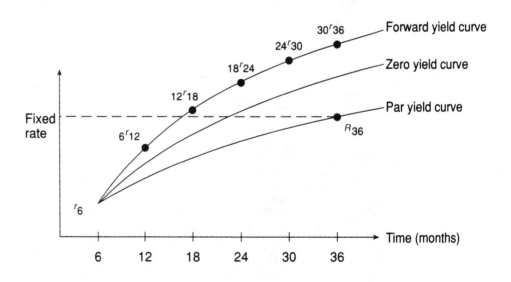

the less creditworthy counterparties have been, by and large, paying cash flows based on a fixed interest rate. Hence, the probability of default for the portfolio of swaps is lower than if the counterparties were reversed.

The credit management systems used by many of the firms that intermediate interest rate swaps actually reflect the impact of the shape of the term structure on the probability of default. In the context of the credit premium matrices noted in Figure 17–10 above, the matrix firms use to reflect the probability of default in an interest rate swap in which the bank receives the fixed rate is different from that used in a swap in which the bank receives the floating rate.

Methods for Reducing Credit Risk

The simplest and most effective means of reducing credit risk is netting. However, other methods can be employed to reduce the credit risk inherent in OTC derivatives transactions.

Termination Provisions

In the case of a specified "credit event," the counterparty that has not experienced the credit event would have the right to terminate the transaction at prevailing market prices. The credit event is typically defined as a downgrade below investment grade for rated counterparties or as violation of regulatory capital or specified net worth for nonrated counterparties.

The problem with termination provisions is that they would be triggered at a time when the counterparty is under financial stress and may be unable to make the termination payment.

Collateral

For any transaction which involves an extension of credit, the credit risk can be reduced by bonding the transaction—requiring that collateral be posted. The collateral is to support *net* exposure; so the counterparties must have in place a master agreement and pledge documentation, and these must be enforceable in the relevant jurisdiction(s).

In the case of OTC derivatives, the transaction is marked-to-market and collateral is posted in accordance with the mark-to-market size of the exposure. Acceptable forms of collateral include not only cash but also mutually acceptable securities. Securities that have been used as collateral include government and agency securities and, possibly with a "haircut" to reflect their credit or liquidity risk, foreign or domestic equities, foreign debt securities, and non-investment-grade debt.

Collateral agreements tend to be bilateral—both parties are required to post collateral when the market value of their side of the contract is negative. However, collateral agreements can be unilateral—only the weaker credit is required to post collateral.

Collateral can be required "up-front." However, to reduce the cost of a collateral arrangement, thresholds for movement of collateral are common. In such a structure, collateral is posted only if the agreement is "triggered." Two kinds of triggers have been observed in the market.

Value trigger. Collateral is posted only if the mark-to-market value of the transaction exceeds a specified threshold. To facilitate transactions between counterparties with different levels of creditworthiness, uneven thresholds can exist—i.e., the threshold for the higher-rated counterparty is set at a higher level.

Event trigger. While value triggers are more common, agreements have been structured such that collateral is required (or the level of collateral is increased) when the counterparty is downgraded or when capital ratios fall below specified levels. Some counterparties use a "tiered" collateral system. Such a system is illustrated in Figure 17–12. As a counterparty's rating declines, the threshold exposure declines, and calls for collateral will occur more frequently. For the worst credits, collateral may be required even though the contract currently has a negative market value.

"Re-hypothecation"—the use of collateral posted by one counterparty to meet collateral obligations to another counterparty—has the effect of increasing the liquidity of the institution. (Note the similarity between re-hypothecation and multilateral netting.)

Finally, we were struck by the differences between the way that a financial institution perceives the effect of collateral on loans versus that on derivatives.[16] This difference in perception is summarized in Figure 17–13.

FIGURE 17–12   Tiered Collateral Agreement

Credit Rating	Threshold Exposure Limit	Minimum Call Amount
AAA	$50,000,000	$10,000,000
AA-	$25,000,000	$5,000,000
A-	$10,000,000	$2,000,000
BBB-	$5,000,000	$1,000,000
Below BBB-	− $5,000,000	$1,000,000
No collateral required for exposures below threshold		

FIGURE 17-13 Perceived Impact of Collateral: Loans vs. Derivatives

	Effect of Collateralization on	
	Exposure	*Perceived Probability of Default*
Collateralize a loan	No change	Decrease
Collateralize a derivative	Decrease	No change

If collateral is posted against a loan, the perception is that the probability of default is reduced. (In most banks, the internal "risk rating" on the loan will usually improve.) However, if collateral is posted against a derivative position, the bank's perception of the probability of default is unchanged; instead, the effect is on the amount at risk.

As an alternative to posting collateral, weaker credits can be supported by letters of credit or guarantees from a third party. Guarantees, or weaker variants such as "keepwell," "support," or "comfort letters," are often required from a counterparty's parent company or affiliate. Less frequently, an unaffiliated third party will guarantee performance of one of the counterparties in a derivative transaction in return for a fee.

Coupon Resets

Coupon resets give the counterparties a way to agree that when the exposure reaches a specified level, the transaction or set of transactions between the counterparties will be restructured so as to reduce the exposure. When the trigger is hit, the "coupon" on the derivative transaction is reset to prevailing market rates and one party pays the other the market value of the transaction.

> For example, in an interest rate swap, the fixed rate on the existing swap would be reset from X percent to the current market swap rate. If X percent is higher (lower) than the current swap rate, the fixed-rate receiver (payer) will make a payment equal to the mark-to-market value of the X percent swap.

The new coupon means that the current exposure is now zero. However, such a device has P&L, tax, and balance sheet consequences.

Instead of resetting the coupon to eliminate all of the exposure, the counterparties agree to cash settle all exposures above a specified level—by resetting the coupons at some specified spread to the market rates. If the mark-to-market value of the transactions exceeds this specified level, one party will have to send cash sufficient to reduce the exposure to the specified level.

Still another form of this agreement is to reset the coupons at intermediate points in the life of the transaction. For example, the counterparties could enter into a five-year transaction in which the coupon is reset annually, thereby effectively reducing the credit exposure to a one-year exposure.

Assignments and Pair-Offs

Transactions Could Be Assigned to a Third Party.   Instead of cash-settling all exposures above a specified level, the counterparties could agree that when the mark-to-market value of the transactions exceeds a specified level, some transactions will be assigned to another counterparty. This structure is only practical when the counterparty's credit is strong.

Transactions Could Be Unwound.   Instead of cash-settling the transactions, the counterparties could put in place a mirror transaction which would have the effect of putting a ceiling on the exposure. (Clearly, such a structure requires that bilateral netting be enforceable.)

Evidence on Defaults for the Risk Management Instruments

If we return to the conceptual discussion at the beginning of this chapter and assume that the underlying financial price for a derivative transaction is uncorrelated with the value of the counterparty's other assets, the probability of default on a derivative transaction would be one half the probability of default for a bond. If the two are independent, in half the cases in which the counterparty would default on a debt obligation, the derivative transaction is generating inflows.

Altman (1989) provides some data that are useful in estimating this likelihood. Examining data from bond issues from 1971 through 1986, he reports cumulative default rates according to the S&P rating for the bond at origination. Ten years after issuance, AAA bonds had a cumulative default rate of 0.13 percent; AA, 2.46 percent; A, 0.93 percent; BBB, 2.12 percent, and BB, 6.64 percent.

As noted above, let's assume that the financial prices underlying swaps are uncorrelated with the values of the counterparties' other assets. If we also assume that the "representative" swap counterparty is a single-A-rated firm, Altman's estimates would suggest that the average probability of default on a swap would be 1/2 of 1 percent.

Moving from the conceptual, let's see what the available data indicate. At the end of 1991, the ISDA surveyed its members on their default experience. Survey respondents accounted for more than 70 percent of the total notional principal outstanding. The results of this survey, provided in Table 17–2, indicate that cumulative

TABLE 17–2   Net Loss by Counterparty Type

	Amount (in millions)	Percent
UK local authorities	$177.7	49.6%
Corporate	94.5	26.4
Other nondealer financial institutions	60.1	16.8
Savings & loans	20.3	5.6
Other governmental entities	3.0	0.8
Non-ISDA dealers	2.0	0.6
ISDA dealers	0.6	0.2
Total	$358.2	100.0%

SOURCE: ISDA.

losses (losses over the respondents' entire history in the swap market) had been $358.36 million. The ratio of these *cumulative* losses to the respondents' notional principal *outstanding at the end of 1991* was 0.0115 percent. Perhaps a more useful ratio is that between these cumulative losses and the market value of the respondents' portfolios at the end of 1991—0.46 percent. As a rough comparison, in 1991 alone, federally insured banks charged off 1.8 percent of year-end loan balances. And the composition of the losses is instructive. Almost half of the total losses were in transactions with UK local authorities—Hammersmith and Fulham.[17]

Settlement Risk[18]

Finally, we have to consider the risks inherent in the settlement system itself. Settlement risk exists when there is a simultaneous exchange required in the transaction.[19]

One aspect of settlement risk results from the fact that few financial transactions are settled on a same-day basis. In United States equity markets, for example, the difference between the trade date and settlement is at present three days. As a result, one party could suffer a loss if the price moved in his favor and the counterparty refused to exchange on the settlement date.[20]

Settlement risk in derivatives is reduced greatly by the widespread use of the payment-netting provisions of master agreements. This reduces the settlement risk of payments made in the same currency. In addition, for many derivative transactions (for example, interest rate swaps), principal amounts are not exchanged on the maturity date.

Payment netting, however, does not address cross-currency settlement risk. The largest source of settlement risk in payment systems is the settlement exposures created by foreign currency trade—spot and short-dated forwards. While derivatives activity would benefit from a reduction of Herstatt risk, it must be noted that the amounts involved in derivatives are very small relative to the amounts involved in traditional foreign exchange activities. It has been estimated by ISDA that daily global cash flows from interest rate swaps and currency swaps average $0.65 billion and $1.9 billion, respectively. In contrast, the BIS Central Bank Survey of Foreign Exchange Market Activity in April 1992 estimated daily global net turnover in foreign exchange spot and forward markets at $400 billion and $420 billion, respectively.

Risk Management in Practice

Settlement Risks for OTC Derivatives

Ronald D. Watson

For those who use derivatives, credit and market risks dominate the list of "downside" concerns—and should! However, "settlement failure" risks also deserve consideration, especially for derivatives strategies based on transactions that settle in over-the-counter markets. "Settlement" is the actual physical or electronic event when a financial exchange occurs and both parties satisfy their obligations under the contract terms created by the derivative transaction. Reliable, timely settlement of contracts is the "plumbing and electrical work" behind financial engineering. It isn't sexy, but the cost of not designing and maintaining it properly can be enormous.

The safest form of transaction clearance occurs in a secure, electronic exchange system where settlement is immediate and guaranteed by a central bank. The Federal Reserve's wire transfer system is ideal for settling transactions that are consummated by a single-payment transfer. Its book-entry system for U.S. Treasury and Agency securities creates a simultaneous exchange of securities and cash (called "deliver versus payment," or DVP). Any departure from this model creates risk for the transacting parties.

There are three sources of risk once settlement starts. One is the failure of either party to deliver cash, FX, a commodity, or securities at settlement. Another is the risk that a settlement agent (the bank, clearinghouse, or exchange being used to execute the money or securities transfers) will fail to perform. Finally, there is a risk that financial markets will encounter difficulties that create "systemic" settlement problems. The chances of any one of these events occurring are very low, but the risk is still real and must be anticipated.

Settlement Risks for OTC Derivatives continued

Counterparty Failure to Perform

Counterparty risk is more than a simple credit risk issue. In transactions such as a foreign exchange forward contract, either party may require special steps to protect its principal from the financial weakness of its counterparty. If failure occurs *before* settlement, and the exchange of payments can't be completed, you may be at risk for the cost of replacing the hedge at current market prices but not for the value of the contract. However, once the settlement date arrives, either party may be exposed for the full value being transferred (unless they have assurance that their counterparty has already made the transfer). The counterparty's failure at this time creates a risk of losing the full transaction amount. Controlling this exposure is a matter of both counterparty credit risk management and diligence in controlling release of your funds only on confirmed completion of the other party's obligations.

Intermediary Agent Performance

To the extent that a derivate contract is structured to use agents to perform any exchanges of value or securities, the parties should monitor the agents' soundness. Securities firms, banks, clearinghouses, and exchanges all perform these "exchange agent" functions. In recent years most exchanges and organized clearinghouses have tightened their rules and operating practices to minimize the risk that they will be unable to settle all transactions entrusted to them. U.S. exchange clearinghouses use a combination of capital requirements for members, security deposits, intraday counterparty exposure limits, margin calls, lines of credit, and other risk-reduction and sharing arrangements to assure their ability to make settlement for all trades on time.

When immediate, irrevocable settlement of each contract is not possible, clearinghouses often settle each business day's transactions at the end of the day. Usually transactions are "netted" to reduce settlement risks. Netting is the process of offsetting the payments obligations of each participant with cash it should receive from the same or other counterparties. Netting the transactions of each pair of participants is called "bilateral" netting, while combining and offsetting the trades of all participants into a single net settlement payment for each is called "multilateral" netting. By netting the projected payments of each participant in the exchange, a clearinghouse can reduce the aggregate number and size of settlement payments. This in turn decreases the liquidity burden of meeting the settlement and increases the probability of a successful settlement. Netting of payments is the norm for all U.S. settlement systems (except the Federal Reserve's), but the practice is not as well established in other parts of the world.

Transactions that are not settled in an exchange's clearinghouse may not enjoy the same multilayered protections. Private settlement arrangements may be efficient (and sophisticated financial firms even engage in bilateral netting with willing counterparties), but they don't operate with the same level of public scrutiny or member oversight as exchanges. The most recent innovations in over-the-counter derivatives contracts may be so specialized that they cannot be handled as "standardized" back-office settlements. *The more that private agents, time-zone differences, currency conversions, different sovereign legal jurisdictions, and special covenants become involved in reaching a proper settlement, the greater the risk.*

Systemic Risk

The least tangible but most troubling risk is the possibility that a single major settlement failure will "domino" throughout our highly interdependent global financial markets and create a series of failures. This can occur if an unforeseen event such as revolution or natural disaster shocks price relationships of major currencies or commodities enough to bankrupt several large players. Their rapid demise could create losses for their creditors, who in turn might then be unable to meet their obligations to others. Financial turbulence tends to produce gridlock in settlement markets as each player waits for the others to release payments first. Central banks would be forced to step in to stabilize markets, but it is virtually certain that large losses would be taken by some private parties before order was restored.

Industry Efforts to Cut Risk

Appreciation of settlement exposure is growing along with the size and complexity of these markets. Central banks of the larger industrialized nations and the international finance trade associations are both taking steps to manage it. At the level of the "deal" itself, considerable private effort is being devoted to defining standardized, court-tested, contract language for these new financial instruments. This is particularly challenging for contracts that require settlements in more than one sovereign jurisdiction, but progress is being made.

The central banks of the G-10 countries have been working on these problems for several years. There is general agreement among the regulators on minimum soundness standards that must be imposed on any private-sector clearing system offering cross-border, multicurrency netting services to its participants. Regulators are also integrating off-balance-sheet risk exposures (including derivatives such as currency, interest rate swaps, and more complex

---

contracts) into their common capital adequacy regulations.

Finally, the private sector is experimenting with clearinghouse arrangements intended to deal with the settlement risks of global finance. In the foreign exchange markets, bilateral trade-matching and netting systems have been created and participation is expanding. In addition, groups of large international banks in North America and in Europe are each creating clearinghouses for multilateral netting of FX trades. Settlements will be guaranteed by the clearinghouses if transactions pass prespecified risk limit tests. These multilateral systems are also being tied into the bilateral netting arrangements to increase coverage.

In summary, efforts to reduce the settlement risks of nonstandard derivative products are under way, but the problems are far from solved. This is an arena in which the global financial services industry and its counterpart family of central banks have a common interest in working in concert to refine the laws, regulations, contract standards, and day-to-day operating procedures of the institutions conducting this business to minimize the risk of financial market disruption and potential for catastrophe.

Ronald D. Watson is the chairman of Custodial Trust Company (CTC), the securities servicing and custody bank of The Bear Stearns Companies, Inc. Before joining CTC he taught at the University of Delaware and spent 17 years at the Federal Reserve Bank of Philadelphia.

Notes

1. *Default risk* and *credit risk* are used interchangeably in the market. However, while default (counterparty) risk could refer to any failure to perform under the contract, credit risk is more specific, referring to a financial inability to pay.
2. Taylor, Parkinson, and White (1987).
3. This discussion of the nature of default risk is adapted from Smith (1993).
4. Johnson (1987) and Stulz (1982) provide a mathematical discussion of these issues.
5. Nor, in truth, are things really that simple for traditional bank products. The exposure to the bank on a transaction like a standby line of credit is neither the total amount of the commitment nor only the amount of the commitment actually used to date. Instead, the amount the bank has at risk is somewhere in between these two—the question is, where in between?
6. Some readers of this chapter disagreed with referring to a zero-coupon loan as a "constant-exposure" instrument. Some noted that the face value of the loan is different from the amount that "walked out of the bank"—i.e., treating the zero-coupon loan as a constant-exposure instrument focuses only on principal repayment and ignores the additional loss the bank will suffer if the borrower fails to repay interest. However, as one bank credit officer noted, the traditional treatment of credit exposure is invariant to the payment of interest. Others noted that as interest rates change, the *present value* of the zero-coupon instrument will change.

7. The variance for the price change for this binomial process is:

$$(P_0)^2[pu^2 + (1 - p)d^2] - (P_0)^2[pu + (1 - p)]d^2$$

8. Indeed, if the underlying distribution is lognormal, the dispersion increases with the square root of time.

9. The "humped" exposure profile is a characteristic of at-market interest rate swaps. If the swap is deep in-the-money, the initial exposure is positive and the hump becomes less pronounced.

10. The staffs of the Federal Reserve System and the Bank of England expressed these two questions as (1) What is the *average* replacement cost over the life of a *matched pair* of swaps? (2) What is the *maximum* replacement cost over the life of a *single* swap? See Board of Governors of the Federal Reserve System and the Bank of England (1987) and Muffett (1986).

11. As this chapter was being assembled, Cliff Smith bridled at using the word *maximum*, correctly arguing that no maximum value exists for the derivative instruments. While he would have preferred using the word *extreme*, we elected to remain with the market convention and use *maximum*. Note further that this "maximum" is different from the "worst-case" exposure measures described in the next section of this chapter.

12. And this prescription is not limited to the derivatives transactions. An excellent example of an instance in which banks were damaged by not using an option-theoretic approach to default is found by looking at nonrecourse real estate development loans.

13. Were a dealer to implement this approach to estimating the exposure to default-induced losses, the dealer should not view the default-risk "option" as a simple option. In fact, as we described at the beginning of this chapter, the valuation of this optionlike construction would be more correctly written as a compound option which depends on (1) the value of the swap contract and (2) the value of the other assets of the counterparty. Hence, the exposure to default-induced losses would be

$$\text{Exposure} = f(r_t, r_0, r, T, \sigma_r, \sigma_{\text{FIRM}}, \sigma_{r,\text{FIRM}})$$

where σ_{FIRM} = volatility of value of counterparty's other assets and $\sigma_{r,\text{FIRM}}$ = covariance between the interest rate and the value of the counterparty's other assets.

14. *Payment netting* is similar to netting by novation. The counterparties agree to net payments (settlements) that are due on the same day and in the same currency—e.g., the settlements in an interest rate swap. According to John Behof (1993), payment netting is accomplished via an unwritten agreement; if the agreement is written, payment netting becomes netting by novation.

15. The impetus toward netting is reinforced by accounting rules. SFAS 105, which went into effect in 1993, requires that gains and losses be reported separately, unless they are netted with an acceptable contract.

16. I am indebted to my colleague Michael Davis for this insight.

17. The losses attributable to the Hammersmith and Fulham transactions are understated in Table 17–2, since one of the major victims, TSB Bank, was not a member of ISDA at the time of the survey.

18. This discussion is adapted from the Report of the Group of Thirty Derivatives Project.

19. Settlement risk is also referred to as *Herstatt risk,* named after the settlement problem which occurred when German regulators closed Bankhaus Herstatt in 1974.

20. This two-sided settlement risk is similar to the two-sided credit risk for forwards and swaps.

18 MANAGING PRICE RISK IN A PORTFOLIO OF DERIVATIVES

To manage the price risk—the market risk—of a portfolio of derivatives, the portfolio must be structured so that its value will not be affected by changes in the underlying price. While this underlying price might be foreign exchange rates or commodity prices, we will, for the purposes of the example used in this chapter, consider interest rates as the underlying price.

Measuring Price Risk: "Fraternity Row"

The first step in managing price risk for a portfolio of derivatives is to *quantify* the risks. Several measures of price risk could be used. However, most portfolio managers[1] now use a series of Greek letters to identify the different risks that will be hedged. We like to refer to these Greek-letter measures of risk as *fraternity row*.

Delta

The first of the Greek letters to be considered—the first house on fraternity row, if you will—is *delta*. In the context of interest rates, delta measures the change in the value of a financial asset as the underlying price (in this example, interest rates) changes.

Graphically, delta is the slope of a value profile. Figure 18–1 illustrates the relation between a long bond position and interest rates: the value of the bond declines as the interest rate rises. Delta is simply the slope of this value profile.

Delta is not a new concept. In the case of interest rates, delta is simply a new name for a concept that has heretofore been referred to by bond traders as

---
FIGURE 18–1   Delta

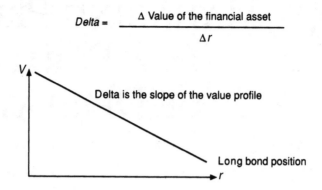

$$Delta = \frac{\Delta \text{ Value of the financial asset}}{\Delta r}$$

Delta is the slope of the value profile

Long bond position

basis-point value or *the value of an 01.* Moreover, delta and *duration* are two measures of the same risk. Indeed, as indicated in the following equation, the calculation of duration embodies delta:

$$\text{Duration} = -\frac{\text{percentage change in the value of the asset}}{\text{percentage change in the discount rate}}$$

$$= -(\Delta V/V) \, / \, [\Delta(1 + r)/(1 + r)]$$

$$= -(\Delta V/\Delta r) \times (1 + r)/V$$

$$= -\text{delta} \times (1 + r)/V$$

In Figure 18–1, we illustrate delta as constant—that is, we drew the value profile as a straight line. However, this need not be the case. The value profile for a short-term, noncallable government bond is well approximated by a straight line. However, as the maturity of the bond gets longer or as the bond incorporates other features (for example, the right to prepay), the value profile becomes increasingly nonlinear. And for options, there is no question that delta is *not* constant. Panel (*a*) of Figure 18–2 illustrates the value profile for a long position in a call option on an interest rate—an interest rate cap. As panel (*a*) illustrates, delta (the slope of the value profile for the option) ranges from zero when interest rates are very low to one when interest rates are very high. Conversely, for the put option on interest rates—an interest rate floor [illustrated in (*b*) of Figure 18–2]—delta would range from negative one when interest rates are very low to zero when interest rates are high.

Gamma

The dramatic change in delta evident for options leads us to the next of the Greek-letter measures of risk (the next house on fraternity row), gamma. Gamma measures the change in delta as the underlying price—in this case, the interest rate—changes.

FIGURE 18–2   Delta for Option Positions

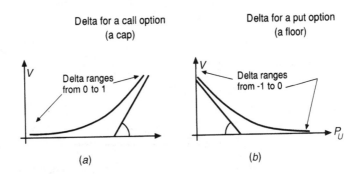

This concept is illustrated in Figure 18–3. As the interest rate moves up and down, the delta for the option position changes; gamma measures this change.

Gamma is not a new concept. In the same way that delta is another name for basis-point value, gamma is another name for *convexity*.

Panel (*a*) of Figure 18–3 illustrates a financial instrument that has a *convex* value profile. Note that when the value profile is convex, gamma is positive. Panel (*b*) illustrates the value profile for a financial instrument that exhibits what the market refers to as *negative convexity*. In this case, gamma is negative.

If the payoff profile were linear, gamma would be zero. Indeed, interest rate futures contracts are constructed so as to have linear payoffs; hence for interest rate futures, gamma equals zero.[2]

While both interest rate forwards (FRAs) and interest rate swaps exhibit gamma, this risk is primarily a characteristic of options.[3] And as Figure 18–4 illustrates,

FIGURE 18–3   Gamma

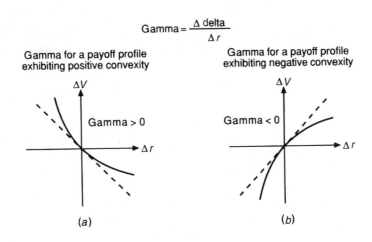

FIGURE 18–4   Gamma for Options

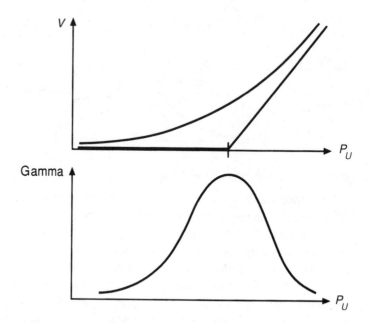

gamma is largest when the option is *at-the-money*. When the option is way out-of-the-money, the slope of the call function is very near zero, and the slope doesn't change very much for small changes in the price of the underlying. Likewise, when the option is way in-the-money, the slope of the call function is very near to one, and small changes in the price of the underlying don't have much of an impact on the slope. Only when the option is at-the-money do small changes in the underlying price have much impact on the slope of the value profile.

Vega (a.k.a. Kappa)[4]

The final house on fraternity row to be considered here is referred to by market practitioners as *vega*. Vega measures the change in the value of the financial instrument that occurs when the *volatility* of interest rates (the underlying price) changes.

$$\text{Vega} = \frac{\Delta \text{ value of financial instrument}}{\Delta \sigma}$$

Of the derivative instruments—forwards, futures, swaps, and options—only the value of options is influenced by volatility. Hence while gamma is a characteristic *primarily* of options, vega is a characteristic *solely* of options.[5]

Figure 18–5 illustrates two option value profiles, one when the volatility of interest rates is σ_1 and the other when volatility is σ_2, where $\sigma_1 < \sigma_2$. The value

Risk Management in Practice

The Curse of Negative Convexity

Kosrow Dehnad

"Buy high and sell low." That sounds like a sure way to the poorhouse. Unfortunately, this is the dilemma managers face when they try to hedge positions after they have sold options. Their ordeal, theoretically, will not be over till they spend the last penny of the option premiums they receive to delta-hedge their positions and to break even at expiration!

The villain is negative convexity—or being "short gamma." With negative convexity, when the option increases in value, losses on the hedge can well offset the gains in the value of the option, and when the option decreases in value, the hedge does not generate enough gains to compensate for the loss.

Adding insult to injury, the hedge often also exhibits slippage because of approximation error resulting from trying to use straight lines (that is, the payoff profile for the hedge instruments) to "synthetically" construct a curve (that is, the payoff profile for the option).

Since a picture is worth a thousand words, let us illustrate the above points graphically.

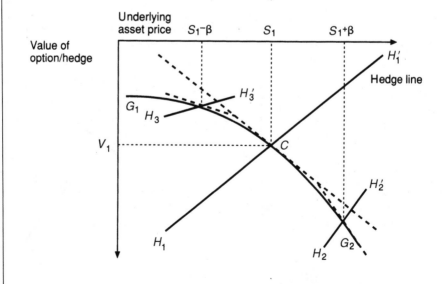

The Curse of Negative Convexity continued

The figure shows the value of a short position in a European call (G_1 G_2) for different values of the underlying asset; for example, when the asset price is S_1, the option value is V_1. To immunize (hedge) our position against small movements in the asset price, we should buy some of the underlying asset.

The size of the hedge, to first approximation, is based on the slope of the tangent to the curve at point C. In fact, the hedge position is given by the line H_1 H_1', which is the reflection of the tangent line about the line parallel to the X-axis and passing through point C. The construction reflects the fact that the hedge position is opposite the option position. So if we are short the call, we should be long the underlying. In other words we approximate our option position for small changes in the price of the underlying by a straight line. The hedge using the stock should be opposite to that, so the hedge position is given by the reflected line.

Should the stock price rise to $S_2 = S_1 + \beta$, the new hedge ratio would the slope of the line H_2 H_2', which indicates that we have to add to our holding of the stock when its price is advancing—that is "buy high."

On the other hand, if the stock goes down to $S_3 = S_1 - \beta$, the new hedge ratio is the slope of H_3 H_3', which indicates that we should reduce our hedge and sell when the price of the stock declines—that is "sell low."

The hedge slippage that can occur because of approximating a curve with a straight line is illustrated below. Suppose the price advances to $S_1 + \beta$ and our

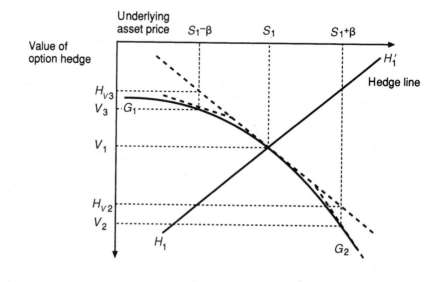

The Curse of Negative Convexity continued

short option position loses $V_2 - V_1$. The hedge position gains only $V_1 - H_{V2}$, that is, less than the loss on the option position; this translates into a slippage of $H_{V2} - V_2$. Similarly, if the stock price falls to $S_1 - \beta$, our short option positions will have a value of V_3 and gains $V_3 - V_1$. On the other hand, the hedge loses $V_1 - H_{V3}$. Once more, the loss on the hedge outweighs the gains on the position and we will experience a slippage of $H_{V3} - V_3$. The reason for slippage is that we are trying to hedge our position that changes nonlinearly as a function of the underlying stock (curve) with an instrument whose value changes linearly as a function of the underlying security—the asset itself or a futures contract on the asset.

All the above phenomena are reversed for the holder of the long option position: by delta-hedging the position, the holder will be selling high and buying low and theoretically should recuperate costs. Moreover, the hedge slippage will also work in the holder's favor. All this because, up front, the holder of the option paid the option premium to buy the call.

Kosrow Dehnad is a vice president and head of Hybrid Product Development and Structuring at Citicorp Securities Inc. Prior to Citicorp, he was a vice president responsible for new product development at the Chase Manhattan Bank. Before joining Chase in 1990, Dr. Dehnad worked at AT&T Bell Laboratories. He is the author of numerous technical articles and of *Quality Control, Robust Design, and the Taguchi Method.* He has served as an adjunct professor at San Jose State University, Rutgers University, and Columbia University. Dr. Dehnad has received two doctorates, one in applied statistics from Stanford University and the other in mathematics from the University of California at Berkeley.

---

for this interest rate option is higher with σ_2 than σ_1 for all interest rates, but the difference in value is greatest when the option is at-the-money—in other words, the magnitude of vega is largest when the option is at-the-money, the same relation we observed for gamma.

Managing the Price Risk in a Simplified Warehouse

Given the measures of risk, we can now consider how to measure and manage the price risk inherent in a warehouse.

Delta-Hedging a Warehouse

Within a bank, a warehouse manager normally begins by hedging the delta risk, the exposure of the warehouse to movements in the underlying price. The manager wants to structure the warehouse so that changes in the underlying price—shifts in the yield curve—will have no impact on the value of the warehouse.

FIGURE 18–5   Vega for Options

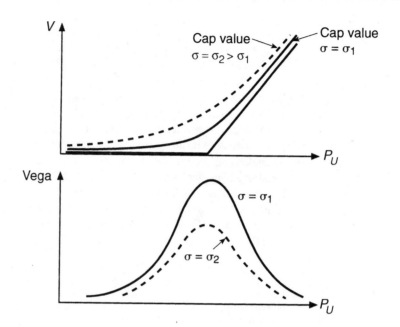

To see how this is accomplished, let's consider the simple warehouse of derivatives provided in Table 18–1.

Continuing to keep this example as simple as possible, let's suppose that it's mid-December, and let's suppose further that a zero-coupon yield curve is the smooth, upward-sloping yield curve illustrated in Figure 18–6. To see how changes in interest rates affect this portfolio of derivatives, let's begin by looking at the transactions, one at a time.

Delta-Hedging a Swap.   Figure 18–7 illustrates the cash flows for swap 1 using the same kind of illustration used in Chapter 8. In Figure 18–7, the convention we use is that arrows pointing up indicate cash flows coming into the bank; arrows pointing down indicate cash flows leaving the bank.

TABLE 18–1   The Warehouse

Swap 1:	2-year maturity $25MM notional principal, bank receives six-month LIBOR, pays fixed semiannual settlement
Swap 2:	1.5-year maturity $10MM notional principal, bank receives fixed, pays six-month LIBOR semiannual settlement
Cap:	Bank has sold a one-year cap on three-month LIBOR. Notional principal $50MM, cap rate 8.5%, quarterly settlement

FIGURE 18–6 A Stylized LIBOR Yield Curve

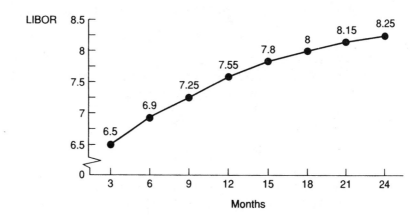

For swap 1, the bank is paying the fixed rate, so the amount that the bank pays at each of the settlement dates—June and December of the upcoming year and June and December of the following year—is the same.

However, the amount the bank will receive is not going to be the same over time. The amount that the bank will receive in June—six months from now—is already known; this cash flow will be determined by the six-month LIBOR rate in effect today and the $25 million notional principal of the swap:

$$[r_6/2 \times \$25MM]$$

But the payments the bank will receive in December of next year, and in June and December of the following year, are not known; they will depend on future

FIGURE 18–7 Swap 1: Cash Flows

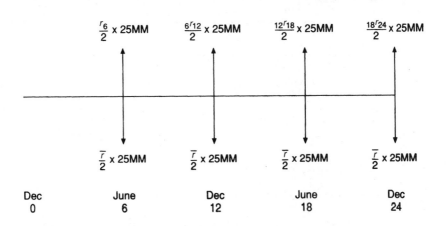

six-month LIBOR rates. The payment the bank will receive in December of next year depends on six-month LIBOR—not the six-month LIBOR rate in effect today, but rather the rate that will be in effect six months from now:

$$[_6r_{12}/2 \times \$25MM]$$

Likewise, the payments the bank will receive in June and December of the next year depend on the 6-month LIBOR rates in effect 12 months and 18 months from now:

$$[_{12}r_{18}/2 \times \$25MM]; \text{ and}$$

$$[_{18}r_{24}/2 \times \$25MM].$$

The cash flows illustrated in Figure 18–7 give us a way to think about the delta for swap 1. A one basis point change in spot rates will have two effects on the value of the swap and hence its delta. First, the floating rate cash flows that have not yet been locked in will be expected to change. Second, both the new floating cash flows and the fixed cash flows must be discounted at the new interest rates. We must take both factors into account in measuring a swap's delta.

Let's first consider the floating cash flows. The floating payments in December of next year and June of the following year are expected to change (the first floating rate cash flow has already been locked in). Since we are increasing all interest rates by one basis point, we might expect that the forward rates would also increase by one basis point. This turns out to be almost, but not exactly, the case. The new forward rates are shown in the second row of Table 18–2. These were calculated as in Chapter 8, "Valuing an Interest Rate Swap." The resulting swap cash flows on the floating side are shown in row three. The floating payment in period 6-12 is now expected to be \$991,977 based on the new forward rate:

$$[0.0793582/2 \times \$25mm = 991,977]$$

TABLE 18–2   Swap 1: Calculation of Delta

Swap Period	*0–6*	*6–12*	*12–18*	*18–24*
New spot rates (+1 bp)	6.91%	7.56%	8.01%	8.26%
New forward rates	n/a	7.93582%	8.28375%	8.04357%
New floating cash flows	862,500	991,977	1,035,469	1,005,446
Fixed cash flows	970,692	970,692	970,692	970,692
Net cash flow per period	−108,192	21,285	64,777	34,754
PV of net cash flows	−104,579	19,789	57,828	29,826
PV of original cash flows	−104,584	18,712	56,884	28,989
Per period change in value (delta)	5	1,077	944	837
Total swap delta	+2,863 = 5 + 1,077 + 944 + 837			

The fourth row of Table 18–2 shows the fixed payments. While the fixed payments are not affected by the change in rates, their present value is. In row five we have calculated the net cash flow (floating payments minus fixed payments) expected in each period. The present value of those flows is shown in row six based on the new spot rates. Finally, to arrive at the swap's delta we calculate the difference in the present values of the new cash flows and those on the original swap. The resulting per period deltas are shown in row seven. Notice that even though the first period's cash flows are not directly affected by the one basis point change in rates, there is a small delta in that period due to the change in discount rates. Summing the per period deltas gives the total delta, i.e., change in value of the swap, for a one basis point increase in rates. This swap is expected to increase in value by $2,863 if rates rise by one basis point.

We will illustrate how the deltas for swap 2 and the cap can be calculated. However, as long as we have the delta for swap 1, let's consider how this swap could be hedged.

Managers of derivatives warehouses use a range of financial instruments to hedge their positions. Swap 1 could be hedged by positions in the cash market (bonds), with forward-rate agreements (FRAs), with other swaps, or with futures contracts. But to keep our example as simple as possible, let's consider hedging the swap using only futures contracts. In this example we will presume that the hedge is managed using Eurodollar futures contracts.

Table 18–3 summarizes the delta-hedge position for swap 1. The first row in Table 18–3 summarizes the delta for swap 1. (This row is taken directly from Table 18–2 except we will ignore the $5 delta in period 0-6, which makes our new swap delta $2,858. In a large warehouse we would have added that delta to other positions or included it in the second swap period.) The delta of $1,077 for month 6 to month 12 is plotted against the time line at month 6, to reflect the time when the exposure is encountered. Similarly, the delta of $944 is plotted at month 12, and the final element of the delta for swap 1, $837, is plotted at month 18.

TABLE 18–3   Swap 1: "Delta-Hedged" Position

	0	3	6	9	12	15	18	21	24	
	D	M	J	S	D	M	J	S	D	
Delta for swap 1			+1,077		+944		+837			+2,858
Delta for one ED futures contract			−25		−25		−25			
Futures hedge			+43 contracts		+38 contracts		+33 contracts			
Delta for futures Contracts			−1,075		−950		−825			−2,850
			+2		−6		+2			+8

This first row indicates that we must use Eurodollar futures that expire in June and December of the next year and in June of the following year. The questions that remain are whether we must buy these futures contracts or sell them, and how many futures contracts we must buy or sell.

The second row in Table 18–3 provides the delta for a Eurodollar futures contract. As we noted in Chapter 6, a Eurodollar futures contract is a cash-settled instrument whose value is determined by the value of a three-month, $1 million Eurodollar deposit. If interest rates rise, the value of this deposit—the value of a very short bond—will fall. More specifically, if interest rates rise by one basis point, the value of a $1 million three-month bond will fall by $25:

$$0.0001/4 \times \$1MM = \$25$$

Hence, the delta for a long position in a Eurodollar futures contract is −$25.

The third row of Table 18–3 describes the hedge. Consider month 6—June of next year. The delta for swap 1 is positive, so the warehouse manager requires an asset with a negative delta in June to establish the hedge. Since the delta for a long position in a Eurodollar futures contract is negative, it follows that the manager must buy futures contracts. How many futures contracts are required? If we divide the June delta for swap 1 ($1,077) by the delta for a single Eurodollar futures contract ($25) and round to the nearest whole number, it follows that the warehouse manager must buy 43 contracts.

$$1,077/25 = 43.08 \rightarrow 43$$

Similarly, to hedge the exposure in December, the manager must buy 38 contracts. And to hedge the exposure next June, the manager must buy 33 contracts that expire in June of the following year.

The fourth row in Table 18–3 summarizes the delta for the futures contracts that the warehouse manager bought, the number of contracts multiplied by −$25. Summing across that row, the delta for the futures contracts purchased is negative $2,850.

It follows then that since the delta for swap 1 is positive $2,858 and the delta for the futures contracts purchased is negative $2,850, the delta for the hedged position is $8.

Table 18–4 describes the delta hedge for swap 2. Note that since the bank pays the floating rate in swap 2, the delta for swap 2 is negative rather than positive (as in Swap 1 there is a small delta (−2) in the first period which we will round to zero for this example). To hedge this swap, the warehouse manager must sell rather than buy Eurodollar futures contracts.

Delta-Hedging a Cap.   The cap that the bank has sold is actually a package of interest rate options—what the practitioner may refer to as "caplets." Three months from now, if the three-month LIBOR rate is above 8.5 percent, the bank will pay to

TABLE 18–4   Swap 2

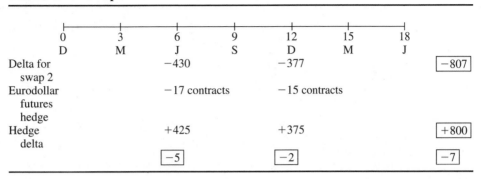

	0	3	6	9	12	15	18	
	D	M	J	S	D	M	J	
Delta for swap 2			−430		−377			−807
Eurodollar futures hedge			−17 contracts		−15 contracts			
Hedge delta			+425		+375			+800
			−5		−2			−7

the holder of this option the difference between the three-month LIBOR rate and 8.5 percent. Likewise, the holder of this option will receive payments from the bank if the three-month LIBOR rate is above 8.5 percent at month 6 and at month 9.

Table 18–5 describes this cap. As noted above, the cap is a strip of three active options: one with a maturity of three months, one with a maturity of six months, and one with a maturity of nine months. The cap rate, the exercise (strike) price for the options, is specified as 8.5 percent. Since these options can be exercised only in the future, the relevant rate to compare with the exercise rate is not the current three-month LIBOR rate but rather the forward rate for three-month LIBOR. These forward three-month LIBOR rates at months 3, 6, and 9 are calculated from the LIBOR yield curve illustrated in Figure 18–6. Using a standard option pricing model, we have valued the three interest rate options. Table 18–5 provides the value of these options, expressed both in basis points and in dollars.

However, the warehouse manager is interested not only in the value of the options but also in the Greek-letter risk measures described earlier. Table 18–6 provides these risk measures for the cap.[6] The first row of Table 18–6 provides the delta for the strip of individual interest rate options that make up the cap and the total for

TABLE 18–5   The Cap = A Package of Interest Rate Options

	0	3	6	9	12
Option maturity		3 month	6 month	9 month	
Cap rate		8.5%	8.5%	8.5%	
Forward rate		$_3r_6 = 7.18\%$	$_6r_9 = 7.68\%$	$_9r_{12} = 8.01\%$	
Option value					
basis points		0.38 bp	8.95 bp	23.89 bp	Total
Dollars		$475	$11,188	$29,863	$41,525

TABLE 18–6   Greek-Letter Risk Measures for the Cap

	3-Month Option	*6-Month Option*	*9-Month Option*	*Total*
Delta	−24	−243	−426	−693
Gamma	−100	−390	−399	−889
Vega	−200	−1,838	−3,075	−5,113

the cap. Note that as the maturity of the interest rate options gets longer, the forward rates are higher, increasing the delta for the options. Likewise, looking at gamma and vega, both of those numbers rise—and rise dramatically—as the options move nearer to the money.

Table 18–7 illustrates how this cap could be delta-hedged using Eurodollar futures contracts. The first row of Table 18–7 is the delta for the cap (taken from Table 18–6). If interest rates rise by one basis point, the value of this cap to the bank that sold it declines by $693. Since the delta is negative, the bank must sell Eurodollar futures contracts to hedge this position. The second row of Table 18–7 summarizes the required number of futures contracts to be sold. The third row of Table 18–7 provides the delta for the Eurodollar futures contracts. The final row summarizes the hedged position, the sum of the delta for the cap itself and the delta for the Eurodollar futures contracts. A one-basis-point increase in interest rates causes the value of the cap to decline by $693. However, once the cap is delta-hedged, a one-basis-point increase in interest rates results in only a $7 increase in the value of the hedged position.

Delta-Hedging a Warehouse.   So far, we've acted as if a portfolio of derivatives would be hedged transaction by transaction. However, it's probably evident that there are portfolio effects to be realized by instead hedging the entire portfolio.

TABLE 18–7   Cap: "Delta-Hedged" Position

	0 D	3 M	6 J	9 S	12 D	
Cap delta		−24	−243	−426		−693
Eurodollar futures hedge		−1	−10	−17		
Hedge delta		+25	+250	+425		+700
		+1	+7	−1		+7

Table 18–8 illustrates the delta for the entire warehouse. The deltas for the warehouse are obtained simply by summing the deltas for the individual transactions. Notice, however, that the magnitude of the total warehouse delta ($1,358) is smaller than the delta for swap 1 ($2,858). That is, by combining these transactions into a portfolio, the overall risk is reduced.

Albeit smaller, the warehouse contains residual risk that remains to be hedged. The method by which this risk is hedged is precisely that used earlier to hedge the individual transactions. At a point in time, if the delta for the warehouse is negative, the manager must sell Eurodollar futures contracts to hedge that position. If, on the other hand, the delta is positive, the manager must buy Eurodollar futures contracts.

Table 18–9 illustrates the delta-hedged warehouse. Consider month 3, March. The delta for the warehouse is a negative $24. To hedge this exposure, the manager sells one Eurodollar futures contract. The delta for short one Eurodollar futures contract is $25, so after the hedge is established, the delta for the warehouse is $404. To hedge this positive delta of $404, the manager buys Eurodollar futures contracts as follows:

$$\$404/25 = 16.16 \rightarrow 16 \text{ Eurodollar futures contracts}$$

The delta for a long position in 16 Eurodollar futures contracts is −$400. Summing the $404 positive delta for the warehouse and the $400 negative delta for the futures contracts, the delta-hedged warehouse has a delta of only $4. This procedure is repeated for each maturity bucket.

Hedging the Warehouse against Risk Other Than Delta

Before the delta-hedge was implemented, the warehouse was quite sensitive to changes in interest rates. A one-basis-point change in interest rate would change the value of the warehouse by $1,358. After the hedge is implemented, the sensitivity

TABLE 18–8   Delta for the Warehouse

	0 D	3 M	6 J	9 S	12 D	15 M	18 J	
Swap 1 delta			+1,077		+944		+837	
Swap 2 delta			−430		−377			
Cap delta		−24	−243	−426				
Warehouse delta		−24	+404	−426	+567	0	+837	+1,358

TABLE 18-9   The Delta-Hedged Warehouse

	0 D	3 M	6 J	9 S	12 D	15 M	18 J	
Swap 1 delta			+1,077		+944		+837	
Swap 2 delta			−430		−377			
Cap delta		−24	−243	−426				
Warehouse delta		−24	+404	−426	+567	0	+837	+1,358
Eurodollars futures contracts		−1	+16	−17	+23	0	+33	
Delta for futures		+25	−400	+425	−575	0	−825	−1,350
Hedged warehouse delta		+1	+4	−1	−8	0	+12	+8

of the hedged warehouse declined dramatically. As indicated in Table 18–9, once the warehouse is hedged, a one-basis-point movement in interest rates changes the value of the warehouse by only $8.

But the delta-hedge is only the beginning. The delta-hedge protects the warehouse against small, parallel shifts in the yield curve. However, the warehouse manager must also protect the warehouse against rotations in the yield curve (yield-curve twists), jumps in interest rates, changes in the volatility of interest rates, and other risks.

Hedging the Warehouse against Term Structure Twists.   To consider how the warehouse could be managed to hedge against rotations in the term structure, consider the delta ladders for warehouse 1 and warehouse 2 illustrated in Figure 18–8.

For both warehouse 1 and warehouse 2, the aggregate delta for the warehouse is zero—that is, the positive delta for some maturity buckets is exactly offset by the negative delta for other maturity buckets. However, the manner in which this aggregate delta of zero is obtained is quite different for the two delta ladders. In panel A-1, warehouse 1 has a very large positive delta for the three-month maturity bucket and a very large negative delta at the five-year maturity bucket. On the other hand, warehouse 2 (panel A-2) has a delta ladder that has positive and negative delta scattered through the maturity buckets.

FIGURE 18–8   Hedging against Rotations of the Term Structure

Consider the delta "ladders" for two warehouses. Both of the warehouses are delta-hedged. Aggregate delta = 0

Panel A–1: Warehouse #1 has positive delta in the 3–month maturity bucket offset by negative delta in the 5–year bucket.

Panel A–2: Warehouse #2 has positive and negative delta interspersed throughout the maturity buckets.

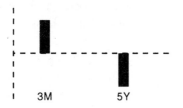

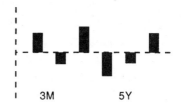

Panel B: Suppose the yield curve steepens—short-term rates fall and long-term rates rise.

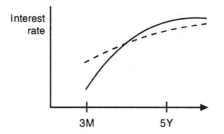

Panel C–1: Warehouse #1 loses value *both* due to the fall of short-term rates and the rise of long-term rates.

Panel C–2: Warehouse #2 is structured so that the rotation in the yield curve has little impact—gains and losses balance out.

	3M	5Y
Delta	+	−
Chg in int rate	↓	↑
Chg in value	↓	↓

	3M					5Y
Delta	+	−	+	−	−	+
Chg in int rate	↓	↓	↑	↑	↑	↑
Chg in value	↓	↑	↑	↓	↓	↑

If the manager's objective is to hedge the warehouse against rotations in the term structure, warehouse 2 is preferred to warehouse 1. To see why this is the case, consider the yield-curve twist illustrated in panel B and the resultant impact on the two warehouses, illustrated in panels C-1 and C-2.

As panel C-1 shows, warehouse 1 would lose value in both the three-month and five-year maturity buckets. Since warehouse 1 has a positive delta at the three-month maturity, the reduction in interest rates at the short end of the yield curve causes a loss in value. And since the warehouse has a negative delta at the five-year maturity bucket, the increase in rates at the long end of the curve also causes a loss in value. So with this twist in the yield curve, the value of warehouse 1 will decline even though the delta is zero.

However, for warehouse 2, the positive and negative deltas in the maturity buckets tend to cancel each other. Consequently, the change in value of the portfolio caused by this twist in the yield curve will be much smaller.

Hedging Gamma and Vega.   When we toured fraternity row, we described the Greek-letter measures of risk: delta, gamma, and vega. However, when we've hedged this warehouse, we've hedged only the delta risk. Any gamma and vega risk in the warehouse remains. Indeed, because this bank has sold an interest rate cap, the warehouse is short both gamma and vega.

Since swaps and FRAs have gamma, the manager could use them to hedge the gamma introduced by selling the cap. (We will return to the implementation of a gamma hedge using swaps and FRAs later.) However, to hedge the vega risk in the warehouse, the warehouse manager has no choice but to buy options. The questions facing the warehouse manager are then: *Which options do I buy? How many options do I buy?*

In many cases, a warehouse manager will elect to hedge residual gamma and vega by purchasing out-of-the-money options. Figure 18–9 illustrates the vega in the warehouse for the out-of-the-money cap; since the bank sold the option, the vega is negative. And since vega is largest when the option is at-the-money, the vega in the warehouse is most negative at interest rates higher than the prevailing rate.

To hedge this vega, the warehouse manager must purchase other options. Suppose that the warehouse manager had implemented the hedge by purchasing options that were even further out-of-the-money than the ones the bank sold. As Figure 18–9 illustrates, vega is now hedged—but only as long as interest rates remain at current levels. In addition, as the contracts age, the vega profile will change even if rates remain constant.

Hedging the Warehouse against Jumps.   So far, we have talked about hedging the warehouse assuming that the market moves continuously. However, there have been times when the market has "jumped" (or "gapped"). One such instance

FIGURE 18–9 Hedging against Jumps

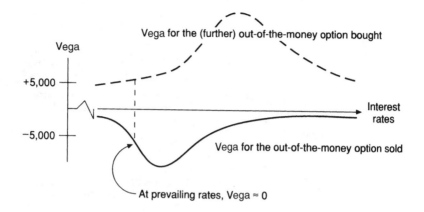

occurred in the foreign exchange markets, when sterling left the ERM in September 1992.[7]

> Liquid, orderly foreign exchange markets temporarily disappeared in September 1992. This was most evident by looking at volatility. Under the ERM, volatility had been low compared with free-floating currencies. For example, before the crisis erupted, one-month UK sterling-deutsche mark volatility was as low as 3.8 percent while one-month U.S. dollar-deutsche mark volatility was in the 12–15 percent range.[8] From the end of August to September 11, one-month implied UK sterling-deutsche mark volatility was around 7 percent. Three days before sterling devalued, implied volatilities had risen to 14–15 percent. On the morning that sterling devalued, implied UK sterling–deutsche mark volatility was as high as 35 percent.
>
> And the turmoil in the currency markets caused huge volatility in the interest rate markets as central banks manipulated short-term rates to defend their ERM parities. Short-term interest rate contracts had unprecedented trading ranges. And highs and lows were often reached within 48 hours of each other. A case in point is the jump in the overnight Swedish krona rate from 24 percent to 500 percent.

To put this into context, consider again the vega hedge described in Figure 18–9. This hedge is valid only if interest rates stay at their prevailing level. If interest rates were to jump up or down, vega is no longer hedged.

To show how this can happen, Figure 18–10 illustrates the net vega for the warehouse. This net vega is obtained by summing the negative vega from the cap that the bank sold and the positive vega obtained when the warehouse manager bought the further out-of-the-money option.

Notice that if rates jump up a little, vega becomes negative. But if rates jump a lot, vega can actually become positive. So the warehouse manager has to consider

---

FIGURE 18–10   Hedging against Jumps, Continued

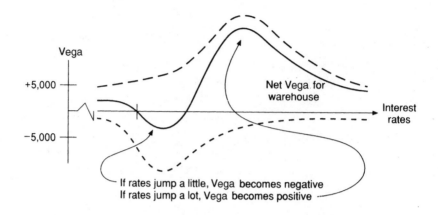

not only what the vega risk is today but also what the vega risk could be tomorrow if interest rates move a little or a lot.

Implementing the Hedge

So far, we have talked about hedging a warehouse (portfolio) of derivatives as if we first hedge delta, then hedge gamma, and finally hedge vega. While this is a logical way to *think* about the necessary hedge, it is not a logical way to *implement* the hedge.

Table 18–10 illustrates the difficulty. Suppose the initial risk parameters of the warehouse are as provided in the first row of the table: delta = +1,750, gamma = −1,000, and vega = −5,000. Suppose that the warehouse manager first uses futures to hedge the delta risk. The results are provided in row 3: delta is zero, gamma and vega are unchanged. So far so good. Now, suppose the manager uses swaps and FRAs to hedge the gamma. As row 5 illustrates, the manager can enter into swaps and FRAs with enough positive gamma to make the gamma of the warehouse zero, but since swaps and FRAs have delta as well as gamma, the warehouse would no longer be hedged with respect to delta. Consequently, the warehouse manager would then have to rehedge delta (see rows 6 and 7). Look what happens if the manager then purchases options to hedge the negative vega. Rows 8 and 9 illustrate that by purchasing the appropriate number of options, the manager could eliminate the vega risk, but since options have both gamma and delta, the warehouse will no longer have zero delta and gamma. Rows 10–15 illustrate the steps that would have to be accomplished to hedge the delta for the options (rows 10 and

TABLE 18–10　The Difficulties Encountered Implementing a Delta-Gamma-Vega Hedge

		Delta	Gamma	Vega
(1)	Initial warehouse	+1,750	−1,000	−5,000
(2)	Hedge delta with futures	−1,750	0	0
(3)	Warehouse after hedge	0	−1,000	−5,000
(4)	Hedge gamma with swaps and FRAs	−5,000	+1,000	0
(5)	Warehouse after hedge	−5,000	0	−5,000
(6)	Hedge delta with futures	+5,000	0	0
(7)	Warehouse after hedge	0	0	−5,000
(8)	Hedge vega with options	+500	+500	+5,000
(9)	Warehouse after hedge	+500	+500	0
(10)	Hedge delta with futures	−500	0	0
(11)	Warehouse after hedge	0	+500	0
(12)	Hedge gamma with swaps and FRAs	+2,000	−500	0
(13)	Warehouse after hedge	+2,000	0	0
(14)	Hedge delta with futures	−2,000	0	0
(15)	Warehouse after hedge	0	0	0

11), to hedge the gamma for the options (rows 12 and 13), and then to rehedge the delta that will be disturbed by hedging the gamma (rows 14 and 15).

As illustrated in Table 18–10, if the warehouse manager attempts to hedge delta and then gamma and then vega, rehedging is constant. If I have delta hedged and I then hedge gamma, I displace the delta hedge; if I hedge vega, I displace both the delta and gamma hedges.

Hence, instead of hedging delta-gamma-vega, the warehouse manager will hedge vega-gamma-delta. This is illustrated in Table 18–11. The manager first uses

TABLE 18–11　Implementing a Vega-Gamma-Delta Hedge

		Delta	Gamma	Vega
(1)	Initial warehouse	+1,750	−1,000	−5,000
(2)	Hedge vega with options	+500	+500	+5,000
(3)	Warehouse after hedge	+2,250	−500	0
(4)	Hedge gamma with swaps and FRAs	−2,500	+500	0
(5)	Warehouse after hedge	−250	0	0
(6)	Hedge delta with futures	+250	0	0
(7)	Warehouse after hedge	0	0	0

options to hedge the vega (rows 2 and 3). The warehouse manager next hedges the remaining gamma with swaps and FRAs (rows 4 and 5). Since these instruments have no vega, hedging the gamma will not displace the vega hedge. Finally, the manager will hedge the remaining delta with futures (rows 6 and 7). Since futures have only delta, this hedge will not displace the existing hedges of gamma and vega.

Hedging beyond Delta-Gamma-Vega

While delta, gamma, and vega are risk measures used by virtually all managers of derivatives warehouses, they are by no means all of the "houses" on fraternity row. In this section we note some of the other risk measures that are commonly employed.

Theta measures the change in value of the financial asset associated with a change in the time to contract maturity. Most trading rooms also refer to theta as "time decay" and track this change in value as part of the daily profit/loss report.

For options other than interest rate options, rho measures the change in the value of the option associated with changes in interest rates. For foreign exchange options, rho would be associated with the domestic interest rate rather than the foreign interest rate.

Lambda measures the change in the value of the options associated with changes in the dividend rate for equity options or the foreign interest rate for foreign exchange options.

The multifactor options we introduced in Chapter 13 require that the manager also measure the risk to the warehouse from a change in the correlation between variables.

Mark Garman suggested some additions to the list of risk measures.[9] Interestingly, this new list of risk parameters potentially reflects a shift in direction for the derivatives business: the language seems to be shifting from fraternity row to the jargon of physics.

As noted, gamma measures the change in delta that will occur as the price of the underlying asset changes.[10] A manager of a large warehouse keeps a close eye on gamma, since this risk measure provides advance warning of the change that will be required in the hedge. Moving a step further, to obtain some advance warning of changes in gamma, some warehouse managers are now tracking the change in gamma as the price of the underlying asset changes. According to Garman, this risk measure is being referred to as *speed*.[11]

On a practical basis, one of the most stressful times for the manager of a warehouse that contains options is just prior to expiration of an option contract. As the time remaining on the option becomes short, the positions tend to become more sensitive to price changes around the exercise price. This increase in sensitivity

The Market Risk Management Process

Peter Hancock

In a modern financial firm, risk management is not the sole responsibility of a single risk management unit within a firm, but is shared among several independent business and control units. On the business side, traders and marketers ("front office"), transaction support ("middle office"), and operations all play crucial roles in risk management. The same is true of independent control units, including financial control, audit, and the corporate risk management group. Each has its own purpose, but the result is to have more than one set of eyes, each of which is accountable to a different reporting line within the firm, looking at risks across portfolios within a business and at risks across businesses.

Risk management begins with articulating a risk management philosophy, which addresses such choices as centralized versus decentralized decision making and accountability for results. Next comes establishing a risk management process. By designating responsibility and accountability for market risk, the process ensures that a firm's activities are consistent with corporate policies and regulatory requirements. At J. P. Morgan, for example, the risk management process attempts to combine risk management by the business units with firmwide risk measurement and monitoring.

A risk management process should reflect a firm's corporate culture and management philosophy. Because no two firms are exactly alike, there is no standard model of a risk management process. The following are elements of the market risk management process at J. P. Morgan; the general headings represent tasks that all institutions should address, although implementation details will differ among firms. The objectives of a risk management process are:

- Risk transparency and effective communication between risk takers and managers.
- Consistent risk methodologies, models, policies, and procedures.
- Timely, useful, and accurate information.
- Measurement and monitoring of all material risks, including "hidden" risk concentrations.
- Avoidance of catastrophic loss due to events of market stress.
- Efficient allocation of risk capital.

The Market Risk Management Process continued

Front-End Controls and Intraday Risk Management

The trading desk is the front line in risk management. Traders are responsible for hedging intraday positions; the middle office is responsible for checking accuracy and completeness of transaction data entry, for verifying compliance with market and credit risk limits, and for monitoring amounts at risk on an ongoing basis. Separation of duties here between traders and the middle office is crucial: inaccurate (or fraudulent) data capture at the front end can seriously compromise the rest of the risk management process.

Limits

The purpose of limits is to prevent excessive concentrations of risk in positions, risk types, markets, and countries. Limit setting is a dynamic process, responding to changes in risk appetite, expected returns, business strategy, and market liquidity. The central corporate risk management group sets global business limits, within which businesses set limits as appropriate. Limits may be set in terms of maximum allowable daily earnings at risk (DEAR)* as well as sensitivity parameters such as gamma and vega; in addition, there are limits on concentrations of risks; finally, liquidity considerations influence limit setting. In order to separate decision management from decision control, limits are subject to approval and monitoring by the corporate risk management function.

After limits are set, businesses and the financial control group monitor "excessions," which are risks or positions that exceed limits. Excessions require the control unit to seek approval or disapproval from the appropriate level of senior management. Approval would lead to ongoing monitoring of the risk. Disapproval would lead not to mechanical "stop-loss" actions but to a search for measures that seek to reduce the risk to an acceptable level; risk-reduction measures could take the form of a hedge, an unwind, or a compensating reduction of other risks.

DEAR Reporting

At J. P. Morgan, DEAR reporting is embodied in the "4:15 report," in which each business reports estimated position, risk, and revenue data at 4:15 each business-day afternoon, which are then discussed and forwarded to senior management. A purpose of such reporting is to identify firmwide risk concentrations that might not be obvious at the business level; another is to provide early warning of increasing risks. Requiring same-day position reporting involves an inevitable trade-off between speed and accuracy, illustrated in the choice between being "approximately right or precisely wrong." Reporting also involves next-day reconciliation of data reported by businesses with books and records of the firm.

New Product Approval

This step in the risk management process is initiated by the business units themselves. Once a business decides to pursue the development of a new product, the independent control groups help identify risks and ensure the risks are understood and reported, verify the adequacy of processing and controls, and assure senior management that risks are consistent with corporate policy and business strategy.

Model and Methodology Management

Model calibration and verification ensure that models are appropriate for their purposes, that they are in line with evolving market practices, and that controls are in place; calibration and verification are necessary both for newly developed models and for models that are already in use. Although businesses develop and maintain the models, the control units are responsible for independent validation and verification. An important consideration is the range in which a model can be trusted to give accurate results. In addition, a pricing model might be verified to a level sufficient to support a trader or marketer in pricing a transaction; a valuation model would undergo validation and verification sufficiently rigorous to compute profit and loss. Finally, a risk management model used for hedging purposes normally requires a far higher level of accuracy than does a risk assessment model used primarily for reporting aggregate portfolio risks.

Back Testing

By comparing risk model predictions with actual profits and losses, back testing seeks to ensure that the DEAR methodology and models capture risk accurately. Back testing results do not simply test the model, however; they also help assess risk capital usage and allocation. If a business unit seldom breaches its risk limits, for example, the implication could be that the business does not have an appetite for taking as much risk as it is allowed. Similarly, if the business frequently breaches its limits, the risk management group might respond by expanding the business's limits while reexamining those of other businesses.

The Market Risk Management Process continued

Stress Testing and Event Risk Analysis

While a DEAR measure focuses on potential losses under normal market conditions, stress testing and event risk analysis concentrate on *tail risks,* which are extreme or low-probability events in the tails of the risk distribution that could lead to catastrophic losses to the business. The objective of stress testing is to analyze the effect of such unlikely events on portfolio value, and then to determine how best to avoid or protect against such events. Stress testing is meant to be a complement to DEAR, and is carried out periodically; it is especially useful for assessing nonlinear risks in complex derivatives portfolios. Response to the results could involve revising business strategy or setting aside additional capital, as deemed appropriate by the business units. Stress limits can also be set to control the tail risks.

Peter Hancock is managing director and head of Global Fixed Income for J. P. Morgan in New York. He joined Morgan in 1980 and worked initially in Corporate Finance at the Petroleum Department in London. In 1984, he joined the Eurobond Syndicate Desk. Two years later, he moved to New York to become manager of the Multi-Currency Asset and Liability desk. In 1987, he joined Swaps as manager of Swap and Interest Rate Derivative Trading. Two years later he headed the New York Swaps group, in 1990 he became head of Global Swaps, and in 1991 he assumed joint management responsibility for FX, Equity and Commodity derivatives. He assumed his current responsibilities in March 1995. Mr. Hancock is a native of England and holds a master of arts degree in politics, philosophy, and economics from Oxford University.

Daily earnings at risk (DEAR) is the name that J. P. Morgan uses to denote its one-day "value-at-risk." Value-at-risk is discussed in detail in Chapter 19.

---

as the time to expiration declines is illustrated in Figure 18–11. With a lot of time remaining to the expiration of the option, changes in the underlying price from below to above the exercise cause delta to change, but the change in delta is relatively smooth; that is, gamma is relatively small. However, when expiration is imminent, changes in the underlying price from below to above the exercise cause delta to change abruptly from very small to very large; that is, gamma is large. Consequently, some warehouse managers are beginning to track not only theta but also two other time effects.

Charm is the name Garman suggested for the change in delta as time to maturity changes. If the manager is attempting to keep the warehouse delta-hedged, the hedge will have to be adjusted day to day even if the underlying price does not change and Charm tells the warehouse manager how much the hedge will change.

Color measures the change in gamma as time to maturity changes. Particularly when expiration is close, the manager will want to know how small changes in the underlying price will impact the hedge.

FIGURE 18–11   Changes in Delta and Gamma as Time to Expiration Changes

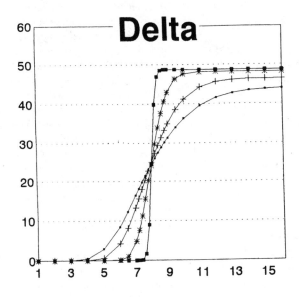

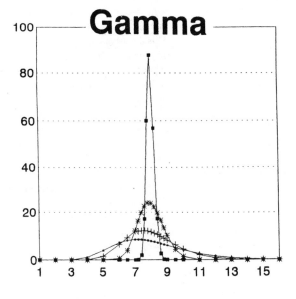

Notes

1. In this chapter we will refer to the "portfolio manager" or the "warehouse manager"; in Chapter 19, we will talk about the "risk manager."

   The portfolio manager's job is to take care of a particular position—e.g., the firm's U.S. dollar interest rate book or the firm's Canadian dollar–UK sterling book. The portfolio manager worries about the impact of movement in financial prices on the value of that portfolio; and if something needs to be done to the portfolio to modify the risk, the portfolio manager is the person who does it.

   The risk manager's job is to oversee the market risk (and perhaps other risks) associated with a number of positions—perhaps even the entire firm. The risk manager worries about the impact of financial price movement on the value of this set of portfolios; but if something needs to be done, the risk manager will not be the one actually doing the action.

2. Interest rate futures were designed to have zero gamma so that the change in the futures price for a given change in interest rates would be invariant to the level of rates. With this convention, a one-basis-point move in three-month LIBOR changes the value of a Eurodollar futures contract on the CME by $25, regardless of whether the move in three-month LIBOR is from 3 percent to 3.01 percent or from 6 percent to 6.01 percent. Similarly, with this convention, there is strict linear relation between interest rate changes and the value of the futures contract—a three-basis-point move will change the value of a Eurodollar futures contract by $75, a 30-basis-point move will change the value of a Eurodollar futures contract by $750, and a 300-basis-point move will change the value of a Eurodollar futures contract by $7,500.

3. Foreign exchange and commodity forward contracts have no gamma; delta is constant. Hence the gamma for FX and commodity swaps would also be zero.

4. There are some who still refer to this risk as "kappa," and even a few who refer to it as "lambda." Since *vega* is not a Greek letter—even though it sounds like one—we have always wondered where it came from. Alan Marshall, our colleague at CIBC, told us that John Hull (at the time at York University, now at University of Toronto) coined the term.

5. As we saw in earlier chapters of this book, changes in volatility change the value of an option but not the values of forwards, futures, or swaps.

   However, there are special cases in which one could argue that financial instruments other than options have vega. For example, suppose that the structure of interest rates follows the Cox-Ingersoll-Ross (1985): Short-term interest rates determine the structure of bond prices. In such an environment, if the volatility of short-term rates rises while the level of the short-term rate is constant, financial instruments that have a nonzero gamma will have a nonzero vega as well.

6. The risk measures and the option valuation measures were obtained using a Black model to value the individual options—the caplets.

7. This discussion is adapted from "Things Fall Apart," an article by Richard Cookson and Lillian Chew that appeared in the October 1992 issue of *Risk*.

8. All volatilities were implied from the value of at-the-money options.

9. Garman (1988).

10. For those of you who like to think about these as mathematical derivatives, gamma is the second derivative of the value of the asset with respect to the price of the underlying asset.

11. If gamma is the second derivative of the value of the asset with respect to the price of the underlying asset, speed is the third derivative.

19 RISK GOVERNANCE

In Chapters 17 and 18, we examined the techniques dealers employ to *manage* risk. In this chapter, we turn our attention to risk *governance*.[1] In the main, risk governance relates to (1) communication from the trading and risk management activities to senior management and the board of directors and (2) senior management/board oversight of the risks that the firm faces and the way that the firm will deal with those risks.

If senior management and the board are to oversee the risks that the firm faces and the way that the firm deals with those risks, some measure of risk needs to be communicated from the trading and risk management activities to senior management and the board. As trading portfolios have become more complex, it has become more difficult for senior management to obtain an *integrated* measure of market risk. The most widely used summary measure is commonly known as *value-at-risk* (VAR).

However, we do not want you to jump to the conclusion that VAR is *the* integrated risk measure. VAR is not the "end of the story"; VAR is where the finance profession is today. Ten years from now, the risk measures that will be used in risk governance are likely to be much different from the techniques we will describe in the following pages.

Not only is VAR *not* the end of the story, but VAR is *not* the beginning of the story. A number of risk measures preceded the VAR measure. So before we begin our discussion of VAR, we will take a moment to review these precursors.

Aside

The Role of the Board of Directors in Risk Governance

There is universal agreement that the role of the board of directors is *crucial*. Likewise, there is essentially universal agreement that it is *not* necessary for the board members to be rocket scientists; instead, the members of the board of directors need to know the right questions to ask.

A former director of the Division of Market Regulation of the U.S. Securities and Exchange Commission provided insight into the way that the SEC might view the responsibilities of directors.* He said that the members of the board of directors must understand clearly the risks associated with the use of financial derivatives and must assume responsibility for making informed decisions about the company's investment and risk management policies. Moreover, directors must have a broad understanding of the credit, market, and operational risks involved and must establish clear guidelines about the way that the company will use derivative instruments. In addition, the former director noted that the board must ensure both that the company has adequate risk management controls and qualified personnel in place to monitor the company's risk position and that the company's investments are in keeping with its overall objectives.

He went on to say:

When defining the company's fundamental risk-management policies, directors should consider its broader business strategies and management expertise and adopt policies consistent with the company's overall business objectives. Directors should require that the board be informed of the company's risk exposure and of the effect adverse market and interest-rate conditions may have on the company's derivatives portfolio. Directors should identify those individuals who will assume responsibility for managing risk as well as those who will have the authority to engage in derivative transactions. . . . Directors must fully understand the corporation's obligations to account for and publicly disclose information about derivatives activities.

The preceding description suggests that the members of boards of directors have, voluntarily or not, accepted four responsibilities. (1) The board must approve the firm's risk management policies and procedures. (2) The board must ensure that the operating management team possesses the requisite technical capabilities† (and is actively communicating with the people implementing the risk management program). (3) The directors must be able to evaluate the performance of the risk management activity. (4) The board must maintain oversight of the risk management activity.

---

*These comments by Brandon Becker, then the director of the Division of Market Regulation of the U.S. Securities and Exchange Commission, were reported in the January–February 1995 issue of the *Harvard Business Review.*

†Technical knowledge is *necessary,* but is not *sufficient;* technical knowledge will never replace good judgment.

Precursors to VAR

VAR was designed to look at market risk. It represents an attempt to measure the risk of loss for a portfolio resulting from movement in market *factors*.[2] However, VAR is not the first such measure.

Interest Rate Sensitivity Measures

Traditional measures of market risk treat one market factor at a time. Many of these precursor measures focused on interest rate risk. In the following, we will look at four interest rate sensitivity measures—maturity gap, value of an 01, duration, and convexity.

Maturity Gap. Unlike the other risk measures we will discuss in this chapter, *maturity gap* is a "flow," rather than "stock," measure. That is, maturity gap focuses on the impact of a change in the interest rate on income and/or expense, rather than on the mark-to-market value of the portfolio. In fact, as we will describe in more detail in Chapter 23, maturity gap analysis is employed primarily by financial institutions to measure the impact of changes in interest rates on their net interest income (NII):

$$\text{Gap} = \Delta\text{NII}/\Delta r \qquad (19\text{--}1)$$

Value of an 01 and Duration. *Value of an 01*[3] measures the change in the value of an asset or liability associated with a one-basis-point parallel shift in the yield curve. That is,

$$\text{Value of 01} = \Delta V/\Delta r \qquad (19\text{--}2)$$

where Δr is defined to be one basis point.

Duration was "discovered" almost simultaneously by Federich Macaulay (1938) and Sir John Hicks (1939). However, these two researchers had very different objectives. Macaulay's goal was to define a measure by which two bonds with common maturity but divergent payment structures could be compared. In the Macaulay sense, duration measures *when,* on average, the value of the bond is received. Hicks attempted to measure interest rate sensitivity for any particular bond. In the tradition of Hicks, duration provides a measure of the exposure of the bond to interest rate risk. Using the Hicks notion of duration, we can define duration (D) as

$$D = -(\text{percentage change in value})/(\text{percentage change in discount rate}) \qquad (19\text{--}3)$$

Since percentage change is simply change over total, we can rewrite Equation 19–3 as

$$D = -(\Delta V/V)/[\Delta r/(1 + r)]$$
$$= -(\Delta V/\Delta r) \times [(1 + r)/V] \qquad (19\text{--}4)$$

Equations 19–2 and 19–4 demonstrate that both the value of 01 and duration are linear measures of risk. In both, the risk measure is the slope of the value profile, $\Delta V/\Delta r$. Figure 19–1 makes this a little more clear. The problem is that the value of an 01 and duration are only linear approximations of the true risk. If interest rates change a lot, the approximation error can be large.

Convexity. Duration is essentially a measure of the slope of the value profile at current interest rates and bond prices. Convexity is a measure of the curvature—the change in slope—of the value profile, again at current interest rates and bond prices.

The user of a convexity measure assumes that the curvature of the value profile will remain the same for all interest rates. So convexity is also an approximation. As Figure 19–2 illustrates, the approximation error can be large for large changes in the interest rate; but the approximation error will be larger than that if the risk manager were to look at duration alone.

Option-Based Sensitivity Measures

The preceding discussion makes the point that the weaknesses in some of the traditional measures of financial price risk result from nonlinearities in the value profiles of the instruments in the trading portfolios. Much of this nonlinearity is the result of options—explicit or embedded. Mortgage-backed securities (MBS) are a good example of financial instruments for which a duration measure (or even duration and convexity together) doesn't work well. This is because MBS contain

---

FIGURE 19–1   Value of an 01 and Duration

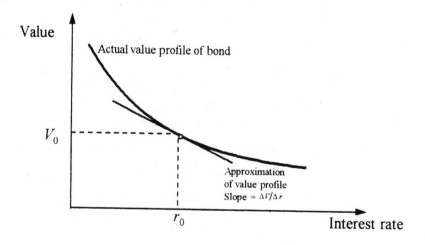

FIGURE 19–2 Convexity

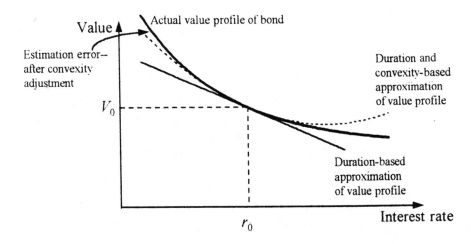

embedded options. U.S. mortgages contain a prepayment option; the home owner has the right to prepay the mortgage at any time, with no penalty. In the main, this prepayment option can be characterized as an interest rate option. The home owner is long a put option on interest rates—if rates fall sufficiently, the home owner will prepay the existing mortgage and refinance the property. Consequently, the holder of the MBS is short the put option on interest rates.

If the problem is the result of optionality, a simple solution would be to use option-based risk measures. In Chapter 18, we introduced three of the option-based risk measures:

Delta—the change in the value of the asset associated with changes in the underlying financial price[4]:

$$\text{Delta} = \Delta V / \Delta P \qquad (19\text{–}5)$$

Gamma—the change in delta associated with changes in the underlying financial price:

$$\text{Gamma} = \Delta \text{delta} / \Delta P \qquad (19\text{–}6)$$

Since delta is the slope of the value profile, gamma measures the change in the slope of the value profile.[5]

Vega—the change in the value of the asset associated with changes in the volatility of the underlying financial price:

$$\text{Vega} = \Delta V / \Delta \sigma_P \qquad (19\text{–}7)$$

The risk manager could measure delta, gamma, and vega for each trading portfolio—e.g., the U.S. dollar interest rate book or the DM/US$ book.

Weaknesses of Traditional Measures

In our opinion, there are three reasons why the traditional measures of risk—the value of an 01, duration, convexity, and option-based measures—proved unsatisfactory.

First, the traditional risk measures cannot be aggregated across types of risk factors. For example, delta and vega risks cannot be aggregated. Moreover, risk factors cannot be aggregated across markets. For example, the delta of a mark call and an equity call are not additive.

Second, the traditional risk measures do not measure capital at risk. Consequently, it is difficult to implement risk-adjusted performance.

Third, the traditional risk measures do not facilitate control. Position limits by factor risk are often not effective.

These problems led risk managers to look for a summary measure of market risk.

Value at Risk—A Summary Measure of Market Risk[6]

Our discussion of VAR begins at the beginning, by describing the VAR *concept*. We next spend a considerable amount of time reviewing the methods currently being used to calculate VAR. We then turn our attention to applications of VAR. First, we look at the extent to which VAR is used by different market participants, i.e., dealers, end users, and regulators. Then we examine some of the issues from the ongoing debate about which firms should use VAR and the "right way" to calculate the risk measure.

The VAR Concept

As illustrated in Figure 19–3, the concept behind VAR is extremely simple. First, as is illustrated at the top of Panel (*a*), value the current portfolio using today's "price list"[7] to obtain the current value of the portfolio, V_0. Then, revalue the current portfolio using a number of "alternative price lists" and calculate the changes in the portfolio value that would result; i.e., the value change i, ΔV_i, would be the difference in the value of the portfolio using today's price list and the value obtained using alternative price list i. Panel (*a*) illustrates using, for purposes of this example, 100 alternative price lists to simulate 100 alternative values for the port-

FIGURE 19–3   The Logic of VAR

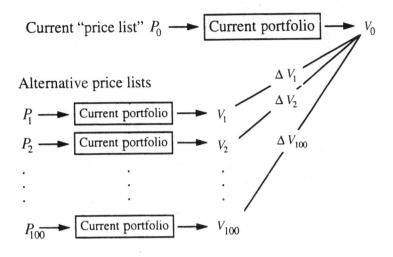

(*a*) Simulate changes in the value of the portfolio

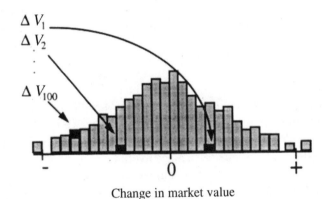

Change in market value

(*b*) Collect the simulated changes to provide
a distribution of changes

folio, from which we obtain 100 ΔV's.[8] Next, as is illustrated in Panel (*b*), we collect the simulated changes in the value of the portfolio—the ΔV's—to provide a distribution of changes in the value of the portfolio.

Given a distribution of value changes like that displayed in Panel (*b*) of Figure 19–3, VAR is specified in terms of a confidence level. The risk manager can calculate the maximum the institution can lose over a specified *time horizon* at a specified *probability level*. For instance, the risk manager can define the maximum loss for a one-day period at a 95 percent probability—i.e., the loss that should be exceeded on only five trading days out of 100.

In general, VAR is a *probability statement* about the potential change in value of a portfolio resulting from changes in market factors over a specified time interval.

Calculating VAR

Implementation of VAR is not quite as simple as the concept. If we knew the distribution of changes in value for the portfolio in question, VAR would be a straightforward calculation. The problem is that we have got to obtain the distribution of value changes, and this means that we must choose a methodology for modeling changes in market factors—i.e., we must define the distribution of market factors. (In the context of the preceding discussion of the VAR concept, this means that we must find a way to obtain a series of vectors of alternative market factors.)

Three methods are currently being used to calculate VAR. The first two are *simulation* methodologies in which the objective is to simulate the value of a market factor τ days in the future—i.e., on day $t + \tau$. In general, if F_t is the value of the market factor on day t, the ith simulated value of the market factor on day $t + \tau$ could be expressed as

$$F_{t+\tau,i} = F_t + \Delta F_i \tag{19–8}$$

where ΔF_i is one of many possible τ-day changes in the market factor. If we want to simulate m values for the market factor, we need m values for the τ-day change in the market factor. The question is where to get these m values for the τ-day change in the market factor. One place to obtain value changes is to look at historical data—i.e., obtain actual τ-day changes. Another place to get these value changes is to simulate them using the techniques of Monte Carlo simulation.

Historical Simulation Method.   Collect the values of the market factors for a particular historical period and calculate the observed changes in them over the time horizon to be used in the VAR calculation.

If a one-day VAR is to be obtained using the past 101 trading days, each of the market factors will have a vector of observed changes that will be made up of the 100 changes in value of the market factor. For example, consider market factor j today (i.e., $t = 0$), $F(j)_0$. The previous 101 values of market factor j generate 100 changes in market factor j:

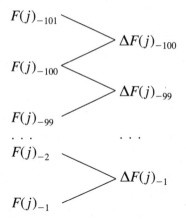

For each of the j market factors, create a vector of alternative values $AF(j)$ by adding each of the values in the vector of observed changes to the current value of the market factor, $F(j)_0$:

$$AF(j)_1 \ = F(j)_0 + \Delta F(j)_{-1}$$
$$AF(j)_2 \ = F(j)_0 + \Delta F(j)_{-2}$$
$$Ú$$
$$AF(j)_{100} = F(j)_0 + \Delta F(j)_{-100}$$

Find the portfolio value V using the current and alternative values for each of the n market factors. Then, calculate the changes in portfolio value between the current value and the alternative values:

Current:

$$F(1)_0, \quad F(2)_0, \quad F(3)_0, \ldots, F(n)_0 \qquad \rightarrow \qquad V_0$$

Alternative:

$$AF(1)_1, \quad AF(2)_1, \quad AF(3)_1, \ldots, AF(n)_1 \qquad \rightarrow \qquad V_1$$

$$AF(1)_2, \quad AF(2)_2, \quad AF(3)_2, \ldots, AF(n)_2 \qquad \rightarrow \qquad V_2$$

$$\ldots \qquad \ldots \qquad \ldots \qquad \ldots$$

$$AF(1)_{100}, AF(2)_{100}, AF(3)_{100}, \ldots, AF(n)_{100} \qquad \rightarrow \qquad V_{100}$$

ΔV_1

ΔV_2

$Ú$

ΔV_{100}

Sort the changes in portfolio value from the lowest value to the highest value and determine VAR based on the desired confidence interval.

Illustration 19–1

Obtaining a Historical Simulation VAR

Our objective is to calculate a one-day, 99 percent confidence-level VAR for a U.S. dollar-denominated portfolio. Let's begin with a simple portfolio containing only one transaction—a US/DM call option.*

As we know from Chapter 11, four market factors impact on the value of this foreign exchange option: spot USD/DM exchange rate, volatility of spot exchange rate, USD interest rates, and DM interest rates. In the interest of simplifying the example and saving space, we will follow only the first two factors—the spot exchange rate and its volatility. (In a real-world application, the other two factors would be included, but, the technique is precisely the same.)

To implement the historical simulation method, we need to collect historical data. Suppose that we collected daily market close values for the spot USD/DM exchange rate and the volatility of the spot exchange rate for the last 101 days. These data are displayed in the first three columns of the following table.

Day	US/DM	Volatility	Change in USD/DM	Change in Volatility
−101	1.4000	0.150		
−100	1.3970	0.149	−0.0030	−0.001
−99	1.3960	0.149	−0.0010	+0.000
−98	1.3973	0.151	+0.0013	+0.002
...	...	...	...	...
−2	1.4015	0.163	+0.0015	+0.005
−1	1.4024	0.162	+0.0007	−0.001

Using the daily data, we can calculate one-day changes in the two factors. (Remember that we are looking for a one-day VAR.) These one-day changes in the two market factors are illustrated in the last two columns of the preceding table.

Using this set of 100 one-day changes, we can simulate 100 values for each of the factors:

	Spot FX Rate	Volatility of Spot FX Rate
Simulated value 1	$FX_0 + \Delta FX_1$	$\sigma_0 + \Delta\sigma_1$
Simulated value 2	$FX_0 + \Delta FX_2$	$\sigma_0 + \Delta\sigma_2$
...	...	...
Simulated value 100	$FX_0 + \Delta FX_{100}$	$\sigma_0 + \Delta\sigma_{100}$

Then we would use these 100 simulated values for the factors in an option pricing model to compute 100 alternative portfolio values.

$$\text{Simulated portfolio value 1} = C(FX_0 + \Delta FX_1, \quad \sigma_0 + \Delta\sigma_1, \quad \ldots)$$
$$\text{Simulated portfolio value 2} = C(FX_0 + \Delta FX_2, \quad \sigma_0 + \Delta\sigma_2, \quad \ldots)$$
$$\ldots \qquad\qquad \ldots$$
$$\text{Simulated portfolio value 100} = C(FX_0 + \Delta FX_{100}, \sigma_0 + \Delta\sigma_{100}, \ldots)$$

Then we compare each of these 100 alternative portfolio values with the current value to generate 100 changes in value of the portfolio.

Current value = \$1.80

Change in USD/DM, ΔFX	Change in Volatility, $\Delta\sigma$	Alternative Value, USD/DM Call	Change from Current Value
−0.0030	−0.001	\$1.75	−\$0.05
−0.0010	+0.000	\$1.73	−\$0.07
+0.0013	+0.002	\$1.69	−\$0.11
...	...	...	...
+0.0015	+0.005	\$1.87	+\$0.07
+0.007	−0.001	\$1.88	+\$0.08

Next we sort the changes from the largest negative change to the largest positive change.

Rank	Change from Current Value
100	−\$0.11
99	−\$0.07
98	−\$0.05
...	...
2	+\$0.07
1	+\$0.08

Given the preceding distribution of value changes, the 99 percent confidence-level VAR is that value for which only 1 percent of the value changes are lower. (In our case where the distribution contains 100 value changes, this means that only one of the value changes will be lower than the 99 percent confidence-level VAR.) In the preceding table, that value would be −$0.07—i.e., the one-day, 99 percent confidence-level VAR for this portfolio is 7 cents.

Now suppose that the portfolio contains two transactions—the US/DM call option and a German bond. As before, let's obtain a one-day, 99 percent confidence-level VAR.

We already have data for the option; we need data for the German bond. The DM value of the bond will be impacted by the DM inter-est rate. But since this is a dollar-denominated portfolio, we also must consider the market factor that will impact on the U.S. dollar value of this bond—the spot USD/DM exchange rate. As we did with the FX option, we collected daily market close values for the spot USD/DM exchange rate and the German interest rate for the last 101 days. We then calculated the one-day changes in these rates. These data are displayed in the first three columns of the following table.

Day	US/DM	German Interest Rate	Change in USD/DM	Change in DM Interest Rate
−100	1.4000	5.250		
−100	1.3970	5.125	−0.0030	−0.125
−99	1.3960	5.125	−0.0010	+0.000
−98	1.3973	5.100	+0.0013	+0.025
...	...	...	...	...
−2	1.4015	4.910	+0.0015	+0.010
−1	1.4024	4.925	+0.0007	+0.015

As we did with the option, we use the two sets of 100 one-day changes to simulate 100 values for the exchange rate and German interest rate and use these 100 simulated values for the factors to simulate 100 values for the German bond. Then we compare each of these 100 alternative portfolio values with the current value to generate 100 changes in value of the German bond. The changes for the value of the USD/DM call option and the German bond are displayed in columns 1 and 2 of the following table.

Change in USD/DM Call	Change in German Bond	Change in Portfolio Value
−$0.05	−$0.03	−$0.08
−$0.07	$0.02	−$0.05
−$0.11	$0.15	+$0.04
...	...	...
$0.07	−$0.12	−$0.05
$0.08	−$0.02	+$0.06

Obtaining a Historical Simulation VAR continued

Shown as column 3 of the preceding table, the changes in the value of the portfolio are simply the sum of the changes in the values of the two transactions that make up the portfolio.

We could sort the changes in the portfolio value from the largest negative change to the largest positive change, as we did for the one-transaction portfolio; or we could simply arrange all of the changes in the value of the portfolio as a histogram.

In the preceding histogram, the 99 percent confidence level would be −$0.05—i.e., the one-day, 99 percent confidence-level VAR for this portfolio is 5 cents.

_____

*The US/DM call option will be valued in U.S. dollars.

For a one-day, 95 percent confidence-level VAR, using the past 101 trading days, the VAR would be the 95th most adverse change in portfolio value.

The pros and cons for the historical simulation method are listed in Table 19–1.

TABLE 19–1   Historical Simulation: Pros and Cons

Pros	*Cons*
• No assumed distributions	• Trends reflected in historical data can distort risk measurement
• Volatility/correlations as they actually occurred	
• Outliers included in price list	• VAR measure sensitive to outliers in data
• Aggregation across markets is straightforward	• Pricing models required for all instruments
• Spreadsheet programmable	• Difficult to conduct sensitivity analyses and stress tests

Monte Carlo Simulation Method.   We find that the easiest way to understand the Monte Carlo simulation method is to think of it as proceeding in four steps:

Step 1—Specify a Probability Distribution for Each Market Factor.   For example, if the value of the portfolio was impacted by the spot USD/DM exchange rate, the volatility of the spot exchange rate, USD interest rates, and DM interest rates, it would be necessary to specify four distributions—one for each of the four relevant market factors.

Step 2—Obtain Estimates of the Parameters for Each of the Distributions Specified in Step 1. And, Obtain Estimates of the Correlation between Pairs of Market Factors.   The most likely place to get these estimates is from historical data.[9] But with the simulation method, the risk manager might also want to specify parameters different from the ones observed historically.

Step 3—Use Monte Carlo Simulation Techniques to Randomly Sample from the Distributions Identified in Steps 1 and 2 to Obtain Simulated Changes in the Market Factors.   Use the distributions in a Monte Carlo simulation to obtain m simulated changes in the n market factors, $S\Delta F(j)_i$, over the time horizon to be used in the VAR calculation:

$$\text{Vector of simulated changes in } F(j)$$

$$S\Delta F(j)_1$$

$$S\Delta F(j)_2$$

$$S\Delta F(j)_3$$

$$\cdots$$

$$S\Delta F(j)_m$$

Step 4—Obtain VAR as in the Historical Simulation Method.   The only difference is that we will replace the historical changes in the market factors with simulated changes.

For each of the market factors, create a vector of alternative values by adding each of the values in the vector of simulated changes to the current value of the market factor, $F(j)_0$:

$$AF(j)_1 = F(j)_0 + S\Delta F(j)_1$$

$$AF(j)_2 = F(j)_0 + S\Delta F(j)_2$$

$$AF(j)_3 = F(j)_0 + S\Delta F(j)_3$$

$$\cdots$$

$$AF(j)_m = F(j)_0 + S\Delta F(j)_m$$

Once this vector of alternative values of the market factors is obtained, calculate the current and alternative values for the portfolio, the changes in the value of the portfolio, and the VAR exactly as in the historical simulation method.

Illustration 19–2

Obtaining a Monte Carlo Simulation VAR

Again consider the simple portfolio containing only one transaction, a US/DM call option. Suppose that we want a one-day, 99 percent confidence-level VAR.

The only difference between this method and the historical simulation method is in the way that we obtain the one-day changes in the factors. In the historical simulation method, we collected historical data and observed historical one-day changes in the factors. In the Monte Carlo simulation method, we simulate them:

Iteration	US/DM	Volatility	Simulated Changes, USD/DM	Simulated Changes, Volatility
100				
99			−0.0030	−0.001
98	*Simulation skips*		−0.0010	+0.000
97	*this step*		+0.0013	+0.002
...	...	...	...	...
2			+0.0015	+0.005
1			−0.0007	−0.001

(Note in the preceding table that there is no reason to simulate the values of the factors. We are not interested in the values, only the one-day changes in values.)

From this point on, the Monte Carlo simulation method is exactly the same as the historical simulation method. Using this set of 100 simulated one-day changes, we can simulate 100 values for each of the factors :

	Spot FX Rate	Volatility of Spot FX Rate
Simulated value 1	$FX_0 + \Delta FX_1$	$\sigma_0 + \Delta\sigma_1$
Simulated value 2	$FX_0 + \Delta FX_2$	$\sigma_0 + \Delta\sigma_2$
...	...	...
Simulated value 100	$FX_0 + \Delta FX_{100}$	$\sigma_0 + \Delta\sigma_{100}$

Then we would use these 100 simulated values for the factors in an option pricing model to compute 100 alternative portfolio values.

Obtaining a Monte Carlo Simulation VAR continued

$$\text{Simulated portfolio value 1} \quad = C(FX_0 + \Delta FX_1, \quad \sigma_0 + \Delta \sigma_1, \ldots)$$
$$\text{Simulated portfolio value 2} \quad = C(FX_0 + \Delta FX_2, \quad \sigma_0 + \Delta \sigma_2, \ldots)$$
$$\ldots \qquad\qquad\qquad\qquad \ldots$$
$$\text{Simulated portfolio value 100} = C(FX_0 + \Delta FX_{100}, \sigma_0 + \Delta \sigma_{100}, \ldots)$$

Then we compare each of these 100 alternative portfolio values with the current value to generate 100 changes in value of the portfolio and then sort the changes from the largest positive change to the largest negative change.

Rank	*Change from Current Value*	
100	−$0.13	Choose a confidence level:
⑨⑨	(−$0.08)	99% in this case
98	−$0.04	
...	...	
2	+$0.10	
1	+$0.12	

Or we could display the 100 changes in the value of the portfolio as a histogram.

Losses greater than -0.08 occur no more than 1% of the time

The more *iterations* in the simulation, the smoother the distribution

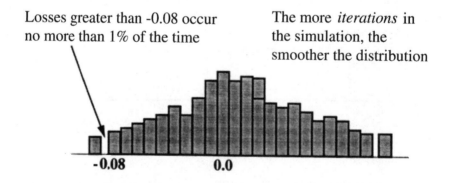

-0.08   **0.0**

In the preceding table or histogram, the one-day, 99 percent confidence-level VAR for this portfolio is 8 cents.

The pros and cons for the Monte Carlo simulation method are listed in Table 19–2.

TABLE 19–2   **Monte Carlo Simulation: Pros and Cons**

Pros	*Cons*
• Specifying distributions builds in more theory • Aggregation across markets is simple and consistent • Ability to do sensitivity analyses and stress tests • Must specify a distribution for each market factor	• Pricing models required for all instruments • Outliers not included in price lists • Simulated prices are one level removed from "real-world" prices • More complex programming

Analytic Variance-Covariance Method.   As you have noted, the historical simulation and Monte Carlo simulation methods are very similar. (They differ only in where you obtain the market factor changes.) The analytic variance-covariance method is very different. As was the case with the Monte Carlo simulation, we find it easiest to think of this process in steps:

Step 1—Specify Distributions and Payoff Profiles.   In the analytic variance-covariance method, the risk manager makes *assumptions* about the shapes of the distributions of the market factors and about the payoff profiles for the transactions in the portfolio.

The best-known and most widely used of the analytic variance-covariance approaches is J. P. Morgan's *RiskMetrics**.[10]

The analytic variance-covariance method assumes that the underlying distributions are *normal* (and that the individual observations are serially independent). With normal distributions, all the historical information is summarized in the means, variances, and covariances of the market factors, so users do not need to keep all the historical data. It also assumes that all the value profiles of the transactions in the portfolio are *linear*. This results in portfolio value changes which are normally distributed. (This assumption leads to a problem with options that we will return to later in this section.)

Step 2—Decompose the Transactions in the Portfolio into Simpler "Standard" Transactions.   The analytic variance-covariance method is based on the idea that the financial instruments in the portfolio can be decomposed—"mapped"—into a set of simpler instruments that are exposed to only one market factor.

---

*RiskMetrics is the registered trademark of Morgan Guaranty Trust Company.

For example, using the techniques one would use to "strip" a Treasury, a two-year U.S. Treasury note can be mapped into a set of zero-coupon bonds, one for each coupon and one for the principal. Each of these zero-coupon bonds is exposed to only one market factor—a specific U.S. zero-coupon interest rate.

Moving to the next level of complexity, a foreign currency–denominated bond can be mapped into a set of foreign currency zero-coupon bonds and a cash foreign exchange amount. Suppose a U.S. portfolio manager holds a two-year deutsche mark–denominated bond with a face value of DM5,000 and a 5.5 percent coupon, paid annually. Suppose further that the one- and two-year deutsche mark zero-coupon rates are 4.45 percent and 5.60 percent, respectively, and that the spot dollar-deutsche mark exchange rate is DM1.45. Figure 19–4 illustrates how this bond can be decomposed into three "standard" transactions: two deutsche mark zero-coupon bonds, the values of which are exposed only to changes in the respective deutsche mark zero-coupon interest rates, and one cash position, the value of which is exposed only to changes in the spot foreign exchange rate.

Step 3—Estimate Variances and Covariances for the Standard Transactions.   In step 2, the risk manager defines a set of instruments that are each exposed to only one market factor. Now, the risk manager must use historical data to estimate the variances and covariances of these instruments.

Step 4—Calculate VAR.   If all the market factors are assumed to be normally distributed and if all the payoff profiles for the transactions in the portfolio are linear, the portfolio—the sum of the individual instruments—can also be assumed to be

FIGURE 19–4   Mapping a German Bond

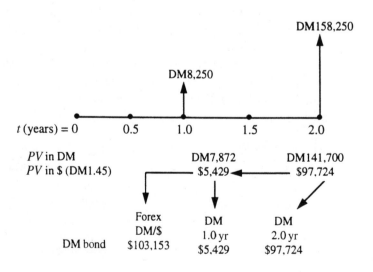

normally distributed. This means that one can calculate the portfolio variance using standard statistical methods, which are reviewed in the following box.

Aside

Analytic Variance-Covariance—General Framework

Use traditional statistics to calculate the standard deviation of a portfolio of securities with normally distributed returns.

Portfolio of normal variables:

$$aX + bY$$

where X and Y are securities whose returns are assumed to be normally distributed, and a

and b are the amounts (i.e., market values of X and Y) contained in the portfolio.

Standard deviation of a portfolio of normal variables:

$$\sigma_P = \sqrt{a^2\sigma_X^2 + b^2\sigma_Y^2 + 2ab\rho_{XY}\sigma_X\sigma_Y}$$

Applying the standard statistical techniques for dealing with portfolios of normally distributed components, VAR can be expressed in terms of the standard deviation of the portfolio:

$$\sigma_P = \sqrt{\alpha_X^2\sigma_X^2 + \alpha_y^2\sigma_Y^2 + 2\alpha_X\alpha_Y\rho_{XY}\sigma_X\sigma_Y} \tag{19–9}$$

where α_j is the home currency present value of the position in market factor j, σ_j^2 is the variance of market factor j, and ρ_{jk} is the correlation coefficient between market factors j and k.

The portfolio VAR is then simply some number of portfolio standard deviations; e.g., 1.65 standard deviations will isolate 5 percent of the area of the distribution in the lower tail.

We decomposed the deutsche mark–denominated bond illustrated in Figure 19–4 into three "standard" transactions—two deutsche mark zero-coupon bonds and one cash position. Hence, the relevant market factors are the spot DM-US$ exchange rate, the one-year deutsche mark zero-coupon interest rate, and the two-year deutsche mark zero-coupon interest rate. Suppose that, using daily historical data, the variance-covariance matrix for the three market factors has been calculated as:

	$/DM	1-Yr DM Zero	2-Yr DM Zero
Dollar/deutsche mark	0.0000185	−0.00000678	−0.00000350
One-year deutsche mark zero	−0.00000678	0.0000250	0.0000161
Two-year deutsche mark zero	−0.00000350	0.0000161	0.0000185

Illustration 19–3

Obtaining an Analytic Variance-Covariance VAR

Let's consider a portfolio made up of five transactions. The home currency of the portfolio is U.S. dollars. Following are the initial and remaining maturities of the five transactions, as well as the face values or notional principals and the current mark-to-market (MTM) values:

Transaction	Initial Maturity	Remaining Maturity	Notional	Current MTM
US$ zero-coupon bond	1 year	1 year	$10,000	$9,440
US$ interest rate swap	3 years	2 years	$1,000,000	$2,243
US$ interest rate swap	2 years	2 years	$1,000,000	$0
German bond	2 years	1.5 years	$103,448	$106,494
US$/DM forward	1 year	1 year	$34,853	$0
Total			$2,148,301	$118,177

Step 1—Specify Distributions and Payoff Profiles

Following RiskMetrics, we assume that all of the distributions are *normal* (and that the individual observations are serially independent). Also following RiskMetrics, we assume that all of the value profiles of the transactions in the portfolio are *linear*.

Step 2—Decompose the Transactions in the Portfolio into Simpler "Standard" Transactions

The mark-to-market values of the five transactions in the portfolio will be affected by United States and German interest rates and the DM/USD exchange rate. The problem is that the instruments are impacted by the *term structures* of interest rates in the United States and Germany, rather than by a single rate. To reflect the term structures, we decided to use four points on the U.S. dollar yield curve and three points on the German deutsche mark yield curve. That is, we will define eight standard instruments:

Spot FX (DM/USD)

Four U.S. dollar, zero-coupon bonds
    Maturities six months, one year, 18 months, and two years

Three DM, zero-coupon bonds
    Maturities six months, one year, and two years

Obtaining an Analytic Variance-Covariance VAR continued

Then we need to decompose each of the five transactions into these eight standard transactions. That is, we need to map the values of the transactions into the eight "buckets," so we need to fill in the following matrix.

	FX DM/$	US$ 0.5 yr	US$ 1.0 yr	US$ 1.5 yr	US$ 2.0 yr	DM 0.5 yr	DM 1.0 yr	DM 2.0 yr
Zero bond								
Swap 1								
Swap 2								
DM bond								
Forward								
Total U.S.$								

Transaction 1—One-Year USD Zero-Coupon Bond. The cash flows for the one-year, USD zero-coupon bond can be illustrated as:

$$\text{1 year U.S. risk-free zero rate} = 5.85\%$$
$$\text{PV of position} = 10,000/\,(1+0.0585/_2)^2 = 9,440$$

The only market factor that impacts on the value of this bond is the one-year USD zero-coupon rate; so the present value of this bond can be mapped into the one-year USD zero-coupon bucket.

	FX DM/$	US$ 0.5 yr	US$ 1.0 yr	US$ 1.5 yr	US$ 2.0 yr	DM 0.5 yr	DM 1.0 yr	DM 2.0 yr
Zero bond			9,440					

Transaction 2—USD Interest Rate Swap— Initial Maturity: Three Years, Remaining Maturity: Two Years.   When it was originated as a three-year swap, the fixed rate was set at 6 percent. For the two years remaining to maturity, the portfolio will receive the 6 percent fixed rate and pay six-month USD LIBOR on the notional amount of $1,000,000, with all payments made on a semiannual basis.

As we demonstrated in Chapter 8, this swap is equivalent to being long a fixed-rate bond and short a floating-rate bond. Consequently, the cash flows could be mapped to the U.S. dollar, zero-coupon bonds as follows:

Var/Cov Buckets	Fixed Cash Flows	PV of Fixed Cash Flows	Floating Cash Flows	PV of Floating Cash Flows	Net Mapped Cash Flows
0.5 years	30,000	29,153	(1,029,040)	(1,000,000)	(970,847)
1.0 years	30,000	28,320	0	0	28,320
1.5 years	30,000	27,508	0	0	27,508
2.0 years	1,030,000	917,261	0	0	917,261

Adding the values from the preceding table to the matrix we are building, we get:

	FX DM/$	US$ 0.5 yr	US$ 1.0 yr	US$ 1.5 yr	US$ 2.0 yr	DM 0.5 yr	DM 1.0 yr	DM 2.0 yr
Swap		(970,847)	28,320	27,508	917,261			

Transaction 3—USD Interest Rate Swap— Initial Maturity: Two Years, Remaining Maturity: Two Years.   The portfolio manager has just booked this swap to close out the swap we designated as Transaction 2. In the Transaction 3 swap, the portfolio pays the at-market swap rate of 5.88 percent and receives six-month USD LIBOR. In a similar fashion to Transaction 2, the cash flows mapped to the U.S. dollar, zero-coupon bonds are:

Var/Cov Buckets	Fixed Cash Flows	PV of Fixed Cash Flows	Floating Cash Flows	PV of Floating Cash Flows	Net Mapped Cash Flows
0.5 year	(29,397)	(29,568)	1,029,040	1,000,000	971,432
1.0 year	(29,397)	(27,751)	0	0	(27,751)
1.5 years	(29,397)	(26,956)	0	0	(26,956)
2.0 years	(1,029,397)	(916,725)	0	0	(916,725)

Transfer the values in the table to the matrix row:

	FX DM/$	US$ 0.5 yr	US$ 1.0 yr	US$ 1.5 yr	US$ 2.0 yr	DM 0.5 yr	DM 1.0 yr	DM 2.0 yr
Swap		971,432	(27,751)	(26,956)	(916,725)			

Transaction 4—18-Month German Bond. This bond had an initial maturity of two years, of which 18 months remain. The bond has a face value of DM150,000 and pays annual coupons at a rate of 5.5 percent. The cash flows for the bond can be illustrated as follows:

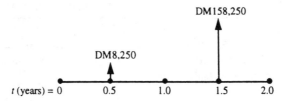

For the USD-denominated portfolio, the value of the German bond could be affected by either (1) changes in German interest rates or (2) changes in the foreign exchange rate.

1. *The riskiness of the bond attributable to the German interest rate*—We need to map the *dollar* values of the cash flows into the available DM interest rate buckets. First let's think about the mapping process itself. We have a German interest rate bucket that corresponds to the six-month cash flow; but, there is no bucket that corresponds to the 18-month DM cash flow. Consequently, this 18-month cash flow must be allocated between the one-year and two-year buckets.* For purposes of this illustration, we have elected to split the DM158,250 equally between the one-year and two-year buckets.

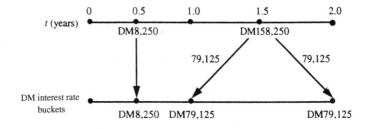

Obtaining an Analytic Variance-Covariance VAR continued

Given that we know which buckets we will put the cash flows in, we now need to calculate the present value of the DM cash flows in the home currency of the portfolio (U.S. dollars) for each of the DM interest rate buckets. With a spot DM/USD exchange rate of 1.45 DM per US$, the resulting present values are:

DM Interest Rate Bucket	DM Zero-Coupon Interest Rate	Present Value of Cash Flow in DM	Present Value of Cash Flow in USD
6 month	4.45%	$DM8,250/(1 + 0.0445/2)^{2*0.5} = DM8,070$	$DM8,070/1.45 = US\$5,566$
1 year	4.75%	$DM79,125/(1 + 0.0475/2)^{2*1.0} = DM75,496$	$DM75,496/1.45 = US\$52,066$
2 years	5.60%	$DM79,125/(1 + 0.0560/2)^{2*2.0} = DM70,850$	$DM70,850/1.45 = US\$48,862$

2. *The riskiness of the bond attributable to the DM/USD exchange rate*—The total value exposed to exchange rate risk is

US$5,566 + US$52,066 + US$48,862 = US$106,494

The "bucketed" cash flows from changes 1 and 2 can be added to the matrix as:

	FX DM/$	US$ 0.5 yr	US$ 1.0 yr	US$ 1.5 yr	US$ 2.0 yr	DM 0.5 yr	DM 1.0 yr	DM 2.0 yr
DM bond	106,494					5,566	52,066	48,862

Transaction 5—One-Year Forward Contract. The portfolio has entered into a forward contract to buy U.S. dollars with DM in one year at a rate of 1.4346 DM per US$. With a notional principal of DM50,000, the transaction can be illustrated as follows:

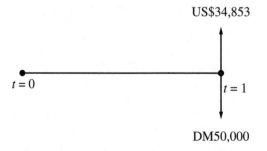

As we discussed in Chapter 4, a forward foreign exchange contract is equivalent to borrowing in one currency and lending in another, plus a long or short foreign currency position (depending on whether the foreign currency is being purchased or sold). The specific forward contract in this portfolio is equivalent to investing US$32,901 for one year at 5.85 percent and borrowing DM47,707 for one year at 4.75 percent:

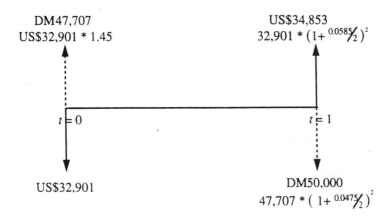

DM47,707
US$32,901 * 1.45

US$34,853
$32,901 * (1 + \frac{0.0585}{2})^2$

$t = 0$

$t = 1$

US$32,901

DM50,000
$47,707 * (1 + \frac{0.0475}{2})^2$

and selling DM47,707 spot (for US$32,901).

The riskiness of the forward contract associated with DM and USD interest rates can be expressed by decomposing the cash flows into positions in US$ and DM one-year, zero-coupon bonds:

	Future Value of Cash flow	*Present Value of Cash Flow in Local Currency*	*Present Value of Cash Flow in USD*
1-year US$: Invest	US$34,853	US$32,901	US$32,901
1-year DM: Borrow	(DM50,000)	(DM47,707)	(US$32,901)

With respect to the foreign exchange rate risk, US$32,901 is exposed.

Obtaining an Analytic Variance-Covariance VAR continued

Adding the "bucketed" cash flows from this one-year forward contract completes the matrix we have been constructing:

	FX DM/$	US$ 0.5 yr	US$ 1.0 yr	US$ 1.5 yr	US$ 2.0 yr	DM 0.5 yr	DM 1.0 yr	DM 2.0 yr
Zero bond			9,440					
Swap 1		(970,847)	28,320	27,508	917,261			
Swap 2		971,432	(27,751)	(26,956)	(916,725)			
DM bond	106,494					5,566	52,066	48,862
Forward	(32,901)		32,901				(32,901)	
Total	73,593	586	42,910	552	537	5,566	19,165	48,862

The values in the row labeled "Total" are simply the (column) sums of the values for the five individual transactions. By doing this summation, the "Total" row represents the decomposition of the portfolio into the eight standard transactions.

From this point on, we will be concerned only with the "Total" row.

Step 3—Estimate Variances and Covariances for the Standard Transactions

Using historical data, we can estimate the variances and covariances for the eight stan-

dard transactions. Using the RiskMetrics convention, we have reported these in terms of volatility and correlation. Also following the RiskMetrics convention, we have scaled up the volatility numbers so that they reflect a 95 percent confidence level—i.e., we multiplied the volatilities by 1.65.

	FX DM/$	US$ 0.5 yr	US$ 1.0 yr	US$ 1.5 yr	US$ 2.0 yr	DM 0.5 yr	DM 1.0 yr	DM 2.0 yr
Volatility	0.71%	1.49%	1.42%	1.31%	1.19%	0.81%	0.83%	0.71%
DM/US$	1	−0.313	−0.312	−0.312	−0.313	−0.541	−0.315	−0.189
US$0.5 yr	−0.313	1	0.996	0.989	0.983	0.704	0.674	0.831
US$1.0 yr	−0.312	0.996	1	0.994	0.988	0.707	0.685	0.827
US$1.5 yr	−0.312	0.989	0.994	1	0.994	0.705	0.667	0.816
US$2.0 yr	−0.313	0.983	0.988	0.994	1	0.702	0.648	0.805
DM0.5 yr	−0.541	0.704	0.707	0.705	0.702	1	0.853	0.635
DM1.0 yr	−0.315	0.674	0.685	0.667	0.648	0.853	1	0.749
DM2.0 yr	−0.189	0.831	0.827	0.816	0.805	0.635	0.749	1

Note: Volatility is 1-day price volatility for 1.65 standard deviations.

Obtaining an Analytic Variance-Covariance VAR continued

Step 4—Calculate VAR

RiskMetrics defines two VAR numbers—*undiversified* and *diversified*.

To calculate the *undiversified* VAR, we ignore the correlation coefficients above and set all of the correlation coefficients to 1.0. (That is, we treat all of the market factors as if they are perfectly positively correlated.) Multiplying each element in the "Total" row by the 95 percent confidence-level volatility of the corresponding standard instrument, we obtain the "position volatility." The *undiversified* VAR of the portfolio is then obtained by applying the standard deviation formula.

Undiversified VAR (No Correlation Benefits)

	FX DM/$	US$ 0.5 yr	US$ 1.0 yr	US$ 1.5 yr	US$ 2.0 yr	DM 0.5 yr	DM 1.0 yr	DM 2.0 yr
Volatility	0.71%	1.49%	1.42%	1.31%	1.19%	0.81%	0.83%	0.71%
Total	73,593	586	42,910	552	537	5,566	19,165	48,862
Position volatility	523	9	609	7	6	45	159	347

Undiversified VAR ($\rho = 1$)

$$\sqrt{(523 + 9 + 609 + 7 + 6 + 45 + 159 + 347)^2} = \text{US\$1,705}$$

To calculate the *diversified* VAR, we use the estimated correlation coefficients. Consequently, the calculation of the standard deviation for the portfolio becomes messier, since the formula will include both volatility and correlation terms:*

Diversified VAR

Volatility	Correlation	
1. FX $= 523$	1. FX/US$ 0.5 yr	$= 73{,}593*586*(-0.313)*0.0071*0.0149$
2. US$0.5 yr $= 9$	2. FX/US$ 1.0 yr	$= 73{,}593*42{,}910*(-0.312)*0.0071*0.0142$
... ...	...	... ...
8. DM 2.0 yr $= 347$	28. DM 1 yr/DM 2 yr	$= 19{,}165*48{,}862*0.749*0.0083*0.0071$
column 1 sum $= x$	column 2 sum $= y$	

Diversified VAR $= \sqrt{x + 2y}$

Diversified VAR $= \text{US\$1,059}$

---

*At this point, you might say, "Why not just set up an 18-month German interest rate bucket?" The problem is that the analytic variance-covariance method is based on defining some *limited number* of standard transactions. Consequently, there will always be some cash flows that do not correspond precisely to a bucket.

For the deutsche mark–denominated bond, the portfolio variance is 349.09; so the standard deviation of the portfolio would be $18.68. A 95 percent, one-day VAR would be $1.65 \times \$18.68 = \$30.82$.

The pros and cons for the analytic variance-covariance method are listed in Table 19–3.

The argument in Table 19–3 that the analytic variance-covariance method "does not provide a reliable risk measure for options" deserves some additional comment. The presence of options in a portfolio results in a nonlinear payoff profile, which violates one of the assumptions of the analytic variance-covariance method. The resulting distribution of portfolio value changes is no longer normally distributed; so the analytic variance-covariance method cannot be applied. However, there are simplifications which permit incorporating options into this method.

The most common approach for incorporating the market risk of option positions in the analytic variance-covariance method is to incorporate a delta-based (i.e., linear) measure of option positions into the mapped cash flows.[11] This method for including options in the analytic method uses an option pricing model to obtain the delta. This hedge ratio is then used to determine the amount of a market factor that must be held to compensate for a small change (usually a one-basis-point move) in the underlying. The present value of the delta-hedge position in the underlying is then mapped into the appropriate cash flow bucket and included in the analytic formula for calculating portfolio variance.

However, a delta-based approach for including options in the analytic variance-covariance VAR calculation does not account for convexity (gamma). Since the option's delta is a linear risk measure *for small changes* in the underlying price, it will result in inaccurate market risk measures for large changes in the price of the underlying—which, by definition, is precisely what VAR is attempting to measure.

Figure 19–5 illustrates the value profile for a long call position. Suppose we measure the delta of the option at the current market price of the underlying (P_0), and use this as the measure of the riskiness of the option for all prices. Figure 19–5 indicates that for large price increases, the delta measure underestimates the increase in the value of the option position; and for large price decreases, the delta measure overestimates the decrease in the value of the option position. Consequently, since VAR is concerned with potential losses, an analytic variance-covariance VAR based on

---

TABLE 19–3   Analytic Variance-Covariance: Pros and Cons

Pros	*Cons*
• No price models required	• Mapping cash flows can become complex
• Data sets available	• Cannot conduct sensitivity analyses
• Off-the-shelf software available	• Does not provide a reliable risk measure for options

FIGURE 19–5

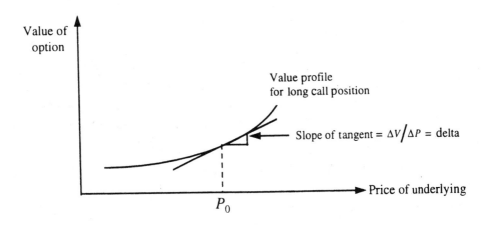

delta will overestimate the riskiness of the long call position. But the bias in an analytic variance-covariance VAR based on delta is not always positive, as it is for a long call position. As summarized in Table 19–4, VARs based on delta will overestimate the risk for long option positions and underestimate the risk for short option positions.[12]

The delta approach can be enhanced by including gamma in the risk measure.[13] Instead of measuring the slope of the option's value curve for a given underlying price, gamma adds an adjustment to compensate for the change in the value curve's slope. As an option pricing model must be used to determine the option's delta, gamma can easily be incorporated. However, since the change in slope or curvature of the option value curve is not constant for different prices of the underlying, the risk measure including gamma will again provide an inaccurate measure of market risk for larger changes in the price of the underlying. Nonetheless, including gamma in the calculation will result in a smaller estimation error for market risk than using delta alone.[14]

TABLE 19–4 Does a Delta-Based Analytic Variance-Covariance VAR Overestimate or Underestimate Riskiness?

Call options	
Long position	Overestimates
Short position	Underestimates
Put options	
Long position	Overestimates
Short position	Underestimates

FIGURE 19–6

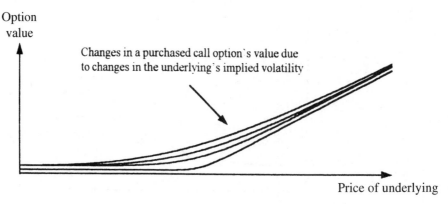

Option
value

Changes in a purchased call option's value due
to changes in the underlying's implied volatility

Price of underlying

Delta-based or delta-gamma–based VARs also do not account for changes in volatility (vega). Figure 19–6 illustrates the fact that delta changes as volatility changes. To include vega in this analytic VAR model, separate buckets measuring the effect of changes in volatility (the volatility of volatility) for specified market factors would have to be included in the variance-covariance matrix. And

---

Risk Management in Practice

"Diversified" versus "Undiversified" VARs

Ziad Zakharia

RiskMetrics draws a distinction between "diversified" VAR and "undiversified" VAR for a given portfolio. The diversified VAR is obtained using the observed correlation coefficients in Equation 19–9, while the undiversified VAR is calculated setting all the correlation coefficients to one.* For example, in Illustration 19–3 the diversified VAR value was $1,059 and the undiversified VAR was $1,705; the portfolio manager obtained a "diversification benefit" of $646, because the market factors were less than perfectly positively correlated.

However, the user is advised to be cautious about the interpretation of diversified and undiversified VARs.

The techniques of RiskMetrics make this distinction between the two VAR values regardless of whether the positions in the underlying standard assets[†] are long or short. However, given the way in which undiversified VAR is defined, a diversification benefit will only be *guaranteed* if all positions are long (or all are short); and only in these instances is it meaningful to talk about diversified and undiversified VARs in the same way that one thinks about diversified and undiversified portfolios.

This result follows from modern portfolio theory where it can be shown that the standard deviation of a portfolio with *positive* weights on all assets is, in general, less than the weighted average of the standard deviations of the individual assets.[‡] In the context of RiskMetrics, since the standard deviation of the portfolio relates to diversified VAR and the weighted average of the standard deviations relates to undiversified VAR,[§] this implies that if the portfolio has *long* positions in all the standard assets, then, in general, the diversified VAR will be less than the undiversified VAR and we can observe the benefits from diversification.

However, if the portfolio has *long* positions in some of the standard assets and *short* positions in others, the relation between diversified and undiversified VARs becomes much less clear.

To illustrate this, consider again the portfolio used in Illustration 19–3, but remove Transaction 3 (the second interest rate swap). The original portfolio had long positions in all eight of the standard assets; thus the new portfolio will have a short position in the 6M USD zero-coupon bond. In such a case, portfolio theory doesn't guarantee that a diversification benefit will be realized (i.e., that the diversified VAR will be less than the undiversified). In this case, the diversified VAR—$3,002—is *larger* than the undiversified VAR—$1,113.

If you work through the calculations, you will note that, without Transaction 3, the portfolio is dominated by the 6M USD and 2Y USD standard assets. Hence, the portfolio can be approximated by a two-standard-asset portfolio, where the portfolio is short the 6M USD zero-coupon bond and long the 2Y USD zero-coupon bond. From portfolio theory, one can show that given two assets (one short and the other long), what we misleadingly term *diversified* VAR will, in general, be *greater* than *undiversified* VAR. Hence, in retrospect, it should come as no surprise to us that the diversified VAR value of $3,002 is greater than the undiversified value of $1,113.

Ziad Zakharia is an associate of CIBC World Markets Financial Products, where he is responsible for financial modeling and the development of educational software for interest rate derivatives, standard options, exotic options, yield-curve analytics, value-at-risk, and credit risk. Mr. Zakharia received his M.S. from M.I.T. and his B.S. from Loyola Marymount University.

*The VAR value of a portfolio is obtained from the portfolio variance. For example, at the 95 percent confidence level, the relation is VAR = 1.65 × (standard deviation).

[†]Standard assets are basically the market factors.

[‡]Elton and Gruber (1995).

[§]See footnote *.

delta-based or delta–gamma-based VAR measures do not account for time decay (theta).[15] However, this is a factor only if the VAR is measured for extended time horizons.

Comparison of Calculated VARs

Comparison of VARs Generated by Different Methods.   Not surprisingly, the three methods described above produce different VAR measures. However, the differences are not necessarily large.

The reason why the differences can be small is that, in truth, the three methods end up using similar data: The historical simulation method collects actual τ-day changes in the market factors using historical data drawn from the last p trading days. The analytic variance-covariance model assumes that all of the market factors are normally distributed; but the parameters of the distributions—variances, and covariances—are obtained using historical data drawn from the last p trading days. The Monte Carlo simulation method simulates the τ-day changes in the market factors, based on specified distributions for the market factors; but in many cases the distributions are assumed to be normal (or lognormal), and the parameters of the distributions are in many cases obtained using historical data drawn from the last p trading days.

Comparisons of Portfolios with Linear Payoff Profiles.   In addition to the preceding, if the portfolio is made up of transactions that have linear payoff profiles, the bias in the analytic variance-covariance method will not be present. James Jordan and Robert Mackay (1997) illustrated this by looking at a portfolio of equities. (The payoff profile for an equity is linear with respect to the price of the underlying equity.) Table 19–5 provides the Jordan and Mackay VAR calculations for a portfolio of five equities. In this case, the differences between the VARs obtained from the analytic variance-covariance method and those obtained from either the historical simulation or the Monte Carlo simulation methods are small.

While the Jordan-Mackay results are informative, one might wonder about their robustness, given that Jordan and Mackay only looked at five portfolios. Darryll

TABLE 19–5   Jordan-Mackay: VAR for Portfolio of Equities (95% Confidence Level)

	Daily	Weekly	Monthly
Historical simulation	$16,142	$33,600	$54,400
Monte Carlo simulation	$16,268	$30,272	$62,427
Analytic variance-covariance	$15,642	$34,236	$54,930

Adapted from Tables 8.3, 8.6, and 8.12 of Jordan and Mackay (1997).

Hendricks (1996) provided that robustness when he compared VARs obtained from the historical simulation method with those obtained using the analytic variance-covariance method.

Hendricks examined 12 VAR measures.

- He calculated VARs for four historical simulation approaches, using the last 125, 250, 500, and 1,250 days.
- He calculated VARs for eight analytic variance-covariance models—of two different types:

  He looked at five analytic variance-covariance models in which the variance-covariance matrix was estimated by equally weighting the historical observations. (This is the approach that was implicitly described in our discussion of the analytic variance-covariance method.) He examined VARs using the past 50, 125, 250, 500, and 1,250 days.

  He looked at three analytic variance-covariance models in which the variance-covariance matrix was estimated by exponentially weighting the historical observations.[16] Exponential weighting has the effect of giving more weight to the more recent observations. (This is the approach actually employed in RiskMetrics.)

  For each of the 12 VAR measures, he calculated one-day VARs for 1,000 randomly selected FX portfolios for 3,005 days.[17]

Like Jordan and Mackay, Hendricks found no significant difference between 95 percent confidence-level VARs obtained using the historical simulation method and those obtained using the analytic variance-covariance method. However, at the 99 percent confidence-level, the VARs obtained using the historical simulation method were larger than those obtained using the analytic variance-covariance method. The reason for this is that the historical simulation method is more sensitive to outliers in the data. (Look again at Table 19–1.)

While Hendricks found that historical simulation VARs are very similar to analytic variance-covariance VARs, he also found that there is considerable variation of the VARs calculated on a given day versus the mean. Table 19–6 indicates that 30–50 percent differences between measures on a given date are not uncommon.

We also examined the VARs generated by different calculation methods by using the Value at Risk Educational Software developed by the CIBC World Markets School of Financial Products.

To further demonstrate that the VARs obtained from the historical simulation, Monte Carlo simulation, and analytic variance-covariance methods can be very similar, we considered a portfolio composed of three instruments with linear (or

TABLE 19–6   Hendricks Comparisons

	Root-Mean-Squared Relative Bias (95% VAR)
Historical Simulation	
125 days	0.14
500 days	0.13
Analytic Variance-Covariance	
Equally weighted	
125 days	0.10
500 days	0.13
Exponentially weighted	
$\lambda = 0.94$	0.18
$\lambda = 0.99$	0.05

nearly linear) payoff profiles: two interest rate swaps and one DM/US$ forward contract.

Interest rate swap 1:	3 years, $1million,	Pay fixed at 7.51%	MTM: ($39,343)
Interest rate swap 2:	1 year, $1 million	Pay fixed at 7.00%	MTM: ($13,272)
DM/US$ forward:	3 years, DM1.8million	Sell DM at 1.56	MTM: ($88,807)
			Total MTM: ($141,422)

The data used for the historical simulation and to estimate the parameters for the Monte Carlo simulation and analytic variance-covariance methods were obtained from the period 12/16/94 to 11/14/96—500 days. The resulting VARs are displayed in Table 19–7.

TABLE 19–7   Comparison of VARs Computed by Different Methods—Linear Portfolio

	Confidence Level		
	99%	*95%*	*90%*
Historical simulation	18,051	11,199	7,543
Monte Carlo simulation*	15,292	9,934	7,729
Analytic variance-covariance	15,240	10,778	8,386

*Number of iterations = 600.

As was the case with the Hendricks results, at the 99 percent confidence level, the VARs obtained using the historical simulation method are larger than those obtained from the other methods. To make sure that this was, in fact, due to outliers in the data set, we computed 95 percent and 90 percent confidence level VARs. As would be expected, the VARs computed using the historical simulation method became more similar to those computed by the other two methods as the confidence level gets smaller (thereby reducing the impact of the outliers).

Absent the effect of the outliers, the differences between the three different methods are small. For example, at the 95 percent confidence level, the percentage difference between the historical simulation and Monte Carlo simulation VARs is 11 percent; the percentage difference between the historical simulation and analytic variance covariance VARs is 4 percent; and the percentage difference between the Monte Carlo simulation and analytic variance covariance VARs is 8 percent.

Comparisons of Portfolios with Nonlinear Payoff Profiles. VARs calculated using the three different methods have the potential to be much more different when the portfolios contain options. As we noted above, the analytic method usually estimates the market risk of option positions based on delta (or delta and gamma). Using only delta to measure the market risk of option positions will result in inaccurate risk estimates for large changes in the price of the underlying. The historic and simulation methods can account for potential changes in all the market factors that affect the price of an option, and the revaluation process allows the market risk of options to be more accurately measured for larger estimated changes in market factors. Therefore, analytic VAR measures can differ substantially from historic and simulation VAR measures for portfolios with substantial option positions.

To illustrate instances in which the VARs generated by different calculation methods can differ, we again used the CIBC World Markets School of Financial Products' Value at Risk Educational Software.

We formed two different nonlinear portfolios—one "weakly nonlinear" and the other "strongly nonlinear."

Weakly Nonlinear Portfolio: To the two-swap and one FX forward portfolio described above, we added an interest rate option and a foreign exchange option:

Interest rate option:	3 years	$1 million	Buy cap at 6.00%	MTM: $9,159
FX option:	3 years	DM180,000	Sell DM at $X = 1.56$	MTM: ($10,817)

With the inclusion of the two options, the MTM changes only slightly—from ($141,422) to ($143,079).

Strongly Nonlinear Portfolio: The strongly nonlinear portfolio contains only the options that we included in the weakly nonlinear portfolio. And we made two changes with respect to the foreign exchange option: (1) we increased the notional principal by a factor of 10, and (2) we bought, rather than sold, the option. (These changes and the resulting change in the mark-to-market of the option are highlighted.)

Interest rate option:	3 years	$1 million	Buy cap at 6.00%	MTM: $ 9,159
FX option:	3 years	DM **1,800,000**	**Buy** DM at $X = 1.56$	MTM: **$108,168**
				Total MTM: $117,327

As before, the data used for the historical simulation and to estimate the parameters for the Monte Carlo simulation and analytic variance-covariance methods were obtained from the period 12/16/94 to 11/14/96—500 days. The resulting VARs are displayed in Table 19–8.

In the case of the weakly nonlinear portfolio, the VARs obtained from the analytic variance-covariance method are quite similar to those obtained using the historical simulation and Monte Carlo simulation methods. The percentage difference between the historical simulation and Monte Carlo simulation VARs is 17 percent; the percentage difference between the historical simulation and analytic variance-covariance (delta only) VARs is 6 percent; and the percentage difference between the Monte Carlo simulation and analytic variance covariance (delta only) VARs is 14 percent.

However, in the case of the strongly nonlinear portfolio, the VARs obtained from the analytic variance-covariance method are quite different from those obtained using the historical simulation and Monte Carlo simulation methods. The percentage difference between the historical simulation and Monte Carlo simulation VARs is 7 percent; but the percentage difference between the historical simulation and analytic variance-covariance (delta only) VARs is 58 percent and that between the Monte Carlo simulation and analytic variance-covariance (delta only) VARs is 50 percent. And, the inclusion of a "gamma correction" doesn't help very

TABLE 19–8   Comparison of VARs Computed by Different Methods—Nonlinear Portfolios
(All 95% Confidence-Level VARs)

	Nonlinearity	
	Weak	*Strong*
Historical simulation	12,749	8,025
Monte Carlo simulation	10,579	8,602
Analytic variance-covariance (delta only)	12,010	12,646
Delta-gamma VAR	12,017	12,464

much. The percentage differences between the historical simulation VAR and the "delta-gamma VAR" is 55 percent (compared with 58 percent) and that between the Monte Carlo simulation VAR and the delta-gamma VAR is 48 percent (compared with 50 percent).

The preceding illustration shows that the degree to which analytic variance-covariance VARs differ from historical simulation and Monte Carlo simulation VARs depends on the "degree of nonlinearity" of the portfolio, which itself depends on two things:

> *Size*—relative magnitude of the linear and nonlinear components of the portfolio. In our weakly nonlinear portfolio the MTM for the nonlinear components was only about 1 percent of the MTM value of the linear components. However, for our strongly nonlinear portfolio the nonlinear components represented 100 percent of the portfolio.
>
> *Sign*—whether or not the option positions "cancel out." In our weakly nonlinear portfolio one option position was long and the other was short; but in our strongly nonlinear portfolio both option positions were long.

Comparison of VARs Generated by the Same Method.   Christopher Marshall and Michael Siegel (1996) did not look at different methods but instead looked at real-world implementations of a single method. Marshall and Siegel focused on J. P. Morgan's RiskMetrics. When they undertook their study in 1995, 17 vendors were known to have incorporated RiskMetrics into their systems. All 17 were asked to participate in the study; 11 agreed to participate.[18]

The 11 vendors were given seven identical portfolios of financial instruments:

- FX forwards (five positions)
- Money market deposits (three positions)
- Forward rate agreements (five positions)
- Government bonds (14 positions)
- Interest rate swaps (eight positions)
- FX options (five positions)
- Interest rate caps and floors (five positions)

The vendors were asked to produce one-day, 95 percent confidence level VARs in U.S. dollars as of 10:30 A.M. EST, September 27, 1995. To minimize differences based on data, the vendors were given identical RiskMetrics data sets.

The results of the Marshall-Siegel survey are presented in Table 19–9.[19] It is interesting to note that no two of the VARs produced by the different vendors matched.

TABLE 19–9   **Vendors' Results**

Implementation	Foreign Exchange Forwards	Money Market Deposits	Forward Rate Agreements	Government Bonds	Interest Rate Swaps	Foreign Exchange Options	Interest Rate Caps and Floors
A	N/A	498,425	N/A	N/A	438,680	N/A	N/A
B	426,288	673,101	426,288	3,808,750	315,177	889,609	416,722
C	N/A	N/A	N/A	5,490,568	N/A	N/A	N/A
D	437,379	668,690	437,379	3,802,820	303,502	N/A	N/A
E	426,000	673,000	426,000	3,754,000	307,000	943,000	N/A
F	425,677	673,034	425,677	3,824,799	425,677	N/A	N/A
G	425,189	671,626	425,189	3,809,410	425,189	501,811	616,145
H	N/A	671,060	N/A	4,823,042	N/A	N/A	N/A
J	425,363	639,968	425,363	3,806,757	425,363	718,846	416,523

Table 19–10 provides more insight about the degree to which the VARs differed. As would be expected, as the portfolios become more complex, the differences between the VARs increased.

Marshall and Siegel proposed a number of reasons for the differences:

- Different vendors used different mapping algorithms for the transactions. To see how this might happen, look back at our mapping of the German bond in Illustration 19–3. We decided to split the 18-month cash flow equally between the one-year and two-year interest rate risk buckets. Had we allocated more of the cash flow to the two-year DM interest rate bucket, the VAR for the bond would have increased (and vice versa).
- Different vendors employed different methods for interpolating the term structures.

TABLE 19–10   **Comparison of One-Day VAR Results**

Portfolio	Mean	Median	Standard Deviation	Standard Dev/Median
FX forwards	427,649	425,839	4,784	1%
Money market deposits	646,113	671,343	60,720	9%
Forward rate agreements	78,856	78,856	7,534	10%
Government bonds	4,140,018	3,809,080	652,762	17%
Interest rate swaps	306,663	311,089	66,648	21%
FX options	763,317	804,228	198,829	25%
Interest rate caps and floors	483,130	416,722	115,194	28%

- Different vendors used different conventions—e.g., day count, valuation date, settlement date, reset date, and holidays.

Choosing among the Methods

The inevitable question is: Which method is best? The answer—also inevitable—is: It depends.

The method utilized should be determined by the composition of the portfolio and the time horizon for the VAR measure. Earlier we noted that the degree to which analytic variance-covariance VARs differ from historical simulation and Monte Carlo simulation VARs depends on the degree of nonlinearity of the portfolio, which itself depends on (1) size, the relative magnitude of the linear and nonlinear components of the portfolio, and (2) sign, whether or not the option positions cancel out. Consequently, it appears that for one-day VARs for portfolios that are weakly nonlinear, the analytic variance-covariance method may well be the best choice. The analytic variance-covariance method is simple, in the sense that it does not require pricing models. Perhaps even more important is that the necessary data are available—J. P. Morgan provides its *RiskMetrics* data on its Internet web site (*www.jpmorgan.com*) at no charge. And as indicated above, a number of software vendors support the analytic variance-covariance method.[20]

If the VAR is for a longer time horizon or if the payoff profile for the portfolio is strongly nonlinear, the historical simulation or Monte Carlo simulation methods may be more appropriate.

The historical simulation method is conceptually simple. And since pricing models for financial products are now readily available as add-ins to a spreadsheet program, it is also easy to implement. However, a significant problem with the historical simulation method is that stress testing and sensitivity analysis are difficult to do.

As we will discuss in the next section, stress testing and sensitivity analysis are desirable—and may become necessary. Consequently, the Monte Carlo simulation method is the most attractive. However, the problem is the implementation of a full Monte Carlo simulation method. In the simulations, you would simulate movements by yield curves, rather than individual interest rates. In a full Monte Carlo, the simulation must be done so that there are no arbitrage opportunities—either on the yield curve for currency X or between the yield curves for currencies X and Y. The result is that a full Monte Carlo simulation model is very complex and the run time for such a model can get very long.

Given the merits of the Monte Carlo simulation method, researchers are turning their attention to ways of having a Monte Carlo simulation run faster or ways of approximating the accuracy of a full Monte Carlo simulation with some simpler technique.

Risk Management in Practice

The Trade-off: Accuracy versus Computational Time

Matthew Pritsker

Good risk management practice requires that VAR figures are both reasonably accurate and available on a timely enough basis to actively manage the firm's risk. This will typically involve a trade-off, because the most accurate methods for computing VAR often require the most time to compute. In a recent article*, I examined the trade-off between VAR accuracy and computational time when calculating VARs for portfolios of European exercise foreign exchange options.

Computational speed and accuracy depend on the distribution assumption for the risk factors and on the method used to reprice the portfolio. I examined six methods of computing VAR:

- The first was the standard *delta* method. This method, described earlier in this volume as part of the discussion on the analytic variance-covariance method, assumes the risk factors are normally distributed and approximates changes in portfolio value as a linear function of the risk factors. This setup produces analytical expressions for VAR, and is hence very fast to compute. However, its linear approximation may not adequately capture the nonlinearities in option portfolios.

- The second method considered was a *full Monte Carlo* method, which uses exact repricing in conjunction with simulation of the future risk factors. Because this method uses exact repricing, it is likely to be the most accurate, but also the most time consuming.

In addition to these, three delta-gamma methods were examined. All of these methods replace the first-order approximation to nonlinearity used in the delta method with a Taylor series expansion that is second order in terms of changes in market factors and first order in terms of the time horizon.

- The *delta-gamma-delta* method employs the additional distributional assumption that the portfolio changes using the second-order Taylor series expansion are normally distributed. This assumption is not correct, because the distribution of the second-order term follows a chi-squared distribution. However, this assumption makes computation of VAR in this method analytically tractable, as in the delta method.

- The *delta-gamma-minimization* method assumes the factors are distributed normally and computes VAR by solving for factors that generate the greatest loss in portfolio value over a constraint set whose size is based on the VAR confidence level. This method, while not analytic, is fairly straightforward to compute, and has the added benefit of generating factor realizations that constitute worst-case scenarios. However, for reasons too complicated to explain here, this method has a very strong tendency to overstate VAR.

- The *delta-gamma Monte Carlo* method involves the sampling of future risk factors, as in the full Monte Carlo approach. The portfolio value change for each sample is then computed using the second-order Taylor series expansion. This is likely to be more time consuming than the other delta-gamma methods, but also makes fewer unrealistic distributional assumptions.

One property of the delta and delta-gamma methods is that they depend on local approximations (i.e., Taylor series) whose errors increase in the size of the risk factor realizations. This is an undesirable feature of these approximation methods because it is the large factor realizations that are probably the most important for VAR computation and are probably of most concern to risk managers.

One method for improving on the local approximation methods used in the delta and delta-gamma methods is to compute VAR using a "grid" Monte Carlo method. This involves repricing the portfolio exactly on the nodes of a grid of factor value realizations, and then repricing for factor realizations that fall between the nodes by using linear interpolation. Market factor changes are then generated as in the *full Monte Carlo* method. The advantage of the grid approach is that it uses an approximation method whose errors depend on the mesh of the grid and the roughness of the pricing functions, but not on the size of the factor realizations. The disadvantage of this approach is that its computational demands grow exponentially in the number of risk factors per instrument. Therefore, I considered the following modification of this approach:

- The *modified-grid Monte Carlo* method is similar to the grid method except that the effects of only those factors that involve the most severe nonlinearities are modeled on a grid; the other factors are modeled using a first-order Taylor series. This keeps the grid from growing too large.

Based on an analysis of 500 randomly chosen portfolios over a VAR time horizon of one day, the ranking of these methods on the basis of accuracy alone was as follows:

Most accurate	Full Monte Carlo
	Delta-gamma Monte Carlo
	Modified-grid Monte Carlo
	Delta-gamma-delta
	Delta
Least accurate	Delta-gamma-minimization

The Trade-off: Accuracy versus Computational Time continued

With respect to computations, I chose a rough yardstick by which one could compare the computational requirements of the different models. Specifically, I differentiated between "complex" computations (e.g., computing the price, delta, or gamma of a derivative instrument) and "simple" computations (e.g., linear interpolation or computing VAR using inputs from complex computations). For example, if the portfolio contains 3,000 instruments—where 1,000 are sensitive to a single factor, 1,000 are sensitive to two factors, and 1,000 are sensitive to three factors—and if the Monte Carlo simulations were based on 300 draws, the number of complex and simple computations required to compute the VAR for the portfolio using the six different methods are as follows:

Method	Number of Complex Computations	Number of Simple Computations
Delta	6,000	1
DGD	23,000	1
DGMin	23,000	1
DGMC	23,000	300
ModGridMC	33,000	300
FullMC	900,000	0

SOURCE: Pritsker (1997), Table 2.

When I examined accuracy and computational time together, two of the methods—delta-gamma-minimization and modified-grid Monte Carlo—were strictly dominated by one or more of the others. The remaining four involve trade-offs between accuracy and time. Based on the rate that I am willing to trade off accuracy for computational time, I believe that the delta-gamma Monte Carlo method had the best performance for the portfolios I examined. However, a firm's "best" method will depend on types of instruments in its portfolio, its time horizon for the VAR computation, and the rate at which it is willing to trade off VAR accuracy against the computational burdens involved in computing VAR.

Matthew Pritsker is an economist at the Board of Governors of the Federal Reserve System where he does research on risk measurement and management. The views expressed here are those of the author, and do not necessarily represent the views of the Board of Governors of the Federal Reserve System or other members of its staff.
*Pritsker (1997).

The Users

The VAR concept is being adopted by dealers and end users and has been embraced by the regulatory community. However, questions still remain about the appropriateness of the tool. To see why VAR may or may not be an appropriate measure for different firms, remember that the VAR concept is based on valuation of the *current portfolio*. Figure 19–7 summarizes the arguments about the kind of firm that will find VAR more or less useful.

The value of some firms is closely related to the current value of their assets. In Figure 19–7, we have proposed such a firm—Acme Securities. The VAR concept is very relevant to firms that look like Acme Securities, which is concerned with managing the volatility of its current asset value.

The value of other firms depends on research and/or investment opportunities—growth options. The value of a firm with significant growth options is tied less closely to the market value of the current portfolio and more closely to the manner in which the firm manages these options. A good example of a company whose value is determined primarily by growth options is a pharmaceutical firm—where research and development investments can be regarded as option premiums. Consequently, in Figure 19–7, the firm we have put on the other end of the spectrum is Acme Pharmaceuticals.[21] The VAR concept is much less relevant to firms that look like Acme Pharmaceuticals, which is more concerned with managing the volatility of its cash flows so it can effectively manage its growth options—exercising them

---

FIGURE 19–7 Applicability of VAR

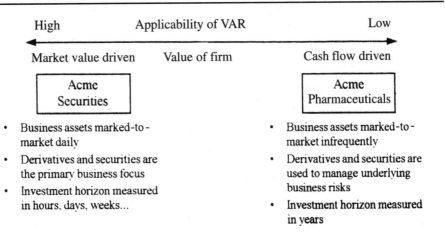

when optimal. (In Chapter 21, we will return to this topic and will describe a cash flow analogue to VAR that we refer to as *cash flow sensitivity analyses.*)

Donald Lessard, a professor of finance at the Sloan School at M.I.T., made this point more elegantly when he noted that:

> VAR appears to be a good system for controlling/allocating capital to cover trading positions. However, it is not a complete methodology for non-financial or less-trading oriented firms. The problem is how to compute the capital at risk associated with economic/operating exposures.... A key difference between financial and non-financial firms is that the former have few ... "natural positions" arising from their business operations and most of these can not be readily marked to market ... VAR works best for more ... liquid positions. Therefore a non-trading entity with longer-term exposures ... might find another method more appropriate for capitalizing its total risk.[22]

With this perspective in mind, let's look at the use of VAR by the participants in the risk management market.

Derivatives Dealers and Other Financial Institutions.   Derivatives dealers and other financial institutions are the real-world "Acme Securities." Data on the use and/or reporting of VAR by dealers and other financial institutions are summarized in Table 19–11.

In a survey by the Group of Thirty's global derivatives project in 1993, 30 percent of dealers said they were using a VAR-like measure of market risk.[23] In the follow-up survey in 1994, 43 percent of dealers reported that they were using some form of VAR measure and 37 percent indicated that they planned to implement VAR by the end of 1995.[24] If we can believe this survey, at least 80 percent of dealers are using VAR as part of their market risk management and governance process.

TABLE 19–11   The Use of VAR by Derivatives Dealers and Other Large Financial Institutions

	1993	*1994*	*1995*
Percentage of Derivatives Dealers Using VAR			
Group of Thirty Global Derivatives Project			
1993 survey	30%		
1994 Follow-up survey—actual		43%	
1994 Follow-up survey—actual plus planned			80%
Percentage of International Banks and Security Firms That Disclosed VAR Data			
BIS/ISOCO Review of Annual Reports			
1995 report	5%	23%	
1996 report			46%

In November 1995, an official review of the annual reports of 67 internationally active banks and 12 securities firms from the Group of 10 countries, carried out by the Basle Committee on Banking Supervision and the technical committee of the International Organization of Securities Commissions,[25] showed that in 1993 only four firms (all U.S. banks) disclosed VAR data; by 1994, this number had risen to 18 firms (all banks). An updated survey was released in November 1996 which indicated that the number of firms disclosing VAR data had risen to 36 (still all banks).

End Users—Institutional Investors. Institutional investors are another real-world example of firms that look like Acme Securities in Figure 19–7. A survey of pension funds' risk management practices by the New York University Stern School of Business asked funds about the techniques they used to assess risk.[26] Sixty percent said they used VAR measures.[27]

End Users—Nonfinancial Corporations. To the best of our knowledge, the first nonfinancial corporations to report VAR measures were British Petroleum (BP) and Mobil Oil Corporation, both of which began reporting VAR in their 1994 annual reports.

In the context of Figure 19–7, British Petroleum looks like *both* Acme Securities *and* Acme Pharmaceuticals. BP trades a portfolio of interest rate, foreign exchange rate, and oil derivatives for profit—like Acme Securities. However, BP also uses interest rate, foreign exchange rate, and oil derivatives to manage the interest rate, foreign exchange rate, and oil price risks in its core business—like Acme Pharmaceuticals. Consequently, BP reports its derivatives positions under two headings—trading and risk management.

Risk Management in Practice

Using Derivatives at British Petroleum

R. K. Hinkley

BP Finance was created in 1985. It coincided with the rapid evolution of the financial marketplace that occurred in the late eighties, notably the development of derivative instruments. BP established its treasury as a profit center: as well as managing the company's natural exposures, it was expected to trade foreign exchange and interest rate products with the intent of contributing to the bottom-line profit. While this approach may not suit many companies, it was a natural evolution for one which was already trading oil and its products. By being an active trader, the company gained ancillary advantages in terms of information flow and transaction execution, which enhanced the management of its considerable natural flows, in addition to the direct contribution made. From the outset, BP Finance established an explicit control environment, consistent with the best practices employed by financial institutions.

BP Finance uses derivatives for a variety of purposes, some related to the delivery of a trading profit, at other times to satisfy the Group's risk management needs. This requires careful recording and monitoring of transactions to ensure that they are consistent with management's intentions. The management of the *trading* activity is, in many respects, the most straightforward. BP Finance's Dealing Rooms in London and Melbourne can trade foreign currency and/or interest rate products—forwards, futures, and options—within defined exposure limits. Whereas originally they were controlled in terms of the outright transaction size, value-at-risk (VAR) has become the measurement standard, in line with the development of market thinking. Activity has historically been focused on the major traded currencies, but is being extended into those of emerging countries, particularly those in which BP may be represented through its primary businesses.

Managing BP's structural financial risks has a number of facets, but broadly the activity can be divided into two categories:

- The hedging of the net long-term financial exposure of the BP Group
- Procurement of foreign currencies and/or the setting of interest expense defined by BP's cash flows

The former derives from the analysis of the company's long-term position (which will be described in Chapter 21 of this text). From that analysis, and as part of a broader financial strategy, policies have been defined which match the structure of the Group's financial liabilities to its assets. Thus notwithstanding that BP is a British company, its borrowing baseline is set in U.S. dollars. And even though its assets are long-lived, their effective duration is much shorter. Hence, the Group has a baseline for its interest rate expense of 65 percent floating: 35 percent fixed, with the fixed element being spread over a 1–10-year horizon. BP is an extensive user of foreign currency and interest rate swaps to decouple the sourcing of its borrowing from the management of financial exposures. Given its status as a profit center, BP Finance has some limited discretion to add value through the management of the associated transactions, but the baseline set by the financial policies establishes a control reference against which performance is continuously measured.

Having set such a reference for the long-term exposure of the Group, policies have also been established to govern the handling of ongoing cash flows. These may be foreign currency requirements created by BP's business units or foreign currency and interest rate setting which arises at the corporate level. A good example is the foreign currency flows which arise from BP's oil production in the United Kingdom. The need to meet outlays for operating expenses, capital expenditures, and taxes requires some U.S. dollars to be converted to sterling. Typically, these flows would be managed over a one-year horizon. The business units involved are obliged to effect these transactions with BP Finance at rates defined by an agreed "template." But consistently with the establishment of BP Finance as a profit center it has discretion to effect the transactions with the market in the way it judges most appropriate. For example, if sterling is perceived to be atypically strong, it will choose to protect itself against an extreme downsize through the use of out-of-the money options, but leave open the possibility of upside should sterling weaken. Conversely, if sterling is weak, it will lock rates through the use of forwards. And in the intermediate zone, cylinders will be used.

BP's approach to managing its treasury has brought a number of advantages:

- It has a professional interface with the market, providing access to new opportunities and timely information on market movements.
- Through the definition of a baseline for each program, the Group can explicitly separate the use of derivatives for profit making from their use in managing structural exposures.
- There is an incentive to add value, both through trading and through efficient execution of transactions associated with risk management.
- There is a transparent basis for control and performance review.

BP also ensures that its use of financial instruments is fully disclosed to shareholders. The table below is extracted from its Annual Report and Accounts for 1996. It summarizes the activity of BP Finance, and its commodities trading arm, Oil Trading International. It is supported by comprehensive notes which describe individual programs.

THE BRITISH PETROLEUM COMPANY p.l.c. AND SUBSIDIARIES

NOTES TO FINANCIAL STATEMENTS (Continued)

Note 24—Derivative financial instruments (continued)

The following table shows a statistically based assessment of market risk, i.e., of exposures to possible future changes in market values over a 24-hour period, under "assessed market risk."

With regard to credit risk, the Group may be exposed to loss in the event of nonperformance by a counterparty. The Group controls credit risk by entering into derivative contracts only with highly credit rated counterparties and through credit approvals, limits, and monitoring procedures and does not usually require collateral or other security. The Group has not experienced material nonperformance by any counterparty.

The table shows the fair value of the asset or liability created by derivatives. This represents the market value at the balance sheet date. Credit exposure at December 31 is represented by the column "Fair value asset."

The table also shows the net carrying amount of the asset or liability created by derivatives. This amount represents the net book value, i.e., market value when acquired or later marked-to-market.

	Gross contract amount	Assessed market risk	Fair value asset ($ million)	Fair value liability	Net carrying amount asset (liability)
At December 31, 1996					
Risk management					
Interest rate contracts ...	3,349	n/a	34	(129)	(37)
Foreign exchange contracts	5,677	n/a	339	(59)	100
Oil price contracts	2,935	n/a	11	(39)	(28)
Trading					
Interest rate contracts ...	130	—	—	—	—
Foreign exchange contracts	2,852	—	24	(19)	5
Oil price contracts	1,692	(1)	70	(68)	2
At December 31, 1995					
Risk management					
Interest rate contracts ...	3,967	n/a	109	(184)	(49)
Foreign exchange contracts	6,018	n/a	278	(107)	86
Oil price contracts	2,212	n/a	133	(148)	(15)
Trading					
Interest rate contracts ...	413	—	—	—	—
Foreign exchange contracts	2,156	(2)	—	(1)	(1)
Oil price contracts	1,095	(1)	102	(97)	5

n/a = not applicable

Using Derivatives at British Petroleum continued

In summary, BP has been an active user of derivatives over many years, tailoring their use appropriately to a variety of purposes. Considerable value has been created for shareholders as a result.

R. K. Hinkley is currently BP's deputy group treasurer. Prior to that, he served in a number of planning, control, and finance posts, including a spell as corporate treasurer for BP Australia during 1988–90 and head of BP's Strategy Team. Before joining British Petroleum, Dr. Hinkley was a member of HM Treasury from 1972 to 1981.

In the table in the preceding box, the column labeled "Assessed Market Risk" is BP's VAR measure.[28] Note that BP reports a VAR measure only for derivatives used for trading—i.e., for the Acme Securities–like portion of its business. This is consistent with our argument that the VAR concept is much less relevant to firms that look like Acme Pharmaceuticals. And, practically, there is no way to really measure the risk for the Acme Pharmaceuticals–like portion of the business, because the derivative positions are hedging cash flows that have not yet been booked.

In contrast to BP, which implicitly divides the firm into the portion that looks like Acme Securities and the portion that looks like Acme Pharmaceuticals, Mobil uses its VAR measure to assess the market risk of positions "that vary from management's defined benchmarks." See Figure 19–8.

In addition to British Petroleum and Mobil, a number of industrial corporations are using—or are considering using—VAR. In the 1995 Wharton/CIBC World Markets Survey of derivatives usage among U.S. nonfinancial firms, 29 percent of respondents indicated that they use VAR for evaluating the risk of derivatives

FIGURE 19–8   Excerpt from Mobil Annual Report 1996

Note 10: Financial Instruments and Risk Management

"Risk Based Measurements—In its risk management activities, Mobil measures its value at risk using simulation techniques that project probability of expected changes in value from market movements on financial exposures that vary from management's defined benchmarks. These benchmarks are standards that have been established by management and represent the risk profile of the environment in which Mobil operates and the assets that one-day market movement in interest and currency rates that would cover 99.7% of all such movements measured against the benchmarks. At December 31, 1995 and 1996, the value benchmark, was $5 million.

VAR—In Their Own Words*

In the November 1995 issue of *Derivatives Strategy,* Beth McGoldrick interviewed a number of industrial corporations about their use of VAR. Following are some of the things that different financial executives had to say about VAR.

Enrique C. Falla, Executive Vice President and CFO, Dow Chemical Co.

Dow has been utilizing value-at-risk as a measurement of financial risk for the last five years. . . . At Dow, this concept has been given several applications. First, assessing risk/ return trade-off of alternative financial strategies; second, delegating authority for financial risk management activities; third, controlling and communicating financial risk on a global basis across foreign exchange and interest rate instruments and exposures. . . . We decided to complement this measure with an assessment of abnormal market fluctuations through the use of stress testing. This measurement covers . . . events like the instability of correlations, market price changes in excess of two standard deviations, volatility changes, yield curve shifts, etc.

Jesse Green, Treasurer, Eastman Kodak

It is true that many non-financial companies don't have to be as rigorous as do financial companies about risk measurement, but it absolutely is useful. We do use the value-at-risk approach. . . . Kodak has no interest rate derivatives right now. . . . Our forex hedges were terminated in 1995. . . . We use VAR to gauge the impact of commodity prices on the company, especially that of silver. . . . At Kodak we do stress testing.

Eugene Beard, Executive Vice President, Finance and Operations, The Interpublic Group of Companies, Inc.

We are aware of VAR and have looked at it, but do not currently utilize it as part of our currency risk management program. We think VAR is more applicable for firms with fixed long-term exposures or companies with very large derivatives portfolios, neither of which applies to Interpublic. Interpublic regularly analyzes the potential impact of currency movement on overseas earnings exposures. . . . Extreme as well as normal market scenarios are included in these analyses. . . . Interpublic's currency hedging program is defensive. Its primary focus is to reduce the impact of currency fluctuations on earnings.

John Cooper, Senior Vice President, Finance, US Generating

We don't use VAR because our use of derivatives is to fix the interest rate on our debt. . . . While we don't see the need for VAR right now, we may someday. As the independent power industry begins to take on more commodity risk, the need will arise. Right now we're pretty well hedged through our power contracts.

---

*McGoldrick (November 1995).

transactions. CIBC World Markets cosponsored a similar survey of Canadian non-financial institutions with the University of Waterloo, in which 47 percent of responding firms said that they use VAR. In a survey of multinational corporations in the June 1995 issue of *Institutional Investor,* 32 percent of firms said they used VAR to measure market risk.[29] A 1995 survey of 250 top UK nonfinancial companies by Record Treasury Management found that 25 percent of the respondents were using VAR to quantify their derivative exposures.

However, as is illustrated in the following, there still remains a considerable range of opinion about VAR from industrial corporations.

Regulators—Bank and Securities Firms Regulators. In December 1995, the governors of the G10 central banks agreed that, beginning in January 1998, banks would be permitted to use their in-house VAR models for measuring the capital they would be required to hold for market risk. However, as is described in the following box, the bank regulators specified the parameters that would be used in the VAR model and provided for a significant cushion.

Aside

The Basle Internal Models Approach

A bank that computes a VAR:

- Must use a one-day, 99 percent (one-tailed) confidence interval.
- Must use a minimum 10-day holding period.*
- Must incorporate a historical observation period of at least one year.
- Could recognize correlation effects within and across† risk factor categories (i.e., interest rates, exchange rates, equity prices, and commodity prices, including related options volatilities in each risk factor category), but would have to aggregate value-at-risk numbers across risk factor categories on a simple sum basis.

Once the VAR is calculated, the capital charge for a bank that uses a proprietary model will be the higher of:

- The previous day's value-at-risk.
- Three times the average of the daily value-at-risk of the preceding 60 business days.

_____

*However, as a way of reducing the calculation burden, the Basle Committee said that banks will be allowed to scale up a one-day VAR measure to arrive at the required 10-day holding period, by multiplying their one-day VAR by the square root of 10.

†For the bank to be able to recognize correlation across factor categories, the bank's supervisory authority must be satisfied that the bank's system for measuring correlations is "sound and implemented with integrity."

The European Union's Capital Adequacy Directive, which came into effect in January 1996, recognizes VAR models as a valid method of calculating capital requirements for foreign exchange. And a recent EU decision has been made to move toward the use of VAR models to calculate other market risk capital requirements.

The U.S. Federal Reserve System is considering even more extensive use of banks' VAR models. In July 1995, the Board of Governors of the U.S. Federal Reserve System released its market risk proposal referred to as "precommitment." The precommitment approach would allow banks to use their own internal models to specify the amount of capital needed to support market risks during a determined time interval and to commit to limiting trading losses over the time interval to an amount less than the specified capital. The length of the time interval utilized by the approach would differ by institution, based on the regulators' assessment of the institution's trading activities and risk management capabilities. A bank would have the option to either increase or decrease the capital commitment at the end of time intervals. Should the amount of trading losses during the time interval exceed the capital allocated to support such losses, a bank would suffer "penalties." The proposal suggests that the severity of penalties should increase with the size of the gap between losses incurred due to market moves and the precommitted capital. Suggested penalties include fines, punitive capital charges, restrictions on future trading activities, public disclosure of excess losses, and loss of the right to implement the precommitment approach to determine regulatory capital.[30]

Regulators—Securities and Exchange Commission. In January 1997, the U.S. SEC issued a final rule designed to enhance the disclosure of market risk inherent in "derivative financial instruments, other financial instruments and derivative commodity instruments." The rule permits publicly traded firms in the U.S. to select VAR as one of three different methods for calculating and disclosing potential loss in earnings, fair values, or cash flows.[31] The VAR disclosure would include both on- and off-balance-sheet financial transactions.

Implementing VAR—Parameter Selection

Once a firm has decided to produce a VAR and has decided which calculation method to use, the next question is one of implementation: What VAR parameters will be used? Of particular interest is the time horizon, the confidence level, and the variance-covariance data.

Time Horizon. Many VAR models use a one-day holding period to measure the amount of risk for the firm. Because these models measure the maximum expected losses for one day, they tend to show relatively small amounts at risk. This assumes that markets are liquid enough to unwind positions in one day. Essentially, they measure expected losses in normal markets.

Nearly all risk managers believe the one-day VAR approach is valid for trading purposes. However, they disagree on the appropriate holding period for the long-term solvency of the institution. One reason that this debate is so lively is that concerns about the appropriate holding period are, in part, due to nonlinearities in value profiles. This problem becomes most evident for short option positions, where much of the attention has been given to "negative gamma."

Supporters of a one-day time horizon argue that they can capture the risk control effects of a longer holding period by multiplying the one-day risk measure by the square root of time.

Aside

Using the Square Root of Time to Scale Up One-Day VARs*

We know that VAR will increase with time, because absolute volatility increases with time. We also know that the standard deviation of an asset's return increases in proportion to SQRT(T).

Since VAR is a multiple of the standard deviation of the portfolio—e.g., in a RiskMetrics framework, the 95 percent confidence-level VAR is 1.65 × (standard deviation of portfolio)—many VAR users obtain a T-day VAR by multiplying the one-day VAR by SQRT(T).

Such a calculation will be precisely correct only if the following conditions are met:

- The underlying factors must be joint normally distributed. (Any linear combination of normally distributed random variables is itself normally distributed.)
- The variance-covariance matrix (i.e., volatility and correlations) must be constant over time. This would imply that the term structure of volatility is flat, something that is not true.
- The underlying factors must exhibit zero drift. This is a reasonable assumption for shorter time horizons, but may not be for longer periods.
- The portfolio must exhibit no optionality.

---

*This discussion is based on Iacono and Skeie (1996).

Opponents agree that such extrapolation works for linear products such as forwards and swaps but is not good enough to capture the behavior of nonlinear products such as options. For example, linear risk measures can underestimate potential loss for portfolios exhibiting negative gamma value profiles.

Some opponents of a one-day holding period argue not only that one must use a longer holding period but also that it is necessary to perform stress tests, i.e., stress simulations on extraordinary scenarios. But others doubt the merits of stress testing. They argue that since valuation models are based on certain behavioral assumptions which may be invalid during market stress, stress testing can generate misleading results.

Confidence Level.   The decision about the appropriate confidence level is one that is made by senior management. However, the risk manager must be able to provide some guidance.

One interesting question is whether an X percent VAR did in fact result in a number that was exceeded only $(100 - X)$ percent of the time. Darryll Hendricks (1996) considered this question. His results on this question are provided in Table 19–12. Note that, in Hendricks's analysis, only the 1,250-day historical simulation attained a 99 percent coverage for all 1,000 portfolios.

Variance-Covariance Data.   In the illustrations we provided, we have been using a data set made up of the last 100 observations. Is 100 large enough? Hendricks looked at the variability of the VAR over time. His results are summarized in Table 19–13. These results suggest that 100 observations is too small; volatility is higher for those VARs that rely more heavily on more recent data.

Beyond the question of the number of observations to use, other crucial questions involve the appropriate degree of correlation to assume between financial prices and the way to aggregate exposures to risk factors. These questions cannot be answered independently. Simple addition of exposures to risk factors is the

TABLE 19–12   Do VARs Cover the Portfolio Outcome They Were Intended to Cover?

	Percentage of Outcomes Covered (95%/99% VAR)	*Multiple Needed to Attain Desired Coverage (95%/99% VAR)*
Historical Simulation		
125 days	94.4/98.3	1.04/1.14
500 days	94.8/98.8	1.01/1.05
Analytic Variance-Covariance		
Equally Weighted		
125 days	95.1/98.4	−/1.13
500 days	95.4/98.4	−/1.13
Exponentially Weighted		
$\lambda = 0.94$	94.7/98.2	1.02/1.14
$\lambda = 0.99$	95.4/98.5	−/1.10

SOURCE: Hendricks (1996).

TABLE 19–13   Tendency for VAR Measure to Fluctuate over Time

	Annualized Percentage Volatility (95% VAR)
Historical Simulation	
125 days	0.40
500 days	0.10
Analytic Variance-Covariance	
Equally Weighted	
125 days	0.19
500 days	0.05
Exponentially Weighted	
$\lambda = 0.94$	0.91
$\lambda = 0.99$	0.16

SOURCE: Hendricks (1996).

most conservative way of aggregating exposures because you end up with the largest total. Simple addition implies that all factors are perfectly positively correlated, i.e., that all factors can (and will) move against your positions at the same time. Most VAR models use historic correlations among risk factors to recognize market diversification. However, the debate is complicated by the fact that historic correlations are unstable. This is most evident when the markets experience stress.

Implementing VAR—Beyond a Single VAR Number

To this point, everything we have discussed has dealt with calculation of *the* VAR. However, calculation of a single VAR number is not sufficient. Successful risk governance will require that the risk manager analyze the sensitivity of and backtest the VAR.

Sensitivity Analysis.   The risk manager will want to know how sensitive the VAR is to the data set used to generate the VAR.

Scenario Analysis.   Suppose the X percent one-day VAR has been calculated to be $$Y$. The risk manager should expect senior management or members of the board to ask questions that could be paraphrased as:

"Is $$Y$ what we can expect to lose if we experience another day like *(fill in the blank)*?"

The date that will be used to fill in the blank will be different for different firms. It might be October 19, 1987, when the equity markets crashed. Or it might be February 4, 1994, when the U.S. Federal Reserve changed direction and started increasing U.S. interest rates. Or it might be December 20, 1994, when the peso was devalued. Or it might be any other day when extreme market movements occurred.

Regardless of the specific date, the most likely answer to the question posed is "no." As we have seen, VAR is based on "standard" movements in the financial prices. It was not designed to deal with days in which the market experiences extreme movements.

Consequently, the risk manager will want to calculate a number of additional VARs. Some of these involve recreating historic market events. Others would involve the risk manager creating new events.

Stress Testing.   Moving beyond the *ad hoc* scenario analysis, the risk manager will want to stress-test the VAR number by changing the parameters of the model. The risk manager will want to see what happens to the VAR number if the values of market factors move outside their current confidence intervals. The risk manager will want to model breakdowns in the correlations reflected in current data.

Part and parcel in this stress testing is to see what happens if conditions are other than "standard." Such an examination becomes more difficult if the risk manager is using a VAR model that presupposes that the underlying market factors are distributed normally. However, one method that has been proposed is to specify one normal distribution in "standard" periods and a different normal distribution for "extreme" periods. This is illustrated in Figure 19–9.[32]

Back Testing.   Perhaps even more important than analyzing the sensitivity of the VAR number is back-testing the VAR to see how it performed relative to *realized* losses. By comparing actual losses to the "extreme" losses generated by the VAR, the risk manager can get some insight into whether the VAR model is appropriate.

In this back testing, one will expect there to be days in which the portfolio will lose more than the VAR. Indeed, if the X percent one-day VAR has been calculated to be $\$Y$, the portfolio should lose more than $\$Y$ on $(100 - X)$ percent of the trading days.

When the actual loss exceeds VAR, the risk manager needs to determine if the VAR measure is flawed or if this is simply one of those times when statistics will mean that the VAR will be exceeded. Some of the questions the risk manager needs to ask include: Does this event represent a "draw" from the "tail" of the distribution; or has the distribution changed? If the distribution changed, is it temporary or permanent?

FIGURE 19-9   Adjusting for "Event Risk"

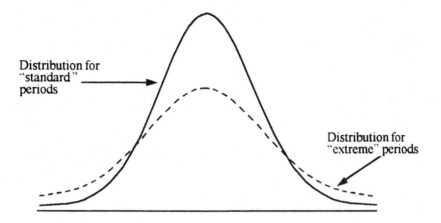

Distribution for "standard" periods

Distribution for "extreme" periods

Finally, the risk manager needs to have an idea about the degree to which actual losses might exceed the VAR. Darryll Hendricks (1996) considered this question as well. His results on this question are provided in Table 19–14.

This table suggests that, on average, a 95 percent VAR could be exceeded by 35 to 48 percent. And, losses as large as four times a 95 percent VAR could be expected to occur in 5 percent of the days that VAR is exceeded.

TABLE 19–14   Size of Outcomes That Exceed VAR

	Average Multiple of Tail Event to VAR (95%/99% VAR)	Maximum Multiple of Tail Event to VAR (95%/99% VAR)
Historical Simulation		
125 days	1.48/1.48	3.91/2.58
500 days	1.44/1.37	4.09/2.48
Analytic Variance-Covariance		
Equally Weighted		
125 days	1.38/1.44	3.59/2.50
500 days	1.38/1.46	3.86/2.70
Exponentially Weighted		
$\lambda = 0.94$	1.41/1.44	3.58/2.48
$\lambda = 0.99$	1.35/1.40	3.55/2.47

SOURCE: Hendricks (1996).

Notes

1. To the best of our knowledge, this "governance" term was first employed by the U.S. Office of the Comptroller of the Currency (OCC).
2. A "market factor" is a price or volatility. For example, the market factors that affect the value of a bond denominated in a foreign currency are the term structure of the foreign interest rate (either points on the zero-coupon curve or the appropriate yield-to-maturity on the par curve) and the exchange rate.
3. *Value of an 01* is also referred to as the *present value of an 01* (PV01), *discounted value of an 01* (DV01), or *basis point value* (BPV).
4. If you compare Equation 19–5 with Equations 19–2 and 19–4, you will see that delta is based on the same concept as are the value of an 01 and duration.
5. Note that gamma is based on the same concept as is convexity.
6. This section is based on two articles Lyle Minton and I wrote for *Risk:* "Value-at-Risk (1): Understanding the Various Ways to Calculate VAR" (January 1996) and "Value-at-Risk (2): The Debate on the Use of VAR" (February 1996).
7. The components of the price list are the "market factors" that affect the transactions included in the portfolio.
8. For expositional simplicity, we use 100 alternative price lists in this example (and in our illustration of the historical and Monte Carlo simulation methods). We will deal with the appropriate number of alternative price lists later in this chapter (where we will decide that 100 alternative price lists are probably too few).
9. Note that in the case of volatilities, you might use historical volatilities or you might use implied volatilities observed from historical data.
10. Strictly speaking, RiskMetrics comprises two methods. The first method, which we term *analytic variance-covariance,* is what Morgan refers to as *analytic: simple VAR.* The second method used by RiskMetrics, which we will cover later, is referred to as *delta-gamma VAR.*
11. While we will continue to refer to this method as the *analytic variance-covariance* method, it might be more precise to call this *analytic:delta-only.*
12. For more on this, see Allen (1994) and Jorion (1997).
13. This delta-gamma VAR is the second of the two methods implemented in RiskMetrics. Including gamma in the analysis introduces nonlinearity into the payoff profile. Hence, this delta-gamma VAR method is distinct from the analytic variance-covariance (or analytic: delta-only) method described above.
14. For a discussion of the application of a delta-gamma method, see Rouvinez (1997).
15. Bob Mark (1995) has developed an approach for measuring gamma over larger changes in the price of the underlying. His technique can be used to incorporate volatility and time-decay risk.
16. The three approaches used values for λ of 0.94, 0.97, and 0.99. (As λ approaches 1.00, exponential weighting approaches equal weighting.)
17. According to my calculator, Hendricks calculated more than 36 million VARs.
18. The 11 participating vendors were Algorithmics, Brady, C-ATS Software, Dow Jones/Telerate, Financial Engineering Associates, Infinity, Price Waterhouse, Renaissance, Softek, True Risk, and Wall Street Systems.
19. While Marshall and Siegel reported that 11 vendors participated in the study, Table 19–10 contains only nine rows. According to Christopher Marshall, two of the vendors were unhappy about their results relative to the mean of the study and pulled their numbers.
20. In addition to the 11 software vendors who participated in their survey, Marshall and Siegel note that the RiskMetrics approach is supported by Barra, EDS, KPMG, LMT, OY Trema, Quantec, and Sailfish. And J. P. Morgan markets its own RiskMetrics software, called "FourFifteen." (The name is taken from the fact that the past chairman of Morgan, Sir Dennis Weatherstone, insisted on receiving the risk measure for the bank no later than 4:15 P.M. EST daily.)
21. Some of you might want to think about a technology firm like Acme Software or Acme Netware.
22. This quote is taken from Neu (May, 1995).
23. Specifically, 30 percent of the respondents indicated that the phrase that best described how they measured and determined limits for market risk was "amount at risk based on specified valuation models using confidence levels."
24. The Group of Thirty follow-up survey included results from 125 dealers from 15 countries.

25. *Public Disclosure of the Trading and Derivatives Activities of Banks and Securities Firms.*

26. The survey was sent to 50 pension funds; the number of responses was not reported.

27. However, only 33 percent of the funds surveyed reported that they had internal risk management systems. Eighty percent of the funds reported that pension consultants provided risk management services.

28. BP's measure of VAR, "assessed market risk," was defined as "a statistically based assessment of market risk, i.e., of exposures to possible future changes in market values over a 24-hour period."

29. A November 1995 survey by Emcor Risk Management Consulting got a similar percentage but gave the survey results a different interpretation: " . . . 66 percent of the respondents . . . said they do not feel that they have 'an adequate understanding or the necessary in-house expertise to effectively utilize the VAR measure.'"

30. At the time this book was going to press, the Federal Reserve, in cooperation with the New York Clearing House, was conducting a test of the precommitment approach.

31. The other two options for disclosure are an analysis of sensitivity to hypothetical changes in market rates and a tabular presentation of expected cash flows and maturity dates. The proposal does not apply to investment firms.

32. The result is a "jump-diffusion" process.

20 RISK MANAGEMENT AND THE VALUE OF A NONFINANCIAL FIRM

When we described the risk management products—forwards, futures, swaps, options, and structured products—we noted that, at origination, the expected net present value of a risk management product is zero. How then can risk management activities increase the value of the firm? It turns out that there are several ways that risk management activities can increase the value of the firm. For ease of exposition, we have divided these into two types—*tactical* and *strategic*.

But before we look at reasons why firms may *want* to use risk management, it might be useful to consider whether firms might actually be *required* to use risk management.

Tactical Risk Management

Over the years, we have heard a lot of conversations about using risk management products to reduce the cost of funding the firm. Once we boiled these conversations down, we concluded that the ways risk management products are used to reduce funding costs can be grouped under four broad headings—acting on a view, arbitraging markets, reducing transactions costs, and selling options.[1] In the next few pages we will examine some of the ways in which risk management products can be used to reduce funding costs.

Using Risk Management to Reduce Funding Cost by Acting on a View

Risk management products can be used to take a view on the *level* of interest rates. If the managers of the firm believe that an interest rate (or the entire term structure) is going to fall, they could act on this view by entering into a "pay-floating" swap. If rates do fall, the firm's interest expense will decline.

Risk Management in Practice

Do Corporations Have a Duty to Hedge?
Brane v. Roth and *In re Compaq*

Daniel P. Cunningham

A 1992 decision by an Indiana court and a class action suit filed in 1991 by the U.S. District Court for the Southern District of Texas have led some to question whether there may exist in some circumstances a duty for corporations to hedge their exposures to changing commodity prices and currency values. Following is an analysis of these two cases and a discussion of how the law should develop on this issue.

Brane v. Roth

In *Brane v. Roth,* 590 N.E. 2d 587 (Ind. Ct. App. 1992), a case decided by the Indiana Court of Appeals in 1992, the plaintiffs held shares in a grain elevator cooperative that received 90 percent of its operating income from the sale of grain. A decline in grain prices resulted in large losses to the cooperative—losses that could have been mitigated through the use of hedging contracts. The Indiana Court of Appeals held that the failure to hedge constituted a breach of the fiduciary duty of care owed by the directors to the cooperative's shareholders.

Absent self-dealing, a corporate director can satisfy his or her fiduciary duty to shareholders by exercising good faith and honest judgment. The business judgment rule provides a presumption that informed decisions made in good faith shall not be judicially reviewed, even if the results of such decisions indicate that the choices were unwise or inexpedient.

The *Brane* court reasoned that the directors of the grain cooperative did not enjoy the protection of the business judgment rule because they failed adequately to inform themselves about the hedging opportunities that could have prevented their losses. In Delaware, there is some argument that directors must be *fully informed* in order to enjoy the protection of the business judgment rule. *See Smith v. Van Gorkom,* 488 A.2d 858 (Del. 1985). New York law also requires that corporate decisions be informed, but the standard is arguably lower, since New York courts will respect business decisions which reflect the "exercise of honest judgment." *See Auerbach v. Bennett,* 419 N.Y.S. 2d 920, 926 (N.Y. 1979). Since the directors in the *Brane* case were found to have breached their fiduciary duty to the shareholders, the directors were liable for the losses incurred due to the failure to hedge.

If read broadly, *Brane* would inject the specter of judicial second-guessing into the day-to-day operational decisions of corporations, because courts would be forced to examine the substance of decisions to hedge or not to hedge. In *Brane,* the grain cooperative derived 90 percent of its income from grain sales, so the court simply assumed that hedging was a necessary activity to reduce the risk of a decline in grain prices. In essence, the court posited the failure properly to hedge as evidence that the managers were ill-informed about hedging, thus giving rise to liability.

The duty of care, however, is violated only by uninformed decisions, and not merely by decisions that have negative results. By blurring the distinction between the procedural steps taken to reach a decision and the substance of the decision itself, *Brane* invites shareholders and judges to substitute their judgment, with the benefit of hindsight, for the judgment of the board of directors. Given these problems, *Brane* may stand alone as an anomalous departure from the mandate of the business judgment rule.

Though *Brane* has prompted some concerns in the financial community, the case has not been cited, favorably or otherwise, by any other court since it was decided in 1992.

In re Compaq

In re Compaq Securities Litigation, 848 F. Supp. 1307 (S.D. Tex. 1993), a class action suit brought by shareholders of Compaq Computer Corporation against that corporation's chief executive officer and chairman of the board of directors, raised many of the same issues as the *Brane* case. The causes of action in *Compaq,* however, were based on alleged violations of Federal securities laws. The plaintiffs had purchased shares of Compaq based on its president's statements regarding the future prospects for the company. Soon thereafter, the stock dropped 20 percent in value in response to a disappointing earnings report. The plaintiffs charged that the public statements made by the president had been materially misleading (within the meaning of Section 10(b) of the Securities Exchange Act of 1934 and Rule 10-b5 promulgated thereunder). The claim was based in part upon the corporation's failure to disclose its lack of adequate foreign currency hedging mechanisms to protect against a drop in value of foreign currencies against the U.S. dollar. The absence of currency hedges allegedly was material because Compaq derived 54 percent of its revenues from foreign markets.

Do Corporations Have a Duty to Hedge? Brane v. Roth and In re Compaq continued

For the court to find in the plaintiff's favor, the plaintiffs in *Compaq* needed to show that the failure to disclose the absence of hedging contracts was "material." Information is material if there is a substantial likelihood that a reasonable shareholder would consider it important in deciding how to invest. The absence of hedging would only be material if the court decided that there was a reason that Compaq should have been hedging. Therefore, though pleaded as a 10b-5 claim, the *Compaq* case, much like *Brane,* gave the court the opportunity to examine the underlying substance of the decision not to hedge and determine the reasonableness of that decision.

However, the court did not decide whether the failure to disclose the absence of foreign exchange hedging was material, and therefore did not examine the reasonableness of Compaq's decision not to hedge. The court granted Compaq's motion for summary judgment on the claim stating that because the market did not rely on Compaq's statements, it did not need to determine whether Compaq's failure to hedge was material. The case was subsequently settled. Accordingly the issue of whether the absence of hedging was material was not resolved.

Analysis

As noted earlier, *Brane* might be limited to its facts and therefore have little significance as precedent. Likewise, because the *Compaq* court did not examine the materiality of Compaq's decision not to hedge, the question of whether such novel claims would be successful still remains unanswered.

Nevertheless, if courts begin to cite *Brane* as meaningful precedent and other plaintiffs litigate the novel claims of *Compaq,* the two cases could lend support to the existence of a duty to hedge against business risks through the use of financial derivatives. Such a duty, however, would represent a significant judicial intrusion into the day-to-day corporate decision-making process. A more narrow reading of the *Brane* ruling and the concerns raised in *Compaq* would not create a two-tiered procedural requirement to be followed by directors in making hedge-related decisions. The following approach most likely would satisfy the requirements of these two cases.

First, at a minimum, directors would need to understand their corporate risks and set up proper mechanisms to address those risks. This requirement would not force *all* corporate directors to become educated in the nuances of financial derivatives; rather, the directors would need to ensure that the responsibility rested with a knowledgeable party who could adequately assess corporate risks and develop proper responses. Directors would be insulated from liability by relying on the decisions and actions of knowledgeable employees, and would

Do Corporations Have a Duty to Hedge? Brane v. Roth and In re Compaq continued

not be confronted with the problem faced by the *Brane* directors, who delegated the hedging issue to an uninformed subordinate. By becoming adequately informed and creating a structure to address risk management issues, directors should enjoy the protection of the business judgment rule, even under an expansive application of *Brane*.

Second, after implementing a system to make informed hedging decisions, directors should disclose those hedging decisions that might be considered material. This disclosure could help to avoid Rule 10b-5 claims from disgruntled shareholders. The required disclosure will differ depending upon the facts, and more disclosure may be necessary if the corporation makes optimistic predictions. In addition, on January 31, 1997, the Securities and Exchange Commission issued final rules (Release No. 33-7386) that clarify and expand disclosure requirements for various financial instruments, including derivatives, for registrants that file reports under the U.S. securities laws.

By making a good faith effort to become informed about corporate risk management, properly delegating the risk assessment and management tasks to qualified employees, and then disclosing hedging decisions that might be considered material to the reasonable investor, corporate directors should be able to avoid the type of liability that arose in *Brane v. Roth* and was argued for in *In re Compaq*.

The duty to hedge or understand derivatives may arise in other circumstances. In a recent case, *Levy v. Bessemer Trust Company, N.A.,* No. 97 Civ. 1785 (JFK), 1997 WL 431079 (S.D.N.Y. July 30, 1997), a court denied a motion to dismiss the negligence claim of a plaintiff based on the failure of an investment advisor to know of and advise the plaintiff of the availability of risk management tools. In the complaint, Levy asserted that he owned approximately 257,000 shares of Corning stock held in an account being managed by Bessemer Trust Company ("BTC"). Levy alleged that he informed BTC that the shares constituted a large portion of his net worth, and that he wanted protection from downside price movements. BTC purportedly advised Levy that there was no way to obtain such protection due to the nature of his shares. Eventually, Levy discovered from an alternate source that there were a variety of hedging possibilities open to him. Levy subsequently moved his account to another firm and hedged the downside price risk. However, the price of Corning stock had already fallen substantially. Levy asserted that BTC was negligent in failing to know of and advise him of the existence of downside protection. BTC moved to dismiss this claim, but the Court denied its motion. While the case has yet to be fully litigated, the plaintiff's allegations, if upheld, suggest that an investment advisor may have a duty to understand, and in some circumstances use, derivatives.

Do Corporations Have a Duty to Hedge? Brane v. Roth and In re Compaq continued

---

Daniel P. Cunningham is a partner of the law firm of Cravath, Swaine & Moore. His corporate finance practice includes derivative instruments, mergers and acquisitions, and receivables finance.

Mr. Cunningham serves as outside counsel to the International Swaps and Derivatives Association (ISDA). In that capacity, he has participated in the preparation of standard master agreements for derivative transactions and has served as legal coordinator for the preparation of memoranda under the laws of 34 jurisdictions, examining the status of the 1987 and 1992 ISDA master agreements with counterparties that have become insolvent under the laws of those nations.

Mr. Cunningham was a member of the Group of Thirty Derivatives Project Working Group.

Mr. Cunningham received a B.A. degree from Princeton University in 1971. In 1975 he graduated from Harvard Law School.

Instead of a view on the level of rates, the firm might take a view on the *shape* of the term structure. A firm might take the view that, in the future, the term structure will be steeper than the current yield curve. In the cash market, such a view would be implemented by borrowing at the short end of the yield curve and investing the proceeds at the long end.

However, this view could be implemented in the swap market by "spreading" longer-term swaps against shorter-term swaps. If I expect the yield curve to steepen, I will want to receive at the long end of the yield curve and pay at the short end. Entering into a swap where I receive a floating rate indexed to a long-term rate (e.g., the 10-year Treasury bond rate) and simultaneously entering into a swap where I pay a floating rate indexed to a short-term rate (e.g., the six-month Treasury bill rate) is a way of implementing this view.

The spreads in the swap market contain information about how the market "expects" the term structure to behave. If the floating rate is indexed to a longer-term rate, the spread on the fixed rate (Treasury + spread) is typically wider than the spread for a swap with the floating rate indexed to a shorter-term interest rate. When the swap spreads for swaps indexed to shorter-term rates widen relative to swaps indexed to longer-term rates, the market is reflecting increased uncertainty about the future shape of the yield curve.

In the late 1990s, the U.S. dollar yield curve steepened dramatically—the spread between the 30-year Treasury bond rate and the three-month Treasury bill rate increased from about 50 basis points to 300 basis points. In the summer of 1991, we witnessed a reversal in the swap spreads: one- to two-year swap spreads became wider than the five-year spreads. The swap market was predicting that the yield curve would flatten out.

A still more subtle way of taking a view is by taking a view about *the relation between the forecasts of future spot rates implied by the yield curve*—the forward rates embedded in the term structure—and actual future spot rates. As we demonstrated in Chapter 8, swaps are priced on the basis of the forward yield curve. So the question is whether interest rates will behave as indicated by the prevailing forward yield curve.

As indicated by the following box, some academic research suggests that forward rates "overforecast" future spot interest rates. If the yield curve is very steep, the firm might then take the view that future interest rates will not be as high as are implied in the yield curve (and, indeed, priced into an interest rate swap).

> In 1992 and 1993, a number of firms implemented such a strategy. Since interest rates were at historic lows, the firms elected to issue long-term debt—20-year, 30-year, 40-year, and even 100-year debt. However, because the yield curve was so steeply sloped, the firms believed that future spot rates would be lower than the rates implied by the forward yield curve. The firms implemented this view by entering into one- to five-year swaps in which the firms would pay a floating rate. The firms ended up with a financing in which the firms paid a floating rate in the early years and fixed rate in the later years.

Using Risk Management to Reduce Funding Cost by "Arbitraging" Markets

In Chapter 8 we noted that the term *arbitrage* has been used widely in connection with the swap market. As we said there, we find little evidence of any sort of textbook arbitrage—simultaneously buy and sell to earn a riskless profit. Rather, the "arbitrage" accessed by the use of swaps is generally the result of asymmetric tax treatments or government regulation.

Sometimes the arbitrage is the result of some barrier to entry to a particular debt market. If an effective barrier exists, the supply of fixed-income securities in that market will be restricted; so the price for securities will be higher than would be the market-determined price. Correspondingly, these securities would carry below-market coupons. The end users who are able to access such an arbitrage are usually sovereigns who have special access (e.g., the World Bank) or extraordinary corporates (i.e., the "supranational" corporates).

At other times, the arbitrage is the result of tax provisions which treat a debt issue differently in one market and another. Such an arbitrage occurred in 1990. A number of U.S. corporations were able to borrow at below-market rates by issuing debt in New Zealand and swapping it back into U.S. dollars. The source of this arbitrage was asymmetric tax treatment. The New Zealand tax authority had imposed a withholding tax. But the withholding tax was only relevant for issuers in the domestic market. This meant that the domestic yield curve for New Zealand was higher than the Euro yield curve for New Zealand dollar–denominated assets. (See Figure 20–1.) Borrowers took advantage of this difference by borrowing in the

Do Forward Rates Predict Future Interest Rates?*

Gregory S. Hayt

The ability of forward premia in interest rates to predict subsequent spot interest rates has been of interest to academics for decades. It is of particular relevance for participants in the derivatives market given the very steep yield curves of recent years.

Under the "pure expectations" hypothesis the variation in forward premia is directly attributable to expected changes in the spot rate. However, early tests of this hypothesis found the slope of the term structure contained very little information about subsequent changes in spot rates.

One explanation for the failure of early studies is that forward premia, in addition to containing a forecast of the expected spot rate, also contain information about the risk premium for holding multiperiod bills. Variation in expected risk premia would tend to obscure the ability of the forward rate to predict the spot rate. Taking variation in risk premia into account, a study by Eugene Fama[†] found that high forward premia on U.S. Treasury bills consistently preceded a rise in spot rates. Spot rates, however, did not change by as much as would have been predicted based on the forward curve. In other words, forward rates were found to be biased predictors of future spot rates.

Fama also found that variation in forward premia did not explain much of the fluctuation in subsequent spot rates. In a statistical analysis, forward premia could account for no more than 29 percent of the variation in the one-month spot rate one month ahead between 1959 and 1982. The ability of forward rates to explain variation in more distant spot rates was considerably lower.

Gregory Hayt is an Executive Director of CIBC Financial Products, where he focuses on teaching and the development of curriculum for the CIBC World Markets School of Financial Products. Prior to joining CIBC, Mr. Hayt was a vice president at Chase Manhattan Bank, where he advised clients on a wide range of risk management issues, from financial modeling and exposure measurement to the design and implementation of risk management policies.

*This originally appeared in *Financial Risk Management,* a newsletter published by the Risk Management Research Center of The Chase Manhattan Bank.

[†]Eugene Fama, "The Information in the Term Structure," *Journal of Financial Economics* 13 (1984).

FIGURE 20–1   A "Tax Arbitrage" Due to the Imposition of a Withholding Tax

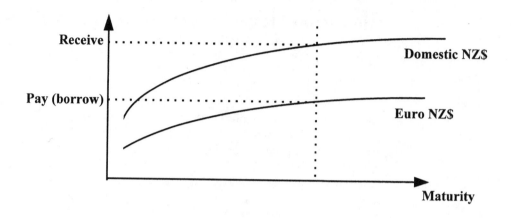

Euro market—i.e., paying the rate on the lower yield curve—and then swapping back into the domestic market—i.e., receiving the rate on the higher yield curve.

Using Risk Management to Reduce Funding Cost by Reducing Transaction Costs

One of the most important (but probably least discussed) ways in which swaps can reduce the cost of funding is by reducing the transaction costs which are a natural consequence of raising funds. In Chapter 9 we noted that these costs include items such as the bid-ask spread, information acquisition, and liquidity. We also outlined how international firms sometimes use excess borrowing capacity in markets where they can raise funds relatively cheaply and use swaps to convert them into synthetic borrowings in markets where they have no special advantages.

Using Risk Management to Reduce Funding Cost by Selling Options

To reduce funding costs a firm might elect to sell rather than buy options. In Chapter 12, we noted that a firm funded with floating-rate debt might buy interest rate caps to protect the firm from rising rates. Alternatively, a firm funded with floating-rate debt might sell an interest rate floor to reduce its funding costs. The premium it receives "lowers" its funding cost.

> Suppose a firm that would normally pay a rate of LIBOR + 50 on three-year debt sells a three-year, 4 percent interest rate floor. Suppose further that the value of the interest rate floor, amortized over three years, is 35 basis points. If LIBOR is 4 percent or above, the firm will pay LIBOR + 50 − 35 = LIBOR + 15; but if LIBOR drops below 4 percent, the firm will pay a flat 4.15 percent.[2] If LIBOR rises, the coupon

the firm must pay will rise. However, the firm will receive the benefit of a declining LIBOR only to the floor rate; below the floor rate, the firm will not benefit from a further lowering of rates.

As we described in detail in Chapter 15, corporations can reduce their funding costs by issuing "hybrid debt." One example of hybrid debt is a debt package which contains an option. The most familiar of this kind of structure is a bond with an equity warrant. This debt instrument can be thought of as containing two components: (1) a standard debt instrument and (2) a call option on the value of the equity of the firm. Purchasers of the debt compensate the firm for this attached option by paying a higher price for the package—which reduces the coupon on the debt. We have also seen options on assets other than the firm's equity attached to a bond. Indexed bonds, as this debt is sometimes called, have been issued which contain options on many different underlying assets: commodities (e.g., gold) and international stock market index (e.g., S&P 500 Index).

And firms sell embedded options to reduce their funding costs. Although embedded options have all the features of standard options, they are not separate instruments, but are part and parcel of the larger contract. In many cases the option embedded in the contract has the same, or similar, payoff characteristics as other options traded on an exchange or over-the-counter. When this is the case, the holder of the option can sell the liquid exchange or OTC counterpart to generate revenue or reduce funding costs. Many everyday business transactions contain embedded options. The right to opt out of a contract—e.g., the right to prepay a mortgage—is just such an embedded option.

Callable corporate debt is another example of a contract which contains an embedded option. From the issuing firm's perspective, callable fixed-rate debt can be thought of as two things combined into one contract: (1) standard fixed-rate debt and (2) an out-of-the-money interest rate option. The callable debt gives the issuer the right to purchase the debt at a fixed price at a specified time in the future (and so it has the same payoff profile as a put option on interest rates). If interest rates decline after the debt is issued, the firm can buy back the debt at a fixed price once the call waiting period has elapsed. This serves as the firm's hedge against a decline in interest rates after it issues debt. There is some evidence that, in the past, investors undervalued the embedded interest rate option. Some firms took advantage of this underpricing by selling a put on interest rates after issuing the bond. Amortizing the premium for the put option sold by the issuing firm resulted in below-market fixed-rate debt.[3]

Strategic Risk Management[4]

If a firm manages its financial price risk, it follows that the volatility of the value of the firm or of the firm's real cash flows will decline. This general relation is illustrated in Figure 20–2.

FIGURE 20–2   The Impact of Risk Management Hedging Is to Reduce the Variance in the Distribution of Firm Value

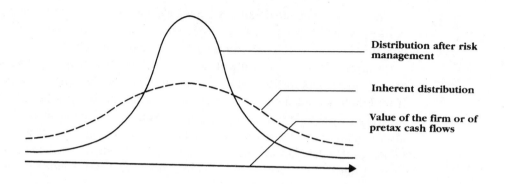

Distribution after risk management

Inherent distribution

Value of the firm or of pretax cash flows

Since the value of a firm is sensitive to movements in interest rates, foreign exchange rates, or commodity prices, a tantalizing conclusion is that the value of the firm will necessarily rise if this exposure is managed. But however appealing, this conclusion does not follow directly. That a firm is confronted with strategic risk is a *necessary* condition for the firm to manage that risk. The *sufficient* condition for a firm to manage risk is that the strategy increase the present value of the expected net cash flows, $E(\text{NFC}_{jt})$, where r_{jt} is the discounted rate.

$$V_j = \sum^t \frac{E(\text{NCF}_{jt})}{(1 + r_{jt})}$$

This equation provides the insight that if the market value of the firm is to increase, the gain must result from either an increase in expected net cash flows or a decrease in the discount rate.

Whether risk management will have an impact on the discount rate—the firm's cost of capital—is an issue we defer until the end of this chapter. One special case should be mentioned now, however. For firms in which the owners do not hold well-diversified portfolios (such as proprietorships, partnerships, and closely held corporations) the risk aversion of the firm's owners can provide an important risk management incentive. At this point, we want to focus on how risk management could increase the value of the firm by increasing the firm's expected net cash flows. Hence, the question that must be answered is, How can hedging, or any other financial policy, have any impact on the real cash flows of the organization?

The relation between the firm's real cash flows and its financial policies was established by Franco Modigliani and Merton Miller in 1958 in what has come to be called the M&M proposition. The M&M proposition would imply that in a world with no taxes, no transaction costs, and a fixed investment policy, investors can create their own "homemade" risk management by holding diversified portfolios.[5] However, the message of the M&M proposition for practitioners becomes evident only when the argument is turned upside down:

> *If* financial policies matter . . . if risk management policies are going to have an impact on the value of the firm,
>
> *then* risk management must have an impact on the firm's taxes, transaction costs, or investment decisions.

Theory 1—Risk Management Can Add Value by Decreasing Taxes

For risk management to produce tax benefits, the firm's effective tax schedule must be *convex.* As illustrated in Figure 20–3, a convex tax schedule is one in which the firm's average effective tax rate rises as pretax (financial statement) income rises. If the firm's effective tax function is convex and if the firm is subject to financial price-induced volatility in its pretax income, it is a mathematical certainty that hedging will reduce the firm's expected taxes.[6] However, instead of resorting to a mathematical proof, we think that this point is demonstrated in Illustration 20–1.

If the firm's effective tax function is convex, risk management can reduce the firm's expected taxes. And the more convex the tax schedule is, the greater the tax benefits are. The obvious question then is, Why would my firm's effective tax function be convex?

The obvious factor that would make a tax schedule convex is *progressivity,* a tax schedule in which the statutory tax rate rises as income rises. Greater progressivity

FIGURE 20–3   **Convexity in the Tax Function**

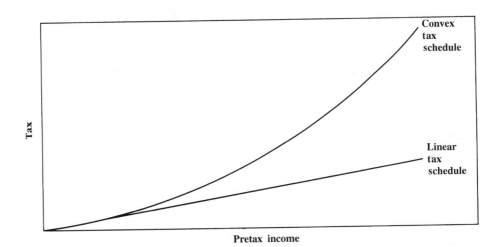

Tax

Convex tax schedule

Linear tax schedule

Pretax income

Illustration 20–1

Reducing Taxes with Risk Management

Consider a firm that is exposed to financial price risk; its pretax income is related to interest rates, foreign exchange rates, or some commodity price. Suppose that if the firm does not hedge, the distribution of its pretax income will be as shown below: for any given year, the firm's pretax income might be low or high, either with a probability of 50 percent.

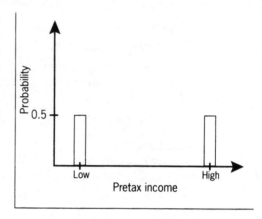

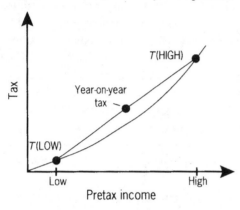

If the firm implements an effective risk management program, the volatility in its pretax income will decline. In the context of our simple distribution, a reduction in volatility means that the pretax income LOW and pretax income HIGH will both move toward the mean. For purposes of illustration, suppose

that the firm hedges completely; in such a case the distribution of the firm's pretax income would be a single point, *MEAN*.

If the firm has the low pretax income, it will pay tax T(LOW); if the firm's pretax income is high, the tax will be T(HIGH). Hence if the firm does not hedge, its expected tax will be the average of these two taxes. In other words, the firm's year-on-year taxes would be on the straight line connecting T(LOW) and T(HIGH), halfway between T(LOW) and T(HIGH).

And as the next illustration shows, the firm will pay a tax that is strictly less if it hedges than if it does not hedge.

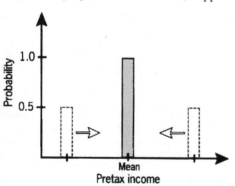

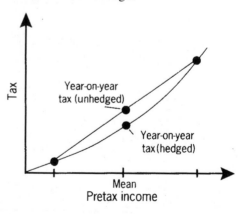

results in a more convex tax schedule. However, since the range of progressivity for corporate income taxes in the United States is relatively small, this factor would not be a significant source of convexity for most large, public industrial corporations.

Another cause of convexity in the effective tax function is *the existence of tax preference items*—for example, tax loss carryforwards and investment tax credits (ITC). Since a firm will always be induced to use the most valuable tax preference items first, these tax shields will result in the firm's effective tax function being convex.[7]

Finally, in the United States, firms that are subject to the alternate minimum tax (AMT) provision face convex effective tax functions. The AMT gives the tax authorities a claim that is similar to a call option on the pretax income of the firm, and so the AMT puts a "kink" in the effective tax function, making it convex.

While the impact of hedging on the firm's taxes is driven by a mathematical relation—the convexity of the effective tax function—the underlying logic is simple, perhaps easiest to see in the case of the tax preference items. If the firm does not hedge, there will be some years in which the firm's income is too low to use (or use completely) the tax preference items, and so the firm would lose a benefit. By reducing volatility in pretax income, hedging reduces the probability that the firm will not be able to take advantage of its tax preference items. In a similar fashion, hedging reduces the probability that the firm pays the higher tax rates specified under a progressive tax schedule or AMT provision.

Theory 2—Risk Management Can Add Value by Decreasing the Cost of Financial Distress

As illustrated in Figure 20–2, risk management reduces the volatility of the value of the firm. Figure 20–4 goes further to show that by reducing volatility, risk management reduces the probability of the firm's encountering financial distress and the consequent costs.

How much risk management can reduce these costs depends on two obvious factors: the probability of encountering distress if the firm does not hedge and the costs if distress occurs. The greater the probability of distress or distressed-induced costs, the greater the firm's benefit from risk management through the reduction in these expected costs.

Default results when a firm's income is insufficient to cover its fixed claims. The probability of financial distress and subsequent default, therefore, is determined by two factors: *fixed-claims coverage* (because the probability of default rises as the coverage of fixed claims declines) and *income volatility* (because the probability of default rises as the firm's income becomes more volatile).

The cost of financial distress has two major components. The first is the direct expense of dealing with a default, bankruptcy, reorganization, or liquidation. The second is the indirect costs arising from the changes in incentives of the firm's various claim holders. For example, if the firm files for bankruptcy and attempts to

---

FIGURE 20–4   Hedging and Financial Distress

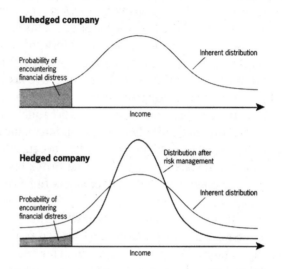

reorganize its business under Chapter 11, the bankruptcy court judge overseeing the case is unlikely to approve nonroutine expenditures. The judge receives little credit if the activities turn out well, but is criticized by creditors with impaired claims if the efforts turn out badly. Thus, firms undergoing reorganizations are likely to pass up positive net-present-value projects systematically because of the nature of the oversight by the bankruptcy court.

But even short of bankruptcy, financial distress can impose substantial indirect costs on the firm.[8] These indirect costs include higher costs to the firm in contracting with its customers, employees, and suppliers.

The impact of financial distress on the cost of contracting with customers is perhaps the easiest to observe. Firms that provide service agreements or warranties make long-term contracts with their customers. As illustrated in the following example, if the firm is less viable, consumers place less value on the service agreements and warranties and are more likely to turn to a competitor.

If the firm can convince potential customers that the likelihood of financial distress has been reduced, the firm can increase consumers' valuation of its service agreements and warranties. And this perceived increase in value will be reflected in the cash flows to the firm and in the price the consumers will be willing to pay for the product. These potential benefits of risk management are likely to be greater for firms that produce "credence goods" and firms whose future existence is more uncertain.

A credence good is one wherein quality is important but is difficult (and in some cases impossible) to determine prior to consumption. A good example is airline travel: quality is crucial, but until the trip is complete and baggage is recov-

---

Illustration 20–2

The Impact of Financial Risk on Sales: The Case of Wang*

As reported in the *Wall Street Journal,* "The biggest challenge any marketer can face [is] selling the products of a company that is on the ropes."

For purchasers of computers, manufacturers' guarantees and warranties (both explicit and implicit) are extremely important. As the *Journal* put it, "Customers . . . want to be sure that their suppliers . . . will be around to fix bugs and upgrade computers for years to come." Not surprisingly, when Wang's leverage got to the point that earnings volatility could put the firm into financial distress, sales turned down. A potential Wang customer put it best when she noted that "before the really bad news, we were looking at Wang fairly seriously [but] their present financial condition means that I'd have a hard time convincing the vice president in charge of purchasing. . . . At some point we'd have to ask 'How do we know that in three years you won't be in Chapter 11?'"

---

*This illustration is from Bulkeley (1989).

---

ered, there is no way for the consumer to judge the quality level. (In contrast, when firms purchase materials—for example, refined copper—they can determine the quality prior to use by assaying a sample.) Thus, firms that produce credence goods would receive a larger benefit from hedging and being able to assure potential customers that they will not depreciate quality.

Consumers are aware that firms approaching financial distress are more likely to cheat on quality than financially healthy firms. So the benefit from hedging would be larger for firms that have a higher probability of encountering financial distress.

Theory 3—Risk Management Can Add Value by Facilitating Optional Investment

The M&M proposition implies that if hedging policy increases firm value, it does so by reducing contracting costs, by reducing taxes, or by controlling investment incentives. We now turn to this last general motive for corporate hedging—dysfunctional investment incentives.

Incentives to turn down positive net-present-value projects also can arise in firms that avoid bankruptcy. These incentives arise because of the conflict between the bondholders and the shareholders resulting from differences in the kind of claims each hold.[9] Bondholders hold fixed claims, while shareholders hold claims that are equivalent to a call option on the value of the firm. The conflict results in a constraint on the debt capacity of the firm (or in the firm's having to pay a higher coupon on its debt).

The severity of the conflict between the shareholders and bondholders is determined primarily by the debt-equity ratio. As debt level in the capital structure rises, the conflict becomes more significant. But other factors, such as the range of investment projects available to the firm, also affect the severity of the bondholder-shareholder conflict. As with any other option, the value of shareholders' equity rises as the variance in the returns to the underlying asset increases. If shareholders switch from low-variance investment projects to high-variance projects, they could transfer wealth from the bondholders to themselves.[10]

Basically, bondholders, or rather, potential bondholders, are concerned about the probability that they will be left holding the bag, that the value of the firm's assets will be insufficient to cover the promised payments in the indenture. In addition to concerns about future market conditions, potential bondholders are concerned about opportunistic behavior on the part of shareholders who might declare a liquidating dividend, burden the firm with extra debt, or select risky investments. Potential bondholders, however, recognize the possibility of opportunistic behavior and protect themselves by lowering the price they are willing to pay for the firm's bonds.

To convince potential bondholders to pay more for bonds, shareholders must assure them that wealth transfers will not occur. These assurances frequently have been given by attaching restrictive covenants to debt issues (restrictions on dividends and debt coverage ratios), issuing a mortgage bond (to preclude asset substitution), making the debt convertible (to align the interest of the bondholders with those of the shareholders), and issuing preferred stock instead of debt (to reduce the probability that future market conditions will lead to default).

The shareholder-bondholder conflict can also be reduced through risk management. Figure 20–4 shows that risk management reduces the probability of default, so potential bondholders will be willing to pay more for the bond. Hence, risk management can increase the debt capacity of the firm.

Likewise, risk management can decrease the coupon the firm will have to pay on its debt.

In addition to increasing the financing cost for investment projects undertaken, volatility in the firm's earnings can even cause the firm to pass up positive NPV projects. Textbook "underinvestment" occurs when the firm is highly levered and the value of the firm's assets is volatile: shareholders may opt not to undertake a positive NPV project because the gains accrue to the bondholders.[11] Perhaps the simplest way to understand this rather complex theoretical argument is with an example.

An instance in which risk management can avoid this type of underinvestment problem occurs in the long-term debt market. As we have noted, if a firm issues long-term debt, its shareholders have the incentive to pass up positive NPV projects or to shift from low-risk to high-risk projects. Recognizing this incentive, bondholders demand a large premium on long-term debt. However, this "opportunistic-behavior premium" is lowered for firms with higher bond ratings, presumably

Illustration 20–3

The Impact of Volatility on Debt Capacity*

As *Corporate Finance* reported, a number of firms realize that "hedging techniques can stabilize a company's net worth and keep it from tripping into technical default . . ." and by doing so, the firm can increase its debt capacity. As a case in point, "Kaiser has effectively increased its debt-carrying capacity by removing volatility from its cost and revenue stream. . . ."

_____

*This illustration is based on "Kaiser and Union Carbide Hedge Their Bets with Their Banks," which appeared in the June 1991 issue of *Corporate Finance*.

Illustration 20–4

Cutting Rate Risk on Buyout Debt: Reducing Shareholder-Debtholder Conflict on the RJR Nabisco Deal*

When Kohlberg, Kravis, Roberts and Co. got ready to issue the senior bank debt for the RJR Nabisco deal, they ran into the shareholder-debtholder conflict head-on. But by using risk management, they were able to reduce the conflict and increase their debt capacity.

The market was concerned about the interest rate risk such a large amount of debt would entail. If the debt carried a floating-rate coupon, and if rates rose substantially, the probability of default would rise dramatically. Therefore, to reduce the shareholder-debtholder conflict, KKR was required to purchase interest rate insurance. As the vice chairman of Chase Manhattan explained, before committing any money to finance a corporate takeover, Chase insists that steps be taken to reduce the interest rate risk.

Consequently, KKR agreed to keep interest rate protection (in the form of swaps or caps) on half the outstanding balance of its bank debt. In this way, KKR was able to borrow $13 billion. Without the rate insurance, the amount the banks would have been willing to lend would have been substantially less.

_____

*Based on Quint (1989).

Illustration 20–5

Controlling Underinvestment with Hedging*

Let's consider a 100 percent equity firm whose value is positively related to oil prices—a small oil producer, for example. The value of the firm in the initial period, Period 1, will be higher if oil prices are high than if they are low. For simplicity, let's suppose that there are only two outcomes, each with a 50 percent probability.[†]

Outcome	Probability	Value of Firm in Period 1
Price of oil high	.5	1,000
Price of oil low	.5	200

While this initial value belongs completely to the shareholders—our simple firm begins as all equity—suppose that the shareholders plan to issue, in Period 1, bonds with *face value* of $500. All the proceeds of the debt issue will be passed directly to the shareholders.

Now suppose that the shareholders of the firm are presented with a riskless investment opportunity: if the shareholders make an outlay of $600 in Period 1 (before the issue of the debt), the investment project will result in an income to the firm of $800 in Period 2 *with certainty*. Logic would suggest that share-holders will always accept a riskless opportunity with a return above the riskless rate, but that's not necessarily how it will work.

As shown in Table 20–1, if the price of oil is low, the shareholders of this firm will pass up this positive NPV project. In other words, if the value of the firm in Period 1 is $200, the shareholders will not undertake the riskless investment project.

The reason for this surprising result is that the volatility in the value of the firm, coupled with a large debt-equity ratio, could transfer wealth from the shareholders to the bond-holders if the shareholders elect to undertake the positive NPV project.

The total value of the shareholders' wealth position is the sum of their equity value in the firm at Period 2 plus the monies they receive from the debt issue. Note that while the *face* value of the debt is $500, the *market* value of the debt—what the potential bondholders will actually pay the shareholders for the debt—is equal to the expected value of the debt:

$$1/2(\$500) + 1/2(\$200) = \$350$$

The expected value of the shareholder's equity in the firm is $1/2(\$700) + 1/2(0) = \$350$; the total value of the shareholders'

because higher-rated firms have established reputations. Lower-rated firms can avoid this premium by issuing short-term debt. But short-term debt could expose the firm to interest rate risk. If, however, the firm issues short-term debt and then swaps the debt into a fixed-rate, the lower-rated firm can control the agency problem while avoiding interest rate risk.[12]

But even without excessive leverage, volatility in earnings can lead to a form of underinvestment.

Controlling Underinvestment with Hedging continued

TABLE 20–1

Period 1		Period 2			
Value of Firm		*Value of Firm*	*Value of Debt*	*Value of Equity*	*Will the Positive NPV Project Be Undertaken?*
$1,000	Undertake project	$1,200	$500	$700	
	Do not undertake project	1,000	500	500	Yes
$200	Undertake project	400*	500†	− 100‡	
	Do not undertake project	200	200	0	No

*If the firm is worth only $200 initially, the shareholders would have to put up another $400 to get the $600 necessary to invest in the riskless project. In Period 2, the firm's treasury would contain the $800 proceeds from the investment project; but $400 of these dollars would be earmarked for return to the shareholders.

†Even though the firm would be worth only $400, the treasury would contain the $800 proceeds from the investment (see * note above). Since the bondholders would have the senior claim, they can take the full $500 face value of the bond from the treasury.

‡The treasury would "owe" $400 to the shareholders (see * note above); but after the bondholders took their $500 from the treasury, only $300 is left.

holdings—the value of shareholders' equity in the firm plus the monies they received from the debt issue—is $350 + $350 = $700.

Now let's look at the impact of risk management on this situation. Suppose the shareholders of the firm hedged its exposure to the price of oil by entering into a simplified commodity swap agreement:

Price of oil high: This firm pays $400.

Price of oil low: This firm receives $400.

Now the value of the firm is hedged against oil price fluctuations. No matter what happens to oil prices, the value of the firm is $600.

As Table 20–2 indicates, with the value of the firm hedged against oil price fluctuations, the positive NPV project will always be undertaken.

With the hedge against oil prices, the total value of the shareholders' wealth is $500 (the proceeds of the debt issue), plus $300 (the value of their equity at Period 2) to give them a total of $800. By hedging, the shareholders would increase the value of their wealth by $100.

Controlling Underinvestment with Hedging continued

TABLE 20–2

Period 1	Period 2			
Value of Firm	Value of Firm	Value of Debt	Value of Equity	Will the Positive NPV Project Be Undertaken?
$600 { Undertake project	$800	$500	$300	Yes
Do not undertake project	600	500	100	

*This illustration is based on Mayers and Smith (1987).

†For tractability, we have created this example with no transactions costs and no taxes and a risk-free interest rate equal to zero. These simplifying assumptions in no way influence the qualitative outcome of the example; but they make the exposition immensely more simple.

Don Chance, Professor of Finance at Virginia Tech, pointed out that the underinvestment problem in this example goes away if the equity holders do not pay themselves a dividend with the money raised with the debt issue. His point is well taken. This stylized example is intended to illustrate the *nature* of the underinvestment problem; for a more complete discussion of this and other agency problems, the reader is referred to Stern and Chew (1986).

Since there is a well-established relation between R&D activity and value for pharmaceutical firms, there was a clear reason Merck would want to manage its foreign exchange risk. However, this form of underinvestment problem is one that a number of firms have encountered. And if risk management permits the firm to undertake positive NPV projects that would otherwise be deferred, its net cash flows will necessarily rise.

Froot, Scharfstein, and Stein (1993) generalized the underinvestment problem introduced by Lewent and Kearney (1990). Noting that firms simultaneously choose the optimal levels of investment and financing (subject to an expected profit constraint), they proposed that financial price risk management should have a single overriding goal: to ensure that a company has the cash available to make value-

---

Illustration 20–6

The Impact of Earnings Volatility on Investment: The Case of Merck*

Since Merck's earnings are denominated in U.S. dollars, its pretax income fluctuates with the value of the dollar. If the dollar is weak, the dollar value of net income received from foreign operations will be high; if the dollar is strong, Merck's dollar income will be low.

Looking at its behavior in the past, Merck discovered that this volatility in earnings had impacted its investment decision. When the dollar was strong and pretax income was low, Merck had cut back the rate of growth of R&D spending.

---

*This illustration is based on Lewent and Kearney (1990).

---

enhancing investments. The risk management paradigm rests on the basic premises that the key to creating corporate value is making good investments and the key to making good investments is generating enough cash internally to fund those investments.

Evidence[13]

The preceding section introduced three theoretical arguments about the way that strategic risk management can increase the firm's net cash flows. However, the question is whether or not the behavior of firms is actually consistent with these theoretical arguments. To answer this question, the theoretical arguments must be translated into testable hypotheses about the determinants of financial price risk management. Table 20–3 summarizes the signs of the determinants that would be predicted by Smith and Stulz (1985) and Froot, Scharfstein, and Stein (1993).

Table 20–4 summarizes the empirical evidence provided by nine empirical studies that have examined the use of risk management by nonfinancial firms: Wall and Pringle (1989), Nance, Smith, and Smithson (1993), Mian (1994), Dolde (1995), Hentschel and Kothari (1997),[14] Tufano (1996),[15] Geczy, Minton, and Schrand (1996),[16] Samant (1996), and Wysocki (1996).

Risk management to reduce taxes. The available evidence is consistent with the Smith and Stulz "tax convexity" argument—firms that have more convex effective tax functions are more likely to use risk management. Dolde (1995) reported a positive and significant relation between tax loss carryforwards and the use of risk management instruments. Both Nance, Smith, and Smithson (1993) and Mian

TABLE 20–3   Theoretical Predictions

	Smith and Stulz	Froot, Sharfstein, and Stein
Risk Management to Reduce Taxes		
Tax loss carryforwards	Positive	Negative
Tax credits	Positive	Negative
Income in progressive region of tax schedule	Positive	Negative
Risk Management to Reduce Cost of Financial Distress		
Interest coverage	Negative	Negative
Interest rate/FX risk	Positive	Positive
Leverage	Positive	Positive
Credit rating	Negative	Negative
Risk Management to Facilitate Optimal Investment		
R&D expenditure	Positive	Positive
Market-to-book value	Positive	Positive

(1994) found a statistically significant positive relationship between tax credits and the use of risk management instruments.

Risk management to reduce the cost of financial distress.   The available evidence is consistent with the arguments by Smith and Stulz and Froot, Scharfstein, and Stein that firms with a higher probability of encountering financial distress are more likely to use risk management products: Mian (1994) and Geczy, Minton, and Schrand (1996) found a statistically significant, positive relation between the level of the firm's foreign operations (a proxy for its foreign exchange rate exposure) and the use of risk management instruments. Dolde (1995) and Samant (1996) both found a statistically significant, positive relationship between the use of risk management and leverage.

Risk management to facilitate optimal investment.   As is predicted by theory, Nance, Smith, and Smithson; Geczy, Minton, and Schrand; and Dolde all found a statistically significant, positive relationship between the firm's R&D expenditure and its use of risk management products. The evidence is mixed with respect to the market-to-book ratio. Samant found a statistically significant positive relationship while, in contrast to the theoretical predictions, Mian reported a statistically significant negative relationship between the market-to-book value ratio and the use of risk management.[17]

Table 20–5 compares the theoretical predictions in Table 20–3 with the empirical evidence in Table 20–4. It shows that firms' behavior is consistent with the theo-

TABLE 20-4 Empirical Results

Author(s) of Study	Wall & Pringle	Nance, Smith, & Smithson	Mian	Dolde	Hentschel & Kothari	Tufano	Geczy, Minton, & Schrad	Samant	Wysocki
Publication (date)	Financial Management (1989)	Journal of Finance (1993)	Working paper (1994)	Journal of Financial Engineering (1995)	Working paper (1995)	Journal of Finance (1996)	Journal of Finance (1997)	Journal of Financial Services Research (1996)	Working paper (1996)
Sample (date)	250 swaps users (1986)	169 of Fortune 500 (1986)	3,022 firms (1992)	244 of Fortune 500 (1992)	325 large U.S. firms (1990–92)	48 North American gold mining firms (1991–93)	372 of Fortune 500 (1991)	354 U.S. firms (1990–92)	403 U.S. firms (1994)
Focus of study	Interest rate swaps	All derivatives	All derivatives	All derivatives	All derivatives	Gold price hedging	FX hedging	Interest rate risk management	All derivatives
Derivatives data source	Footnotes to ann. reports	Survey	Footnotes to ann. reports	Survey	Footnotes to ann. reports	Survey	Footnotes to ann. reports	Footnotes to ann. reports	Footnotes to ann. reports
Risk Management Determinant									
To reduce taxes									
Tax loss carryforwards	Negative	Negative	Negative	Positive*		Positive	Positive		Positive
Tax credits	Positive*	Positive*	Positive*						Positive
Income in progressive region of tax schedule	Positive	Positive	Positive						
To reduce cost of financial distress									
Interest coverage	Negative	Negative							Positive
Interest rate/FX risk			Positive*	Positive*			Positive*		
Leverage	Negative	Negative	Positive		Positive	Positive	Negative	Positive*	Negative
Credit rating	Negative								
To reduce agency costs									
R&D	Positive*	Positive*		Positive*			Positive*		
Market/book value			Negative*				Positive	Positive*	Negative

NOTE: An asterisk (*) indicates that estimate is statistically significant.

retical predictions. The available empirical evidence provides a crucial link: theory indicates how firms should be behaving if they are increasing shareholder value via risk management; the empirical evidence indicates that they are behaving in that manner.

However, the evidence reported must be regarded as indirect. It demonstrates that firms are behaving as if they are increasing value, but it does not directly demonstrate the relation between the use of risk management and increased share value. Empirical evidence on whether risk management increases shareholder value is not yet available, but some evidence is beginning to suggest that risk management may actually have an impact on the firm's beta.

If financial price risks are diversifiable, the capital asset pricing model (CAPM) would predict that financial price risk management would have no effect on beta. However, in their survey of empirical work on the effects of the introduction of derivative securities on the underlying assets, Aswath Damodaran and Marti G. Subrahmanyam (1992) note evidence that when derivatives on individual equities are introduced, *the beta for the involved firm declines.*

Using data on 32 stocks for the period 1970–76, Gary Trennepohl and William Dukes (1979) find that after options were listed on the stocks, the beta for the individual stock declined. Robert Klemkosky and Terry Maness (1980) had similar results for a sample of 40 stocks over the period 1972–79. However, as noted in Table 20–6, the more recent studies do not find any statistically significant changes in beta.[18]

TABLE 20–5   Comparison

	Prediction	Estimate
Risk Management to Reduce Taxes		
Tax loss carry forwards	?	+
Tax credits	?	+
Income in progressive region of tax schedule	?	+ (ns)
Risk Management to Reduce Costs of Financial Distress		
Interest coverage	−	?
Interest rate or FX risk	+	+
Leverage	+	+
Credit rating	−	−(ns)
Risk Management to Facilitate Optimal Investment		
R&D expenditure	+	+
Market value/book value	+	?

NOTE: (ns) = estimate not statistically significant; ? = evidence was ambiguous.

TABLE 20–6   **The Impact of the Introduction of Options on Individual Shares on the Beta for the Shares**

Study	Number of Shares/ Period Examined	Impact on Beta of Individual Share
Trennepohl and Dukes (1979)	32/1970–76	Declined
Klemkosky and Maness (1980)	40/1972–79	Declined
Skinner (1988)		No change
Damodaran and Lim (1991)	200/1973–85	No change

Notes

1. However, in some instances, the decision to sell an option is simply another way to "act on a view."

2. The 4 percent floor plus the 15-basis-point spread.

3. We also addressed this topic in Chapter 14 when we discussed swaptions.

4. This section is adapted from Rawls and Smithson (1990).

5. The original M&M proposition focused on the firm's debt-equity ratio (Modigliani and Miller, 1958). The rationale is that because (under their assumptions) leverage by an individual is a perfect substitute for corporate leverage, an investor will not pay the firm for corporate leverage. The M&M proposition was extended to dividends in Modigliani and Miller (1961), with the argument that "homemade" dividends can be created as the investor sells the firm's stock.

6. Indeed, the mathematical paradigm that makes this happen even has a name: *Jensen's inequality.*

7. A substantial body of evidence demonstrates that tax preference items will result in the effective tax function being convex. For example, see Siegfried (1974), Zimmerman (1983), and Wilkie (1988).

8. The work of Jerry Warner suggests that the direct costs of bankruptcy are small in relation to the value of the firm (Warner 1977b). However, his evidence suggests that there are scale economies in this cost function, so avoiding these costs is potentially more important for smaller firms.

9. This conflict has been discussed under the rubric of agency problems. The agency problem refers to the conflicts of interest that occur in virtually all cooperative activities among self-interested individuals. The agency problem was introduced by Jensen and Meckling (1976).

10. The problem referred to as *asset substitution* is a case in point. A firm can increase the wealth of its shareholders at the expense of its bondholders by issuing debt with the promise of investing in low-risk projects and then investing the proceeds in high-risk projects.

11. Myers (1977).

12. Wall (1989).

13. This section is adapted from a column I wrote for *Risk:* "Theory v. Practice: Does Financial Risk Management Increase Shareholder Value?" (Smithson, 1996a).

14. Rather than focus on the determinants listed in Table 20–3, the principal focus of the Hentschel and Kothari paper was on testing the hypothesis that derivatives are used to "hedge," not to "speculate." (Hentschel and Kothari were unable to reject the null hypothesis that firms are hedging.)

15. As will be described later in this section, the principal focus of Tufano's paper was on the relation between share holding and the use of risk management.

16. The Geczy, Minton, and Schrand empirical analysis summarized in Table 20–4 evolved from a paper they published in 1995. Their 1995 paper examined a larger number of firms (411 rather than 372) and considered interest rate and commodity-price risk management, in addition to foreign exchange risk management.

17. The positive relation between the firm's market-to-book ratio and its use of risk management reported by Geczy, Minton, and Schrand becomes stronger when that variable is interacted with leverage. Geczy, Minton, and Schrand interpret this to mean that firms with more growth opportunities and more constraints on financing are more likely to use derivatives.

18. As Damodaran and Subrahmanyam point out, the difference may be that the more recent studies correct for nontrading problems in estimating beta.

21

MEASURING A NONFINANCIAL FIRM'S EXPOSURE TO FINANCIAL PRICE RISK

At the outset of this book, we stressed that the volatility of interest rates, foreign exchange rates, and commodity prices is greater today than it has been in the past and that this increased volatility has put some otherwise well-managed firms into financial distress.

While a firm's CEO or CFO might find this discussion of the altered financial environment intellectually appealing, managers tend to be more pragmatic, reacting with more specific questions:

Is *my* firm one that can be put out of business by this increased volatility? To what degree is my firm exposed to interest rates? Foreign exchange rates? Commodity prices?

These are the questions this chapter addresses.

In this chapter, we describe methods of measuring a firm's exposure. We first look at the ways in which financial price risk would be reflected in the firm's annual report. We then look at methods used to obtain external—market-price-based—measures of exposures. We conclude by looking at internal measures of financial price risk.

Before we begin, let's put this in perspective by looking at the experience of one large multinational firm.

Financial Price Risk Reflected in the Firm's Financial Statements

Perhaps the first place to examine the impact of volatility in interest rates, commodity prices, and foreign exchange rates on a firm is in the firm's financial statements. In this section, we describe some of the ways in which financial price risk

Risk Management in Practice

Risk Management at British Petroleum

R. K. Hinkley

The formation of BP Finance in 1985 raised the profile of financial risk management across the BP Group. Subsequently a risk management unit was created, with the aim of capitalizing on the company's experience using financial products to manage foreign exchange, interest rate, and commodity-price risks. BP had proven trading expertise in these areas but saw further opportunity in a more systematic approach to the management of its longer-term, structural exposures.

Such an approach clearly begs the question of defining the underlying exposures. While the financial services sector has been very proficient in developing products to manage risk, it has not always been as helpful in giving treasurers the necessary understandings to use them efficiently. In BP, we sought to resolve such concerns by commissioning extensive research of our financial risks, using external help for specific aspects where our own expertise was limited.

At the heart of this study lay two empirical studies:

1. An analysis of BP's historical cash flows, testing their correlation with key financial variables.
2. An analysis of BP's historical share prices, also testing their correlation with key financial variables.

As well as providing insight into BP's long-term exposures, comparison of the two sets of results indicated whether the market's perceptions of risk matched those based on recent performance.

The issues surrounding statistical analysis of this kind are well aired (in the textbooks). For us, the problems were compounded by the significant changes to the Group's portfolio that had occurred. However, we were able to derive a number of key conclusions.

The cash flow analysis highlighted the expected exposure to crude oil and product prices, but it was weaker than expected. It confirmed the use of the U.S. dollar base, but the interest rate exposure was lower than we had anticipated. Two important aspects of risk management were brought out in this work.

1. Correlations among financial variables. While it may be possible to isolate, say, a pure exchange risk in the short run and hedge it in a

straightforward way using a forward or option, over the long term the correlations, for example, between exchange rates and oil prices, must be taken into account. This has obvious implications for financial strategy and the design of risk management products.

2. The significance of tax regimes. A good part of BP's North Sea revenues is paid to the UK government as royalties and taxes. Much of the tax rate is directly related to the oil price. BP is more exposed to this regime than its competitors. The outcome is that BP's oil price exposure is lower than its relative asset mix might imply, reflecting the offset through the tax system.

The share price analysis was conducted using an estimation equation similar to that provided in the final section of this chapter. As anticipated, the UK stock market proved to be a strong driver of BP's share price behavior over the period tested, but oil and product prices, and the dollar-pound exchange rate, also had significant explanatory power. This suggests that the market was differentiating BP according to its exposure to these variables. In principle, this kind of information should help the design of investor relations programs.

A potential weakness of both studies was that they were backward looking. Markets and company portfolios are subject to change. One way to help overcome such difficulty is through the use of forward-looking simulation models that can be tested and improved in real time.

Overall, the work put BP's risk management onto a sounder foundation. We are conscious of the limitations of the research, but our experience suggests that complete accuracy, if such a thing even exists, is not necessary. Having stable policies that are broadly correct is enough.

R. K. Hinkley is currently BP's Deputy Group Treasurer. Prior to that he served in a number of planning, control, and finance posts, including a spell as Corporate Treasurer for BP Australia during 1988–90 and Head of BP's Strategy Team. Prior to joining British Petroleum, Dr. Hinkley was a member of HM Treasury from 1972 to 1981.

is reflected in the firm's balance sheet, statement of consolidated income, and statement of changes in financial position. We also note the one place the firm's annual report might reflect the firm's economic exposure.

The Balance Sheet

The balance sheet (including the notes) provides insight into a number of questions.

What Is the Firm's Liquidity?   Some indicators of liquidity are the *current ratio* (current assets divided by current liabilities), which measures the ability of the firm to cover its bills within one year, and the *quick ratio* (cash, short-term investments, and net receivables divided by current liabilities), which measures the firm's ability to cover its bills immediately.

Liquidity can substitute for risk management. Some firms—notably German industrial corporations—have so much liquidity that the impact of volatility in their cash flows induced by financial prices can be cushioned. This was the case for Japanese firms as well until the dramatic decline in Japanese equity values absorbed this liquidity. U.S. firms tend to have a much smaller liquidity cushion.

How Highly Leveraged Is the Firm?   How much debt exists? How is the debt structured—for example, what percentage is fixed rate, floating rate, convertible, or some other form? Indicators of leverage include the firm's debt-equity ratio or the ratio of debt to debt plus current assets. Note also that some firms have material levels of off-balance-sheet leverage through leases that are reported in footnotes to the financial statements.

Does the Company Have Foreign Exchange Translation Exposures?   The indicator of a translation exposure is the existence of foreign subsidiaries or foreign operations.

Does the Company Have Foreign Exchange Transaction Exposures?   The balance sheet (or the notes) may indicate receivables or payables whose value will change if the foreign exchange changes. Transaction exposures generally occur when there is a mismatch between currency received and the currency being paid out. Companies often think that as long as they can adjust their selling price for adverse changes in exchange rate fluctuations, they have no exposure. But companies often are exposed because they are not able to react quickly enough. Many corporations use a bulletin system for posting their prices. By the time they get around to making a change in the printed prices, a year may have passed. During this period, competitors may have entered the firm's domestic market, pricing their products lower because exchange rates moved in their favor.

Does the Company Have a Long-Term Foreign Exchange Exposure?   A firm may wish to repatriate profits made through its overseas operations in the form of dividends, royalties, or intercompany transfers. The case for such repatriation is especially strong in countries where the company forecasts a continuing decline in the value of the local currency. And while U.S. companies traditionally hedge only those profits remitted to the parent, they should consider hedging the portion they do not. The argument for doing so is especially compelling for highly leveraged companies facing a potential ratings downgrade and those thinking of using stock in making future acquisitions, either at home or abroad.

Is the Company Exposed to Interest Rate Risk?   The first place to look is at the firm's debt. If the firm has floating-rate debt, changes in short-term interest rates will result in changes in the firm's expenses. However, changes in interest rates will also change the cash flows received from (or the value of) the firm's investments.

Is the Firm Exposed to Commodity-Price Changes?   In addition to reflecting the firm's exposures to financial price risk, the balance sheet sometimes provides insights into the firm's rationale for using risk management. For example, the balance sheet will show whether the firm has investment tax credits or tax loss carry-forwards whose value could be increased through risk management instruments. As we noted in Chapter 20, if the firm's pretax income is volatile because of changes in exchange rates, interest rates, or commodity prices, the firm can increase its value by hedging.

Statement of Consolidated Income and Statement of Changes in Financial Position

A balance sheet is limited in what it reveals about financial price risk. It is like a snapshot: it shows only what the firm's financial status was at one point in time. The balance sheet does not indicate whether the financial health of the firm is improving, getting worse, or developing a condition that could put the firm in distress.

To evaluate financial changes over time and the impact they have on a firm's risk profile, additional information is necessary, information that portrays the firm's financial health as both a snapshot and a movie (in financial jargon, both *flows* and *stocks*). That leads us to the firm's statement of consolidated income and statement of changes in financial position.

Statement of Consolidated Income.   This account provides data on the state of the core business—the demand for the firm's products and the pattern of costs—and facilitates analysis of the firm's current financial health. From this baseline, one can identify the financial risks that could jeopardize or enhance the firm's position. This checklist indicates some of the questions analysts would ask and the line items they would examine:

What is the State of the Market for This Firm's Output?   Is the core business expanding or eroding? Some of the indicators are change in net sales and the inventory-turnover ratio.

Illustration 21–1

Looking for Financial Price Risk in the Firm's Balance Sheet

Below is a balance sheet for a hypothetical corporation that is a composite of a number of balance sheets from U.S. industrial corporations to illustrate how financial price risks might appear. The balance sheet itself tells us something about liquidity and leverage.

XYZ Corporation: Consolidated Balance Sheet

(In Millions) Assets		November 30, 1988 Liabilities & Shareholders' equity	
Current assets		Current liabilities	
Cash and short-term investments	$213	Accounts payable	$686
Receivables, net	314	Notes payable	493
Prepaid expenses	136	Accrued liabilities	650
Deferred income tax benefit	67	Other current liabilities	236
Inventories	452		
		Total current liabilities	2,065
Total current assets	1,182		
		Long-term debt	1,115
Property, buildings, and equipment			
Property	937	Deferred income taxes	388
Buildings	1,363		
Equipment	3,052	Other liabilities	374
Construction in progress	166		
Total prop, bldgs, equip at cost	5,518		
less accumulated depreciation	(1,876)	Shareholders' equity	
		Preferred stock	234
Total net prop, bldgs, equip	3,642	Common stock	788
		Retained earnings	1,434
Other noncurrent assets	189	Less com. stock in treasury	(394)
		Cumulative foreign	
		Currency adjustment	(8)
Other assets			
Intangible assets	65	Total shareholders' equity	2,054
Investments in affiliates (foreign & domestic)	629		
Miscellaneous assets	289		
Total other assets	983		
		Total liabilities and	
Total assets	$5,996	shareholders' equity	$5,996

Handwritten annotations:

Quick ratio: (213 + 314) / 2,065

Current ratio: 1,182 / 2,065

FX translation Exposure?

Debt-Equity Ratio: (2,065 + 1,115 + 374) / 2,054

Looking for Financial Price Risk in the Firm's Balance Sheet continued

Liquidity

XYZ's balance sheet indicates some liquidity concerns. Its "current ratio" (current assets divided by current liabilities) is just 0.57, which means it can pay back roughly half of what it owes currently. (A less risky ratio would be 1.5–2.0.) Its "quick ratio" (cash and short-term investments and net receivables divided by current liabilities), a measure of the firm's ability to cover its bills now if it had to, is just 0.25. (A more desirable ratio would fall somewhere between 0.75 and 1.0.)

Leverage

For XYZ, the ratio of debt to equity assets

$$\frac{2,065 + 1,115 + 374}{2,054} = 1.73$$

is high enough to raise the eyebrows of ratings agencies.

In the case of XYZ, the notes to the balance sheet tell us even more than does the balance sheet itself:

Notes to the Consolidated Financial Statement

Possible A/L (interest rate) Exposures

Significant Accounting Policies

A. **Principals of Consolidation**—The consolidated financial statement includes the accounts of XYZ Corporation, a holding company, and its domestic and foreign subsidiaries at the close of our fiscal year which occurred on 11/30/88. Due to the dissimilar nature of its operations, **XYZ's wholly owned finance subsidiary** is included here on the equity basis. Hereafter XYZ Corporation will be known as "Parent Company," . . .

Commodity Price Exposure

C. **Inventories**—The LIFO method is used to value all inventories. Copper, a primary component for the manufacture of the latest design . . . and is among inventory . . .

F. **Income Taxes**—The provision for income taxes is based on pretax financial income which differs from taxable income. Differences generally arise because certain items, such as depreciation and write-downs of certain assets, are reflected in different time periods for financial and tax purposes. At XYZ Corporation, we chose to use the flow-through method of accounting for investment tax credits. This method enables a firm to recognize investment tax credits as a reduction of income tax expense in the year the qualified investments were made. The statutory Federal income tax rate for 1987 and 1988 was reduced by the Tax Reform Act of 1986. However, the effective income tax rate for 1987 actually increased due to the repeal of the investment tax credit (although some credits were allowed in 1986 under the transition rules) and a higher capital gains tax rate.

G. **Property, Plant & Equipment**—Recorded at cost . . .

FX Exposures

J. **Foreign Currency Transition—The local currency of the foreign subsidiary is the functional currency.** The rate of exchange in effect on the balance sheet is used to translate the value of the assets and liabilities. Operating results are converted to U.S. dollars by averaging the prevailing exchange rates during the period. Gains or losses due to currency translations over the period have been captured in a special equity retained account.

L. **Research & Development**—New product development . . .

Foreign Operations

FX Exposures

Sales from consolidated foreign operations were 15.5% of the total sales for 1988. Net income of consolidated foreign companies totaled $106MM in 1988. Net foreign assets consist of manufacturing facilities in Ireland, Spain, Italy and Taiwan.

Commitments, Contingent Liabilities, and Restrictions on Assets

On November 30, 1988 commitments for capital expenditures in progress were approximately . . .

Looking for Financial Price Risk in the Firm's Balance Sheet continued

Discontinued Operations

During the second quarter of 1988, our southwestern manufacturing operations were discontinued. The net assets of these operations have been consolidated in this balance sheet. Additional after tax charges from these discontinued operations have been recorded.

The adjustments are the result of the anticipated effects of the 1986 Tax Reform Act, additional estimated tax costs and some other minor adjustments to reserves.

Supplemental Disclosures to Statements of Cash Flow

Interest and taxes have been classified . . .

Cash and Short-Term Investments

Figures for cash and short-term investments consist of commercial paper, loan participations, certificates of deposit, and bankers' acceptances. All short-term investments are considered cash equivalents for purposes of disclosure in this balance sheet. The wholly owned finance subsidiary, XYZ Finance, purchases nearly all notes receivable resulting from domestic operations. **Foreign subsidiaries sell certain receivables to a non-affiliated finance company.**

erest Rate Expo-sure

Legal Proceedings

The matters cited below . . .

Preferred Shares of Stock

In 1985, the Parent Company issues 2,340,000 shares of **Adjustable Rate Cumulative Preferred Stock,** at face value of $100 per share. The annualized dividend rate for the initial dividend periods ended January 15, 1986, and April 15, 1986, was 10%. Thereafter, dividends have been set quarterly at an annualized rate of 1.85% less than the highest of the U.S. Treasury three-month, 10-year or 20-year maturity rates, which rate may not be less than 6.75% nor greater than 14.0%. The preferred stock is redeemable, in part or in whole, at the option of the Parent Company.

Foreign Exchange Exposures

XYZ's balance sheet suggests the company may face significant foreign exchange trans-

lation exposures. The notes tell us that XYZ's net asset translation exposures consist of manufacturing facilities in Ireland, Spain, Italy, and Taiwan.

Because foreign sales make up only 15.5 percent of the company's total, XYZ may be less concerned about foreign exchange transaction exposures. Nevertheless, exchange rate fluctuations may affect the company's ability to compete against foreign manufacturers.

Interest Rate Exposures

Investments—XYZ's current assets include $123 million in cash and short-term investments, which include commercial paper, loan participations, certificates of deposit and bankers' acceptances. The company should consider the yield erosion that would occur on these instruments if rates decline.

Gap—Because the finance subsidiary purchases receivables from domestic operations, it must fund those purchases, presumably through long-term debt. The result is an interest rate funding/lending gap.

Commodity-Price Exposures

The notes to XYZ's balance sheet indicate the company is exposed to changing copper prices, referring to "copper [as] a primary component for the manufacturing component of the latest design."

XYZ has a hidden interest rate exposure in the capital structure. In 1985, XYZ issued 2.34 million shares of adjustable-rate preferred stock that pays a dividend tied to an interest rate index. Consequently, XYZ has an interest rate exposure. Moreover this preferred is "dividend-constrained," guaranteeing that the

---

Looking for Financial Price Risk in the Firm's Balance Sheet continued

preferred dividend payouts will be within specified range—between 6.75 percent and 14 percent. The net result is that, by issuing this form of preferred stock, XYZ has sold an interest rate collar.

Are there investment tax credits and tax loss carryforwards that can be accessed via risk management instruments? Leveraged companies such as XYZ should be doing everything possible to reduce their tax burden and preserve cash, and one way to do that is via tax planning. It is essential for XYZ to use its investment tax credits (ITCs) and tax loss carryforwards (TLCFs). XYZ's balance sheet suggests the company might take advantage of both ITCs and TLCFs.

Are the Company's Costs Changing Relative to Income? Indicators include cost of goods sold; selling, administrative, and general costs; and gross margin.

Are There Foreign Exchange Exposures? The income statement will provide information about currencies in which the firm buys or sells, and the analyst will want to look at transactional foreign exchange gains or losses.

How Well Is the Firm Carrying Its Debt? And are there year-to-year changes in the levels or the sensitivities of that debt? The indicators to focus on are times interest earned and debt coverage ratios.

Statement of Changes in Financial Position. More subjective evaluations of this statement are required. Fewer accounting ratios can be used as a basis for objective evaluations. Nevertheless, two issues tend to be stressed:

Quality of Earnings. An analyst looks beyond the funds a firm may be accumulating. After all, it can be doing so while going out of business. The more relevant question: Do the firm's earnings result from ongoing operations or do the earnings reflect short-term fixes?

Pension Fund Policies. Who manages the pension fund? What are the policy guidelines? What is in the portfolio? Are there substantial unfunded liabilities?

The Letter to the Shareholders in the Annual Report

So far, we have illustrated how changes in exchange rates, interest rates, or commodity prices can affect the value of the firm or the company's net income through changes in the value of assets or liabilities (known as *translation exposures*) or through firm commitment *transaction exposures*.

Illustration 21–2

Looking for Financial Price Risk in the Firm's Statement of Consolidated Income

Applying the preceding questions to the statement of consolidated income for XYZ Corporation yields some interesting results.

XYZ Corporation: Statement of Consolidated Income (in millions of U.S. dollars, except per share data)

| | Fiscal Year Ended | |
	11/30/88	11/30/87
Net sales	12,595	10,313
Costs and expenses:		
Costs of goods sold	7,808	5,672
Selling, administrative, & general costs	3,230	3,106
Interest expense	463	403
Pension expense	80	69
Foreign currency expense	232	206
Depreciation	113	103
Total costs and expenses	11,926	9,559
Income from continuing operations before taxes	669	754
Income taxes (U.S. & foreign)	122	176
Income from continuing operations	547	578
Income per share— continuing operations	$8.29	$8.76
Discontinued operations after taxes	34	—
Net income	581	578
Net income per share	$8.81	$8.76
Average number of common shares	66	66

Margin notes (left): Net sales are up by 22% / Selling costs have risen by only 4% / But... Cost of goods sold increased dramatically. / Interest and FX expenses are both up dramatically.

The income statement indicates that sales and administration are doing well:

• XYZ's products are selling well. Net sales reflect an increase in revenues of about 22 percent. And even after adjusting for the 4.8 percent inflation rate in 1988, XYZ has experienced a real increase in sales growth of roughly 17.2 percent.

• With such an increase in sales, many firms have had troubles keeping their people motivated: with sales increasing, the staff often begins to take life too easy. But the income statement indicates that no one at XYZ is living "high on the hog." Selling, administrative, and general costs have risen by only 4 percent, a much smaller percentage than the increase in sales, indicating the sales representatives continue to fly coach and stay in Motel 6, while the office staff watches the paper clips.

But something is wrong in production and in finance:

• Costs of goods sold increased dramatically, rising from 55 percent of net sales in 1987 to 62 percent in 1988. A footnote to the financial statements addressed this, noting that most of this increase was attributable to a rise in the price of copper, a primary input in the production of XYZ's output. (In light of this copper price change, the performance of both side and S&A expenses should be reinterpreted; neither is particularly spectacular.)

• Interest expense is up. (The source of this increase will be discussed when we look at the statement of changes in financial position.) With this increase in interest expense,

Looking for Financial Price Risk in the Firm's Statement of Consolidated Income continued

Costs of Goods Sold.
In 1988, the average price of electrolytic copper rose to 122.66¢ per lb. from 84.80¢ per lb. in 1987. Since copper is a primary input in producing XYZ's products, this 45% increase in copper prices had a significant impact on cost of goods sold.

...and a significant portion of our problems can be laid at Washington's doorstep. Over the past three years, the dollar lost almost one-fourth of its value relative to the yen as the dollar fell from 168 yen per dollar in 1986 to 144 yen in 1987 and 128 yen in 1988. Since XYZ sources a significant amount of components from Asia, this decline in the value of the dollar has hit us hard ...Furthermore, Washington's failure to negotiate down Japan's (and others') protective tariffs has severely limited our ability to recoup the high expense with export revenues...

service on the firm's debt is becoming increasingly troublesome: times interest earned has declined from 1.88 times in 1987 to 1.51 times in 1988.

• As the value of the dollar continued its decline in 1988, XYZ's foreign currency expense increased markedly. The chief executive officer of XYZ mentioned this problem explicitly in his letter to the shareholders, as he complained about the monetary policies of the G-7 and about U.S. trade policies ... And the result is reduced performance at XYZ.

• XYZ's net profit margin fell from 6 percent in 1987 to 4 percent in 1988.

But changes in financial prices can also have an impact on the value of a firm through transactions not yet booked, so the firm must also consider what we call *contingent exposures.* Changes in exchange rates, interest rates, or commodity prices can influence a firm's sales and market share, so it's worthwhile for treasury executives to consider their competitive exposures as well.

As we illustrated earlier, anyone wishing to identify and quantify a firm's translation and transaction exposures will find plenty of helpful information in the firm's financial statements. The annual report, its income statement, and statement of changes in financial position all contain valuable information that can be used to measure risk.

Illustration 21–3

Looking for Financial Price Risk in the Firm's Statement of Changes in Financial Position

Applying these general guidelines to XYZ, several conclusions are obvious.

XYZ Corporation: Statement of Changes in Financial Position
(in millions of U.S. dollars)

	Fiscal Year Ended	
	11/30/88	11/30/87
Funds provided (used) by operations:		
Net income	581	578
Depreciation	113	103
Deferred income tax	67	58
Accounts and notes receivable	(56)	(40)
Deferred pension plan costs	50	40
Accounts payable—trade	38	29
Funds provided by operating activities	793	768
Funds provided by discontinued operations	9	—
Funds provided by extraordinary items	3	—
Total funds provided by continuing operations	805	768
Funds provided (used) by investment activities: special pension funding	(37)	(25)
Total funds provided by investment activities	(37)	(25)
Funds provided (used) by financing activities:		
Short-term debt incurred	51	19
Short-term debt paid	(149)	(82)
Long-term debt paid	(220)	(142)
Dividend paid	(122)	(120)
Total funds provided by financing activities	(440)	(325)
Increase in cash and short-term investments	(6)	8
Net increase (decrease)	322	426

The quality of XYZ's earnings has declined:
• Comparing the 1988 financials with those for 1987, XYZ posted increases both in net income (from $578 million to $581 million) and in total funds provided by continuing operations (from $768 million to $805 million). Unfortunately, these aggregate figures disguise the fact that the "quality" of XYZ's earnings declined in 1988.
• The gain in total funds is overstated by two one-time, non-operation transactions: as recorded in the footnotes to the financial statements, XYZ benefited from the sale of a facility.

Discontinued Operations.
During the second quarter of 1988, XYZ sold its Ohio assembly operation to reduce operating costs and eliminate duplicated work responsibilities. Funds provided by this discontinued operation after taxes amounted to $9 million.

Handwritten margin notes:
Net income increased.

But all of the increase is offset by one-time transactions.

The firm is adding short-term debt.

The firm is less liquid.

Looking for Financial Price Risk in the Firm's Statement of Changes in Financial Position continued

And from the settlement of a lawsuit.

> *Extraordinary Items.*
> *A favorable judgment for XYZ Corp. was found after several years of dispute over a matter of unfair competition. The suit was initiated by XYZ against ABC Corp. in 1986. An award in the amount of $3 million was granted by the Appellate Court to XYZ during the first quarter of this year...*

• Even more telling, net income represents a smaller percentage of total funds provided by continuing operations in 1988 than it did in 1987, falling from 75 percent to 72 percent.

There are problems in the investment division:

• According to a footnote, a special pension funding was required in 1988.

> *Retirement Benefits.*
> *XYZ Corp. increased funds allocated to the special pension account to offset losses in the internally managed fixed-income portfolio. The special pension fund is protected by internal policy which determines the funding limits...*

Losses in the fixed-income portfolio were the result of rising interest rates.

The structure of XYZ's financing has changed:

• As indicated in the funds provided (used) by financing activities section, XYZ incurred almost three times more short-term debt in 1988 than it did in 1987. Because the market value of its shares declined in 1988 and it issued no new shares in 1988, this increase in debt means that XYZ's debt-equity ratio has risen.

• The footnotes indicate that most of XYZ's debt is short-term, floating-rate debt.

> *Cash, Short-Term Investments.*
> *During the third and fourth quarters of fiscal year 1988, the management at XYZ saw it necessary to add $24.9 million in floating rate, short-term debt to the total debt outstanding... Total floating rate, short-term debt for the year amounted to $38.5 million while total fixed-rate debt equalled $12.50 million.*

XYZ is less liquid.

• Apparently, as XYZ has increased its marketing effort, it has had more trouble collecting its receivables from customers: accounts and notes receivable rose by 40 percent, about twice the increase in sales.

Looking for Financial Price Risk in the Firm's Statement of Changes in Financial Position continued

• Increase in cash and short-term investments shows XYZ decreased its holding of short-term financial assets in 1988.

Not surprisingly, these same problems have been noted by the rating agencies. Early in 1989, XYZ Corporation appeared in Standard & Poor's *CreditWeek* in a way it would have liked to avoid.

XYZ Corp. (revised to negative).

Credit implications are revised to negative from "developing" on XYZ Corp.'s 'A' senior debt and 'A – ' subordinated debt ratings . . .

It is somewhat difficult, but certainly not impossible, to find information about a firm's strategic exposures. A company's letter to shareholders in its annual report often contains clues. (See Illustration 21–4.)

External Measures of Financial Price Risk

Since "external" measures of financial price risk rely on values obtained in the market, they could also be called "market-based measures." To give you some idea of how different external measures of risk fit together, we can look at the external measures as different factor models.

We can write a general linear factor model as

$$R_{it} = \sum_j b_{ij} F_{jt} + e_{it} \qquad (21-1)$$

where R_i is the rate of return on financial instrument i—it could be a bond or a deposit or a share of stock—F_j is the jth "factor," b_{ij} is the weighting coefficient for the jth factor, and e_i is the residual variation. In the sense of a risk measure, the coefficient b_{ij} measures the financial instrument's sensitivity to—exposure to—the jth factor.

Illustration 21–4

Looking for Financial Price Risk
in the Letter to the Shareholders

The letter to the shareholders from the president of XYZ Corporation reiterates some of the exposures identified in its accounting statements, but it also mentions some contingent and competitive exposures.

XYZ Corporation: Letter to shareholders

Pursuing total quality in everything we do is the key to creating value—value for our shareholders, for our customers, and for our employees.

This year's results

Commodity Price Exposure

The year's results met the challenging goal of maintaining the Corporation's record of growth with an increase of sales of 22%. Our products showed excellent improvements in sales worldwide.

Corporate earnings, however, declined to an unsatisfactory level due greatly to unexpectedly sharp increases in the cost of copper and fierce competition which inhibited recovery of these costs. In addition to this raw materials price increase, we have continued to see price increases on intermediate products; and a significant portion of our problems can be laid at Washington's doorstep. Over the past three years the dollar lost almost one-fourth of its value relative to the yen as the dollar fell from 168 yen per dollar in 1986 to 144 yen in 1987 and 128 yen in 1988. Since XYZ sources a significant number of components from Asia, this decline in the value of the dollar has hit us hard.

FX Exposure

In response to the severe foreign currency moves seen over the past several years, we have stepped up efforts to increase productivity and cut costs.

Tempered optimism

Our longer-term outlook, while optimistic, is tempered by the knowledge that we face substantial challenges: the need to increase our investment in product and facility improvements, higher customer expectations, competitive pressures on margins and substantial marketing costs. Furthermore, Washington's failure to negotiate down Japan's (and others') protective tariffs has severely limited our ability to recoup the high expense with export revenues. Only the strongest performers will survive in the highly competitive years ahead, and we intend to be one of them. To do so, we must provide high-quality products that exceed our customers' expectations, instill a people-oriented culture throughout the company, and implement the most cost-efficient operating and business processes possible.

If we focus on these priorities, and if we apply ourselves diligently to the basics of running the business, we will maintain our momentum and will continue to perform strongly in the years ahead.

John B. Doe

For the Board of Directors
Chairman and Chief Executive Officer

Looking for Financial Price Risk in the Letter to the Shareholders continued

Commodity Price Exposure

XYZ's exposure to copper prices, which appeared in the "cost of goods sold" footnote to the statement of consolidated income, is highlighted in the letter to the shareholders.

Foreign Exchange Exposures

It's not unusual to see poor earnings blamed on foreign exchange: Caterpillar, for ex-

ample, said in its 1982 annual report that "the strong dollar is a prime factor in Caterpillar's reduced sales and earnings. . . ." Like Caterpillar, XYZ also faces transaction and contingent exposures: a weak dollar has made its input costs more expensive—and they may become even more expensive in the future.

By regressing the rate of return to a particular equity (R_i) against the return for a market portfolio (R_m)

$$R_{it} = \alpha_i + \beta_i R_{mt} + e_{it} \tag{21-5}$$

one obtains estimates of beta (β)—a measure of the firm's market risk.[1]

Using a technique much like that by which analysts obtain the firm's beta, it is possible to measure the market's perception of the sensitivity of the value of the firm to changes in interest rates, foreign exchange rates, and commodity prices. Our task is to decompose the variation in the share price return and to determine how much of the variation is attributable to movements in specific financial price. We do so by adding the financial prices to the market model.

Our approach follows the work of earlier researchers who added interest rates (bond prices) or foreign exchange rates to examine interest rate and foreign exchange exposures:

Mark Flannery and Christopher James (1984) added the rate of return from holding a constant-maturity, default-free bond (R_b) to the market model,[2]

$$R_{it} = \alpha_i + \beta_i R_{mt} + \gamma_{Bi} R_{Bt} + e_{it} \tag{21-6}$$

to examine the interest rate exposure reflected in equity prices for banks and S&Ls. In Equation 21–6, γ_{Bi} measures the bond price exposure (interest rate exposure) faced by financial institution i. Sweeney and Warga (1986) used much the same model, substituting the change in the interest rates (Δr) for the rate of return calculated from bond prices,

$$R_{it} = \alpha_i + \beta_i R_{mt} + \gamma_{ri}(\Delta r_t) + e_{it} \tag{21-7}$$

Aside

Duration in the Context of a Factor Model

While factor models are normally associated with the equity market, the first factor model used in finance appeared in the bond market—the duration model.

As we showed in Chapter 19, duration was "discovered" almost simultaneously by both Frederick Macaulay (1938) and Sir John Hicks (1939). Macaulay's goal was to define a measure by which two bonds with common maturity but divergent payment structures could be compared. In the Macaulay sense, duration measures when, on average, the value of the bond is received. Hicks attempted to measure interest rate sensitivity for any particular bond. In the tradition of Hicks, duration provides a measure of the exposure of the bond to interest rate risk.

In the context of a factor model, duration provides a measure of the relation between the rate of return on bond i and the percentage change in $(1 + r)$—the discount factor,*

$$R_{it} = b_i \left[\frac{\Delta r_t}{(1 + r_t)} \right] + e_{it} \quad (21\text{–}2)$$

In the preceding factor model, the coefficient b_i is the "duration" of bond i.[†] Rearranging the terms of Equation 21–2,

$$b_i = \text{duration} = R_{it} / [\Delta r_t / (1 + r_t)] \quad (21\text{–}3)$$

and since the rate of return on the bond, R, is simply the percentage change in the value of the bond ($\Delta V/V$), we can express duration in more familiar terms:

$$\text{Duration} = \frac{\left(\begin{array}{c} \text{percentage change} \\ \text{in value of the bond} \end{array} \right)}{\text{percentage change in } (1 + r)}$$

$$(21\text{–}4)$$

---

*This interpretation follows Hopewell and Kaufman (1973).

[†]If we refer to Macaulay measure as "duration," the measure in Equation 21–3 would be referred to as "modified duration." For a development of the relation between duration and modified duration, see Bierwag, Kaufman and Toevs (1983)

---

to examine the interest rate exposure reflected in equity prices for nonfinancial corporations—measured by γ_{ri}.

Jorion (1990) added the rate of change in a foreign exchange rate ($\Delta P_{FX}/P_{FX}$) to the market model,

$$R_{it} = \alpha_i + \beta_i R_{mt} + \gamma_{FXi} \left(\frac{P_{FX}}{P_{FX}} \right)^t + e_{it} \quad (21\text{–}8)$$

to examine the exchange rate exposure reflected in equity prices for U.S. multinationals. This exposure to foreign exchange rates is measured by γ_{FXi} in Equation 21–8.

Since we are interested in the exposure of financial and nonfinancial firms to movements in interest rates, foreign exchange rates, and commodity prices, our model incorporates the Flannery-James and Jorion models by including both the rate of change in interest rates ($\Delta r/r$) and the rate of change in exchange rates ($\Delta P_{FX}/P_{FX}$) as independent variables. Moving one step further to provide estimates of the firm's exposure to commodity-price risk, we add the rate of change of commodity prices ($\Delta P_c/P_c$). Hence, the equation we consider is

$$R_{it} = \alpha_i + \beta_i R_{mt} + \gamma_{ri}\left(\frac{\Delta r}{r}\right)^t + \gamma_{FXi}\left(\frac{\Delta P_{FX}}{P_{FX}}\right)^t + \gamma_{Ci}\left(\frac{\Delta P_c}{P_c}\right)^t + e_{it} \quad (21\text{-}9)$$

where β reflects the firm's exposure to the market and γ_{ri}, γ_{FXi}, and γ_{ci} reflect the exposure of firm i to interest rate risk, foreign exchange risk, and commodity-price risk, respectively.

Moving toward a more concrete illustration, suppose we wished to determine the sensitivity of some firm to

- three-month LIBOR,
- the 10-year Treasury bond rate,
- the deutsche mark-dollar exchange rate,
- the pound sterling-dollar exchange rate,
- the yen-dollar exchange rate, and
- the price of oil.

Using Equation 21–9, we could address this question by estimating the regression equation

$$\begin{aligned}
R_{it} = \alpha_i &+ \beta_i R_{mt} \\
&+ \gamma_{3M}(\Delta r_{3M}/r_{3M})_t + \gamma_{10Y}(\Delta r_{10Y}/r_{10Y})_t \\
&+ \gamma_{DM}(\Delta P_{DM}/P_{DM})_t + \gamma_{\pounds}(\Delta P_{\pounds}/P_{\pounds})_t + \gamma_{\yen}(\Delta P_{\yen}/P_{\yen})_t \\
&+ \gamma_{Oil}(\Delta P_{Oil}/P_{Oil})_t + e_t,
\end{aligned} \quad (21\text{-}10)$$

where R_{it} is the rate of return for holding a share of the firm's stock, R_{mt} is the rate of return for holding the market portfolio, $\Delta r_{3M}/r_{3M}$ is the percentage change in three-month LIBOR, and $\Delta r_{10Y}/r_{10Y}$ is the percentage change in the 10-year Treasury bond rate; $\Delta P_{DM}/P_{DM}$, $\Delta P/P_{\pounds}$, and $\Delta P_{\yen}/P_{\yen}$ are the percentage changes in the dollar prices of the three foreign currencies; and $\Delta P_{Oil}/P_{Oil}$ is the percentage change in the price of crude oil. The estimate of γ_{3M} and γ_{10Y} provides measures of the sensitivity to the exchange rates; and γ_{Oil} estimates the sensitivity to the oil price.

These coefficients actually measure elasticities. Further, had we used the percentage change in (1 + interest rate) instead of the percentage change in the interest rates themselves, the coefficients γ_{3M} and γ_{10y} could be interpreted as "duration" measures. Specifically, we could modify the estimation equation to provide a measure of "the duration of equity."

Another application of these techniques is to examine market-based measures of exposures for the firm's major competitors. This exercise can provide useful insight into the nature of the competition and the structure of the industry. Examining competitors' exposures can be especially valuable if the firm is private and thus lacks the return data to estimate its exposures directly. Finally, note that these approaches are not mutually exclusive. In fact, our experience suggests a comparison of the results from the different methods yields a much richer understanding of the firm's exposure.

Internal Measures of Financial Price Risk

The internal measures of financial price risk are concerned with flows: how sensitive are revenues and expenses to changes in interest rates, foreign exchange rates, and/or commodity prices? Over the past several years, we have worked with a number of firms to quantify their exposures to financial prices. Our experience is that firms use one of two methods to obtain an internal measure of financial price risk.

Statistical Analysis of Revenues and Expenses

For many firms, the likely first step is to look at the behavior of accounting data—revenue and expense data. This is accomplished by using regression to estimate the historical relation between the relevant financial prices and important internal data on revenues and expenses (as well as more disaggregated items such as capital expenditures). Using historical accounting data, managers can estimate models of the following form:

$$\text{Revenue}_t = a_0 + \Sigma\, a_i(\text{financial price})_{it} + e_{rt}$$
$$\text{Expense}_t = b_0 + \Sigma\, b_i(\text{financial price})_{it} + e_{rt}$$

Regression analysis is by definition an historical measure of a firm's sensitivity to financial prices. Although relatively simple to implement, the value of the results depends on historical relations holding true in the future. Therefore, for a firm entering new markets, these estimates of historical sensitivities are less informative than for a firm planning to maintain its current market position. In addition, accounting data will not necessarily reflect the true economic relations underlying the firm's financial price exposures. For example, accounting data typically do not reflect opportunity costs.

Simulation Analyses—Cash Flow Sensitivity[3]

As we will describe in more detail in Chapter 22, risk management practice in leading nonfinancial firms has been evolving from a focus on individual price exposures—interest rate, foreign exchange, or commodity—to the management of the firm's exposure to financial prices as a portfolio of interrelated risks.

Attaining the goal of a unified risk measure has been difficult for nonfinancial firms. Ideally, the firm would be able to sidestep the more market-specific terms and directly capture the effect of price changes on projected cash flows.

VAR Doesn't Fit Many Nonfinancial Firms.   The desire of nonfinancial firms to find an aggregate exposure measure is similar to the problem faced by derivatives dealers when it became clear that oversight by individual market or risk parameter was an ineffective means of controlling risk. As we described in Chapter 19, to address this problem, dealers have now largely adopted a set of aggregate exposure measures, broadly referred to as value-at-risk (VAR) measures, which ease the communication of exposure and acceptable limits between market professionals and senior management.

However, as we discussed in Chapter 19, VAR is not a suitable risk measure for most nonfinancial businesses. In contrast to dealers of derivatives, the nonfinancial end users have balance sheets that contain physical assets and intangible assets—e.g., capitalized research and development and brand names. For these nonfinancial firms, mark-to-market (or liquidation) values are relevant for, at best, a small portion of the balance sheet; instead, the focus is on projected cash flows over a multiyear planning horizon.

A natural definition of aggregate exposure for firms that manage cash flows over long horizons relates the size and timing of inflows to a firm's contractual commitments and investment objectives. This idea, which is becoming widely accepted, has been elegantly expressed by Kenneth Froot, David Scharfstein, and Jeremy Stein (1993). The *1994 Wharton Survey of Derivatives End-Users* also supports this notion, finding that 62 percent of nonfinancial firms report reducing cash flow volatility as their primary risk management objective.

The Logic of the Cash Flow Sensitivity Approach.   Our cash flow–based measure of exposure, *cash flow sensitivity,* defines a firm's consolidated exposure to financial prices as the probability that the firm will fail to meet financial performance targets as the result of unexpected changes in the financial prices.

The trick in implementing such a measure is in building a model that takes as its input uncertain financial and product prices and produces the desired probability-based exposure measure. To accomplish this linkage requires a model of the firm that is rich enough in detail to capture the effect of changes in market prices on production quantities and product markups.

As illustrated in Figure 21–1, we believe the foundation upon which to build this cash flow sensitivity model is the firm's existing budget or planning model. While not sufficient by itself to capture the firm's exposures, it serves as a firmwide risk management "circuit diagram," capturing relationships between commodity inputs, product prices, foreign and domestic operations, and contractual commitments such as debt and lease payments, to name but a few. Furthermore, the accounting framework is the logical choice for communicating exposure and setting overall risk management objectives that can be communicated both internally to managers and externally to investors, regulators, and rating agencies.

FIGURE 21–1   The Evolution of Corporate Risk Management

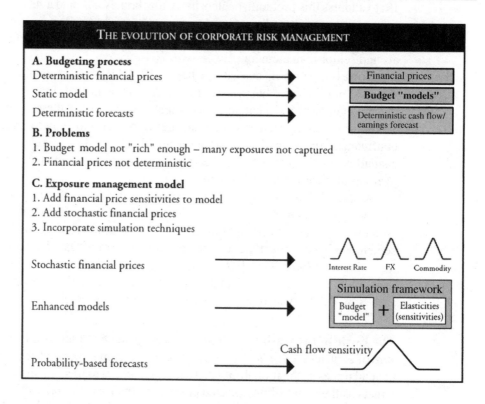

To move from the budget model to a cash flow sensitivity model requires addressing the two major shortcomings of the budgeting framework.

First, the firm's risk manager must develop a method of explicitly expressing the relationship between financial prices and changes in the firm's operating cash flows. For example, a change in a foreign exchange rate not only may affect the home currency value of an order book in the short run but also may affect the firm's market share in the long run as competitive advantage shifts between producers. Incorporating changes in operating variables requires managers to quantify, if only approximately, their response to changing financial prices.

Second, the firm's risk manager must replace the deterministic financial prices contained in the budget model with stochastic financial prices. Stochastic financial prices can be obtained using simulation software and models of how financial prices change over time. (The use of a simulation platform and models of financial price changes adds some complexity to the process; but it means management can be confident that the price scenarios fed into the model have the necessary realism.)

Defining Exposures. Building a model of exposure that goes beyond the base accounting model will be easier for some firms than others. Commodity-driven firms, single-product firms, and firms with relatively little direct or indirect foreign exchange exposure will have an easier time than multinational firms with global production and competition. However, in all cases the firm will want to identify two types of cash flow exposure.

The first type will arise from fixed contractual obligations: foreign currency accounts receivable, the amount of foreign currency debt, or an obligation to purchase a fixed amount of a commodity. For example, in the case of a U.S. firm with a German subsidiary, a change in the US$/DM exchange rate will not affect the local (DM) value of a receivable, but it will affect its value in terms of the home currency (US$). The home currency value of contractual obligations in a foreign currency will change in value one-for-one with the exchange rate; therefore, contractual exposures have an elasticity of one.

The second cash flow exposure arises from changes in the firm's operating cash flows as the result of financial price changes—i.e., operating exposures. Contractual cash flows will be fixed in the local currency (or units of a commodity), and only their nominal value in the home or base currency will change as prices change. Operating cash flows, however, will fluctuate because the amount of product the firm sells or quantity of resources consumed will vary along with the price. In other words, operating cash flows are subject to both price and quantity uncertainty.[4]

There are many approaches one can take to linking financial prices to changes in contractual and operating cash flows. One method is to incorporate an economic pricing model into the budget framework. For example, a refiner or specialty chemical manufacturer might have a pricing model that it uses to determine the prices and quantities of its outputs given a set of input prices. Similarly, some multinational firms model the price and demand for their products given foreign exchange rates and their competitors' pricing policies. Ideally these economic models, which capture both price and quantity variations, can be incorporated into the framework of the risk management model.

However, most firms will not have such detailed models or the resources to build them. Rather than model price and quantity sold directly, these firms will find a useful simplification in the idea of revenue and cost elasticities. *Elasticity* is simply the percentage change in one variable given a 1 percent change in another. If, for example, a firm's dollar revenues increase by 10 percent when the deutsche mark appreciates by 10 percent against the dollar, then the elasticity of dollar revenue with respect to the mark is one. As illustrated in the following box, elasticities can capture a wide variety of exposure situations whether arising from contractual or operating exposures.

Aside

Framing Exposures

Operating exposures are often referred to as competitive exposures. Consider again a U.S. firm with a German subsidiary. The subsidiary's local currency (DM) cash flows might depend on the value of the deutsche mark relative to one or more currencies. The value of the DM affects the competitive position of the subsidiary in Germany and other markets in which it operates. Since exchange rates will affect both the local currency cash flow and the conversion of the cash flow back to dollars, the total effect of an exchange rate change in terms of the home currency (dollar) could be larger or smaller than one-for-one. In other words, operating exposure *elasticities* could be larger or smaller than unity.

Framing operating exposures is a critical step in cash flow modeling. Inaccurate or incomplete characterization of the firm's exposure could do more harm than good. There are several ways a firm might develop good elasticity estimates. A domestic firm selling a product in a foreign market can base an elasticity estimate on how much of an exchange rate change it can "pass through" in the local currency price of its product without changing the quantity sold. Thus a U.S.-based firm selling into a highly competitive German market might be able to pass through only 10 percent of an adverse move in the dollar-deutsche mark exchange rate in its local (deutsche mark) price without affecting the quantity sold. If the firm's policy is to maintain market share, then revenue elasticity (in the short run) would be 0.9 (90 percent of the depreciation in the foreign currency is reflected in home currency revenue).

Another estimate of revenue (or cost) elasticity can be obtained from an analysis of the historical relationship between exchange rates and revenues (or costs). Revenue elasticity is sometimes called an exposure beta, because it is the same concept as an equity beta. Given good accounting data, one could use a regression of the percentage change in monthly home currency revenues as a function of the percentage change in one or more foreign exchange rates. Accounting data do not always cooperate with statistical analyses, but a regression might be a starting point.

Elasticity is a powerful exposure measurement tool. While we know that a change in foreign exchange rates might affect both the quantity of a product sold in a foreign market and its price, the elasticity concept captures the net effect of both the price and quantity change. How firms arrive at elasticity estimates will vary. Some may use economic models, but others will take a less technical approach. Asking operating managers to estimate the impact of various foreign exchange rate scenarios on their revenues and costs can lead to direct estimates of elasticities. These estimates can then be "tried on" with historical accounting results and exchange rates for fine tuning.

Elasticity also makes it easier to express the effect of a change in foreign exchange rates on revenue from domestic operations (the elasticity concept is not limited to foreign exchange—for example, one could calculate a commodity-price elasticity). A purely domestic manufacturing firm facing local competition from a foreign competitor can use elasticity to express its competitive exposure. If, historically, a 10 percent depreciation of the foreign currency causes domestic revenues to decline by 2 percent, then the domestic firm's exposure elasticity will be 0.2.

The determination of exposure elasticities should recognize links between pricing in the domestic and a foreign market. Pricing cannot become completely disconnected between the two markets because of the possibility of third parties shipping a firm's goods across borders to arbitrage price differentials. In a similar vein, a firm's response to foreign exchange rate changes will not necessarily be linear. A small change in the exchange rate may cause one response; a large change may cause another.

The translation of financial price changes into changes in operating performance is by far the most difficult task of cash flow modeling. However, the challenge should not be a deterrent since the issue, i.e., how the firm responds to changes in prices, exists whether the firm uses traditional characterizations of exposure or simulation-based methods. A distinct advantage of the modeling approach is that it forces managers to be explicit about their operating assumptions, and these assumptions can be examined in light of the model.

Simulating Financial Prices. Moving from a planning model based on fixed prices to a simulation based on a realistic model of financial prices has become significantly easier with the improvement of spreadsheet programs and the availability of software "add-ins" expressly designed for this purpose. Indeed, the knowledge of how to build a simulation model of the firm has been around for years; the renewed interest in the technique is driven by the combination of more powerful desktop computers and new insights into the uses of modeling for risk assessment and policy formulation.

Figure 21–2 illustrates the mechanical process of running the budget model with exposure measurement enhancements to generate a probability distribution

FIGURE 21–2   Monte Carlo Simulation

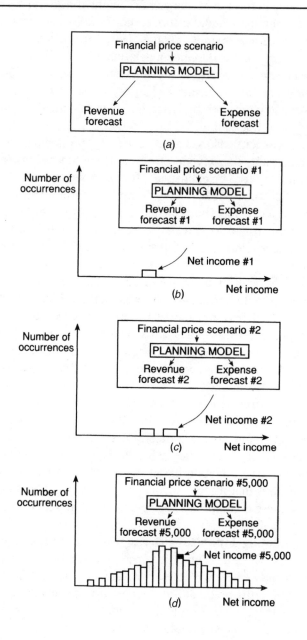

(a)

(b)

(c)

(d)

for cash flow. One can run the model several thousand times, each time feeding the model a different series of financial prices, e.g., one set of prices for each quarter over a three-year period. Each turn of the model generates another revenue and expense forecast, quarter by quarter, for the next three years. The histogram constructed in Figure 21–2 shows different realizations of cash flow at a given point in time, e.g., at the end of the second year.

At each iteration the model needs a new input for each financial price incorporated into the model. Thus, from an initial starting value of six-month LIBOR or the DM/US\$ exchange rate, or the price of West Texas Intermediate crude oil, we need a series of quarter-by-quarter price changes. A spreadsheet will generate normally distributed random changes in prices quite easily, but a realistic simulation requires using random changes in conjunction with a model of how interest rates, foreign exchange rates, and commodity prices change together.

In the simulation of interest rates and foreign exchange rates, it is important to use an economic model that ensures that interest rates and foreign exchange rates maintain a realistic relationship with each other during the planning horizon. In particular, the interest rate model will generate a yield curve for each quarter that will be realistic in the sense that there will be no arbitrage opportunities between points on the curve. Two-factor models have the added realism of also being able to generate inverted and "humped"-shaped curves.[5]

If the simulation incorporates yield curves in two or more currencies, it will be necessary to generate simulated foreign exchange rates that are consistent with the interest rates in each currency. Interest rates and foreign exchange rates are linked by an arbitrage relationship known as *covered interest parity*. Given the short-term interest rate in each currency and the spot foreign exchange rate, the covered interest parity relation we described in Chapter 4 defines the forward foreign exchange rate:

$$F_0 = S_0[(1 + r_{DM}) / 1 + r_{US\$}]$$

We can use this relationship to create a forward foreign exchange rate for each period that relates to the current state of interest rates. In a simple model, the next period's spot foreign exchange rate can be centered on the forward rate for that quarter with a normally distributed error. While not perfectly realistic, this technique ensures that interest rates and foreign exchange rates remain in economically reasonable relationships.

Implementing one of the yield-curve models requires some programming, but the resulting realism in the simulated rates and prices is worth the investment. The interest rate and foreign exchange rate simulation should be done carefully, but it should also be remembered that uncertainty in the firm's basic exposure model will be likely to swamp the subtleties in the most sophisticated yield curve models.

Extensions.   In the preceding example, the firm was concerned about *per-period* cash flow. Other firms view their exposure in terms of *cumulative* cash flow or balance sheet ratios (e.g., interest coverage). A major strength of the cash flow sensitivity approach is that these and other exposure definitions can be accommodated, so long as they can be expressed in terms of the balance sheet or income statement.

If the probability of failing to meet defined goals is too high, the firm can use the cash flow sensitivity model to determine how this probability might be lowered. For example, the simulation software we used has features to help identify those sources of uncertainty, e.g., interest rates or commodity prices, that had the great-

---

Illustration 21–5

Cash Flow Sensitivity for a Hypothetical Manufacturing Firm

To illustrate the use of a cash flow sensitivity model, we built a simple model around the consolidated financial statements of a hypothetical manufacturing firm assumed to be exposed to a single currency. Foreign exchange and commodity exposures were added as elasticities, and the firm's short-term debt was repriced each quarter at the prevailing short-term interest rate in each of two currencies.

The distribution of the firm's total cash flow on a quarterly basis for three years was simulated using a spreadsheet and an add-in Monte Carlo simulation function. There are several ways to express the output of the model. The following two-dimensional histogram shows the distribution of net cash flow for the eighth quarter, i.e., at the end of the second year.

Cash Flow Distribution of Year 2

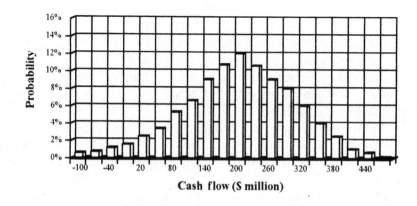

Cash Flow Sensitivity for a Hypothetical Manufacturing Firm continued

Combining all 12 quarterly cash flow estimates yields the following three-dimensional plot.

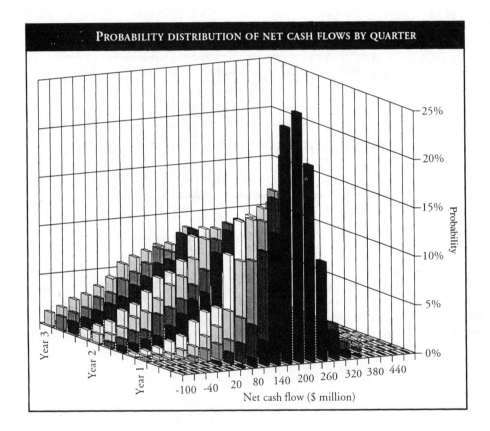

PROBABILITY DISTRIBUTION OF NET CASH FLOWS BY QUARTER

The quarter-by-quarter forecasts illustrate the increasing amount of uncertainty (width of the distribution) as cash flows are forecasted further into the future. Alternatively, one could plot the cumulative cash flow by quarter.

Given the information about the distribution of cash flow (or some other variable of interest), the senior management of the firm must decide whether the existing degree of uncertainty is acceptable. This requires a definition of a minimum performance level by the board of directors. For example, the firm could define a minimum level of cash flow by adding contractual interest and principal repayments (net of rollovers), current

Cash Flow Sensitivity for a Hypothetical Manufacturing Firm continued

dividends, and planned research and development spending. If cash flow falls below this level, the firm will have to increase debt, cut its dividend, or forgo planned investment.

Risk of Not Achieving Target

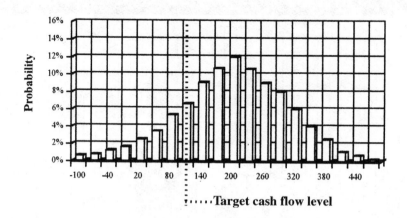

The preceding figure shows a bar superimposed on the histogram defining this level of critical cash flow. The probability of falling below this level is one possible measure of exposure. If this probability is too high, alternative strategies can be developed to bring in the left-hand tail of the distribution.

On a quarter-by-quarter basis the cash flow necessary to meet the firm's financial plan defines a level at which the firm is in "distress." The following figure illustrates the probability of failing to meet cumulative cash flow targets by quarter for three years.

est impact on performance. Using this feature helps focus the risk management discussion on the prices and markets with the greatest impact on performance. And it may highlight the fact that the firm needs only actively manage one or two critical exposures. Using the hypothetical manufacturing firm in Illustration 21–5, Figure 21–3 illustrates the relative impact of eliminating uncertainty in one price at a time by plotting the reduction in the upper and lower 95 percent confidence bounds on cash flow. For this example, almost nothing is to be gained in terms of performance by hedging the first three sources of uncertainty since the tails of the distribution are only marginally impacted. However, hedging financial prices 3 and 4 signifi-

Cash Flow Sensitivity for a Hypothetical Manufacturing Firm continued

Probability of Distress

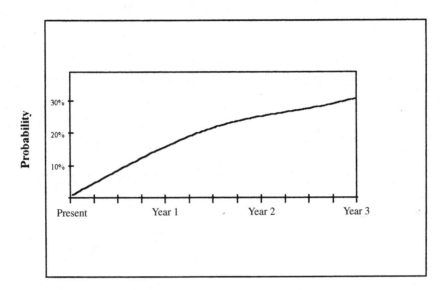

This concise way of displaying exposure information can be extended to include multiple objectives, e.g., cash flow, earnings, and interest coverage. By plotting multiple performance goals on the same chart, the firm can identify those areas where risk management may be most valuable.

cantly reduces uncertainty—suggesting risk management strategy should primarily address those two prices.

Having isolated the critical sources of uncertainty, the model can be used to try out alternative strategies, whether on balance sheet or off balance sheet. For example, returning to the hypothetical manufacturing firm in Illustration 21–5, Figure 21–4 illustrates the change in second-year cash flow as the result of locking in one of the critical financial prices for three years via a swap. The shaded bars indicate the new cash flow distribution after locking in prevailing forward prices for a part of the firm's exposure. Thus, hedges placed in specific markets can be viewed in terms of their impact on the chosen measure(s) of aggregate exposure.

FIGURE 21–3   Marginal Effect of "Freezing" Different Financial Prices on the Upper and Lower Confidence Bands

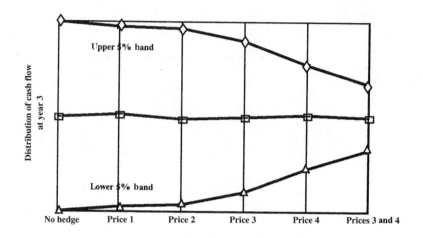

FIGURE 21–4   Cash Flow Distribution After Hedging

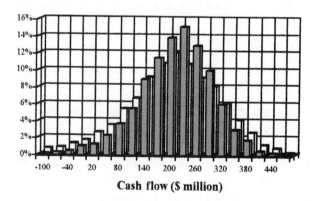

Notes

1. For our purposes, Equation 21–5 can best be viewed as a variance decomposition, with the parameter beta measuring the share of the total variation in the share return that is attributable to variation in returns to holding the market portfolio.
2. Note the relation between this specification and the definition of duration.
3. This section is adapted from a paper that my School of Financial Products colleagues Gregory Hayt and Shang Song wrote for *Risk:* "Handle with Sensitivity" (September 1995).
4. For a discussion of contractual and economic exposures, see Flood and Lessard (Spring 1986).
5. We have used the model proposed by Longstaff and Schwartz (1992).

22 | IMPLEMENTING A RISK MANAGEMENT PROGRAM

Lessons Learned from the Events of 1994

Losses by Industrial Corporations

1994 was a difficult year for users and sellers of derivatives. Prior to 1994, *derivatives* had been almost a "nerdy" word; in 1994, it became almost a dirty word, as a number of firms reported derivatives-related losses. Let's take a minute to review some of the most widely reported losses reported by industrial corporations—most of which were precipitated by an unexpected rise in U.S. dollar interest rates in February 1994:

Codelco.[1]   In January 1994, Codelco, Chile's national copper company, announced that it lost $207 million because of unauthorized trading on the London Metals Exchange by its chief futures trader. According to the trader's lawyer, the trouble began when the trader incorrectly entered a series of buy and sell orders into his computer and then traded against the erroneous positions, resulting in an initial $30 million loss. Instead of admitting the losses, the trader attempted to recover them in a frenzy of trading. Between September 1993 and January 1994, the trader executed more than 5,000 futures transactions, resulting in a $163.9 million loss in copper, a $30.6 million loss in silver, and a $12.2 million loss in gold.

Gibson Greetings.   In March 1994, Gibson Greetings Inc. announced that it incurred a $3 million loss as a result of "unauthorized" interest rate swaps. The Cincinnati-based greeting card and wrapping paper company said the transactions involved "aggressive forms of derivatives." Gibson indicated that the $3 million loss will be offset by a $2 million deferred gain from earlier interest rate swaps.[2]

In April 1994, Gibson Greetings Inc. announced an additional charge against earnings of $16.7 million for the first quarter—in addition to the $3 million realized loss announced in March. Gibson again said that the loss resulted from "unauthorized" interest rate swaps.[3]

Aside

Leveraged Swaps

1994 was the year the phrase *leveraged swaps—* or more broadly, *leveraged derivative transaction**—entered the jargon of derivatives. Earlier in the book, we noted that in the last half of 1993, many people believed that U.S. dollar interest rates in 1994 would be lower than the rates forecasted by the yield curve. And many of those people acted on that view.

If I believe that the future spot rate is going to be less than the rate implied by the forward rate, I can implement my belief:

> Enter into an interest rate swap. Receive a fixed rate and pay a floating rate. Define the notional principal on the swap to be *X.*

If I *really* believe that the future spot rate is going to be less than the rate implied by the forward rate, I can implement my belief:

> Enter into the same receive-fixed/pay-floating swap but *increase the notional principal from X to 2X.*

If I am constrained by the amount of notional principal I can transact, I can change the terms of the preceding slightly:

> Enter into a swap with a notional principal of *X.* Receive an above-market fixed rate and *pay two times the prevailing floating rate.* Such a swap has come to be called a *leveraged swap.*

If I *really, really* believe that the future spot rate is going to be less than the rate implied by the forward rate, I can enter into a *leveraged* swap, but one with more leverage applied:

> Enter into a swap with a notional principal of *X.* Receive a much-above-market fixed rate and *pay n times the prevailing floating rate.*

If I *really, really, really* believe that the future spot rate is going to be less than the rate implied by the forward rate,

> Enter into a swap with a notional principal of *X.* Receive a much-much-above-market fixed rate and *pay the square of the prevailing floating rate.* Such a swap has come to be called a *LIBOR-squared swap.*

Note to the Reader: The "aggressive forms of derivatives" Gibson Greetings referred to (see above) was a LIBOR-squared swap.

While the preceding might seem kind of silly, it does highlight two points. First, notional principal is not useful in controlling a firm's

---

risk management activities. Second, the stand-alone concept of leverage is likely to turn out to be a *red herring*. "Leverage" as a stand-alone concept doesn't seem all that useful—particularly when options are added to the structure. Were I buying a complex structure, I would want to know about possible changes in *cash flows* and *mark-to-market value.*

———

*This phrase is the one used by the New York Fed in its December 1994 "written agreement" with Bankers Trust.

Procter & Gamble.   In April 1994 Procter & Gamble Co. said it would take a one-time pretax charge of $157 million in its fiscal third quarter to close out two risky interest rate swap contracts that were walloped by rising interest rates in the United States and Germany. P&G referred to the transactions as "leveraged swap transactions."[4]

Mead[5].   In April 1994, when it reported first-quarter earnings, Mead Corporation reported a loss of $7.4 million on the closeout of "a unique leveraged interest rate swap transaction."

Air Products[6].   In May 1994, Air Products & Chemicals Inc. took a $60 million after-tax charge to reflect the declining value of five interest rate swaps. Later that month, Air Products announced an additional after-tax charge of $9 million on the same swap transactions (reflected in third-quarter earnings).[7]

Federal Paper[8].   In July 1994, Federal Paper Board Co. announced a $19 million pretax loss associated with foreign currency contracts.

Caterpillar[9].   In August 1994, Caterpillar Financial Services Corporation, a financial services unit of Caterpillar Inc., announced that it had lost $13.2 million in the first six months of 1994 selling interest rate caps and swaptions.

Lessons Learned

Despite the widely publicized losses, firms did not stop using derivatives. As Moody's Investors Service put it: "For most companies the question is how to be involved with derivatives, not whether to be involved."[10] In its October 1994 cover story, *Business Week* indicated that industrial corporations "are beginning to realize that the only way to stem the tide of financial calamities is by fundamentally overhauling the way they deal with risks" and that "they now recognize that the effectiveness of their risk-management program can determine whether they flourish or wither and die."[11]

But the events of 1994 had taught industrial firms some very important lessons. The lessons learned are probably best exemplified by the public statements of Gerald A. White, the CFO of Air Products.

> Air Products had used interest-rate swap contracts since the late 1980s to manage the risk associated with and lower the interest cost of its $1.3 billion debt portfolio. In the fall of 1993, Air Products entered into five interest-rate swap contracts "with the same motivation as the other contracts, to lower our interest cost at a reasonable level of risk." However, the 1993 contracts weren't the "plain vanilla" investments that the company normally used, but included "significant leverage features that magnify the downside loss exposure," Mr. White said. "In hindsight, our risk analysis was faulty. . . . We absolutely aren't doing these kind of transactions in the future." Mr. White said the five leveraged transactions were uncovered in an audit performed after Procter & Gamble announced its big loss. Mr. White went on to say that the transactions were not adequately disclosed to top management and not fully understood by the Air Products financial staff who bought the swap contracts.[12]

I think that the lessons Mr. White described can be reduced to two simple rules:

Rule 1: Make Sure You Know How Much Is at Risk. The firm needs to have a measure of what will happen if financial prices change. This rule is important if the firm is using derivatives to reduce risk, in which the firm will probably want to have a measure that shows what the exposure was before the derivatives were put in place and what the exposure is with the derivatives. However, this rule is *critical* if the firm is using derivatives to take a position—as Air Products was doing when it was using derivatives to reduce its interest cost. If the firm has put on a position, the firm must have a measure of the magnitudes of potential gains or losses if the financial price moves.

Rule 2: Make Sure That Everyone Is on the Same Page. Senior management must know what to expect. If the treasury of the firm has modified the firm's exposure to a financial price and especially if the treasury has put on a position, it is essential that senior management know what will happen to the firm's cash flows if the financial price rises or falls.

One way that firms can make sure that these rules are being adhered to is by designing effective policies and procedures for using derivatives.

Defining Effective Policies and Procedures

While effective risk management policies and procedures can take many different forms, the risk management cycle illustrated in Figure 22–1 has proved to be a useful organizing structure for a number of firms. This cycle illustrates that, in putting together policies and procedures, the firm must carefully consider four issues.

FIGURE 22–1   The Risk Management Cycle

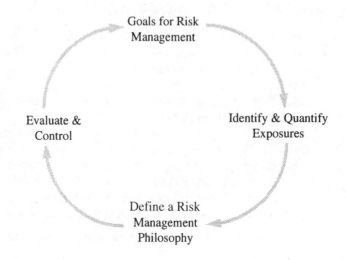

Goals for Risk Management

The firm must specify its goals—what it intends to accomplish with a risk management program.

In some cases, the goal is to seek additional profits by trading derivatives. If this is the firm's goal, the firm will need to decide how much of its capital it wishes to put at risk and how large a return it is attempting to earn. In October 1995 U.S. nonfinancial corporations were surveyed about their use of derivatives by the Wharton School at the University of Pennsylvania (see Bodnar and Marston, 1996); the survey was funded by CIBC World Markets. Figure 22–2 suggests that a relatively small percentage of nonfinancial firms "frequently" actively take a position; but a more substantial percentage "sometimes" actively take a position.

In many cases, firms specify the goal of their risk management program as the reduction in some form of volatility—e.g., the volatility of its cash flows, the volatility of its earnings, or the volatility in its market value. Figure 22–3 summarizes results from the 1995 Wharton/CIBC World Markets Survey of U.S. Derivatives End-Users which indicate that firms are most likely to reduce cash flow or earnings volatility. However, if the goal is to reduce volatility, the directors and managers need to be clear about *why* they are doing so: they need to spell out how volatility reduction is going to increase the value of the firm.

Of late, we have witnessed something akin to "moral judgments" being made about the two goals. We have seen some people argue that volatility reduction (a.k.a. *hedging*) is "good" and trading for profit (a.k.a. *speculation*) is "evil."[13] We do not agree. Firstly, on a philosophical level, there is nothing "evil" about trading for

FIGURE 22–2   Frequency with Which Derivatives Users Actively Take Positions

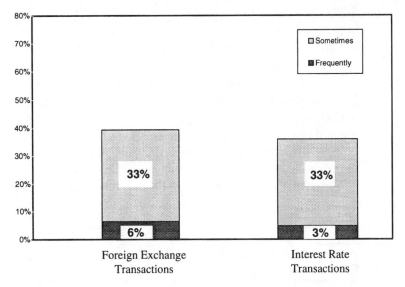

SOURCE: Wharton/CIBC World Markets 1995 Survey of Derivatives Usage by U.S. Non-Financial Firms.

FIGURE 22–3   "Most Important" Objective in Using Derivatives to Hedge

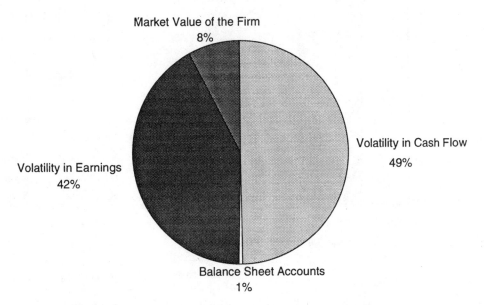

SOURCE: Wharton/CIBC World Markets 1995 Survey of Derivatives Usage by U.S. Non-Financial Firms.

profit. Seeking additional profits from the use of derivatives may be an appropriate goal for a particular company; *but since it is a completely different objective from volatility reduction, it must be managed differently.* Secondly, on a more pragmatic level, our observation is that most firms act on their views about the future path of interest rates or foreign exchange rates or some other financial price. While Figure 22–2 suggested that relatively few U.S. nonfinancial firms are using derivatives to actively trade, Figure 22–4 suggests a substantial number *do* implement their views about future rates or prices by altering the timing or size of their hedges. Do such changes in timing and/or size represent "hedging" or "speculation"? We would suggest that they are *both* and *neither.* Indeed, the recent use of the words *hedge* and *speculation* has been such that neither word has general meaning anymore.[14]

FIGURE 22–4   Does "Market View" Impact FX and Interest Rate Derivatives Transactions Decisions?

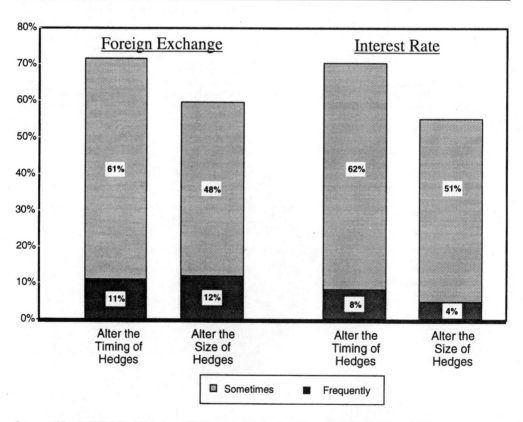

SOURCE: Wharton/CIBC World Markets 1995 Survey of Derivatives Usage by U.S. Non-Financial Firms.

Identify and Quantify Exposures

In order to manage risks, the firm must know what risks it faces and how big they are. Consequently, the firm must implement a "system" for measuring risk. It is essential for this system to be able to keep track of how big the risks were before the risk management program was implemented and how big they are after the program is put in place.

Currently, a lot is being heard about VAR, but VAR is not the only measure of market risk that is currently being used. Figure 22–5 summarizes the results obtained from the 1995 CIBC World Markets/Wharton Survey of U.S. Derivatives End-Users when the respondents were asked what methods they used to evaluate market risk.[15]

And we are not convinced that VAR or any of the other measures depicted in Figure 22–5 are the *right* one for a nonfinancial corporation. All of those measures are "stock" measures; they indicate how a change in the financial price will impact on the *present value* of an asset, a liability, or a portfolio. In contrast, most nonfinancial firms are managed to "flows"; the important measure is how changes in a financial price will impact on the firm's cash flows or earnings. We believe that over the next few years, we will see a movement toward "cash flow–at–risk."[16]

FIGURE 22–5   Methods Used for Evaluating Market Risk

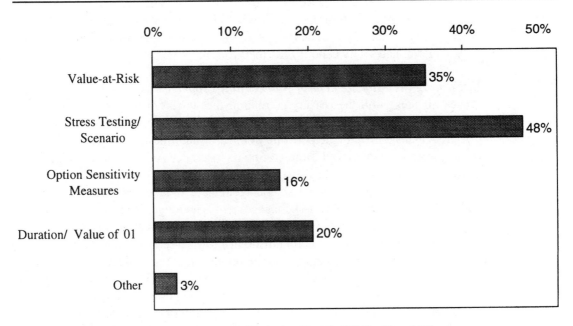

SOURCE: Wharton/CIBC World Markets 1995 Survey of Derivatives Usage by U.S. Non-Financial Firms.

Define a Risk Management Philosophy

To effectively manage financial price risks, the firm must have a risk management "philosophy"; and then it must turn this philosophy into an action plan via some careful operating rules.

"One-Off" or "Integrated" Risk Management?[17]

"Integrated risk management" is the phrase of the day in the financial community—but what exactly does it mean? In practice, it means different things to different firms. There are at least three ways in which a nonfinancial end user could think about achieving integration.

Integrating the Management of Different Market Risks. Nonfinancial firms are working to integrate the management of interest rate, foreign exchange rate, commodity price, and equity price risks in a portfolio. Some firms have adopted a portfolio approach to manage financial price risks. In the 1980s and early 1990s, many corporates created "netting centers" or "internal banks" to net financial exposures, e.g., Asea Brown Boveri, Hewlett-Packard, Intel, TNT, and Valeo. Earlier this year, it was reported that Hyundai Group was establishing a universal risk management strategy, integrating the management of interest rate and foreign exchange rate risks.

But only one third of U.S. nonfinancial firms say they are looking at any type of portfolio measures of risk, according to the 1995 Wharton/CIBC World Markets survey of derivatives use.[18] Two thirds of end users of derivatives are still looking at risk on a transaction-by-transaction basis. This implication is reinforced by another survey, which showed that in 1996, of more than 500 multinational firms, only a quarter had "fully centralized" their treasuries.[19]

Integrating the Management of Market and Property/Casualty Risk. This involves linkages within the treasury, combining the two risk management functions—finance and insurance. It is already under way: Union Carbide has added financial price risk management to the portfolio of the assistant treasurer responsible for the firm's insurance. Honeywell is integrating its insurance activities with its financial price risk management and has also added political and environmental risks.

Both users and providers of risk management recognize that the distinction between insurance and financial risk management is no longer appropriate. Insurance providers have recognized this partly because their traditional market is shrinking; firms are moving away from buying insurance toward self-insuring (Mello, 1996). Insurance companies have begun to write policies that resemble options on financial price variables. For example, XL Insurance and Cigna Property & Casualty as well as Swiss Re are offering to write insurance policies on losses the firm might experience due to movement in foreign exchange rates or commodity prices.[20]

Integrating the Management of Market Risk throughout the Firm. This is what we referred to as *strategic risk management* in Chapter 20; it involves linking the treasury with the firm's core businesses—manufacturing and marketing. In Chapter 20 we noted that the most well-known example of strategic risk management in practice is Merck & Company. But Merck is not the only firm to adopt strategic risk management. Australian gold producers have increased production by integrating finance with production and marketing. Financial price risk management gave them more certainty about price, allowing them to concentrate on locating and extracting gold.

Implementation. The first two types of integration involve linkages within the treasury and can therefore be accomplished without worrying about the organization of the wider firm. However, the third type—integrating risk management throughout the firm—requires the treasury function to be an integral part of managing the firm, rather than simply providing the financing once the investment decisions are made.

Derivatives versus "Natural" Hedges. If the firm decides to manage financial price risk, one of the first questions it must answer is how. The firm could use derivative instruments to transfer the risk to other parties; or it could create "natural" hedges, for example, by matching the currencies of costs and revenues.

Periodically, press reports will describe companies with global operations that manage their currency exposure in part by choosing sourcing and production locations.[21] Examples of firms that have worked to match currency "footprints" by locating production or sourcing in their overseas markets include Toyota, Honda, BMW, Mercedes-Benz, General Motors, Ford, and IBM. Writing in *Treasury & Risk Management,* Linda Corman described how Phelps Dodge (the Phoenix, Arizona–based copper mining company) manages its foreign exchange rate risk.

> Phelps Dodge uses forward contracts, puts, calls and other derivatives whenever it finds itself vulnerable to currency fluctuations and where there is a liquid market in that currency. However, in some Latin American countries, where the markets for the local currency are not sufficiently developed, the company will hedge its foreign exchange risk by borrowing in the local currency. When the local currency falls relative to the dollar, the US dollar value of the cash flows to the US parent will decline; but the US dollar value of the payments on debt borrowed in local currency will also diminish.

However, we would be remiss if we left you with the opinion that all market observers agree that risk management using derivatives and risk management via matching currencies are substitutes for each other.

Aside

Arguments against Managing FX Risk by Matching Currencies

Trevor Harris, Nahum Melumad, and Toshi Shibano (1996) argue that while matching currency footprints reduces profit variability, this practice can also cause reductions in expected profitability. They argue that "the expected profit effects of matching depend on the trade-off between possible expected cost savings of sourcing abroad versus the loss of what we refer to as 'strategic flexibility' in responding to competitors' pricing and quantity decisions."

Antonio Mello, John Parsons, and Alexander Triantis (1996) make a similar argument. They argue that firms place a positive value on the ability to respond rapidly to changes in the economic environment. Indeed they would argue that one of the reasons that firms create global networks of production sites is to take advantage of fluctuating exchange rates—i.e., the firm has the option of shifting production to the lowest cost site. According to Mello, Parsons, and Triantis, being long this flexibility option means that the firm's costs will, on average, be lower than its competitors' through a wide range of exchange rates, because the firm with operations in different countries can always produce at the cheapest cost regardless of how exchange rates move. If the firm uses these production locations as a hedge against exchange rate fluctuations, the firm loses the flexibility option.

Passive versus Active Risk Management.   The philosophy should provide the firm's perspective on the markets, including the firm's beliefs about the degree to which financial prices can be forecasted. And the decision concerning "active" versus "passive" hedging (see the following box) should follow directly from the firm's beliefs about market efficiency.

Aside

"Active" Hedging

Writing for the Association of Corporate Treasurers (UK), Richard Cookson noted that there may be reasons for allowing treasuries some leeway. For example, a company might take a view that it can create value for its shareholders by locking in some of the company's debt at what it considers low interest rates, or it might take a view on what it thinks is an overvalued or undervalued currency. However, *active* risk management does involve taking a view. Is this hedging or speculation? As Arvind Sodhani (vice president and treasurer of Intel Corporation) put it in the *Harvard Business Review,* "[t]he board must be aware that, while risk management can be good and prudent business, it can turn into speculation."

Which Instruments? For What Purposes? By Whom? In What Amounts?

The operating rules should define "what can be used" and "for what purposes." Different firms use different sets of financial instruments. Figure 22–6 summarizes the results obtained from the 1995 Wharton/CIBC World Markets Survey of U.S.

FIGURE 22–6 "Most Important" Derivatives Used to Manage Underlying Financial Exposures

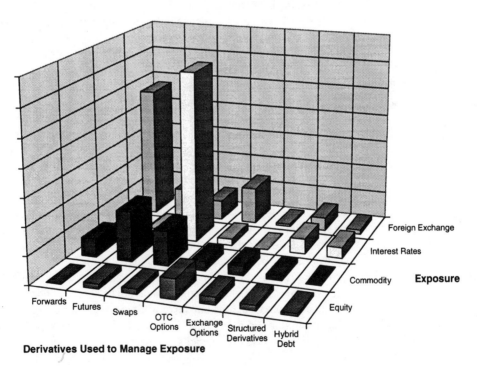

SOURCE: Wharton/CIBC World Markets 1995 Survey of Derivatives Usage by U.S. Non-Financial Firms.

Risk Management in Practice

Hedging Interest Rate Risk without Using Up Bank Lines*

Roger Burge

The original debt for the Channel Tunnel was a six-tranche syndicated loan of £6.8 billion raised in 1987 and 1990. This debt was entirely floating-rate debt. There was, however, the possibility for Eurotunnel to use drawings from four of the six tranches as letters of credit. The purpose was for Eurotunnel to approach long-term lending institutions for fixed-rate funding, which would be guaranteed by letters of credit issued by some participants in the 220-bank syndicate. The European Investment Bank (EIB) committed a £1 billion letter of credit–backed loan facility, which would enable Eurotunnel to fix around 15% of the debt portfolio. In 1990 and 1991, the EIB and the European Coal and Steel Community (ECSC) committed a further £500 million of direct lending, bringing the fixed-rate debt available to £1.5 billion out of a total of £7.3 billion.

As more debt was drawn, the medium-term financial stability of the project became increasingly exposed to interest rate risk. The Board and senior management were increasingly keen to reduce exposure to this risk.

The limited amount of fixed-rate debt available meant that interest rate swaps were the only way to reduce the exposure. The problem was that the risk-weighting applied by banks to the interest rate swap facilities that Eurotunnel was seeking equated to significant further lending on their part.

Since the project financing did not provide any committed hedging facilities, Eurotunnel sought to obtain from the syndicate banks unsecured facilities outside the framework of the main financing structure. In 1990 and 1991 Eurotunnel obtained limited facilities from some of its main relationship banks and used these lines to lock in rates for a two-year period. By late 1992 sterling medium-term rates had fallen significantly (following the UK's exit from the ERM in September of that year). The two-year swaps entered into in 1990 and 1991 would roll off in the near future, and finding a way to lock in rates at the new, lower levels became an increasingly urgent priority.

Since the banking syndicate was heavily committed in funding the project itself, it became clear that Eurotunnel would not be able to obtain sufficient unsecured facilities to reach its objective of fixing a substantial part of the debt. During discussions with a number of banks, the idea of collaterizing the swaps emerged. In this way, Eurotunnel's counterparty banks would be exposed to minimal risk. If interest rates fell, the value of the Eurotunnel pay-fixed swaps would increase; but the banks would reduce this increased credit risk by calling for collateral payments.

Any cash paid out by Eurotunnel would eventually be recouped over the life of the deal, either through swap rates subsequently rising or through paying a lower fixed rate. However, there was a risk that considerable amounts of cash could be tied up for long periods. With uncollateralized swaps, if rates fell during the life of the swap, Eurotunnel would suffer only an opportunity loss. However, with this collateralized structure, Eurotunnel also faced the prospect of significant cash outflows if rates fell. In effect, part of the swap net interest payments would have to be paid in advance. Although the swaps would enable Eurotunnel to achieve the objective of fixing a substantial part of its financing costs, short-term cash flows could become volatile as a result of potentially large and unpredictable mark-to-market payments.

The key question was how much of the debt could be safely hedged within the constraints of the funds available. Due to Eurotunnel's particular situation, there were cash constraints on three distinct time horizons:

First, the amount of cash float that Eurotunnel was permitted to carry was capped under the terms of the credit agreement waiver of conditions precedent in place at the time.

Second, in order to draw down more funds, 10 business days' notice had to be given, due to the size and diversity of the syndicate.

Third, it was starting to become clear that further funding was going to be needed to take Eurotunnel through to cash flow breakeven. Significant cash outflows from margin payments would bring forward unpredictably the date of exhaustion of borrowing facilities.

In order to assess the cash flow risk a simple matrix was created showing, for different combinations of principal amounts and swap maturities, how much cash would be paid out for given falls in swap rates. Sensitivities were then run at different yield-curve levels and with different-shaped curves. With falls in rates of 75–100 basis points combined with the £2 billion or so of swaps needed to achieve the new target level of 75 percent fixed-rate sterling debt, the cash outflows could have been in excess of £100 million.

It was then necessary to assess the likelihood of such large falls in rates actually occurring. To achieve an objective view of the true extent of the cash flow risk, historic measures were used. Interest rate volatility figures from the previous four years made it possible to work out the principal amount that could safely be transacted within a statistical confidence level of two standard deviations. Then, the largest swap rate movements historically seen on a single day and over a 10-day period were studied.

This analysis effectively set the parameters from a historical viewpoint. The most optimistic economists' predictions for medium-term rates were then factored into the equation. With the results of this analysis, it was possible for treasury to recommend a "safe" level of swaps that could be undertaken. This safe level was set well within the two-standard-deviation confidence levels, where the cash position would not be unduly threatened by extreme short-term swap rate movements, or by medium-term sterling rates falling as low as 5 percent over a longer period.

Several months were needed to agree on the documentation for the first £500 million facility, [and] obtain approval from the Eurotunnel's Risk Management Committee and Board and from the agent banks for the syndicate to go ahead with these deals. Getting the first facility up and running was critical, as we were sure that other banks would deal on a similar basis once we could show them that the structure was working. This was indeed what happened, and within three months, more than £2 billion of lines were available to Eurotunnel with very little risk for the providers.

By the time Eurotunnel first dealt in September 1993, four-year sterling rates had fallen to 6.75 percent. Dealing continued and rates carried on falling through to January 1994, by which time £1 billion of swaps had been transacted. During this period there were a few nervous moments, as by January, the earliest deals were a full 1 percent out-of-the-money, and over £16 million had been paid out in margin calls.

A month later, sterling swap rates moved sharply upwards after the Fed raised U.S. interest rates, and all the cash paid out was quickly recovered. After that, no more margin payments were made. Through the use of derivatives, Eurotunnel met its objective of increasing the certainty of debt service costs. This was achieved without the use of costly option products, and with very limited use of bank facilities.

Roger Burge is the deputy treasurer for Eurotunnel. Prior to joining Eurotunnel in 1992, Mr. Burge worked at Spie Batignolles and Natwest Treasury. Mr. Burge holds an honours degree in European business administration from Middlesex Polytechnic (London) and CESEM Reims (France).

*This discussion is excerpted from an article by the same name that appeared in *Uses of Derivatives,* David Creed and Jeremy Wagener, eds., Business of Finance Series, Association of Corporate Treasurers (UK), 1997

Derivatives End-Users when the respondents were asked which derivatives were "most important" for the management of foreign exchange rate, interest rate, commodity price, and equity price exposures.

In addition to "what can be used" and "for what purposes," the operating rules should define "by whom" and "in what amounts." The firm needs to be clear on what instruments are authorized for use for what application. Within the firm, it should be clear who is authorized to transact derivative contracts and what their transaction limits are.

Counterparties: Who? How Much Exposure?   Since derivatives contracts involve promises of future performance, they are credit instruments; so the firm must set the criteria for dealers with whom they are prepared to deal, review the criteria frequently, and ration the amount of exposure which they have to any one dealer. Figure 22–7 summarizes the results obtained from the 1995 Wharton/CIBC World Markets Survey of U.S. Derivatives End-Users when the respondents were asked about the lowest counterparty rating they would accept for derivative transactions with maturities of one year or less and with maturities of more than one year.

And the firm must track its credit exposures to its counterparties. As we noted in Chapter 17, market participants differentiate between the credit risk that exists

FIGURE 22–7   Lowest-Rated Counterparty for Derivative Transactions

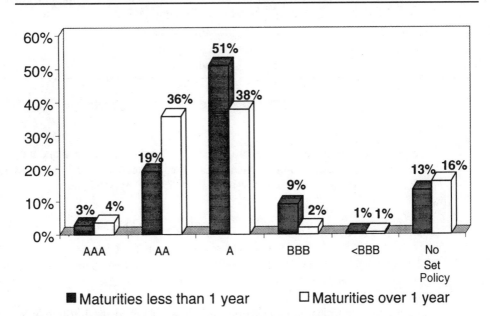

Source: Wharton/CIBC World Markets 1995 Survey of Derivatives Usage by U.S. Non-Financial Firms.

prior to contract settlement—presettlement risk—and the credit risk that exists when the contract matures or reaches a settlement date and the counterparties would be required to pass payments to each other—settlement risk. In Chapter 17 we also noted that the degree of presettlement credit risk is a function of three determinants: (1) exposure—the amount at risk; (2) recovery—the amount that would be recovered in event of default; and (3) probability of default—the likelihood of a loss. Market practice is to treat the three determinants as independent, in which case expected default-induced loss can be expressed as

$$\text{(Exposure net of recovery)} \times \text{(probability of default)}$$

In this discussion we focus on the measurement of presettlement exposure. Since an OTC derivatives transaction implies an extension of credit to the dealer on the other side of the transaction, end users recognize the need to track their credit exposures to their dealers. Our experience suggests that end users continue to wrestle with quantifying those exposures.

Since the focus for an end user is on the allocation of credit, rather than pricing credit risk, end users are most interested in a measure of maximum exposure. Such a measure should incorporate both current and potential exposure and should reflect the impact of both diffusion and amortization on the future mark-to-market of the contract.

Three approaches are widely used to measure maximum total exposure—simulation, scenario, and factor. To demonstrate how these approaches work, we will continue an example we began in Chapter 17.

Aside

Calculating Credit Exposures

The purpose of this example is to compare alternative approaches to estimating the maximum expected exposure measures for two transactions:

Transaction 1–a five-year, $10 million interest rate swap in which the end user is paying fixed at 8.18 percent (semiannual) and receiving six-month dollar LIBOR.

Transaction 2–a five-year, $10 million currency swap in which the end user is paying fixed deutsche mark at 6 percent (semiannual) and receiving fixed dollar at 6.55 percent (semiannual).

Simulation Approach

As we noted in Chapter 17, most dealers use Monte Carlo simulations to provide exposure measures that accurately reflect both the amortization and diffusion effects. In Chapter 17, we obtained the illustrative simulation-based exposure measure shown in the following table by assuming that dollar and deutsche mark interest rates and the deutsche mark-dollar exchange rate were distributed lognormally. We estimated the variances of the distributions using data from the preceding 100 days. We simulated 500 random changes in the spot foreign exchange rate and the yield curves (assuming parallel shifts) at half-yearly intervals up to five years. At each six-month point, we calculated the market value of the swaps (assuming they had aged accordingly), setting any negative values to zero; and from the 500 values, we identified the 98th percentile value. The value reported in the table below is the "expected maximum" over the life of the transaction, i.e., the average of the ten 98th percentile values.

Comparison of Alternative Approaches for Calculating Credit Exposures
(98% Confidence-Level Exposures)

	Simulation Approach	Scenario Approach		Factor Approach
		Worst Case	*Mod. Worst Case*	
Interest rate swap	536,558	953,766	479,507	900,000
Currency swap	1,748,674	3,361,009	4,561,914	2,200,000

Scenario Approach

Instead of simulating a full distribution of values for the underlying financial price over time, the end user could consider a limited number of scenarios about the behavior of the financial price. As with the simulation approach, the replacement cost for the OTC derivative can be tracked over time to determine the maximum cost of replacing the cash flows if the counterparty were to default.

Our experience suggests that end users are using various forms of the scenario approach. In the accompanying table, we have illustrated two:

"Worst Case"*

This approach, discussed in Chapter 17, is a conservative assessment of the credit risk associated with an OTC derivative that is obtained by assuming the "worst" outcome from both the diffusion and amortization processes. We calculated the exposure displayed in column 2 of the table above by assuming that, immediately after inception of the transaction, all of the underlying financial price shifted two standard deviations (corresponding to a 98 percent one-tail confidence level) in the direction that would maximize the value of the transaction. Obviously, one could define more extreme moves leading to still worse cases.

Modified Worst Case

The exposure reported in column 3 of the table differs from the "worst case" exposure in two ways.

First, changes in the financial prices are assumed to occur over time instead of all at once. To obtain the rate at year *t,* the initial rate would be shifted by two standard deviations multiplied by the square root of *t*. For example, if six-month dollar LIBOR was initially 6 percent and its standard deviation was 15 percent, six-month LIBOR at the two-year point would be 6 percent $\times \{1 + [2.00 \times 0.15 \times$ SQRT $(2)]\} = 7.63$ percent.

Second, the modified worst case recognizes the fact that contracts age (the amortization effect) by calculating the mark-to-market value of the transaction at six-month intervals. The value reported in column 3 is the average of the 10 mark-to-market values obtained by projecting financial prices at six-month intervals from contract initiation to maturity. In the case of currency swaps, where the amortization effect is minimal, the modified worst-case approach will lead to very large changes in rates and hence very large exposure measures.

Factor Approach

In this approach, the current exposure of the OTC derivative is again calculated as the maximum of the current mark-to-market or zero. The potential exposure for the transaction is approximated as

$$\text{Notional principal} \times \text{factor}$$

where the "factor" is a percentage that could be obtained, for example, from simulations of

standard OTC derivatives transactions or from regulatory authorities.

The exposures presented in column 4 of the table illustrate what might be obtained by applying factors to the notional amount of each swap. These factors were obtained from Canadian Imperial Bank of Commerce.

The simulation approach is, without question, the most comprehensive and realistic approach of the methods presented and is the most appropriate approach for dealers. But the accuracy of the simulation approach is less crucial for an end user. From a practical standpoint, since total credit risk is small for a typical end user, the cost of wrongly estimating the exposure would be small as well.

The table illustrates the range of exposures which might be obtained from various methods. In many cases, the factor and simulation approaches will lead to similar results since the factors are based on simulations of standard contracts. The worst case and modified worst case can produce reasonable results as well, but they should be used with an understanding of their limitations—in particular, when each method will understate or overstate exposure.

---

*The market refers to this approach as "worst case" because of the assumption of instantaneous adverse movement in the underlying financial price, not because it is truly the worst possible case.

Evaluate and Control

As with any other business activity, the risk management function must be evaluated (and the people involved must be compensated). The recent experiences of Barings, Sumitomo, and others highlight two things that are crucial to effective evaluation and control. First, the evaluation-control function must be *independent* from the activity itself.[22] Second, in order to avoid "surprises," the management of the firm must always know the value of the firm's portfolio of risk management instruments.[23]

To accomplish the evaluation-control function, the system for managing risk noted above must be expanded to reflect the impact of risk management on the firm's inherent exposures. The firm must have a common framework to report and evaluate compliance with the risk management plan. Measurement tools will have to be developed. If the firm is trying to reduce volatility in some financial measure (e.g., cash flow) in order to increase the value of the firm (e.g., by ensuring that funds are available to make investments at the most effective time), it will be necessary to measure (1) the degree to which volatility declined relative to what it would have been in the absence of any hedge, (2) the monetary cost paid to obtain this volatility reduction, and (3) the degree to which the *real* goal (e.g., accomplishing the firm's investment program) was attained. If the firm is going to employ active risk management, it will be necessary to design benchmarks that will tell the firm what a passive strategy would have achieved.

The Role of the Board of Directors

As we noted in Chapter 19, the members of boards of directors have, voluntarily or not, accepted four responsibilities: (1) approve the firm's risk management policies and procedures, (2) ensure that the operating management team possesses the requisite technical capabilities[24] (and is actively communicating with the people implementing the risk management program), (3) evaluate the performance of the risk management activity, and (4) maintain oversight of the risk management activity.

In this section, we will examine each of these four responsibilities. We will then "operationalize" our discussion by providing some of the items that we think should be on a "directors' checklist."

Responsibility 1—Approve Policies

Every authority we surveyed started with the board's responsibilities with respect to *policies*. In its report to the U.S. Congress, the General Accounting Office (GAO) determined that the board of directors "should be responsible for approving the risk management policies and controls." Indeed, the importance of this responsibility is evidenced by the fact that it was made recommendation 1 in the report on derivatives produced by the Global Derivatives Project sponsored by the Group of Thirty (G-30).

G-30 Recommendation 1

Dealers and end-users should use derivatives in a manner consistent with the overall risk management and capital policies approved by their boards of directors. These policies should be reviewed as business and market circumstances change. Policies governing derivatives use should be clearly defined, including the purposes for which these transactions are to be undertaken . . .

Responsibility 2—Ensure Capability

As we noted above, the members of the board need not be rocket scientists; they do not need to be aware of or understand the mechanics of each trade. However, their general duty of care requires that the board members be satisfied that management is adequate to implement board policy decisions.

They should ask senior managers to verify that training and software systems are up to the job.[25] Writing in the *Harvard Business* Review, Cheryl Francis (treasurer of FMC Corporation) reinforced this view: "One of the keys to using derivatives properly is education and training. Managers must know how to identify risks and communicate them."

The problem is deciding what education to provide.[26] It's one thing to know that the people in treasury need to be "capable"; but it's quite another to know what it is they need to be capable *about*. To provide some insights to the issues that were concerning the people who were doing derivatives in 1995—issues that might merit additional education—we have summarized in Figure 22–8 the ranking of 12 issues thought to be of concern to derivatives users.

Responsibility 3—Evaluate Performance

The tools that will be used to evaluate the performance of the risk management function will be provided in the evaluation section of the firm's *Policies & Procedures*. Our belief is that if the evaluation section is *consistent* with the goals section, everything else will follow. However, this consistency between goals and evaluation rules is not as easy to attain as it might first seem. Indeed, in the early 1990s, a number of firms had goal statements which talked about minimizing risk, while the evaluation of the risk management function was based on measuring the performance of the treasury against investment or funding "bogeys" (e.g., LIBOR).

FIGURE 22–8   **Significant Concerns about Derivative Transactions**

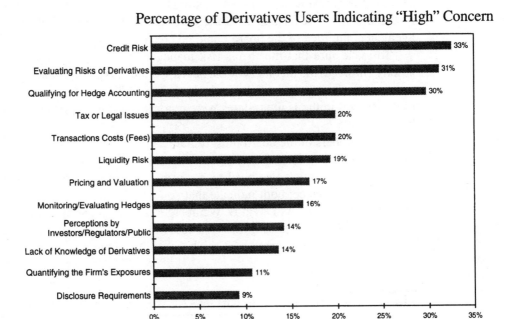

Percentage of Derivatives Users Indicating "High" Concern

SOURCE: Wharton/CIBC World Markets 1995 Survey of Derivatives Usage by U.S. Non-Financial Firms.

The goal statement implied that the firm wanted the treasury to *reduce variance;* but since beating the evaluation bogey required increasing expected returns, the evaluation section was actually implying that the firm wanted the treasury to *increase variance.*[27]

If the goal of the firm is to reduce volatility in cash flows or earnings, the members of the board must be convinced not only that the reduction in volatility occurred but also that the reduction in volatility actually led to the increase in firm value that was presupposed.

If the firm is using active risk management, the members of the board need to be convinced that, with the active management, the company ended up better off than it would have with a more mechanistic (passive) approach.

Responsibility 4—Maintain Oversight

The GAO report noted earlier also determined that the board of directors "is ultimately accountable for risk assumed by the firm." Consequently, it is the responsibility of the board to make sure that the firm's risk management policy is fully explained and strictly enforced.

It may be useful for the board of directors to delegate the continuing oversight role to a committee of the board (which would then be accountable to the full board). It could be handled by an existing committee (e.g., the audit committee); or if the firm's risk management activities are sufficiently complex, a risk management committee of the board could be created.

To make sure that the firm's risk management policy is fully explained and strictly enforced, the members of the board—or the members of the oversight committee of the board—need to be in the loop. Figure 22–9 indicates how often users of derivatives in the United States were reporting risk management activity to the board in 1995.

The members of the board must remain alert for "surprises"—any kind of surprises. *Unanticipated* results are the most dangerous results for a risk management program. And unanticipated positive performance is as dangerous as unanticipated negative performance; both indicate that some aspect of the activity has not been properly understood. As David B. Weinberger, a managing director of Swiss Bank Corporation, wrote in the *Harvard Business Review:* "Used properly, derivative instruments don't create surprises. They help minimize them."

FIGURE 22–9   Frequency of Reporting Risk Management Activity to the Board

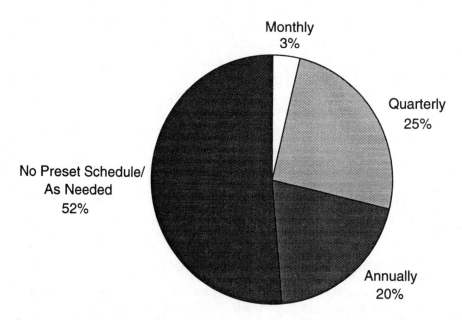

SOURCE: Wharton/CIBC World Markets 1995 Survey of Derivatives Usage by U.S. Non-Financial Firms.

Some Items for a "Directors' Checklist"

As we noted, one of the most important things a member of a board should know is the right questions to ask. Former U.S. Securities and Exchange Commission Chairman Richard Breeden suggested a few questions:

> *Do we know what our risks are?*
>
> *Do we know what our positions are, right now?*
>
> *How effective are our controls?*
>
> *How much does our compensation system encourage perverse behavior?*
>
> *Who is responsible for making sure we know what we're doing?*

However, most of us are less comfortable with a list of questions than we are with a checklist. In Figure 22–10 we have provided some suggestions for items that would be included on a "directors' checklist." In a real sense, these checklist items summarize—and operationalize—the preceding discussion.

In sum, our evaluation of the material available on this subject leads us to conclude that there are two main themes for directors—*knowledge* and *accountability*. Directors should be able to fulfill their obligations by (1) becoming informed about risk management and how it relates to the firm's overall business strategies, (2) delegating the management, monitoring, and control functions to competent staff, and (3) establishing a periodic review process which enables them to understand and assess the risks facing the firm.

FIGURE 22–10   Some Items That Ought to Be Included on the Directors' Checklist

RESPONSIBILITY #1 – APPROVAL OF POLICIES

Define Goals
- The firm intends to Trade for Profit ❑ -OR- Reduce Volatility in Cash flows❑   Earnings ❑   Market Value ❑
- If the firm intends to reduce volatility, identify the benefits to be obtained from volatility reduction   ❑
- Determine the extent of "active" risk management to be permitted
        None ❑   Treasury Permitted to Trade in "Bands" ❑   Treasury to Operate as Profit Centre ❑

Identify and Quantify Exposures
- Identify the financial prices to which the firm is exposed   ❑
    - Determine volatility of relevant financial prices   ❑
    - Determine which of the financial prices have a <u>material</u> impact on the firm's performance   ❑
- Implement a technology for quantifying the firm's exposures ("risk quantification system")   ❑
    - Establish procedures for vetting models and assumptions   ❑
    - Establish procedures for stress-testing the risk quantification system   ❑

Define a Risk Management Philosophy and Execution Plan
- If "active" risk management is permitted, define the market inefficiencies to be exploited   ❑
- Define the authorized instruments and the authorized uses for the instruments   ❑
- Implement and document Controls and Procedures
    - Determine who is authorized to enter into a transaction (and in what amounts)   ❑
    - Determine who is responsible for recording and confirming   ❑
    - Determine limits for credit, market, liquidity, and operations risks   ❑
    - Determine acceptable counterparties and exposure limits for each   ❑

Evaluate and Control
- Ensure that the risk quantification system is capable of measuring pre/post impact of risk mgmt transactions   ❑
- Establish techniques for evaluating risk management transactions   ❑
    - If goal of program is to reduce volatility: Degree of reduction ❑ Impact of volatility reduction on performance ❑
    - If active risk management is permitted: Risk-adjusted return measure ❑   Comparison to passive benchmark ❑

RESPONSIBILITY #2 – ENSURING CAPABILITY
- Verify that expertise exists within the firm to implement and control a risk management program   ❑
- Put in place education programs for staff and senior management   ❑
- Obtain external validation of models used to value risk management transactions   ❑

RESPONSIBILITY #3 – EVALUATION
- Confirm that the results of the risk management program are consistent with the firm's overall goals   ❑
- Confirm that the program did not impose undue regulatory costs and/or constraints on the firm   ❑
- Confirm that the market accurately perceives the intent and effect of the risk management program   ❑

RESPONSIBILITY #4 – CONTINUING OVERSIGHT
- Ensure that a risk management committee is established and is functioning   ❑
    - Risk management strategy in place   ❑
    - Risk management goal and strategy communicated throughout firm   ❑
    - Procedures in place for periodic review and evaluation of risk management activity   ❑
- Ensure implementation of <u>independent</u> monitor of risk management function   ❑

Notes

1. "Another Trader Runs Amok," *Derivatives Strategy,* February 20, 1994.

2. Stern (March 7, 1994).

3. "Gibson Greetings Sets an Additional Charge for the First Quarter" (1994).

4. Stern and Lipin (1994).

5. Falloon (1994).

6. Miller (1994).

7. Goodwin (1994). This article also reported that Air Products' third-quarter charge would increase from $9 million to $14 million. The additional $5 million was due to the termination of two nonleveraged contracts. Because the two contracts were hedging currency risk associated with anticipated chemical exports, rather than actual sales, they were subject to mark-to-market accounting.

8. "Federal Paper Takes Special Charge; Profit Falls from Year Ago" (1994).

9. "Caterpillar Losses on Derivatives" (1994).

10. Herman (1994).

11. *Business Week* (1994).

12. Hansell (1994).

13. Writing in *Derivatives for Directors,* Richard Cookson probably represents something very near an end point with respect to trading for profit: "Any board considering using its treasury as a profit center should ask itself if its treasury really has an edge over banks and securities firms which speculate full time. Many companies that have come a-cropper with derivatives—Showa Shell, Kashima Oil, Volkswagen, and Allied Lyons (now Allied-Domecq) to name but a few—used their treasuries as profit centers."

14. Consequently, if a firm uses these words in its policies, we suggest that the firm carefully define what it means by *hedging* and *speculation.*

15. This figure is intended to illustrate the range of market risk measurement methods currently being used. The question that the respondents were asked was: "Does your firm use any of the following methods for evaluating the riskiness of specific derivatives transactions or portfolios? *a.* "Value at Risk," *b.* Stress testing or scenario analysis, *c.* Option sensitivity measures, *d.* Price value of a basis point or duration, or *e.* Other."

16. For an introduction to "cash flow–at–risk," or what we call "cash flow sensitivity," see Hayt and Song (1995).

17. This discussion is based on Smithson (1997).

18. The survey asked respondents to "indicate which statement best describes your firm's philosophy for managing your derivatives positions." Some 67 percent responded with "individual derivative transactions linked to specific corporate exposures," 18 percent with "as a portfolio linked to aggregate corporate exposures," and 15 percent with "as a stand-alone portfolio for some purposes and as individual transactions linked to specific corporate exposures for other purposes." None responded with "as a stand-alone portfolio."

19. The 1995/96 Price Waterhouse/Treasury Management Association survey covering 566 multinationals in 17 countries. The survey found that 95 percent of firms establish policies and objectives at the corporate treasury level. However, the majority delegate many day-to-day responsibilities to regional treasuries or operating companies. The survey noted that the activities that tend to be centralized at the corporate treasury level include bank relationship management, capital expenditure decision making, foreign exchange translation exposure management, interest rate exposure management, and investment management.

20. Banham (1996) says AIG, Zurich Insurance Group, Munich Re, Chubb, Liberty Mutual, Ace, and Lloyd's of London all plan to have such policies available.

21. See, for example, "Business Risk: As US Firms Gain on Rivals, the Dollar Raises Pesky Questions" (1996).

22. One way to put this is that you can have *player-coaches,* but *player-referees* are another matter altogether.

23. Regardless of whether the firm marks-to-market for accounting, the firm must know the value of the risk management instruments (and this valuation must be independent from the trader's valuation).

24. Technical knowledge is *necessary,* but is not *sufficient;* technical knowledge will never replace good judgment.

25. And the more active the firm is—either in the *magnitude* of transactions or in the *complexity* of transactions—the more expertise the firm must possess.

26. And once you have decided what to educate about, you have to decide how much education to provide and in what format.

27. And in some very well-publicized instances in 1994, that "increase variance" outcome is precisely what the firms got.

23

Uses of Risk Management Products by Banks and Other Financial Institutions

Townsend Walker, a senior vice president at the Bank of America, noted that for most companies, interest rate risk is something to be managed while they go about their primary business of making cars or computers or soap; but for banks and other financial institutions, interest rate risk is at the core of their business and managing it successfully is central to whether or not they make money.[1] Not surprisingly, financial institutions devote a lot of resources and effort to the management of their interest rate risk. However, financial institutions also face other risks that can be managed with derivatives, the most significant of which is credit risk.

In the following, we will look at three areas where we see banks and other financial institutions *using* financial price risk management products (in contrast to financial institutions as the dealers of the products). Financial institutions make extensive use of interest rate derivatives as part of their asset-liability management programs. Financial institutions use interest rate and foreign exchange rate derivatives and structured notes in their investment portfolios. And banks are beginning to make use of credit derivatives to manage their loan portfolios.

Asset-Liability Management

While the values of and cash flows from assets and liabilities could be affected by all of the financial prices, asset-liability management is normally thought of in terms of interest rate risk. In order to *do* asset-liability management, the institution first needs to know how much interest rate risk it faces; so it is with measures of interest rate risk that we will begin.

Measuring the Institution's Exposure to Interest Rate Risk

Changes in interest rates affect both the cash flows from and the value of assets and liabilities. Consequently, banks look at both cash flow and value measures of interest rate risk.

Cash Flow Exposures—Maturity Gap. As we noted in Chapter 19, the maturity gap measure of interest rate risk is concerned with the impact of a change in the interest rate on income and/or expense. Financial institutions use maturity gap to measure the impact of changes in interest rates on their net interest income (NII).

$$\text{Gap} = \Delta\text{NII}/\Delta r \tag{23-1}$$

Maturity gap is probably easiest to explain via an example:

Illustration 23–1

Using Financial Statement Data to Quantify the Impact of Interest Rate Changes on a Bank's Net Interest Income: The "Gap" Methodology

Most financial institutions still use the maturity gap approach to measure their exposure to interest rate changes.* The approach gets its name because it measures the "gap" between the dollar amounts of rate-sensitive assets and rate-sensitive liabilities (i.e., assets and liabilities that will reprice during the gapping period).

$$\text{Gap} = \text{RSA} - \text{RSL}$$

Changes in interest rates affect a financial institution by changing the institution's net interest income (NII). Once the gap is known, the impact on the firm of changes in the interest rate is given by

$$\Delta\text{NII} = (\text{gap}) * (\Delta r)$$

To see how this works, consider the two hypothetical banks presented below. Bank 1 is a "standard bank." Its assets are primarily busi-

Bank 1 (All Values in $ Millions)

Assets		Liabilities	
3 month or less	100	3 month or less	400
6 month	100	6 month	300
12 month	400	12 month	200
Over 12 month	400	Over 12 month	100
	1,000		1,000

ness and mortgage loans with maturities of one year and longer, while the bank's liabilities are primarily demand and savings deposits with maturities less than a year. Within the one-year gapping period, the assets that are rate sensitive—assets that will reprice—are the three-month assets ($100), the six-month assets ($100) and the 12–month assets ($400), so RSA = $600. Within the one-year gapping period, the liabilities that are rate sensitive are the three-month liabilities ($400), the six-month liabilities ($300), and the 12-month liabilities ($200); so RSL = $900. Hence Bank 1 has a negative gap of −$300 million:

Bank 1: Gap = RSA − RSL

$$= \$600 - \$900 = -\$300$$

Bank 2 has precisely the same distribution of assets, but this bank has concentrated on funding itself with one-year and longer CDs.

Bank 2 (All Values in $ Millions)

Assets		Liabilities	
3 month or less	100	3 month or less	100
6 month	100	6 month	100
12 month	400	12 month	300
Over 12 month	400	Over 12 month	500
	1,000		1,000

Consequently, the RSA for this bank remain at $600; but the liabilities that are rate sensitive during the one-year gapping period decline to $500—$100 in three-month liabilities, $100 in six-month liabilities, and $300 in 12-month liabilities. Hence, Bank 2 has a positive gap of $100 million,

Bank 2: Gap = RSA − RSL

$$= \$600 - \$500 = \$100$$

Once the gap is known, the impact of changes in the interest can be calculated directly using the relation between NII, gap, and the change in interest rate specified above. For instance, if interest rates increase by 1 percent (100 basis points), the NII for Bank 1 will decrease by $3 million,

Bank 1
$$\Delta r = 0.01 \rightarrow \Delta \text{NII} = (-300) * (0.01) = -3$$

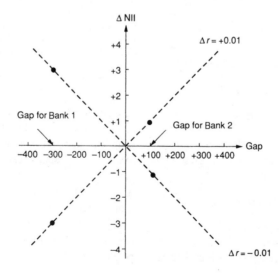

Using Financial Statement Data to Quantify the Impact of Interest Rate Changes on a Bank's Net Interest Income: The "Gap" Methodology continued

while the NII for Bank 2 increases by $1 million:

Bank 2
$$\Delta r = 0.01 \rightarrow \Delta \text{NII} = (+100) * (0.01) = +1$$

Conversely, if interest rates decrease by 1 percent, the NII for Bank 1 will increase by $3 million while the NII for Bank 2 will decrease by $1 million.

These changes in NII for Banks 1 and 2 can be displayed in a *gap diagram* that shows the changes in NII that will occur for particular changes in interest rates (e.g., up 1 basis point or down 1 basis point) for various asset–liability structures (e.g., a negative gap of $300 or a positive gap of $100).

The *risk profile* shows the changes in the value of the bank with respect to changes in interest rates *for a given asset–liability structure.* In essence, the risk profile is like a "slice" of the gap diagram. For example, "slice" the gap diagram at the −$300 gap position: a 100-basis-point increase in the interest rate will decrease NII by $3; a 100-basis-point decrease in the interest rate will increase NII by $3. This "slice" of the gap diagram—the interest rate risk profile for Bank 1—is illustrated below.

---

*Our discussion of the maturity gap model is taken from Alden Toevs (1984). In this discussion, we consider only the basic model. See Toevs for extensions to the periodic gap model or simulation models.

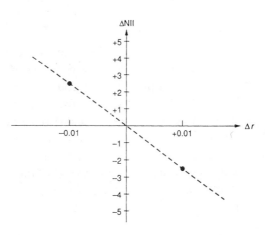

Value Exposures—Duration and Convexity.   We noted in Chapter 19 that there are actually two definitions of *duration.* One of these is attributable to Frederick Macaulay (1938) and the other to Sir John Hicks (1939).

In the concept attributable to Macaulay, duration is a measure by which two bonds with common maturity but divergent payment structures could be compared.

In the Macaulay sense, duration measures when, on average, the value of the bond is received. Macaulay duration is calculated as

$$D_M = \frac{\sum_{t}^{T} CF_t \times (1 + r)^{-t} \times t}{P_0} = \frac{\sum_{t}^{T} PV(CF_t) \times t}{P_0} \qquad (23\text{-}2)$$

The effect of the preceding calculation is to be able to regard the bond in question as a "zero-coupon bond equivalent." That is, if the Macaulay duration of a bond is calculated to be 4.5, it means that the bond behaves like a zero-coupon bond of maturity 4.5 years.

The duration concept attributable to Hicks is a measure of interest rate sensitivity for any particular bond. In the tradition of Hicks, duration provides a measure of the exposure of the bond to interest rate risk. Using the Hicks notion of duration, we can define duration (D) as

$$D = -(\text{percentage change in value})/(\text{percentage change in discount rate}) \quad (23\text{-}3)$$

Since percentage change is simply change over total, we can rewrite Equation 23–3 as

$$D = -(\Delta V/V)/[\Delta r/(1 + r)]$$
$$= -(\Delta V/\Delta r) \times [(1 + r)/V] \qquad (23\text{-}4)$$

The Hicks duration tells the user about the sensitivity of the value of an asset or liability to changes in the interest rate. For example, if the duration of a bond is calculated to be 4.5, it means that if the discount factor increases by 1 percent— e.g., if the interest rate rose 106 basis points from 6.00 percent to 7.06 percent, the discount factor $(1 + r)$ would rise by 1 percent (from 1.0600 to 1.0706)—the value of the bond would fall by 4.5×1 percent = 4.5 percent.

The problem with duration is that it is a linear measure of risk—i.e., duration is a linear approximation of the true value profile of the asset or liability. If the true value profile is nonlinear and if the change in interest rates is large, the approximation error can be large. Consequently, most financial institutions would also measure convexity.

As we noted in Chapter 19, duration is essentially a measure of the slope of the value profile at current interest rates and bond prices. Convexity is a measure of the curvature—the change in slope—of the value profile, again at current interest rates and bond prices. Figure 23–1 illustrates duration and duration-convexity measures.

The bond illustrated in Figure 23–1 exhibits positive convexity. In Figure 23–2, we have illustrated three bond value profiles: a linear profile (#1), a profile exhibiting positive convexity (#2), and a profile exhibiting negative convexity (#3).

Illustration 23–2

Using Market Data to Quantify the Impact of Interest Rate Changes on the Value of a Bank's Portfolio or Equity*

Consider a stylized bank balance sheet.

Assets		Liabilities	
Cash	100	1-year CD	600
Business loans	400	5-year CD	300
Mortgage loans	500	Equity	100
	1,000		1,000

Let's calculate the duration of the five-year CD and the business loan. The cash flows for these two instruments are illustrated below.

The CD

The CD is simple. Since it is a zero-coupon instrument, in a Macaulay sense all of the

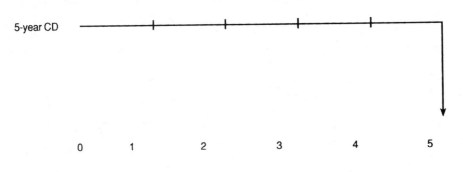

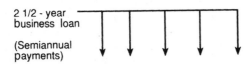

value is received at maturity. Hence, the duration of the five-year CD is five years.

The Business Loan

Suppose that the business loan has a maturity of 2.5 years and is amortizing (has a sinking fund). As the cash flows presented above illustrate, value is received prior to maturity, so the duration of the instrument must be less

than 2.5 years. To find out how much less, we need to ask, "When on average is the present value received?" The following table provides the answer.

Columns 1–4 provide the value of the bond. Column 1 gives time that the cash flows in column 2 are paid. Using the discount rates[†] in column 3, the present values are determined—column 4—and the sum of these present values yield the $400 value of this

(1) Time to Receipt (years)	(2) Cash Flow	(3) Discount Rate	(4) PV	(5) Weight	(6) Weight × Time
0.5	90	7.75%	86.70	0.22	0.11
1.0	90	8.00	83.33	0.21	0.21
1.5	90	8.25	79.91	0.20	0.30
2.0	90	8.35	76.66	0.19	0.38
2.5	90	8.50	73.40	0.18	0.46
			400.00		1.46

loan. To determine when, on average, the present value was received, we need to calculate the weighted average time of receipt. Column 5 provides the weights—for example, at time 0.5 year, $86.70/400 = 0.22 of the total present value of the instrument was received. Multiplying these weights (column 5) by the times the cash flows are received (column 1) and summing gives the weighted average time of receipt—the duration of this business loan—as 1.46 years.[‡]

As we noted earlier, duration provides a means of relating changes in interest rates to changes in the value of the security:

$$D = -\frac{\Delta V}{\Delta r} \times \frac{(1 + r)}{V}$$

where D is the duration of the security as calculated above, V is the market value of the security, and r is the interest rate. Rewriting this equation, we can express the percentage change in the value of the security in terms of the percentage change in the discount rate—$(1 + r)$—and the duration of the security,

$$\frac{\Delta V}{V} = -\frac{\Delta(1 + r)}{(1 + r)} \times D$$

For example, if the discount rate increases by 1 percent—that is, if $\Delta(1 + r)/(1 + r) = 0.01$—the market value of the five-year CD will decrease by 5 percent:

$$\Delta V/V = -(0.01)(5.0) = -0.05$$

However, the same increase in the discount rate would decrease the value of the 2.5-year business loan by only 1.46 percent:

$$\Delta V/V = -(0.01)(1.46) = -0.0146$$

And since duration is additive, the duration technique can be expanded to deal with the impact changes in interest rates on the value of the entire firm. For a portfolio with n assets having market values V_i and durations D_i, the duration of the portfolio is

$$D_{portfolio} = \frac{\Sigma\, V_i D_i}{\Sigma V_i}$$

We can use this equation to examine the duration of the assets of the bank in question. We already know that the duration of the business loan is 1.46 years. Suppose that the duration of the mortgage loans was calculated as 6.84 years. And by definition, the duration of the cash is zero. Hence, the duration of the assets is

$$D_A = \frac{(100 \times 0.0) + (400 \times 1.46) + (500 \times 6.84)}{1,000} = 4.0$$

Likewise, we can examine the duration of the deposits. We have CDs with durations of one and five years, so

$$D_D = \frac{(600 \times 1.0) + (300 \times 5.0)}{900} = 2.33$$

Combining the preceding, we can calculate the duration of the equity—the sensitivity of the value of the firm to changes in the discount rate $(1 + r)$.

$$D_{equity} = \frac{(V_A \times D_A) - (V_D \times D_D)}{V_E}$$

$$= \frac{(1,000 \times 4.0) - (900 \times 2.33)}{100} = 19.03$$

Therefore, if the discount rate increases by 1 percent, the value of the equity of this bank will decline by 19.03 percent.

---

*Our discussion of duration is based on George G. Kaufman, "Measuring and Managing Interest Rate Risk: A Primer," *Economic Perspectives,* Federal Reserve Bank of Chicago.

†These discount rates are zero-coupon rates that include the risk premium appropriate for this instrument.

‡In algebraic form, the duration, D, is calculated as

$$D = \sum_{t=1}^{T} \left(\frac{PV_t}{V}\right) \cdot t$$

where PV_t is the present value of the cash flow received in time period t and V is the market value of the instrument.

FIGURE 23–1   Duration and Convexity

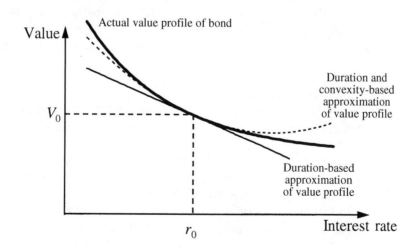

Value

Actual value profile of bond

Duration and convexity-based approximation of value profile

V_0

Duration-based approximation of value profile

r_0

Interest rate

FIGURE 23–2   The Impact of Positive and Negative Convexity

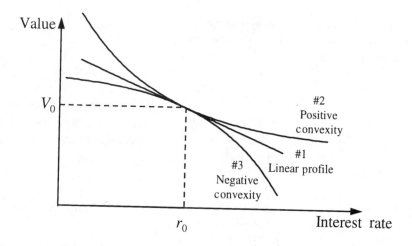

Figure 23–2 illustrates that if the portfolio exhibits positive convexity, any "surprises" are "good surprises": A portfolio manager who is using duration is implicitly assuming that value of the portfolio will follow a linear payoff profile like #1. If the portfolio contains bonds with positive convexity, interest rate increases will lead to decreases in the value of the portfolio that are smaller than would be predicted by duration. On the other hand, if interest rates decrease, a portfolio that has positive convexity will gain more than would be predicted by duration.

However, as Kosrow Dehnad described in "The Curse of Negative Convexity" in Chapter 18, the "surprises" would be much less pleasant if the portfolio exhibits negative convexity. Figure 23–2 illustrates that if the portfolio contains bonds with negative convexity, interest rate increases will lead to decreases in the value of the portfolio that are larger than would be predicted by duration. And if interest rates decrease, a portfolio that has negative convexity will gain less than would be predicted by duration.

Managing Cash Flow Risk[2]

The rates to which assets and liabilities are indexed can create exposures if the underlying indexes are different or if the maturities are different.

Rate Mismatches.   In the United States, prime loans are normally funded by Eurodollar deposits, federal funds, and bank CDs. If the spread between the asset index and the liability index is volatile, the financial institution's income (i.e., spread on the loan) will be volatile. A solution to this exposure is a basis swap, in which the bank pays out prime and receives LIBOR (or federal funds or the T-bill rate). Figure 23–3 shows how a basis swap can be used to maintain a constant spread.

FIGURE 23–3 Using a Prime-LIBOR Basis Swap to Stabilize Spread Income

	Scenario 1 *Prime is 9%* *LIBOR is 6%*	*Scenario 2* *Prime is 11%* *LIBOR is 10%*
Loan interest (prime)	9.00%	11.00%
Funding cost (LIBOR)	(6.00)	(10.00)
Spread without swap	300 basis points	100 basis points
Basis swap		
Swap outflow (prime—250)	(6.50)	(8.50)
Swap inflow (LIBOR)	6.00	10.00
Net lending spread	250 basis points	250 basis points

Instead of locking in the spread with a swap, the bank could protect against declines in the spread while still being able to benefit from increases in the spread by purchasing a floor on prime and a cap on LIBOR. The floor and cap premiums could be offset by selling a cap on prime and selling a floor on LIBOR.

Maturity Mismatches. Banks often resort to "short funding"—e.g., fund six-month loans with one-month deposits. Such a strategy will lead to volatility in the bank's income if the rates do not move together.

Such an exposure can be managed with short-term interest rate swaps. In the swaps we looked at in Chapter 8, the fixed rate was a multiyear rate and the floating rate was a six- or three-month rate. A short-term swap works exactly the same way, except that the rates are much shorter—e.g., the fixed rate might be based on a six-month rate and the floating rate based on a one-month rate.

The exposure resulting from a maturity mismatch can also be hedged with a strip of futures contracts.

Managing Value Risk

Changing the Duration of the Portfolio. The duration of the portfolio is simply the weighted average of the durations of the assets and liabilities.

$$D_P = [D_A \times (\text{value of assets}) - D_L \times (\text{value of liabilities})]/(\text{value of portfolio})$$
$$(23–5)$$

Many financial institutions face volatility in the value of their portfolios, because the duration of their assets is greater than the duration of their liabilities. In this case, if interest rates rise, the present value of the assets will decrease more than the decrease in value of the liabilities. To immunize the portfolio against interest rate risk—i.e., the value of the portfolio is invariant to interest rate movement—the value-weighted durations of assets and liabilities would be equal:

$$D_A \times \text{(value of assets)} = D_L \times \text{(value of liabilities)} \qquad (23\text{--}6)$$

Derivatives can be used to manage asset-liability mismatches. By entering into an interest rate swap (or by buying or selling futures contracts), the duration of the portfolio can be modified.

In Chapter 8, we showed that an interest rate swap can be viewed as equivalent to long and short positions in fixed- and floating-rate bonds. Hence, the duration of a swap can be calculated as

$$D_{\text{SWAP}} = D_{\text{FIXED}} - D_{\text{FLOATING}} \qquad (23\text{--}7)$$

For example, the duration of a five-year interest rate swap in which the fixed rate is 6 percent and the floating rate is six-month LIBOR can be calculated as:

Duration of fixed leg	4.48 years
Duration of floating leg	0.50 years
Duration of swap	3.98 years

To increase the duration of a portfolio, you would want to be long the swap—i.e., receive the fixed rate and pay the floating rate. To reduce the duration of a portfolio, you would want to be short the swap—i.e., pay the fixed rate and receive the floating rate.

Illustration 23–3

Using an Interest Rate Swap to Change the Duration of a Portfolio

Consider an insurance company that sells annuity contracts. The company invests the proceeds of the premiums it receives in bonds; so the balance sheet would have bonds on the asset side and annuity contracts on the liability side. To make the example simple, let's consider the case where the firm has only one bond and one annuity.

Bond	*Annuity*
$50,000	$10,000/year
5-year maturity	5 years
9% coupon	yield = 8%
Annual pay	Annual pay
Option free	Option free
$D = 4.24$	$D = 2.625$

Using an Interest Rate Swap to Change the Duration of a Portfolio continued

The insurance company's surplus is $6,705. The duration of the surplus can be calculated as

$$Ds = [50,000 \, (4.24) - 43,295 \, (2.625)]/$$
$$6,705 = 14.67$$

Such a large duration is likely to be deemed unacceptably risky by the management of the insurance company.

The surplus could be immunized by entering into an interest rate swap. Suppose that the current 5-year swap rate is 7 percent. Which side of the swap should the insurance company take? And how large should the notional principal be to immunize the surplus?

Since swaps can be viewed as equivalent to long and short positions in fixed- and floating-rate bonds, the duration of a swap can be calculated as

$$D_{SWAP} = D_{FIXED} - D_{FLOATING}$$

For the swap in question, the duration of a 5-year, fixed-rate bond with 7 percent semi-annual coupons is 4.3 and the duration of a floating-rate note that resets semiannually is 0.5; so, the duration of the swap is 3.8.

To hedge the surplus the insurance company will need to be short the swap—i.e., pay the fixed rate and receive the floating rate. The notional principal (NP) of the swap would be given by

$$14.67 \, (6,705) - 3.8 \, (NP) = 0$$

Solving the preceding equation for NP, the notional principal of the swap would be $25,884.83.

Changing the Convexity of the Portfolio.   As we noted earlier, the bonds that can result in "unpleasant surprises" are those that exhibit negative convexity. Because an increase in interest rates will have the largest effect on the most distant cash flows, the duration of a "plain vanilla" bond will decrease as interest rates rise—i.e., plain vanilla bonds exhibit positive convexity. Two debt instruments that exhibit negative convexity and are widely held by banks and other financial institutions are callable bonds and mortgages (or mortgage-backed securities).

Hedging Callable Bonds.   At low interest rates, callable bonds exhibit negative convexity. To see why this is the case, remember from Chapter 15 that we described a callable bond as being equivalent to a plain vanilla bond plus selling a put option on interest rates. This equivalence is illustrated in Figure 23–4. At interest rates below the exercise rate for the option, the positive convexity of the plain vanilla bond is overwhelmed by the negative convexity of the short option position. So the callable bond will exhibit negative convexity at low rates and positive convexity at high rates. To hedge the callable bond, the portfolio manager can reverse Figure 23–4—i.e., buy a call option like that embedded in the callable bond.

FIGURE 23–4   **Payoff Profile for a Callable Bond Is Convex at Low Interest Rates**

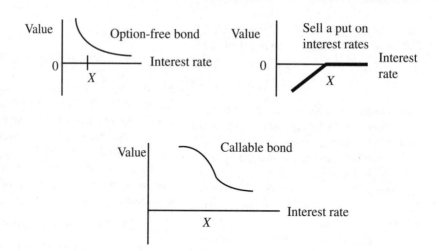

Hedging Mortgages or Mortgage-Backed Securities.   Negative convexity is of special importance with mortgages or mortgage-backed securities (MBS). As interest rates fall, mortgage prepayments increase and the duration of the mortgage or MBS decreases. As with the callable bonds, the holder of the mortgage or MBS is short an interest rate option.

As with the callable bond, the bank or financial institution could hedge the exposure to the prepayment risk by purchasing an interest rate put option. (More likely, the bank would purchase a floor—i.e., a package of interest rate puts.) However, the bank might use a variant on the index-amortization swap (IAS). In Chapter 14, we described an index amortizing swap as one in which the notional principal changes as interest rates change—the notional principal of the swap increases (decreases) as the specified interest rate increases (decreases). An index accreting swap is one in which the relation between the notional principal and the specified interest rate is negative, rather than positive—i.e., the notional principal of the swap increases (decreases) as the specified interest rate index decreases (increases).

The accretion schedule is specified as part of the terms of the swap transaction. An accretion schedule might look like the following:

Change in Index	Accretion of Notional Amount
−1%	110%
−2%	125%
−3%	140%

As with the index amortizing swap, the index accreting swap is made up of a standard swap and a package of options, more specifically swaptions. The fixed rates in an index accreting swap would be lower than that in a plain vanilla swap to pay for the interest rate options embedded in the index accreting swap.

To hedge a mortgage portfolio, the bank or financial institution would enter into an index accreting swap in which the bank will receive the fixed rate. If interest rates decline and the mortgages begin prepaying, the reduced principal will be offset by an increase in the notional principal on the swap.

The Impact on the Financial Institution

Elijah Brewer, Bernadette Minton, and James Moser (1996) examined the effects of the use of interest rate derivative products on the commercial and industrial (C&I) lending activity of U.S. commercial banks. They found that C&I loan growth is positively related to the use of interest rate derivatives—swaps and exchange-traded futures. These results suggest that interest rate derivatives allow commercial banks to lessen their systematic exposures to changes in interest rates, thereby increasing their ability to provide more intermediation services.

Brewer, Minton, and Moser interpret the positive relation between derivatives use and C&I loan growth as being consistent with the notion that derivatives markets allow banks to increase lending activities at a rate greater than they would otherwise. However, it is possible that a bank's C&I activity might affect its decision to use derivatives.

The Investment Portfolio

In addition to using interest rate derivatives for asset-liability management, banks and other financial institutions also use other derivatives to manage their investment portfolios in the same way that institutional investors do. To avoid repetition, we will defer discussion of most of these investor applications to Chapter 24. However, the use of hybrid securities—a.k.a. *structured notes*—in the investment portfolios of banks is something that deserves particular mention.

In 1993 and into the beginning of 1994, sales of structured notes boomed; many dealers claimed that their business rose fivefold over the 1992 level. *Euromoney* suggested that, in 1993, some $60–$70 billion of structured notes were issued—a substantial percentage of the medium-term-note market. The structured note market boomed in large part because U.S. dollar interest rates were so low in 1993 and into 1994. The rates available in 1993 meant that investors were replacing maturing assets which had been yielding 8 percent with new securities which were offering something like 4 percent. Investors wanted to "enhance yield"; and to do so they either had to move down the credit spectrum or had to accept more market risk. Many chose the latter route.[3]

In its *July 1994 Advisory Letter*,[4] the OCC noted most of the structured notes purchased by U.S. banks were issued by U.S. government-sponsored enterprises (GSEs)—the Federal Home Loan Banks, Federal National Mortgage Association, Student Loan Marketing Association, Federal Farm Credit Bank, and Federal Home Loan Mortgage Corporation. The OCC listed six "common structured notes"—all of which we described in Chapter 15.

Step-up bonds initially pay the investor an above-market yield for a short noncall period and then, *if not called*, "step up" to a higher coupon rate. If the bond is not called, the stepped-up coupon would be below then current market rates (if not, the bond would have been called). The investor initially receives a higher yield because of having implicitly sold a call option.

Index amortizing notes (IANs) repay principal according to a predetermined amortization schedule that is linked to the level of a specific index (usually LIBOR). As market interest rates increase (or prepayment rates decrease), the maturity of an IAN extends, similar to that of a collateralized mortgage obligation.

Dual-index notes have coupon rates that are determined by the difference between two market indexes, typically the constant-maturity Treasury rate (CMT) and LIBOR.

Leveraged bonds pay investors according to a formula that is based upon a multiple of the increase or decrease in a specified index, such as LIBOR, the CMT rate, or the prime rate. For example, the coupon might be 1.5 × 10-year CMT + 150 basis points. The leveraging multiplier (1.5) causes the coupon to magnify movements in market yields. A *deleveraged bond* would involve a multiplier less than 1.

Inverse floaters have coupons that increase as rates decline and decrease as rates rise.

Range notes were designed to allow an investor to profit from a very specific view—i.e., that interest rates will stay within a narrow band. As long as the interest rate stays within a specified range, interest accrues at an above-market rate; if, however, the interest rate moves outside the range, no interest is accrued. As the OCC noted in its *July Advisory Letter*, range notes were often structured to reflect an investor's view that is contrary to the "rate forecast" embedded in the yield curve. In January 1994, *Swaps Monitor* called range notes—a.k.a. *corridor* or *accrual notes*—"the latest innovation in the options market."[5] *Euromoney* suggested that, in contrast to 1993 where most of the "plays" were directional plays done via "inverse floaters," January 1994 witnessed a surge of range notes.[6] Given the behavior of interest rates in 1994, the original range notes turned out to be terrible investments. Many "busted" through their ranges and paid no interest after March.[7] Consequently, range notes were singled out by regulators as "inappropriate investments" for banks and mutual funds. One of the SEC's concerns was that the notes did not "reset to pay" and thus violated certain provisions of the legislation that determines what investments mutual funds can purchase. As a result, one-month reset structures appeared. These structures are far less risky and may qualify under SEC provisions regarding resets to par.[8]

With respect to the purchase of structured notes, the Federal Reserve, the OCC, and the FDIC issued specific guidance for banks.[9] As with derivatives in general, the Board of Directors must approve policies that address the goals and objectives expected to be achieved and that set limits on the degree of acceptable price risk, as well as on the amount of funds that may be committed to them. However, the regulators went further, requiring bank management to be able to "understand the risks of structured notes and be able to explain how such securities accomplish strategic portfolio objectives." Indeed, the regulators required that "redemption-linked notes" or notes that contain leverage be specifically authorized in written policy.

The Credit Portfolio

For years, credit risk has been treated as if it is somehow "different." This treatment is in the process of changing. It will change everywhere, but one of the first and most dramatic changes will occur in the way that banks evaluate and manage their loan books.

Applying Modern Portfolio Theory to the Loan Book

To date, the loan books at most banks have been managed as what might be described as "originate and hold" portfolios. The ability of the credit manager to manage the portfolio has been severely limited: *The relationship manager comes to the bank's credit officer with the proposal to lend $X to company XYZ at a price of LIBOR + Y percent. The credit officer then has a "yes" or "no" decision.*

Such a form of management is very different from that suggested by modern portfolio theory. Modern portfolio theory would have the portfolio manager form an efficient portfolio by considering the return on the asset in question, the riskiness of the asset (the standard deviation of its return), and the correlation between the return on the asset and the returns on the other assets in the portfolio. As the asset in question becomes a larger percentage of the portfolio or as the correlation between the returns on the asset and those of the other assets in the portfolio is higher, the required return for the asset must increase: *The relationship manager comes to the bank's credit portfolio manager with a proposal to lend $X to company XYZ at a price of LIBOR + Y percent. The credit portfolio manager responds that given the* *inherent riskiness of company XYZ and given the current composition of the loan book, the necessary return for the proposed transaction is LIBOR + Z percent.*

In order to manage a loan book as a true portfolio, several types of data are necessary.

- The nominal return for lending to company XYZ.
- The percent of the loan amount that the bank would expect to recover if company XYZ defaulted on the loan.
- The riskiness of company XYZ. At one level, this is simply the probability that company XYZ will default on the loan. At a more subtle level, this would also include the probability that company XYZ's credit rating declines over the term of the loan.
- The correlation between the riskiness of company XYZ and that of other companies to which the bank has made loans.

Banks know the interest rate at which they lent money. Using internal data or data from Moody's or Standard & Poor's, the bank can obtain an estimate of the recovery rate on different types of loans and the bank can obtain estimates of the riskiness of company XYZ. The missing data had been the correlation between the riskiness of various credits. In 1997, J. P. Morgan provided the first such data set in what they called *CreditMetrics.**

Aside

CreditMetrics

CreditMetrics is a portfolio model developed by J. P. Morgan to evaluate credit risk. It provides a measure of value-at-risk due to credit caused not only by defaults, but also by credit upgrades and downgrades. CreditMetrics consists of a methodology for assessing portfolio risk due to changes in obligor credit quality and a data set—as well as software that can be purchased to implement the methodology. The CreditMetrics methodology is comparable to the RiskMetrics methodology we described in Chapter 19, in the sense that it constructs a distribution of market or credit outcomes.

Other approaches have been proposed for modeling credit risk.

- *Binomial model*—a tree is constructed with two states at each step: default and no default. This approach ignores changes in value that would be

---

*CreditMetrics is a registered trademark of Morgan Guaranty Trust.

CreditMetrics continued

recognized in a mark-to-market framework.

- *RAROC model*—risk is the observed volatility of corporate bond values within each credit rating category, maturity band, and industry grouping. The results are significantly influenced by credit events that occur (or do not occur) during the observation period.

In contrast, CreditMetrics looks at upgrades and downgrades, not just defaults. And as is illustrated in the following figure, the volatility estimates are based on the likelihood of migrating between credit ratings.

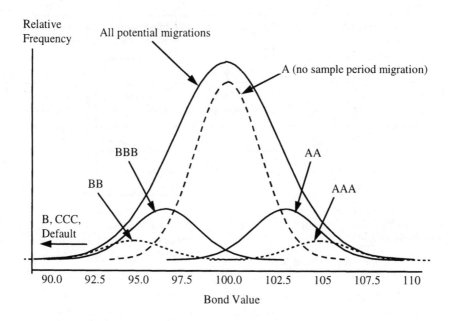

The following flowchart summarizes the CreditMetrics methodology. It comprises three elements which we can think of as proceeding in three steps:

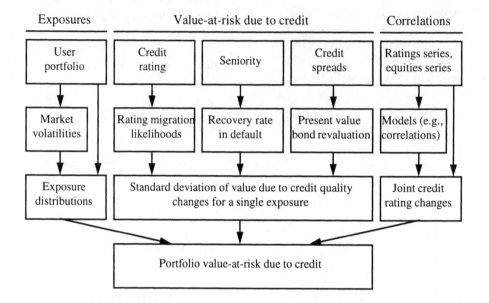

Step 1—Establish the Exposure Profile of Each Obligor in the Portfolio

CreditMetrics is capable of incorporating a range of financial instruments: bonds, loans, commitments, letters of credit, commercial contracts (e.g., receivables), and market-driven instruments, including derivatives. The calculation of exposures differs by the type of instrument:

- *Bonds and loans:* Either treated as market-driven instruments or taken at par. The present value of remaining cash flows is obtained using discount rates appropriate for the rating category.
- *Commitments:* Exposures are computed using three measures: (1) amount currently drawn, (2) expected changes in drawn amount due to credit rating changes, or (3) spreads and fees needed to revalue drawn and undrawn portions.
- *Financial letters of credit:* Full face amount.
- *Receivables:* Full face amount.
- *Market-driven instruments:* Expected exposures at the risk horizon are computed externally and imported into CreditMetrics.

Step 2—Compute Volatility in the Value of Each Instrument Due to Possible Upgrades, Downgrades, and Defaults

A transition matrix is used to determine the probabilities of the issuer (at the senior unsecured level) either defaulting or migrating to

CreditMetrics continued

other credit ratings. Using this transition matrix, the exposure is revalued at the risk horizon. (In default, the seniority of the exposure determines its recovery rate; for upgrades or downgrades, the forward curve appropriate to the credit rating category is used to revalue the exposure.) The resulting revaluations produce a distribution of values due to credit quality changes. The following figure illustrates the methodology for a credit currently rated BBB.

Current state

BBB

8 possible states one year hence

AAA	AA	A	BBB	BB	B	CCC	Default

Transition probabilities

0.02%	0.33%	5.95%	86.93%	5.30%	1.17%	0.12%	0.18%

×

Bond revaluations

$109.37	$109.19	$108.66	$107.55	$102.02	$98.10	$83.64	$51.13

EXPECTED VALUE

$$\mu_T = \sum_{i=1}^{s} p_i \mu_i = \$107.09$$

STANDARD DEVIATION OF VALUE

$$\sigma_T = \sqrt{\sum_{i=1}^{s} p_i \left(V_i - \mu_T\right)^2} = \$2.99$$

Step 3—Using the Correlations between the Credit Events for a Particular Counterparty, Aggregate the Volatilities of the Individual Instruments into a Volatility for the Portfolio

There are a variety of techniques to estimate correlation factors:

- *Actual rating and default correlations:* The problem exists that the data sets are sparse and that all obligors within a given credit rating are treated the same.
- *Bond spread correlations:* Data quality problems exist.

- *Uniform constant correlation:* This approach is easy to use, but it does not permit analysis of concentrations by industry, country, etc.
- *Equity price correlations:* This approach is forward-looking and good data are available, but heavy processing is required to extract credit quality correlations.

CreditMetrics relies on equity price correlations. The value of any firm can be thought of as being characterized by some distribution and that there is some value, below which the firm will default on its obligations.

CreditMetrics continued

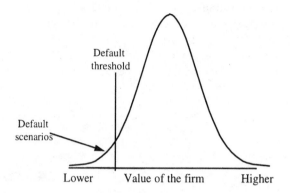

This single-firm distribution can be generalized to represent a firm from a specific rating category and to include not only a default threshold but also thresholds for downgrades and upgrades.

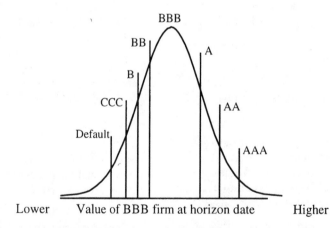

A Methodological Note: So far, CreditMetrics has been described as if it uses an individual firm—XYZ Corp. or ABC Corp.—as the unit of observation. Such an approach—which would require volatilities for each firm and correlations between all firms—would require a huge amount of data. To reduce the data requirement, individual firms are mapped to industries and countries, in the same way that, in RiskMetrics, the transactions are mapped to a standard set of transactions. In the following, the sensitivity of XYZ Corp.'s performance can be attributed to countries—75 percent from the United States, 15 percent from the UK, and

CreditMetrics continued

10 percent from Germany—and to industry sectors—35 percent in finance, 40 percent in technology, and 25 percent in autos. The residual component of the firm's performance that cannot be explained by country and industry sector allocations is assigned to firm-specific risk—in the case of XYZ Corp., 15%.

The CreditMetrics software uses the data generated by the three steps to simulate the mean, variance, skewness, and kurtosis of the value distribution of the portfolio. It also computes the value changes in the portfolio relating to specified percentile levels. Finally, it provides the marginal risk contribution of each transaction in the portfolio.

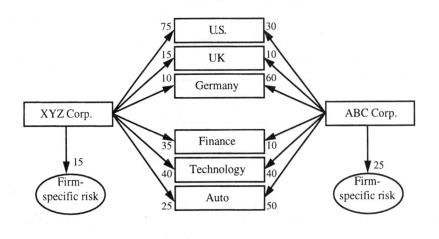

Using Credit Derivatives to Restructure the Loan Book

In Chapter 14, we described the *credit derivatives.* In addition to loan sales or loan securitization, these credit derivatives could be used to restructure the loan book.

For example, suppose that the credit portfolio manager has determined that the bank's loan book has too much exposure to XYZ Corporation. Figure 23–5 illustrates how the credit portfolio manager could synthetically transfer the credit risk of a $20 million loan to a derivatives dealer (who would then transfer this exposure to a third party).

FIGURE 23–5   Hedging a Bank Loan with a Total Return Swap

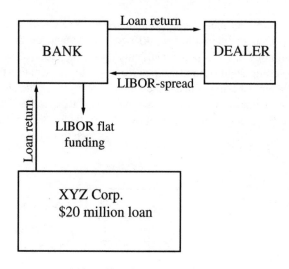

Notes

1. Walker (1997).
2. This section is based on Walker (1997).
3. Bennett (March 1994).
4. Office of the Comptroller of the Currency (1994).
5. "Range Notes Are Latest Options Innovation" (1994).
6. Bennett (March 1994).
7. "US Derivatives: Range Notes with 1-Month Resets Said to Sell Well" (1994).
8. "US Derivatives: Range Notes with 1-Month Resets Said to Sell Well" (1994).
9. See Office of the Comptroller of the Currency (1994), Federal Deposit Insurance Corporation, *Examination Guidance for Structured Notes* (August 1994), and Federal Reserve Board, *Supervisory Memo on the Purchase of Structured Notes* (August 1994).

24

USES OF RISK MANAGEMENT PRODUCTS BY INSTITUTIONAL INVESTORS*

"Institutional investors" include not only investment managers, mutual funds, pension funds, hedge funds, and commodity trading advisers (CTAs), but also banks and thrifts, bank trusts, insurance companies, corporations, and municipalities. Some institutional investors manage to the value of assets. Examples of investors that manage to value include investment managers, mutual funds, hedge funds, CTAs, bank trusts, and corporations. Other institutional investors manage to the "surplus"—i.e., the market value of the assets minus the present value of the liabilities. Examples of institutional investors that manage to the surplus include pension funds, insurance companies, and banks and thrifts.

Institutional investors face a number of risks. In 1995, Joseph Slunt, a student at the NYU Stern School, surveyed relatively small pension and endowment funds (i.e., with assets ranging from $0.3 to $2.3 billion) to get some perspective on the risks they face. His survey results are summarized in Figure 24–1.

Figure 24–1 suggests that fund managers are most concerned about the volatility in the value of their assets or their surplus due to risk factors, including:

- *Interest rate risk*   In the vein of our discussion in Chapter 23, we will treat the *prepayment risk* inherent in mortgages and mortgage-backed securities as a special type of interest rate risk.
- *Foreign exchange rate risk*   Note that in Figure 24–1, this risk is called *currency risk*.
- *Risk associated with the value of the underlying asset*   This risk goes by several names. In an equity portfolio, it is usually referred to as *equity price*

---

*I want to thank my colleague François Gagnon for his assistance with this chapter.

FIGURE 24–1   Principal Risks Facing Institutional Investors, Percent of Survey Respondents

---

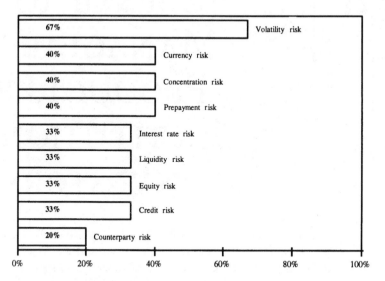

SOURCE: "Survey of Risk Management Practices for Pension Funds," Joseph Slunt, NYU Stern School of Business, Spring 1995.

risk. In a bond portfolio, the same risk is referred to as *credit risk.* (Note that credit risk can lead to one form of *concentration risk.*) And it is sometimes referred to as *event risk* (or what regulators might call *specific risk*).

The *Managing Financial Risk Yearbook* that the CIBC School of Financial Products publishes annually to update this book generally contains "surveys of surveys" of institutional investors.[1] The *1997 Yearbook* examined a total of 13 surveys of institutional investors. These surveys are described in Table 24–1.

The percentages of the survey respondents reporting that they use derivatives are shown in Table 24–2. It is interesting to note that the survey evidence provided by Greenwich Associates suggests that U.S. institutional investors use derivatives less than do investors in Europe and Japan.[2] It is also interesting to note that the NAPF survey asked respondents whether they were prohibited from using derivatives. In 1996, 31 percent of the private plans and 25 percent of the public plans were not authorized to use derivatives.

The reasons the institutional investors gave for using derivatives are summarized in Table 24–3. The most widely offered reason for using derivatives was "risk reduction" (which would include "cash flow management"). However, Table 24–3 indicates that institutional investors also use derivatives for other reasons. Derivatives

TABLE 24-1 Surveys of Institutional Investors

Sponsor	Focus	Survey Date	Samples
International			
Greenwich Associates	Trends in end-user usage	Nov. 94 to Mar. 96	Interviews with 4,000 + users and potential users in North America, Europe, and Asia (2,207 nonfinancial users and liability managers; 1,962 taxable fixed-income and equity investors)
Institutional Investor	Derivative practices	1995	Quarterly surveys of corporate and public pension plan sponsors
Ernst & Young	Derivative practices	1995	143 investment management complexes with combined assets of more than $535 billion
North America			
Record Treasury Management	International investing and currency management strategies	Summer 1996	Top 200 U.S. pension plans
Derivative Sales Alert	Derivative use by the U.S. branches and agencies of foreign banks	Summer 1996	Analysis of filings with bank regulators

TABLE 24-1 (*continued*)

Sponsor	Focus	Survey Date	Samples
Record Treasury Management	International investing, currency management strategies, and derivative practices	Spring 1995	Top U.S. pension plans
New York University Stern School of Business	Institutional investor risks	Spring 1995	Pension and endowment funds with assets ranging from $0.3 to $2.3 billion
Europe			
Wall Street Journal/Watson Wyatt	Use of passive management by pension funds	Mar. 96	68 European pension funds
University of Manchester National Association of Pension Funds	Impact of foreign exchange Benefits provided and investment strategies of UK pension funds	Jan. 96 Dec. 96	192 UK institutional investors, 36 responses 750 UK pension funds
London International Financial Futures and Options Exchange (LIFFE) Wall Street Journal/Watson Wyatt	Derivative usage among UK insurance companies Derivative usage	Aug. 96 Spring 1995	55 largest UK life insurance companies 44 pension funds in 10 European countries with combined assets of more than $300 billion
Asia			
Nippon Credit Bank	Derivative use by Japanese regional financial institutions	1996	49 regional banks 48 "second-tier" regional banks 185 credit associations 301 laborers' credit corporations

---

TABLE 24–2   **Percentage of Institutional Investors Surveyed That Use Derivatives**

Survey Sponsor	Percent Responding That They Use Derivatives
International	
Greenwich Associates	
Fixed-Income Managers:	
United States	289/798 = 36%
Europe/Middle East	575/597 = 96%
Asia	57/141 = 40%
Japan (international investors)	73/139 = 52%
Japan (domestic investors)	56/135 = 41%
Institutional Investor	52%
Ernst & Young	31%
North America	
Derivative Sales Alert*	
Interest rate derivatives	46%
Foreign exchange derivatives	43%
New York University	67%
Stern School of Business	
Europe	
National Association of Pension Funds	
Private plan	70%
Public plan	50%
London International Financial Futures and	71%
Options Exchange (LIFFE)	
Wall Street Journal/Watson Wyatt (1995)	In excess of 54%
Asia	
Nippon Credit Bank	In excess of 48%

* The Derivative Sales Alert only report the number of users—interest rate derivatives, 236, and foreign exchange rate derivatives, 221. Information provided by the Federal Reserve Bank on the number of foreign bank agencies (135) and foreign bank branches in the United States (374) was used to calculate the percentages displayed in the table.

are used to facilitate the construction of the optimal portfolio by using "asset allocation," doing "indexing," and providing "access to international markets." (If the principles of modern portfolio theory are ignored and an ill-diversified portfolio is created, the result is another form of *concentration risk*, alluded to in Figure 24–1.) And derivatives are used for "return enhancement" either via "market timing" or by "creating synthetic securities."

TABLE 24-3 **Reasons Institutional Investors Use Derivatives**

Survey Sponsor	Risk Reduction	Return Enhancement	Market Timing	Cash Flow Management	Create Synthetic Securities	Asset Allocation	Indexing	Access to International Markets
International								
Institutional Investor	35%	29%				35%		
North America								
Greenwich Associates								
U.S. taxable fixed income	79%	13%	26%		29%	24%		
U.S. equity derivative specialists	60%	52%	18%	10%		43%	40%	24%
Record Treasury Management (1996)	62%	25%						
Record Treasury Management (1995)	31%	28%				30%		
New York University Stern School of Business	70%	20%				60%		
Europe								
London International Financial Futures and Options Exchange (LIFFE)								
Nonlinked funds	33%	40%		36%		85%		
Linked funds	20%	0%		57%		56%		
Watson Wyatt	54%					25%		

Table 24–3 reinforces the notion that institutional investors think about using derivatives to reduce the riskiness of their portfolios or to enhance the return to their portfolios as separate issues. In the following, Lisa Polsky points out that institutional investors must move toward thinking about the two issues together, in terms of risk-adjusted returns.[3]

Finally, the types of derivatives that are used are reported in Table 24–4.

Risk Management in Practice

Integrating Risk Management and Strategy

Lisa K. Polsky

Traditionally, risk and return have been treated as separate issues. What is needed is an integration of the two by thinking in terms of risk-adjusted returns. Integrating risk management into the investment process is not an alternative to setting up a risk monitoring function but, rather, a complementary process in which investors and managers consider both return generation and risk management.

For many years the funds management business was focused only on measuring performance. Even as risk management has become more of a focus, many firms attempt to bifurcate risk and return into two separate processes, with one group looking at returns and another looking at risk. The focus needs to be on risk-adjusted returns, a subject that is still discussed less in the funds management industry than it should be.

Risk means different things to different managers—and may mean different things to the investor or plan sponsor than it does to the money manager. But while there are many different measures of risk, they all share one thing in common—the concern about losing money.

At the microlevel, the individual portfolio manager may think of managing risk in terms of an effective sell discipline or in terms of moving into cash when the manager expects adverse market moves. This could be looked at as a form of risk-controlled tactical asset allocation. Buying an option is a dynamic form of risk-controlled TAA: when the market goes against you, you are effectively moving into cash dynamically (the delta gradually goes toward zero); and when the market goes in your favor, you are increasing your investment (the delta goes toward 100 percent invested in the market).

At the macrolevel, the investor or plan sponsor thinks about risk management in terms of asset allocation—i.e., achieving targeted returns while minimizing risk through diversification. Traditional asset allocation involves forecasting returns, but uses historical volatility and correlation as estimates of future risk. But this approach has you only changing your investments when your expectations for returns change. If your expectations for returns in a market are constant but volatility in that market is skyrocketing, shouldn't you reduce your investment? To do this you have to move from a static to a dynamic definition of risk.

Think about February 1994 when the Fed raised interest rates. Most investors held steadfast to their view that interest rates would continue to fall; i.e., their expectations of returns didn't change. So investors steadfastly held their bond positions. But volatility in the bond market was soaring. Expected returns were constant, but risk was increasing. Managers who integrated return generation with risk management would have cut their positions, and avoided a lot of subsequent pain.

In traditional asset allocation, investors diversify risk by diversifying asset classes. But different asset classes may share the same types of risk. Convertible bonds, for example, have both equity and fixed-income risk. Even "plain vanilla" U.S. active equity managers may buy Telemex, creating Latin American risk in the U.S. equity portfolio. To really use asset allocation as a risk management technique, it is useful to take it down two or three levels and break the asset classes down into their smallest components of risk. Equity portfolio risks, for example, may include market directional risk, dividend risk, interest rate risk, currency risk and credit risk. Fixed-income portfolios also can be broken down into directional risk, yield-curve risk, currency risk, and credit risk. It is useful to combine the risks which overlap in the investment portfolio to assess whether or not you are truly diversified.

Once you've unbundled the risks in traditional investments, they can be recombined, hedged, and managed to create the exact profile that optimizes the combination of your market views (i.e., expected returns) and your tolerance for risk.

Take a simple product—say, IBM bonds. If a Japanese investor does not want the exchange rate risk, an instrument can be created by buying more yen as the price of the bond goes up and selling yen as the bond price goes down. This tactic can be carried out dynamically by changing the amount of yen in the portfolio relative to the value of the bond through a quanto option. The term *quanto* means quantity-adjusted, and most applications of quantos center on immunizing the currency risk when purchasing an asset in a currency different from the purchaser's home currency. The quanto option takes the risk of dollars and translates it back into yen by adjusting the quantity of the foreign exchange purchased according to changes in the value of the underlying asset.

Integrating risk management into investment strategies is fundamentally about managing your portfolio dynamically on both the return dimension and the risk dimension. It's not about creating risk reports which get filed in your drawer—it's about creating the highest risk-adjusted returns.

Lisa Polsky is a managing director at Morgan Stanley & Company where she serves on the firm's Risk Advisory Board. She is the global risk manager for the Equity Division and is responsible for equity-structured products and product development.

TABLE 24-4 Derivative Instruments Used by Institutional Investors—Survey Responses

Survey Sponsor	Over-the-Counter Products							Exchange-Traded Products		
	Interest Rate Products		Currency Products		Equity Products	Asset Swaps	Structured Investments	Interest Rate Products	Currency Products	Equity Products
	Swap and Forwards	IR and Bond Options	Swaps and Forwards	Options						
International										
Institutional Investor	10%		43%	34%	16% (options) 5% (swaps)		12%	26%	19%	52%
Ernst & Young	36%		61%		6% (swaps)		41%	53%	30%	56%
Greenwich Associates										
United States	11%	22%	2%			4%	8%		16%	
Europe/Middle East	26%	38%	14%			19%	20%		55%	
Asia	30%	29%	18%			26%	19%		38%	
Japan (international)	28%		9%			32%	20%		35%	
Japan (domestic)	16%	11%	1%			6%	6%		51%	
Europe										
Watson Wyatt	16%		44%		3% (swaps)			>27%	>44%	>41%
London International Financial Futures and Options Exchange	(All OTC products)							No asset class specified		
Nonlinked funds	47%							Futures 82%		Options 47%
Linked funds	41%							53%		29%
University of Manchester			86%	92%					Futures 92%	

Most of this chapter will deal with the *uses* of derivatives by institutional investors. We begin by looking at the use of derivatives in portfolio construction. However, from that point, the discussion might seem somewhat schizophrenic. We just noted that risk and return *should be* considered *jointly,* but the discussion to follow will consider them *separately*—i.e., we look at the use of derivatives to reduce the riskiness of the portfolio and then look at the use of derivatives to increase the expected return of the portfolio. Let me be clear on this: portfolio managers deal with risk and return jointly; the only reason they are separated here is that it makes it easier to explain the techniques.

After looking at uses, we turn to the ways that institutional investors control derivatives activities. We conclude this chapter with a provocative look at the question of whether fund managers are *obliged* to use risk management.

Using Derivatives in Portfolio Construction

In Table 24–3, we noted that derivatives have been widely used in asset allocation. We first look at the use of derivatives for strategic asset allocation and then turn to their use in tactical and insured asset allocations.

Using Derivatives in Strategic Asset Allocation

The strategic asset allocation is the long-run mix of equity, fixed-income, and other asset classes that best meets the investor's risk-return preferences, as well as satisfying any constraints faced by the investor. The investor's strategic asset allocation is concerned with long-run mixes of assets, and therefore should not fluctuate with short-run capital market conditions. Determination of the strategic asset allocation assumes a long-run level of risk tolerance (that will remain unchanged).

Using Derivatives for Portfolio Rebalancing.   Above we probably should have said that the investor's *targeted* strategic asset allocation will not be changed by changing (short-term) capital market conditions. But short-term changes in the capital markets will certainly change the investor's *realized* asset allocation; e.g., if prices in the equity market are rising relative to prices in the bond market or other markets, the realized percentage of the investor's portfolio in equity will rise. To reestablish the targeted strategic asset allocation, the investor will have to make changes in the portfolio composition. These changes could be made via derivatives.

Suppose that an investor's strategic allocation between equity and fixed-income investments is 70–30 and that the investor has $100,000,000 to invest. For simplicity, let's regard the S&P 500 as the market portfolio and limit the choice of fixed-income instruments to U.S. Treasury bills. The allocation would be

| S&P 500 | $70,000,000 | (70%) |
| T-bills | $30,000,000 | (30%) |

By definition, the market portfolio has a beta of 1.0. Treating the yield on a T-bill as uncorrelated with the return on the market portfolio, the beta for the T-bills would be 0.0. so the beta for the target portfolio is 0.7.

$$\text{Target portfolio beta} = 0.7\,(1.0) + 0.3\,(0.0) = 0.7$$

If values in the equity market were to fall by 10 percent, the actual allocation of the portfolio will change to:

| Stocks | $63,000,000 | (67.74%) |
| T-bills | $30,000,000 | (32.26%) |

And the (realized) beta for the portfolio will change as well.

$$\text{Portfolio beta} = 0.6774\,(1.0) + 0.3226\,(0.0) = 0.6774$$

The investor can rebalance the portfolio in the cash market by selling T-bills and buying the market portfolio. Or the investor can rebalance the portfolio using derivatives.

For instance, the investor might reestablish the strategic asset allocation by using S&P 500 futures contracts. Suppose that S&P futures are currently trading at 600; i.e., the dollar value of the 500 shares would be $500 \times \$660 = \$300,000$. Since the target beta for the portfolio is 0.7, a little bit of algebra tells us that the investor will need to purchase six futures contracts.

Aside

Using Derivatives to Rebalance a Portfolio

The $63 million of the portfolio that is invested in the market portfolio has a beta of 1.0; the $30 million invested in bonds has a beta of zero. We have assumed that the S&P 500 is the market portfolio; so the beta for the S&P 500 Index is 1.0 and the beta for the S&P 500 futures contract is $500 \times 1.0 = 500$. If the investor holds n S&P futures contracts which are currently trading at $660, the beta for the futures contracts is $n \times \$660 \times 500$. At the end, the total portfolio ($93 million) is to have a beta of 0.7.

$63,000,000 \times 1.0 + $30,000,000 \times 0.0$
$+ n \times $660 \times 500 = $93,000,000 \times 0.7$

Solving the preceding equation for n, we get

$n = 6.36$

So the investor will need to purchase six contracts.

Instead of futures contracts, an equity swap could be used to obtain the strategic asset allocation. As Figure 24–2 illustrates, an equity swap could be structured so that the investor would pay the return on the existing portfolio and receive the return on the target portfolio.

FIGURE 24-2   **Using an Equity Swap to Rebalance a Portfolio**

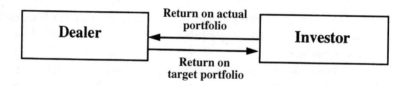

Using Derivatives for Alpha Transport.   *Alpha transport* is a strategy designed to separate the returns generated by the portfolio manager's security selection decisions (alpha) from either overall market effects (beta) or the effect of interest rates or foreign exchange rates. As the following Aside explains, alpha is a measure of excess return.

Aside

Alpha

In the context of the capital asset pricing model (CAPM), the expected return to portfolio P is

$$r_P = r_f + (r_M - r_f)\beta_P$$

where r_f is the risk-free return, r_M is the return to the market portfolio, and β_P is the beta for the portfolio being considered. This equation can be rearranged into the "excess returns" form of the CAPM:

$$r_P - r_f = (r_M - r_f)\beta_P$$

Ex post, a portfolio will be said to have "outperformed" the market if its return exceeded the expected return from the CAPM. Relative outperformance (or underperformance) is measured by alpha:

$$\alpha = r_{P,\text{ACTUAL}} - R_{P,\text{EXPECTED}}$$

To measure alpha, one will typically examine the *ex post* relation between the actual return for the portfolio being considered and the *average* risk-free return and return to the market portfolio over some period,

$$r_P - r_f = \alpha + (r_M - r_f)\beta_P$$

___

*This discussion is adapted from Sharpe and Alexander.

Alpha transport is employed when an institutional investor wishes to separate the performance of the manager from market performance. For example, consider the situation in which a pension fund sponsor decides to reallocate funds from the U.S. stock market into international equities. Suppose the fund sponsor has a U.S. manager whom it regards to be a good stock picker—in the jargon of the market, this U.S. manager has "positive alpha"—but the fund sponsor does not have the same level of trust in any foreign equity manager. A possible solution to this dilemma is to keep the investment with the U.S. fund manager and enter into an equity swap in which the fund will pay on the basis of the return on an appropriate U.S. equity index (e.g., the S&P 500) and receive on the basis of the return to an index in the desired foreign equity market. This strategy moves the directional risk from the U.S. market to the desired foreign market, but the fund is able to keep the positive alpha being generated by the U.S. portfolio manager.

Using Derivatives to Satisfy Constraints. While the objective of the portfolio manager is to maximize risk-adjusted return, most portfolios are subject to constraints on their activities. Some of the constraints may be imposed by external regulatory authorities; others are internally imposed. A common constraint is liquidity; e.g., insurance companies and some other investors must keep a portion of the assets in cash or near-cash. Russell Gregory-Allen (TIAA-CREF Investment Management, Inc.) proposed the following example of how derivatives could be used to satisfy a liquidity constraint.[4]

The portfolio manager would like the investment portfolio to be fully invested in the U.S. equity market, but $20 million must be kept in cash. To achieve the objective, while still satisfying the constraint, the portfolio manager could hold the $20 million in short-term highest-grade commercial paper or Treasuries and establish the equity position synthetically via an equity swap or futures. For example, in August 1995, the capitalization-weighted average price of a share of stock in the S&P 500 was a little over $56 and the price for the December S&P 500 futures contract was $565. The dollar value of each December futures contract was $500 \times 565 = \$282,500$; so to get the desired $20 million exposure to the U.S. equity market, the portfolio manager would buy 70 futures contracts. The combined package of the cash position (the commercial paper or Treasuries) and futures behaves almost identically to the S&P 500 Index itself. In terms of return, the investment fund matches the S&P exactly. (And as we will discuss later, the change to transaction costs for this strategy may be lower than they would be for the equivalent cash transaction.)

Risk Management in Practice

Using Derivatives to Optimize a Portfolio

Claude R. Lamoureux and Robert G. Bertram

The Ontario Teacher's Pension Plan (Teachers') has a mandate to deliver defined pension benefits to 300,000 members, including active, retired, and deferred members, at an acceptable level of cost and risk. Provision of these benefits is currently estimated to cost 16 percent of pay based on the assumption that the plan will earn a real rate of return in excess of 4.5 percent above the rate of inflation. The benefits are fully indexed to the Consumer Price Index.

Teachers' manages about 85 percent of the assets and almost all of the derivative programs internally. The fund's investment team has set its asset-mix policy at three quarters equity and one quarter fixed-income securities. Asset-mix studies and models of the liabilities show that this is the optimal asset mix for enhancing the security of pension benefits and keeping the fund in a sound financial position. It invests the equity portion in domestic stocks and real estate and in non-Canadian stocks worldwide. Teachers' invests the fixed-income portion into bonds and debentures, cash, and real-rate bonds.

In 1990, when the Ontario government allowed the fund to diversify, Teachers' inherited nonmarketable Ontario debentures. Initially, Teachers' invested the fund through derivatives to change its asset mix. Derivatives allowed Teachers' to change the mix without selling the nonmarketable Ontario debentures and in a much more timely manner than it would take using the cash market.

Using Derivatives to Optimize a Portfolio continued

The fund managers use derivatives extensively to shift the asset mix between fixed income and equity, to manage interest rate volatility and foreign exchange exposures, and to enhance returns. Canadian pension funds are restricted from borrowing, so all derivatives are supported or collateralized by underlying assets; i.e., they employ no leverage. Nevertheless, Teachers' has dramatically transformed the economic exposure of its plan's assets through the use of derivatives.

At market value, the plan owns about C$50 billion of physical securities of which C$20 billion consists of nonmarketable Ontario debentures. These debentures have relatively high coupons, have an above-average term to maturity, and still represent about 40 percent of the assets. These debentures, combined with other fixed-income securities, overweight the fund to fixed income compared with the optimal asset mix. The fund uses derivatives to manage the returns on the debentures by swapping them to equity equivalents. The result is a better match between assets and liabilities.

In order to maintain an asset-mix target of 75 percent equity, Teachers' currently exchanges the interest income on about C$10 billion of the nonmarketable debentures for floating-rate exposures using interest rate swaps. It then uses equity swaps on a similar amount to exchange floating-rate interest exposure for equity returns.

While the primary markets for both equity and fixed income remain Canadian, Teachers' also invests over 35 percent of its assets outside of Canada as part of its risk management and diversification strategy. Teachers' diversifies its equity exposure through the use of both cash and derivative investments. The Canadian government imposes a 20 percent foreign content limit on tax-assisted savings. Teachers' investors have used derivatives to gain greater foreign exposure, in economic terms, above the 20 percent limit without violating the cash limitations on content.

Whether domestic or foreign, Teachers' gains a large part of its fund's equity exposure through the use of indexation investment in equity markets. Typically, the fund managers use cash investments either to invest in the indexes of markets that have poorly developed derivative markets or to invest in individual assets in markets that provide excess rewards for individual asset selection. Where well-developed derivative markets are available, or where rewards from asset selection are more illusory, Teachers' uses index funds obtained through the application of derivatives as a substitute for cash investments. For example, Teachers' gains over 95 percent of its U.S. equity exposure by swapping for returns of the S&P 500 Index.

In addition to investing in foreign equity markets through the use of derivatives, the Teachers' fund also established a foreign exchange policy that requires

Using Derivatives in Tactical or Insured Asset Allocation

As we noted, an investor's *strategic* asset allocation does not change in response to short-term changes in the prices of the underlying assets. However, there are other forms of asset allocation that do change when asset prices change.

Tactical Asset Allocation.   *Tactical asset allocation* refers to changing the strategic mix to exploit perceived market opportunities—e.g., overweighting stocks (increasing the allocation to stocks and reducing the allocation to bonds) when stocks are expected to do particularly well. Tactical asset allocation is driven by changes in predictions concerning returns to an asset class. Tactical asset allocation is often based on the assumption that markets overreact; and therefore generates a "contrary" pattern of buying and selling—i.e., tactical asset allocation would call for selling when prices rise and buying when prices fall. As was the case with strategic allocation, tactical asset allocation presumes that investor risk tolerance is unaffected by price changes.

Note that tactical asset allocation is a form of "implementing a view." Later in this chapter we will return to the way that derivatives can be used to implement a view.

Insured Asset Allocation (a.k.a. *Portfolio Insurance*). For both strategic and tactical asset allocations, the investor's risk tolerance is invariant to the prices of the assets. Insured asset allocation assumes that the investor's risk tolerance is sensitive to the current value of the assets; it assumes that risk tolerance is equal to zero when assets reach some minimum value and that investor risk tolerance increases as asset values increase. Consequently, insured asset allocation simplifies reducing (increasing) the investor's exposure to riskier assets as the prices of the riskier assets decline (increase). In contrast to tactical asset allocation, insured asset allocation reinforces market moves; i.e., insured asset allocation would call for selling when prices fall and buying when prices rise.

To illustrate how insured asset allocation differs from strategic asset allocation, let's return to our original portfolio:

S&P 500	$70,000,000	(70%)
T-bills	$30,000,000	(30%)

But this time let's treat the equity portfolio as an insured portfolio. As we noted above, insured asset allocation calls for preserving some "floor" value of the portfolio,

$$V_P = \text{Min [floor, (stocks + T-bills)]}$$

This is accomplished by reducing (increasing) the investor's exposure to the riskier asset—in this case the stocks—as the price of the stocks falls (rises). So the value of the portfolio can be expressed as

$$V_P = (\text{stocks}/M) + \text{floor}$$

where M is a constant. For our illustrative portfolio, let's define the floor value to be $60,000,000. Using the preceding equation, we can solve for the value of M.

$$\$100,000,000 = (\$70,000,000/M) + \$60,000,000$$

$$M = 1.75$$

Now, if the values in the equity market fall by 15 percent, the actual allocation of the portfolio will change to:

Stocks	$59,500,000	(66.5%)
T-bills	$30,000,000	(33.5%)

With the new portfolio value of $89,500,000, insured asset allocation implies that the value of the stocks in the portfolio should be reduced from $59,500,000 to

$$1.75 \times (89,500,000 - 60,000,000) = \$51,625,000$$

which is 57.7 percent of the value of the portfolio. Consequently, the target portfolio beta is 0.577.

As in the case of strategic asset allocation, the target beta could be attained via the cash market or the derivatives market—e.g., futures contracts. If the investor used S&P 500 futures, which were trading at the time at 660, the investor would need to sell 24 S&P futures contracts.

Aside

Using Derivatives in Insured Asset Allocation

The $59.5 million of the portfolio that is invested in the market portfolio has a beta of 1.0; the $30 million invested in bonds has a beta of zero. As before, we assume the beta for the S&P 500 Index is 1.0 and the beta for the S&P 500 futures contract is $500 \times 1.0 = 500$. If the investor holds n S&P futures contract which are currently trading at $660, the beta for the futures contracts is $n \times \$660 \times 500$. At the end, the total portfolio ($89.5 million) is to have a beta of 0.577.

$$\$59,500,000 \times 1.0 + \$30,000,000 \times 0.0 + n \times \$660 \times 500 = \$89,500,000 \times 0.577$$

Solving the preceding equation for n, we get

$$n = -23.8$$

So the investor will need to sell 24 contracts.

The most familiar form of insured rebalancing is *portfolio insurance*—a strategy that was widely used in the mid-1980s. The portfolio insurer is trying to put a floor on the value of the portfolio; so the payoff profile for a successful portfolio insurance program would be equivalent to a long call position.

Portfolio insurance as practice in the 1980s was normally implemented by selling futures as stocks fall and buying futures as stocks rise. Such a strategy has three weaknesses. First, if there are more buyers of insurance than sellers (the natural counterparties are tactical asset allocators), contract liquidity may dry up. Second, a short futures position will limit the investor's gain if the market reverses its course and moves up (at least until the short futures position is removed). Third, stock price changes may be sudden and discontinuous, and so there may not be time to rebalance the portfolio.

The third weakness of portfolio insurance became painfully evident during the market crash in October, 1987. When the cash equity market "gapped" down, the synthetic call portfolio went from being hedged to having far too many long futures positions; and the portfolio insurer was faced with selling futures in a falling market. (To make the portfolio insurer's problems even worse, the cash market and futures markets became disconnected.)

The experiences of 1987 caused the 1980s form of portfolio insurance to disappear. However, Figure 24–3 provides the alternative to portfolio insurance—purchase a put option. In contrast to portfolio insurance, the put does not have the liquidity issue and is not confronted by problems associated with market discontinuity. If the market falls, the option may be exercised, sold, or held. If the market rebounds, the option may be allowed to expire.

FIGURE 24–3   Long Equity + Long Put = Long Call

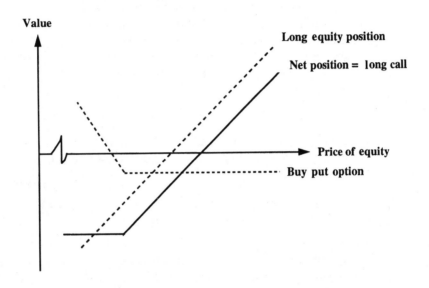

Using Derivatives to Reduce the Riskiness of the Portfolio

This section, in large part, repeats things we have studied earlier in this book. Investors, like nonfinancial corporations or financial institutions, can use derivatives to reduce the exposure to interest rate, foreign exchange rate, commodity, and/or equity price risk. In the following, we will look at a few examples of the ways that derivatives are used to reduce risk for a portfolio.

Using Derivatives to Reduce Interest Rate Risk

There are several different ways in which investors might want to protect the portfolio against movements in interest rates. Some investors, e.g., insurance companies, are constrained by cash flow considerations. Investors that manage to the value of the portfolio assets will want to protect these assets from changes in interest rates.

Investors that manage to the surplus will employ asset-liability management like those we described in Chapter 23.

Protecting Future Cash Flows.   Changes in interest rates can impact on the cash flows to or from an investment portfolio. Consider the simple case where an investor expects a cash flow of $1 million in three months. When received, the funds will be invested in T-bills for three months. She wishes to lock in the current rate.

This lock could be accomplished via the forward-rate agreement (FRA) we described in Chapter 4. Or it could be accomplished via a futures contract. Suppose that the current International Monetary (IMM) T-bill futures index is 95. The investor can take a long futures position, which would commit the investor to purchase $1 million in face value of three-month T-bills at an annualized yield of 5.00 percent. Suppose that, in three months, the index value is 96. The owner of the futures contract has received $25 $\times$ 100 basis points, or $2,500, over the course of the contract in market-to-market settlements. At the time the contract settles, the investor (the owner of the futures contract) must pay the seller

$$\$1,000,000(1 - 0.04 \times 91/360) = \$989,890$$

The net price is $989,890 − $2,500 = $987,390. The resulting three-month Treasury bill should produce a return that approximates the 5 percent return originally sought:

$$[1 - (\$987,390/\$1,000,000)]/(360/91) = 4.99\%$$

A different sort of protection could be accomplished via options—either an OTC option on interest rates (in which case, the investor will want to buy a call) or an option on an interest rate futures contract (in which case, the investor will want to buy a put). In this instance the investor will have to pay a premium; but if the T-bill rate falls dramatically, there is no FRA or long futures position to incur losses.

For longer exposures, the investor might use a forward starting swap or a swaption to manage the cash flow exposure to interest rates.

Protecting the Value of a Bond.   If the investor is managing to the value of the assets, the investor may wish to employ derivatives to protect the value of bonds from increases in interest rates.

Suppose an investor is holding bonds currently valued at $50,000,000 and is concerned about an increase in interest rates. Looking at the value of an 01 or the duration of the bond, the investor expects that if interest rates increase by 100 basis points across all maturities, the portfolio will lose $4.005 million (8.01 percent).

This exposure to interest rates could be managed via bond futures traded on the Chicago Board of Trade. This futures contract is based on 8 percent coupon, 20-year bonds (100 bonds per contract). The market price of the contract bonds is $1,090. Using the techniques we described in Chapter 7, the appropriate hedge would be to sell 572 contracts. Table 24–5 illustrates how the futures contract will hedge the value of the bond, if indeed rates did rise by 100 basis points.

TABLE 24–5   **Hedging the Value of Bonds with Bond Futures**

	Initial Value	Value after Interest Rate Rises by 100 bp	Change in Value
Bonds	50,000,000	45,995,000	(4,005,000)
572 bond futures (short)	(62,805,000)	(58,801,600)	4,004,000
			(1,000)

And the bond value could be hedged via an OTC derivative, e.g., a swap or an option. A duration-adjusted swap locks the value of a bond. Any gain or loss on the bond value is exactly offset by an opposite change in the swap value. An option delta-hedges the value of the bond—a small gain or loss on the bond value is exactly offset by an opposite change in the option value.[5] In this instance, where the investor is concerned about an increase in interest rates, an option might be the better choice. In the event of a significant decrease in interest rates, a locking swap would result in a large loss, while the loss on the option would be limited to the premium paid. However, the option has drawbacks, including (1) the cash outlay required to pay the premium up front, (2) the increased monitoring activity necessary to adjust the delta, and (3) the risk that interest rates will move by a large amount suddenly.

Asset-Liability Management.   If the institutional investor is managing the portfolio surplus (i.e., the market value of the assets minus the present value of the liabilities), the problem facing the investor is precisely the same as that facing a financial institution. In Chapter 23, we discussed the ways that derivatives could be used for asset-liability management. These techniques are equally applicable for an investor.

Using Derivatives to Reduce Foreign Exchange Rate Risk

Contradictory views exist on the way that currency risk should be treated in the context of international investment. Some investors try to immunize their portfolios from foreign exchange rate risk. Others explicitly include stand-alone foreign exchange positions in their portfolios.

At the core of the debate is the question of whether currency should be regarded as an asset class. The difficulty with treating currency as an asset class is that, in contrast to equity or bonds, the available empirical evidence suggests that currency positions do not generate a stable return premium. In the following, Ron Layard-Liesching argues that currency should be treated as a *tactical* asset class—i.e., an exposure in which there is no *intrinsic* return, but rather the potential of return through active management.

Risk Management in Practice

Should FX Be Treated as an Asset Class?

Ronald G. Layard-Liesching

Investment normally is conceived of as placing actual capital in assets that offer positive expected long-term return. The Ibbotsen and Sinquefield studies provide extensive empirical support for the existence of long-term return premiums over cash for assets such as equities and bonds. The currency exposure associated with international investment does not fulfill the usual requirements to be considered as an asset when viewed in isolation. Capital is not necessary to take currency positions; currency positions do not offer intrinsic return; and there is no stable risk premium.

Instead, currency can be defined as a *tactical* asset class. The characteristics of tactical assets are very different from those of strategic assets.

Strategic Asset	*Tactical Asset*
• Stable risk premium	• No stable risk premium
• Positive expected return	• No expected return to passive investment
• Capital employed	• Net capital not required
• Return to passive investment	• Return from active management
• High confidence of decade-long return	• Uncertainty of return even over three years

Another term for tactical assets might be "pure management alpha" assets. Tactical assets exhibit three investment attributes: (1) low correlation with strategic asset returns, (2) positive projected return, and (3) low actual capital requirement. Not surprisingly, with these attributes, a mean-variance model will allocate into such tactical assets. They appear to be truly diversifying assets and thus have the potential to significantly enhance risk return for the total plan.*

There are two key points: First, regarding currency as an asset class leaves totally unaddressed the management of existing currency risk created by international investment. Second, it is intrinsic to all tactical assets that there is no certainty that, even with superior knowledge and managers, there will be any return available to be captured at all. Tactical assets do not always provide return opportunities that the active manager may, or may not, be able to capture.

Should FX Be Treated as an Asset Class? continued

Tactical assets offer a different risk-return trade-off than is seen in conventional, strategic assets. In conventional, strategic asset classes, the well-known risk (equals volatility) versus expected return diagram is applied. In contrast, for a tactical asset class, there is no intrinsic expected return. The appropriate trade-off to analyze is the acceptable loss versus the percentage of available return opportunity that could be captured—if return is available.

Ronald G. Layard-Liesching is a partner and director of research of Pareto Partners.
*But there are portfolio optimizers who have no common sense. As so little capital is required relative to the projected returns, the optimizer left unconstrained would wish to lever up the fund in order to benefit from the tactical asset returns. Hence, in currency-as-an-asset class it is common to find promises of returns of 300–500 basis points per annum.

An investor who elects to treat foreign exchange as an asset class would be tempted to employ the principles of portfolio management to determine the optimal foreign exchange rate positions for his portfolio. However, Layard-Liesching argues that this simple approach might not work. First, the behavior of foreign exchange rates can be characterized by "uncertainty"—in contrast to the "risk" which we have talked about to this point in this text. We have characterized risk by using a distribution; uncertainty is said to exist when the information available is less precise than can be presented by an analytic distribution. The modern portfolio management presumes that there is no uncertainty; i.e., the mean-variance approach is based on the returns being normally distributed. Layard-Liesching argues that we do not know how to specify the models for currency outcomes; at a minimum, long-term currency risk cannot be described by a stable normal distribution of outcomes.[6]

The appropriate course of action for those investors who do not treat currency as an asset class is equally unclear. Portfolio diversification introduces foreign exchange risk into the portfolio. That is, when the investor buys foreign equities or bonds or other assets to diversify the portfolios, the return on these foreign assets is in a currency other than the investor's home currency. What should the investor do with the resulting foreign exchange exposure?

Some would argue that the investor should "do nothing," because the lack of stable currency risk premium means that currency returns will "wash out" in the long run. Layard-Liesching asserts that both theory and evidence contradict this argument. Economic theory holds that exchange rates would be impacted by factors which cannot be forecasted with consistency. And at least over a five-year horizon, there is no empirical evidence that exchange rates revert to some stable equilibrium level.

Forwards, futures, swaps, and options could be used to reduce or eliminate the foreign exchange rate risk.

Russell Gregory-Allen notes that many investment funds that hold securities denominated in currencies other than the investor's home currency use forward currency contracts to hedge against foreign currency movements that might occur between the time a security trades and the time it settles. This could be important, because a trade is "booked" to the account in the home currency on the trade date, but money actually flows on settlement date in the foreign currency, and the time from trade date to settlement date can be quite long.

Illustration 24–1*

Using Derivatives to Hedge Currency Risk

Suppose a U.S. investor desires to sell 10,000 shares of stock in the French company Beghin-Say. That decision is made on the basis of the current price in U.S. dollars, which is based on the current exchange rate. If the price decreases before settlement due to the exchange rate, the investor would receive less. Indeed, the U.S. dollar price could be sufficiently low that the sale is no longer desirable.

For example, on August 2, 1995, Beghin-Say was selling for 775 French francs, and the exchange rate was 4.7545 francs/$US, making the stock worth $163.00. Since French stocks settle at the end of the month, the settle date would be August 31, 1995. By then the exchange rate was 5.043 francs/$US, making the selling price $153.68. The exchange rate change would cost the investor $93,216. To avoid this, the U.S. investor could have arranged a currency forward. On August 2, 1995, a 30-day forward on the French franc cost 4.7591. This would have locked in a price of $162.85—the 0.15 per share "cost" is the price of insurance against exchange.

---

* This illustration is taken from Gregory-Allen (1995).

Protection could be achieved via currency swaps or foreign exchange options. And if the investor wishes to gain exposure to assets denominated in other currencies, without accepting any foreign exchange rate risk, the investments could be made using the quanto form of swaps and options we discussed in Chapters 13 and 14.

Using Derivatives to Reduce Asset Price Risk–Equity Price Risk

The investor could use financial derivatives to protect the portfolio against movements in the underlying asset price.

Suppose an investor holds DM40,000,000 in large-capitalization German stocks, e.g., a DAX portfolio. Suppose further that the investor is worried about the performance of the German stock market over the next two years. To protect the value of the portfolio for two years, the investor may enter into an DM-denominated equity swap like the one illustrated in Figure 24–4. In this swap the investor pays semiannual cash flows determined by the return to the DAX and receives cash flows determined by six-month LIBOR. The notional principal of the swap is variable; it begins at DM40,000,000 and then changes as the value of the portfolio changes.

FIGURE 24–4

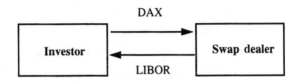

For purposes of this example, let's suppose that, over the two-year life of the swap, the DAX index and six-month LIBOR behave as follows:

Month	DAX	% Change in DAX	LIBOR
0	2,500		6%
6	2,750	10%	5.5%
12	2,650	−3.6%	5.25%
18	2,600	−1.9%	6%
24	2,400	−7.7%	6.25%

With the preceding changes in the value of the DAX and six-month LIBOR rates, the payments paid and received by the investor are presented below.

Month	Notional Principal of Swap	Investor Pays Indexed to Chng in DAX	Investor Receives Indexed to LIBOR	Net Received (Paid) by Investor
6	40,000,000	(4,000,000)	1,200,000	(2,800,000)
12	44,000,000	1,584,000	1,210,000	2,794,000
18	42,416,000	805,904	1,113,420	1,919,324
24	41,610,096	3,203,977	1,248,303	4,452,280

At the first settlement date (month 6), the investor will pay a payment determined by the initial notional principal (DM40,000,000) and the 10 percent increase in the value of the DAX:

$$\text{Amount paid at month } 6 = 40{,}000{,}000 \times 0.10 = 4{,}000{,}000$$

The amount received by the investor at month 6 is determined by the initial notional principal (DM40,000,000) and one half of the six-month LIBOR rate at contract origination (0.5×6 percent $= 3$ percent):

$$\text{Amount received at month } 6 = 40{,}000{,}000 \times 0.03 = 1{,}200{,}000$$

And at month 6, the notional principal of the swap increases from DM40,000,000 to DM44,000,000 to reflect the 10 percent increase in the value of the portfolio.

At the second settlement date (month 12), the investor will pay a payment determined by the current notional principal (DM44,000,000) and the 3.64 percent decrease in the value of the DAX:

$$\text{Amount paid at month } 12 = 44{,}000{,}000 \times -0.036 = -1{,}584{,}000$$

Note that since the DAX decreased, the investor will *receive* rather than pay the DM1,584,000.

The amount received by the investor at month 12 is determined by the current notional principal (DM44,000,000) and one half of the six-month LIBOR rate at month 6 (0.5×5.5 percent $= 2.75$ percent):

$$\text{Amount received at month } 12 = 44{,}000{,}000 \times 0.0275 = 1{,}210{,}000$$

And the notional principal of the swap will be decreased from DM44,000,000 to DM42,416,000 to reflect the 3.6 percent decrease in the value of the portfolio.

The net result of the swap will be to stabilize the value of the portfolio. Instead of swaps (or forwards or futures), the portfolio could be protected with options. As is illustrated in Figure 24–5, the simplest ways to protect the value of the portfolio is by purchasing a put option.

To illustrate how a purchased put option strategy might work, consider an investor who owns 10,000 shares that are trading at $54. The investor is worried about a potential decrease in the stock price and has reasons to believe that the drop is imminent. Suppose that a three-month, $50 put option is available at a price of $1. Let's suppose that the delta for the put is $- 0.4$. To hedge the 10,000 shares, the investor would want to purchase puts. But the question is how many? If the delta of the option is $- 0.4$, the hedge ratio will be $1/0.4 = 2.5$; so the investor will want to purchase $10{,}000 \times 2.5 = 25{,}000$ puts. Let's see what happens if, two days after the investor purchases the puts[7], the stock price falls to $53:

Loss on stock position	10,000 shares × (−$1) = −$10,000
Gain on put position	5,000 puts × ($0.40) = $10,000
Hedge costs	25,000 puts × ($1) = $25,000

FIGURE 24–5 Protecting the Portfolio by Buying a Put

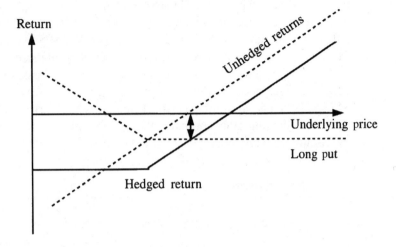

The protective put strategy establishes a floor at the cost of the premium paid for the put options.

While a purchased put strategy will protect the value of the portfolio, the cost of purchasing puts may be prohibitive. As an alternative, the investor could use a collar. As is illustrated in Figure 24–6, with a collar the investor uses the proceeds from the sale of a call (cap) to reduce the out-of-pocket expense of purchasing a put (floor).

FIGURE 24–6 Protecting the Portfolio with a Collar

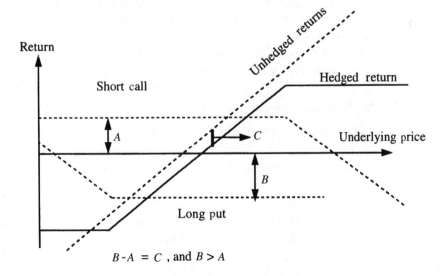

To illustrate how a collar might work, consider an investor who owns 1,000 shares of a stock that is trading at $100. Suppose that the investor was worried about the near-term prospects for the stock. At the time the strategy was put in place, a three-month call option with an exercise price of $105 was available at $1.2392 and a three-month put option with an exercise price of $95 was available at $0.9972.[8] The investor would want to buy 1,000 puts. The cost of these puts would be 1,000 $\times$ $0.9972 = $997.20. To offset the cost of the puts, the investor could sell 100 of the $105 call. The income received from selling the calls would be 100 $\times$ $1.2392 = $123.92. The net premium paid for the collar is $997.20 − $123.92 = $873.28.

The following table compares the results with the collar strategy in place with the results from an unhedged stock position.[9]

Strategy Results

	Unhedged Stock Position		Stocks Plus Equity Collar	
Stock Price Change	−$10.00	+$10.00	−$10.00	+$10.00
Stock Change	($10,000)	$10,000	($10,000)	$10,000
Collar Cost	N/A	N/A	($873.28)	($873.28)
Put Change	N/A	N/A	$4,683.70	($935.80)
Call Change	N/A	N/A	$118.63	($515.06)
Net Change	($10,000)	$10,000	($6,070.95)	$7,675.86
Portfolio Value	$90,000	$110,000	$93,929.05	$107,675.86

Note: Data in the preceding table are based on the presumption that the price variations occur days after the collar implementation.

Using Derivatives to Increase the Expected Return of the Portfolio

As we noted in the survey results presented at the beginning of this chapter, investors also employ derivatives to enhance the return on the portfolio. Derivatives can increase the expected return in one of four ways: (1) by reducing transaction costs, (2) by exploiting mispricings, i.e., arbitrage (3) by accessing otherwise unavailable assets, or (4) by using derivatives to implement a view more effectively.

By Reducing Transaction Costs

As we have described throughout this book, derivatives can be used as a substitute for cash transactions. For example, Professor Jay Light at the Harvard Business School listed 11 ways to buy the S&P 500 Index[10]:

1. Purchase every one of the 500 stocks in the index.
2. Buy a unit investment trust that holds the S&P 500—e.g., a SPDR.
3. Buy an OTC forward contract on the index.

4. Buy a futures contract on the S&P 500.

5. Enter into an equity swap in which you receive the rate of return on the S&P 500.

6. Buy a call option on the S&P 500.

7. Buy the 500 stocks in the index and buy a put option. Put-call parity requires that this would result in the same payoff profile as buying a call option.

8. Deposit money into an equity-linked certificate of deposit that will pay a guaranteed minimum rate; but if the S&P 500 increased over a certain level, the interest rate would be tied to that increase.

9. Buy a guaranteed investment contract with the same linkage from a life insurance company.

10. Buy a bond convertible into the S&P 500 at face value.

11. Buy a structured note with an interest rate tied to the return on the S&P 500.

Professor Light's "way 1" is the cash market transaction. His "way 2" is the securitized form of a derivative we described in Chapter 15. "Way 3" through "way 7" are straight derivative transactions. Professor Light's "way 8" through "way 11" are hybrid structures.

Since derivative transactions could substitute for cash transactions, derivatives can be used as an alternative way of constructing a portfolio. But the question is why someone would elect to use a derivative transaction, rather than the cash transaction. One reason could be that the derivative transactions have lower transaction costs—either in terms of out-of-pocket costs or in the speed with which the portfolio strategy could be implemented.

In some instances, the cost differences are in commission costs. Earlier in this chapter, we recounted a case proposed by Russell Gregory-Allen in which an investor used derivatives to establish a position in the equity market while maintaining liquidity.[11] Instead of using derivatives, that position in the equity market could have been established via the cash market—i.e., invested $20 million in a broad variety of U.S. stocks, say, the S&P 500. At the end of August 1995, the capitalization-weighted average price of a share of stock in the S&P 500 was a little over $56. At $56 per share and 6 cents round-trip transaction costs, the manager could buy (and later sell) about 356,760 shares, for total transaction costs of about $21,406. Establishing the same position via futures, the futures transaction costs are about $12 per contract for the 70 futures contracts that would have been required; so the total transaction costs would have been only $840—about 25 times cheaper than buying and selling the stocks.

Moving beyond anecdotal evidence, it would be useful to compare commission rates in the cash and derivatives markets. While the highly negotiated nature of commissions makes direct comparison difficult, we can provide some representative data for the U.S. equities. For a round-trip transaction in the cash market, the cost depends on who the investor is and what services the investor requires—retail: 30–40 bp, "full-service" institutional: 15–20 bp, "bare-bones" institutional: 8–10 bp. In the derivatives market, the cost of an equity swap on a single share is approximately 10 bp and the cost of a futures contract on a market index is less than 0.5 bp.[12]

In other cases, the difference in the transaction cost are the result of regulatory costs. In some cases, regulatory costs add to the direct cost of the transaction. In other cases, regulations can make the price in one or another of the markets effectively infinite; i.e., the transaction is not possible at any price. Peter Lewis (1997) argued that a case in point was India in the late 1990s. Local stock in Bombay is only available to designated foreign institutional investors (FIIs). Investors not designated as FIIs are effectively precluded from the cash market; so they have turned to derivatives as a way of implementing the position.

And the transaction costs in the cash and derivatives markets can differ due to the time required to complete the transaction. In the cash equity market, a large cash transaction may take several days to complete. A rule of thumb that is used by traders in the equity market is that about 20–25 percent of daily volume can be executed each day. If the transaction is done via futures and/or options on indexes, it could be accomplished more quickly.

By Exploiting Mispricings, i.e., Arbitrage

Investors are adept at recognizing and exploiting arbitrage opportunities. If the identical asset is traded in more than one market and if the prices of the asset are different in the two markets, an investor can simultaneously buy the asset in the market where it is cheap and sell it in the market where it is dear, thereby earning a risk-free return.[13]

The pricing differences could be between the price in the cash market and that implied in the futures market. As an illustration, we have put together a simplified example—which ignores bid-ask spreads.

Instead of arbitrages between cash and futures prices, the arbitrage could be based on differences in the price implied by two derivative positions—e.g., arbitrage between futures and swaps.

Arbitrage opportunities like that in the preceding example are attractive; in practice, they are difficult for an investor to accomplish for a number of reasons. First, a lot of traders (and their computers) are watching for these arbitrage opportunities. The market is therefore very efficient; these arbitrage opportunities appear and disappear quickly. Second, because the opportunities are so short-lived, the calculations and the execution must be done at very high speed. Third, this type of

Using Derivatives to Exploit Mispricings

Suppose that we observe the following prices for the S&P 500 in the cash and futures markets:

Spot price	666.70
Price of two-month futures contract	670
Price of five-month futures contract	676

For simplicity, let both the two-month and five-month interest rates be 5 percent and let the dividend rate for the S&P 500 be 2 percent. Using the cash-and-carry arbitrage relation we described in Chapter 6, we find that the two-month forward price for the S&P 500 would be

$$666.70 \, (1 + 0.05 - 0.02)^{1/6} = 669.99$$

So there is no mispricing between the cash price and the two-month futures price. Using the same cash-and-carry relation, we can calculate the five-month forward price for the S&P 500:

$$666.70 \, (1 + 0.05 - 0.02)^{5/12} = 674.96$$

The cash-and-carry relation indicates that the five-month futures contract is overpriced; i.e., it should be trading at 675, rather than 676. The investor takes advantage of this opportunity by selling the futures and buying the cash position. At origination of the strategy:

Borrow $666.70 (at 5%)	+666.70
Buy the S&P 500	−666.70
Sell the five-month futures contract	0
Net cash flow	0

In five months,

Sell the S&P 500 shares	$S\&P\,500 + [(5/12) \times (0.02) \times 666.70 =$	$S\&P\,500 + \$5.56$
Settle the futures contract		$676 - S\&P\,500$
Repay the loan	$-666.70 \, (1 + 0.05)^{5/12} =$	-680.39
Net cash flow		1.17

With no initial outlay, the investor has earned an arbitrage profit of $1.17.

activity requires very accurate inputs and calculations. In the preceding example, if the dividend rate is 0.01579 instead of 0.02, then the arbitrage opportunity disappears. Compounding this problem is the fact that the dividend yield is difficult to estimate. Hull (1997) notes that the dividend yield on the portfolio underlying an index varies week by week throughout the year.

By Accessing Otherwise Unavailable Assets

The essence of modern portfolio theory is that, by diversifying the portfolio, an investor can reduce the riskiness of the portfolio (holding expected return constant); or—turning this around—with the same level of risk, portfolio diversification could result in a higher expected return. Consequently, investors are always searching for assets that will have strong diversification effects (i.e., assets that have low correlation with the other assets in their portfolio).

In the 1990s, investors became interested in Eastern European equity and debt. However, as Ted Kim (1997) noted, an investor needed a strong stomach to venture into the cash markets in Eastern Europe because of complex transactional, custodial, and counterparty risks. Consequently investors gained access to Eastern European debt and equity via derivatives. For example, derivatives dealers offered options on baskets of equities. An OTC variant was a European-style call option on a basket made up of the common shares of five regional utility companies in Russia. An exchange-listed variant of this type of product is found on the Austrian Futures and Options Exchange (OTOB) which trades futures and options on the Hungarian Traded Index (HTX), a basket of 11 shares that make up more than 90 percent of the market capitalization and trading volume of the Budapest Stock Exchange.

Instead of providing access to products that already exist, derivatives can be used to create products that previously did not exist. Many of the hybrid securities we described in Chapter 15 were developed in response to investor needs.

By Using Derivatives to Implement a View More Effectively

It goes almost without saying that if an investor (1) has a view, (2) acts on that view, and (3) is correct, the return to the portfolio will increase. Derivatives are not necessary for an investor to act on a view. However, derivatives give investors the ability to act on a view *more effectively.*

With derivatives, the investor can leverage the position.   If an investor has a view on price and implements that view in the cash market—e.g., if the investor believes that the price of an asset will rise and so buy the asset—the investor has to fund that position completely; but if the position is implemented in the derivative market, the investor will not have to fund the position.

With derivatives, the investor can "fine-tune" the position by selling options, rather than buying or selling the underlying asset in the cash market. The investor might decide to sell covered calls. Such a strategy is illustrated in Figure 24–7. In this case, the investor who owns the underlying asset believes that the asset price will not rise above P_H. To implement this view, the investor could sell a call option on the asset, with the strike price set so that the sum of the value, net of the premium received, is zero when the asset price is P_H. As long as the price of the asset is below P_H, the return of the "covered-call-writing" strategy exceeds that of the cash market position.

A much riskier strategy is for the investor to sell "naked" options—e.g., sell calls without having a long position in the asset or sell puts without having a short position in the asset. (Such strategies expose the investor to virtually unlimited losses.) Figure 24–8 illustrates a situation in which an investor has a "sell target" of P_{SELL}. The investor could implement this strategy in the cash market (the dashed line in Figure 24–8); or the investor could implement this strategy by selling a naked call option with the exercise price set at P_{SELL}.

Figure 24–9 illustrates a situation in which an investor has a "buy target" of P_{BUY}. The investor could implement this strategy in the cash market (the dashed line in Figure 24–9); or the investor could implement this strategy by selling a naked put option with the exercise price set at P_{BUY}.

FIGURE 24–7   Selling Covered Calls to Implement a View

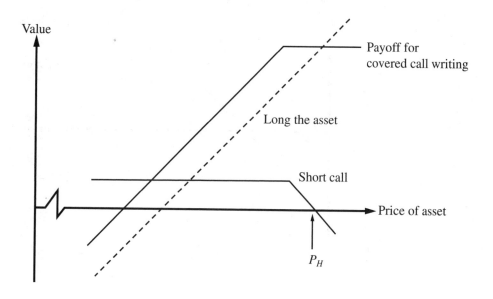

FIGURE 24–8   Selling Naked Call Options to Implement a View

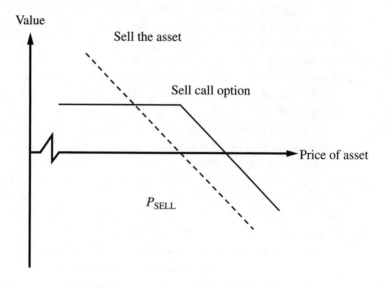

FIGURE 24–9   Selling Naked Put Options to Implement View

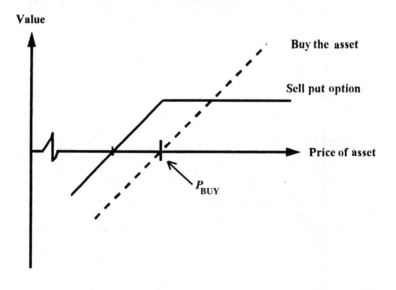

Or it could be the case that the investor believes that the asset will trade in a range; i.e., the price of the asset will fall no lower than P_L and will rise no higher than P_H. As is illustrated in Figure 24–10, the investor might elect to implement this view by selling a call with an exercise price of P_H and selling a put with an exercise price P_L. As long as the price stays within the range, this strategy—referred to in the options markets as *selling a strangle* (see Chapter 14)—will enhance the investor's return.

The problem with the "sell a strangle" strategy is what can happen if the view turns out to be wrong. If the price of the underlying asset trades outside the specified range, the investor's loss could be extremely large. Consequently, the investor might elect to implement this strategy via binary options, as is illustrated in Figure 24–11.

With derivatives, the investor can "fine-tune" the position via strategies like alpha separation. Earlier in this chapter we looked at alpha transport. Alpha transport is a special case of what market participants refer to as *alpha separation*—i.e., strategies designed to separate security selection decisions (alpha) from overall markets effects. Alpha separation implies that the portfolio is constructed so that it is neutral with respect to overall market moves but is exposed to the security selection decision. Following are two examples of alpha separation strategies.

Example 1: The manager of a mutual fund might be optimistic about the U.S. equity market but bearish on the near-term prospects for the health-care sector. The

---

FIGURE 24–10   Selling Naked Calls and Puts to Implement a View

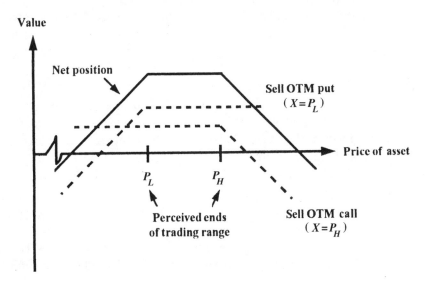

FIGURE 24–11   Selling Naked Binary Calls and Puts to Implement a View

---

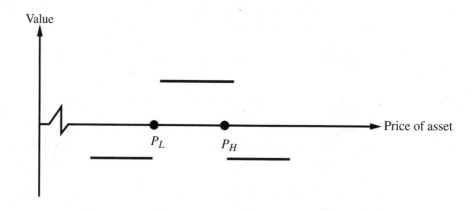

fund manager could implement this view via alpha separation in one of two ways. The manager could hold the S&P 500 (our proxy for the market portfolio) and buy puts on health-care stocks (incurring a premium cost and risking loss of premium if the market moves up). Or the manager could short a basket of health-care stocks and enter into an equity swap on the S&P 500 Index paying a variable rate and receiving the change in the index.

Example 2:   A fixed-income manager believes quality spreads will narrow but is concerned about a general increase in interest rates. To implement this view, the investor would purchase a basket of lower-quality bonds and short a basket of higher-quality bonds. To clean up the duration effect that comes into play if the bonds are pegged to different US Treasury notes, the investor would sell T-bond futures. The result is a pure spread play—without any exposure to interest rates.

Concluding Remarks

At the outset of this chapter we looked at some survey data to see what derivatives investors were using and why. We return to that survey data, but this time we want to focus on the concerns investors have about using derivatives. Figure 24–12 summarizes the concerns, as expressed in the 1995 *Institutional Investor* survey.

Controls

The types of concerns reflected in Figure 24–12 have led institutional investors to put in place guidelines to control the usage of derivatives. Figure 24–13 summarizes the results of the responses received by Record Treasury Management when it surveyed U.S. pension funds in 1995. Going a step further, Figure 24–14

FIGURE 24–12   Concerns about Using Derivatives

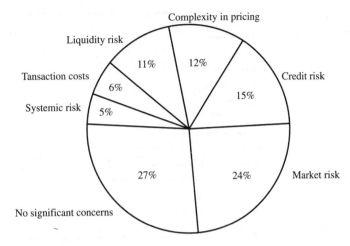

SOURCE: "Devoted to Derivatives," Pensionforum, *Institutional Investor,* 1995.

FIGURE 24–13   Guidelines in Place to Control the Usage of Derivatives

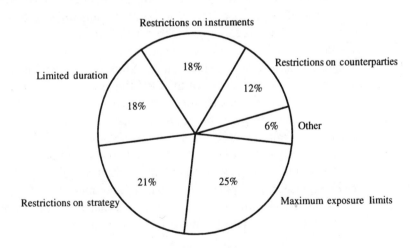

SOURCE: "US Pension Fund Survey," Record Treasury Management, Spring 1995.

FIGURE 24–14   "Sign-Off" Required Prior to Commencing Derivative Trading

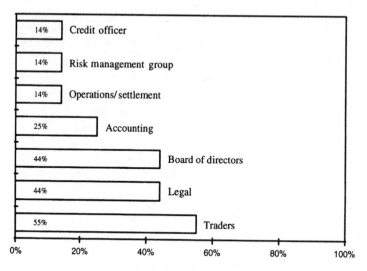

SOURCE: "Derivatives Usage by Investment Funds," Ernst & Young, LLP, 1995.

summarizes the responses received by Ernst & Young when it asked investment funds what "sign-offs" they required.

And in 1994, the Investment Company Institute (ICI) provided guidance for the boards of directors of those investment companies that use derivatives as investments. The ICI recommended that the board not only review and approve policies developed by the investment adviser and other service providers but also oversee the performance of their duties. Moreover, depending upon the context and the particular circumstances of the fund (including the level, types, and objectives of a fund's derivative instruments), the board should (1) understand generally the type of instruments and nature of associated risks, (2) request, receive, and review information from the investment adviser about the adviser's overall strategy with respect to derivatives, (3) review the fund's valuation procedures, (4) consider the adequacy of disclosure, and (5) obtain assurances from the adviser as to the derivatives expertise of its portfolio managers and analysts, its operational capacities, and its internal controls (including how risk management responsibilities are allocated and how risk management principles are applied).

Obligations?

So far, we have provided some reasons why fund managers and other institutional investors may want to use risk management instruments and some evidence about the behavior of institutional investors. An interesting question is whether fund managers are under any *obligation* to use risk management.

Risk Management in Practice

A Fiduciary Duty to Use Derivatives?

George Crawford

The Trustee's Dilemma and the Rejected Derivative Solution

The ticking of the antique clock was the only sound in Frank's wood-paneled bank office as he stared open-mouthed at the papers he had just received. Sued! Over derivatives!

Frank was being sued for failing to use options to reduce the risk of his client's investment portfolio.

A Simple Trust. The trust had seemed so simple, so routine. Barbara had come into the bank with her sister Alice. Barbara was in her eighties and had been diagnosed with Alzheimer's disease. Barbara had given her sister Alice a power of attorney to handle her affairs. Alice didn't have any financial expertise and came to the bank for help. She wanted the bank to manage Barbara's stocks and bonds, and make investment decisions for Barbara, who could no longer depend on her own financial and investment acumen.

Naturally, Frank suggested placing Barbara's assets in a trust, with the bank as trustee.

At the time, Barbara had accumulated an estate of over $2,000,000. There were bonds totaling about $200,000, thirty different stock certificates totaling $700,000, and stock certificates for Philip Morris Company totaling $1,500,000.

The Need for Diversification. Frank knew that diversification was the key to any portfolio's safety. Aside from the fact that diversification made good business sense, Frank knew that a lack of diversification involved legal risks. The bank's attorney had explained to him that federal law specified that pension funds be diversified, and she had given him a copy of the new version of the Prudent Investor Act, recommended to state legislatures by the American Bar Association, which states: "The long familiar requirement that fiduciaries diversify their investments has been integrated into the definition of prudent investing."

With over 60 percent of Barbara's assets tied up in a single stock, Philip Morris, Frank understood that Barbara's portfolio was exposed to considerable risk. He also knew that at Barbara's age she needed safety, not risk.

The Obstacle to Diversification: Taxes.   As he pondered diversifying Barbara's portfolio, Frank considered the tax consequences. Barbara began investing in the early 1930s, some 60 years before her affairs were turned over to the bank. Frank calculated that if all her stocks were sold, the total bill in federal and state income taxes would have come to 40 percent of the $2,050,000 gain, or $82,000, thereby reducing the size of her estate from $2,400,000 to $1,580,000. Frank also realized that whatever remained of Barbara's estate would be taxed upon her death. However, if the stock remained in her estate until after her death, the cost basis of the stock could be automatically adjusted upward to its value on the date of her death. Then, it could be sold the next day with no income tax payable at all. Thus, the $820,000 income tax bill that would be incurred by selling the stock now could be completely avoided.

As Frank thought it all over, selling the Philip Morris stock now would permit diversification of the trust assets, but payment of income taxes would considerably reduce the income on which Barbara depended.

Frank decided to talk the situation over with Alice, who held Barbara's power of attorney. Faced with a difficult choice, she and Frank did nothing. Frank was happy enough with this, since he had involved Alice in the decision, and it would be harder for her to blame him if it proved to be the wrong one.

The Proposed Solutions: Options, Hedges, and Swaps.   Alice mentioned the meeting to her sister Edna, who noticed a simple explanation of options by the *Wall Street Journal* which seemed to offer a solution to the issue raised by Frank. Alice wrote Frank a note, in which she suggested that the bank consider buying puts as a means of insuring against a big drop in the value of the Philip Morris stock.

Frank called and thanked Alice for the note, but did nothing about it because he considered the cost of buying the puts too high.

Several months later, Edna saw an article in *Forbes* which specifically used Philip Morris stock as an example of derivative hedging with options. Alice saw another article in *Business Week,* entitled "When Your Eggs Are All in One Stock," which suggested the use of an equity swap to avoid underdiversification without paying taxes. Alice clipped out both articles and sent them to Frank.

A Fiduciary Duty to Use Derivatives? continued

The Rejection of the Solution.   Despite a follow-up letter from Alice, the bank never implemented any of the strategies that were so clearly presented to it. Frank simply checked on the bank's view of Philip Morris stock and wrote Alice a note thanking her for the articles, stating that the bank's investment department was still positive on Philip Morris stock, reminding her of the adverse tax consequences of a sale, and concluding that the bank believed it was imprudent to use derivatives. In fact, Frank simply thought that derivatives were dangerous and that there might be risks he didn't fully understand, and didn't want to take the trouble to check out the possibilities.

The Loss and the Lawsuit.   Philip Morris stock was selling at about $78 per share at the time Alice sent the articles to the bank. Upon Barbara's death, Philip Morris stock was selling at about $52. Now that there was no longer any tax reason to continue to hold the stock, Alice demanded that it be sold now, and the sale was executed at $52 per share. The next thing Frank knew, he was holding in his hands the papers filed by the attorney probating Barbara's estate. The suit charged the bank with breach of trust by reason of imprudent investment, lack of due care in failing to preserve the principal of the trust, and negligently wasting the assets of the trust.

A Trustee's Fiduciary Duties

Although the use of derivatives as a hedge may be permitted in a trust, Frank may argue that he was under no duty to use them and, therefore, cannot be held liable. This argument implies that Frank's fiduciary duty did not require him to adjust his investment strategy to accommodate innovations in the financial markets. Evaluation of such an argument requires a careful examination of both (1) the Prudent Investor Rule, which defines generally a trustee's duties, and (2) the way that courts have interpreted a fiduciary's duties when confronted with "new" investment choices.

Did Frank Have a Fiduciary Duty to Use Derivatives?

There are currently no reported judicial decisions holding a trustee liable for failing to use derivatives, though at least one bank was sued on these grounds and settled before trial. There is a great deal of legal authority for the proposition that trustees should not run the risks of an undiversified portfolio. Any court would take this authority into account, as well as the changes in contemporary standards and practices discussed above. Frank will have to explain why he maintained so large an investment in Philip Morris stock in the face of diversification requirements. His explanation that a sale would have incurred onerous tax burdens will be met with the argument that there were many ways to use derivatives to diminish the risk without incurring the tax burden.

Frank never held himself out to be an expert at every kind of investment vehicle available, but he was a trustee. Under the traditional formulation of the Prudent Investor Rule he had a duty to "observe" how others manage their affairs, and any such observation would have disclosed the articles and advertisements seen by Edna in the public press, as well as in more specialized financial journals. Frank might at least have contacted other investment managers to find out if, and how, they were using derivatives. At a minimum, Frank could have contacted his own bank's treasurer and fund managers, as well as trust officers at other banks.

Conclusion.   Since 1830, investors of other people's money have been subject to the legal requirement that they "observe" current financial practices and apply them in the management of the money entrusted to their care. Today the colossal scale and widespread use of derivatives requires "observation" of their potential uses by fiduciaries.

The newest restatements of the Prudent Investor Rule, as formulated in the federal regulations governing pension fund investment, and in the Prudent Investor Act propounded for state legislation, make it clear that every category of investment is permitted, including derivatives, so long as it pays an appropriate part in a diversified portfolio whose potential returns are balanced against a level of risk suitable for the beneficiaries.

In the context of fiduciary investing, fiduciaries such as bank trust officers can use derivatives as a pure hedge. Fiduciaries may even be required to use derivatives to hedge against risk in cases where the best result for the beneficiaries can be achieved in no other way.

Fiduciaries may now have a duty to understand enough of this great, new fact of life to make safe use of derivatives to obtain advantages otherwise unavailable to their beneficiaries, as well as to avoid their risky use for highly leveraged investment where those risks are unauthorized, undisclosed, and unsuitable.

George Crawford is a consulting professor at Stanford Law School, an investment adviser, and a director of the Fiduciary Foundation. After Harvard College and Law School, where he was president of the *Harvard Law Review,* he served as law clerk to Justice White at the U.S. Supreme Court, as a member of the White House staff, and as a partner at the Jones Day law firm.

This discussion is excerpted from "A Fiduciary Duty to Use Derivatives?" which appeared in the *Stanford Journal of Law, Business & Finance,* Spring 1995.

Notes

1. For information about the *Managing Financial Risk Yearbook,* see the CIBC School of Financial Products web site—www.schoolfp.cibcwm.com.

2. One could argue that the Derivative Sales Alert and the New York University/Stern School of Business surveys show otherwise. However, since the Derivative Sales Alert survey was of U.S. branches of foreign entities, it may be that the foreign parent company dictates the policies pertaining to derivatives; so these results could not be interpreted as representing the behavior of U.S. investors. As for the New York University/Stern School of Business study, the sample reduces the scope of its results because it is composed of relatively small pension and endowment funds.

3. Francois Gagnon reminded me that, in addition to modern portfolio theory, expected utility maximization provides another reason for arguing that investors will think about returns on a risk-adjusted basis. Modern portfolio theory and the expected utility framework yield virtually the same results (i.e., same portfolio) if the utility preferences are quadratic or if the returns are normally distributed (Mossin, 1973). Since the expected utility framework is based on "economic rationality" (i.e., a set of logical axioms), considering risk and returns jointly is rational in the economic sense.

4. See Gregory-Allen (1995).

5. For significant and sudden price variations, the number of options will have to be adjusted to account for the changing delta.

6. In addition, from a practical standpoint, Layard-Liesching points out that the mean-variance approach to portfolio construction is highly sensitive to changes in forecast returns. As Layard-Liesching pointed out in the box above, there is uncertainty of return even over three years. Compounding this particular problem is the weakness of the existing econometric models of exchange rates; they do not consistently predict the direction the exchange rate will take when a particular shock occurs in one of the explanatory variables.

7. In order to simplify the example, we will assume that relatively little time has passed; so the delta of the option will not have changed significantly.

8. The calls and puts were priced assuming the volatility of the stock to be 15 percent, the dividend yield to be 5 percent, and the risk-free interest rate to be 6 percent.

9. For simplicity, we assume that the price changes occur two days after the options are originated.

10. See Minehan and Simmons (1995). We have re-ordered Professor Light's ways to conform to the order in which we introduced the products in this book.

11. See Gregory-Allen (1995).

12. See Ritchken (1996), p. 300.

13. The return is risk free in the market—price—sense; the transaction may mean that the investor is accepting counterparty credit risk.

REFERENCES

"How Sir Freddie Shot Himself Down," *Business Week,* February 22, 1982.

"A Way for U.S. Companies to Make 'Free Money'," *Business Week,* October 29, 1984, p. 58.

"Chocks Away for New Market in Oil Hedging" (1988). *Corporate Finance,* November.

"Behind the Mirror" (1989). *Risk 2,* no. 2 (February): 17–23.

"First Boston Snares Ford Credit with Swaption-Linked Deal" (1989, January 16). *Investment Dealer's Digest,* pp. 42–43.

"Hedging Seasonal Borrowing" (1989, September). *Corporate Risk Management.*

"Burns & McBride Hedges a White Christmas" (1990). *Corporate Risk Management,* December.

"Falcon Cable Foils Risk" (1990, November). *Corporate Risk Management.*

"Hartmarx Buttons Down an Interest Rate Collar" (1990, November). *Corporate Cashflow.*

"Kraft: The Well-Processed Spreadsheet" (1990). *Corporate Finance,* September.

"Qualex Protects Its Silver Lining" (1990). *Corporate Cashflow,* September.

"How Muzak Stays in Tune with Interest Rates" (1990). *Corporate Cashflow,* March.

"Applied Power Hedges a Strategic Acquisition" (1991). *Corporate Cashflow,* August.

"Buy Now, Pay Later" (1991). *Risk,* November.

"Corporate Risk Management's 'Done Deals'" (1991). *Corporate Risk Management,* January.

"FMC Uses Metal Swaps to Lock in Margins" (1991). *Corporate Risk Management,* January.

"Goldman Sachs Offers a First: Inflation Friendly Notes" (1991). *The Wall Street Journal,* October 25.

"Hedging during Market Backwardation" (1991). From "Corporate Risk Management's Done Deals," *Corporate Risk Management,* January.

"The P&L Railroad Keeps Its Fuel Costs on Track" (1991). *Corporate Cashflow,* March.

"Biosystems Is Ready for the Dollar's Rebound" (1992). *Corporate Finance,* September.

"Curves and the Fuller Figure" (1992). *Risk,* May.

"Texas Parries" (1992). *Risk,* September.

"UBS Profiting from Derivatives" (1992). *American Banker,* December 15.

"Another Trader Runs Amok" (1994). *Derivatives Strategy,* February 20.

Business Week (1994). October 31.

"Caterpillar Losses on Derivatives" (1994). *The New York Times,* August 11.

"Federal Deposit Insurance Corporation (1994). *Examination Guidance for Structured Notes,* August.

"Federal Paper Takes Special Charge; Profits Fall from Years Ago" (1994). *The Wall Street Journal,* July 12.

Federal Reserve Board (1994). *Supervisory Memo on the Purchase of Structured Notes,* August.

"Home in the Range" (1994). *Risk,* April.

"Range Notes Are Latest Innovation" (1994). *Swaps Monitor,* January 17.

"Gibson Greetings Sets an Additional Charge for the First Quarter" (1994). *The Wall Street Journal,* April 20.

"U.S. Derivatives: Range Notes with 1-Month Resets Said to Sell Well" (1994). *Knight-Ridder Money-Center News,* #304, November 18.

"The Dreaded D-word" (1995). *Institutional Investor,* June.

"Forex" (1995). *IFR Swaps,* May 17.

"Using Derivatives: What Senior Managers Must Know" (1995). *Harvard Business Review,* January–February.

"The World According to Richard Breeden" (1996). *Derivatives Strategy,* March.

"Business Risk: As U.S. Firms Gain on Rivals, the Dollar Raises Pesky Questions" (1996). *The Wall Street Journal,* August 16.

"Options and Volatility: A Quick History of the Academic Literature" (1997). *Derivatives Strategy,* June.

"Rate Swaps Added to Jazz Up Credit Card-Backed Securities" (1997). *American Banker,* August 13.

"Risk Innovations: Latest Techniques for Better Hedging" (1997). *Corporate Finance,* June.

Alderson, Michael, and Don Fraser (1993). "Financial Innovations and Excesses Revisited: The Case of Auction Rate Preferred Stock." *Financial Management* 22, Summer.

Allen, Michael (1994). "Building a Role Model." *Risk* 7, no. 9, September.

Allman, El (1989). "Measuring Corporate Bond Mortality and Performance." *Journal of Finance* 44.

American Institute of Certified Public Accountants Financial Instruments Task Force (1994). *Detailed Questions about Derivatives,* June.

American Stock Exchange (1994). "New Interest in AMEX'S Oil Index with Merrill Lynch Smart Notes." News release, March 25.

Angel, James; Gary L. Gastineau; and Clifford J. Weber (1997). "Using Exchange-Traded Equity FLEX Put Options in Corporate Stock Repurchase Programs." *Journal of Applied Corporate Finance,* Spring.

Arak, Marcelle; Arturo Estrella; Laurie Goodman; and Andrew Silver (1988). "Interest Rate Swaps: An Alternative Explanation." *Financial Management* 17 (Summer): 12–28.

Arak, Marcelle; Laurie S. Goodman; and Arthur Rones. "Credit Lines for New Instruments: Swaps, Over-the-Counter Options, Forwards and Floor-Ceiling Agreements." *Bank Structure and Competition,* pp. 437–56.

Association of Corporate Treasurers (U.K.) (1994). *Guide to Risk Management and Control of Derivatives.*

Bachelier, Louis (1900). "Theorie de la Speculation." *Annales de l'Ecole Normale Superieure* 17: 21–86. English translation by A. J. Boness in *The Random*

Character of Stock Market Prices, ed. Paul H. Cootner. Cambridge, Mass.: M.I.T. Press, 1964, pp. 17–78.

Banham, R. (1996). "More Coverage under One Roof." *Treasury & Risk Management,* October.

Bank for International Settlements (1987). *Proposals for International Convergence of Capital Measurement and Capital Standards,* December.

Bankers Trust Insurance Merchant Bank (1995). "Act of God Bonds." *Derivatives Week,* August 14.

Bansal, V. K.; S. W. Pruitt; and K. C. John Wei (1989). "An Empirical Reexamination of the Impact of CBOE Option Initiation on the Volatility and Trading Volume of the Underlying Equities: 1973–1986." *The Financial Review* 24: 19–29.

Barber, Brad M. (1993). "Exchangeable Debt." *Financial Management* 22, Summer.

Barone-Adesi, Giovanni, and Robert E. Whaley (1987). "Efficient Analytic Approximation of American Option Values." *Journal of Finance* 42 (June): 301–20.

Bartov, Eli; Gordon M. Bodnar; and Aditya Kaul (1992). "Exchange Rate Volatility and the Riskiness of U.S. Multinational Firms: Evidence from the Breakdown of the Bretton Woods System." Working Paper, 1993.

Basle Committee on Banking Supervision and the Technical Committee of the International Organization of Securities Commissions (1996). *Survey of Disclosures about Trading and Derivatives Activities of Banks and Securities Firms,* November.

Becker, Brandon (1995). *Harvard Business Review,* January–February.

Beder, Tanya Styblo (1995). "VAR: Seductive but Dangerous." *Financial Analysts Journal,* September–October.

Behof, John P. (1993). "Reducing Credit Risk in the Over-the-Counter Derivatives." Federal Reserve Bank of Chicago *Economic Perspectives,* January/February.

Beidleman, Carl, ed. (1992). "Government Use of Cross Currency Swaps." *Cross Currency Swaps.* Business One Irwin.

Belcher, Sophie (1997). "Swiss Re Readies First Investment Grade Earthquake Bond." *Derivatives Week,* May 26.

Bennett, Rosemary (1994). "Why Everyone Seems to Win with Structured Deals." *Euromoney,* March.

Bergsman, Steve (1994). "Occidental's North of the Border Twist." *FW's Corporate Finance,* Summer.

Bierman, H., Jr. (1967). "The Valuation of Stock Options, *Journal of Financial and Quantitative Analysis* 2: 327–34.

Bierwag, G. O.; George G. Kaufman; and Alden Toevs (1983). "Immunization Strategies for Funding Multiple Liabilities." *Journal of Financial and Quantitative Analysis* 18, no. 1, pp. 113–23.

Black, Fischer (1976). "The Pricing of Commodity Contracts." *Journal of Financial Economics* 3.

Black, Fischer; Emanuel Derman; and William Toy (1990). "A One-Factor Model of Interest Rates and Its Application to Treasury Bond Options." *Financial Analysts Journal* (January–February): 33–39.

Black, Fischer, and Myron Scholes (1973). "The Pricing of Options and Corporate Liabilities," *Journal of Political Economy* 81: 637–59.

Block, S.B., and T. J. Gallagher (1986). "The Use of Interest Rate Futures and Options by Corporate Financial Managers." *Financial Management* 15: 73–78.

Board of Governors of the Federal Reserve System and the Bank of England (1987). "Potential Credit Exposure on Interest Rate and Foreign Exchange Rate Related Instruments." Joint Working Paper.

Bodnar, Gordon, and Richard Marston (1996). *1995 Wharton/CIBC Wood Gundy Survey of Derivative Use by U.S. Nonfinancial Corporations.* The Wharton School, University of Pennsylvania, April. Another report on these survey results was provided by Charles Smithson in Chapter 9 of the *1996 Managing Financial Risk Yearbook,* CIBC Wood Gundy (February 1996).

Boness, A. James (1964). "Elements of a Theory of Stock-Option Value." *Journal of Political Economy* 72 (April): 163–75.

Booth, J. R.; R. L. Smith; and R. W. Stolz (1984). "The Use of Interest Rate Futures by Financial Institutions." *Journal of Bank Research* 15: 15–20.

Bortz, Gary A. (1984). "Does the Treasury Bond Futures Market Destabilize the Treasury Bond Cash Market?" *Journal of the Futures Markets,* Vol. 4, No. 1, pp. 25–38.

Boyle, Phelim P. (1977). "Options: A Monte Carlo Approach." *Journal of Financial Economics* 4 (May): 323–38.

Boyle, Phelim P (1986). "Option Valuation Using a Three Jump Process." *International Options Journal.*

Branch, B., and J. E. Finnerty (1981). "The Impact of Option Listing on the Price and Volume of the Underlying Stock." *Financial Review* 16: 1–15.

Brealey, Richard, and Stewart Meyers (1988/3rd edition) *Principles of Corporate Finance.* New York: McGraw-Hill.

Breeden, Richard C. (1994). "Directors, Control Your Derivatives." *The Wall Street Journal,* March 7.

Brennan, Michael J. (1986). "A Theory of Price Limits in Futures Markets." *Journal of Financial Economics* 16 (June).

Brennan, Michael, and Eduardo Schwartz (1978). "Finite Difference Method and Jump Processes Arising in the Pricing of Contingent Claims." *Journal of Financial and Quantitative Analysis* 13 (September): 461–74.

Brewer, Elijah III; Bernadette A. Minton; and James T. Moser (1996). "Interest-Rate Derivatives and Bank Lending," Working Paper, December.

British Bankers' Association (1985). *Forward Rate Agreements.* London, August.

Bulkeley, William H. (1989). "Tough Pitch: Marketing on the Defense." *The Wall Street Journal,* October 18.

Capatides, Michael G. (1988). *A Guide to the Capital Markets Activities of Banks and Bank Holding Companies.* W. C. Brown and Co.

Chan, K., and C. Turner (1994). "The Evolution Continues: Engineering New Instruments for Risk Management." *Financial Risk Management,* Fall: 4–6.

Chen, Andrew H., and K. C. Chen (1995). "An Anatomy of ELKS." *Journal of Financial Engineering* 4, December.

Chen, Andrew H.; John Kensinger; and Hansong Pu (1994). "An Analysis of PERCS." *Journal of Financial Engineering,* June.

Chen, Andrew H., and John W. Kensinger (1988). "Puttable Stock: A New Innovation in Equity Financing." *Financial Management* 17 (Spring).

Chen, K. C., and R. Stephen Sears (1990). "Pricing the SPIN." *Financial Management,* Summer.

Chesler-Marsh, Caren (1992). "Nightmare on Wall Street." *Euromoney,* February.

Chew, Lillian (1992). "A Bit of a Jam." *Risk* 5 (September).

Chicago Board of Trade (1988). "Futures: The Realistic Hedge for the Reality of Risk."

Conrad, J. (1989). "The Price Effect of Option Introduction." *Journal of Finance* 44: 487–98.

Cookson, Richard. *Derivatives for Directors,* The Association of Corporate Treasurers.

Cookson, Richard, and Lillian Chew (1992). "Things Fall Apart." *Risk,* October 1992.

Cooper, Ian A., and Antonio S. Mello (1991). "The Default Risk of Swaps." *The Journal of Finance* 46, June.

Coopers & Lybrand (1996). *Generally Accepted Risk Principles,* January.

Corgel, John B., and Gerald D. Gay (1984), "The Impact of GNMA Futures Trading on Cash Market Volatility," *AREUEA Journal,* Vol. 12, No. 2, pp. 176–90.

Corman, Linda (1997). "Hedging Risk without Derivatives." *Treasury & Risk Management,* April.

Courtadon, Georges (1982). "A More Accurate Finite Difference Approximation for the Valuation of Options." *Journal of Financial and Quantitative Analysis* 17 (December): 697–703.

Cox, C. C. (1976). "Futures Trading and Market Information." *Journal of Political Economy* 84: 1215–37.

Cox, John; Jonathan Ingersoll; and Stephen A. Ross (1985). "A Theory of the Term Structure of Interest Rates." *Econometrica* 53 (March).

Cox, John A.; Jonathan E. Ingersoll; and Stephen A. Ross (1981). "The Relations between Forwards Prices and Futures Prices." *Journal of Financial Economics* 9.

Cox, John C., and Stephen A. Ross (1976). "The Valuation of Options for Alternative Stochastic Processes." *Journal of Financial Economics* 3 (January–March): 145–66.

Cox, John C.; Stephen A. Ross; and Mark Rubinstein (1979). "Options Pricing: A Simplified Approach." *Journal of Financial Economics,* September.

———. (1985). *Options Markets.* Englewood Cliffs, N.J.: Prentice-Hall.

Dale, Charles, and Rosemarie Workman (1981), "Measuring Patterns of Price Movements in the Treasury Bill Futures Market," *Journal of Economics and Business,* Vol. 33, pp. 81–87.

Damodaran, A. (1990). "Index Futures and Stock Market Volatility." *Review of Futures Markets* 9.

Damodaran, A., and J. Lim (1991). "The Effects of Option Listing on the Underlying Stocks' Return Processes." *Journal of Banking and Finance* 15: 647–64.

Damodaran, Aswath, and Marti G. Subrahmanyam (1992). "The Effects of Derivative Securities on the Markets for the Underlying Assets in the United States: A Survey." *Financial Markets, Institutions, and Instruments,* December.

Das, S. R. (1995a). "Credit Risk Derivatives." *The Journal of Derivatives,* Spring.

Das, Satyajit (1995b). "Path-ology." *IFR Financial Products,* May 17.

Dattatreya, Rowi E., and Kensuke Hotta (1994). *Advanced Interest Rate and Currency Swaps.* Chicago, Illinois, Cambridge, England: Probus Publishing Company.

DeMarzo, P., and D. Duffie (1991). "Corporate Financial Hedging with Proprietary Information." *Journal of Economic Theory* 45: 261–286.

DeTemple, J., and D. Jorion (1990). "Option Listing and Stock Returns." *Journal of Banking and Finance* 14: 781–802.

DeTemple, J., and P. Jorion (1990). "Option Listing and Stock Returns." *Journal of Banking and Finance,* 14.

Dickins, Paul (1988). "Fast Forward with FRAs." *Corporate Finance,* April.

Dolde, W. (1995). "Hedging, Leverage and Primitive Risk." *Journal of Financial Engineering* 4.

Drabenstott, Mark, and Anne O'Mara McDonley (1984). "Futures Markets: A Primer for Financial Institutions." *Economic Review,* Federal Reserve Bank of Kansas City, November.

Edwards, Franklin R. (1988). "Futures Trading and Cash Market Volatility: Stock Index and Interest Rate Futures," *Journal of Futures Markets,* Vol. 8, No. 4, pp. 421–439.

Elton, J. E., and M. J. Gruber (1995). *Modern Portfolio Theory and Investment Analysis,* Wiley. *Draft: Spring 1996.*

Esterle, Celine, and Erica Robb (1995). "Buba Options." *IFR Swaps,* May 17.

Fabozzi, Frank J., and T. Dessa Fabozzi (1991). *The Handbook of Fixed Income Securities,* 3rd ed. New York: McGraw-Hill.

Falloon, William (1994). "Black Eye, Red Ink." *Risk,* May.

Fedenia, Mark, and Theocharry Grammatikos (1992). "Options Trading and the Bid-Ask Spread of the Underlying Stocks." *Journal of Business* 65 (July): 335–51.

Federal Reserve Bank of Chicago (1986). "Credit Lines for New Instruments: Swaps, Over-the-Counter Options, Forwards, and Floor-Ceiling Agreements."

Proceedings of a Conference on Bank Structure and Competition, Federal Reserve Bank of Chicago.

Ferron, Mark, and George Handjinicolaou (1987). "Understanding Swap Credit Risk: The Simulation Approach." *Journal of International Security Markets* (Winter): 135–48.

Figlewski, S. (1981). "The Informational Effects of Restrictions of Short Sales: Some Empirical Evidence." *Journal of Financial and Quantitative Analysis* 16: 463–76.

Figlewski, Stephen (1986). *Hedging with Financial Futures for Institutional Investors: From Theory to Practice.* Cambridge, Mass.: Ballinger.

Finnerty, John D. (1988). "Financial Engineering in Corporate Finance: An Overview." *Financial Management* 17 (Winter).

Finnerty, John D. (1992). "An Overview of Corporate Securities Innovation." *Journal of Applied Corporate Finance,* Winter.

Finnerty, John D. (1993). "Interpreting SIGNs." *Financial Management* 22, Summer.

Finnerty, John D. (1994). "Range Floaters: Pricing, i.e., A Bet on the Future Course of Short-Term Interest Rates." *Financier,* November.

Fitch (1995). *Special Report on Managing Derivatives Risk,* February.

Flood, Eugene, and Donald Lessard (1986). "On the Measurement of Operating Exposure Subject to Exchange Rates: A Conceptual Approach." *Financial Management,* Spring 1986.

Frances, C. *Harvard Business Review.*

Francis, Jack Clark, William W. Toy, and J. Gregg Whittaker, eds. (1995). *Handbook of Equity Derivatives.* New York: McGraw-Hill.

French, Kenneth R. (1983). "A Comparison of Futures and Forward Prices." *Journal of Financial Economics* 12, November.

Friedman, Avner (1975). *Stochastic Differential Equations and Applications.* New York: Academic Press.

Froewiss, Kenneth C. (1978). "GNMA Futures: Stabilizing or Destabilizing?" *Economic Review,* Federal Reserve Bank of San Francisco, Spring, pp. 20–29.

Froot, K.; D. Scharfstein; and J. Stein (1993). "Risk Management: Co-ordinating Corporate Investment and Financing Policies." *Journal of Finance* 48. A more accessible version of this paper appeared as "A Framework for Risk Management" in *Harvard Business Review,* November–December 1994.

Frye, Jon (1992). "Underexposed and Overanxious." *Risk* 5, March.

Furbush, Dean, and Michael Sackheim (1991). "U.S. Hybrid Instruments: Evolving Legal and Economic Issues." *Butterworth's Journal of International Banking and Financial Law,* September.

Garber, Peter M. (1986). "The Tulipmania Legend." Center for the Study of Futures Markets Working Paper #CSFM–139, August.

Garman, Mark B. (1988). "Charm School." *Risk* (October): 16–19.

Garman, Mark B., and Steven W. Kohlhagen (1983). "Foreign Currency Option Values." *Journal of International Money and Finance* 2, December.

Geczy, C.; B. Minton; and C. Schrand (1996). "Why Firms Use Currency Derivatives." *Journal of Finance.*

Geske, Robert (1979a). "The Valuation of Compound Options." *Journal of Financial Economics* 7 (March): 63–81.

———. (1979b). "A Note on an Analytic Valuation Formula for Unprotected American Call Options on Stocks with Known Dividends." *Journal of Financial Economics* 7 (December): 375–80.

Goldman, M. Barry; Howard B. Sosin; and Mary Ann Gatto (1979). "Path Dependent Options: Buy at the Low, Sell at the High." *Journal of Finance* 34, No. 5 (December): 1111–27.

Goodwin, William (1994). "Air Products Drops 2 Currency Hedges in Sing of Skittishness over Derivatives." *American Banker,* June 2.

Government Accounting Office (1994). *Report on Financial Derivatives,* May.

Grabbe, J. Orlin (1983). "The Pricing of Call and Put Options on Foreign Exchange." *Journal of International Money and Finance* 2 (December): 239–53.

Gray, Roger W. (1963). "Onions Revisited," *Journal of Farm Economics,* May 1963, pp. 273–276.

Gregory-Allen, Russell (1995). "Derivatives Do Have a Place in Prudent Investing." *The Financier* 5, December.

Grindal, Izabel (1988). "Flexible Risk Control and Arbitrage." *Futures and Options World,* June.

Group of Thirty, Global Derivatives Study Group (1993). *Derivatives: Practices and Principles—Survey of Industry Practice,* Washington, D.C., July.

Group of Thirty, Global Derivatives Study Group (1993). *Report of the Derivatives Study Group,* Washington, D.C., July.

Group of Thirty, Global Derivatives Study Group (1994). *Derivatives: Practices and Principles—Follow-Up Survey of Industry Practice,* December.

Gutscher, Cecile (1997a). "Can Wall Street Find Buyers for Bonds Tied to Hurricanes and Earthquakes?" *The Wall Street Journal,* May 30.

Gutscher, Cecile (1997b). "Bonds Are Sold Tied to Quake on West Coast." *Wall Street Journal,* June 20.

Hakansson, Nils H. (1976). "The Purchasing Power Fund: A New Kind of Financial Intermediary." *Financial Analysts Journal,* November/December.

Hansell, Saul (1994). "Dervatives and the Fall Guy: Excuses, Excuses." *The New York Times,* October 2.

Harris, L. (1989). "S&P 500 Cash Stock Price Volatilities." *Journal of Finance* 44: 1155–76.

Harris, Trevor S.; Nahum D. Melumad; and Toshi Shibano (1996). "An Argument against Hedging by Matching the Currencies of Costs and Revenues." *Journal of Applied Corporate Finance,* Fall.

Harty, Emmett J., "Americus Trust's PRIMEs, and SCOREs: Precursors to LEAPS, PERCS, ELKS, YEELDS, CHIPS, and Super Trust." in *The Handbook of Equity Derivatives.*

Hayes, S. I., and M. E. Tennenbaum (1979). "The Impact of Listed Options on the Underlying Shares." *Financial Management* 8, No. 4: 72–76. Winter.

Hayt, Gregory (1997). "Electricity Derivatives: Deregulation of the Power Industry around the World Is Creating a Huge New Derivatives Market." *Risk* 10, No. 1, January.

Hayt, Gregory, and Shang Song (1995). "Handle with Sensitivity." *Risk* 8, No. 9, September.

Healy, James P. (1993). "Working Paper of the Credit Risk Measurement and Mangement Subcommittee." The Group of Thirty Global Derivatives Study, July.

Heath, David; Robert Jarrow; and Andrew Morton (1990). "Bond Pricing and the Term Structure of Interest Rates." *Journal of Financial and Quantitative Analysis* 25 (December).

Heath, David; Robert Jarrow; and Andrew Morton (1992). "Bond Pricing and the Term Structure of Interest Rates: A New Methodology for Contingent Claims Valuation." *Econometrica* 60: 77–105.

Hendricks, Darryll (1996). "Evolution of Value-at-Risk Models Using Historical Data." *FRBNY Economic Policy Review,* April.

Henry, Emmett J. (1995). "Americus Trust's Primes and Scores: Precursor to LEAPs, PERCS, ELKS, YEELDS,

and SuperTrust." *Handbook of Equity Derivatives,* eds. Jack Clark Francis, William Toy, and Gregg Whittaker.

Hentschel, Ludger and S. P. Kothari (1997), "Are Corporations Reducing or Taking Risks with Derivatives?" Working Paper, William E. Simon Graduate School of Business Administration, University of Rochester.

Herman, Robert (1994). "U.S. Swaps: Colgate Makes Money with Defined Derivative Strategy." *Knight Ridder Financial News,* October 5.

Hicks, J. R. (1939). *Value and Capital.* Cambridge: Oxford University Press.

Ho, Thomas S. Y., and Sang-Bin Lee (1986). "Term Structure Movements and Pricing Interest Rate Contingent Claims." *Journal of Finance* 41: 1011–29.

Holappa, Hal (1995). "Credit Derivatives: What Are These Youthful Instruments and Why Are They Used?" *Risk,* December.

Holappa, Hal, and Shaun Rai (1996). "Credit Dervatives (2): A Look at the Market, Its Evolution and Current Size." *Risk,* June.

Hopewell, Michael, and George Kaufman (1973). "Bond Price Volatility and Term to Maturity: A Generalized Respecification." *American Economic Review,* 62 (September).

———. (1974). "The Cost of Inefficient Coupons on Municipal Bonds." *Journal of Financial and Quantitative Analysis* 9, No. 2: 155–64.

Houston, Carol Olson, and Gerhard G. Mueller (1988). "Foreign Exchange Rate Hedging and SFAS no. 52: Relatives or Strangers?" *Accounting Horizons* 2, No. 4 (December): 50–57.

Howard, Kerrin (1995). "Cliquet Options and Ladder Options," Learning Curve column in *Derivatives Week,* May 22, 1995.

Hull, John (1989). *Options, Futures, and Other Derivative Securities.* Englewood Cliffs, N.J.: Prentice-Hall.

Hull, John, and Alan White (1987). "The Pricing of Options on Assets with Stochastic Volatilities." *Journal of Finance* 42: 281–300.

———. (1990a). "Pricing Interest Rate Derivative Securities." *Review of Financial Studies* 3.

———. (1990b). "Valuing Derivative Securities Using the Explicit Finite Difference Method." *Journal of Financial and Quantitative Analyses* 25, No. 1 (March): 87–100.

———. (1992a). "The Impact of Default Risk on the Prices of Options and Other Derivative Securities." Unpublished manuscript, May.

————. (1992b). "The Price of Default." *Risk* 5, September.

Hutchins, Dexter (1986). "Caterpillar's Triple Whammy." *Fortune,* October 27.

Huynh, C. (1994). "Back to Baskets." *Risk* (May): 59–61.

Iacono, Frank, and David Skeie (1996). "Translating VaR Using SQRT(T)." *Derivatives Week,* October 14.

Iben, Benjamin, and Rupert Brotheron-Ratcliffe (1991). "Principals at Stake." *Risk* 5, December/January.

Ingersoll, Jonathan (1976). "A Theoretical and Empirical Investigation of the Dual Purpose Funds: An Application of Contingent Claims Analysis." *Journal of Financial Economics* 3 (January–March).

International Chamber of Commerce (1986). *Futures and Options Trading in Commodity Markets,* Paris.

Investment Company Institute (1994). *Memorandum on Investments in Derivatives by Registered Investment Companies,* August.

Jarrow, Robert, and Andrew Rudd (1982). "Approximate Option Valuation for Arbitrary Stochastic Processes." *Journal of Financial Economics* 10 (November): 347–69.

Jarrow, Robert A., and George S. Oldfield (1981). "Forward Contracts and Futures Contracts." *Journal of Financial Economics* 9.

Jarrow, Robert, and Stuart Turnbull (1990). "The Pricing and Hedging of Options on Financial Securities Subject to Credit Risk: The Discrete Time Case." Unpublished manuscript.

————. (1992). "Drawing the Analogy," *Risk* 5 (October).

Jennings, R. H., and L. T. Stark (1981). "Earnings Announcements, Stock Price Adjustment and the Existence of Options Markets." *Journal of Finance* 41: 43–61.

Jensen, Michael C., and William H. Meckling (1976). "Theory of the Firm: Managerial Behavior, Agency Costs, and Capital Structure." *Journal of Financial Economics* 3.

Johnson, H. (1987). "Options on the Maximum or the Minimum of Several Assets." *Journal of Financial and Quantitative Analysis* 22, No. 3: 277–83.

Jordan, James; Robert Mackay; and Eugene Moriarty (1990). "The New Regulation of Hybrid Debt Instruments." *Journal of Applied Corporate Finance,* Winter.

Jordan, James V., and Robert Mackay (1997). "Assessing Value-at-Risk for Equity Portfolios: Implementing Alternative Techniques." *Derivatives Handbook: Risk Management and Control,* eds. Robert Schwartz and Clifford W. Smith, Jr.

Jorion, Philippe (1990). "The Exchange-Rate Exposures of U.S. Multinationals." *Journal of Business* 63.

————. (1997). *Value at Risk: The New Benchmark for Controlling Market Risk.* New York: The McGraw-Hill Companies.

Kemna, A. G. Z., and A. C. F. Vorst (1990). "A Pricing Method for Options Based on Average Asset Values." *Journal of Banking and Finance* 14 (March).

Keslar, Linda (1996). "The View from the Boardroom: Under Control." *Derivatives Strategy,* March.

Keynes, John Maynard (1930) *Treatise on Money.* London: Macmillan.

Kim, Ted (1997). "Emerging Markets: Positive Equities." *Equity & Risk Management Investment,* a supplement to *Futures & Options World,* May.

Kirzner, Eric (1995). "Index Participation Units." *The Handbook of Equity Derivatives,* eds. Jack Clark Francis, William W. Toy, and J. Gregg Whittaker. Irwin.

Kleinbard, Edward D. (1991). "Equity Derivative Products: Financial Innovation's Newest Challenge to the Tax System." *Texas Law Review* 69 (May): 1319–68.

Klemkosky, Robert C., and T. S. Maness (1980). "The Impact of Options on the Underlying Securities." *Journal of Portfolio Management* 7: 12–18.

Krzyzak, Krystyna (1988). "Don't Take Swaps at Face Value." *Risk* 11, November.

Lacey, James (1996). "The Consultants' Verdict: Still in Trouble." *Derivatives strategy,* March.

Lamoureux, Claude (1995). "Derivatives: Beauty or the Beast?" The Role of Directors and Senior Management, University of Waterloo Conference, May 8.

Lane, Karen (1994). "Property Seen as Tortoise in the Derivatives Race." *Knight-Ridder MoneyCenter News* #13209, November 28.

Leander, Ellen (1996). "When the Insurance Salesman Is an Investment Banker." *Global Finance,* March.

Lewent, Judy C., and A. John Kearney (1990). "Identifying, Measuring, and Hedging Currency Risk at Merck." *Journal of Applied Corporate Finance,* Winter.

Lewis, Peter (1997). "Emerging Markets: Enter Equity Swaps." *Equity & Risk Management Investment,* a supplement to *Futures & Options World,* May 1997.

Loeys, Jan (1985). "Interest Rate Swaps: A New Tool for Managing Risk." *Business Review,* Federal Reserve Bank of Philadelphia (May/June): 17–25.

Longstaff, Francis, and Eduardo Schwartz (1992). "Interest Rate Volatility and the Term Structure: A Two-Factor General Equilibrium Model." *Journal Finance* 47: 1259–1282.

Lucchetti, Aaron (1997). "Two Exchanges Seek Launch of Less-Regulated Markets." *The Wall Street Journal,* April 21.

Ma, C. K., and R. P. Rao (1986). "Market Characteristics, Option Trading and Volatility of the Underlying Stock." *Advances in Futures and Options Research* 1: 193–200.

———. (1988). "Information Asymmetry and Options Trading." *The Financial Review* 23: 39–51.

Macaulay, F. R. (1938). *Some Theoretical Problems Suggested by the Movement of Interest Rates, Bond Yields, and Stock Prices Since 1856.* New York: National Bureau of Research.

Macmillan, Lionel W. (1986). "Analytic Approximation for the American Put Options." *Advances in Futures and Options Research* 1: 119–39.

Margrabe W. (1988). "The Value of an Option to Exchange One Asset for Another." *Journal of Finance* 33, No. 1: 177–86.

Margrabe, William (1978). "The Value of an Option to Exchange One Asset for Another," *Journal of Finance,* March 1978, pp. 177–186.

Mark, R. (1995). "Integrated Credit Risk Measurement." *Derivative Credit Risk: Advances in Measurement and Management,* Risk Publications.

Mark R. (1997). "Risk Oversight for the Senior Manager: Controlling Risk in Dealers." *Derivatives: Risk Management and Control,* ed. Robert Scwartz and Clifford Smith. Wiley.

Marshall, Christopher, and Michael Siegel (1996). "Value at Risk: Implementing a Risk Measurement Standard." *MIT Finance Research Center.*

Mayers D., and C. W. Smith (1990). "On the Corporate Demand for Insurance: Evidence from the Reinsurance Market." *Journal of Business* 63: 19–40.

McConnell, John J., and Eduardo S. Schwartz (1982). "The Origin of LYONs: A Case Study in Financial Innovation." *Journal of Applied Corporate Finance,* Winter.

McConnell, John J., and Eduardo S. Schwartz (1986). "LYON Taming." *Journal of Finance,* 41.

McCulloch, J. Huston (1980). "The Ban on Indexed Bonds." *American Economic Review,* 70 (December).

McGoldrick, Beth (1995). "Corporates Talk about Value-at-Risk." *Derivatives Strategies,* November.

Mello, Antonio; John Parsons; and Alexander Triantis (1996). "Flexibility or Hedging?" *Risk,* October.

Mello, J. (1996). "Calculated Risks." *CFO,* September.

Merton, Robert C. (1973). "Theory of Rational Option Pricing." *Bell Journal of Economics and Management Science* 4 (Spring): 141–83.

———. (1976). "Option Pricing When Underlying Stock Returns Are Discontinuous." *Journal of Financial Economics* 3 (January–March): 125–44.

———. (1992). "Financial Innovation and Economic Performance." *Journal of Applied Corporate Finance,* Winter.

Mian, S. (1994). "Evidence on the Determinants of Corporate Hedging Policy." Emory University Working Paper.

Miller, Gregory (1986). "When Swaps Unwind." *Institutional Investor,* November.

Miller, James P. (1994). "Air Products Takes a Charge of $60 Million." *The Wall Street Journal,* May 12. Draft: Spring 1996.

Miller, Merton (1992). "Financial Innovation: Achievements and Prospects." *Journal of Applied Corporate Finance,* Winter.

Millman, Gregory J. (1988). "How Smart Competitors Are Locking in the Cheap Dollar." *Corporate Finance,* December.

———. (1991). "Kaiser and Union Carbide Hedge Their Bets with Their Banks." *Corporate Finance,* June.

Minehan, Cathy E., and Katerina Simmons (1995). "Managing Risk in the '90s: What Should You Be Asking about Derivatives?" *New England Economic Review,* September/October.

Modigliani, Franco, and Merton Miller (1958). "The Cost of Capital, Corporation Finance, and the Theory of Investment." *American Economic Review,* 48 (June).

———. (1961). "Dividend Policy, Growth and the Valuation of Shares." *Journal of Business* 34, October.

Moriarity, E. J. and P. A. Tosini (1985). "Futures Trading and Price Volatility of GNMA Certificates—Further Evidence. *Journal of Futures Markets* 5: 633–41.

Mossin, Jan. *Theory of Financial Markets.* Prentice Hall: Englewood Cliffs, N.J., 1973.

Muffett, Mark (1986). "Modelling Credit Exposure on Swaps." *Proceedings of a Conference on Bank*

Structure and Competition. Federal Reserve Bank of Chicago, pp. 473–96.

Myers, S. C. (1977). "The Determinants of Corporate Borrowing." *Journal of Financial Economics,* 5, November.

Nance, Deana R.; Clifford W. Smith, Jr.; and Charles W. Smithson (1993). "On the Determinants of Corporate Hedging." *The Journal of Finance* 48: 267–84.

Neal, Kathleen, and Katerina Simons (1988). "Interest Rate Swaps, Currency Swaps and Credit Risk." *Issues in Bank Regulation,* Spring: 26–29.

Neal, R. (1987). "Potential and Actual Competition in Equity Options." *Journal of Finance* 42: 511–32.

Neu, Joseph (1995). "VAR & Corporate In-House Banks." *International Treasurer,* May.

Nusbaum, David (1997). "Hurricane Bond Storms Wall Street." *Risk,* July.

Office of the Comptroller of the Currency (1994). AL 94–2, OCC Advisory Letter, July 21, 1994, Subject: Purchases of Structured Notes, TO: Chief Executive Officers of all National Banks, OCC Department and Division Heads, and All Examining Personnel.

Polsky, Lisa K. (1995). "Integrating Risk Management and Strategy." *Risk Management,* AIMR, October 10.

Powers, M. J. (1970). "Does Futures Trading Reduce Price Fluctuations in the Cash Markets?" *American Economic Review* 60: 460–64.

Price Waterhouse and the Treasury Mangement Association (1996). *Corporate Treasury Control and Performance Standards,* November.

Pritsker, Matthew (1997). "Evaluating Value at Risk Methodologies: Accuracy versus Computational Time." *Journal of Financial Services Research* 12 no. 2/3, October/December.

Putman, Bluford, and D. Sykes Wilford, eds. (1986). *The Monetary Approach of International Adjustment.* New York: Praeger.

Pye, Gordon (1966). "A Markov Model of the Term Structure." *Quarterly Journal of Economics* 25 (February).

Quint, Michael (1989). "Reducing Shareholder-Debtholder Conflict on the RJR Nabisco Deal," in "Talking Deals." *The New York Times,* February 16.

Ramaswamy, Krishna, and Suresh M. Sundaresan (1986). "The Valuation of Floating Rate Instruments: Theory and Evidence." *Journal of Financial Economics* 17: 251–72.

Ravindran, K. (1994). "Exotic Options." *Advanced Interest Rate and Currency Swaps; State-of-the-Art Products, Strategies & Risk Management Applications,* eds. Ravi E. Dattatreya and Kensuke Hotta. Chicago: Probus Publishing.

Rawls, S. Waite III, and Charles W. Smithson (1989). "The Evolution of Risk Management Products." *Journal of Applied Corporate Finance,* Winter: 18–26.

———. (1990). "Strategic Risk Management." *Journal of Applied Corporate Finance,* 2, No. 4, Winter.

Record Treasury Management (1995). Dervatives Survey, Summer.

Reiner, E. (1992). "Quanto Mechanics." *Risk* (March): 59–63.

Rendleman, Richard J., Jr., and Brit J. Barter (1979). "Two-State Option Pricing." *Journal of Finance* 34 (December): 1093–10.

Reynolds, Katherine M. (1997). "House Panel Begins Hearings on Futures Exchange Deregulation." *The Bond Buyer,* April 16.

Ritchken, Peter. *Dervatives Markets: Theory, Strategy and Applications.* 1996, CIBC World Markets Financial Products.

Roll, Richard (1977). "An Analytical Formula for Unprotected American Call Options on Stocks with Known Dividends." *Journal of Financial Economics* 5 (November): 251–58.

Rombach, Ed (1991). "The Cost of Insurance." *Risk* 4, No. 5 (May): pg. 12.

Rouvinez, Christophe (1997). "Going Greek with VAR." *Risk,* February.

Rubinstein, Mark (1995). "Supershares." *Handbook of Equity Derivatives,* eds. Jack Clark Francis, William Toy, and Gregg Whittaker.

Samant, A. (1996). "An Empirical Study of Interest Rate Swap Usage by Nonfinancial Corporate Business." *Journal of Financial Services Research* 10.

Samuelson, Paul A. (1965). "Rational Theory of Warrant Pricing." *Industrial Mangement Review* 6: 13–31.

Samuelson, P. A., and R. C. Merton (1969). "A Complete Model of Warrant Pricing that Maximizes Utility." *Industrial Management Review* 10: 17–46.

Santomero, A. (1997). "Commercial Bank Risk Management: An Analysis of the Process." *Journal of Financial Services Research,* 1997, forthcoming.

Santoni, G. J. (1987). "Has Programmed Trading Made Stock Prices More Volatile?" *Economic Review,* Federal Reserve Bank of St. Louis, May, pp. 18–29.

Schacter, B. (1988). "Open Interest in Stock Options around Quarterly Earnings Announcements." *Journal of Accounting Research* 26: 353–72.

Schuyler, K. Henderson (1985). "The Constraints on Trading Swaps." *Euromoney,* May.

Schwartz, Eduardo (1977). "The Valuation of Warrants: Implementing a New Approach." *Journal of Financial Economics* 4 (January): 79–93.

Scott, Louis (1987). "Option Pricing When the Variance Changes Randomly: Theory, Estimation, and an Application." *Journal of Financial and Quantitative Analysis* 22: 419–38.

Seltzer, Jeffrey L. (1995). "A View for the Top: The Roleof the Board of Directors and Senior Managment in the Derivatives Business." Chapter 1 in *Derivatives Risk and Responsibilities,* ed. Robert A. Klein and Jess Lederman. New York: McGraw-Hill.

Sharpe, William F. (1978, 1985). *Investments,* 3rd ed. Englewood Cliffs, N.J.: Prentice-Hall.

———. (1987). "Integrated Asset Allocation." *Financial Analysts Journal,* September/October.

Sharpe, William F., and G. S. Alexander. *Investments,* 4th ed. Upper Saddle River, N. J.: Prentice-Hall.

Siegfried, J. J. (1974). "Effective Average U.S. Corporation Income Tax Rates." *National Tax Journal,* June.

Simpson, W. Gary, and Timothy C. Ireland (1985). "The Impact of Financial Futures on the Cash Market for Treasury Bills." *Journal of Financial and Quantitative Analysis,* Vol. 20, No. 3, pp. 371–379.

Singleton, J. Matthew (1991). "Hedge Accounting: A State-of-the-Art Review." *Bank Accounting and Finance* 5, No. 1. Fall: 26–32.

Skinner, D. (1989). "Option Markets and Stock Return Volatility." *Journal of Financial Economics* 24: 61–78.

Slunt, J. (1995). "Survey of Risk Management Practices for Pension Funds." New York University Stern School of Business, Spring.

Smith, C., Jr. and R. Stulz (1985). "The Determinants of Firms' Hedging Policies." *Journal of Financial and Quantitative Analysis* 20.

Smith, Clifford W., Jr. (1976). "Option Pricing: A Review." *Journal of Financial Economics* 3, January–March.

Smith, Clifford W., Jr. (1993). "A Building-Block Approach to the Credit Risk for OTC Derivatives." Working paper, William E. Simon Graduate School of Business, University of Rochester.

Smith, Clifford W., Jr., and D. Mayers (1987). "Corporate Insurance and the Underinvestment Problem." *Journal of Risk and Insurance* 54 (March).

Smith, Clifford W., Jr., and Charles W. Smithson (1989). "Derivatives and Volatility." *Intermarkets,* July.

Smith, Clifford W., Jr.; Charles W. Smithson, and Lee M. Wakeman (1986). "The Evolving Market for Swaps." *Midland Corporate Finance Journal,* Winter.

———. (1988). "Analyzing the Credit Risk of Swaps." *Simon Management Review,* Winter.

Smith, Clifford W., Jr.; Charles W. Smithson and Lee M. Wakeman (1988). "The Market for Interest Rate Swaps." *Financial Management,* Vol. 17, No. 2, pp. 34–44.

Smith, Clifford, W., Jr., and Jerold B. Warner (1979). "On Financial Contracting: An Analysis of Bond Covenants." *Journal of Financial Economics* 7.

Smith, Clifford W., Jr., and David Watts (1987). "Corporate Insurance and the Underinvestment Problem." *Journal of Risk and Insurance,* LIV, No. 1, (March): 45–54.

Smithson, Charles W. (1987). " A LEGO Approach to Financial Engineering: An Introduction to Forwards, Futures, Swaps, and Options." *Midland Corporate Finance Journal* 4, Winter.

———. (1991). "Wonderful Life." *Risk,* 4, No. 9. (October): 37–44.

Smithson, Charles W. (1996a). "Theory v. Practice: Does Financial Risk Management Increase Shareholder Value?" *Risk* 9, no. 9, September.

Smithson, Charles W. (1996b). "Exposure Measures: How to Measure the Credit Risk Exposure Associated with OTC Derivatives Transactions." *Risk* 9, No. 10, October.

Smithson, Charles W. (1997). "Firm-Wide Risk Management: How Firms Are Integrating Risk Management." *Risk* 10, No. 3, March.

Smithson, Charles W., and William Chan (1997). "Multifactor Options: Definitions and Categorisation." *Risk* 10, No. 5, May.

Smithson, Charles W., and William Chan (1997). "Path-Dependency: Defining and Categorising Path-Dependent Options." *Risk* 10, No. 4, April.

Smithson, Charles W., and Donald H. Chew, Jr. (1992). "The Uses of Hybrid Debt in Managing Corporate Risk." *Journal of Applied Corporate Finance* 4, no. 4 (Winter): 79–89.

Smithson, Charles W., and Hal Holappa (1995). "Credit Derivatives: What Are These Youthful Instruments and Why Are They Used?" *Risk* 8, no. 12, December.

Smithson, Charles W., Hal Holappa, and Shaun Rai (1996). "Credit Derivatives (2): A Look at the Market, Its Evolution and Current Size." *Risk* 9, No. 6, June.

Smithson, Charles W., and Lyle Minton (1996). "Value-at-Risk (1): Understanding the Various Ways to Calculate VAR." *Risk* 9, no. 1, January.

Smithson, Charles W., and Lyle Minton (1996). "Value-at-Risk (2): The Debate on the Use of VAR." *Risk* 9, No. 2, February.

Smithson, Charles W., and Shang Song (1995a). "Extended Family (I): Keeping Track of Option Valuation Models." *Risk* 8, no. 10, October.

Smithson, Charles W., and Shang Song (1995b). "Extended Family (II)." *Risk* 8, no. 11, November.

Smithson, Charles W., and Christopher M. Turner (1994). "Financial Price Risk Evidenced in Share Price Behavior." Risk Management Research Working Paper, the Chase Manhattan Bank.

Spahr, R. W.; M. A. Sunderman; and C. Amalu (1991). "Corporate Bond Insurance: Feasibility and Insurer Risk Assessment." *Journal of Risk and Insurance* 58, September.

Sprenkle, Case M. (1964). "Warrant Prices as Indicators of Expectations and Preferences." *The Random Character of Stock Market Prices,* ed. Paul H. Cootner. Cambridge, Mass.: M.I.T. Press, pp. 412–74.

St. Goar, Jenny (1994). "Freeport-McMoran's Silver Lining." *FW's Corporate Finance,* Summer.

Stern, Gabriella, and Steven Lipin (1994). "Procter & Gamble to Take a Charge to Close Out Two Interest-Rate Swaps." *The Wall Street Journal,* April 13.

Stern, Joel M. and Donald H. Chew, Jr. (1986). *The Revolution in Corporate Finance,* Basil Blackwell.

Sterngold, James (1993). "Rising Yen Rings Alarms in Tokyo." *The New York Times,* April 6.

Stevenson, Merril (1987). "The Risk Game: A Survey of International Banking." *The Economist,* March 21.

Stoll, Hans, and Robert Whaley (1987). "Expiration Date Effects of Index Options and Futures." *Financial Analysts Journal,* Vol. 43, pp. 16–28.

Stovall, Robert H. (1991). "PERCing Up Equities." *Financial World,* October 15.

Street, Andrew (1992). "Stuck up a Ladder?" *Risk* 5, No. 5, May.

Stultz, Rene (1982). "Options on the Minimum or the Maximum of Two Risky Assets," *Journal of Financial Economics* 10: 161–85.

Sullivan J. (1988). "The Application of Mathematical Programming Methods to Oil and Gas Field Development Planning." *Mathematical Programming* 42: 199–200.

Sweeney, Richard J., and Arthur D. Warga (1986). "The Possibility of Estimating Risk Premia in Asset Pricing Models." *The Financial Review* 21, No. 2: 299–308.

Taylor, Gregory S., and Raymond M. Leuthold (1974). "The Influence of Futures Trading on Cash Cattle Price Variations." *Food Research Institute Studies,* Vol. 13, pp. 29–35.

Taylor, Spillenkothen; Parkinson, Spindler; and White (1987). "Uses of Interest Rate and Exchange Rate Contracts by U.S. Banking Organizations." Appendix C to "Treatment of Interest Rate and Exchange Rate Contracts in the Risk Asset Ratio." Staff Report, Federal Reserve System, March 2.

Teweles, Richard J., and Frank J. Jones (1987). *The Futures Game,* 2nd ed. New York: McGraw-Hill.

Thorpe, E. O. (1973). "Extensions of the Black-Scholes Option Model," *39th Session of the International Statistical Institute* (Vienna, Austria), pp. 522–529.

Thorpe, E. O., and S. T. Kassouf (1967). *Beat the Market.* New York: Random House.

Thomas, Bryan (1994). "Something to Shout About." *Risk* 6, No. 5, May.

Thompson, Peter (1995). "Double Barrier Options." *Derivatives Week,* June 19.

Todd, Steven (1997). "The Impact of Financial Intermediation on Consumer Mortgage Financing Costs." Working Paper, University of Washington, April 15.

Toevs, Alden (1984–85). "Interest Rate Risk and Uncertain Lives." *Journal of Portfolio Management* 11, No. 3: 45–46.

Treaster, Joseph B. (1977). "Even Nature Can Be Turned into a Security." *The New York Times,* August 6.

Treasury Management Association (1995). *Voluntary Principles and Practices: Guidelines for End Users of Derivatives,* October.

Trennepohl, Gary L., and W. P. Dukes (1979). "CBOE Options and Stock Volatility." *Review of Business and Economic Research* 18: 36–48.

Tufano, Peter (1989a). "Three Essays on Financial Innovation." Ph.D. dissertation, Harvard University.

———. (1989b). "Financial Innovation and First-Mover Advantages." *Journal of Financial Economics* 25.

Tufano, Peter (1995). "Securities Innovations: A Historical and Functional Perspective." *Journal of Applied Corporate Finance,* Winter.

Tufano, Peter (1996). "Who Manages Risk?" An Empirical Examination of Risk Management Practices in the Gold Mining Industry." *Journal of Finance.*

Turnbull, S., and L. Wakeman (1991). "A Quick Algorithm for Pricing European Average Options." *Journal of Financial and Quantitative Analysis,* 26, No. 3 (September): 377–89.

Vasicek, Oldrich (1977). "An Equilibrium Characterization of the Term Structure." *Journal of Financial Economics* 5, November.

Walker, Townsend (1997). "Managing Bank Asset Liability Exposure." *Derivatives Strategy,* May.

Wall, Larry (1989). "Interest Rate Swaps in an Agency Theoretic Model with Uncertain Interest Rates." *Journal of Banking and Finance* 13.

Wall, Larry D., and John J. Pringle (1988). "Interest Rate Swaps: A Review of the Issues." *Economic Review,* Federal Reserve Bank of Atlanta, November/December.

———. (1989). "Alternative Explanations of Interest Rate Swaps: An Empirical Analysis." *Financial Management* 18: 59–73.

Warner, Jerry (1977a). "Bankruptcy, Absolute Priority, and the Pricing of Risky Debt Claims." *Journal of Financial Economics* 13, May.

———. (1977b). "Bankruptcy Costs: Some Evidence." *Journal of Finance* 32, May.

Weinberger, David B. *Harvard Business Review.*

Wessel, David (1997). "US Will Auction Five-Year Notes Tied to Inflation." *The Wall Street Journal Europe,* June 9.

Whaley, Robert (1981). "On the Valuation of American Call Options on Stock with Known Dividends." *Journal of Financial Economics,* Vol. 9, pp. 207–212.

Whaley, Robert E. (1986). "Valuation of American Futures Options: Theory and Empirical Evidence." *Journal of Finance* 41 (March): 127–50.

Wheat, A. (1995). "Developments in the OTC Derivatives Market." *Financial Derivatives and Risk Management,* May.

Whiteside, M. M.; W. P. Dukes; and P. M. Dunne (1983). "Short-Term Impact of Option Trading on Underlying Securities." *Journal of Financial Research* 6: 313–21.

Whittaker, J. Gregg (1987). "Interest Rate Swaps: Risk and Regulation." Federal Reserve Bank of Kansas City. *Economic Review,* March.

Wiggins, James (1987). "Option Values under Stochastic Volatility: Theory and Empirical Evidence." *Journal of Financial Economics* 19 (December): 351–72.

Wilkie P. J. (1988). "Corporate Average Effective Tax Rates and Inferences about Relative Tax Preferences." *Journal of American Taxation Association,* Fall.

Wilmot, P.; J. Dewynne; and S. Howison (1994). *Options Pricing: Mathematical Models and Computation,* Oxford Financial Press.

Wittaker, J. Gregg, and Janet Kim (1995). "Structured Equity Derivative Products." *The Handbook of Equity Derivatives,* eds. Jack Clark Francis, William W. Toy, and J. Gregg Whittaker. New York: McGraw-Hill.

Wood, Jeremy (1994). "A Twinkle in the Eye." *Risk,* November.

Working, Holbrook (1960). "Price Effects of Futures Trading." *Food Research Institute Studies* 1: 3–31.

Wysocki, P. (1996). "Managerial Motives and Corporate Use of Derivatives: Some Evidence." Simon School of Business, University of Rochester, Working Paper.

Yang, W., and P. Zhang (1995). "Basket Digital Options." *Derivatives Week* (September 18): 9.

Zimmerman, J. L. (1983). "Taxes and Firm Size." *Journal of Accounting and Economics* (August): 119–49.

Zukerman, Gregory (1997). "Inflation Bond Is Still Getting Cool Response." *The Wall Street Journal,* July 10.

Index

AAA subsidiaries, 363
Accrual notes, 341
Acting on a view, 497, 498, 632–636
Active hedging, 562, 563
Adjustable-rate convertible debt, 353
Adjustable-rate convertible notes, 326, 327
Adjustable-rate preferred stock, 343
Adjustment speed, 48
Agented arrangement, 323
Air Products–Chemicals Inc., 554
Alexander, G. S., 613
All-or-nothing options, 285
Alpha separation, 635
Alpha transport, 612, 613
Alternative minimum tax (AMT), 506
American calls, 214–216
American options, 191, 214–217
American puts, 216
Americus trusts, 344
Amortization effect, 378, 379
AMT, 506
Analytic approximation models, 238
Analytic variance-covariance method, 464, 499
Analytical models, 227–233
Angel, James, 257
Applied Biosystems, 253
Applied Power, Inc., 249
Arak, Marcelle, 155

Arbitrage, 500, 630
Arbitrage portfolio, 202, 219
Arbor, Patrick, 53
Asset substitution, 353, 518n
At-market forward contract, 56
At-maturity trigger forward, 292, 294
At-the-money option, 37
Auerbach v. Bennett, 493
Average rate (price) options, 269, 270

Bachelier, Louis, 238
Back-end-set swap, 298
Back testing:
    DEAR methodology, 428
    VAR, 488
Back-to-back loans, 142–144
Backwardation, 108
Balance sheet, 522–527
Bank insolvencies, 391–393
Bank of Credit and Commerce International (BCCI), 391–393
Bankruptcy-remote subsidiaries, 363
Banks (*see* Financial institutions (as users))
Bansal, Vipul, 50
Barber, Brad, 331
Barone-Adesi, Giovanni, 238
Barrier options, 270–273
Bartter, Brit, 234

Basis, 109
Basis-point value (BPV), 406, 490n
Basis swap, 147, 148, 586
Basket options, 282
Basle Accord, 370–372
BCCI case, 391–393
Beard, Eugene, 482
Becker, Brandon, 434
Behof, John, 365
Benzoe Corporation, 119, 246
Bermuda options, 266
Bertram, Robert G., 614, 616
Beta, 518
Better-of options, 279
Bid-ask spreads:
    derivatives, and, 49
    foreign exchange forwards, 66
    forward-rate agreements, 69, 70
    swaps, 162
Bierwag, G., 536
Bilateral netting, 389
Binary options, 285
Binomial models, 233–235, 594
Binomial option pricing model, 201
Black, Fischer, 30, 36, 202, 218, 230
Black-Derman-Toy model, 236
Black model, 236
Black-Scholes option pricing model, 218–226
Board of directors, 434, 571–576

Bodnar, Gordon, 556
Bond with equity warrants, 327
Bondholder-shareholder conflict, 509, 510
Bonds with indexed principal, 328–331
Boness, James, 239
Boost, 343
Boundary condition, 224
Bounding value of option, 197–200
Boutross, Denise M., 381, 384
Boyle, Phelim, 235
Brane v. Roth, 493–496
Break forwards, 290, 291
Breeden, Richard, 575
Brennan, Michael, 235
Bretton Woods system, 3
Brewer, Elijah, 591
British Petroleum (BP), 477–481, 521, 522
Building blocks, 39, 40
    (*See also* Financial engineering)
Bulkeley, William H., 508
Bullet, 323
Burge, Roger, 564, 566
Burns–McBride, 264
Butterfly, 296, 297

C-R-R approach, 201, 233
Call option, 34, 190
Callable bonds, 589, 590
Callable corporate debt, 502
Callable debt, 331
Cancelable swaps, 294
Capital adequacy standards, 370–372
Capped options, 273
Caps, 244, 249
CAPS, 358n
Captions, 306
Cash flow sensitivity analysis, 539–550
Catastrophe bonds, 335
Catastrophe insurance futures/options, 307
Caterpillar, 8
Caterpillar Financial Services Corporation, 554
CBOT, 90, 91, 100, 101
CFTC-SEC jurisdictional disputes, 347, 348
Chan, William, 266n
Chance, Don, 513
Charles, Edwin, 119, 120, 246–248

Charm, 430
Chen, Andrew, 350
Chew, Donald H., Jr., 319n, 513
Chicago Board of Trade (CBOT), 90, 91, 100, 101
CHIPS, 358n
Cho-ai-mai, 23
Chooser options, 283
Claims-distribution problem, 353
Clearinghouse, 94–97
Cliquet options, 284
Closeout netting, 389
Codelco, 552
Collapsible swaps, 294
Collars, 245
    (*See also* Zero-cost collars)
Collateral, 395–397
Color, 430
Combinations, 288–298
Comfort letters, 397
Commodity derivatives, 309
Commodity Futures Trading Commission (CFTC), 89
Commodity interest-indexed bonds, 338–340
Commodity-price risk, 11, 14
    options, and, 253–257
    swaps, and, 174–176
Commodity-price risk management products, 22, 23
Company's letter to shareholders, 533–535
Compaq case, 494–496
Comparative advantage, 153
Competitive exposures, 7
Compound options, 305, 306
Compounding, 166
Concerns about using derivatives, 637
Condor, 298
Conrad, Jennifer, 47
Consol, 25
Constructive sales, 260
Contango, 108
Continental Airlines, 14, 15
Contingent premium options, 286
Continuation structures, 363
Continuous Ito process, 219, 220
Contract price, 54
Controlling usage of derivatives, 636–638
Convertible adjustable preferred stock (CAPS), 358n
Convertible bonds, 328

Convertible preferred, 344
Convexity, 407, 436, 437, 582, 586
Cookson, Richard, 562
Cooper, John, 482
Corman, Linda, 561
Correlation, 287n
Correlation risk, 283
Corridor notes, 341
Cost-effective pricing, 322, 323
Cost of carry model, 101–105
Cotton bonds, 24, 25
Cotton-indexed bond, 320
Counterparty rating, 567
Counterparty risk, 401
Coupon resets, 397, 398
Courtadon, Georges, 235
Covered-interest arbitrage, 62
Covered interest parity, 545
Cox, John C., 201, 205, 229, 233
Cox, Ross, Rubinstein (C-R-R) approach, 201, 233
Crawford, George, 639, 642
Credit arbitrage, 151, 152
Credit derivatives, 312–316
Credit equivalent exposure, 371
Credit event, 318n
Credit premium matrices, 390, 393, 395
Credit risk, 403n
    (*See also* Default risk)
Credit swaps, 313, 314
CreditMetrics, 594–599
Creed, David, 566
Cross-currency swap, 146
Cross-hedging, 112, 113, 127–133
Cross-indexed swaps, 299
Cross-product netting, 389
Cumulative interest rate cap, 270
Cumulative options, 270
Cunningham, Daniel P., 391, 393, 493
Currency swaps:
    creation, 144, 145
    foreign exchange rate risk, and, 173, 174
    FX swap, contrasted, 146
    growth of, 173
    McDonald's, and, 179
    origins, 18
Currency-as-an-asset class, 622, 623
Current ratio, 523
Current replacement cost, 376, 377

Daily earnings at risk (DEAR), 428–430

Damodaran, Aswath, 44, 47–50, 518

Das, Satyajit, 276

Dattatreya, Ravi, 284

Dealers (*see* Derivatives dealers)

DEAR methodology, 428–430

Debe, A. Joseph, 344

Debt capacity:
   options, and, 261, 262
   swaps, and, 181–184

Decomposition, 322, 323

DECS, 350

Default-contingent forward, 312

Default risk, 370–404
   amortization effect, 378, 379
   amortization/diffusion effect
      combined, 381, 382
   assignment/pair-offs, 398
   bank insolvencies, 391–393
   capital adequacy standards, 370–372
   collateral, 395–397
   coupon resets, 397, 398
   CreditMetrics, 594–599
   current replacement cost, 376, 377
   diffusion effect, 379–381
   empirical evidence, 398, 399
   expected exposure, 384, 385
   exposure, 375–385
   exposure measurement, 385–390
   loans, and, 375, 388
   mathematical formula, 374
   maximum exposure, 383, 384
   netting, 389, 395, 401
   options, and, 372, 373
   potential credit exposure, 377, 378
   probability of default, 390–395
   process (approach), 374, 375
   reducing the risk, 395–398
   settlement risk, 400–403
   swaps, and, 373
   swaps/loans, contrasted, 388
   termination provisions, 395

Dehnad, Kosrow, 409, 411

Delayed LIBOR reset swap, 300

Delayed-reset swap, 298, 299

Delayed-start swap, 288, 289

Deleveraged notes/bonds, 325, 592

Deliver versus payment (DVP), 400

Delta, 405–407

Delta-hedging, 411–420

Derivative product companies
   (DPCs), 363

Derivatives dealers, 360–369

functions, 366, 367

integrated risk management, and,
   367–369

largest 100 dealers, 361, 362

SPVs, 363–365

VAR, and, 476

Derivatives-related losses, 552–554

Derman, Emanuel, 236

Diff swaps, 299–303

Difference check, 145

Differential equations, 224

Differential swaps, 299–303

Diffusion effect, 379–381

Directors, board of, 434, 571–576

Disaster insurance, 286

Discounted value of an 01 (DV01),
   435, 490n

Discrete compounding, 166

Diversified VAR, 459, 462, 463

Dividend enhanced convertible stock
   (DECS), 350

Dolde, W., 515–517

Double barrier options, 273

Double trigger forward, 294

Down-and-out options, 270, 271

Dual-currency bond, 324

Dual-index notes, 325, 592

Dukes, William, 518

Duration, 406, 435, 536, 581–585

Durrant, Jim, 287n

Duty to hedge/use derivatives:
   corporations, 493–497
   fund managers, 639–642

DVP, 400

Earthquake bonds, 337

Economic exposures, 7

Efficient market, 16

Elasticity, 542, 543

Electricity derivatives, 310

Electricity futures, 308, 309

ELKS, 349, 350

Elton, J. E., 463

Embedded options, 501, 502

Energy swap, 175

Engineering new products (*see* Financial
   engineering)

Equity index swap, 149

Equity price risk:
   options, and, 257–261
   swaps, and, 176, 177

Equity-linked securities (ELKS),
   349, 350

Esterle, Celine, 272

Estrella, Arturo, 155

European options, 191

Eurotunnel, 564–566

Evaluation-control function, 571

Event trigger, 396

Evolution of risk management products,
   1–26
   commodity-price risk management
      products, 22, 23
   exchange rate risk management
      products, 18–20
   hybrid securities, 320, 321
   interest rate risk management
      products, 20–22
   swap contracts, 140–149

Exchange rate risk, 7–11
   (*See also* Foreign exchange rate risk)

Exchange rate risk management
   products, 18–20

Exchange-traded multifactor
   options, 283

Exchangeable bonds, 328

Exchangeable debt, 331

Exercise price, 191

Exotic options, 266–287

Expectations model, 106–108

Expected exposure, 384, 385

Expiration date, 191

Exposure, 375–385

Exposure beta, 542

Exposure measurement, 385–390

Extendable debt, 331

Extensions to Black-Scholes model,
   230–233

Extremum-dependent options,
   270–277

Factor approach of measuring
   exposure, 570

Factor immobility, 153

FALCON, 358n

Falcon Cable, 244

Falla, Enrique C., 482

Falloon, William, 301

Fama, Eugene, 499

Fedenia, Mark, 49

Federal Paper Board Co., 554

Ferron, Mark, 386

Fiduciary duty to use derivatives, 639–642
Figlewski, Stephen, 108, 109, 113
Financial building blocks, 39, 40
Financial distress, 506–508, 515
Financial engineering, 288–317
  break forward, 290, 291
  butterfly, 296, 297
  cancelable swaps, 294
  catastrophe insurance futures/options, 307
  combinations, 288–298
  commodity derivatives, 309
  compound options, 305, 306
  credit derivatives, 312–316
  delayed reset swaps, 298, 299
  derivatives on emerging country debt, 311
  diff swaps, 299–303
  double trigger forward, 294
  electricity derivatives, 310
  electricity futures, 308
  forward swap, 288, 289
  futures/options on commodity indexes, 307
  futures/options on financial instruments of emerging economies, 307, 308
  index amortizing swaps, 294, 295
  new underlying products, 306–316
  participating forward, 292, 293
  range forward, 290, 291
  real estate swaps, 311
  restructurings, 298–306
  semifixed swaps, 295, 296
  straddles, 296, 297
  strangles, 296, 297
  swaptions, 303–305
  trigger forward, 292, 294
Financial institutions (as users), 578–600
  asset-liability management, 578–591
  callable bonds, 589, 590
  cash flow risk, 586, 587
  convexity of portfolio, 589–591
  credit derivatives, 599, 600
  credit portfolio, 593–600
  duration/convexity, 581–586
  duration of portfolio, 587–589
  gap methodology, 579–581
  interest rate risk, 579–586
  investment portfolio, 591

  maturity mismatches, 587
  mortgages/mortgage-backed securities, 590, 591
  rate mismatches, 586, 587
  short funding, 587
  structured notes, 591–593
  value risk, 587
Financial price risk (*see* Measures of exposure to financial price risk)
Finite difference models, 235
Finnerty, John, 319n, 341
First Union Bank, 245
Fixed quanto, 287n
Flannery, Mark, 535
Flexo quanto, 287n
Floating-rate loans, 20, 153
Floored floating-rate bonds, 340
Floors, 245
Floortions, 306
Ford Motor Credit Corporation, 304
Forecasting, 15–18
Foreign exchange forwards, 60, 61
  bid-ask spreads, 66
  contract, 61
  hedging transaction exposures, 81–83
  markets, 74–76
  pricing, 62–64
  trading, 77–79
Foreign exchange rate risk, 7–11
  institutional investors, and, 621–624
  options, and, 250–253
  swaps, and, 173, 174
Foreign exchange swap, 88n
Forward agreements, 312
Forward contracts, 54–88
  building blocks, as, 39
  default risk, and, 60, 373
  defined, 54–56
  features, 30
  foreign exchange forwards (*see* Foreign exchange forwards)
  FRAs (*see* Forward-rate agreements (FRAs))
  hedging, and, 81–87
  markets, 74–76
  origins, 18, 25
  payoff profile, 29, 57
  risk-neutral valuation, 211, 212
  trading, 77–81
Forward foreign exchange rate, 62
Forward-forward contracts, 69
Forward interest rate, 68

Forward price, 54
Forward-rate agreements (FRAs):
  bid-ask spreads, 69, 70
  contract, 67
  forward interest rate, 67, 68
  hedging interest rate risk, 83–87
  insurance companies, 86, 87
  markets, 76
  pricing, 71, 72
  S&Ls, 83–85
  trading, 79–81
Forward rates and future interest rates, 499
Forward start options, 284
Forward swap, 288, 289
Francis, Cheryl, 572
François, George, 71, 72
FRAs (*see* Forward-rate agreements (FRAs))
Fraternity row, 405–411, 426
Froot, Kenneth, 514, 515, 539
Funding costs, 497–502
Futures contracts, 89–139
  basis, 109–112
  building blocks, as, 39
  clearinghouse, 94–97
  cost of carry, 101–105
  credit risk, and, 91
  cross-hedging, 112, 113, 127–133
  daily settlement, 91–93
  example (foreign exchange hedge), 136–139
  example (hedge/basis risk), 123, 124
  example (simple hedge), 122, 123
  exchanges, 100, 101
  expectations model, 106–108
  features, 30, 31
  hedging, and, 116–139
  items traded, 89, 90
  long hedge, 116, 121
  margin requirements, 30, 31, 93, 94
  origins, 23, 90, 91
  payoff profile, 31
  price limits, 96–99
  prices, 101–113
  regulatory body, 89
  rolling hedge, 124–127
  short hedge, 116, 121
  standardized contracts, 100
  strip hedge, 124, 125
  tailing the hedge, 133–136
  trading volume, 116–118
FX swap, 146

Gagnon, François, 601n
Gamma, 406–408
Gamma-hedging, 422
Gap methodology, 579–581
Garman, Mark, 231, 426, 432n
Garman-Kohlhagen model, 231
Gastineau, Gary, 257, 319n
Gatto, Mary Ann, 232
Geczy, C., 515, 516
Generalist approach, 29
Generalizations of Black-Scholes model, 227–230
Geske, Robert, 232
Gibson Greetings Inc., 552, 553
Goals of risk management, 556–558
Gold-indexed bond, 320
Golden Nugget, 43
Goldman, Barry, 232
Goldman Sachs Commodity Index (GSCI), 307, 330
Goodman, Laurie, 155
Grabbe, Orlin, 232
Grammatikos, Theocharry, 49
Greek-letter measures of risk, 405–411, 426
Green, Jesse, 482
Gregory-Allen, Russell, 613, 624
Gruber, M. J., 463
GSCI, 307, 330
Guarantees, 397

Hancock, Peter, 427, 430
Handjinicolaou, George, 386
Hankus, Frank, 181
Harris, Trevor, 562
Hartmarx Corporation, 249, 250
Hayt, Gregory S., 210, 499
Heat-exchange equation, 225
Heat rate, 310
Heath, David, 236
Heath-Jarrow-Morton model, 236
Hedge ratio, 202
Hedging:
    active, 562, 563
    callable bonds, and, 589, 590
    cross-hedging, 112, 113, 127–133
    delta-hedging, 411–420
    duty to hedge (*see* Duty to hedge/use derivatives)
    financial distress, and, 506–508, 515
    foreign exchange futures, and, 81–83
    FRAs, and, 83–87

futures contracts, and, 116–139
    gamma-hedging, 422
    jumps, and, 422–424
    mortgages/mortgage-backed securities, 590, 591
    options, and, 244–257
    rolling hedge, 124–127
    strip hedge, 124, 125
    swaps, and, 170–189
    tailing the hedge, 133–136
    taxes, and, 503–506, 515
    term structure twists, and, 420–422
    underinvestment, 509–514, 517
    vega-hedging, 422
Hendricks, Darryll, 465, 486, 487, 489
Hentschel, Ludger, 515, 516
Herstatt risk, 399, 404n
Hicks, Sir John, 435, 536, 582
Hicks duration, 435, 582
Hinkley, R. K., 477, 481, 521
Historical simulation method of calculating VAR, 440–445
History (*see* Evolution of risk management products)
Ho, Thomas, 236
Ho-Lee option pricing model, 236
Hopewell, Michael, 536
Hosp, Walter D., 322, 323
Hotta, Kensuke, 284
Hull, John, 230, 233, 235, 236, 632
Hull-White model, 236
Hurricane bonds, 337
Hutchins, Dexter, 8
Hybrid securities, 319–359
    debt and derivatives, 321
    debt plus forward contract, 324
    debt plus one option, 326–338
    debt plus package of options, 338–343
    debt plus swap, 325, 326
    decomposition, 322, 323
    economic rationale for, 351–354
    equity and derivatives, 343
    equity plus option, 344–351
    equity plus swap, 343
    evolution of, 320, 321
    investor strategies, 354–356
    origins, 21, 23, 25, 319, 320

Iacono, Frank, 485
IANs, 341, 592
ICI recommendation, 638
ICON, 330

Impact of introduction of derivatives, 42–53
    adjustment speed, 48
    bid-ask spread, 49
    economy, 51, 52
    OTC derivatives vs. exchange-traded derivatives, 52, 53
    price volatility, 42–48
    trading volume of underlying, 49, 50
Implementation of risk management system (*see* Risk management cycle)
In re Compaq Securities Litigation, 494–496
In-arrears swap, 298
Index accreting swap, 590, 591
Index amortizing notes (IANs), 341, 592
Index amortizing swap, 294, 295
Index participations (IPs), 348
Indexed currency option note (ICON), 330
Indexed principal swap, 294, 295
Inflation-rate interest-indexed bonds, 343
Information asymmetries, 155, 156
Ingersoll, Jonathan, 227
Initial margin, 94
Inside barriers, 272
Institutional investors, 601–643
    accessing unavailable assets, 632
    acting on a view, 632–636
    alpha transport, 612, 613
    arbitrage opportunities, 630–632
    asset price risk/equity price risk, 624–628
    concerns about using derivatives, 637
    controlling usage of derivatives, 636–638
    fiduciary duty to use derivatives, 639–642
    foreign exchange rate risk, 621–624
    insured asset allocation, 616–619
    interest rate risk, 619–621
    liquidity constraint, 613, 614
    portfolio construction, 610–619
    portfolio insurance, 618, 619
    portfolio rebalancing, 610–612
    reducing transaction costs, 628–630
    risk/return (joint consideration), 607, 608, 610

risks faced by, 601, 602
   strategic asset allocation, 610–616
   survey results, 602–609, 636, 637
   tactical asset allocation, 616
Insurance companies and FRAs, 86, 87
Insured asset allocation, 616–619
Integrated hedges, 310
Integrated risk management, 367–369, 560, 561
Interest rate cap, 244
Interest rate floors, 245
Interest rate parity, 62, 64
Interest rate risk, 11
   FRAs, and, 83–87
   institutional investors, and, 619–621
   options, and, 244–250
   swaps, and, 171, 172
Interest rate risk management products, 20–22
Interest rate sensitivity measures, 435, 436
Interest rate swap, 32, 146, 147
International bank insolvencies, 391–393
Inverse floating-rate notes, 185, 325
Investment Company Institute recommendations, 638
IPs, 348
Ito process, 220
Ito's Lemma, 221

J. P. Morgan, 427–430, 594
James, Christopher, 535
Jarrow, Robert, 230, 236
Jennings, Robert, 48
Jensen's inequality, 503, 518n
Jensen, Michael, 353
Johnson, Phillip, 347
Joint quanto, 281
Jordan, James, 464
Jorion, Philippe, 536
Jurisdictional disputes, 347, 348

Kaiser Aluminum, 181
Kappa, 408
Kaufman, George G., 536, 585
Kawaller, Ira G., 119, 120, 136, 246
Kearney, A. John, 514
Keepwell letters, 397
Kensinger, John, 350
Keynes, John Maynard, 107, 108

Kim, Ted, 632
Klemkosky, Robert, 518
Knobler, Joanna, 136–139
Knock-in options, 271
Knock-out cap, 272
Knock-out options, 270, 271
Kohlhagen, Steven, 231
Kothari, S. P., 515, 516
Kraft, 172
Kvaerner, 258

L.L. Bean, 244
Ladder options, 274–276
Laker, Freddie, 7
Laker Airlines, 7, 8
Lambda, 426
Lamoureux, Claude R., 614, 616
Lattice approach, 233
Layard-Liesching, Ronald G., 622, 623
Leander, Ellen, 336
LEAPS, 345
Lee, Sang-Bin, 236
Lehn, Kenneth, 347, 348
Leigh-Pemberton, Robin, 151
Lessard, Donald, 476
Letter *de faire*, 25
Letter to shareholders, 533–535
Letters of credit, 397
Leveraged notes/bonds, 325, 592
Leveraged swaps, 553
Levy v. Bessemer Trust Company, 496
Lewent, Judy C., 514
Lewis, Peter, 630
Light, Jay, 628
Lim, J., 44, 47–50, 518
Limited exercise options, 287n
Liquid yield option note (LYON), 332–335, 354
Loeys, Jan, 154, 156
Long straddle, 296
Long-term equity anticipation securities (LEAPS), 345
Lookback options, 274, 276
Losses by industrial corporations, 552–554
LYON, 332–335, 354

M&M proposition, 503
Macaulay, Frederick, 435, 536, 581
Macaulay duration, 435, 581, 582
Mackay, Robert, 464

Macmillan, Lionel, 238
Magma Copper's senior subordinated notes, 262, 338, 339
Maintenance margin, 94
Maness, Terry, 518
Margin, 93
Margrabe, William, 233
Market factor, 490n
Marking the swap to market, 167–169
Markov process, 220
Marshall, Christopher, 469, 470
Marston, Richard, 556
Matching currency footprints, 521, 562
Maturity date, 191
Maturity gap, 435, 579–581
Max option, 280
Maximum exposure, 383, 384
Mayers, D., 513
MBS, 436, 437
McDonald's Corporation, 178, 181
McGoldrick, Beth, 482
Mead Corporation, 554
Mean-dependent options, 267–270
Measures of exposure to financial price risk, 520–551
   balance sheet, 522–527
   cash flow sensitivity analysis, 539–550
   external measures, 533–538
   internal measures, 538–550
   letter to shareholders, 533–535
   statement of changes in financial position, 528–533
   statement of consolidated income, 524, 528–530
   statistical analysis of revenues/expenses, 538
   VAR, 539
Meckling, William, 353
Mello, Antonio, 562
Mello, J., 560
Melumad, Nahum, 562
Merck, 514
Merton, Robert, 227, 228, 230
Metropolitan Atlanta Rapid Transit Authority (MARTA), 175, 176
Mexicana de Cobre (Mexocobre), 181–184
Mian, S., 515, 516
Mid-Atlantic options, 287n
Mid-rates, 66
MidWest Banc, 79, 80
Miller, Merton, 51, 503
Millman, Gregory, 8, 181

Min option, 280
Minton, Bernadette, 515, 516, 591
Mirror swap, 151
Mobil, 481
Modified worst case exposure measures, 569, 570
Modigliani, Franco, 503
Monetizing equity positions, 259, 260
Monte Carlo simulations, 235
    cash flow sensitivity analysis, 544
    exposure measures, 387
    VAR, 446–449
Mortgage-backed securities (MBS), 436, 437, 590
Morton, Andrew, 236
Moser, James, 591
Multibranch netting agreements, 392
Multifactor options, 278–283
Multilateral netting, 389
Muzak, 248

n-color rainbow option, 279
Nance, Deana R., 515, 516
Neal, Robert, 49
Negative convexity, 407, 409–411, 586
Net interest income (NII), 83
Netting, 389, 390, 395, 401
Netting by novation, 389
New products (*see* Financial engineering)
1994 Wharton Survey of Derivatives End-Users, 539
Normal backwardation, 108
Normal contango, 108
Notional principal:
    forward contracts, 56
    swap contracts, 144
Numerical models, 233–237

Oil swap, 148, 149
Ontario Teacher's Pension Plan, 614–616
Operational risk, 368
Operational VAR, 369n
Option-based sensitivity measures, 436–438
Option buyer, 190
Option maker, 190
Option payoff diagram, 204, 205
Option seller, 190
Option spreads, 254
Option writer, 190

Options, 34–39, 190–287
    activity levels, 242, 243
    analytic approximation models, 238
    analytical models, 227–233
    Black-Scholes option pricing model, 218–226
    bounding value of option, 197–200
    combinations, 290–298
    commodity-price risk, and, 253–257
    competitive tool, as, 263, 264
    debt capacity, and, 261, 262
    default risk, 372, 373
    equity price risk, and, 257–261
    exercise styles, 266
    family tree, 218, 238, 239
    foreign exchange rate risk, and, 250–253
    governmental use, 256, 257
    graphics of, 191–195
    hedging, 244–257
    innovative products, 264
    interest rate risk, and, 244–250
    numerical models, 233–237
    option contracts, 190, 191
    origins, 18, 19, 21, 25
    payoff profiles, 34, 35, 204, 205
    put-call parity, 195–197
    quotes (*Wall Street Journal*), 192
    reducing funding costs, and, 501, 502
    restructurings, 303–306
    risk-neutral valuation, 212, 213
    similarity to other instruments, 38, 39
    time effects (as expiration approaches), 426, 430
    types (*see* Types of options)
    valuation, 195–214
Ordinary differential equation, 224
Out-of-the-money option, 37
Outperformance options, 279, 280
Outside barriers, 272

Paducah & Louisville (P&L) Railroad, 255
Parallel loan agreements, 142–144
Parsons, John, 562
Partial differential equation, 224
Participating forward, 292, 293
Path-dependent floater, 340
Path-dependent options, 267–278
Pay-now—choose-later option, 283

Payer swaptions, 303
Payment netting, 399, 404n
Payoff profiles, 40
PEACs, 358n
Pearl, Carleton Day, 178, 181
PERCS, 349, 350, 352
Periodic caps/floors, 284
PERLS, 324
PERQS, 358n
Petrobonds, 324
Phelps Dodge, 269, 561
PINC property contracts, 317n
Plain vanilla interest rate swap, 167
Po, Tyrone, 333, 335
Polsky, Lisa K., 607, 608
Portfolio construction, 610–619
Portfolio insurance, 618, 619
Portfolio manager, 432n
Portfolio rebalancing, 610–612
Positive convexity, 586
Potential credit exposure, 377, 378
Precommitment, 484
Predictions, 15–18
Preference equity redemption cumulative stock (PERCS), 349, 350, 352
Present value of an 01 (PV01), 435, 490n
Presettlement risk, 370, 568
Price risk:
    charm, 430
    color, 430
    delta, 405, 406
    delta-hedging, 411–420
    gamma, 406–408
    gamma-hedging, 422
    hedging against jumps, 422–424
    implementing the hedge, 424–426
    lambda, 426
    rho, 426
    speed, 426
    term structure rotations, 420–422
    theta, 426
    vega, 408, 411
    vega-hedging, 422
    (*See also* Measures of exposure to financial price risk)
PRIME, 344
Principal exchange rate linked security (PERLS), 324
Pringle, John J., 515, 516
Pritsker, Matthew, 472, 474
Probability of default, 390–395
Procter & Gamble, 554

Property futures contracts, 317n
Pruitt, Stephen, 50
Pure diffusion process, 229
Pure expectations hypothesis, 499
Put-call parity, 38, 195–197
Put option, 35, 190
Puttable debt, 331

Qualex, 255
Qualified financial contracts, 392
Quality spread, 152–154
Quanto options, 280, 281
Quanto swaps, 299
Quasi-American options, 287n
Quick ratio, 523
Quint, Michael, 510

R&D expenditures, 509–514
Rainbow options, 279
Range forward, 290, 291
Range notes, 341–343, 592
RAROC model, 595
Ratchet options, 284
Rawls, S. Waite, III, 1n
Re-hypothecation, 396
Real estate swaps, 311
Real yield securities (REALS), 343
Receiver swaptions, 303
Regression analysis, 538
Rendleman, Richard, 234
Rendleman-Bartter model, 234, 235
Restructured swaps, 298–303
Restructurings, 298–306
Revenue elasticity, 542
Reverse PERLS, 324
Revolving credit lines, 248
Rho, 426
Ring-fencing approach, 391
Risk-free interest rate, 203
Risk governance, 433, 434
    (*See also* Value-at-risk (VAR))
Risk management and value of firm,
    492–519
    acting on a view, 497, 498
    arbitraging markets, 500
    decreasing taxes, 503–506, 515
    empirical evidence, 515–518
    investment decisions, and,
        509–514, 517
    reducing probability of financial
        distress, 506–508, 515

reducing transaction costs, 501
selling options, 501, 502
strategic risk management, 502–518
tactical risk management, 497–502
Risk management cycle
    evaluation-control function, 571
    goals for risk management, 556–558
    identify/quantify exposures, 559
    overview, 556
    risk management philosophy,
        560–568
Risk management philosophy, 560–568
Risk management process, 427–430
Risk manager, 432n
Risk measures, 405–411, 426
Risk-neutral valuation, 210–214
Risk profile, 27
Risk/return (joint consideration), 607,
    608, 610
RiskMetrics, 449, 471, 490n
Robb, Erica, 272
Roll, Richard, 232
Roll-down calls, 272
Roll-up puts, 272
Rolling hedge, 124–127
Ross, Stephen A., 201, 205, 229, 233
Rozario, John, 45, 46
Rubinstein, Mark, 201, 205, 233
Rudd, Andrew, 230

S&P 500 index subordinated notes
    (SPINs), 331
Samant, A., 515–517
Samuelson, Paul, 239
Sandner, John F., 52
Santomero, Anthony, 368
SAPCO property contracts, 317n
Savings and loan associations (S&Ls),
    11, 13, 83–85
Scenario exposure measures, 385–387,
    569, 570
Scharfstein, David, 514, 515, 539
Scholes, Myron, 36, 202, 218
School of Financial Product, 465
Schrand, C., 515, 516
Schwartz, Eduardo, 235
SCORE, 344
Scott, Louis, 230
SEC-CFTC jurisdictional disputes,
    347, 348
Second-generation options, 266–287
Sell a strangle strategy, 635

Semifixed swap, 295, 296
Settlement risk, 372, 400–403
Shad, John, 43, 347
Shad-Johnson agreement, 347
Share repurchase program, 257, 258
Shareholder-bondholder conflict,
    509, 510
Sharpe, William, 98, 201, 613
Shibano, Toshi, 562
Short against the box, 260
Short funding, 587
Shout options, 275–277
Siegel, Michael, 469, 470
SIGNs, 331
Silver, Andrew, 155
Silver-indexed bonds, 328, 329
Simulation exposure measures, 387,
    568, 569
    (*See also* Monte Carlo simulations)
Single equity swap, 149
Single-payout options, 285, 286
Skeie, David, 485
Skinner, Douglas, 44, 48, 50, 518
Slunt, Joseph, 601, 602
SMART notes, 340
Smith v. Van Gorkom, 493
Smith, Clifford W., Jr., 140n, 218n, 353,
    513, 515, 516
Smithson, Charles W., 1n, 27n, 140n,
    218n, 515, 516
Sodhani, Arvind, 563
Sonatrach hybrid, 335, 336
Song, Shang, 218n
Sosin, Howard, 232
Spark spreads, 310
Special purpose vehicles (SPVs),
    363–365
SPECs, 358n
Speed, 426
Speed of price adjustment, 48
Spiders, 346
SPINs, 331
SPRDRs, 346
Spread options, 287n, 314
Standard–Poor's depositor receipts
    (SPDRs), 346
Stark, Laura, 48
Statement of changes in financial
    position, 528–533
Statement of consolidated income, 524,
    528–530
Statistical analysis of revenues/
    expenses, 538

Stein, Jeremy, 514, 515, 539
Step-up bonds, 340, 341, 592
Stern, Joel M., 513
Stock index growth notes (SIGNs), 331
Stock market annual reset term
    (SMART) notes, 340
Stock repurchase program, 257, 258
Stock upside note securities (SUNS), 340
Straddles, 296, 297
Strangles, 296, 297
Strategic asset allocation, 610–616
Strategic assets, 622
Strategic risk management, 502–518
Stress testing:
    DEAR methodology, 429
    VAR, 488
Strike price, 191
Strip hedge, 124, 125
Structured notes, 591–593
Stulz, René, 233, 515
Subrahmanyam, Marti G., 518
SUNS, 340
SuperTrust, 345, 346
Support letters, 397
Surety bond, 93
Swap contracts, 140–189
    building blocks, as, 39
    commodity-price risk, and,
        174–176
    credit arbitrage, 151, 152
    debt capacity, and, 181–184
    default risk, and, 373
    delta-hedging, 412–416
    difference check, 145
    differential cash flow packages,
        154, 155
    equity price risk, and, 176, 177
    evolution of, 140–149
    evolution of products/participants,
        150, 151
    example (McDonald's), 178–181
    example (Mexcobre), 181–184
    foreign exchange rate risk, and,
        173, 174
    growth of swap market, 151–162
    hedging, 170–189
    information asymmetries,
        155, 156
    interest rate risk, and, 171, 172
    intermediaries, 150, 151
    marking the swap to market,
        167–169
    notional principal, 144

origins, 140
overview, 31–34
pricing/valuing swaps, 162–169
quality spreads, 152–154
synthetic instruments, and, 162,
    184–188
tax and regulatory arbitrage,
    156–161
transaction costs, and, 177
types (*see* Types of swaps)
Swaptions, 303–305
Sweeney, Richard J., 535

Tactical asset allocation, 616
Tactical assets, 622, 623
Tactical risk management, 497–502
Tailing the hedge, 133–136
Tax and regulatory arbitrage,
    156–161
Tax arbitrage, 500
Tax preference items, 506
Taxes, 503–506, 515
Taxpayer Relief Act of 1997, 260
Termination provisions, 395
Termination structures, 365
Texas, 256, 257
Theta, 426
Tiered collateral agreement, 396
Tierny, Jacques, 185, 188
Time-dependent options, 283, 284
Toevs, Alden, 536, 581
Total return swaps, 313
Toy, William, 236
Trading volume of underlying assets,
    49, 50
Transaction costs, 177, 501, 628–630
Transaction exposures, 6, 7
Translation exposure, 8
Treatise on Money (Keynes), 107
Trennepohl, Gary, 518
Triantis, Alexander, 562
Trigger forward, 292
Triggering an agreement, 396
Trilobyte Corporation, 136–139
Trinomial lattice approach, 235
Triple-witching hour, 45, 46
True quanto, 287n
Tufano, Peter, 515, 516
Tulipmania, 23
Turnbull, Stuart, 278
Two-color rainbow, 279
Types of options:

all-or-nothing, 285
American, 191, 214–217
Asian, 267–269
average rate (price), 267–269
average strike, 269, 270
barrier, 270–273
basket, 282
basket-digital, 306
Bermuda, 266
better-of/worse-of, 279
binary, 285
capped, 273
chooser, 283
cliquet, 284
compound, 305, 306
contingent premium, 286
cumulative, 270
double barrier, 273
down-and-out, 270, 271
European, 191
exotic, 266–287
extremum-dependent,
    270–277
forward start, 284
knock-in, 271
knock-out, 270, 271
ladder, 274–276
lookback, 274, 276
mean-dependent, 267–270
min/max, 280
multifactor, 278–283
outperformance, 279, 280
path-dependent, 267–278
quanto, 280, 281
rainbow, 279
ratchet, 284
second-generation, 266–287
shout, 275–277
single-payout, 285, 286
spread, 314
swaptions, 303–305
time-dependent, 283, 284
up-and-out, 270, 271
Types of swaps:
    basis, 147, 148
    cancelable, 294
    credit, 313, 314
    cross-currency, 146
    currency, 144–146
    delayed-reset, 298, 299
    diff, 299–303
    energy, 175
    equity, 176, 177

equity index, 149
forward, 288, 289
FX, 146
index amortizing, 294, 295
interest rate, 146, 147
mirror, 151
oil, 148, 149
real estate, 311
restructured, 298–303
semifixed, 295, 296
single equity, 149
total return, 313

Unbundled stock units (USUs),
   344, 345
Underinvestment, 511–514
Underinvestment problem, 353
Underwriting fees, 323
Undiversified VAR, 459, 462, 463
Up-and-out options, 270, 271
USUs, 344, 345

Value-at-risk (VAR), 433–491
   accuracy vs. computational time
      tradeoff, 472–474
   analytic variance-covariance method,
      449–464
   applicability of VAR, 475, 476
   back testing, 488
   Bank internal models approach, 483
   calculation methods, 440–464
   choosing a calculation method, 471
   comparison of calculation methods,
      464–471
   confidence level, 486
   derivatives dealers, and, 476, 477
   diversified VAR, 459, 462, 463

historical simulation method,
   440–445
implementation, 484–489
institutional investors, and, 477
losses which exceed VAR, 489
Monte Carlo simulation method,
   446–449
nature of, 438–440
nonfinancial businesses, and, 539
nonfinancial corporations, and,
   477–483
precursors to, 435–438
regulators, and, 483, 484
RiskMetrics, 449, 471, 490n
scenario analysis, 487
sensitivity analysis, 487
square root of time, and, 485
stress testing, 488
time horizon, 484–486
undiversified VAR, 459, 462, 463
usage, 559
uses, 475–484
variance-covariance data,
   486, 487
Value at Risk Educational Software, 465
Value of an 01, 406, 435
Value of firm (*see* Risk management and
   value of firm)
Value trigger, 396
VAR (*see* Value-at-risk (VAR))
Variation margin, 94
Vega, 408, 411
Vega-hedging, 422
Volatility, 520
   commodity prices, of, 4, 5
   derivatives, and, 42–48
   foreign exchange rates, of, 3
   interest rates, of, 4
Volcker, Paul, 4

Wagener, Jeremy, 566
Wakeman, Lee MacDonald,
   140n, 278
Walker, Townsend, 578
Wall, Larry D., 515, 516
Warga, Arthur D., 535
Warner, Jerry, 353
Watson, Ronald D., 400, 403
Weber, Clifford, 257
WEBS, 346
Wei, John, 50
Weinberger, David B., 574
Whaley, Robert, 233, 238
Wharton Financial Institutions
   Center, 368
Wharton Survey of Derivatives End-
   Users, 539
Wheat, Allen, 315
White, Alan, 230, 235, 236
White, Gerald A., 555
Wiggins, James, 230
Wilford, D. Sykes, 74n
Witching hours, 45, 46
"Wonderful Life," 218n
World equity benchmark shares
   (WEBS), 346
Worse-of options, 279
Worst-case exposure measures, 386,
   387, 569
Wysocki, P., 515, 516

YEELDS, 358n
Yield-curve notes, 325

Zakharia, Ziad, 462, 463
Zero-cost collars, 248, 249, 254